ATHLETIC SCHOLARSHIPS

ATHLETIC SCHOLARSHIPS 3RD EDITION

Thousands of Grants—and over $400 Million—
for College-Bound Athletes

ANDY CLARK AND AMY CLARK

ATHLETIC SCHOLARSHIPS 3rd Edition: Thousands of Grants—and over $400 Million—for College-Bound Athletes

Facts On File, Inc.
460 Park Avenue South
New York NY 10016

Library of Congress Cataloging-in-Publication Data

Clark, Andy, 1958–
Athletic scholarships: Thousands of grants—and over $400 million—for college-bound athletes / Andy Clark and Amy Clark. — 3rd ed.
p. cm.
Rev. ed. of: The directory of athletic scholarships / by Alan Green, c1987.
Includes bibliographical references (p.) and index.
ISBN 0-8160-2892-3. — ISBN 0-8160-2893-1 (pbk.)
1. Sports—Scholarships, fellowships, etc.—United States—Directories. 2. Universities and colleges—United States—Directories. I. Clark, Amy Holsapple. II. Green, Alan, 1950– Directory of athletic scholarships. III. Title.
GV583.G72 1994 93-16812
796'.079'73—dc20

A British CIP catalogue record for this book is available from the British Library.

Facts On File Books are available at special discounts when purchased in bulk quantities for businesses, associations, institutions or sales promotions. Please call our Special Sales Department in New York at 212/683-2244 or 800/322-8755.

Text design bt Ellen Levine
Jacket design by Ellie Nigretto
Composition and manufacturing by the Maple-Vail Book Manufacturing Group
Printed in the United States of America

10 9 8 7 6 5 4 3 2 1

This book is printed on acid-free paper

CONTENTS

ACKNOWLEDGMENTS

We would like to thank our three children: Andy, Aaron, and Amelia. The oldest just turned seven and Amelia is two. In their own special way, each helped us complete this book.

The student-athletes who use this book deserve respect and recognition. You are the ones who really put in the effort to compete in sports and to succeed academically. We wish you success in all your endeavors!

This book was definitely a team effort! We really appreciate and thank all of those wonderful contacts at the colleges and universities who were kind enough to provide the valuable information necessary to compile this book. Two other team members are also to be thanked. Gary M. Krebs, associate editor at Facts On File, Inc., provided an incredible level of support throughout the project. Traci Cothran did a very thorough job of copyediting, which really enhanced the accuracy of the information. Thanks again, team!

INTRODUCTION

You do not need to be a football hero to win an athletic scholarship. This book details over $400 million of athletic scholarship aid (with even more that is not specified) available in sports from Alpine Skiing to Wrestling . . . and everything in between. It also provides information that will enhance your chances of obtaining an athletic award to help defray the cost of a college education.

Each year, the nation's colleges and universities award millions of dollars in grants-in-aid to student-athletes. And each year, a significant percentage of available assistance is not awarded—partly because recruiters and coaches, with limited budgets, are unable to locate qualified students, and partly because qualified students are either unaware of all the potential opportunities or uncertain about how to go after them.

Undoubtedly, the easiest way to win an athletic scholarship is to be a star, particularly in "major" sports like football or basketball, which get considerable coverage in local newspapers. The word on top "talent" is never kept secret and an outstanding high school or junior college athlete will find the mailbox overflowing, the telephone ringing off the hook, the stands filled with interested coaches and, where permitted by association rules, a long line of recruiters waiting to ring the doorbell.

But if you are not a star, if you are an average or above-average athlete, you may never see or hear from a recruiter, despite the fact that you may be scholarship material. As such, you will have to actively look for financial aid. The problem, though, is that most student-athletes do not know how to go about it, and the majority of campaigns end up haphazard and often unproductive.

This book explains the process that is often used in awarding athletic scholarship aid and it provides the essential tools needed to pursue it. There is a comprehensive directory of four-year and junior colleges, showing you which schools offer athletic aid and approximate amounts, if available. The directory is accompanied by a sport-by-sport appendix to help identify the colleges that offer programs in your sport. This information will allow you to focus your energy on obtaining the athletic scholarship aid you deserve and it will maximize the probability of a winning effort.

The Game Plan

Perhaps the best way to go about formulating a strategy for winning an athletic scholarship is to first understand how the recruiters and coaches in search of athletic talent operate. When you have a line on their moves, you can pattern your offense accordingly.

For example, take a sports program at a Division I Eastern University. Being with a state school, the coaches are always getting reports about local talent—from high school coaches, alumni, newspapers and that good old established standby, the grapevine.

The cycle begins in the spring when the coaches read through the recruiting services' scouting reports and files on young talent. In March or April, the school will send out questionnaires to potential prospects, asking them general questions about their physical attributes and athletic background. During the summer, the coaches will head for some sports camps, where they will have a chance to evaluate talent from all over. In addition to the camps, they will spend time sizing up players in summer league competitions, keeping notes on prospective talent.

By the end of the summer, the staff might have a list of 400 names to whom questionnaires were sent. Those players who did not respond will receive telephone calls to determine whether they might be interested in the school. In September the field will be narrowed down to include only those students who could possibly fit into the program and the coaches will arrange to start visiting them at their high schools or junior colleges.

When this list is complete, the coaches will begin their travels, which last until mid-October. They will visit with students and make presentations about their institution and its sports program. Generally, the students who receive visits are those the coaches believe they might be able to attract to the institution.

But once that visit is over, the student-athlete is not forgotten. Periodic mailings are sent out about the program and how the team is shaping up. During the last three weeks in December, the coaches are out on the road again, this time watching the talent in action. A transcript request form may be sent to a student-athlete's high school, so the coaches can decide whether it is feasible to continue with the recruitment process.

As the season progresses, the coaches will begin trying to determine who may give them a commitment. If the coaches are especially interested in certain players, they will try to get to all their games—even those 150 or 200 miles away. If they like what they see, they will try to assess what an athlete is thinking, perhaps by talking to friends or high school coaches. If the student-athlete is leaning in their direction, they will invite him or her to up to the school for a visit.

In February, they will have a better idea about a student-athlete's grades and how interested he or she really is in the school. The coach's office might now resemble a field general's headquarters, with a large board sitting in one corner listing the names of prospective student-athletes. Names are moved around or dropped off, depending on how the coaches assess each prospect.

The coaches will try to develop a rapport with the student-athlete and/or anyone who might be able to influence his or her decision. At the same time, they will be trying to establish exactly what their needs are and what sorts of players they would most like to have. As the school year draws to a close, the coaches will try to persuade the student-athletes they are interested in to sign letters of intent. Offers of financial aid are made at this time. The coaches, with an idea of what the team will look like the following season, then start the process all over, sending out questionnaires, reading scouting reports and adding new names to their lists. In other words, the recruiting process never ends.

Not every school works exactly this way, but it is typical of a big-time program. Coaches at smaller schools, which generally put less emphasis on sports, may visit fewer camps each summer, talk to fewer high school coaches about their talent, and watch fewer interscholastic games, but the methods are essentially the same. In the end, all roads lead in the same direction: Where possible, go out and see the talent in action.

At smaller schools, the recruiting budgets may not allow coaches to cover much territory. Nevertheless, these are the schools that provide the best scholarship opportunities for most students. So if you are interested in such a school, it is your job to make sure they know about you.

Collaborating with Your Coach

Do not rule yourself out of athletic scholarship aid. Talk with your coach about the matter. Ask for an honest assessment of your chances of obtaining athletic aid and ask how he or she can help you with the effort. Even if you do not like what you are hearing, hold any comments until the coach is finished speaking. Try to keep all discussions constructive by limiting discussion of past events and focusing on any areas in need of improvement. Before you leave, be sure to thank the coach for taking the time to talk with you.

The point cannot be overemphasized that a high school coach is crucial to the whole process of winning an athletic scholarship. Many times, college coaches will go directly to your high school coach for information about your ability and interest without your ever knowing about it. Such calls to your coach could come as a result of your initial contact, an alumni suggestion or a scouting report. If your coach is aware of your ambitions and interest in athletic scholarship aid, it will make matters easier for all concerned. Eventually, college coaches are going to get to your high school coach for information, so it is wise to work with that coach from the very beginning of your search.

Correspondence

It can be difficult for students to get athletic scholarships on their own. A coach who leads the way and makes contact can be an enormous asset. But coaches cannot do everything for you, and you are going to have to do your own investigation of where you might like to go and narrow down choices without much assistance from your coach. This is particularly true if you are investigating colleges outside your state or region.

Most college athletic departments have available general literature about their programs and obtaining it is often a good first step in the selection process. Schools send this information to anyone who calls or writes, but you will want your initial contact to be more than a simple request for a brochure. For that first contact, a letter is usually better than a telephone call because what is said over the telephone may be forgotten, while a letter will probably go right into a permanent file. An initial letter to a college coach will tell a lot about you, so make certain you get off on the right foot.

A form letter will suffice if you have a general interest in the school (see Sample Letter #1), but if for some reason you are really enthusiastic about the institution, a personal letter explaining your interest is definitely more appropriate (see Sample Letter #2). Include in the letter if your parents or other relatives are alumni of the school or if you have friends who play sports there. The letter should be addressed to the appropriate coach; if you do not know the coach's name, you can contact the college for it or you can simply write to the Athletic Director.

It is a good idea to include a brief resume with your first letter. A one-page description of yourself will quickly give a coach an idea of whether you may be the sort of athlete the team needs. Make copies of your resume to send to all the schools you are investigating. But do not spread your focus too wide; a blanket mailing to every school you have heard of is of little value. The schools you should generally contact are the ones you are interested in attending and the ones that could be interested in you, given your athletic and academic credentials.

The resume should have all pertinent data, including your grade-point average, SAT scores, the sport(s) you play, awards and honors received, personal statistics, volunteer activities and other associations you have, along with some names, addresses and telephone numbers of a few athletic and personal references. Where appropriate, include your time for sprints and longer distances. A field hockey coach, for example, may be impressed with the way you handle a stick, but that coach may be even more impressed to learn how well you move—and how long you can continue moving.

The sample resume shown here does not have to be followed exactly, but yours should contain similar information. The idea behind a resume is to quickly give coaches an idea of who you are, what you have done and what your potential may be. If you play a sport such as tennis, by all means include your ranking. And if you have any press clippings, send copies along. Also, it is not a bad idea to include a copy of your upcoming game schedule, if available. A coach who is interested in your credentials will probably want to see you in action.

Neatly organize copies of all your correspondence. This will help greatly when you need to refer back to it. One way to do this is to punch holes in the copies and place them in a notebook with dividers for each school. Let your high school coach know which institutions you are contacting and who has responded. In many cases, it helps to run your correspondence past the coach or another guidance resource before mailing.

A word of caution: A number of athletic departments operate under the assumption that if they have not already heard of you, they are probably not interested. At such schools, a letter touting your abilities might be placed in the trash can. They may rely entirely on their paid recruiters to find talent. So do not be totally put off if you never hear back from a school you contact. You can never be certain about its needs and recruitment strategies, but there is never any harm in trying.

Obtaining athletic aid is much like a search for any other job. The superstars and well connected rarely have to look too hard . . .their main problem is choosing from among the offers. But, for most of us, it is hard work. The correspondence skills that have been described here are almost identical to those used when looking for employment, and the tactics you will learn from your efforts will provide valuable skills.

SAMPLE LETTER #1

Ralph Seidner
278 Perlov Street
Worcester, MA 01610
April 2, 19xx

Soccer Coach
University of Vermont
Patrick Gymnasium
Burlington, VT 05401

Dear Coach:

I am a junior at MacNeice High School, where I have played soccer for the last three years. I am in the process of investigating colleges and am interested in the University of Vermont. I am particularly interested in exploring the possibility of an athletic scholarship, as I believe I can be an asset to the team.

I have enclosed a brief resume outlining my accomplishments along with some newspaper clippings. I would appreciate it if you would provide me with information about your soccer program and scholarship opportunities. Thank you very much.

Sincerely,

Ralph Seidner

SAMPLE LETTER #2

Ralph Seidner
278 Perlov Street
Worcester, MA 01610
April 2, 19xx

Mr. Gary Prushansky
Soccer Coach
Gussie State College
San Diego, CA 92109

Dear Coach:

I am a junior at MacNeice High School, where I have played soccer for the last three years. As a freshman, I was the leading scorer on the junior varsity team with 11 goals and 21 assists. In my sophomore year, playing right wing for the varsity, I scored nine goals and had 24 assists, and was named Honorable Mention All-County. This past season, I led the league in scoring with 23 goals and was named third team All-State. Next year, I expect to do even better.

I am in the process of investigating colleges and am interested in Gussie State. Having grown up in the San Diego area, I am aware of the college's fine reputation. I am particularly interested in exploring the possibility of an athletic scholarship, as I believe I can be an asset to the Gussie State team.

I should add that I am quite familiar with the athletic program at Gussie State. My brother, Michael, graduated two years ago and was one of your top wrestlers.

I have enclosed a brief resume outlining my career to date, along with some newspaper clippings. I would appreciate it if you would provide me with information about the soccer program and the opportunities for athletic scholarship assistance. Thank you very much.

Sincerely,

Ralph Seidner

Sample Resume

RALPH SEIDNER
278 Perlov Street
Worcester, MA 01610
(617) 555-2345

ACADEMIC INFORMATION

MacNeice High School
Worcester, MA
Expected Graduation: June 19xx
PSAT scores: 594 (verbal) 636 (math)
GPA: 87
Expected field of study: Engineering
Student council treasurer, junior year.

PERSONAL STATISTICS

Date of birth: November 12, 19xx
Height: 5'9"
Weight: 164
40 yard time: 4.95
100 yard time: 10.9
Mile time: 5.12

ATHLETIC HISTORY

Soccer, freshman year: left wing, junior varsity; 11 goals, 21 assists. Team finished second in league, 12-4.
Soccer, sophomore year: right wing, varsity; 9 goals, 24 assists. Team finished first in league; named Honorable Mention All-County.

Track, sophomore year: quarter mile, best time 52.8.
All-American Soccer Camp, Sutton, N.H., summer of sophomore year.
Soccer, junior year: right wing, varsity; 23 goals, 19 assists. Team made it to state quarter finals; named to third team All-State. Elected team captain for senior year.

REFERENCES

Charlie Russo, Varsity soccer coach, MacNeice High
Jerrold Schoenholtz, J.V. soccer coach, MacNeice High
Peter Goldwater, director, All-American Soccer Camp

Your Ticket to College Scholarship Awards

Getting seen in action by the college coaches and/or their recruiters will really enhance your chances of obtaining athletic scholarship assistance. Your letters will result in opportunities, and there are additional methods to gain exposure. College coaches rely heavily on films, which is another reason to work closely with your high school coach, who can see to it that a college receives any available footage of you in action.

Although not all sports are filmed, there are other opportunities for college coaches to get to see you play. One way is at a summer camp. Camps offer an excellent chance not only for you to be seen, but also to help improve your skills and to have fun. Just as there are scholarships available for college, athletic scholarship aid to summer camp is available. Recruiters also keep a close eye on summer leagues, so get involved with one of these, if possible. Your high school coach will be able to provide more information about camps and summer leagues.

Some schools, particularly junior and smaller four-year schools, allow walk-ins, where anyone can try out for the team. If the coach likes what he or she sees, you may end up with a scholarship, although chances are it will not be for the first year, after which time they are certain of your value to the team.

Be sure to thoroughly investigate other aid that an institution may offer. Virtually all institutions of higher education have very extensive need-based and merit-based aid programs. The cumulative value of non-athletic aid far exceeds the value of athletic aid.

Generally, steer clear of outside services that offer to match you up with athletic scholarship aid for a fee. These services rarely do anything that you are not completely capable of doing yourself and some have been known to be unscrupulous. With the help of your high-school coaches and other resources, you can write the same letters, make the same contacts and get the same (or better) results without spending money that should be earmarked for college.

Key Points

1. Do not wait until your senior year to get the process going. As pointed out, the recruiting process is a long one. You should start pursuing athletic scholarship assistance at the beginning of your junior year or even by the middle of your sophomore year in high school. If you are already past that point, your effort will need to be more intense.
2. Work closely with your high school coach. He or she cannot completely read your intentions and interests. Respectfully seek their guidance and assistance, but do not rely on them to make decisions for you.
3. Be seen as often as possible. In most cases, the bottom line in obtaining athletic scholarship aid is being seen in action in your sport by college coaches and recruiters.
4. Explore all of your options. While this book focuses on athletic scholarship aid, there is an incredible level of nonathletic aid available as well.

Peptalk

The keys to winning anything are hard work and a good attitude. You are already ahead of the competition. By using this book, your search is on and it is up to you to win both the athletic and non-athletic college scholarship aid you need and deserve.

The work you put into the search in high school will probably take many, many hours over a long period of time. But all of those hours are nothing compared with the time you would have work to earn the money at a job or when compared with the work needed to pay off college loans. When pursuing college scholarship aid, consider it among your most important jobs while in high school and make appropriate sacrifices so you have the time to find the financial assistance you need to *finish* college.

Don't get discouraged. Some doors will close but others will open. Be positive, active and upbeat. Every letter you write, every call you make, every good grade you get and every game you play are all steps towards your goal of a college education. Just take enough steps—you *will* reach that goal!

Understanding the State-by-State Listings

The directory is broken down by state and colleges are shown in alphabetical order within each state. The college name, address and telephone number appear first in each record. Most of the telephone numbers will connect you to the Athletic Information Office, often to the individual listed as a contact. In other cases, they connect you with a main switchboard. The name given is the one provided by the college as a primary contact for student-athlete inquiries or the one that was on file from previous research. Some of the records do not have contact names, in which case contact the college and ask for the Athletic Information Office for further details. In any case, it is vital to verify the contact information before sending a letter, as the staffing situation at most colleges is subject to change.

The colleges were asked to provide approximate numbers of athletic scholarships awarded during the most recent year and the approximate dollar value of the aid. This information can be used to gauge the level of athletic aid awarded by a particular school. Many colleges chose to keep this information confidential; in those cases it is noted that unspecified athletic scholarship aid is available.

Some colleges provided notes or restrictions that may be applicable to their programs, which are included. Two-year colleges are specified; the rest are four-year institutions.

The athletic programs offered by the school come next. Programs in which athletic awards *are* available are listed for both men (M) and women (W). Men's and women's non-scholarship aid sports programs are also listed for each school, where applicable.

Again, it is important to confirm all information when making contact with the college. Every effort was made to ensure the accuracy of the information, however unintentional errors are still possible.

STATE BY STATE LISTINGS

Alabama

ALABAMA A & M UNIVERSITY
P.O. Box 306
Huntsville, AL 35762
(205) 851-5368 Contact: Antoine Bell
Men's Aid (#/$): 45/$144,051
Women's Aid (#/$): 29/$69,484
M: basketball, cross country, football, indoor track, soccer, tennis, track & field, volleyball
W: basketball, cross country, indoor track, track & field

ALABAMA STATE UNIVERSITY
Box 271
Montgomery, AL 36101-0271
(205) 293-4507 Contact: Jack Jeffery
Unspecified athletic aid available
M: basketball, football. Men's Non-aid: baseball, cross country, golf, indoor track, tennis, track & field
W: basketball. Women's Non-aid: cross country, indoor track, tennis, track & field, volleyball

ATHENS STATE COLLEGE
300 North Beaty Street
Athens, AL 35611
2-year college
(205) 233-8143 Contact: Barry DeVine
Men's Aid (#/$): 13/unspecified $
Women's Aid (#/$): 13/unspecified $
M: basketball
W: softball

AUBURN UNIVERSITY
P.O. Box 351
Auburn, AL 36831
(205) 844-9800 Contact: David Housel
Men's Aid (#/$): 158/$1,127,724
Women's Aid (#/$): 81/$605,178
Restrictions and notes: Athletic aid averages 40% of costs.
M: baseball, basketball, cross country, diving, football, golf, indoor track, swimming, tennis, track & field
W: basketball, cross country, diving, golf, gymnastics, indoor track, swimming, tennis, track & field, volleyball

AUBURN UNIVERSITY (MONTGOMERY)
Atlanta Highway
Montgomery, AL 36193-0401
(205) 271-9300 Contact: James D. Berry
Unspecified athletic aid available

M: baseball, basketball, cheerleading, soccer, tennis
W: basketball, cheerleading, tennis

BIRMINGHAM-SOUTHERN COLLEGE
Arkadelphia Road
Birmingham, AL 35254
(205) 226-4688 Contact: Ron Elmore
Men's Aid (#/$): 37/$559,007
Women's Aid (#/$): 7/$66,345
M: baseball, basketball, soccer, tennis
W: tennis

CHATTAHOOCHEE VALLEY COMMUNITY COLLEGE
2602 College Drive
Phenix City, AL 36869
2-year college
(205) 291-4908 Contact: Doug Key
Men's Aid (#/$): 33/$13,200
Women's Aid (#/$): 30/$12,000
M: baseball, basketball
W: basketball, softball

ENTERPRISE STATE JUNIOR COLLEGE
P.O. Box 1300
Enterprise, AL 36331
2-year college
(205) 347-2623 Contact: Chip Quisenberry
Unspecified athletic aid available
M: baseball, basketball, tennis
W: softball, tennis

FAULKNER UNIVERSITY
5345 Atlantic Highway
Montgomery, AL 36109-3398
(205) 272-5820 X. 148 Contact: J.T. Harrison
Unspecified athletic aid available
M: baseball, basketball, cheerleading
W: cheerleading, softball

GADSDEN STATE COMMUNITY COLLEGE
P.O. Box 227
Gadsden, AL 35999-0227
2-year college
(205) 549-8310 X. 317 Contact: Riley Whitaker
Unspecified athletic aid available
M: baseball, basketball
W: basketball, softball

GEORGE C. WALLACE COMMUNITY COLLEGE
Route 6, Box 62
Dothan, AL 36303
2-year college
(205) 983-3521 X. 216 Contact: Mary Bubbett
Men's Aid (#/$): 51/$58,146
Women's Aid (#/$): 50/$53,240
M: baseball, basketball, golf
W: basketball, softball

HUNTINGDON COLLEGE
1500 East Fairview Avenue
Montgomery, AL 36106-2148
(205) 265-0511 Contact: Matt Clark
Men's Aid (#/$): 24/unspecified $
Women's Aid (#/$): 22/unspecified $
Restrictions and notes: Highest award level is for tuition only. All scholarships are partial.
M: baseball, golf, soccer, tennis
W: soccer, softball, tennis, volleyball

JACKSONVILLE STATE UNIVERSITY
Pelham Road
Jacksonville, AL 36265
(205) 782-5377 Contact: Mike Galloway
Men's Aid (#/$): 75/unspecified $
Women's Aid (#/$): 42/unspecified $
M: baseball, basketball, football, golf, riflery, tennis
W: basketball, softball, tennis, volleyball

JEFFERSON DAVIS JUNIOR COLLEGE
Alco Drive
Brewton, AL 36426
2-year college
(205) 867-4832 Contact: Dr. Virgil Warren
Unspecified athletic aid available

M: baseball, basketball, tennis
W: basketball, softball, tennis

JEFFERSON STATE JUNIOR COLLEGE
2601 Carson Road
Birmingham, AL 35215
2-year college
(205) 853-1200 Contact: Don Coleman
Unspecified athletic aid available
M: baseball, basketball, tennis
W: tennis

JOHN C. CALHOUN STATE COLLEGE
P.O. Box 2216
Decatur, AL 35609-2216
2-year college
(205) 353-3102 Contact: Mickey Sutton
Men's Aid (#/$): 38/$51,300
Women's Aid (#/$): 35/$47,250
M: baseball, basketball
W: basketball, softball

JUDSON COLLEGE
P.O. Box 120
Marion, AL 36756
(205) 683-6161 X. 837 Contact: Doris A. Wilson
Women's Aid (#/$): 16/$57,800
Restrictions and notes: Up to full tuition only, based on skills and academic qualifications.
W: basketball, golf, tennis

LIVINGSTON UNIVERSITY
LU Station 6
Livingston, AL 35470
(205) 652-9661 Contact: Mr. Dee Outlaw
Men's Aid (#/$): 60/$250,560
Women's Aid (#/$): 20/$83,520
M: baseball, basketball, football, tennis
W: basketball, softball, tennis, volleyball

MARION MILITARY INSTITUTE
Washington Street
Marion, AL 36756
2-year college
(205) 683-2359 Contact: Tommy Murfee
Unspecified athletic aid available
M: baseball, football, golf, tennis.
Men's Non-aid: riflery

MILES COLLEGE
5500 Myron Massey Boulevard
Birmingham, AL 35208
(205) 923-2771 Contact: Willie K. Patterson Jr.
Unspecified athletic aid available
M: baseball, basketball, cross country, track & field
W: basketball, cross country, track & field, volleyball

MOBILE COLLEGE
P.O. Box 13220
Mobile, AL 36663-0220
(205) 675-5990 Contact: Curt Berger
Unspecified athletic aid available
M: baseball, basketball, cross country, golf, soccer, tennis
W: baseball, crew, sailing, soccer, synchronized swimming

NORTHWEST ALABAMA STATE COMMUNITY COLLEGE
Route 3, Box 77
Phil Campbell, AL 35581
2-year college
(205) 993-5331 Contact: Charles Taylor
Unspecified athletic aid available
M: baseball, basketball
W: basketball, softball

SAMFORD UNIVERSITY
800 Lakeshore Drive
Birmingham, AL 35229
(205) 870-2966 Contact: Paul South
Unspecified athletic aid available
M: baseball, basketball, cross country, golf, indoor track, track & field, volleyball. Men's Non-aid: football
W: cross country skiing, gymnastics, indoor track, softball, track & field, volleyball

SELMA UNIVERSITY
1501 Lapsley Street
Selma, AL 36701

2-year college
(205) 872-9745 Contact: Homer Davis, Jr.
Unspecified athletic aid available
M: baseball, basketball, bowling
W: basketball

SNEAD STATE COMMUNITY COLLEGE
P.O. Drawer D
Boaz, AL 35957
2-year college
(205) 593-5120 Contact: David Wilson
Men's Aid (#/$): 55/$86,000
Women's Aid (#/$): 55/$86,000
Restrictions and notes: School also provides aid for their athletic management/trainer program.
M: baseball, basketball, cheerleading, golf, tennis
W: basketball, cheerleading, softball, tennis, volleyball. Women's Non-aid: cross country

SOUTHERN UNION STATE JUNIOR COLLEGE
Robert Street
Wadley, AL 36276
2-year college
(205) 395-2211 Contact: Joe Jordan
Unspecified athletic aid available
M: baseball, basketball
W: basketball

SPRING HILL COLLEGE
Office of Financial Aid
4000 Darphin Street
Mobile, AL 36608
(205) 460-2140 Contact: Betty Harlan
Men's Aid (#/$): 14/$58,096
Women's Aid (#/$): 9/$37,875
M: baseball, basketball, golf, softball, tennis
W: basketball, tennis

TALLADEGA COLLEGE
627 West Battle Street
Talladega, AL 35160
(205) 362-0206 Contact: Wylie N. Tucker
Men's Aid (#/$): 20/unspecified $
Women's Aid (#/$): 20/unspecified $
M: baseball, basketball, cross country, golf, indoor track, tennis, track & field
W: basketball, cross country, indoor track, tennis, track & field, volleyball

TROY STATE UNIVERSITY
Athletic Department
Davis Field House
Troy, AL 36082
(205) 670-3480 Contact: Tom Ensey
Unspecified athletic aid available
M: baseball, basketball, cheerleading, cross country, football, golf, indoor track, tennis, track & field
W: cheerleading, cross country, indoor track, softball, tennis, track & field, volleyball

TUSKEGEE UNIVERSITY
321 James Center
Tuskegee, AL 36088
(205) 727-8150 Contact: Arnold L. Houston
Men's Aid (#/$): 53/$82,000
Women's Aid (#/$): 4/$18,000
M: basketball, football. Men's Non-aid: baseball, cross country, indoor track, tennis, track & field
W: basketball. Women's Non-aid: cross country, indoor track, tennis, track & field, volleyball

UNIVERSITY OF ALABAMA (BIRMINGHAM)
115 UAB Arena
Birmingham, AL 35294-1160
(205) 934-0722 Contact: Grant Shingleton
Men's Aid (#/$): 14/$33,724
Women's Aid (#/$): 12/$35,166
M: baseball, basketball, cross country, golf, riflery, soccer, tennis, volleyball
W: basketball, cross country, golf, tennis, track & field, volleyball

UNIVERSITY OF ALABAMA (HUNTSVILLE)
205 Spragins Hall
Huntsville, AL 35899

(205) 895-6144 Contact: Julie Woltjen
Unspecified athletic aid available
M: basketball, crew, cross country, golf, ice hockey, soccer, tennis
W: basketball, crew, cross country, tennis, volleyball

UNIVERSITY OF ALABAMA (TUSCALOOSA)
P.O. Box 870391
Tuscaloosa, AL 35487-0391
(205) 348-6084 Contact: Larry White
Men's Aid (#/$): 54/$285,149
Women's Aid (#/$): 49/$190,778
M: baseball, basketball, cross country, football, golf, indoor track, swimming, swimming-diving, tennis, track & field
W: basketball, cross country, golf, gymnastics, indoor track, swimming, swimming-diving, tennis, track & field, volleyball

UNIVERSITY OF MONTEVALLO
Station 6229
Montevallo, AL 35115
(205) 665-6599 Contact: Ron Holsombeck
Men's Aid (#/$): 28/$149,576
Women's Aid (#/$): 24/$128,208
M: baseball, basketball, golf
W: basketball, volleyball. Women's Non-aid: cheerleading

UNIVERSITY OF NORTH ALABAMA
Box 5038
Florence, AL 35632-0001
(205) 760-4595 Contact: Ande Jones
Men's Aid (#/$): 68/$295,664
Women's Aid (#/$): 24/$104,352
M: baseball, basketball, cross country, football, golf, tennis
W: basketball, cross country, softball, tennis, volleyball

UNIVERSITY OF SOUTH ALABAMA
1107 HPELS Building
Mobile, AL 36688
(205) 460-7035 Contact: Fred Huff
Unspecified athletic aid available
M: baseball, basketball, cross country, golf, indoor track, soccer, tennis, track & field
W: basketball, cross country, golf, indoor track, tennis, track & field, volleyball

WALLACE COMMUNITY COLLEGE SELMA
P.O. Box 1049
Selma, AL 36702-1049
2-year college
(205) 875-2634 Contact: Roland Maxwell/Coach: Lothian Smallwood
Men's Aid (#/$): 45/$67,500
Women's Aid (#/$): 32/$48,000
M: baseball, basketball, cheerleading, tennis
W: cheerleading, softball, tennis

WALLACE STATE COMMUNITY COLLEGE
P.O. Box 2000
Hanceville, AL 35077-2000
2-year college
(205) 352-6403 Contact: Dr. James E. Van Horn
Unspecified athletic aid available
M: baseball, basketball, golf
W: basketball

Alaska

SHELDON JACKSON COLLEGE
801 Lincoln Street
Sitka, AK 99835
(907) 747-5241 Contact: Len Nardone
Men's Aid ($): $60,000
Women's Aid ($): $60,000
M: basketball
W: basketball

UNIVERSITY OF ALASKA
3211 Providence Drive
Anchorage, AK 99508
(907) 786-1230 Contact: Tim McDiffett

Men's Aid (#/$): 79/$346,722
Women's Aid (#/$): 46/$178,748
M: alpine skiing, basketball, cross country, cross country skiing, ice hockey, swimming, swimming-diving
W: alpine skiing, basketball, cross country skiing, gymnastics, volleyball

UNIVERSITY OF ALASKA (FAIRBANKS)
101 Patty Center
Fairbanks, AK 99775-0240
(907) 474-6812 Contact: Karen J. Morris
Men's Aid (#/$): 31/$237,212
Women's Aid (#/$): 20/$157,052
M: basketball, cross country, cross country skiing, ice hockey, riflery
W: basketball, cross country, cross country skiing, riflery, volleyball

UNIVERSITY OF ALASKA SOUTHEAST
11120 Glacier Highway
Juneau, AK 99801-8697
(907) 789-4463 Contact: Bruce Gifford
Unspecified athletic aid available
M: alpine skiing, basketball. Men's Non-aid: riflery
W: alpine skiing, basketball. Women's Non-aid: riflery

Arizona

ARIZONA STATE UNIVERSITY
ICA
First Floor
Tempe, AZ 85287-2505
(602) 965-6592 Contact: Mark Brand
Men's Aid (#/$): 79/$193,750
Women's Aid (#/$): 50/$106,250
M: archery, badminton, baseball, basketball, cross country, football, golf, gymnastics, indoor track, swimming, swimming-diving, tennis, track & field, wrestling
W: archery, badminton, basketball, cross country, diving, golf, gymnastics, indoor track, softball, swimming, swimming-diving, tennis, track & field, volleyball

CENTRAL ARIZONA COLLEGE
8470 North Overfield Road
Coolidge, AZ 85228
2-year college
(602) 426-4289 Contact: Gary Heintz
Unspecified athletic aid available
M: baseball, basketball, cross country, rodeo, track & field
W: basketball, rodeo, softball, volleyball

COCHISE COUNTY COMMUNITY COLLEGE
Highway 80 West
Douglas, AZ 85607
2-year college
(602) 364-0295 Contact: Charles Rodgers
Unspecified athletic aid available
M: baseball, basketball
W: basketball, volleyball

GLENDALE COMMUNITY COLLEGE
6000 West Olive Avenue
Glendale, AZ 85302
2-year college
(602) 435-3000 Contact: David Grant
Unspecified athletic aid available
M: archery, baseball, basketball, cross country, football, golf, soccer, tennis, track & field
W: archery, basketball, cross country, softball, tennis, track & field, volleyball

GRAND CANYON COLLEGE
3300 West Camelback
Phoenix, AZ 85017-1097
(602) 589-2529 Contact: Bob Beynon
Unspecified athletic aid available
M: baseball, basketball, golf, soccer, tennis
W: tennis, volleyball

MESA COMMUNITY COLLEGE
1833 West Southern Avenue
Mesa, AZ 85202
2-year college
(602) 461-7542 Contact: Gerald Smith
Unspecified athletic aid available
Men's Non-aid: baseball, basketball, cross country, golf, soccer, tennis, track & field
W: basketball, softball, tennis, volleyball. Women's Non-aid: cross country, track & field

NAVAJO COMMUNITY COLLEGE
Box 804
Tsailc, AZ 86556
2-year college
(602) 724-3311 Contact: Edward McCombs
Unspecified athletic aid available
M: archery, basketball, cross country, rodeo
W: archery, basketball, cross country, rodeo, volleyball

NORTHERN ARIZONA UNIVERSITY
Box 15400
Flagstaff, AZ 86001
(602) 523-6791 Contact: Wylie Smith
Unspecified athletic aid available
M: basketball, cross country, football, ice hockey, indoor track, swimming, tennis, track & field, wrestling
W: basketball, cross country, diving, indoor track, swimming, swimming-diving, tennis, track & field, volleyball

PHOENIX COLLEGE
1202 West Thomas Road
Phoenix, AZ 85013
2-year college
(602) 285-7197 Contact: Fred Moore
Men's Aid (#/$): 236/$23,600
Women's Aid (#/$): 142/$14,200
M: baseball, basketball, cross country, football, golf, soccer, tennis, track & field, wrestling
W: basketball, cross country, golf, softball, tennis, track & field, volleyball

PIMA COMMUNITY COLLEGE
2202 West Anklam Road
Tucson, AZ 85709
2-year college
(602) 884-6710 Contact: Mike Lopez
Unspecified athletic aid available
M: archery, baseball, basketball, cross country, golf, tennis, track & field, wrestling
W: archery, basketball, cross country, softball, tennis, track & field, volleyball

UNIVERSITY OF ARIZONA
229 McKale Center
Tucson, AZ 85721
(602) 621-4163 Contact: Orville (Butch) Henry III
Men's Aid (#/$): 31/$123,725
Women's Aid (#/$): 10/$49,520
M: baseball, basketball, cross country, football, golf, swimming-diving, tennis, track & field
W: basketball, cross country, golf, gymnastics, softball, swimming-diving, tennis, track & field, volleyball

YAVAPAI COLLEGE
1100 East Sheldon Street
Prescott, AZ 86301
2-year college
(602) 776-2235 Contact: Lynn Merritt
Unspecified athletic aid available
M: baseball
W: basketball, volleyball

Arkansas

ARKANSAS COLLEGE
2300 Highland Road
Batesville, AR 72501
(501) 698-4220 Contact: Kevin Jenkins
Men's Aid (#/$): 12/$120,000
Women's Aid (#/$): 12/$120,000
M: basketball. Men's Non-aid: baseball, cross country, golf, indoor track, tennis, track & field
W: basketball. Women's Non-aid: cross

country, golf, indoor track, tennis, track & field

ARKANSAS STATE UNIVERSITY
P.O. Box 1000
State University, AR 72467
(501) 972-3702 Contact: Neil Brooks
Men's Aid ($): $653,690
Women's Aid ($): $165,150
M: baseball, basketball, cross country, football, golf, indoor track, track & field
W: basketball, cross country, golf, indoor track, tennis, track & field, volleyball

ARKANSAS TECH UNIVERSITY
Tucker Coliseum
Russellville, AR 72801
(501) 968-0645 Contact: Larry G. Smith
Men's Aid (#/$): 45/$3,970
Women's Aid (#/$): 24/$3,970
Restrictions and notes: In-state, 1 year athletic aid only.
M: basketball, football. Men's Non-aid: baseball, golf, tennis
W: basketball, volleyball. Women's Non-aid: tennis

CENTRAL BAPTIST COLLEGE
1501 College Avenue
Conway, AR 72032
(501) 329-6872 Contact: Mark Hamby
Men's Aid (#/$): 15/$26,117
Women's Aid (#/$): 1/$1,000
M: basketball
W: basketball

GARLAND COUNTY COMMUNITY COLLEGE
One College Drive
Hot Springs, AR 71913
2-year college
(501) 767-9371 Contact: Susan Cathey
Men's Aid (#/$): 6/$6,000
Women's Aid (#/$): 6/$6,000
M: tennis
W: tennis

HARDING UNIVERSITY
P.O. Box 765
Searcy, AR 72143
(501) 279-4760 Contact: Bryan Phillips
Men's Aid (#/$): 45/$360,000
Women's Aid (#/$): 24/$192,000
M: basketball, football. Men's Non-aid: baseball, cross country, golf, indoor track, tennis, track & field
W: basketball, volleyball. Women's Non-aid: cross country, indoor track, tennis, track & field

HENDERSON STATE UNIVERSITY
Box 7518
Arkadelphia, AR 71923
(501) 246-5511 Contact: Steve Eddington
Men's Aid (#/$): 46/$42,400
Women's Aid (#/$): 25/$29,380
M: basketball, football. Men's Non-aid: baseball, cross country, diving, golf, indoor track, swimming, swimming-diving, tennis
W: basketball, volleyball. Women's Non-aid: cross country, equestrian, swimming, swimming-diving, tennis

JOHN BROWN UNIVERSITY
2000 University Street
Siloam Springs, AR 72761
(501) 524-3131 Contact: Tom Elgie
Unspecified athletic aid available
M: basketball, soccer, swimming, tennis
W: basketball, swimming, tennis, volleyball

NORTH ARKANSAS COMMUNITY COLLEGE
420 Pioneer Ridge
Harrison, AR 72601
2-year college
(501) 743-3000 Contact: Dorm Saylors
Unspecified athletic aid available
M: baseball, basketball
W: basketball, volleyball

OUACHITA BAPTIST UNIVERSITY
OBU Box 3761
Arkadelphia, AR 71923

(501) 246-4531 X. 208 Contact: Mac Sisson
Men's Aid (#/$): 45/$382,500
Women's Aid (#/$): 24/$204,000
M: basketball. Men's Non-aid: baseball, cross country, diving, golf, indoor track, swimming, swimming-diving, tennis, track & field
W: basketball, volleyball. Women's Non-aid: diving, swimming, swimming-diving, tennis

SCOTTSDALE COMMUNITY COLLEGE

9000 East Chaparral Road
Scottsdale, AR 85256-2699
2-year college
(602) 423-6629 Contact: John Kazanas
Unspecified athletic aid available
M: baseball, basketball, cross country, football, golf, soccer, tennis, track & field. Men's Non-aid: archery, bowling, fencing, racquetball
W: basketball, cross country, softball, tennis, track & field, volleyball. Women's Non-aid: archery, bowling, fencing, racquetball

SHORTER COLLEGE

604 Locust Street
North Little Rock, AR 72114
2-year college
(501) 374-6305
Unspecified athletic aid available
M: baseball, basketball, golf, tennis
W: basketball. Women's Non-aid: softball

SOUTHERN ARKANSAS UNIVERSITY

P.O. Box 1420
Magnolia, AR 71753
(501) 235-4104 Contact: Houston Taylor
Men's Aid (#/$): 15/$17,396
Women's Aid (#/$): 6/$9,603
M: basketball, football, rodeo. Men's Non-aid: baseball, cross country, golf, indoor track, tennis, track & field
W: basketball, rodeo, volleyball. Women's Non-aid: tennis

UNIVERSITY OF ARKANSAS (FAYETTEVILLE)

Broyles Athletics Complex
Fayetteville, AR 72701
(501) 575-2751 Contact: Rick Schaeffer
Unspecified athletic aid available
M: baseball, basketball, cross country, football, golf, indoor track, swimming, tennis, track & field
W: basketball, cross country, diving, indoor track, soccer, swimming, tennis, track & field

UNIVERSITY OF ARKANSAS (LITTLE ROCK)

2801 South University
Little Rock, AR 72204
(501) 569-3449 Contact: Will Hancock
Unspecified athletic aid available
M: baseball, basketball, diving, golf, soccer, swimming, tennis. Men's Non-aid: water polo
W: swimming, tennis, volleyball. Women's Non-aid: cross country

UNIVERSITY OF ARKANSAS (MONTICELLO)

UAM Box 3589
Monticello, AR 71655
(501) 460-1074 Contact: James Brewer
Men's Aid (#/$): 13/$22,860
Women's Aid (#/$): 13/$22,860
M: basketball, football. Men's Non-aid: baseball, cross country, golf, track & field
W: basketball. Women's Non-aid: cross country, golf, track & field

UNIVERSITY OF ARKANSAS (PINE BLUFF)

134 UAPB
Pine Bluff, AR 71601
(501) 541-6549 Contact: Carl Whimper
Men's Aid (#/$): 45/$160,000
Women's Aid (#/$): 18/$97,000
M: basketball, football. Men's Non-aid: cross country, golf, tennis, track & field

W: basketball, cross country, indoor track, track & field, volleyball

UNIVERSITY OF CENTRAL ARKANSAS
P.O. Box 5004
Conway, AR 72032
(501) 450-5743 Contact: Bob Valentine
Unspecified athletic aid available
M: basketball, football. Men's Non-aid: baseball, cross country, diving, golf, indoor track, swimming, tennis, track & field
W: basketball, volleyball. Women's Non-aid: cross country, diving, indoor track, swimming, tennis, track & field

UNIVERSITY OF THE OZARKS
415 College Avenue
Clarksville, AR 72830
(501) 754-3839 Contact: Sonja McCuen
Men's Aid (#/$): 12/$6,870
Women's Aid (#/$): 12/$6,870
M: basketball
W: basketball

WESTARK COMMUNITY COLLEGE
P.O. Box 3649
Fort Smith, AR 72913
2-year college
(501) 785-4241 Contact: Jim Wyatt
Men's Aid (#/$): 30/$38,000
Women's Aid (#/$): 12/$12,000
M: baseball, basketball
W: basketball

California

AZUSA PACIFIC UNIVERSITY
P.O. Box 7000
Azusa, CA 91702
(818) 812-3025 Contact: Nick Dawson
Unspecified athletic aid available
M: baseball, basketball, cross country, football, indoor track, soccer, track & field
W: basketball, cross country, indoor track, softball, track & field, volleyball

BARSTOW COLLEGE
2700 Barstow Road
Barstow, CA 92311
2-year college
(619) 252-2411 Contact: Ray Perea
Men's Non-aid: baseball, basketball, cheerleading, cross country, tennis
Women's Non-aid: cheerleading, softball, tennis, volleyball

BIOLA UNIVERSITY
13800 Biola Avenue
La Mirada, CA 90639
(310) 903-4889 Contact: John Baker
Unspecified athletic aid available
M: baseball, basketball, cross country, soccer, track & field
W: basketball, tennis, volleyball

BUTTE COLLEGE
3565 Butte Campus Drive
Oroville, CA 95265
2-year college
(916) 895-2521 Contact: Mike Liddell
Men's Non-aid: baseball, basketball, cross country, football, golf, tennis, track & field, wrestling
Women's Non-aid: basketball, cross country, softball, tennis, track & field, volleyball

CABRILLO COLLEGE
6500 Soquel Drive
Aptos, CA 95003
2-year college
(408) 479-6409 Contact: Dale Murray
Men's Non-aid: baseball, basketball, cross country, football, golf, soccer, swimming, swimming-diving, tennis, track & field, water polo
Women's Non-aid: basketball, cross country, softball, swimming, track & field, volleyball

CALIFORNIA BAPTIST COLLEGE
8432 Magnolia Avenue
Riverside, CA 92504

(714) 689-5771 Contact: Vandella McCombs
Unspecified athletic aid available
M: baseball, basketball, soccer
W: basketball, softball, volleyball

CALIFORNIA INSTITUTE OF TECHNOLOGY

1201 East California Boulevard
Pasadena, CA 91125
(818) 356-6146 Contact: Karen Nilsen
Men's Non-aid: baseball, basketball, cross country, fencing, golf, sailing, soccer, softball, swimming-diving, tennis, track & field, water polo, wrestling
Women's Non-aid: cross country, fencing, golf, sailing, soccer, swimming-diving, tennis, track & field, water polo

CALIFORNIA LUTHERAN UNIVERSITY

60 West Olsen Road
Thousand Oaks, CA 91360
(805) 493-3115 Contact: Betsy Kocher
Men's Aid (#/$): 36/$46,107
Women's Aid (#/$): 17/$30,203
M: baseball, basketball, cross country, football, golf, soccer, tennis, track & field
W: basketball, cross country, softball, tennis, track & field, volleyball

CALIFORNIA MARITIME ACADEMY

200 Maritime Academy Drive
Vallejo, CA 94590
(707) 648-4261 Contact: Harry Diavatis
Men's Non-aid: basketball, crew, sailing, soccer, volleyball, water polo

CALIFORNIA POLYTECHNIC STATE UNIVERSITY

1 Grand Avenue
Attn: Financial Aid
San Luis Obispo, CA 93407
(805) 756-2927 Contact: Diane Ryan
Aid (#/$): 428/$435,000 (M&W)
M: baseball, basketball, cross country, football, tennis, track & field, wrestling.
Men's Non-aid: soccer
W: basketball, cross country, gymnastics, softball, tennis, track & field, volleyball

CALIFORNIA STATE POLYTECHNIC UNIVERSITY

3801 West Temple Avenue
Pomona, CA 91768
(714) 869-3700 Contact: Al Aldino
Men's Aid (#/$): 63/$101,569
Women's Aid (#/$): 61/$125,548
M: baseball, basketball, cross country, soccer, tennis, track & field
W: basketball, cross country, soccer, softball, tennis, track & field, volleyball

CALIFORNIA STATE UNIVERSITY

801 West Monte Vista Avenue
Turlock, CA 95380
(209) 667-3168 Contact: Will Keener
Men's Non-aid: baseball, basketball, cross country, golf, soccer, track & field
Women's Non-aid: basketball, cross country, softball, track & field, volleyball

CALIFORNIA STATE UNIVERSITY (CHICO)

Financial Aid Office
Chico, CA 95929-0705
(916) 898-6451 Contact: David G. Cook
Men's Non-aid: baseball, basketball, cross country, football, soccer, swimming-diving, track & field, wrestling
Women's Non-aid: basketball, cross country, field hockey, gymnastics, soccer, softball, swimming-diving, track & field, volleyball

CALIFORNIA STATE UNIVERSITY (DOMINGUEZ HILLS)

1000 East Victoria
Carson, CA 90747-0005
(213) 516-3764 Contact: Kevin Gilmore
Men's Aid (#/$): 36/unspecified $
Women's Aid (#/$): 39/unspecified $
M: baseball, basketball, golf, soccer

W: basketball, soccer, softball, volleyball

CALIFORNIA STATE UNIVERSITY (FRESNO)
Fresno, CA 93740-0064
(209) 278-2182 Contact: Joseph Heuston
Unspecified athletic aid available
M: baseball, basketball, cross country, football, golf, indoor track, soccer, swimming, tennis, track & field, water polo, wrestling
W: basketball, cross country, indoor track, softball, swimming, tennis, track & field, volleyball

CALIFORNIA STATE UNIVERSITY (FULLERTON)
800 North State College Boulevard
Fullerton, CA 92634-9480
(714) 773-3057 Contact: Christine McCarthy
Men's Aid (#/$): 115/$360,000
Women's Aid (#/$): 80/$215,000
M: baseball, basketball, cross country, football, soccer, track & field, wrestling. Men's Non-aid: cheerleading, fencing
W: basketball, cross country, gymnastics, softball, tennis, track & field, volleyball. Women's Non-aid: cheerleading, fencing

CALIFORNIA STATE UNIVERSITY (HAYWARD)
Athletic Department
Hayward, CA 94542-3062
(510) 881-3528 Contact: Marty Valdez
Men's Non-aid: baseball, basketball, cross country, diving, football, soccer, swimming, swimming-diving, tennis, track & field
Women's Non-aid: basketball, cross country, diving, soccer, softball, swimming, swimming-diving, tennis, track & field, volleyball

CALIFORNIA STATE UNIVERSITY (LONG BEACH)
1250 Bellflower Boulevard
Long Beach, CA 90840
(310) 985-8403 Contact: Dr. Gloria Kapp
Unspecified athletic aid available
M: baseball, basketball, football, golf, swimming, swimming-diving, tennis, volleyball, water polo. Men's Non-aid: archery, badminton, cross country, fencing, rugby
W: basketball, golf, gymnastics, softball, swimming, swimming-diving, tennis, volleyball. Women's Non-aid: archery, badminton, cross country, fencing, soccer

CALIFORNIA STATE UNIVERSITY (LOS ANGELES)
5151 State University Drive
Los Angeles, CA 90032-8240
(213) 343-3198 Contact: John Czimbal
Unspecified athletic aid available
M: baseball, basketball, cross country, diving, soccer, swimming, swimming-diving, tennis, track & field, volleyball
W: basketball, cross country, diving, swimming, swimming-diving, tennis, track & field, volleyball

CALIFORNIA STATE UNIVERSITY (NORTHRIDGE)
18111 Nordhoff Street
Northridge, CA 91330
(818) 885-3243 Contact: Barry Smith
Men's Aid (#/$): 55/$377,855
Women's Aid (#/$): 28/$189,264
M: baseball, basketball, football, golf, soccer, swimming-diving, track & field, volleyball
W: basketball, softball, swimming-diving, tennis, track & field, volleyball

CALIFORNIA STATE UNIVERSITY (SACRAMENTO)
600 J Street
Sacramento, CA 95819-6073
(916) 278-6896 Contact: Jeff Minahan
Unspecified athletic aid available
M: basketball, football. Men's Non-aid: baseball, cross country, diving, golf, soccer, swimming, swimming-diving, track & field
W: basketball, softball, volleyball.

Women's Non-aid: cross country, diving, golf, gymnastics, swimming, swimming-diving, track & field

CALIFORNIA STATE UNIVERSITY (SAN BERNARDINO)

5500 University Parkway
San Bernardino, CA 92407
(714) 880-5012 Contact: Dave Beyer
Men's Non-aid: baseball, basketball, cross country, golf, soccer, tennis
Women's Non-aid: basketball, cross country, softball, tennis, volleyball

CALIFORNIA STATE UNIVERSITY AT BAKERSFIELD

9001 Stockdale Highway
Bakersfield, CA 93311
(805) 664-3071 Contact: Joni Jones
Men's Aid (#/$): 105/$271,800
Women's Aid (#/$): 66/$109,500
M: basketball, soccer, swimming, swimming-diving, track & field, wrestling
W: softball, tennis, track & field, volleyball

CERRITOS COLLEGE

11110 East Alondra Boulevard
Norwalk, CA 90650
2-year college
(310) 860-2451 X. 705 Contact: John Van Gaston
Men's Non-aid: baseball, basketball, cross country, football, golf, soccer, swimming, swimming-diving, tennis, track & field, water polo, wrestling
Women's Non-aid: cross country, softball, swimming, swimming-diving, tennis, track & field, volleyball

CHAFFEY COLLEGE

5885 Haven Avenue
Rancho Cucamonga, CA 91701-3002
2-year college
(714) 387-3702 Contact: James Bryant
Men's Non-aid: baseball, basketball, diving, football, golf, swimming, swimming-diving, track & field, water polo
Women's Non-aid: diving, golf, softball, swimming, swimming-diving, tennis, track & field, volleyball

CHAPMAN UNIVERSITY

333 North Glassell
Orange, CA 92666
(714) 997-6900 Contact: Derek Anderson
Men's Non-aid: baseball, basketball, cross country, soccer, tennis, water polo
Women's Non-aid: basketball, soccer, softball, volleyball

CITY COLLEGE OF SAN FRANCISCO

50 Phelan Avenue
San Francisco, CA 94112
2-year college
(415) 239-3412 Contact: Ernest Domecus
Men's Non-aid: baseball, basketball, crew, cross country, football, soccer, swimming-diving, tennis, track & field, volleyball
Women's Non-aid: baseball, basketball, crew, cross country, swimming-diving, tennis, track & field, volleyball

COLLEGE OF NOTRE DAME

1500 Ralston Avenue
Belmont, CA 94002
(415) 508-3590 Contact: Virginia Babel
Men's Non-aid: basketball, cross country, soccer, tennis, track & field
Women's Non-aid: basketball, cross country, softball, tennis, track & field, volleyball

COLLEGE OF THE DESERT

43-500 Monterey Avenue
Palm Desert, CA 92260
2-year college
(619) 773-2581 Contact: John Marman
Restrictions and notes: State champions in tennis and golf.
Men's Non-aid: baseball, basketball, cross country, football, golf, soccer, tennis, track & field
Women's Non-aid: basketball, cross

country, softball, tennis, track & field, volleyball

COLLEGE OF THE REDWOODS
7351 Tompkins Hill Road
Eureka, CA 95501-9302
2-year college
(707) 445-6926 Contact: Don Terbush
Men's Non-aid: baseball, basketball, cross country, football, golf, track & field
Women's Non-aid: basketball, cross country, softball, track & field, volleyball

COMPTON COMMUNITY COLLEGE
1111 East Artesia Boulevard
Compton, CA 90221
2-year college
(310) 637-2660 Contact: William Thomas
Men's Non-aid: baseball, basketball, cross country, football, track & field
Women's Non-aid: basketball, cross country, track & field

CONTRA COSTA COLLEGE
2600 Mission Bell Drive
San Pablo, CA 94806
2-year college
(510) 235-7800 X. 310 Contact: Phil Clifton
Men's Non-aid: baseball, basketball, cross country, football, tennis, track & field
Women's Non-aid: basketball, tennis, track & field

COSUMMES RIVER COLLEGE
8401 Center Parkway
Sacramento, CA 95823
2-year college
(916) 688-7261 Contact: Marlin Davies
Men's Non-aid: baseball, basketball, cross country, soccer, tennis, track & field
Women's Non-aid: cross country, softball, tennis, track & field, volleyball

CUESTA COLLEGE
P.O. Box 8106
San Luis Obispo, CA 93403-8106
2-year college
(805) 546-3211 Contact: Mike Robles
Men's Non-aid: baseball, basketball, cross country, golf, swimming-diving, tennis, track & field, water polo, wrestling
Women's Non-aid: basketball, cross country, softball, swimming-diving, tennis, track & field, volleyball

DE ANZA COMMUNITY COLLEGE
21250 Stevens Creek Boulevard
Cupertino, CA 95014
2-year college
(408) 864-8751 Contact: Bob Mazzuca
Men's Non-aid: baseball, basketball, cross country, diving, football, golf, soccer, swimming, tennis, track & field, water polo
Women's Non-aid: basketball, cross country, diving, swimming, synchronized swimming, tennis, track & field

DIABLO VALLEY COMMUNITY COLLEGE
321 Golf Club Road
Pleasant Hill, CA 94523
2-year college
(510) 685-1230 Contact: Mike Maramonte
Men's Non-aid: baseball, basketball, cross country, diving, football, swimming, tennis, track & field, water polo, wrestling
Women's Non-aid: cross country, diving, softball, swimming, track & field, volleyball

DOMINICAN COLLEGE
50 Acacia Avenue
San Rafael, CA 94901-8008
(415) 485-3230 Contact: Bill Fusco
Men's Aid (#/$): 15/$50,825
Women's Aid (#/$): 20/$52,535
Restrictions and notes: Partial athletic scholarships available.

M: basketball, cross country, tennis.
Men's Non-aid: fencing
W: archery, tennis, volleyball.
Women's Non-aid: fencing

EAST LOS ANGELES COMMUNITY COLLEGE
1301 Brooklyn Avenue
Monterey Park, CA 91754
2-year college
(213) 265-8713 Contact: Gil Rozadilla
Men's Non-aid: baseball, basketball
Women's Non-aid: basketball, cross country, track & field, volleyball

EL CAMINO COLLEGE
16007 Crenshaw Boulevard
Torrance, CA 90506
2-year college
(310) 715-3548 Contact: Mary Ann Keating
Men's Non-aid: baseball, basketball, cross country, diving, football, golf, soccer, swimming, swimming-diving, tennis, track & field, volleyball, water polo
Women's Non-aid: basketball, cross country, diving, soccer, softball, swimming, swimming-diving, tennis, track & field, volleyball

FOOTHILL COLLEGE
12345 El Monte Road
Los Altos Hills, CA 94022
2-year college
(415) 949-7222 Contact: Bill Abbey
Men's Non-aid: baseball, basketball, cross country, golf, soccer, tennis, track & field
Women's Non-aid: basketball, cross country, softball, tennis, track & field, volleyball

FRESNO CITY COLLEGE
1101 East University Avenue
Fresno, CA 93741
2-year college
(209) 442-8229 Contact: Woody Wilk
Men's Non-aid: baseball, basketball, cross country, football, golf, soccer, tennis, track & field, wrestling
Women's Non-aid: basketball, cross country, soccer, softball, tennis, track & field, volleyball

FRESNO PACIFIC COLLEGE
1717 South Chestnut Avenue
Fresno, CA 93702
(209) 453-2009 Contact: Bruce Watts
Men's Aid (#/$): 21.75/$178,350
Women's Aid (#/$): 16/$131,200
Restrictions and notes: Tuition scholarships—not inclusive of room & board.
M: basketball, cross country, indoor track, soccer, track & field
W: basketball, cross country, indoor track, track & field, volleyball

FULLERTON COLLEGE
321 East Chapman Avenue
Fullerton, CA 92634
2-year college
(714) 992-7391 Contact: Ken Hill
Men's Non-aid: baseball, basketball, cross country, football, golf, soccer, swimming, swimming-diving, tennis, track & field, water polo
Women's Non-aid: basketball, cross country, softball, swimming, swimming-diving, tennis, track & field, volleyball

GLENDALE COMMUNITY COLLEGE
1500 North Verdugo Road
Glendale, CA 91208
2-year college
(818) 240-1000 Contact: Merry Shelburne
Men's Non-aid: baseball, basketball, cross country, football, soccer, tennis, track & field
Women's Non-aid: basketball, cross country, tennis, track & field

GOLDEN WEST COLLEGE
15744 Golden West Street
Huntington Beach, CA 92647-0592

2-year college
(714) 895-8344 Contact: Eric Maddy
Unspecified athletic aid available
M: baseball, basketball, cross country, football, golf, soccer, swimming, swimming-diving, tennis, track & field, volleyball, water polo, wrestling
W: basketball, cross country, soccer, softball, swimming, swimming-diving, tennis, track & field, volleyball

HUMBOLDT STATE UNIVERSITY
Arcata, CA 95521
(707) 826-3631 Contact: Tom Trepiak
Men's Non-aid: basketball, cross country, football, soccer, track & field, wrestling
Women's Non-aid: basketball, cross country, swimming, tennis, track & field, volleyball

LONG BEACH CITY COLLEGE
4901 East Carson Street
Long Beach, CA 90808
2-year college
(310) 420-4243 Contact: Miles Logan Beam
Men's Non-aid: baseball, basketball, cross country, football, golf, soccer, swimming, tennis, track & field, volleyball, water polo
Women's Non-aid: basketball, cross country, soccer, softball, swimming, swimming-diving, tennis, track & field, volleyball

LOS ANGELES PIERCE JUNIOR COLLEGE
6201 Winnetka Avenue
Woodland Hills, CA 91371
2-year college
(818) 719-6421 Contact: Bob O'Connor
Men's Non-aid: baseball, basketball, cross country, football, golf, soccer, swimming-diving, tennis, track & field, volleyball, water polo, wrestling
Women's Non-aid: basketball, cross country, gymnastics, softball, swimming-diving, tennis, track & field, volleyball

LOS ANGELES VALLEY COLLEGE
5800 Fulton Avenue
Van Nuys, CA 91401
2-year college
(818) 781-1200 X. 210 Contact: Mark Buryoynoni
Men's Non-aid: baseball, basketball, cross country, football, swimming, track & field, water polo
Women's Non-aid: cross country, softball, swimming, track & field

LOS MEDANOS COLLEGE
2700 East Leland Road
Pittsburg, CA 94565
2-year college
(510) 439-2181 Contact: Shirley Baskin
Men's Non-aid: baseball, basketball, football, soccer
Women's Non-aid: basketball, softball

LOYOLA MARYMOUNT UNIVERSITY
Loyola Boulevard and West 80th Street
Los Angeles, CA 90045
(310) 338-2765 Contact: Bruce Meyers
Men's Aid (#/$): 30.5/$555,100
Women's Aid (#/$): 23/$418,600
M: baseball, basketball, volleyball.
Men's Non-aid: crew, cross country, golf, soccer, tennis, water polo
W: basketball, tennis, volleyball.
Women's Non-aid: crew, cross country, soccer, softball, swimming

MARYMOUNT COLLEGE
30800 Palos Verdes Drive East
Rancho Palos Verdes, CA 90274-6299
2-year college
(310) 377-5501 X.352 Contact: Jim Masterson
Men's Non-aid: soccer, tennis
Women's Non-aid: soccer, tennis

MASTER'S COLLEGE
21726 West Placerita Canyon
Santa Clarita, CA 91321
(805) 259-3540 Contact: Chris Harrison
Men's Aid (#/$): 9/$38,630

Women's Aid (#/$): 3/$6,000
M: baseball, basketball, soccer. Men's Non-aid: cross country
W: basketball, soccer, volleyball. Women's Non-aid: cross country

MIRACOSTA COLLEGE
One Barnard Drive
Oceanside, CA 92056
2-year college
(619) 757-2121 Contact: Clete Adelman
Men's Non-aid: basketball, tennis
Women's Non-aid: cross country, track & field

MODESTO JUNIOR COLLEGE
College Avenue
Modesto, CA 95350
2-year college
(209) 575-6399 Contact: Doug Hodge
Men's Non-aid: baseball, basketball, cross country, football, golf, soccer, swimming-diving, tennis, track & field, water polo, wrestling
Women's Non-aid: basketball, cross country, soccer, softball, swimming-diving, tennis, track & field, volleyball

MOORPARK COLLEGE
7075 Campus Road
Moorpark, CA 93021
2-year college
(805) 378-1410 Contact: Aaron Gold
Men's Non-aid: alpine skiing, badminton, baseball, basketball, bowling, cross country, equestrian, field hockey, football, golf, soccer, softball, tennis, track & field, volleyball, weightlifting, wrestling
Women's Non-aid: alpine skiing, badminton, baseball, basketball, bowling, cross country, equestrian, field hockey, golf, soccer, softball, tennis, track & field, volleyball, weightlifting, wrestling

MT. SAN ANTONIO COLLEGE
1100 North Grand Avenue
Walnut, CA 91789
2-year college
(714) 594-5611 X. 4630 Contact: Micol Coppock
Men's Non-aid: baseball, basketball, cross country, diving, football, golf, soccer, swimming, swimming-diving, tennis, track & field, volleyball, water polo, wrestling
Women's Non-aid: basketball, cross country, soccer, softball, swimming, swimming-diving, synchronized swimming, track & field, volleyball

OCCIDENTAL COLLEGE
1600 Campus Road
Los Angeles, CA 90041
(213) 259-2699 Contact: Jim Kerman
Men's Non-aid: baseball, basketball, cross country, diving, football, golf, soccer, swimming, swimming-diving, tennis, track & field, water polo
Women's Non-aid: basketball, cross country, diving, soccer, swimming, swimming-diving, tennis, track & field, volleyball

ORANGE COAST COLLEGE
2701 Fairview Road
Costa Mesa, CA 92628-0120
2-year college
(714) 432-5175 Contact: Jack Shinar
Men's Non-aid: baseball, basketball, crew, cross country, diving, football, golf, sailing, soccer, swimming, swimming-diving, tennis, track & field, volleyball, water polo
Women's Non-aid: basketball, crew, cross country, diving, football, golf, sailing, soccer, softball, swimming, swimming-diving, tennis, track & field, volleyball

OXNARD COLLEGE
4000 South Rose Avenue
Oxnard, CA 93033
2-year college
(805) 986-5825 Contact: Office of Public Information
Men's Non-aid: baseball, basketball, cross country, soccer, track & field

Women's Non-aid: basketball, cross country, track & field, volleyball

PADUCAH COMMUNITY COLLEGE
Alben Barkley Drive
Paducah, CA 42001
2-year college
(502) 554-9200 Contact: Tony McClure
Unspecified athletic aid available
M: baseball, basketball, golf, tennis
W: basketball, softball, tennis

PALOMAR COLLEGE
1140 West Mission Road
San Marcos, CA 92069
2-year college
(619) 744-1150 Contact: John Strey
Men's Non-aid: baseball, basketball, diving, football, golf, soccer, swimming, swimming-diving, tennis, water polo, wrestling
Women's Non-aid: basketball, diving, soccer, softball, swimming, swimming-diving, tennis, volleyball

PEPPERDINE UNIVERSITY
24255 Pacific Coast Highway
Malibu, CA 90263
(310) 456-4333 Contact: Michael Zapolski
Men's Aid (#/$): 47/$987,000
Women's Aid (#/$): 37/$729,000
Restrictions and notes: Women's soccer with scholarship available Fall 1993. Full grant: $21,000, Tuition Grant: $15,000
M: baseball, basketball, golf, tennis, volleyball, water polo. Men's Non-aid: cross country
W: basketball, golf, soccer, swimming, tennis, volleyball. Women's Non-aid: cross country

POINT LOMA NAZARENE COLLEGE
3900 Lomaland Drive
San Diego, CA 92106
(619) 221-2411 Contact: Dan Van Ommen
Unspecified athletic aid available
M: baseball, basketball, cross country, golf, soccer, tennis, track & field
W: basketball, cross country, tennis, track & field

POMONA-PITZER COLLEGES
220 East 6th Street
Claremont, CA 91711
(714) 621-8119 Contact: Kirk Reynolds
Men's Non-aid: baseball, basketball, cross country, diving, football, golf, soccer, swimming, swimming-diving, tennis, track & field, water polo
Women's Non-aid: basketball, cross country, diving, soccer, softball, swimming, swimming-diving, tennis, track & field, volleyball, water polo

RANETTO SANTIAGO COLLEGE
17th & Bristol Street
Santa Ana, CA 92706
2-year college
(714) 564-6475 Contact: Dave Ruite
Men's Non-aid: baseball, basketball, cross country, diving, football, golf, soccer, swimming, swimming-diving, tennis, track & field, water polo, wrestling
Women's Non-aid: basketball, cross country, diving, softball, swimming, swimming-diving, tennis, track & field, volleyball

RIVERSIDE COLLEGE
4800 Magnolia Avenue
Riverside, CA 92506
2-year college
(714) 684-3240 Contact: Robert Schmidt
Men's Non-aid: baseball, basketball, cross country, football, golf, swimming-diving, tennis, track & field, water polo
Women's Non-aid: basketball, cross country, softball, swimming-diving, tennis, track & field, water polo

SADDLEBACK COLLEGE
28000 Marguerite Parkway
Mission Viejo, CA 92692
2-year college

(714) 582-4530 Contact: Jerry Hannula
Men's Non-aid: baseball, basketball, cross country, diving, football, golf, swimming, swimming-diving, tennis, track & field, water polo
Women's Non-aid: basketball, cross country, diving, softball, swimming, swimming-diving, tennis, track & field, volleyball

SAINT MARY'S COLLEGE OF CALIFORNIA
P.O. Box 5100
Moraga, CA 94575
(415) 631-4402 Contact: Claude Hagopian
Men's Aid ($): $800,000
Women's Aid ($): $700,000
M: baseball, basketball, cross country, football, golf, soccer, tennis. Men's Non-aid: crew, lacrosse, rugby
W: basketball, cross country, soccer, softball, tennis, volleyball. Women's Non-aid: crew, lacrosse

SAN BERNARDINO COMMUNITY COLLEGE
701 South Mt. Vernon Avenue
San Bernardino, CA 92410
2-year college
(714) 888-6511 X. 1370 Contact: Willie Ellison
Men's Non-aid: baseball, basketball, cross country, football, golf, swimming, tennis, track & field, volleyball, wrestling
Women's Non-aid: basketball, cross country, softball, swimming, tennis, track & field, volleyball

SAN DIEGO CITY COLLEGE
1313 12th Avenue
San Diego, CA 92101
2-year college
(619) 230-2486 Contact: Dave Evans
Men's Non-aid: baseball, basketball, cross country, football, golf, soccer, tennis, track & field, volleyball, wrestling
Women's Non-aid: basketball, cross country, golf, softball, tennis, track & field, volleyball

SAN DIEGO MESA COLLEGE
7250 Mesa College Drive
San Diego, CA 92111
2-year college
(619) 627-2600 Contact: Dr. Judy Stamm
Men's Non-aid: badminton, baseball, basketball, bowling, cross country, diving, fencing, football, golf, gymnastics, racquetball, soccer, softball, swimming, swimming-diving, tennis, track & field, volleyball, water polo
Women's Non-aid: badminton, baseball, basketball, bowling, cross country, diving, fencing, football, golf, gymnastics, racquetball, soccer, softball, swimming, swimming-diving, tennis, track & field, volleyball, water polo

SAN DIEGO STATE UNIVERSITY
San Diego, CA 92182
(619) 594-5163 Contact: John Rosenthal
Unspecified athletic aid available
M: baseball, basketball, football, soccer, tennis, volleyball. Men's Non-aid: cross country
W: basketball, soccer, softball, tennis, track & field, volleyball. Women's Non-aid: cross country

SAN FRANCISCO STATE UNIVERSITY
1600 Holloway Avenue
San Francisco, CA 94132
(415) 338-1579 Contact: Kyle McRae
Men's Non-aid: baseball, basketball, cross country, football, soccer, swimming, track & field, wrestling
Women's Non-aid: basketball, cross country, soccer, softball, swimming, track & field, volleyball

SAN JOAQUIN DELTA COLLEGE
5151 Pacific Avenue
Stockton, CA 95207-6370

2-year college
(209) 474-5176 Contact: Ernie Marcopulos
Men's Non-aid: baseball, basketball, cross country, football, golf, soccer, swimming, tennis, track & field, water polo, wrestling
Women's Non-aid: basketball, cross country, softball, swimming, tennis, track & field, volleyball

SAN JOSE STATE UNIVERSITY
1 Washington Square
San Jose, CA 95192
(408) 924-1217 Contact: Lawrence Fan
Men's Aid (#/$): 24/$50,250
Women's Aid (#/$): 13/$24,750
M: baseball, basketball, cross country, football, golf, gymnastics, soccer, tennis, track & field, wrestling
W: basketball, field hockey, golf, gymnastics, softball, swimming, tennis, volleyball

SANTA BARBARA CITY COLLEGE
721 Cliff Drive
Santa Barbara, CA 93109-2394
2-year college
(805) 965-0581 Contact: Jim Williams
Men's Non-aid: baseball, basketball, cross country, football, golf, soccer, tennis, track & field, volleyball
Women's Non-aid: basketball, cross country, soccer, tennis, track & field, volleyball

SANTA CLARA UNIVERSITY
Toso Pavilion
Santa Clara, CA 95053
(408) 554-4661 Contact: Jim Young
Men's Aid (#/$): 59.66/$907,884
Women's Aid (#/$): 37.50/$502,755
M: baseball, basketball, football, soccer. Men's Non-aid: crew, cross country, golf, tennis, water polo
W: basketball, soccer, volleyball. Women's Non-aid: crew, cross country, golf, softball, tennis

SANTA MONICA COLLEGE
1900 Pico Boulevard
Santa Monica, CA 90405
2-year college
(310) 452-9310 Contact: John Secia
Men's Non-aid: baseball, basketball, cross country, football, soccer, swimming, tennis, track & field, volleyball, water polo
Women's Non-aid: baseball, basketball, cross country, softball, swimming, tennis, track & field, volleyball

SANTA ROSA JUNIOR COLLEGE
1501 Mendocino Avenue
Santa Rosa, CA 95401
2-year college
(707) 527-4237 Contact: Arlene Greenamyre
Men's Non-aid: baseball, basketball, cross country, football, golf, soccer, swimming, tennis, track & field, water polo, wrestling
Women's Non-aid: basketball, cross country, soccer, softball, swimming, tennis, track & field, volleyball

COLLEGE OF THE SEQUOIAS
915 South Mooney Boulevard
Visalia, CA 93277
2-year college
(209) 730-3911 Contact: Harry Kargenian
Men's Non-aid: baseball, basketball, cross country, diving, football, golf, swimming, swimming-diving, tennis, track & field, water polo
Women's Non-aid: basketball, cross country, diving, softball, swimming, swimming-diving, tennis, track & field, volleyball

SIERRA COLLEGE
5000 Rocklin Road
Rocklin, CA 95677
2-year college
(916) 781-0455 Contact: Nancy Ackley
Men's Non-aid: alpine skiing, baseball, basketball, cross country, cross country skiing, diving, football, golf, swimming, swimming-diving, tennis, water polo, wrestling
Women's Non-aid: alpine skiing, basketball, cross country, cross country

skiing, diving, golf, softball, swimming, swimming-diving, tennis, volleyball

SIMPSON COLLEGE
Redding, CA 96003
(916) 222-6360 Contact: Chris Kinnier
Men's Non-aid: baseball, basketball, cross country, football, golf, indoor track, tennis, track & field, wrestling
Women's Non-aid: basketball, cross country, golf, indoor track, softball, tennis, track & field, volleyball

SKYLINE COLLEGE
3300 College Drive
San Bruno, CA 94066
2-year college
(415) 738-4271 Contact: Samuel Goldman
Men's Non-aid: baseball, basketball, cross country, soccer, track & field, wrestling
Women's Non-aid: cross country, softball, track & field, volleyball

SOLANO COMMUNITY COLLEGE
4000 Suisun Valley Road
Suisun City, CA 94585
2-year college
(707) 864-7126 Contact: Bob Myers
Men's Non-aid: baseball, football, softball, swimming, track & field
Women's Non-aid: softball, swimming-diving, track & field, volleyball

SOUTHERN CALIFORNIA COLLEGE
55 Fair Drive
Costa Mesa, CA 92626
(714) 556-3610 X. 361 Contact: Matthew J. Fogelsong
Unspecified athletic aid available
M: baseball, basketball, cross country, soccer
W: basketball, cross country, softball, volleyball

SOUTHWESTERN COLLEGE
900 Otay Lakes Road
Chula Vista, CA 92010
2-year college
(619) 421-0595 Contact: Bob Mears
Men's Non-aid: baseball, basketball, football, soccer, track & field
Women's Non-aid: basketball, softball, tennis, track & field, volleyball

STANFORD UNIVERSITY
Sports Information Office
Stanford, CA 94305
(415) 723-4418 Contact: Bob Vazquez
Men's Aid (#/$): 192/unspecified $
Women's Aid (#/$): 74/unspecified $
M: baseball, basketball, football, golf, gymnastics, soccer, swimming-diving, tennis, track & field, volleyball, water polo. Men's Non-aid: crew, fencing, sailing, wrestling
W: basketball, golf, gymnastics, soccer, swimming-diving, tennis, track & field, volleyball. Women's Non-aid: crew, fencing, field hockey, sailing, softball

TAFT COLLEGE
P.O. Box 1437
Taft, CA 93268
2-year college
(805) 763-4282 Contact: Dennis McCall
Unspecified athletic aid available
Restrictions and notes: "Our financial aid package is considered one of the best in the state among community colleges and overall fees are among the lowest."
M: baseball, cross country, football, golf, track & field
W: cross country, softball, track & field, volleyball

UNIVERSITY OF CALIFORNIA (BERKELEY)
210 Memorial Stadium
Berkeley, CA 94720
(510) 642-5363 Contact: Kevin Reneau
Unspecified athletic aid available
M: baseball, basketball, cross country, football, gymnastics, soccer, swimming-diving, tennis, track & field, water polo. Men's Non-aid: crew, golf, rugby
W: basketball, cross country, diving, field hockey, gymnastics, soccer,

softball, swimming, tennis, track & field, volleyball. Women's Non-aid: crew

UNIVERSITY OF CALIFORNIA (DAVIS)
116 A Street
Davis, CA 95616
(916) 752-3505 Contact: Jim Doan
Men's Non-aid: baseball, basketball, cross country, football, golf, soccer, swimming-diving, tennis, track & field, water polo, wrestling
Women's Non-aid: basketball, cross country, gymnastics, soccer, softball, swimming-diving, tennis, track & field, volleyball

UNIVERSITY OF CALIFORNIA (IRVINE)
Crawford Hall
Irvine, CA 92717
(714) 856-5814 Contact: Bob Olson
Men's Aid (#/$): 107/$359,256
Women's Aid (#/$): 50/$169,252
M: basketball, diving, soccer, swimming-diving, tennis, water polo. Men's Non-aid: crew, cross country, golf, sailing, track & field, volleyball
W: basketball, cross country, diving, soccer, swimming-diving, tennis, track & field, volleyball. Women's Non-aid: crew, sailing

UNIVERSITY OF CALIFORNIA (RIVERSIDE)
Riverside, CA 92521
(714) 787-5438 Contact: Tom Phillips
Unspecified athletic aid available
M: baseball, basketball, tennis, track & field. Men's Non-aid: cross country, diving, swimming, swimming-diving, volleyball, water polo
W: basketball, softball, volleyball. Women's Non-aid: cross country, diving, swimming, swimming-diving, tennis, track & field, water polo

UNIVERSITY OF CALIFORNIA (SAN DIEGO)
Intercollegiate Athletics 0905
9500 Gilman Drive
La Jolla, CA 92093-0905
(619) 534-4211 Contact: Bill Gannon
Men's Non-aid: baseball, basketball, crew, cross country, diving, fencing, golf, rugby, sailing, soccer, swimming, swimming-diving, tennis, track & field, volleyball, water polo
Women's Non-aid: basketball, crew, diving, fencing, golf, sailing, soccer, softball, swimming, swimming-diving, tennis, track & field, volleyball, water polo

UNIVERSITY OF CALIFORNIA (SANTA BARBARA)
Robertson Gym, 302 B
Santa Barbara, CA 93106
(805) 893-3428 Contact: Bill Mahoney
Men's Aid (#/$): 46/$408,782
Women's Aid (#/$): 43/$370,282
M: baseball, basketball, diving, golf, gymnastics, soccer, swimming, swimming-diving, tennis, track & field, volleyball, water polo. Men's Non-aid: cross country
W: basketball, gymnastics, soccer, softball, swimming, swimming-diving, tennis, track & field. Women's Non-aid: cross country, diving

UNIVERSITY OF CALIFORNIA (SANTA CRUZ)
1156 High Street
Santa Cruz, CA 95064
(408) 459-3362 Contact: Cheryl Jones
Men's Non-aid: basketball, cross country, sailing, soccer, tennis, volleyball
Women's Non-aid: basketball, cross country, sailing, tennis, volleyball

UNIVERSITY OF CALIFORNIA (UCLA)
405 Hilgard Avenue
Morgan Center
Los Angeles, CA 90024
(310) 206-6831 Contact: Marc Dellins
Men's Aid (#/$): 175/$2,159,117
Women's Aid (#/$): 85/$913,300
M: baseball, basketball, cross country, diving, football, golf, gymnastics,

soccer, swimming, swimming-diving, tennis, track & field, volleyball. Men's Non-aid: water polo
W: basketball, cross country, diving, golf, gymnastics, softball, swimming, swimming-diving, tennis, track & field, volleyball

UNIVERSITY OF LA VERNE
1950 Third Street
La Verne, CA 91750
(714) 593-3511 X. 4261 Contact: Pam Maunakea
Men's Non-aid: baseball, basketball, cross country, football, golf, soccer, tennis, track & field, volleyball, wrestling
Women's Non-aid: basketball, cross country, softball, tennis, track & field, volleyball

UNIVERSITY OF REDLANDS
1200 East Colton Avenue
Redlands, CA 92373-0999
(909) 793-2121 X. 4004 Contact: Chuck Sadowski
Men's Non-aid: baseball, basketball, crew, football, golf, soccer, swimming, tennis, track & field, water polo
Women's Non-aid: baseball, basketball, crew, soccer, softball, swimming, tennis, track & field, volleyball

UNIVERSITY OF SAN DIEGO
Alcala Park
San Diego, CA 92110
(619) 260-4803 Contact: Ted Gosen
Men's Aid (#/$): 16/$118,055
Women's Aid (#/$): 6/$82,480
M: baseball, basketball, tennis. Men's Non-aid: crew, cross country, football, golf, soccer
W: basketball, swimming, tennis, volleyball. Women's Non-aid: crew, cross country, softball

UNIVERSITY OF SAN FRANCISCO
2130 Fulton Street
San Francisco, CA 94117-1080
(415) 666-6161 Contact: Peter H. Simon
Men's Aid (#/$): 35.75/$654,000
Women's Aid (#/$): 27.25/$498,000
M: baseball, basketball, golf, soccer, tennis. Men's Non-aid: cross country, riflery
W: basketball, golf, soccer, tennis, volleyball. Women's Non-aid: cross country, riflery

UNIVERSITY OF SOUTHERN CALIFORNIA
University Park
Los Angeles, CA 90089-0601
(213) 740-8480 Contact: Tim Tessalone
Men's Aid (#/$): 150/$3,000,000
Women's Aid (#/$): 50/$1,000,000
M: baseball, basketball, cross country, diving, football, golf, indoor track, swimming, tennis, track & field, volleyball, water polo. Men's Non-aid: crew, sailing
W: basketball, cross country, diving, golf, indoor track, swimming, tennis, track & field, volleyball. Women's Non-aid: crew, sailing

UNIVERSITY OF THE PACIFIC
3601 Pacific Avenue
Stockton, CA 95211
(209) 946-2479 Contact: Kevin Messenger
Unspecified athletic aid available
M: baseball, basketball, football, golf, swimming, tennis, water polo. Men's Non-aid: crew, lacrosse, rugby, soccer
W: basketball, field hockey, softball, swimming, tennis, volleyball. Women's Non-aid: crew, cross country

VENTURA COLLEGE
4667 Telegraph Road
Ventura, CA 93003
2-year college
(805) 644-6462 Contact: Karen McKean
Men's Non-aid: baseball, basketball, cross country, football, golf, swimming, tennis, track & field, water polo
Women's Non-aid: basketball, cross country, gymnastics, softball, swimming, tennis, track & field, volleyball

WESTMONT COLLEGE
955 La Paz Road
Santa Barbara, CA 93108
(805) 565-6010 Contact: John Kirkgard
Unspecified athletic aid available
M: baseball, basketball, cross country, soccer, tennis, track & field
W: cross country, soccer, tennis, track & field, volleyball

WHITTIER COLLEGE
13406 Philadelphia Street
Whittier, CA 90608
(310) 907-4271 Contact: Rock Carter
Men's Non-aid: baseball, basketball, cross country, diving, football, golf, lacrosse, soccer, swimming, swimming-diving, tennis, track & field, water polo
Women's Non-aid: basketball, cross country, diving, soccer, softball, swimming, swimming-diving, tennis, track & field, volleyball, water polo

YUBA COMMUNITY COLLEGE
2088 North Beale Road
Marysville, CA 95901
2-year college
(916) 741-6779 Contact: Joe McCarron
Men's Non-aid: baseball, basketball, football, tennis, track & field
Women's Non-aid: softball, tennis, track & field, volleyball

Colorado

ADAMS STATE COLLEGE
Box B
Richardson Hall
Alamosa, CO 81102
(719) 589-7121 Contact: Lloyd Engen
Men's Aid (#/$): 40/$32,400
Women's Aid (#/$): 25/$29,200
M: basketball, cross country, football, indoor track, track & field, wrestling.
Men's Non-aid: golf
W: basketball, cross country, gymnastics, indoor track, softball, track & field, volleyball

COLORADO CHRISTIAN UNIVERSITY
180 South Garrison
Lakewood, CO 80226
(303) 238-5386 Contact: Judy Vaughn
Unspecified athletic aid available
M: basketball, soccer
W: basketball, volleyball

COLORADO COLLEGE
14 East Cache La Poudre
Colorado Springs, CO 80903
(719) 389-6755 Contact: Dave Moross
Men's Aid (#/$): 18/$340,200
Women's Aid (#/$): 10/$189,000
M: ice hockey. Men's Non-aid: baseball, basketball, cross country, football, golf, indoor track, lacrosse, soccer, swimming, swimming-diving, tennis, track & field
W: soccer. Women's Non-aid: basketball, cross country, indoor track, swimming, swimming-diving, tennis, track & field, volleyball

COLORADO NORTHWESTERN COMMUNITY COLLEGE
500 Kennedy Drive
Rangely, CO 81648
2-year college
(303) 675-2261 Contact: Ron Hill
Unspecified athletic aid available
M: baseball, basketball, wrestling
W: basketball, softball, volleyball

COLORADO SCHOOL OF MINES
1500 Illinois Street
Golden, CO 80401
(303) 273-3300 Contact: Steve Smith
Men's Aid (#/$): 40/$100,000
Women's Aid (#/$): 15/$38,000
M: baseball, basketball, cross country, diving, football, golf, indoor track, lacrosse, soccer, swimming, swimming-diving, tennis, track & field, wrestling.
Men's Non-aid: alpine skiing, bowling, cross country skiing
W: baseball, basketball, cross country, diving, football, golf, indoor track, softball, swimming, swimming-diving, tennis, track & field, volleyball.

Women's Non-aid: alpine skiing, bowling, cross country skiing

COLORADO STATE UNIVERSITY
214-D Moby Arena
Fort Collins, CO 80523
(303) 491-5067 Contact: Gary Ozzello
Unspecified athletic aid available
M: basketball, cross country, football, golf, tennis, track & field
W: basketball, cross country, diving, golf, swimming, swimming-diving, tennis, track & field, volleyball

FORT LEWIS COLLEGE
1000 Rim Drive
Durango, CO 81301-3999
(303) 247-7441 Contact: Chris Aaland
Men's Aid (#/$): 85/$82,500
Women's Aid (#/$): 32/$43,000
M: basketball, cross country, football, golf, soccer, wrestling
W: basketball, cross country, softball, volleyball. Women's Non-aid: alpine skiing

LAMAR COMMUNITY COLLEGE
2401 South Main
Lamar, CO 81052-3999
2-year college
(303) 336-2248 Contact: David Leenhouts
Unspecified athletic aid available
M: baseball, basketball
W: basketball

MESA STATE COLLEGE
1175 Texas Avenue
Grand Junction, CO 81502
(303) 248-1396 Contact: Phillip W. Swille
Men's Aid (#/$): 73/$104,536
Women's Aid (#/$): 27/$38,664
M: baseball, basketball, football, tennis, wrestling
W: cross country, cross country skiing, softball, tennis, volleyball

METROPOLITAN STATE COLLEGE
P.O. Box 173362
Denver, CO 80227-3362
(303) 556-3431 Contact: Greg Smith
Unspecified athletic aid available
M: baseball, basketball, soccer, swimming, tennis
W: basketball, soccer, softball, swimming, tennis, volleyball

NORTHEASTERN JUNIOR COLLEGE
100 College Drive
Sterling, CO 80751
2-year college
(303) 522-6600 X. 605 Contact: Keith Bowers
Unspecified athletic aid available
M: basketball, cross country, indoor track, riflery, tennis, track & field
W: basketball, cross country, indoor track, riflery, softball, tennis, track & field, volleyball

OTERO JUNIOR COLLEGE
1802 Colorado Avenue
La Junta, CO 81050
2-year college
(719) 384-6831 Contact: Dr. Joe M. Treece
Unspecified athletic aid available
M: baseball, basketball, rodeo
W: basketball, rodeo, volleyball

REGIS UNIVERSITY
3333 Regis Boulevard
Denver, CO 80221-1099
(303) 458-4070 Contact: Mike Grose
Men's Aid (#/$): 20/unspecified $
Women's Aid (#/$): 20/unspecified $
M: baseball, basketball, golf, soccer, tennis
W: basketball, soccer, softball, tennis, volleyball

TRINIDAD STATE JUNIOR COLLEGE
600 Prospect Street
Trinidad, CO 81082
2-year college
(719) 846-5510 Contact: Jim Toupal
Unspecified athletic aid available
M: baseball, basketball, golf
W: golf, volleyball

UNIVERSITY OF COLORADO
Campus Box 357
Boulder, CO 80309
(303) 492-5626 Contact: David Plati
Men's Aid (#/$): 174/$1,327,937
Women's Aid (#/$): 66/$567,046
M: alpine skiing, basketball, cross country, cross country skiing, football, golf, indoor track, tennis, track & field
W: alpine skiing, basketball, cross country, cross country skiing, indoor track, tennis, track & field, volleyball

UNIVERSITY OF COLORADO (COLORADO SPRINGS)
Colorado Springs, CO 80933
(719) 593-3460 Contact: Lee Ingalls
Men's Aid (#/$): 30/$27,492
Women's Aid (#/$): 34/$34,556
Restrictions and notes: Part of aid from a state merit award. Transfer students must have at least 2.5 GPA to qualify for athletic aid.
M: basketball, golf, soccer, tennis
W: basketball, softball, tennis, volleyball

UNIVERSITY OF DENVER
2201 East Asbury
Denver, CO 80208
(303) 871-3399 Contact: Rita Campbell
Men's Aid (#/$): 30/$228,000
Women's Aid (#/$): 30/$152,000
M: alpine skiing, baseball, basketball, ice hockey, soccer, swimming, tennis.
Men's Non-aid: golf, lacrosse
W: alpine skiing, basketball, gymnastics, soccer, swimming, tennis, volleyball

UNIVERSITY OF NORTHERN COLORADO
Butler-Hancock Hall
Greeley, CO 80639
(303) 351-2534 Contact: Sue Jacobson
Men's Aid (#/$): 61.75/$416,091
Women's Aid (#/$): 28/$183,478
M: baseball, basketball, football, indoor track, tennis, track & field, wrestling
W: basketball, indoor track, soccer, swimming-diving, tennis, track & field, volleyball

UNIVERSITY OF SOUTHERN COLORADO
2200 North Bonforte Boulevard
Pueblo, CO 81001
(719) 549-2753 Contact: Gina Mestas
Unspecified athletic aid available
M: basketball, cross country, golf, indoor track, soccer, tennis, track & field, wrestling
W: basketball, cross country, indoor track, tennis, track & field, volleyball

WESTERN STATE COLLEGE
Gunnison, CO 81231
(303) 943-3035 Contact: J.W. Campbell
Unspecified athletic aid available
M: alpine skiing, basketball, cross country, cross country skiing, football, golf, track & field, wrestling
W: alpine skiing, basketball, cross country, cross country skiing, swimming-diving, track & field, volleyball

Connecticut

CENTRAL CONNECTICUT STATE UNIVERSITY
1615 Stanley Street
New Britain, CT 06050
(203) 827-7636/7824 Contact: Brent Rutkowski
Unspecified athletic aid available
M: baseball, basketball, cross country, diving, football, golf, indoor track, soccer, swimming, swimming-diving, tennis, track & field, wrestling
W: basketball, cross country, diving, indoor track, softball, swimming, swimming-diving, tennis, track & field, volleyball

CONNECTICUT COLLEGE
113 Fanning Hall
Mohegan Avenue

New London, CT 06514
(203) 439-2501 Contact: Becker House
Men's Non-aid: basketball, crew, cross country, ice hockey, lacrosse, sailing, soccer, tennis, track & field
Women's Non-aid: basketball, crew, cross country, field hockey, gymnastics, lacrosse, sailing, soccer, swimming, tennis, track & field, volleyball

EASTERN CONNECTICUT STATE UNIVERSITY
83 Windham Street
Willimantic, CT 06226-2295
(203) 456-5483 Contact: Robert Molta
Men's Non-aid: baseball, basketball, cross country, soccer, track & field
Women's Non-aid: baseball, basketball, cross country, soccer, softball, track & field, volleyball

FAIRFIELD UNIVERSITY
North Benson Road
Fairfield, CT 06430
(203) 254-4116 Contact: Victor D'Ascenzo
Men's Aid ($): $349,569
Women's Aid ($): $322,679
M: baseball, basketball, lacrosse, soccer. Men's Non-aid: alpine skiing, crew, cross country, diving, fencing, golf, ice hockey, rugby, sailing, swimming, swimming-diving, tennis
W: basketball, soccer, softball, volleyball. Women's Non-aid: alpine skiing, crew, cross country, diving, fencing, field hockey, lacrosse, sailing, swimming, swimming-diving, tennis

MANCHESTER COMMUNITY TECHNICAL COLLEGE
60 Bidwell Street
Manchester, CT 06040
2-year college
(203) 646-6059 Contact: J. Pat Mistretta
Men's Non-aid: baseball, basketball, soccer
Women's Non-aid: basketball, softball

MITCHELL COLLEGE
437 Pequot Avenue
New London, CT 06320
2-year college
(203) 443-2811 Contact: Dan Mara
Men's Aid (#/$): 30/$110,000
Women's Aid (#/$): 30/$110,000
M: baseball, basketball, field hockey, soccer, tennis. Men's Non-aid: golf, sailing
W: soccer, softball, volleyball.
Women's Non-aid: golf, sailing

QUINNIPIAC COLLEGE
New Road
Hamden, CT 06518
(203) 281-8625 Contact: Bill Chaves
Unspecified athletic aid available
M: baseball, basketball, cross country, golf, ice hockey, lacrosse, soccer, tennis
W: basketball, cheerleading, cross country, soccer, softball, tennis, volleyball

SACRED HEART UNIVERSITY
5151 Park Avenue
Fairfield, CT 06432-1000
(203) 371-7970 Contact: Don Harrison
Unspecified athletic aid available
M: baseball, basketball, soccer, volleyball. Men's Non-aid: cross country
W: softball, volleyball. Women's Non-aid: cross country

SOUTHERN CONNECTICUT STATE UNIVERSITY
501 Crescent Street
New Haven, CT 06515
(203) 397-4225 Contact: Rick Leddy
Men's Non-aid: baseball, basketball, cross country, football, golf, gymnastics, soccer, softball, swimming-diving, tennis, track & field, wrestling
Women's Non-aid: badminton, baseball, cross country, field hockey, gymnastics, softball, swimming-diving, tennis, track & field, volleyball

TEIKYO POST UNIVERSITY
Waterbury, CT 06723
(203) 755-0121 Contact: Claire Dwyer
Men's Aid (#/$): 28/$112,005

Women's Aid (#/$): 24/$92,113
M: baseball, basketball, equestrian, soccer, softball
W: baseball, basketball, equestrian, soccer, softball

TRINITY COLLEGE
79 Vernon Street
Hartford, CT 06106
(203) 297-2137 Contact: Christopher Brown
Men's Non-aid: baseball, crew, cross country, fencing, football, golf, ice hockey, indoor track, lacrosse, rugby, soccer, squash, swimming, swimming-diving, tennis, track & field, water polo, wrestling
Women's Non-aid: crew, cross country, fencing, field hockey, indoor track, lacrosse, rugby, soccer, softball, squash, swimming, swimming-diving, tennis, track & field, volleyball, water polo

UNIVERSITY OF BRIDGEPORT
120 Waldemere Avenue
Bridgeport, CT 06601
(203) 576-4918 Contact: Scott Rice
Men's Aid (#/$): 10/$127,404
Women's Aid (#/$): 9/$55,471
M: basketball, soccer. Men's Non-aid: baseball, golf, tennis, volleyball
W: basketball, gymnastics, softball. Women's Non-aid: soccer, tennis, volleyball

UNIVERSITY OF CONNECTICUT
U-78, 2111 Hillside Road
Storrs, CT 06269-3078
(203) 486-3531 Contact: Tim Tolokan
Unspecified athletic aid available
M: baseball, basketball, cross country, diving, football, golf, ice hockey, indoor track, soccer, swimming-diving, tennis, track & field
W: basketball, cross country, field hockey, gymnastics, indoor track, soccer, softball, swimming-diving, tennis, track & field, volleyball

UNIVERSITY OF HARTFORD
200 Bloomfield Avenue
West Hartford, CT 06117
(203) 243-4620 Contact: James R. Keener, Jr.
Men's Aid (#/$): 16/$191,000
Women's Aid (#/$): 16/$191,000
M: baseball, basketball, cross country, golf, lacrosse, soccer, tennis, track & field
W: basketball, cross country, golf, soccer, softball, tennis, track & field, volleyball

UNIVERSITY OF NEW HAVEN
300 Orange Avenue
West Haven, CT 06516
(203) 932-7025 Contact: Jack Jones
Unspecified athletic aid available
M: baseball, basketball, cross country, football, indoor track, soccer, track & field. Men's Non-aid: lacrosse
W: basketball, softball, tennis, volleyball

WESLEYAN UNIVERSITY
161 Cross Street
Freeman Athletic Center
Middletown, CT 06457
(203) 347-9411 Contact: Brian Katten
Men's Non-aid: baseball, basketball, crew, cross country, football, golf, ice hockey, indoor track, lacrosse, soccer, squash, swimming, tennis, track & field, wrestling
Women's Non-aid: basketball, crew, cross country, field hockey, ice hockey, indoor track, lacrosse, soccer, softball, squash, swimming, tennis, track & field, volleyball

WESTERN CONNECTICUT STATE UNIVERSITY
181 White Street
Danbury, CT 06810
(203) 797-2777 Contact: Scott Ames
Men's Non-aid: baseball, basketball, fencing, football, golf, soccer, tennis
Women's Non-aid: basketball, fencing, field hockey, softball, tennis, volleyball

YALE UNIVERSITY
Undergraduate Financial Aid Office
143 Elm Street
New Haven, CT 06520
(203) 432-0360 Contact: Jim Tilton
Men's Non-aid: baseball, basketball, crew, cross country, diving, fencing, football, golf, ice hockey, indoor track, lacrosse, soccer, squash, swimming, swimming-diving, tennis, track & field, water polo, wrestling
Women's Non-aid: basketball, crew, cross country, diving, fencing, field hockey, football, golf, gymnastics, ice hockey, indoor track, lacrosse, soccer, softball, squash, swimming, swimming-diving, tennis, track & field, volleyball

Delaware

DELAWARE STATE COLLEGE
1200 North Dupont Highway
Dover, DE 19901
(302) 739-4926 Contact: Matt Santo
Unspecified athletic aid available
M: basketball, cross country, football, indoor track, track & field, wrestling. Men's Non-aid: tennis
W: basketball, cross country, indoor track, track & field. Women's Non aid: tennis

GOLDEY-BEACOM COLLEGE
4701 Limestone Road
Wilmington, DE 19808
(302) 998-8814 Contact: Neal Isaac
Men's Aid (#/$): 14/$15,000
Women's Aid (#/$): 14/$15,000
M: soccer
W: softball

UNIVERSITY OF DELAWARE
Bob Carpenter Center
Newark, DE 19716-2010
(302) 831-2186 Contact: Scott Selheimer
Unspecified athletic aid available
M: baseball, basketball, football, lacrosse, soccer. Men's Non-aid: cross country, golf, indoor track, swimming-diving, tennis, track & field
W: basketball, field hockey, lacrosse, soccer, softball, volleyball. Women's Non-aid: cross country, indoor track, swimming-diving, tennis, track & field

WESLEY COLLEGE
P.O. Box B-4
Dover, DE 19901
(302) 736-2354 Contact: Richard Biscayart
Men's non-aid: baseball, basketball, cheerleading, football, golf, lacrosse, soccer, tennis
Women's non-aid: basketball, cheerleading, softball, tennis

WILMINGTON COLLEGE
320 DuPont Highway
New Castle, DE 19720
(302) 328-9401 Contact: Craig Wolfe
Men's Non-aid: baseball, basketball, cross country, football, golf, soccer, tennis, track & field, wrestling
Women's Non-aid: basketball, soccer, softball, track & field, volleyball

District of Columbia

THE AMERICAN UNIVERSITY
4400 Massachusetts Avenue NW
Washington, DC 20016
(202) 885-3032 Contact: Joan Von Thron
Unspecified athletic aid available
M: baseball, basketball, cross country, golf, soccer, swimming-diving, wrestling. Men's Non-aid: tennis
W: basketball, cross country, field hockey, swimming-diving, tennis, volleyball

CATHOLIC UNIVERSITY OF AMERICA
620 Michigan Avenue NE
Washington, DC 20064

(202) 319-5000 Contact: Gabe Romano
Men's Non-aid: baseball, basketball, cross country, football, golf, lacrosse, soccer, tennis, track & field
Women's Non-aid: basketball, cross country, field hockey, softball, tennis, track & field, volleyball

GEORGE WASHINGTON UNIVERSITY
600 22nd Street, NW
Washington, DC 20052
(202) 994-8604 Contact: Betsy Barrett
Men's Aid (#/$): 104/$1,800,000
Women's Aid (#/$): 104/$1,800,000
M: baseball, basketball, crew, cross country, diving, golf, soccer, swimming, tennis, water polo
W: basketball, crew, cross country, diving, gymnastics, soccer, swimming, tennis, volleyball

GEORGETOWN UNIVERSITY
37th and "O" Streets
Washington, DC 20057
(202) 687-2435 Contact: Joe Lang
Men's Aid (#/$): 30/$690,000
Women's Aid (#/$): 30/$690,000
M: basketball, cross country, golf, indoor track, lacrosse, sailing, track & field
W: basketball, cross country, indoor track, sailing, tennis, track & field, volleyball

HOWARD UNIVERSITY
511 Gresham Place
Drew Hall
Washington, DC 20059
(202) 806-7182/7184 Contact: Edward Hill, Jr.
Unspecified athletic aid available
M: baseball, basketball, football, soccer, swimming, tennis, track & field, wrestling
W: basketball, swimming, tennis, track & field, volleyball

UNIVERSITY OF THE DISTRICT OF COLUMBIA
4200 Connecticut Avenue NW
Washington, DC 20008
(202) 282-3174 Contact: Angela M. Mason
Unspecified athletic aid available
M: basketball, cross country, football, soccer, tennis, track & field
W: basketball, cheerleading, cross country, tennis, track & field, volleyball

Florida

BARRY UNIVERSITY
11300 Second Avenue NE
Miami Shores, FL 33161
(305) 899-3553 Contact: Mike Bunting
Unspecified athletic aid available
M: baseball, basketball, cross country, golf, soccer, tennis
W: cross country, soccer, softball, tennis

BETHUNE-COOKMAN COLLEGE
640 Second Avenue
Daytona Beach, FL 32015
(904) 255-1401 X. 303 Contact: Joseph Coleman
Men's Aid (#/$): 18/$107,902
Women's Aid (#/$): 4/$22,954
M: baseball, basketball, football. Men's Non-aid: cross country, golf, indoor track, tennis, track & field
W: basketball. Women's Non-aid: cross country, golf, indoor track, softball, tennis, track & field

BREVARD COLLEGE
1519 Clearlake Road
Cocoa, FL 32922
2-year college
(407) 632-1161 X. 3750 Contact: Angie Powers
Unspecified athletic aid available
M: baseball, basketball, cross country, indoor track, soccer, swimming, track & field
W: basketball, cross country, indoor track, soccer, softball, swimming, track & field, volleyball

BROWARD COMMUNITY COLLEGE
3501 Davie Road
Ft. Lauderdale, FL 33314
2-year college
(305) 475-6523 Contact: Tom Ryan
Men's Aid (#/$): 70/$62,909
Women's Aid (#/$): 48/$43,401
M: baseball, basketball, diving, golf. Men's Non-aid: bowling, racquetball, sailing, softball, swimming, swimming-diving, tennis, volleyball, weightlifting
W: baseball, basketball, diving, golf. Women's Non-aid: bowling, racquetball, sailing, softball, swimming, swimming-diving, tennis, volleyball, weightlifting

CENTRAL FLORIDA COMMUNITY COLLEGE
P.O. Box 1388
Ocala, FL 34478
2-year college
(904) 237-2111 Contact: Mike McGinnis
Men's Aid (#/$): 33/unspecified $
Women's Aid (#/$): 27/unspecified $
M: baseball, basketball
W: basketball, softball

CHIPOLA JUNIOR COLLEGE
College Street
Mariannna, FL 32446
2-year college
(904) 526-2761 Contact: Milton H. Johnson
Unspecified athletic aid available
M: baseball, basketball
W: basketball

DAYTONA BEACH COMMUNITY COLLEGE
P.O. Box 1111
Daytona Beach, FL 32015
2-year college
(904) 255-8131 X. 3302 Contact: Thomas Schlageter
Men's Aid (#/$): 12/$59,800
Women's Aid (#/$): 18/$53,200
M: basketball
W: softball

ECKERD COLLEGE
P.O. Box 12560
St. Petersburg, FL 33733-2560
(813) 864-8251 Contact: Bill Thornton
Men's Aid (#/$): 39/$150,000
Women's Aid (#/$): 16/$80,000
Athletic programs not specified.

EDISON COMMUNITY COLLEGE
8099 College Parkway
Fort Myers, FL 33907
2-year college
(813) 489-9277 Contact: Hilary Allen
Unspecified athletic aid available
M: basketball. Men's Non-aid: baseball, golf
W: basketball, softball, volleyball

EDWARD WATERS COLLEGE
1658 Kings Road
Jacksonville, FL 32209
(904) 355-3030 X. 214 Contact: Lorenzo Woodward
Unspecified athletic aid available
M: baseball, basketball, cross country, indoor track, track & field
W: basketball, cross country, indoor track, softball, track & field

FLAGLER COLLEGE
King Street
St. Augustine, FL 32084
(904) 829-6481 X. 225 Contact: Reuben D. Sitton
Men's Aid (#/$): 18/$137,520
Women's Aid (#/$): 10/$78,310
M: baseball, basketball, cross country, golf, soccer, tennis
W: basketball, cross country, tennis, volleyball

FLORIDA A & M UNIVERSITY
P.O. Box 982, FAMU
Tallahassee, FL 32307
(904) 599-3200 Contact: Alvin Hollins
Unspecified athletic aid available
M: baseball, basketball, cross country, football, indoor track, swimming, tennis, track & field. Men's Non-aid: golf

W: basketball, cross country, indoor track, softball, swimming, tennis, track & field, volleyball

FLORIDA ATLANTIC UNIVERSITY

500 NW 20th Street
Boca Raton, FL 33431-0991
(407) 367-3163 Contact: Katrina McCormick
Unspecified athletic aid available
M: baseball, cross country, fencing, golf, soccer, tennis
W: basketball, cross country, fencing, swimming-diving, tennis

FLORIDA COLLEGE

119 Glen Arven Avenue
Temple Terrace, FL 33617-5578
2-year college
(813) 988-5131 Contact: Dr. Daniel W. Petty
Men's Aid (#/$): 11/$70,098
M: baseball, basketball, golf
Women's Non-aid: cross country

FLORIDA INSTITUTE OF TECHNOLOGY

Country Club Road
Melbourne, FL 32901
(407) 768-8000 X. 8070 Contact: Leonard E. Gude
Unspecified athletic aid available
M: baseball, basketball, cheerleading, crew, cross country, tennis
W: basketball, cheerleading, cross country, softball, volleyball

FLORIDA INTERNATIONAL UNIVERSITY

Athletic Department
Golden Panther Arena
University Park Campus
Miami, FL 33199
(305) 348-2756 Contact: Stuart Davidson
Unspecified athletic aid available
M: baseball, basketball, cross country, golf, soccer, tennis
W: basketball, cross country, golf, soccer, tennis. Women's Non-aid: volleyball

FLORIDA MEMORIAL COLLEGE

15800 N.W. 42nd Avenue
Miami, FL 33054
(305) 626-3690 Contact: Alfred Parker
Unspecified athletic aid available
M: baseball, basketball, cross country, indoor track, track & field. Men's Non-aid: tennis
W: basketball, cross country, indoor track, softball, track & field, tennis

FLORIDA SOUTHERN COLLEGE

111 Lake Hollingsworth Drive
Lakeland, FL 33801-5698
(813) 644-1480 Contact: Joe Labat
Men's Aid (#/$): 158/$1,403,522
Women's Aid (#/$): 82/$860,079
M: baseball, basketball, cross country, football, golf, indoor track, swimming-diving, tennis, track & field
W: basketball, cross country, golf, indoor track, softball, swimming-diving, tennis, track & field, volleyball

FLORIDA STATE UNIVERSITY

P.O. Drawer 2195
Tallahassee, FL 32316
(904) 644-1402 Contact: Wayne Hogan
Unspecified athletic aid available
M: baseball, basketball, cross country, diving, football, golf, swimming, swimming-diving, tennis, track & field. Men's Non-aid: indoor track, rugby, soccer, water skiing
W: basketball, cross country, diving, golf, swimming, swimming-diving, tennis, track & field, volleyball. Women's Non-aid: handball, indoor track, rugby, soccer, synchronized swimming, water skiing

GULF COAST COMMUNITY COLLEGE

5230 West Highway 98
Panama City, FL 32401
2-year college
(904) 872-3831 Contact: William Frazier
Unspecified athletic aid available
M: baseball, basketball
W: softball

HILLSBOROUGH COMMUNITY COLLEGE
P.O. Box 30030
Tampa, FL 33630
2-year college
(813) 253-7446 Contact: Joe Patton
Men's Aid (#/$): 36/$30,510
Women's Aid (#/$): 44/$37,290
M: baseball, basketball
W: basketball, softball, tennis, volleyball

INDIAN RIVER COMMUNITY COLLEGE
3209 Virginia Avenue
Fort Pierce, FL 34981-5599
2-year college
(407) 462-4772 Contact: Bob Bottger
Unspecified athletic aid available
M: baseball, basketball, golf, swimming-diving, tennis
W: basketball, swimming-diving, tennis, volleyball

JACKSONVILLE UNIVERSITY
2800 University Boulevard North
Jacksonville, FL 32211
(904) 744-3950 X. 3402 Contact: Gary Izzo
Unspecified athletic aid available
M: baseball, basketball, crew, cross country, golf, riflery, soccer, tennis. Men's Non-aid: crew
W: crew, cross country, golf, riflery, soccer, tennis, volleyball. Women's Non-aid: crew

LAKE-SUMTER COMMUNITY COLLEGE
5900 Highway 441 South
Leesburg, FL 32788
2-year college
(904) 787-3747 Contact: Jon Scarbrough
Unspecified athletic aid available
M: basketball, golf
W: golf, volleyball

LYNN UNIVERSITY
3601 North Military Trail
Boca Raton, FL 33431
(407) 994-0770 Contact: Jim Blankenship
Men's Aid (#/$): 53/$465,819
Women's Aid (#/$): 25/$197,870
M: baseball, golf, soccer, tennis
W: golf, soccer, tennis

MIAMI-DADE COMMUNITY COLLEGE NORTH
11380 NW 27th Avenue
Miami, FL 33167
2-year college
(305) 237-1362 Contact: Jay Rokeach
Men's Aid (#/$): 38/$50,000
Women's Aid (#/$): 38/$50,000
M: baseball, basketball, tennis. Men's Non-aid: fencing, gymnastics, martial arts
W: basketball, softball, tennis. Women's Non-aid: fencing, gymnastics, martial arts

MIAMI-DADE COMMUNITY COLLEGE SOUTH
11011 SW 104 Street
Miami, FL 33176
2-year college
(305) 347-2309 Contact: James Carrig
Unspecified athletic aid available
M: baseball, basketball, diving, soccer, swimming, tennis, track & field
W: basketball, diving, softball, swimming, tennis, volleyball

MIAMI-DADE JUNIOR COLLEGE
300 NE Second Avenue
Miami, FL 33132
2-year college
(305) 347-3083 Contact: Al Schlazer
Unspecified athletic aid available
M: baseball, tennis
W: tennis, volleyball

NORTH FLORIDA JUNIOR COLLEGE
1000 Turner Davis Drive
Madison, Fl 32340
2-year college
(904) 973-2288 Contact: Clyde Alexander

Men's Aid (#/$): 25/unspecified $
Women's Aid (#/$): 12/unspecified $
M: baseball, basketball
W: basketball

NOVA UNIVERSITY
Fort Lauderdale, FL 33314
(305) 475-7067 Contact: Geri Castora
Men's Aid (#/$): 76/$285,961
Women's Aid (#/$): 14/$38,900
M: baseball, basketball, cross country, golf, soccer
W: cross country, tennis, volleyball

OKALOOSA-WALTON JUNIOR COLLEGE
100 College Boulevard
Niceville, FL 32578
2-year college
(904) 729-5358 Contact: Mickey Englett
Men's Non-aid: tennis
Women's Non-aid: tennis

PALM BEACH ATLANTIC COLLEGE
P.O. Box 24708
West Palm Beach, FL 33416-4708
(407) 835-4320 Contact: Donna Coons
Men's Non-aid: baseball, basketball, soccer
Women's Non-aid: cheerleading, volleyball

PALM BEACH COMMUNITY COLLEGE
4200 Congress Avenue
Lake Worth, FL 33461
2-year college
(407) 439-8067 Contact: Hamid Saquir
Men's Aid (#/$): 35/unspecified $
Women's Aid (#/$): 38/unspecified $
M: baseball, basketball, tennis
W: basketball, softball, tennis

PENSACOLA JUNIOR COLLEGE
1000 College Boulevard
Pensacola, FL 32504
2-year college
(904) 484-1304 Contact: Larry Bracken
Unspecified athletic aid available
M: baseball, basketball
W: basketball, volleyball

POLK COMMUNITY COLLEGE
999 Avenue "H," NE
Winter Haven, FL 33880
2-year college
(813) 297-1007 Contact: Bill Moore
Unspecified athletic aid available
M: baseball, basketball
W: basketball, volleyball

ROLLINS COLLEGE
1000 Holt Avenue-2730
Winter Park, FL 32789-4499
(407) 646-2663 Contact: Fred Battenfield
Men's Aid (#/$): 34/$618,630
Women's Aid (#/$): 21/$382,095
M: baseball, basketball, golf, soccer, tennis. Men's Non-aid: crew, cross country, sailing, water skiing
W: basketball, golf, tennis, volleyball. Women's Non-aid: crew, cross country, sailing, softball, water skiing

SAINT LEO COLLEGE
P.O. Box 2038
St. Leo, FL 33574
(904) 588-8221 Contact: Fran Reidy
Unspecified athletic aid available
M: baseball, basketball, soccer, tennis. Men's Non-aid: cross country
W: basketball, softball, tennis, volleyball. Women's Non-aid: cheerleading, cross country

SAINT THOMAS UNIVERSITY
16400 NW 32nd Avenue
Miami, FL 33054
(305) 628-6676 Contact: Dr. Andrew L. Kreutzer
Men's Aid (#/$): 28/$178,000
Women's Aid (#/$): 17/$122,000
M: baseball, basketball, soccer. Men's Non-aid: golf, lacrosse
W: soccer, softball, tennis

SANTA FE COMMUNITY COLLEGE
3000 NW 83rd Street
Gainesville, FL 32606-6200

2-year college
(904) 395-5535 Contact: Kenny Drost
Men's Aid (#/$): 30/$48,000
Women's Aid (#/$): 30/$48,000
Restrictions and notes: Athletic aid applies to tuition and books only.
M: baseball, basketball
W: basketball, softball

SEMINOLE COMMUNITY COLLEGE
Sanford, FL 32771
2-year college
(305) 323-1450 Contact: Joe Sterling
Unspecified athletic aid available
M: baseball, basketball, cross country, tennis, track & field
W: basketball, softball, tennis, volleyball

SOUTH FLORIDA COMMUNITY COLLEGE
600 West College Drive
Avon Park, FL 33825
2-year college
(813) 453-6661 X. 120 Contact: Dr. Aubrey Gardner
Men's Aid (#/$): 12/$31,152
Women's Aid (#/$): 12/$31,152
M: basketball
W: volleyball

ST. JOHNS RIVER COMMUNITY COLLEGE
5001 St. Johns Avenue
Palatka, FL 32177
2-year college
(904) 328-1571 Contact: William H. Tuten
Unspecified athletic aid available
M: baseball, basketball
W: softball

ST. PETERSBURG JUNIOR COLLEGE
P.O. Box 13489
St. Petersburg, FL 33733
2-year college
(813) 791-2662 Contact: Edward J. Long
Men's Aid (#/$): 37/$53,872
Women's Aid (#/$): 34/$49,504
M: baseball, basketball, golf, swimming-diving
W: basketball, softball, swimming-diving

STETSON UNIVERSITY
Campus Box 8317
Deland, FL 32720-3756
(904) 822-8100 Contact: Bob Jacoby
Men's Aid (#/$): 32/$510,000
Women's Aid (#/$): 22/$319,000
M: baseball, basketball, cross country, golf, soccer, tennis, track & field
W: basketball, cross country, golf, soccer, softball, tennis, track & field, volleyball

TAMPA COLLEGE
3319 West Hillsborough Ave.
Tampa, FL 33614
(813) 879-6000 Contact: Office of Admissions
Unspecified athletic aid available
M: baseball, basketball, cross country, golf, soccer, swimming, tennis
W: basketball, cross country, softball, swimming, tennis, volleyball

UNIVERSITY OF CENTRAL FLORIDA
Orlando, FL 32816
(407) 823-2464 Contact: Art Zeleznic
Unspecified athletic aid available
M: baseball, basketball, cross country, football, golf, soccer, tennis, track & field
W: basketball, cross country, golf, soccer, tennis, track & field, volleyball

UNIVERSITY OF FLORIDA
P.O. Box 11485
Florida Field
Gainesville, FL 32604-2485
(904) 375-4683 Contact: John Humenik
Men's Aid (#/$): 154/$954,000
Women's Aid (#/$): 81/$458,575
M: baseball, basketball, football, golf, swimming-diving, tennis, track & field

W: basketball, cross country, golf, gymnastics, swimming-diving, tennis, track & field, volleyball

UNIVERSITY OF MIAMI
P.O. Box 248167
Coral Gables, FL 33124
(305) 284-3244 Contact: Linda Venzon
Unspecified athletic aid available
M: baseball, basketball, diving, football, golf, swimming, swimming-diving, tennis. Men's Non-aid: cross country
W: basketball, diving, golf, swimming, swimming-diving, tennis. Women's Non-aid: cross country

UNIVERSITY OF NORTH FLORIDA
4567 St. Johns Bluff Road South
Jacksonville, FL 32224
(904) 646-2833 Contact: Bonnie Senappe
Unspecified athletic aid available
M: cross country, golf, indoor track, tennis, track & field
W: cross country, indoor track, tennis, track & field

UNIVERSITY OF SOUTH FLORIDA
PED 214
Tampa, FL 33620
(813) 974-2125 Contact: John Gerdes
Unspecified athletic aid available
M: baseball, basketball, cross country, golf, indoor track, soccer, tennis, track & field
W: basketball, cross country, golf, indoor track, softball, tennis, track & field, volleyball

UNIVERSITY OF TAMPA
401 West Kennedy Boulevard
Tampa, FL 33606-1490
(813) 253-6241 Contact: Gil Swalis
Men's Aid (#/$): 20/$94,050
Women's Aid (#/$): 20/$76,950
M: baseball, basketball, golf, soccer, swimming, tennis. Men's Non-aid: crew, cross country
W: basketball, swimming, tennis, volleyball. Women's Non-aid: crew, cross country, softball

UNIVERSITY OF WEST FLORIDA
11000 University Parkway
Pensacola, FL 32514-5750
(904) 474-2400 Contact: Dr. Ray Bennet
Men's Aid (#/$): 1/$1,000
Women's Aid (#/$): 1/$1,000
M: baseball, golf, tennis
W: basketball, softball, tennis

VALENCIA COMMUNITY COLLEGE
P.O. Box 3028
Orlando, FL 32802
2-year college
(407) 299-5000 X. 1408 Contact: Don Rutledge
Men's Aid (#/$): 32/$44,800
Women's Aid (#/$): 33/$46,200
M: baseball, basketball
W: basketball, softball

WARNER SOUTHERN COLLEGE
5301 U.S. Highway 27 South
Lake Wales, FL 33853
(813) 638-1426 Contact: Doug Cleary
Unspecified athletic aid available
M: baseball, basketball, soccer. Men's Non-aid: cheerleading
W: basketball, volleyball. Women's Non-aid: cheerleading

WEBBER COLLEGE
P.O. Box 96
Babson Park, FL 33827-0096
(813) 638-1431 Contact: Nancy Nichols
Unspecified athletic aid available
Restrictions and notes: 150 athletes average $1,200 athletic aid each.
M: basketball, crew, cross country, golf, soccer, tennis
W: basketball, crew, cross country, soccer, softball, tennis, volleyball

Georgia

AGNES SCOTT COLLEGE
East College Avenue
Decatur, GA 30030
(404) 371-6393 Contact: Tansill H. Hille
Women's Non-aid: cross country, tennis

ALBANY STATE COLLEGE
504 College Drive
Albany, GA 31705
(912) 430-4672 Contact: Rickey Walker
Unspecified athletic aid available
M: basketball, cross country, football, track & field. Men's Non-aid: tennis
W: basketball, track & field. Women's Non-aid: tennis

ANDREW COLLEGE
413 College Street
Cuthbert, GA 31740-1395
2-year college
(912) 732-2171 Contact: Ruth Eliason
Unspecified athletic aid available
M: baseball, cross country, soccer, tennis
W: cross country, soccer, tennis

ARMSTRONG STATE COLLEGE
11935 Abercorn Extension
Savannah, GA 31419-1997
(912) 927-5336 Contact: Darrell Stephens
Men's Aid (#/$): 17/$155,979
Women's Aid (#/$): 10/$92,400
M: baseball, basketball, cross country, tennis
W: basketball, cross country, tennis, volleyball

AUGUSTA COLLEGE
2500 Walton Way
Augusta, GA 30910
(706) 737-7925 Contact: Nicky Zuber
Unspecified athletic aid available
M: baseball, basketball, cross country, golf, soccer, tennis
W: basketball, cross country, softball, swimming, swimming-diving, tennis, volleyball

BERRY COLLEGE
P.O. Box 279
Mount Berry, GA 30149
(706) 236-2226 Contact: R.G. Smithson
Unspecified athletic aid available
M: baseball, basketball, cross country, golf, soccer, tennis
W: basketball, cross country, soccer, tennis

BRENAU UNIVERSITY
1 Centennial Circle
Gainesville, GA 30501
(706) 534-6152 Contact: Pam Barret
Women's Aid (#/$): 8/$51,000
W: tennis

BREWTON PARKER COLLEGE
Vidalia Road
Highway 280
Mt. Vernon, GA 30445-0197
(912) 583-2241 Contact: Dr. Donald Weber
Men's Aid (#/$): 26/$56,813
Women's Aid (#/$): 35/$25,790
M: baseball, basketball, soccer, tennis
W: basketball, softball, tennis

BRUNSWICK JUNIOR COLLEGE
Fourth & Altama
Brunswick, GA 31523
2-year college
(912) 264-7224 Contact: Dr. Scott Staples
Unspecified athletic aid available
M: basketball, tennis
W: tennis

CLARK ATLANTA UNIVERSITY
Atlanta, GA 30314
(404) 880-8065 Contact: Shelia Brown
Unspecified athletic aid available
M: basketball, football, tennis, track & field
W: basketball, cheerleading, cross country, tennis, track & field, volleyball

COLUMBUS COLLEGE
13600 Algonquin Drive
Columbus, GA 31907-2079
(706) 568-2036 Contact: John W. Rogers
Unspecified athletic aid available
M: baseball, basketball, cross country, golf, soccer, tennis
W: softball, tennis, volleyball

COVENANT COLLEGE
Scenic Highway
Lookout Mountain, GA 30750
(706) 820-1560 Contract: Jenny Gienapp
Unspecified athletic aid available
M: basketball, soccer. Men's Non-aid: cross country
W: basketball. Women's Non-aid: cross country, volleyball

DALTON COLLEGE
213 North College Drive
Dalton, GA 30720
2-year college
(706) 272-4436 Contact: Phil Hall
Men's Non-aid: archery, badminton, bowling, fencing, golf, racquetball, soccer, swimming, tennis, volleyball, weightlifting, wrestling
Women's Non-aid: archery, badminton, bowling, fencing, golf, racquetball, soccer, swimming, tennis, volleyball, weightlifting

EMORY UNIVERSITY
Woodruff P.E. Center
Atlanta, GA 30322
(404) 727-6553 Contact: John Arenberg
Men's Non-aid: crew, cross country, soccer, swimming-diving, tennis, track & field
Women's Non-aid: cross country, swimming-diving, tennis, track & field

FORT VALLEY STATE COLLEGE
1005 State College Drive
Fort Valley, GA 31030-3298
(912) 825-6437 Contact: Russell Boone, Jr.
Unspecified athletic aid available
M: baseball, basketball, football, tennis, track & field. Men's Non-aid: baseball, track & field
W: basketball, tennis, track & field. Women's Non-aid: track & field, volleyball

GEORGIA COLLEGE
Athletic Department
Milledgeville, GA 31061
(912) 453-5149 Contact: Aurelia M. Dykes
Men's Aid (#/$): 21/$19,087
Women's Aid (#/$): 11/$12,722
M: baseball, basketball, golf, soccer, tennis
W: basketball, gymnastics, softball, tennis

GEORGIA INSTITUTE OF TECHNOLOGY
190 Third Street, NW
Atlanta, GA 30332
(404) 894-4160 Contact: Curley Williams
Unspecified athletic aid available
M: baseball, basketball, cross country, football, golf, indoor track, tennis, track & field
W: basketball, cross country, softball, tennis, track & field, volleyball

GEORGIA MILITARY COLLEGE
201 East Greene Street
Milledgeville, GA 31061
2-year college
(912) 454-2700 Contact: Robert Nunn
Unspecified athletic aid available
M: football, tennis

GEORGIA SOUTHERN UNIVERSITY
Landrum Box 8085
Statesboro, GA 30460
(912) 681-5239 Contact: Matt Rogers
Men's Aid (#/$): 94/$535,000
Women's Aid (#/$): 35/$200,000
M: baseball, basketball, cross country, football, golf, soccer, swimming-diving, tennis

W: basketball, cross country, softball, swimming-diving, tennis, track & field, volleyball

GEORGIA SOUTHWESTERN COLLEGE
Wheatley Street
Americus, GA 31709
(912) 928-1378 Contact: Rebecca L. McNeill
Unspecified athletic aid available
M: baseball, basketball, tennis. Men's Non-aid: football
W: basketball, softball, tennis

GEORGIA STATE UNIVERSITY
University Plaza
Atlanta, GA 30303-3083
(404) 651-2071 Contact: Martin Harmon
Men's Aid ($): $402,000
Women's Aid ($): $401,000
M: baseball, basketball, cross country, golf, soccer, tennis, wrestling
W: basketball, cross country, golf, softball, tennis, volleyball

KENNESAW STATE COLLEGE
P.O. Box 444
Marietta, GA 30061
(404) 423-6074 Contact: Thomas I. Patterson
Men's Aid (#/$): 10/$15,000
Women's Aid (#/$): 10/$15,000
M: baseball, basketball, cross country, golf, soccer. Men's Non-aid: track & field
W: basketball, cross country, softball. Women's Non-aid: track & field

MERCER UNIVERSITY
1400 Coleman Avenue
Macon, GA 31207
(912) 752-2670 Contact: Carol Williams
Men's Aid (#/$): 35.7/$506,154
Women's Aid (#/$): 33.2/$470,709
M: baseball, basketball, cross country, golf, soccer, tennis
W: basketball, cross country, golf, sailing, softball, tennis, volleyball

MOREHOUSE COLLEGE
Atlanta, GA 30314
(404) 681-2800 Contact: Craig Cason
Unspecified athletic aid available
M: baseball, basketball, football, tennis, track & field

MORRIS BROWN COLLEGE
643 Martin Luther King Drive
Atlanta, GA 30314
(404) 220-0367/0368 Contact: Cecil McKay
Men's Aid (#/$): 115/$325,000
Women's Aid (#/$): 50/$115,000
Athletic programs not specified

NORTH GEORGIA COLLEGE
Dahlonega, GA 30597
(706) 864-1411 Contact: W. Arnold Hulsey
Unspecified athletic aid available
M: basketball, riflery, soccer. Men's Non-aid: tennis
W: basketball, riflery. Women's Non-aid: softball, tennis

OGLETHORPE UNIVERSITY
4484 Peachtree Road NE
Atlanta, GA 30319
(404) 261-1441 Contact: Pam Beaird
Men's Non-aid: baseball, basketball, cross country, soccer, tennis
Women's Non-aid: basketball, cross country, soccer, tennis, volleyball

PAINE COLLEGE
1235 15th Street
Augusta, GA 30910-2799
(404) 821-8264 Contact: Robert G. Skinner
Unspecified athletic aid available
M: baseball, basketball, cross country, track & field
W: basketball, cross country, track & field, water polo. Women's Non-aid: softball

PIEDMONT COLLEGE
Demorest, GA 30535
(706) 778-3000 Contact: Dr. Ralph B. Singer, Jr.

Men's Aid (#/$): 44/$55,800
Women's Aid (#/$): 27/$37,500
M: baseball, basketball, cross country, golf, soccer, tennis
W: basketball, cross country, golf, soccer, softball, tennis

SAVANNAH STATE COLLEGE
P.O. Box 20427
Savannah, GA 31404
(912) 356-2191 Contact: Lee Grant Pearson
Men's Aid (#/$): 54/unspecified $
Women's Aid (#/$): 20/unspecified $
M: baseball, basketball, football, track & field
W: basketball, cross country, tennis, volleyball

SHORTER COLLEGE
Rome, GA 30161-4298
(706) 291-2121 Contact: Rondall H. Day
Men's Aid (#/$): 24/$178,200
Women's Aid (#/$): 10/$98,900
M: baseball, basketball, cross country, golf, tennis
W: basketball, softball, tennis.
Women's Non-aid: cross country

SOUTHERN COLLEGE OF TECHNOLOGY
1000 South Marietta Parkway
Marietta, GA 30060-2896
(404) 528-7290 Contact: Dr. Emerelle McNair
Men's Aid (#/$): 34/$47,763
M: baseball, basketball, tennis
Women's Non-aid: tennis

TOCCOA FALLS COLLEGE
P.O. Box 800266
Toccoa Falls, GA 30598
(706) 886-6831 Contact: Charles Temple
Men's Non-aid: baseball, basketball, cross country, soccer
Women's Non-aid: basketball, volleyball

TRUETT-MCCONNELL JUNIOR COLLEGE
Clarksville Highway
Cleveland, GA 30528
2-year college
(706) 865-5608 Contact: Todd Smyly
Unspecified athletic aid available
M: baseball, basketball, soccer, tennis
W: basketball, softball, tennis, volleyball

UNIVERSITY OF GEORGIA
P.O. Box 1472
Athens, GA 30613
(404) 542-1621 Contact: Claude Felton
Unspecified athletic aid available
Restrictions and notes: Athletic aid limited to NCAA maximums
M: baseball, basketball, cross country, diving, football, golf, indoor track, swimming, swimming-diving, tennis, track & field
W: cross country, diving, golf, gymnastics, indoor track, swimming, swimming-diving, tennis, track & field, volleyball

VALDOSTA STATE COLLEGE
North Patterson Street
Valdosta, GA 31698
(912) 333-5890 Contact: Steve Roberts
Unspecified athletic aid available
M: baseball, basketball, cross country, football, golf, tennis
W: basketball, cross country, softball, tennis

WEST GEORGIA COLLEGE
1600 Maple Street
Carrollton, GA 30118
(404) 836-6542 Contact: Dan Minish
Men's Aid (#/$): 61.2/$290,215
Women's Aid (#/$): 19.1/$90,661
M: baseball, basketball, cross country, football, golf, tennis

W: basketball, cross country, softball, tennis, volleyball

Hawaii

BRIGHAM YOUNG UNIVERSITY
P.O. Box 1824
BYU-HC
Laie, HI 96762
(808) 293-3912 Contact: Ken Brown
Unspecified athletic aid available
M: basketball, cross country, tennis. Men's Non-aid: rugby
W: cross country, tennis, volleyball

CHAMINADE UNIVERSITY
3140 Walalae Avenue
Honolulu, HI 96816
(808) 735-4790 Contact: Chuck English
Men's Aid (#/$): 25/$213,080
Women's Aid (#/$): 21/$136,100
M: basketball, cross country, tennis, water polo
W: cross country, softball, tennis, volleyball

HAWAII PACIFIC UNIVERSITY
1060 Bishop Street PH
Honolulu, HI 96813
(808) 544-0221 Contact: Russ Dung
Men's Aid (#/$): 9/$36,360
Women's Aid (#/$): 5/$20,260
M: baseball, basketball, cross country, soccer, squash, swimming, tennis
W: cross country, softball, swimming, volleyball

UNIVERSITY OF HAWAII (HILO)
Hilo, HI 96720-4091
(808) 933-3324 Contact: Jean Coffman
Unspecified athletic aid available
M: baseball, basketball, cross country, golf, tennis
W: cross country, tennis, volleyball

UNIVERSITY OF HAWAII (MANOA)
1337 Lower Campus Road
Honolulu, HI 96822-2370
(808) 948-7523 Contact: Ed Inouye
Unspecified athletic aid available
M: baseball, basketball, football, golf, swimming-diving, tennis, volleyball. Men's Non-aid: sailing
W: basketball, cross country, golf, softball, swimming-diving, tennis, volleyball. Women's Non-aid: sailing

Idaho

ALBERTSON COLLEGE
Caldwell, ID 83605
(208) 459-5308 Contact: Scott Arnold
Unspecified athletic aid available
M: alpine skiing, baseball, basketball, soccer, tennis
W: alpine skiing, volleyball

BOISE STATE UNIVERSITY
1910 University Drive
Boise, ID 83725
(208) 385-1515 Contact: Max Corbet
Men's Aid (#/$): 114/unspecified $
Women's Aid (#/$): 67/unspecified $
M: basketball, football, golf, tennis, track & field, wrestling
W: basketball, golf, gymnastics, tennis, track & field, volleyball

THE COLLEGE OF IDAHO
2112 Cleveland Boulevard
Caldwell, ID 83605
(208) 459-5512 Contact: Dave Hahn
Unspecified athletic aid available
M: baseball, basketball, cross country skiing, soccer
W: cross country skiing, tennis, volleyball

COLLEGE OF SOUTHERN IDAHO
315 Falls Avenue
Twin Falls, ID 83303-1238
2-year college
(208) 733-9554 Contact: Karl Kleinkoph
Unspecified athletic aid available
M: baseball, basketball, cross country, rodeo, track & field

W: basketball, cross country, rodeo, track & field, volleyball

IDAHO STATE UNIVERSITY
P.O. Box 81241 SU
Pocatello, ID 83209
(208) 236-3651 Contact: Glenn Alford
Unspecified athletic aid available
M: basketball, cross country, football, golf, indoor track, track & field
W: basketball, cross country, indoor track, tennis, track & field, volleyball

LEWIS CLARK STATE COLLEGE
6th Street and 8th Avenue
Lewiston, ID 83501
(208) 799-2224 Contact: Steven Bussolini
Unspecified athletic aid available
M: baseball, basketball, tennis
W: basketball, tennis, volleyball

NORTH IDAHO COLLEGE
1000 West Garden
Coeur d'Alene, ID 83814
2-year college
(208) 769-3315 Contact: Erna Rhinehart
Restrictions and notes: 190 aid recipients received $157,294 total.
M: baseball, basketball, cheerleading, cross country, track & field, wrestling,
W: cheerleading, cross country, track & field, volleyball

NORTHWEST NAZARENE COLLEGE
623 Holly Street
Nampa, ID 83686
(208) 467-8396 Contact: Rich Sanders
Men's Aid (#/$): 15/$120,000
Women's Aid (#/$): 15/$120,000
M: baseball, basketball, soccer, track & field
W: basketball, tennis, track & field, volleyball

RICKS COLLEGE
Hart Building
Rexburg, ID 83460-0900
2-year college
(208) 356-2113 Contact: Lori Woodland
Unspecified athletic aid available
M: baseball, basketball, cross country, football, track & field, wrestling. Men's Non-aid: indoor track
W: basketball, cross country, track & field, volleyball. Women's Non-aid: indoor track

UNIVERSITY OF IDAHO
Kibbie Activity Center
Moscow, ID 83843
(208) 885-0211 Contact: Rance Pugmire
Unspecified athletic aid available
M: basketball, cross country, football, golf, indoor track, tennis, track & field
W: basketball, cross country, indoor track, tennis, track & field, volleyball

Illinois

AUGUSTANA COLLEGE
639 38th Street
Rock Island, IL 61201
(309) 794-7265 Contact: David Wrath
Men's Non-aid: baseball, basketball, cross country, diving, football, golf, soccer, swimming-diving, tennis, track & field, wrestling
Women's Non-aid: basketball, cross country, softball, swimming-diving, tennis, track & field, volleyball

AURORA UNIVERSITY
347 South Gladstone
Aurora, IL 60506
(708) 844-5479 Contact: Dave Beyer
Men's Non-aid: baseball, basketball, football, golf, soccer, tennis
Women's Non-aid: basketball, golf, softball, tennis, volleyball

BELLEVILLE AREA COLLEGE
4950 Maryville Road
Granite City, IL 62040
2-year college
(618) 931-0600 Contact: Mary Brown

Unspecified athletic aid available
M: baseball, basketball, tennis
W: basketball, softball, tennis, volleyball

BLACKBURN COLLEGE
700 College Avenue
Carlinville, IL 62626
(217) 854-3231 Contact: Cheryl Gardner
Men's Non-aid: baseball, basketball, cross country, golf, soccer, softball, swimming-diving, tennis, track & field
Women's Non-aid: basketball, cross country, softball, swimming-diving, tennis, track & field, volleyball

BLACK HAWK COLLEGE
6600 34th Avenue
Moline, IL 61265
2-year college
(309) 796-1311 Contact: Bob Eggdson
Men's Non-aid: baseball, basketball, golf
Women's Non-aid: basketball, volleyball

BLACK HAWK COLLEGE
South Route 78
Kewanee, IL 61443
2-year college
(309) 852-5671 Contact: Nelson Lay
Men's Aid (#/$): 11/unspecified $
Women's Aid (#/$): 11/unspecified $
Restrictions and notes: Athletic aid is in the form of tuition waivers.
M: basketball, track & field
W: basketball, track & field

BRADLEY UNIVERSITY
1501 West Bradley Avenue
Peoria, IL 61625
(309) 677-2624 Contact: Joe Dalfonso
Men's Aid (#/$): 44/$622,336
Women's Aid (#/$): 52/$608,192
M: baseball, basketball, cross country, golf, soccer, softball, swimming, tennis, volleyball
W: basketball, cross country, golf, soccer, softball, swimming, tennis, volleyball

CHICAGO STATE UNIVERSITY
9501 South King Drive
Chicago, IL 60628
(312) 995-2217 Contact: Lisette Allison-Moore
Unspecified athletic aid available
M: baseball, basketball, golf, soccer, tennis, track & field, wrestling. Men's Non-aid: cross country, indoor track
W: basketball, softball, track & field, volleyball. Women's Non-aid: cross country, indoor track

COLLEGE OF ST. FRANCIS
500 North Wilcox Street
Joliet, IL 60435
(815) 740-3842 Contact: Dave Laketa
Men's Aid (#/$): 204/$795,600
Women's Aid (#/$): 100/$239,000
M: baseball, basketball, football, golf, soccer, tennis
W: basketball, cheerleading, cross country, softball, tennis, volleyball

CONCORDIA UNIVERSITY
7400 Augusta Street
River Forest, IL 60305
(708) 209-3113 Contact: Thomas O. Faszholz
Men's Non-aid: baseball, basketball, cross country, football, tennis, track & field, wrestling
Women's Non-aid: basketball, cross country, softball, tennis, track & field, volleyball

DANVILLE AREA COMMUNITY COLLEGE
2000 East Main Street
Danville, IL 61832
2-year college
(217) 443-8780 Contact: John Spezia
Men's Aid (#/$): 22/$33,000
Women's Aid (#/$): 19/$28,500
M: basketball, cross country, golf
W: basketball, cross country, golf

DEPAUL UNIVERSITY
1011 West Belden Avenue
Chicago, IL 60614

(312) 362-8350 Contact: John H. Schoultz
Unspecified athletic aid available
M: basketball, cross country, golf, indoor track, riflery, soccer, tennis, track & field
W: basketball, cross country, indoor track, riflery, softball, tennis, track & field, volleyball

EASTERN ILLINOIS UNIVERSITY
Lantz Gym
Charleston, IL 61920
(217) 581-6408 Contact: David Kidwell
Unspecified athletic aid available
M: baseball, basketball, cross country, football, indoor track, soccer, track & field. Men's Non-aid: diving, swimming, tennis
W: basketball, cross country, indoor track, softball, track & field, volleyball, wrestling. Women's Non-aid: diving, swimming, tennis

ELGIN COMMUNITY COLLEGE
1700 Spartan Drive
Elgin, IL 60123
2-year college
(708) 697-1000 X. 371 Contact: Gayle Saunders
Men's Non-aid: baseball, basketball, golf, tennis
Women's Non-aid: basketball, golf, softball, tennis, volleyball

ELMHURST COLLEGE
190 Prospect
Elmhurst, IL 60126
(708) 617-3142 Contact: Chris Ragsdale
Men's Non-aid: baseball, basketball, cross country, football, golf, indoor track, tennis, track & field, wrestling
Women's Non-aid: basketball, cross country, indoor track, softball, tennis, track & field, volleyball

EUREKA COLLEGE
300 East College Street
Eureka, IL 61530
(309) 467-6310 Contact: Martin Stromberger
Men's Non-aid: basketball, diving, football, golf, swimming, swimming-diving, tennis, track & field
Women's Non-aid: basketball, diving, softball, swimming, swimming-diving, tennis, track & field, volleyball

GREENVILLE COLLEGE
315 East College Avenue
Greenville, IL 62246
(618) 664-1840 Contact: Lynn Adams
Men's Non-aid: baseball, basketball, cross country, golf, soccer, tennis, track & field
Women's Non-aid: basketball, softball, tennis, track & field, volleyball

HARPER WILLIAM RAINEY COLLEGE
Algonquin & Roselle Roads
Palatine, IL 60067
2-year college
(708) 397-3000 Contact: Ron Lanham
Men's Non-aid: baseball, basketball, cross country, diving, football, racquetball, swimming, swimming-diving, tennis, track & field, wrestling
Women's Non-aid: basketball, cross country, diving, softball, swimming, swimming-diving, synchronized swimming, tennis, volleyball

ILLINOIS BENEDICTINE COLLEGE
5700 College Road
Lisle, IL 60532
(312) 960-1500 X. 293 Contact: Randa Duncan
Men's Non-aid: baseball, basketball, cross country, diving, football, golf, indoor track, soccer, swimming, tennis, track & field
Women's Non-aid: basketball, cross country, diving, golf, indoor track, softball, swimming, tennis, track & field, volleyball

ILLINOIS CENTRAL COLLEGE
One College Drive
East Peoria, IL 61635
2-year college

(309) 694-5595 Contact: Louise Heimann
Men's Non-aid: baseball, basketball, golf
Women's Non-aid: basketball, softball, volleyball

ILLINOIS COLLEGE
1101 West College Avenue
Jacksonville, IL 62650
(217) 245-3048 Contact: James T. Murphy
Men's Non-aid: baseball, basketball, cross country, football, golf, indoor track, soccer, tennis, track & field, wrestling
Women's Non-aid: basketball, cross country, golf, indoor track, soccer, softball, tennis, track & field, volleyball

ILLINOIS INSTITUTE OF TECHNOLOGY
3040 South Wabash
Chicago, IL 60616
(312) 567-3296 Contact: Chris Meyer
Unspecified athletic aid available
M: baseball, basketball, cross country, diving, swimming, swimming-diving, tennis, volleyball
W: basketball, cross country, diving, softball, swimming, swimming-diving, tennis, volleyball

ILLINOIS STATE UNIVERSITY
123 Horton Field House
Normal, IL 61761-6901
(309) 438-3825 Contact: Kenny Mossman
Unspecified athletic aid available
M: baseball, basketball, cross country, football, golf, indoor track, soccer, tennis, track & field, wrestling
W: basketball, cross country, golf, gymnastics, indoor track, softball, swimming-diving, tennis, track & field, volleyball

ILLINOIS VALLEY COMMUNITY COLLEGE
2578 East 350th Road
Oglesby, IL 61348-1099
2-year college
(815) 224-2720 Contact: Francis Brolley
Men's Non-aid: baseball, basketball, football, tennis, track & field
Women's Non-aid: basketball, softball, tennis, track & field, volleyball

ILLINOIS WESLEYAN UNIVERSITY
P.O. Box 2900
Bloomington, IL 61702-2900
(309) 556-3206 Contact: Stew Salowitz
Men's Non-aid: baseball, basketball, cross country, diving, football, golf, indoor track, soccer, swimming, swimming-diving, tennis, track & field
Women's Non-aid: basketball, cross country, diving, softball, swimming, swimming-diving, tennis, track & field, volleyball

KANKAKEE COMMUNITY COLLEGE
Box 888
Kankakee, IL 60901
2-year college
(815) 933-0234 Contact: Denny Lehnus
Unspecified athletic aid available
M: basketball. Men's Non-aid: baseball, tennis
Women's Non-aid: basketball, softball, volleyball

KASKASKIA COMMUNITY COLLEGE
Shattuc Road
Centralia, IL 62801
2-year college
(618) 532-1981 Contact: Dave Kreps
Men's Non-aid: baseball, basketball, tennis
Women's Non-aid: softball, tennis, volleyball

KISHWAUKEE COLLEGE
Malta Road
Malta, IL 60150
2-year college
(815) 825-2086 Contact: Gregg Gierke
Men's Non-aid: baseball, basketball, golf, soccer

Women's Non-aid: basketball, golf, softball, volleyball

KNOX COLLEGE
South Street
Galesburg, IL 61401
(309) 343-0112 X. 269 Contact: Jay D. Redfern
Men's Non-aid: baseball, basketball, cross country, diving, football, golf, indoor track, soccer, swimming-diving, tennis, track & field, wrestling
Women's Non-aid: basketball, cross country, diving, indoor track, softball, swimming-diving, tennis, track & field, volleyball

LAKE FOREST COLLEGE
555 North Sheridan Road
Lake Forest, IL 60045
(708) 234-3100 Contact: Gordon E. White
Men's Non-aid: basketball, diving, football, handball, ice hockey, lacrosse, soccer, swimming, swimming-diving, tennis
Women's Non-aid: basketball, diving, handball, soccer, softball, swimming, swimming-diving, tennis, volleyball

LAKE LAND COLLEGE
5001 Lake Boulevard
Mattoon, IL 61938
2-year college
(217) 235-3131 X. 333 Contact: Pam Crimson
Men's Aid (#/$): 53/unspecified $
Women's Aid (#/$): 42/unspecified $
M: baseball, basketball, cross country, tennis
W: basketball, cross country, softball, volleyball

LEWIS UNIVERSITY
Route 53
Romeoville, IL 60441
(815) 838-0500 X. 247 Contact: Mike Altobella
Unspecified athletic aid available
M: baseball, basketball, cross country, golf, soccer, tennis, track & field
W: basketball, cross country, soccer, softball, tennis, volleyball

LEWIS AND CLARK COMMUNITY COLLEGE
5800 Godfrey Road
Godfrey, IL 62035
2-year college
(618) 466-3411 Contact: George C. Terry
Unspecified athletic aid available
M: baseball, basketball, soccer, tennis
W: basketball, tennis, volleyball

LINCOLN CHRISTIAN COLLEGE
100 Campus View Drive
Lincoln, IL 62656
(217) 732-3168 Contact: Thomas G. Ewald
Unspecified athletic aid available
M: baseball, basketball, soccer, tennis
Women's Non-aid: basketball, volleyball

LINCOLN COLLEGE
300 Keokuk Street
Lincoln, IL 62656
2-year college
(217) 732-3155 Contact: Allen Pickering
Unspecified athletic aid available
M: baseball, basketball, cross country, golf, soccer, swimming, swimming-diving, tennis, wrestling
W: basketball, softball, swimming, swimming-diving, tennis, volleyball

LINCOLN LAND COMMUNITY COLLEGE
Shepherd Road
Springfield, IL 62794-9256
2-year college
(217) 786-2426 Contact: Richard Dhabalt
Unspecified athletic aid available
M: baseball, basketball, cross country, golf, indoor track, soccer, track & field
W: basketball, softball, volleyball

LINCOLN TRAIL COLLEGE
Rural Route 3
Robinson, IL 62454

2-year college
(618) 544-8657 Contact: P.D. Highsmith
Unspecified athletic aid available
M: basketball, golf
W: basketball, softball, volleyball

LOYOLA UNIVERSITY
6525 North Sheridan Road
Chicago, IL 60626
(312) 508-2566 Contact: Lisa Mikolai
Men's Aid (#/$): 11/$81,527
Women's Aid (#/$): 14/$111,903
Restrictions and notes: Scholarship amounts vary permissibly.
M: basketball, cross country, golf, indoor track, soccer, swimming, track & field
W: basketball, cross country, indoor track, soccer, track & field, volleyball

MCHENRY COUNTY COLLEGE
8900 U.S. Highway 14
Crystal Lake, IL 60012-2761
2-year college
(815) 455-8550 Contact: Wally Reynolds
Men's Aid (#/$): 13/$10,500
Women's Aid (#/$): 13/$10,500
Restrictions and notes: Athletic aid only for McHenry County H.S. or district residents.
M: baseball, basketball, soccer, tennis
W: basketball, softball, tennis, volleyball

MCKENDREE COLLEGE
701 College Road
Lebanon, IL 62254
(618) 537-4481 X. 117 Contact: Tamie Comley
Men's Aid (#/$): 60/$126,500
Women's Aid (#/$): 21/$58,000
M: baseball, basketball, golf, soccer
W: basketball, golf, softball, volleyball

MILLIKIN UNIVERSITY
1184 West Main Street
Decatur, IL 62522
(217) 424-6350 Contact: Mickey Smith
Men's Non-aid: baseball, basketball, cross country, diving, football, golf, indoor track, soccer, swimming, tennis, track & field, wrestling
Women's Non-aid: basketball, cross country, indoor track, softball, swimming-diving, tennis, track & field, volleyball

MONMOUTH COLLEGE
700 East Broadway
Monmouth, IL 61462
(309) 457-2176 Contact: Richard L. Partin
Men's Non-aid: baseball, basketball, cross country, football, indoor track, soccer, track & field, wrestling
Women's Non-aid: basketball, cross country, indoor track, softball, track & field, volleyball

MOODY BIBLE INSTITUTE
820 North LaSalle Street
Chicago, IL 60610
(312) 329-4451 Contact: Sheldon Bassett
Men's Non-aid: basketball, soccer
Women's Non-aid: basketball, volleyball

MORAINE VALLEY COMMUNITY COLLEGE
10900 South 88th Avenue
Palos Hills, IL 60465
2-year college
(708) 974-4300 Contact: Barbara Wilcox
Men's Non-aid: baseball, basketball, football, golf, soccer, tennis
Women's Non-aid: basketball, softball, tennis, volleyball

MORTON COLLEGE
3801 South Central Avenue
Cicero, IL 60650
2-year college
(708) 656-8000 X. 370 Contact: Robert Slivovsky
Men's Aid (#/$): 10/unspecified $
Women's Aid (#/$): 6/unspecified $
Restrictions and notes: Athletic aid restricted to students who live in college district.

M: baseball, basketball, cross country, golf
W: basketball, cross country, softball

NATIONAL-LOUIS UNIVERSITY
2840 Sheridan Road
Evanston, IL 60201
(708) 256-5150 X. 2264 Contact: Myra Minuskin
Unspecified athletic aid available
M: soccer
W: basketball, softball, volleyball

NORTH CENTRAL COLLEGE
P.O. Box 3063
Naperville, IL 60565-7063
(708) 420-3441 Contact: Tom Carlton
Men's Non-aid: baseball, basketball, cross country, football, golf, indoor track, soccer, swimming, tennis, track & field, wrestling
Women's Non-aid: basketball, cross country, indoor track, softball, swimming, tennis, track & field, volleyball

NORTHEASTERN ILLINOIS UNIVERSITY
5500 North St. Louis Avenue
Chicago, IL 60625
(312) 794-6241 Contact: Tom Lake
Unspecified athletic aid available
M: baseball, basketball, cross country, football, golf, tennis
W: basketball, cross country, softball, tennis, volleyball

NORTHERN ILLINOIS UNIVERSITY
112 Evans Field House
De Kalb, IL 60115
(815) 753-1706 Contact: Michael Korcek
Men's Aid (#/$): 132.75/$975,700
Women's Aid (#/$): 85.15/$625,850
M: baseball, basketball, football, golf, soccer, swimming-diving, tennis, wrestling
W: basketball, golf, gymnastics, soccer, softball, swimming-diving, tennis, volleyball

NORTHWESTERN UNIVERSITY
1501 Central Street
Evanston, IL 60201
(708) 491-7503 Contact: Tim Clodjeaux
Unspecified athletic aid available
M: baseball, basketball, cross country, football, golf, swimming-diving, tennis, track & field, wrestling. Men's Non-aid: fencing, indoor track, soccer
W: basketball, cross country, field hockey, softball, swimming-diving, tennis, track & field, volleyball. Women's Non-aid: fencing, indoor track, lacrosse

OAKTON COMMUNITY COLLEGE
1600 East Golf Road
Des Plaines, IL 60016
2-year college
(708) 635-1753 Contact: Cindy Doubek
Men's Non-aid: baseball, basketball, cross country, golf, indoor track, tennis, track & field, wrestling
Women's Non-aid: basketball, cross country, indoor track, softball, tennis, track & field, volleyball

OLIVET NAZARENE UNIVERSITY
P.O. Box 592
Kankakee, IL 60901
(815) 939-5249 Contact: Laurel Hubbard
Men's Aid (#/$): 168/$415,786
Women's Aid (#/$): 33/$40,182
M: baseball, basketball, cross country, football, golf, soccer, softball, tennis, track & field, wrestling
W: basketball, cross country, tennis, track & field, volleyball

OLNEY CENTRAL COLLEGE
Olney, IL 62450
2-year college
(618) 395-4351 Contact: Dennis Conley
Unspecified athletic aid available
M: baseball, basketball
W: basketball, softball

PARKLAND COLLEGE
2400 West Bradley Avenue
Champaign, IL 61821

2-year college
(217) 351-2226 Contact: Jim Reed
Unspecified athletic aid available
M: baseball, basketball, cross country, golf, indoor track, softball, tennis, track & field, volleyball. Men's Non-aid: cheerleading
W: basketball, cross country, indoor track, softball, track & field, volleyball. Women's Non-aid: cheerleading

PARKS COLLEGE OF ST. LOUIS UNIVERSITY
500 Falling Springs Road
Cahokia, IL 62206
(618) 337-7575 Contact: Jerry Kurfman
Women's Non-aid: basketball, soccer

PRINCIPIA COLLEGE
Elsah, IL 62028
(618) 374-5310 Contact: Phil Webster
Men's Non-aid: baseball, basketball, cross country, diving, football, soccer, swimming, swimming-diving, tennis, track & field
Women's Non-aid: basketball, cross country, diving, soccer, swimming, swimming-diving, tennis, track & field, volleyball

QUINCY COLLEGE
1800 College Avenue
Quincy, IL 62301
(217) 228-5275 Contact: Jim Naumovich
Men's Aid (#/$): 31/$363,766
Women's Aid (#/$): 19.5/$250,107
M: baseball, basketball, soccer
W: basketball, soccer, softball, volleyball

REND LAKE
Rural Route 1
Ina, IL 62846
2-year college
(618) 437-5321 Contact: Bob Kelley
Men's Aid (#/$): 26/unspecified $
Women's Aid (#/$): 20/unspecified $
M: baseball, basketball, golf
W: baseball, softball

ROOSEVELT UNIVERSITY
430 South Michigan Avenue
Chicago, IL 60605
(312) 341-3565 Contact: Stephen Bellin
Unspecified athletic aid available
M: basketball, golf, soccer, tennis. Men's Non-aid: badminton, bowling, cross country, martial arts, swimming, tennis, track & field, weightlifting
Women's Non-aid: badminton, bowling, martial arts, swimming, tennis, track & field, volleyball

ROSARY COLLEGE
7900 West Division Street
River Forest, IL 60305
(312) 366-2490 Contact: Hildegarde Schmidt
Men's Aid (#/$): 30/$175,000
Women's Aid (#/$): 37/$215,000
M: baseball, basketball, soccer, tennis. Men's Non-aid: track & field
W: basketball, tennis, volleyball

SAINT XAVIER UNIVERSITY
3700 West 103rd Street
Chicago, IL 60655
(312) 298-3000 Contact: Lynn O'Linski
Men's Aid (#/$): 60/$240,000
Women's Aid (#/$): 40/$160,000
M: baseball, basketball, soccer
W: softball, volleyball

SAUK VALLEY COLLEGE
173 Illinois Route 2
Dixon, IL 61021-9110
2-year college
(815) 288-5511 Contact: Ralph Gelander
Unspecified athletic aid available
M: basketball, golf, soccer, tennis
W: basketball, tennis, volleyball

SOUTHEASTERN ILLINOIS COLLEGE
3575 College Road
Harrisburg, IL 62946
2-year college
(618) 252-6376 Contact: Britton Blair
Unspecified athletic aid available
M: baseball, basketball
W: basketball, softball

SOUTHERN ILLINOIS UNIVERSITY
SIU Arena/Lingle Hall
Carbondale, IL 62901
(618) 453-7235 Contact: Fred Huff
Men's Aid (#/$): 177/$889,225
Women's Aid (#/$): 114/$562,475
M: baseball, basketball, cross country, football, golf, indoor track, swimming-diving, tennis, track & field
W: basketball, cross country, golf, indoor track, softball, swimming-diving, tennis, track & field, volleyball

SOUTHERN ILLINOIS UNIVERSITY (EDWARDSVILLE)
Box 1027
Edwardsville, IL 62026
(618) 692-3608 Contact: Eric Hess
Men's Aid (#/$): 74/$154,196
Women's Aid (#/$): 48/$77,799
M: baseball, basketball, cross country, golf, soccer, tennis, track & field, wrestling
W: basketball, cross country, soccer, softball, tennis, track & field

SPOON RIVER COLLEGE
Rural Route 1
Canton, IL 61520
2-year college
(309) 647-4645 Contact: Ed Georgieff
Men's Aid (#/$): 30/$42,120
Women's Aid (#/$): 30/$42,120
M: baseball, basketball, cross country, golf, indoor track, track & field
W: basketball, cross country, golf, indoor track, softball, track & field, volleyball

TRINITY CHRISTIAN COLLEGE
6601 West College Drive
Palos Heights, IL 60463
(708) 598-1600 Contact: Steve Hilbelink
Men's Non-aid: baseball, basketball, soccer, track & field
Women's Non-aid: basketball, softball, track & field, volleyball

TRINITY COLLEGE
2077 Halfday Road
Deerfield, IL 60015
(708) 948-8980 Contact: David Seilf
Men's Non-aid: baseball, crew, cross country, fencing, football, golf, ice hockey, indoor track, lacrosse, rugby, soccer, squash, swimming, swimming-diving, tennis, track & field, water polo, wrestling
Women's Non-aid: crew, cross country, fencing, field hockey, indoor track, lacrosse, rugby, soccer, squash, softball, swimming, swimming-diving, tennis, track & field, volleyball, water polo

TRITON COLLEGE
2000 North Fifth Avenue
River Grove, IL 60171
2-year college
(708) 456-0300 Contact: Ed Schaffer
Men's Non-aid: baseball, basketball, football, indoor track, soccer, swimming-diving, track & field, wrestling
Women's Non-aid: basketball, indoor track, softball, swimming-diving, track & field, volleyball

UNIVERSITY OF CHICAGO
5640 University Avenue
Chicago, IL 60637
(312) 702-7681 Contact: Chuck Sadowski
Men's Non-aid: baseball, basketball, cross country, diving, fencing, football, indoor track, swimming, swimming-diving, tennis, track & field, wrestling
Women's Non-aid: basketball, cross country, diving, fencing, indoor track, softball, swimming, swimming-diving, tennis, track & field, volleyball

UNIVERSITY OF ILLINOIS
Box 4348 M/C 196
Chicago, IL 60680
(312) 996-5882 Contact: Dave Mateer
Unspecified athletic aid available
M: basketball, cross country, diving, fencing, football, golf, gymnastics, indoor track, swimming, swimming-diving, tennis, track & field, wrestling
W: basketball, cross country, diving,

golf, gymnastics, indoor track, swimming, swimming-diving, tennis, track & field, volleyball

UNIVERSITY OF ILLINOIS (URBANA-CHAMPAIGN)
1800 South First Street
115 Assembly Hall
Champaign, IL 61820
(217) 333-1390 Contact: Mike Pearson
Unspecified athletic aid available
M: basketball, cross country, diving, fencing, football, golf, gymnastics, indoor track, swimming, swimming-diving, tennis, track & field, wrestling
W: basketball, cross country, diving, golf, gymnastics, indoor track, swimming, swimming-diving, tennis, track & field, volleyball

WABASH VALLEY COLLEGE
2200 College Drive
Mt. Carmel, IL 62863
2-year college
(618) 262-8641 Contact: Bill Hackler
Unspecified athletic aid available
M: baseball, basketball, golf, tennis
W: basketball, softball, volleyball

WAUBONSEE COLLEGE
Route 47 at Harter Road
Sugar Grove, IL 60554
2-year college
(312) 466-4811 Contact: Adrian Montgomery
Men's Non-aid: baseball, basketball, cross country, golf, soccer, tennis, wrestling
Women's Non-aid: basketball, softball, tennis, volleyball

WESTERN ILLINOIS UNIVERSITY
Western Hall 234
Macomb, IL 61455
(309) 298-1964 Contact: Kathy Orban
Men's Aid (#/$): 113/$598,000
Women's Aid (#/$): 52/$295,000
Restrictions and notes: Aid numbers based on full equivalents.
M: baseball, basketball, cross country, golf, indoor track, soccer, swimming-diving, tennis, track & field
W: basketball, cross country, indoor track, softball, swimming-diving, tennis, track & field, volleyball

WHEATON COLLEGE
501 East College Avenue
Wheaton, IL 60187
(708) 752-5747 Contact: Steve Schwepker
Men's Non-aid: baseball, basketball, cross country, football, golf, indoor track, soccer, swimming, tennis, track & field, wrestling
Women's Non-aid: basketball, cross country, indoor track, soccer, softball, swimming, tennis, track & field, volleyball

WILLIAM RAINEY HARPER COLLEGE
1200 West Algonquin Road
Palatine, IL 60067-7398
2-year college
(708) 397-3000
Men's Non-aid: baseball, basketball, football, golf, soccer, swimming-diving, tennis, track & field, wrestling
Women's Non-aid: basketball, softball, swimming-diving, tennis, track & field, volleyball

Indiana

ANDERSON UNIVERSITY
1100 East Fifth Street
Anderson, IN 46012
(317) 641-4495 Contact: Marcie Taylor
Men's Non-aid: baseball, basketball, cross country, football, golf, indoor track, soccer, tennis, track & field
Women's Non-aid: basketball, cross country, indoor track, tennis, track & field, volleyball

BALL STATE UNIVERSITY
HP 120
Muncie, IN 47306-0929

(317) 285-8242 Contact: Joe Hernandez
Unspecified athletic aid available
M: baseball, basketball, cross country, football, golf, indoor track, swimming-diving, tennis, track & field, volleyball. Men's Non-aid: ultimate frisbee
W: basketball, cross country, field hockey, gymnastics, indoor track, softball, swimming-diving, tennis, track & field, volleyball. Women's Non-aid: lacrosse

BETHEL COLLEGE
1001 McKinley Avenue
Mishawaka, IN 46545
(219) 259-8511 Contact: Guy A. Fisher
Unspecified athletic aid available
M: baseball, basketball, cross country, golf, soccer, tennis
W: basketball, cross country, softball, tennis, volleyball

BUTLER UNIVERSITY
4600 Sunset Avenue
Indianapolis, IN 46208
(317) 283-9375 Contact: Jim McGrath
Unspecified athletic aid available
M: basketball, cross country, golf, indoor track, lacrosse, soccer, tennis, track & field. Men's Non-aid: football
W: basketball, cross country, indoor track, soccer, softball, swimming, tennis, track & field, volleyball

DE PAUW UNIVERSITY
300 East Seminary Street
Greencastle, IN 46135
(317) 658-4630 Contact: Bill Wagner
Men's Non-aid: baseball, basketball, cross country, football, golf, soccer, softball, swimming-diving, tennis, track & field, wrestling
Women's Non-aid: baseball, basketball, cross country, field hockey, golf, softball, swimming-diving, tennis, track & field, volleyball

EARLHAM COLLEGE
National Road West
Richmond, IN 47374
(317) 983-1298 Contact: Pat Thomas
Men's Non-aid: baseball, basketball, cross country, football, golf, soccer, tennis, track & field
Women's Non-aid: basketball, cross country, field hockey, lacrosse, softball, tennis, track & field, volleyball

GOSHEN COLLEGE
1700 S. Main Street
Goshen, IN 46526
(219) 535-7525 Contact: Walter Schmucker
Men's Aid (#/$): 8/$4,150
Women's Aid (#/$): 4/$3,000
M: baseball, basketball, cross country, soccer, tennis, track & field
W: basketball, cross country, soccer, tennis, track & field, volleyball

GRACE COLLEGE
200 Seminary Drive
Winona Lake, IN 46590
(219) 372-5575 Contact: Matt Delong
Unspecified athletic aid available
M: baseball, basketball, golf, soccer, tennis, track & field
W: basketball, softball, track & field, volleyball

HANOVER COLLEGE
P.O. Box 108
Hanover, IN 47243-0108
(812) 866-7010 Contact: Carter J. Cloyd
Men's Non-aid: baseball, basketball, cross country, football, golf, soccer, tennis, track & field
Women's Non-aid: basketball, cross country, field hockey, softball, tennis, track & field, volleyball

HUNTINGTON COLLEGE
2303 College Avenue
Huntington, IN 46750
(219) 356-6000 X. 1015 Contact: Sharon R. Woods
Men's Aid (#/$): 64/$111,791
Women's Aid (#/$): 63/$125,840
M: baseball, basketball, cross country, golf, soccer, tennis, track & field

W: basketball, cross country, softball, tennis, track & field, volleyball

INDIANA INSTITUTE OF TECHNOLOGY
1600 East Washington Boulevard
Fort Wayne, IN 46803
(219) 422-5561 Contact: Teresa M. Vasquez
Unspecified athletic aid available
M: basketball
W: basketball

INDIANA STATE UNIVERSITY
Room 118B
Indiana State Arena
Terre Haute, IN 47809
(812) 237-4160 Contact: Jackie Fischer
Unspecified athletic aid available
M: baseball, basketball, cross country, football, indoor track, tennis, track & field. Men's Non-aid: archery, bowling
W: basketball, bowling, cross country, softball, tennis, track & field, volleyball. Women's Non-aid: archery, gymnastics

INDIANA UNIVERSITY
17th and Fee Lane
Assembly Hall
Bloomington, IN 47405
(812) 855-2421 Contact: Kit Klingelhoffer
Men's Aid (#/$): 180/$1,608,676
Women's Aid (#/$): 82/$747,608
M: baseball, basketball, football, golf, soccer, swimming, tennis, track & field, wrestling
W: basketball, golf, softball, swimming, tennis, track & field, volleyball

INDIANA UNIVERSITY (SOUTH BEND)
South Bend, IN 46634
(219) 237-4372 Contact: Jerry Jones
Men's Aid (#/$): 8/$15,000
Women's Aid (#/$): 8/$15,000
Restrictions and notes: Partial scholarships only.
M: basketball
W: basketball

INDIANA UNIVERSITY-PURDUE UNIVERSITY
901 West New York Street
Suite 105
Indianapolis, IN 46202-5193
(317) 274-0620 Contact: Greg Taylor
Men's Aid (#/$): 30/$60,000
Women's Aid (#/$): 30/$60,000
M: baseball, basketball, soccer, tennis
W: basketball, softball, volleyball

INDIANA UNIVERSITY-PURDUE UNIVERSITY (FORT WAYNE)
2101 Coliseum Boulevard East
Fort Wayne, IN 46805-1499
(219) 481-6646 Contact: David Hilbert
Men's Aid (#/$): 89/$130,000
Women's Aid (#/$): 62/$80,000
M: baseball, basketball, cross country, golf, soccer, tennis, volleyball
W: basketball, cross country, softball, tennis, volleyball

INDIANA WESLEYAN UNIVERSITY
4201 South Washington Street
Marion, IN 46953
(317) 677-2114 Contact: Kathy J. Street
Men's Aid (#/$): 80/$97,000
Women's Aid (#/$): 70/$90,000
M: baseball, basketball, cross country, golf, soccer, tennis, track & field
W: basketball, cross country, soccer, softball, tennis, track & field, volleyball

MANCHESTER COLLEGE
604 College Avenue
North Manchester, IN 46962
(219) 982-2141 Contact: Greg Miller
Men's Non-aid: baseball, basketball, cross country, football, golf, indoor track, soccer, tennis, track & field
Women's Non-aid: basketball, cross country, indoor track, softball, tennis, track & field, volleyball

MARIAN COLLEGE
Indianapolis, IN 46222
(317) 929-0234 Contact: John E. Shelton
Men's Aid (#/$): 77/$113,391
Women's Aid (#/$): 30/$74,978
M: baseball, basketball, cross country, golf, soccer, tennis, track & field
W: basketball, cross country, softball, tennis, track & field, volleyball

OAKLAND CITY COLLEGE
Lucretia Street
Oakland City, IN 47660
(812) 749-1266 Contact: Denise Sandifar
Unspecified athletic aid available
M: baseball, basketball
W: basketball, volleyball

PURDUE UNIVERSITY
West Lafayette, IN 47907
(317) 494-5050 Contact: Joyce Hall
Men's Aid (#/$): 47/$323,292
Women's Aid (#/$): 28/$77,115
M: baseball, basketball, cross country, football, golf, indoor track, swimming-diving, tennis, track & field, wrestling
W: basketball, cross country, field hockey, golf, indoor track, swimming-diving, tennis, track & field, volleyball

PURDUE UNIVERSITY (CALUMET)
2233 171st Street
Hammond, IN 46323-2094
(219) 989-2309 Contact: Paul Belmanger
Men's Aid (#/$): 13/$20,000
Women's Aid (#/$): 16/$18,000
M: basketball, soccer
W: basketball, volleyball

ROSE-HULMAN INSTITUTE OF TECHNOLOGY
5500 Wabash Avenue
Terre Haute, IN 47803
(812) 877-8418 Contact: Dale Long
Men's Non-aid: baseball, basketball, cross country, diving, football, golf, indoor track, riflery, soccer, swimming, swimming-diving, tennis, track & field, wrestling

SAINT FRANCIS COLLEGE
2701 Spring Street
Fort Wayne, IN 46808
(219) 434-3283 Contact: Cynthia Tremain
Men's Aid (#/$): 39/$96,480
Women's Aid (#/$): 25/$47,520
M: baseball, basketball, soccer, softball, swimming-diving, tennis. Men's Non-aid: cross country, water polo
W: basketball, swimming-diving, volleyball. Women's Non-aid: cross country, tennis

SAINT JOSEPH'S COLLEGE
Rensselaer, IN 47978
(219) 866-7111 Contact: Charles Schuttrow
Unspecified athletic aid available
M: baseball, basketball, cross country, football, golf, soccer, tennis, track & field
W: basketball, cross country, softball, tennis, track & field

SAINT MARY'S COLLEGE
Angela Athletic Facility
Notre Dame, IN 46556-5001
(219) 284-5548 Contact: Jo-Ann Nester
Women's Non-aid: basketball, fencing, soccer, softball, swimming-diving, tennis, track & field, volleyball

TRI-STATE UNIVERSITY
Hershey Hall
Angola, IN 46703-0307
(219) 665-4840 Contact: Jean Deller
Unspecified athletic aid available
M: baseball, basketball, fencing, golf, indoor track, soccer, tennis, track & field, volleyball
W: basketball, cross country, fencing, indoor track, soccer, softball, tennis, track & field, volleyball

UNIVERSITY OF EVANSVILLE
1800 Lincoln Avenue
Evansville, IN 47722

(812) 479-2350 Contact: Bob Boxell
Unspecified athletic aid available
M: baseball, basketball, cross country, soccer, swimming, tennis
W: basketball, cross country, soccer, softball, swimming, tennis, volleyball

UNIVERSITY OF INDIANA SOUTHEAST

4201 Grantline Road
New Albany, IN 47150
(812) 941-2246 Contact: Patricia King
Men's Aid (#/$): 26/$24,007
Women's Aid (#/$): 15/$8,850
Restrictions and notes: Maximum award equals in-state tuition cost.
M: baseball, basketball. Men's Non-aid: cheerleading
W: basketball, volleyball. Women's Non-aid: cheerleading

UNIVERSITY OF INDIANAPOLIS

1400 East Hanna Avenue
Indianapolis, IN 46227-3697
(317) 788-3494 Contact: Joe Gentry
Unspecified athletic aid available
M: baseball, basketball, cross country, football, golf, soccer, swimming-diving, tennis, track & field, wrestling
W: basketball, cross country, golf, softball, swimming-diving, tennis, track & field

UNIVERSITY OF NOTRE DAME

Joyce Center
Notre Dame, IN 46556
(219) 631-7516 Contact: John Heisler
Men's Aid (#/$): 153/$2,940,966
Women's Aid (#/$): 66/$1,268,652
Restrictions and notes: Only about 38% of Notre Dame undergraduate students are women, and total athletic aid is allocated accordingly.
M: baseball, basketball, cross country, fencing, football, golf, ice hockey, indoor track, soccer, swimming-diving, tennis, track & field. Men's Non-aid: lacrosse
W: basketball, cross country, fencing, golf, indoor track, soccer, softball, swimming-diving, tennis, track & field, volleyball

UNIVERSITY OF SOUTHERN INDIANA

8600 University Boulevard
Evansville, IN 47712
(812) 464-1767 Contact: James M. Patton
Men's Aid (#/$): 16/$25,261
Women's Aid (#/$): 12/$11,775
M: baseball, basketball, cross country, golf, soccer, tennis
W: basketball, cross country, softball, tennis, volleyball

VALPARAISO UNIVERSITY

Recreation Center
Valparaiso, IN 46383
(219) 464-5232 Contact: Bill Rogers
Unspecified athletic aid available
M: baseball, basketball, cross country, diving, football, golf, soccer, swimming, swimming-diving, tennis, track & field, wrestling. Men's Non-aid: indoor track
W: basketball, diving, field hockey, gymnastics, softball, swimming, swimming-diving, tennis, volleyball

VINCENNES UNIVERSITY JUNIOR COLLEGE

1002 North First Street
Vincennes, IN 47591
2-year college
(812) 885-4511 Contact: Dan Sparks
Unspecified athletic aid available
M: baseball, basketball, bowling, cross country, diving, golf, indoor track, swimming, swimming-diving, tennis, track & field. Men's Non-aid: soccer
W: basketball, bowling, cross country, diving, indoor track, swimming, swimming-diving, track & field, volleyball

WABASH COLLEGE

P.O. Box 352
Crawfordsville, IN 47933-0352
(317) 364-4364 Contact: Jim Amidon

Men's Non-aid: baseball, basketball, cross country, diving, football, golf, soccer, swimming, swimming-diving, tennis, track & field, wrestling

Iowa

BRIAR CLIFF COLLEGE

P.O. Box 2100
Sioux City, IA 51104-2100
(712) 279-5440 Contact: Don Duzik
Men's Aid (#/$): 10/$8,901
Women's Aid (#/$): 12/$7,773
M: baseball, basketball, golf
W: basketball, golf, softball, volleyball

BUENA VISTA COLLEGE

610 West 4th Street
Storm Lake, IA 50588
(712) 749-2253 Contact: Jim Hershberger
Men's Non-aid: baseball, basketball, cross country, diving, football, golf, swimming, swimming-diving, tennis, track & field, wrestling
Women's Non-aid: basketball, cross country, diving, golf, softball, swimming, swimming-diving, tennis, track & field, volleyball

CENTRAL COLLEGE

812 University Avenue
Pella, IA 50219
(515) 628-5278 Contact: Larry Happel
Men's Non-aid: baseball, basketball, cross country, football, golf, indoor track, tennis, track & field, wrestling
Women's Non-aid: basketball, cross country, golf, indoor track, softball, tennis, track & field, volleyball

CLINTON COMMUNITY COLLEGE

1000 Lincoln Boulevard
Clinton, IA 52732
2-year college
(319) 242-6841 Contact: Bob Walker
Men's Aid (#/$): 5/$4,000
Women's Aid (#/$): 4/$1,800
Restrictions and notes: Tuition awards only.
M: basketball
W: volleyball

COE COLLEGE

1220 First Avenue NE
Cedar Rapids, IA 52402
(319) 399-8570 Contact: Alice Davidson
Restrictions and notes: Wide variety of non-athletic aid available.
Men's Non-aid: baseball, basketball, cross country, football, golf, indoor track, soccer, swimming, track & field, wrestling
Women's Non-aid: basketball, cross country, football, indoor track, soccer, softball, swimming, tennis, volleyball, wrestling

CORNELL COLLEGE

Sports Center
Mount Vernon, IA 52314
(319) 895-4483 Contact: Mick Kulikowski
Men's Non-aid: baseball, basketball, cross country, football, golf, ice hockey, indoor track, soccer, swimming, swimming-diving, tennis, track & field, wrestling
Women's Non-aid: basketball, cross country, indoor track, soccer, softball, swimming, swimming-diving, tennis, track & field, volleyball

DES MOINES AREA COMMUNITY COLLEGE

1125 Hancock Drive
Boone, IA 50036
2-year college
(515) 432-7203 Contact: Harold Johnson
Men's Aid (#/$): 20/$10,000
Women's Aid (#/$): 20/$10,000
M: baseball, basketball
W: basketball, softball

DRAKE UNIVERSITY

Drake Fieldhouse
Des Moines, IA 50311

(515) 271-3012 Contact: Mike Mahon
Men's Aid (#/$): 52/$814,004
Women's Aid (#/$): 51/$814,698
M: basketball, cross country, golf, indoor track, soccer, tennis, track & field, wrestling. Men's Non-aid: football
W: basketball, cross country, indoor track, softball, tennis, track & field

GRACELAND COLLEGE
700 College Avenue
Lamoni, IA 50140
(515) 784-5136 Contact: Nancy Wolff
Men's Aid (#/$): 216/$474,823
Women's Aid (#/$): 104/$171,217
M: baseball, basketball, cross country, football, soccer, tennis, track & field, volleyball
W: basketball, cross country, softball, tennis, track & field, volleyball

GRAND VIEW COLLEGE
1200 Grand View
Des Moines, IA 50316
(515) 263-2897 Contact: Lou Yaciniat
Unspecified athletic aid available
M: baseball, basketball, golf, soccer, tennis. Men's Non-aid: cross country, track & field
W: basketball, golf, softball, tennis, volleyball. Women's Non-aid: cross country, track & field

GRINNELL COLLEGE
P.O. Box 805
Grinnell, IA 50112-8012
(515) 269-3832 Contact: Andy Hamilton
Men's Non-aid: baseball, basketball, cross country, diving, football, golf, indoor track, soccer, swimming, swimming-diving, tennis, track & field
Women's Non-aid: basketball, cross country, diving, indoor track, softball, swimming, swimming-diving, tennis, track & field, volleyball

INDIAN HILLS COMMUNITY COLLEGE
721 North First Street
Centerville, IA 52544-1223
2-year college
(515) 856-2143 Contact: Dick Sharp
Unspecified athletic aid available
M: baseball, basketball

IOWA STATE UNIVERSITY OF SCIENCE AND TECHNOLOGY
1802 South Fourth Street
Ames, IA 50010
(515) 294-3372 Contact: Dave Starr
Unspecified athletic aid available
M: baseball, basketball, cross country, football, golf, gymnastics, swimming, track & field, wrestling
W: basketball, cross country, golf, gymnastics, softball, tennis, track & field, volleyball

IOWA WESLEYAN COLLEGE
601 North Main
Mount Pleasant, IA 52641
(319) 385-6301 Contact: Randy Novotny
Unspecified athletic aid available
M: baseball, basketball, cross country, football, indoor track, track & field. Men's Non-aid: swimming
W: basketball, cross country, indoor track, softball, track & field, volleyball. Women's Non-aid: swimming

KIRKWOOD COMMUNITY COLLEGE
Box 2068
Cedar Rapids, IA 52406
2-year college
(319) 398-4909 Contact: Ted Oglesby
Unspecified athletic aid available
M: baseball, basketball, wrestling
W: basketball, softball

LORAS COLLEGE
1450 Alta Vista
Dubuque, IA 52001
(319) 588-7407 Contact: Howard Thomas
Men's Non-aid: baseball, basketball, cross country, diving, football, golf, lacrosse, martial arts, soccer, swimming, swimming-diving, tennis, track & field, wrestling

Women's Non-aid: basketball, cross country, diving, golf, indoor track, martial arts, softball, swimming, swimming-diving, tennis, track & field

LUTHER COLLEGE
700 College Drive
Decorah, IA 52101
(319) 387-1586 Contact: Dave Blanchard
Men's Non-aid: baseball, basketball, cross country, football, golf, indoor track, swimming-diving, synchronized swimming, tennis, track & field, wrestling
Women's Non-aid: basketball, cross country, field hockey, golf, indoor track, softball, swimming-diving, tennis, track & field, volleyball

MORNINGSIDE COLLEGE
1501 Morningside Avenue
Sioux City, IA 51106
(712) 274-5127 Contact: Mark Gambaina
Unspecified athletic aid available
M: baseball, basketball, football, softball, track & field. Men's Non-aid: golf, tennis
W: baseball, basketball, softball, volleyball. Women's Non-aid: golf, tennis

MOUNT MERCY COLLEGE
1330 Elmhurst Drive
Cedar Rapids, IA 52402
(319) 363-8213 Contact: Paul Gavin
Restrictions and notes: All aid is in the form of academic scholarships and grants for those who qualify.
Men's Non-aid: baseball, basketball, cross country, golf, soccer, track & field
Women's Non-aid: basketball, cross country, golf, softball, track & field, volleyball

NORTH IOWA AREA COMMUNITY COLLEGE
500 College Drive
Mason City, IA 50401
2-year college
(515) 421-4281 Contact: Jerry Dunbar
Unspecified athletic aid available
M: baseball, basketball, football, softball. Men's Non-aid: cross country skiing, golf, volleyball, weightlifting
W: basketball, softball. Women's Non-aid: cross country skiing, volleyball

NORTHWESTERN COLLEGE
Seventh Street South
Orange City, IA 51041
(712) 737-4821 Contact: Bill Boote
Men's Aid (#/$): 49/$38,084
Women's Aid (#/$): 32/$18,900
M: baseball, basketball, cross country, football, indoor track, wrestling. Men's Non-aid: golf, tennis
W: basketball, cross country, indoor track, softball, volleyball. Women's Non-aid: golf, tennis

SAINT AMBROSE COLLEGE
518 West Locust Street
Davenport, IA 52803
(319) 383-8943 Contact: Don White
Unspecified athletic aid available
M: baseball, basketball, cross country, football, golf, tennis
W: basketball, golf, softball, tennis, volleyball

SOUTHEASTERN COMMUNITY COLLEGE
1015 South Avenue
West Burlington, IA 52665
2-year college
(319) 752-2731 Contact: Curtis A. Blom
Unspecified athletic aid available
M: basketball. Men's Non-aid: baseball, bowling, golf
W: basketball

TEIKYO MARYCREST UNIVERSITY
1607 West 12th Street
Davenport, IA 52804
(319) 326-9201 Contact: Betty Albrecht
Unspecified athletic aid available

M: baseball, basketball, cross country, soccer
W: basketball, cross country, soccer, softball, volleyball

TEIKYO WESTMAR UNIVERSITY

1002 Third Avenue SE
Le Mars, IA 51031
(712) 546-7081 X. 216 Contact: Dennis J. Mertes
Men's Aid (#/$): 178/$339,186
Women's Aid (#/$): 64/$99,200
Restrictions and notes: In addition to listed sports, this school offers women's aid in Danceline.
M: baseball, basketball, football, golf, indoor track, soccer, tennis, track & field, wrestling
W: basketball, indoor track, soccer, softball, track & field, volleyball. Women's Non-aid: golf

UNIVERSITY OF DUBUQUE

2000 University Avenue
Dubuque, IA 52001
(319) 589-3230 Contact: Jay Schiesl
Men's Non-aid: baseball, basketball, cross country, football, golf, tennis, track & field, wrestling
Women's Non-aid: basketball, cross country, golf, softball, tennis, track & field, volleyball

UNIVERSITY OF IOWA

205 Carver-Hawkeye Arena
Iowa City, IA 52242
(319) 335-9411 Contact: George Wine
Unspecified athletic aid available
M: baseball, basketball, cross country, diving, field hockey, football, golf, gymnastics, indoor track, softball, swimming, swimming-diving, tennis, track & field, volleyball, wrestling
W: basketball, field hockey, golf, gymnastics, softball, swimming-diving, tennis, track & field, volleyball

UNIVERSITY OF NORTHERN IOWA

NW Upper UNI-Dome
Cedar Falls, IA 50614-0314
(319) 273-6354 Contact: Nancy Justis
Unspecified athletic aid available
M: baseball, basketball, cross country, football, indoor track, track & field, wrestling. Men's Non-aid: golf, swimming-diving, tennis
W: basketball, cross country, golf, indoor track, softball, swimming-diving, tennis, track & field, volleyball

UPPER IOWA UNIVERSITY

P.O. Box 1857
Fayette, IA 52142
(319) 425-5266 Contact: Sandy Miller
Men's Non-aid: baseball, basketball, cross country, football, golf, tennis, track & field, wrestling
Women's Non-aid: basketball, cross country, golf, softball, tennis, track & field, volleyball

WALDORF COLLEGE

106 South Sixth Street
Forest City, IA 50436
2-year college
(515) 582-8206 Contact: Julie Lentz
Men's Aid (#/$): 113/$173,760
Women's Aid (#/$): 67/$59,060
M: baseball, basketball, football, golf, wrestling
W: basketball, golf, softball, volleyball, cheerleading

WARTBURG COLLEGE

222 Ninth Street NW
P.O. Box 1003
Waverly, IA 50677-0903
(319) 352-8277 Contact: Duane Schroeder
Men's Non-aid: baseball, basketball, cross country, football, golf, indoor track, soccer, tennis, track & field, wrestling
Women's Non-aid: basketball, cross country, golf, indoor track, softball, tennis, track & field, volleyball

WILLIAM PENN COLLEGE

201 Trueblood Avenue
Oskaloosa, IA 52577

(515) 673-1079 Contact: John Eberline
Men's Non-aid: baseball, basketball, cross country, football, golf, indoor track, tennis, track & field, wrestling
Women's Non-aid: basketball, cross country, golf, indoor track, softball, tennis, track & field, volleyball

Kansas

ALLEN COUNTY COLLEGE

1801 North Cottonwood
Iola, KS 66749
2-year college
(316) 365-5116 Contact: John Masterson
Men's Aid (#/$): 74/$30,640
Women's Aid (#/$): 37/$15,647
M: baseball, basketball, cross country, golf, soccer, track & field
W: basketball, cross country, softball, track & field, volleyball

BAKER UNIVERSITY

Eighth and Grove
P.O. Box 65
Baldwin, KS 66006
(913) 594-6451 x. 588 Contact: Brian Borland
Men's Aid (#/$): 77/unspecified $
Women's Aid (#/$): 22/unspecified $
M: baseball, basketball, cross country, football, golf, indoor track, soccer, tennis, track & field
W: basketball, cross country, indoor track, soccer, softball, tennis, track & field, volleyball

BARTON COUNTY COLLEGE

Route 3
Great Bend, KS 67530
2-year college
(316) 792-2701 Contact: Lynn Lichter
Men's Aid (#/$): 94/unspecified $
Women's Aid (#/$): 85/unspecified $
M: baseball, basketball, cross country, golf, indoor track, track & field
W: basketball, cross country, indoor track, softball, tennis, track & field, volleyball

BENEDICTINE COLLEGE

1020 North Second
Box N-75
Atchison, KS 66002
(913) 367-5340 Contact: Drew Shin
Unspecified athletic aid available
M: baseball, basketball, football, golf, indoor track, soccer, tennis, track & field
W: basketball, golf, indoor track, soccer, softball, tennis, track & field, volleyball

BETHANY COLLEGE

425 North First Street
Lindsborg, KS 67456
(913) 227-3311 X. 275 Contact: A. John Pearson
Men's Non-aid: baseball, basketball, cross country, football, golf, soccer, softball, swimming-diving, tennis, track & field
Women's Non-aid: baseball, basketball, cross country, field hockey, golf, softball, swimming-diving, tennis, track & field, volleyball

BETHEL COLLEGE

300 East 27th Street
North Newton, KS 67117
(316) 283-2500 Contact: Dick Koontz
Unspecified athletic aid available
M: basketball, football, tennis, track & field. Men's Non-aid: indoor track, soccer
W: basketball, tennis, track & field, volleyball. Women's Non-aid: soccer

BUTLER COUNTY COMMUNITY COLLEGE

901 South Haverhill Road
El Dorado, KS 67042
2-year college
(316) 321-5083 Contact: Kristin J. Blomquist
Men's Non-aid: baseball, basketball, golf, racquetball, tennis

Women's Non-aid: softball, tennis, volleyball

CENTRAL COLLEGE
1200 South Main Street
McPherson, KS 67460
2-year college
(316) 241-0723 Contact: Gary Turner
Men's Non-aid: baseball, basketball, cross country, football, golf, indoor track, tennis, track & field, wrestling
Women's Non-aid: basketball, cross country, golf, indoor track, softball, tennis, track & field, volleyball

CLOUD COUNTY COMMUNITY COLLEGE
P.O. Box 1002
Concordia, KS 66901-1002
2-year college
(913) 243-1435 Contact: Rod Stacken
Unspecified athletic aid available
M: baseball, basketball, cross country, golf, indoor track, soccer, tennis, track & field
W: basketball, cross country, indoor track, softball, tennis, track & field, volleyball

COFFEYVILLE COMMUNITY COLLEGE
11th and Willow
Coffeyville, KS 67337
2-year college
(316) 251-7700 Contact: Nancy Misch
Unspecified athletic aid available
M: baseball, basketball, football, golf, tennis, track & field
W: basketball, tennis, track & field, volleyball

COLBY COMMUNITY COLLEGE
1255 South Range
Colby, KS 67701
2-year college
(913) 462-3984 Contact: Jason Nuss
Men's Aid (#/$): 60/$60,000
Women's Aid (#/$): 40/$40,000
M: baseball, basketball, cross country, indoor track, rodeo, track & field, wrestling
W: basketball, cross country, indoor track, rodeo, softball, track & field, volleyball

COWLEY COUNTY COMMUNITY COLLEGE
P.O. Box 1147
Arkansas City, KS 67005-1147
2-year college
(316) 442-0430 X. 268 Contact: Larry Grose
Unspecified athletic aid available
M: baseball, basketball, tennis
W: basketball, softball, volleyball

DODGE CITY COMMUNITY COLLEGE
2501 North 14th Avenue
Dodge City, KS 67801
2-year college
(316) 225-1321 Contact: Howie Smith
Men's Aid (#/$): 95/unspecified $
Women's Aid (#/$): 55/unspecified $
M: baseball, basketball, football, golf, rodeo
W: basketball, softball, volleyball

EMPORIA STATE UNIVERSITY
200 Commercial Street
Emporia, KS 66801
(316) 343-5454 Contact: Dan Ballou
Unspecified athletic aid available
M: baseball, basketball, cross country, football, golf, indoor track, tennis, track & field
W: basketball, cross country, indoor track, softball, tennis, track & field, volleyball

FORT HAYS STATE UNIVERSITY
600 Park Street
Hays, KS 67601
(913) 628-4408 Contact: Karl Metzger
Men's Aid (#/$): 196/$311,254
Women's Aid (#/$): 70/$94,265
M: baseball, basketball, cross country, football, golf, indoor track, track & field, wrestling
W: basketball, cross country, indoor track, tennis, track & field, volleyball

FORT SCOTT COLLEGE
2108 South Horton
Fort Scott, KS 66701
2-year college
(316) 223-2700 Contact: John Beal
Unspecified athletic aid available
M: baseball, basketball, football, indoor track, rodeo, track & field
W: basketball, rodeo, tennis, volleyball

FRIENDS UNIVERSITY
2100 University
Wichita, KS 67213
(316) 261-5850 Contact: Anita K. Curry
Unspecified athletic aid available
M: baseball, basketball, football, soccer
W: basketball, softball, volleyball

GARDEN CITY COMMUNITY COLLEGE
801 Campus Drive
Garden City, KS 67846
2-year college
(316) 276-7611 Contact: Dennis Perryman
Restrictions and notes: 333 scholarships total.
M: basketball, cross country, football, golf, indoor track, soccer, track & field, wrestling
W: basketball, cross country, indoor track, track & field, volleyball

HASKELL INDIAN JUNIOR COLLEGE
P.O. Box 461207
Lawrence, KS 66046
2-year college
(913) 749-8459 Contact: Gerald L. Tuckwin
Men's Non-aid: basketball, cross country, football, golf, track & field
Women's Non-aid: basketball, cross country, golf, track & field

HIGHLAND COMMUNITY COLLEGE
Box 68
Highland, KS 66035
2-year college
(913) 442-3238 Contact: Tom Smith
Unspecified athletic aid available
M: baseball, basketball, cross country, football, indoor track, track & field
W: basketball, cross country, indoor track, softball, track & field, volleyball

HUTCHINSON COLLEGE
1300 North Plum
Hutchinson, KS 67501
2-year college
(316) 665-3530 Contact: Jack Morris
Unspecified athletic aid available
M: baseball, basketball, cross country, football, golf, tennis, track & field
W: basketball, tennis, track & field, volleyball

JOHNSON COUNTY COMMUNITY COLLEGE
12345 College at Quivira
Overland Park, KS 66210
2-year college
(913) 469-3886 Contact: J. Michael Yasko
Unspecified athletic aid available
M: baseball, basketball, cross country, golf, indoor track, soccer, tennis, track & field. Men's Non-aid: weightlifting
W: basketball, cross country, indoor track, softball, tennis, track & field, volleyball

KANSAS CITY KANSAS COMMUNITY COLLEGE
7250 State Avenue
Kansas City, KS 66112
2-year college
(913) 334-1100 Contact: Alan Hoskins
Unspecified athletic aid available
M: baseball, basketball, cross country, golf, tennis, track & field
W: basketball, cross country, softball, track & field, volleyball

KANSAS NEWMAN COLLEGE
3100 McCormick Avenue
Wichita, KS 67213
(316) 942-4291 X. 118 Contact: Paul Sanagorski

Unspecified athletic aid available
Restrictions and notes: 90% of all athletes receive some assistance.
M: baseball, golf, soccer
W: basketball, soccer, softball, volleyball

KANSAS STATE UNIVERSITY
1800 College Avenue
Bramlage Coliseum
Manhattan, KS 66502-3355
(913) 532-6735 Contact: Ben Boyle
Men's Aid (#/$): 194/$912,805
Women's Aid (#/$): 70/$347,298
M: baseball, basketball, football, golf, indoor track, track & field
W: basketball, cross country, golf, indoor track, tennis, track & field, volleyball

KANSAS WESLEYAN COLLEGE
100 East Claflin
Salina, KS 67401
(913) 827-5541 X. 217 Contact: Glenna Alexander
Unspecified athletic aid available
M: baseball, basketball, cross country, football, indoor track, track & field
W: basketball, cross country, indoor track, softball, track & field, volleyball

LABETTE COMMUNITY COLLEGE
200 South 14th Street
Parsons, KS 67357
2-year college
(316) 421-0911 Contact: Tom Hilton
Unspecified athletic aid available
M: basketball, volleyball. Men's Non-aid: baseball, wrestling
W: basketball, tennis, volleyball

MCPHERSON COLLEGE
1600 East Euclid
McPherson, KS 67460
(316) 241-0731 Contact: Glen E. Snell
Unspecified athletic aid available
M: basketball, cross country, football, golf, indoor track, tennis
W: basketball, cross country, golf, indoor track, tennis, volleyball

MIDAMERICA NAZARENE COLLEGE
2030 East College Way
Olathe, KS 66062-1899
(913) 782-3750 Contact: Rick Fields
Men's Aid (#/$): 48/$47,500
Women's Aid (#/$): 8/$9,000
M: baseball, basketball, cross country, football, indoor track, soccer, track & field
W: basketball, cross country, indoor track, softball, track & field, volleyball

OTTAWA UNIVERSITY
10th and Cedar
Ottawa, KS 66067
(913) 242-5200 X. 235 Contact: Ron Yingling
Unspecified athletic aid available
M: basketball, cross country, football, golf, soccer, tennis, track & field
W: basketball, cross country, golf, tennis, track & field, volleyball

PITTSBURG STATE UNIVERSITY
1701 South Broadway
Pittsburg, KS 66762
(316) 235-4122 Contact: Shawn Ahearn
Men's Aid (#/$): 68/$335,036
Women's Aid (#/$): 24/$118,248
M: baseball, basketball, cross country, football, golf, indoor track, track & field
W: basketball, cross country, indoor track, softball, track & field, volleyball

PRATT COMMUNITY COLLEGE
North Highway 61
Pratt, KS 67124
2-year college
(316) 672-5641 Contact: Don Schwartz
Men's Aid (#/$): 115/$123,000
Women's Aid (#/$): 65/$68,000
Restrictions and notes: Athletic aid covers tuition and books only.
M: baseball, basketball, cheerleading, cross country, indoor track, rodeo, tennis, track & field
W: basketball, cheerleading, cross country, indoor track, rodeo, tennis, track & field, volleyball

SAINT MARY COLLEGE
Leavenworth, KS 66048
(913) 682-5151 Contact: Judy Wiedower
Men's Aid (#/$): 20/$9,450
Women's Aid (#/$): 18/$10,550
M: basketball, soccer
W: soccer, softball, volleyball

SEWARD COUNTY COMMUNITY COLLEGE
1801 North Kansas
Liveral, KS 67901
2-year college
(316) 624-1951 Contact: Richard Robinson
Unspecified athletic aid available
M: baseball, basketball, tennis
W: basketball, tennis, volleyball

SOUTHWESTERN COLLEGE
100 College Street
Winfield, KS 67156
(316) 221-4150 Contact: Margaret Robinson
Unspecified athletic aid available
M: basketball, cross country, football, golf, indoor track, tennis, track & field
W: basketball, cross country, golf, indoor track, tennis, track & field, volleyball

STERLING COLLEGE
Broadway and Cleveland
Sterling, KS 67579
(316) 278-4277 Contact: Jim Woudstra
Unspecified athletic aid available
M: baseball, basketball, football, softball, tennis, track & field
W: baseball, basketball, softball, tennis, track & field, volleyball

TABOR COLLEGE
400 South Jefferson
Hillsboro, KS 67063
(316) 947-3121 Contact: Karl Kliewer
Unspecified athletic aid available
M: baseball, basketball, football, soccer, tennis
W: basketball, softball, tennis, volleyball

UNIVERSITY OF KANSAS
202 Allen Fieldhouse
Lawrence, KS 66045-8881
(913) 864-3417 Contact: Doug Vance
Men's Aid (#/$): 217/$1,764,800
Women's Aid (#/$): 114/$697,900
M: baseball, basketball, cross country, diving, football, golf, indoor track, swimming, swimming-diving, tennis, track & field
W: basketball, cross country, diving, golf, indoor track, softball, swimming, swimming-diving, tennis, track & field, volleyball

WASHBURN UNIVERSITY
1700 College
Topeka, KS 66621
(913) 295-6334 Contact: Mary Beth Brutton
Men's Aid (#/$): 26/$53,551
Women's Aid (#/$): 11/$22,950
M: baseball, basketball, football, golf, tennis
W: basketball, softball, tennis, volleyball

WICHITA STATE UNIVERSITY
Campus Box 18
Wichita, KS 67208
(316) 689-3265 Contact: Scott Schumacher
Men's Aid (#/$): 48/$330,000
Women's Aid (#/$): 57/$356,000
M: baseball, basketball, cross country, golf, indoor track, tennis, track & field
W: basketball, cross country, golf, indoor track, softball, tennis, track & field, volleyball

Kentucky

ALICE LLOYD COLLEGE
Purpose Road
Pippa Passes, KY 41844
(606) 368-2101 X. 4801 Contact: Nancy Melton
Men's Aid (#/$): 4/$33,064

Women's Aid (#/$): 5/$41,330
M: baseball, basketball. Men's Non-aid: tennis
W: basketball. Women's Non-aid: softball

ASBURY COLLEGE
North Lexington Avenue
Wilmore, KY 40390-1148
(606) 858-3511 X. 2149 Contact: Troy R. Martin
Restrictions and notes: No athletic scholarships. Full program of need and merit based aid.
Men's Non-aid: baseball, basketball, cross country, soccer, swimming, tennis
Women's Non-aid: basketball, cross country, softball, swimming, tennis, volleyball

BELLARMINE COLLEGE
Newburg Road
Louisville, KY 40205
(502) 452-8380 Contact: Charles Just
Men's Aid (#/$): 23/$55,000
Women's Aid (#/$): 22/$29,314
Restrictions and notes: Men's basketball, 12 full grants. Women's basketball, 10. Partial tuition grants available in all other sports.
M: baseball, basketball, cross country, golf, soccer, tennis. Men's Non-aid: indoor track, track & field
W: basketball, cross country, field hockey, soccer, softball, tennis, volleyball. Women's Non-aid: indoor track, track & field

BRESCIA COLLEGE
717 Frederica Street
Owensboro, KY 42301
(502) 685-3131 Contact: Catharine P. Howell
Unspecified athletic aid available
M: basketball, golf, soccer
W: basketball, volleyball

CAMPBELLSVILLE COLLEGE
200 West College Street
Campbellsville, KY 42718-1657
(502) 789-5213 Contact: Mark Whitt
Men's Aid (#/$): 61/$107,422
Women's Aid (#/$): 26/$60,043
M: baseball, basketball, cross country, golf, soccer, swimming, tennis. Men's Non-aid: football
W: basketball, cross country, golf, softball, swimming, tennis

CUMBERLAND COLLEGE
P.O. Box 7881
Williamsburg, KY 40769
(606) 549-2200 X. 4364 Contact: Bill Sergent
Unspecified athletic aid available
M: baseball, basketball, cross country, golf, tennis. Men's Non-aid: football, track & field
W: basketball, softball, tennis, volleyball

EASTERN KENTUCKY UNIVERSITY
Lancaster Avenue
Richmond, KY 40475
(606) 622-1253 Contact: Martha Mullins
Men's Aid (#/$): 107/$549,690
Women's Aid (#/$): 49/$328,666
M: baseball, basketball, cross country, football, golf, indoor track, tennis, track & field
W: basketball, cross country, indoor track, softball, tennis, track & field, volleyball

GEORGETOWN COLLEGE
400 East College Street
Georgetown, KY 40324-1696
(502) 863-8027 Contact: Debra Covert
Men's Aid (#/$): 137/$406,804
Women's Aid (#/$): 27/$56,753
M: baseball, basketball, cross country, football, golf, soccer, tennis
W: basketball, cross country, softball, tennis, volleyball

KENTUCKY CHRISTIAN COLLEGE
617 North Carol Malone Boulevard
Grayson, KY 41143-1199
(606) 474-6613 X. 3215 Contact: Bruce W. Dixon

Men's Non-aid: baseball, basketball, soccer
Women's Non-aid: basketball

KENTUCKY STATE UNIVERSITY
East Main Street
Frankfort, KY 40601
(502) 227-6509 Contact: Frank McGowan
Unspecified athletic aid available
M: baseball, basketball, cross country, football, indoor track, track & field. Men's Non-aid: golf, tennis
W: basketball, indoor track, track & field, volleyball. Women's Non-aid: cross country, golf, softball, tennis

KENTUCKY WESLEYAN COLLEGE
3000 Fredrica Street
Owensboro, KY 42301-1039
(502) 683-4795 Contact: Roy Pickerill
Men's Aid (#/$): 72/$152,092
Women's Aid (#/$): 68/$24,720
M: baseball, basketball, golf, soccer. Men's Non-aid: football
W: basketball, softball, tennis, volleyball

LEES JUNIOR COLLEGE
601 Jefferson
Jackson, KY 41339
2-year college
(606) 666-7521 Contact: Susan Herald
Men's Aid (#/$): 24/$34,000
Women's Aid (#/$): 14/$22,500
M: baseball, basketball. Men's Non-aid: cross country
W: basketball, softball. Women's Non-aid: cross country

MOREHEAD STATE UNIVERSITY
UPO 1023
Morehead, KY 40351
(606) 783-2500 Contact: Randy Stacy
Unspecified athletic aid available
M: baseball, basketball, football, golf, tennis. Men's Non-aid: cross country, diving, soccer, swimming, swimming-diving
W: basketball, softball, tennis, volleyball. Women's Non-aid: cross country, diving, soccer, swimming, swimming-diving

MURRAY STATE UNIVERSITY
Stewart Stadium
Room 211
Murray, KY 42071
(502) 762-4271 Contact: Jimmy Wilder
Unspecified athletic aid available
M: baseball, basketball, cross country, football, golf, indoor track, riflery, tennis, track & field
W: basketball, cross country, indoor track, riflery, tennis, track & field, volleyball

NORTHERN KENTUCKY UNIVERSITY
Louise B. Nunn Drive
Highland Heights, KY 41076
(606) 572-5470 Contact: J.D. Campbell
Unspecified athletic aid available
M: baseball, basketball, cross country, golf, soccer, tennis
W: basketball, cross country, softball, tennis, volleyball

PIKEVILLE COLLEGE
Sycamore Street
Pikeville, KY 41501
(606) 432-9382 Contact: Bobby G. Price
Men's Aid (#/$): 9/$36,000
Women's Aid (#/$): 10/$36,000
M: basketball. Men's Non-aid: baseball
W: basketball. Women's Non-aid: softball

ST. CATHERINE COLLEGE
Bardstown Road
Springfield, KY 40061
2-year college
(606) 336-9303 Contact: Pat Smith
Unspecified athletic aid available
M: basketball. Men's Non-aid: cross country
W: basketball

SUE BENNETT COLLEGE
101 College Street
London, KY 40741

2-year college
(606) 864-6621 Contact: Gene McSweeney
Men's Aid (#/$): 17.5/$122,500
Women's Aid (#/$): 22.5/$157,500
M: baseball, basketball, cross country, soccer, softball
W: basketball, cheerleading, cross country, soccer, softball, volleyball

THOMAS MORE COLLEGE

333 Thomas More Parkway
Crestview Hills, KY 41017
(606) 344-3673 Contact: Ted Kiep
Unspecified athletic aid available
M: baseball, basketball, tennis
W: basketball, volleyball. Women's Non-aid: softball

TRANSYLVANIA UNIVERSITY

300 North Broadway
Lexington, KY 40508-1797
(606) 233-8120 Contact: Sarah Emmons
Men's Aid (#/$): 52/$255,109
Women's Aid (#/$): 57/$143,055
M: basketball, golf, soccer, swimming, tennis
W: basketball, field hockey, softball, swimming, tennis

UNION COLLEGE

310 College Street
Barbourville, KY 40906
(606) 546-4151 Contact: Scott Cummings
Unspecified athletic aid available
M: baseball, basketball, swimming, swimming-diving, tennis
W: basketball, softball

UNIVERSITY OF KENTUCKY

Memorial Coliseum
Room 23
Lexington, KY 40506-0019
(606) 257-3838 Contact: Chris Cameron
Men's Aid (#/$): 204/$1,106,367
Women's Aid (#/$): 82/$543,432
M: baseball, basketball, cross country, diving, football, golf, indoor track, soccer, swimming, swimming-diving, tennis, track & field. Men's Non-aid: riflery
W: basketball, cross country, diving, golf, gymnastics, indoor track, soccer, swimming, swimming-diving, tennis, track & field, volleyball. Women's Non-aid: riflery

UNIVERSITY OF LOUISVILLE

Floyd and Brandeis Street
Louisville, KY 40292
(502) 588-6581 Contact: Kenny Klein
Men's Aid (#/$): 231/$1,232,332
Women's Aid (#/$): 95/$449,050
M: baseball, basketball, cross country, diving, football, golf, indoor track, soccer, swimming, tennis, track & field
W: basketball, cross country, diving, field hockey, indoor track, soccer, swimming, tennis, track & field, volleyball

WESTERN KENTUCKY UNIVERSITY

Wetherby Administration Building
Bowling Green, KY 42101
(502) 745-4295 Contact: Paul Just
Unspecified athletic aid available
M: baseball, basketball, cross country, diving, football, golf, indoor track, soccer, swimming, swimming-diving, tennis, track & field
W: cross country, golf, indoor track, tennis, track & field, volleyball

Louisiana

CENTENARY COLLEGE

P.O. Box 41188
Shreveport, LA 71134-1188
(318) 869-5092 Contact: Steve Murray
Men's Aid (#/$): 42/$464,207
Women's Aid (#/$): 25/$275,438
M: baseball, basketball, cross country, golf, riflery, soccer, tennis
W: cross country, gymnastics, riflery, soccer, softball, tennis, volleyball

DELGADO COLLEGE
615 City Park Avenue
New Orleans, LA 70119
2-year college
(504) 483-4381 Contact: Tommy Smith
Unspecified athletic aid available
M: baseball, basketball
W: basketball

DILLARD UNIVERSITY
2601 Gentilly Boulevard
New Orleans, LA 70122
(504) 283-8822 Contact: Mary Horne
Unspecified athletic aid available
M: basketball
W: basketball

GRAMBLING STATE UNIVERSITY
P.O. Box N
Grambling, LA 71245
(318) 274-2761 Contact: Stanley O. Lewis
Men's Aid (#/$): 118/unspecified $
Women's Aid (#/$): 46/unspecified $
M: baseball, basketball, football, golf, tennis, track & field
W: basketball, cross country, golf, indoor track, tennis, track & field, volleyball

LOUISIANA COLLEGE
P.O. Box 584
Pineville, LA 71359-0584
(318) 487-7194 Contact: Derald Harris
Men's Aid (#/$): 12/$96,000
Women's Aid (#/$): 10/$80,000
M: basketball, cheerleading
W: basketball, cheerleading

LOUISIANA STATE UNIVERSITY
P.O. Box 25095
Baton Rouge, LA 70894-5095
(504) 388-8226 Contact: Herb Vincent
Men's Aid (#/$): 73/$299,154
Women's Aid (#/$): 34/$159,444
M: baseball, basketball, cross country, diving, football, golf, indoor track, swimming, tennis, track & field
W: basketball, cross country, diving, golf, gymnastics, indoor track, swimming, tennis, track & field, volleyball

LOUISIANA STATE UNIVERSITY (ALEXANDRIA)
Alexandria, LA 71301
2-year college
(318) 473-6453 Contact: Michael Medill
Unspecified athletic aid available
M: baseball, basketball, cross country, diving, football, golf, indoor track, swimming, tennis, track & field
W: basketball, cross country, diving, golf, gymnastics, indoor track, swimming, tennis, track & field, volleyball

LOUISIANA TECH UNIVERSITY
P.O. Box 3046
Tech Station
Ruston, LA 71272
(318) 257-3144 Contact: Keith Prince
Men's Aid (#/$): 126/$581,616
Women's Aid (#/$): 48/$221,000
M: baseball, basketball, cross country, football, golf, indoor track, track & field. Men's Non-aid: power lifting, racquetball, soccer
W: basketball, cross country, indoor track, softball, tennis, track & field, volleyball. Women's Non-aid: power lifting, racquetball, soccer

MCNEESE STATE UNIVERSITY
P.O. Box 92735
Lake Charles, LA 70609
(318) 475-5207 Contact: Louis Bonnette
Men's Aid (#/$): 109/$558,995
Women's Aid (#/$): 36/$184,284
M: baseball, basketball, cross country, football, golf, track & field
W: basketball, cross country, softball, track & field, volleyball

NICHOLLS STATE UNIVERSITY
P.O. Box 2032
Thibodaux, LA 70301
(504) 446-8111
Men's Aid (#/$): 127/$216,617
Women's Aid (#/$): 66/$90,401

M: baseball, basketball, cross country, football. Men's Non-aid: riflery, soccer
W: basketball, cross country, softball, tennis, track & field, volleyball

NORTHEAST LOUISIANA UNIVERSITY
100 Stadium Drive
Monroe, LA 71209
(318) 342-5460 Contact: Bob Anderson
Men's Aid (#/$): 130/$642,000
Women's Aid (#/$): 50/$232,000
M: baseball, basketball, cross country, diving, football, golf, indoor track, softball, swimming, tennis, track & field
W: basketball, cross country, diving, indoor track, softball, swimming, track & field, volleyball

NORTHWESTERN STATE UNIVERSITY OF LOUISIANA
Athletic Department
Athletic Fieldhouse
Natchitoches, LA 71497
(318) 357-4272 Contact: Jack Freeman
Men's Aid (#/$): 111/$498,380
Women's Aid (#/$): 42/$188,580
M: baseball, basketball, football, golf, track & field
W: basketball, softball, tennis, track & field, volleyball

SOUTHEASTERN LOUISIANA UNIVERSITY
Box 880
Hammond, LA 70402
(504) 549-2341 Contact: Larry Hymel
Men's Aid (#/$): 49.5/$202,950
Women's Aid (#/$): 51/$209,100
M: baseball, basketball, cross country, golf, indoor track, tennis, track & field
W: basketball, cross country, indoor track, softball, tennis, track & field, volleyball

SOUTHERN UNIVERSITY AND A & M COLLEGE
Baton Rouge, LA 70813
(504) 771-2796 Contact: Cynthia Taiver
Unspecified athletic aid available
M: baseball, basketball, cross country, football, golf, indoor track, tennis, track & field
W: basketball, cross country, indoor track, track & field, volleyball. Women's Non-aid: tennis

TULANE UNIVERSITY
New Orleans, LA 70118
(504) 865-5723 Contact: Tom Lovett
Unspecified athletic aid available
M: baseball, cross country, football, golf, swimming, tennis, track & field
W: basketball, cross country, swimming, tennis, track & field, volleyball

UNIVERSITY OF NEW ORLEANS
Lakefront Arena
New Orleans, LA 70148-1613
(504) 286-6284/7027 Contact: Ed Cassiere
Men's Aid (#/$): 33.2/$188,481
Women's Aid (#/$): 18.2/$121,737
M: baseball, basketball, cross country, golf, indoor track, swimming-diving, track & field
W: basketball, cross country, indoor track, swimming-diving, tennis, track & field, volleyball

UNIVERSITY OF SOUTHWESTERN LOUISIANA
P.O. Box 41206
Lafayette, LA 70504
(318) 231-6498 Contact: Gracie Guillory
Men's Aid (#/$): 133/unspecified $
Women's Aid (#/$): 50/unspecified $
M: baseball, basketball, cross country, football, golf, indoor track, tennis, track & field
W: basketball, cross country, indoor track, softball, tennis, track & field, volleyball

XAVIER UNIVERSITY OF LOUISIANA
7325 Pine Palmetto
New Orleans, LA 70125

(504) 486-7411 X. 329 Contact: Richard Tucker
Men's Aid (#/$): 15/$100,000
Women's Aid (#/$): 15/$100,000
M: basketball
W: basketball

Maine

BATES COLLEGE
News Bureau
Lewistown, ME 04240
(207) 786-6330 Contact: Anne Whittemore
Men's Non-aid: alpine skiing, baseball, basketball, cross country, cross country skiing, football, golf, indoor track, lacrosse, soccer, squash, swimming-diving, tennis, track & field
Women's Non-aid: alpine skiing, basketball, cross country, cross country skiing, field hockey, golf, indoor track, lacrosse, soccer, softball, squash, swimming-diving, tennis, track & field, volleyball

BOWDOIN COLLEGE
Public Relations Office
Brunswick, ME 04011
(207) 725-3326 Contact: Sidney J. Watson
Restrictions and notes: No athletic scholarships available.
Men's Non-aid: alpine skiing, baseball, basketball, cross country, cross country skiing, diving, football, golf, ice hockey, indoor track, lacrosse, sailing, soccer, squash, swimming, swimming-diving, tennis, track & field, wrestling
Women's Non-aid: alpine skiing, basketball, cross country, cross country skiing, diving, field hockey, golf, ice hockey, indoor track, lacrosse, sailing, soccer, squash, softball, swimming, swimming-diving, tennis, track & field, volleyball

HUSSON COLLEGE
One College Circle
Bangor, ME 04401
(207) 947-1121 X. 227 Contact: Robert L. Caswell
Men's Non-aid: baseball, basketball, golf, soccer
Women's Non-aid: basketball, softball, volleyball

THOMAS COLLEGE
West River Road
Waterville, ME 04901
(207) 873-0771 X. 313 Contact: Jim Evans
Men's Non-aid: baseball, basketball, golf, soccer, softball, tennis
Women's Non-aid: baseball, basketball, golf, soccer, softball, tennis

UNITY COLLEGE
HC 78, Box 1
Unity, ME 04988
(207) 948-3131 X. 200 Contact: Carol Bradstreet
Unspecified athletic aid available
M: basketball, cross country, soccer
W: volleyball

UNIVERSITY OF MAINE
186 Memorial Gym
Orono, ME 04469
(207) 581-1086 Contact: Matt Burque
Unspecified athletic aid available
M: baseball, basketball, cheerleading, cross country, diving, football, golf, ice hockey, soccer, swimming, tennis, track & field
W: basketball, cheerleading, cross country, diving, field hockey, swimming, tennis, track & field

UNIVERSITY OF MAINE (FORT KENT)
Pleasant Street
Fort Kent, ME 04743
(207) 834-3162 X. 132 Contact: James J. Grandmaison
Men's Non-aid: basketball

Women's Non-aid: basketball, soccer, volleyball

UNIVERSITY OF MAINE (MACHIAS)
9 O'Brien Avenue
Machias, ME 04654
(207) 255-3313 X. 203 Contact: Stephanie Armstrong
Men's Non-aid: basketball, soccer
Women's Non-aid: basketball, soccer, volleyball

UNIVERSITY OF MAINE (PRESQUE ISLE)
Presque Isle, ME 04769
(207) 764-0311 X. 213 Contact: Barbara J. Bridges
Men's Aid (#/$): 3/$5,289
Women's Aid (#/$): 4/$4,519
Restrictions and notes: Tuition waivers also available to qualified student-athletes.
M: baseball, basketball, cross country, soccer
W: basketball, cross country, soccer, softball

UNIVERSITY OF NEW ENGLAND
11 Hills Beach Road
Biddeford, ME 04005
(207) 283-0171 X. 342 Contact: Daniel V. Pinch III
Unspecified athletic aid available
M: basketball, lacrosse, soccer
W: basketball, softball, volleyball

Maryland

BALTIMORE CITY COMMUNITY COLLEGE
2901 Liberty Heights Avenue
Baltimore, MD 21215
2-year college
(410) 333-5372 Contact: Elliott Oppenheim
Unspecified athletic aid available
M: baseball, basketball, cross country, indoor track, track & field
W: basketball, cross country, indoor track, track & field

BOWIE STATE UNIVERSITY
Bowie, MD 20715
(301) 464-6683 Contact: Donald Kish
Men's Aid (#/$): 80/$135,629
Women's Aid (#/$): 31/$28,957
M: baseball, basketball, cross country, football, indoor track, track & field
W: basketball, cross country, indoor track, softball, track & field, volleyball

CATONSVILLE COMMUNITY COLLEGE
800 South Rolling Road
Baltimore, MD 21228
2-year college
(410) 455-4197 Contact: Gary Keedy
Unspecified athletic aid available
M: baseball, basketball, bowling, cross country, diving, indoor track, lacrosse, soccer, swimming, swimming-diving, tennis, track & field
W: basketball, bowling, cross country, diving, indoor track, soccer, softball, swimming, swimming-diving, tennis, track & field, volleyball

CECIL COMMUNITY COLLEGE
1000 North East Road
North East, MD 21901
2-year college
(410) 287-6060 Contact: Tom Wilhide
Unspecified athletic aid available
M: baseball, basketball, soccer
W: basketball, softball, volleyball

CHARLES COUNTY COMMUNITY COLLEGE
Mitchell Road
La Plata, MD 20646
2-year college
(301) 934-2251 Contact: Chad Norcross
Men's Aid (#/$): 28/$12,188
Women's Aid (#/$): 18/$7,515

M: baseball, basketball, golf, soccer, tennis
W: softball, tennis, volleyball

COLLEGE OF NOTRE DAME OF MARYLAND
701 North Charles Street
Baltimore, MD 21210
(410) 532-3588 Contact: Donna M. Ledwin
Men's Non-aid: basketball, cross country, soccer
Women's Non-aid: cross country, softball, volleyball

COLUMBIA UNION COLLEGE
Takoma Park, MD 20912
(301) 891-4005 Contact: Alice Willsey
Unspecified athletic aid available
M: basketball, cross country, soccer, tennis, track & field
W: basketball, cross country, softball, tennis, track & field, volleyball

COPPIN STATE COLLEGE
2500 W. North Avenue
Baltimore, MD 21216
(410) 333-5642 Contact: Michael Preston
Unspecified athletic aid available
M: basketball, indoor track, track & field, wrestling. Men's Non-aid: baseball, cross country, soccer, tennis
W: basketball, indoor track, track & field. Women's Non-aid: cross country, tennis, volleyball

DUNDALK COMMUNITY COLLEGE
7200 Sollers Point Road
Baltimore, MD 21222
2-year college
(410) 522-5711 Contact: Lou Hammen
Unspecified athletic aid available
M: baseball, basketball, soccer, tennis
W: basketball, bowling, soccer, softball, tennis, volleyball

ESSEX COMMUNITY COLLEGE
7201 Rossville Boulevard
Baltimore, MD 21237
2-year college
(410) 522-1379 Contact: Tim Puls
Unspecified athletic aid available
M: baseball, basketball, bowling, cross country, golf, indoor track, lacrosse, softball, tennis, track & field
W: basketball, bowling, cross country, field hockey, lacrosse, tennis, track & field, volleyball

FREDERICK COMMUNITY COLLEGE
7932 Opossumtown Pike
Frederick, MD 21702
2-year college
(301) 846-2500 Contact: David G. Clark
Men's Non-aid: basketball, golf, softball, tennis, track & field, volleyball
Women's Non-aid: baseball, basketball, golf, soccer, tennis, track & field, wrestling

GARRETT COMMUNITY COLLEGE
Mosser Road
McHenry, MD 21541
2-year college
(410) 387-6666 Contact: Elizabeth Fawcett
Unspecified athletic aid available
M: baseball, basketball
W: basketball, volleyball. Women's Non-aid: softball

GOUCHER COLLEGE
1021 Dulaney Valley Road
Towson, MD 21204
(410) 337-6141 Contact: Faye W. Perry
Men's Non-aid: archery, badminton, basketball, bowling, equestrian, fencing, field hockey, golf, racquetball, sailing, swimming, synchronized swimming, tennis, volleyball
Women's Non-aid: archery, badminton, basketball, bowling, equestrian, fencing, field hockey, golf, lacrosse, racquetball, sailing, soccer, swimming, synchronized swimming, tennis, volleyball

HAGERSTOWN JUNIOR COLLEGE
11400 Robinwood Drive
Hagerstown, MD 21742-6590

2-year college
(301) 790-2800 X. 367 Contact: Kevin Smoot
Unspecified athletic aid available
M: baseball, basketball, cross country, indoor track, soccer, track & field
W: basketball, cross country, indoor track, softball, track & field, volleyball

HARFORD COMMUNITY COLLEGE
401 Thomas Run Road
Bel Air, MD 21014
2-year college
(410) 836-4226 Contact: Jack Nichols
Men's Aid (#/$): 30/$9,600
Women's Aid (#/$): 30/$9,600
M: baseball, basketball, lacrosse, soccer. Men's Non-aid: tennis
W: basketball, field hockey, lacrosse, softball. Women's Non-aid: tennis

HOOD COLLEGE
Rosemont Avenue
Frederick, MD 21701
(301) 663-3131 X. 351 Contact: Richelle Emerick
Women's Non-aid: basketball, diving, field hockey, lacrosse, swimming, tennis, volleyball

JOHNS HOPKINS UNIVERSITY
Charles and 34th Streets
Baltimore, MD 21218
(410) 516-7490 Contact: Tom Calder
Unspecified athletic aid available
Restrictions and notes: Athletic aid only in men's lacrosse. Beginning with 93-94 season, will award 12.6 men's lacrosse grants.
M: lacrosse. Men's Non-aid: archery, badminton, baseball, basketball, crew, indoor track, power lifting, riflery, soccer, swimming, swimming-diving, tennis, track & field, water polo, wrestling
Women's Non-aid: basketball, crew, cross country, diving, fencing, field hockey, indoor track, lacrosse, riflery, soccer, squash, swimming, swimming-diving, tennis, track & field, volleyball, water polo

LOYOLA COLLEGE
4501 North Charles Street
Baltimore, MD 21210
(410) 617-2777 Contact: Steve Jones
Men's Aid (#/$): 12/$70,500
Women's Aid (#/$): 18/$111,180
M: basketball, lacrosse, soccer. Men's Non-aid: cross country, diving, golf, swimming, tennis
W: basketball, lacrosse, soccer, volleyball. Women's Non-aid: cross country, diving, swimming, tennis

MONTGOMERY COLLEGE
7600 Takomo Avenue
Takoma Park, MD 20912
2-year college
(301) 650-1447 Contact: Al Murray
Men's Non-aid: basketball, diving, soccer, swimming, tennis
Women's Non-aid: diving, swimming, tennis, volleyball

MORGAN STATE UNIVERSITY
1700 East Cold Spring Lane
Baltimore, MD 21239
(410) 319-3831 Contact: Joe McIver
Unspecified athletic aid available
M: basketball, cross country, football, indoor track, track & field, wrestling. Men's Non-aid: baseball, riflery, tennis
W: basketball, cross country, indoor track, track & field, volleyball. Women's Non-aid: riflery, tennis

MOUNT ST. MARY COLLEGE
Route 15
Emmitsburg, MD 21727
(301) 447-5384 Contact: Dave Reeder
Men's Aid (#/$): 28.5/$468,112
Women's Aid (#/$): 22.5/$369,562
M: baseball, basketball, cross country, indoor track, lacrosse, soccer, tennis, track & field. Men's Non-aid: golf
W: basketball, cross country, indoor track, soccer, tennis, track & field. Women's Non-aid: softball

PRINCE GEORGE'S COMMUNITY COLLEGE
301 Largo Road
Largo, MD 20772
2-year college
(301) 322-0512 Contact: Ronald Mann
Unspecified athletic aid available
M: baseball, basketball, bowling, soccer. Men's Non-aid: golf, tennis
W: basketball, bowling, softball, volleyball. Women's Non-aid: tennis

SAINT MARY'S COLLEGE
St. Mary's City, MD 20686
(301) 862-0323 Contact: Pam Wojnar
Men's Non-aid: baseball, basketball, lacrosse, sailing, soccer, swimming, tennis
Women's Non-aid: basketball, lacrosse, sailing, soccer, swimming, tennis, volleyball

TOWSON STATE UNIVERSITY
Towson Center
Towson, MD 21204-7097
(410) 830-2232 Contact: Peter Schlehr
Unspecified athletic aid available
M: baseball, basketball, football, lacrosse, soccer, swimming-diving, tennis. Men's Non-aid: cross country, golf, indoor track, track & field
W: basketball, field hockey, gymnastics, lacrosse, softball, tennis, volleyball. Women's Non-aid: cross country, indoor track, swimming-diving, track & field

UNIVERSITY OF MARYLAND
College Park, MD 20740
(301) 314-7076 Contact: Sue Tyler
Men's Aid (#/$): 193.5/$1,682,369
Women's Aid (#/$): 107/$702,999
Restrictions and notes: Partials to fulls available in various sports.
M: baseball, basketball, cross country, diving, football, golf, indoor track, lacrosse, soccer, swimming, swimming-diving, tennis, track & field, wrestling
W: basketball, cross country, diving, field hockey, gymnastics, indoor track, lacrosse, soccer, swimming, swimming-diving, tennis, volleyball

UNIVERSITY OF MARYLAND (BALTIMORE COUNTY)
5401 Wilkens Avenue
Baltimore, MD 21228
(410) 455-2126 Contact: Steve Levy
Men's Aid (#/$): 90/$350,000
Women's Aid (#/$): 90/$350,000
M: baseball, basketball, cross country, diving, golf, indoor track, lacrosse, soccer, swimming, swimming-diving, tennis, track & field
W: basketball, cross country, diving, indoor track, lacrosse, soccer, softball, swimming, swimming-diving, tennis, track & field, volleyball

UNIVERSITY OF MARYLAND (EASTERN SHORE)
Princess Anne, MD 21853
(410) 651-2200 Contact: Dr. Hallie Gregory
Unspecified athletic aid available
M: baseball, basketball, cross country, golf, indoor track, tennis, track & field
W: basketball, cross country, golf, indoor track, tennis, track & field, volleyball

WASHINGTON COLLEGE
Washington Avenue
Chestertown, MD 21620
(410) 778-7238 Contact: Sarah Feyerherm
Men's Non-aid: baseball, basketball, crew, lacrosse, soccer, swimming, tennis
Women's Non-aid: basketball, field hockey, lacrosse, softball, swimming, tennis, volleyball

WESTERN MARYLAND COLLEGE
2 College Hill
Westminster, MD 21157-4390
(410) 857-2291 Contact: Scott Deitch
Men's Non-aid: baseball, basketball, cross country, football, lacrosse, soccer, swimming, tennis, track & field, wrestling

Women's Non-aid: basketball, cross country, field hockey, golf, lacrosse, soccer, softball, swimming, tennis, track & field, volleyball

Massachusetts

AMERICAN INTERNATIONAL COLLEGE

1000 State Street
Springfield, MA 01109
(413) 737-6344 Contact: Frank Polera
Unspecified athletic aid available
M: baseball, basketball, football, ice hockey. Men's Non-aid: golf, soccer, tennis
W: basketball, softball, volleyball. Women's Non-aid: soccer, tennis

AMHERST COLLEGE

P.O. Box 2202
Public Affairs Office
Amherst, MA 01002
(413) 542-2321 Contact: Doug Battema
Men's Non-aid: baseball, basketball, cross country, football, golf, ice hockey, indoor track, lacrosse, soccer, squash, swimming, swimming-diving, tennis, track & field
Women's Non-aid: basketball, cross country, field hockey, golf, indoor track, lacrosse, soccer, squash, swimming, swimming-diving, tennis, track & field, volleyball

ASSUMPTION COLLEGE

500 Salisbury Street
Worcester, MA 01609
(508) 752-5615 X. 240 Contact: Steve Morris
Men's Aid (#/$): 12/unspecified $
Women's Aid (#/$): 12/unspecified $
M: basketball
W: basketball

ATLANTIC UNION COLLEGE

South Lancaster, MA 01561
(919) 237-3161 Contact: W. A. Deitemeyer
Unspecified athletic aid available
M: basketball, soccer
W: volleyball

BABSON COLLEGE

Athletic Department
Babson Park, MA 02157
(617) 239-4553 Contact: Christine M. Merlo
Men's Non-aid: baseball, basketball, cross country, diving, golf, ice hockey, lacrosse, soccer, swimming, tennis
Women's Non-aid: basketball, cross country, diving, field hockey, lacrosse, soccer, softball, swimming, tennis, volleyball

BECKER COLLEGE

3 Paxton Street
Leicester, MA 01524
2-year college
(508) 892-9471 Contact: Herbert Whitworth
Men's Aid (#/$): 75/unspecified $
Women's Aid (#/$): 60/unspecified $
M: baseball, basketball, soccer, tennis. Men's Non-aid: equestrian
W: field hockey, soccer, softball, volleyball. Women's Non-aid: basketball, equestrian

BENTLEY COLLEGE

175 Forest Street
Waltham, MA 02154-4705
(617) 891-2334 Contact: Dick Lipe
Unspecified athletic aid available
M: basketball. Men's Non-aid: baseball, cross country, golf, ice hockey, indoor track, soccer, tennis, track & field
W: basketball. Women's Non-aid: cross country, field hockey, indoor track, softball, tennis, track & field, volleyball

BOSTON COLLEGE

321 Conte Forum
Chestnut Hill, MA 02167
(617) 552-3004 Contact: Reid Oslin
Men's Aid (#/$): 36/$610,753
Women's Aid (#/$): 18/$156,244
M: basketball, cross country, football, ice hockey, indoor track, soccer, track

& field. Men's Non-aid: alpine skiing, baseball, diving, golf, lacrosse, sailing, swimming, swimming-diving, tennis, wrestling
W: basketball, cross country, diving, field hockey, indoor track, lacrosse, soccer, softball, swimming, swimming-diving, tennis, track & field, volleyball. Women's Non-aid: alpine skiing, fencing, golf, sailing

BOSTON UNIVERSITY
285 Babcock Street
Boston, MA 02215
(617) 353-2872 Contact: Ed Carpenter
Men's Aid (#/$): 302/$3,200,280
Women's Aid (#/$): 129/$1,310,452
M: basketball, crew, cross country, diving, football, ice hockey, indoor track, soccer, swimming, track & field, wrestling. Men's Non-aid: baseball, golf, tennis
W: basketball, crew, cross country, diving, field hockey, indoor track, softball, swimming, tennis, track & field

BRANDEIS UNIVERSITY
Swing Center
Waltham, MA 02254
(617) 736-3631 Contact: Jack Molloy
Men's Non-aid: baseball, basketball, cross country, fencing, indoor track, sailing, soccer, swimming, swimming-diving, tennis, track & field
Women's Non-aid: basketball, cross country, fencing, indoor track, sailing, soccer, softball, swimming, swimming-diving, tennis, track & field

BRIDGEWATER STATE COLLEGE
Financial Aid Office
Bridgewater, MA 02325
(508) 697-1341 Contact: Doreen Rose
Men's Non-aid: baseball, basketball, cross country, football, soccer, swimming, tennis, track & field, wrestling
Women's Non-aid: basketball, cross country, field hockey, lacrosse, soccer, swimming, tennis, track & field, volleyball

BUNKER HILL COMMUNITY COLLEGE
250 Rutherford Avenue
Charlestown, MA 02129
2-year college
(617) 241-8600 Contact: Peter Siatta
Men's Non-aid: baseball, basketball, soccer, softball
Women's Non-aid: baseball, basketball, soccer, softball

CLARK UNIVERSITY
950 Main Street
Kneller Athletic Center
Worcester, MA 01610
(508) 793-7164 Contact: Kathryn D. Smith
Men's Non-aid: baseball, basketball, crew, cross country, diving, golf, soccer, swimming, swimming-diving, tennis, track & field
Women's Non-aid: basketball, crew, cross country, diving, field hockey, golf, soccer, softball, swimming, swimming-diving, tennis, track & field, volleyball

CURRY COLLEGE
1071 Blue Hill Avenue
Milton, MA 02186
(617) 333-0500 X. 2330 Contact: Troy Watkins
Men's Non-aid: baseball, basketball, football, ice hockey, lacrosse, soccer, tennis
Women's Non-aid: basketball, soccer, softball, tennis

DEAN JUNIOR COLLEGE
99 Main Street
Franklin, MA 02038-1994
2-year college
(508) 528-9100 X. 213 Contact: Mary Anne Dean
Men's Non-aid: baseball, basketball, football, lacrosse, soccer, tennis
Women's Non-aid: basketball, field hockey, soccer, softball, tennis

EASTERN NAZARENE COLLEGE
23 East Elm Avenue
Quincy, MA 02170
(617) 773-6350 X. 347 Contact: Carolyn Morse
Men's Non-aid: baseball, basketball, cross country, soccer, tennis
Women's Non-aid: basketball, cross country, softball, tennis, volleyball

EMERSON COLLEGE
100 Beacon Street
Boston, MA 02116
(617) 578-8690 Contact: James Peckham
Men's Non-aid: baseball, basketball, golf, ice hockey, soccer, wrestling
Women's Non-aid: basketball, softball, tennis, volleyball

FITCHBURG STATE COLLEGE
160 Pearl Street
Fitchburg, MA 01420
(508) 345-2151 X. 3343 Contact: Dave Marsh
Men's Non-aid: baseball, basketball, cross country, football, ice hockey, soccer, track & field
Women's Non-aid: basketball, cross country, field hockey, softball, track & field, volleyball

GORDON COLLEGE
255 Grapevine Road
Wenham, MA 01984
(508) 927-2300 X. 3217 Contact: Mark Sylvestor
Men's Non-aid: baseball, basketball, cross country, soccer, tennis
Women's Non-aid: basketball, cross country, field hockey, soccer, softball, tennis, volleyball

GREENFIELD COMMUNITY COLLEGE
One College Drive
Greenfield, MA 01301
2-year college
(413) 774-3131 Contact: John H. Palmer
Men's Non-aid: baseball, basketball, cross country, golf, soccer, volleyball
Women's Non-aid: basketball, cross country, golf, soccer, softball, volleyball

HARVARD UNIVERSITY
60 Kennedy Street
Cambridge, MA 02138
(617) 495-2206 Contact: John Veneziano
Men's Non-aid: alpine skiing, baseball, basketball, crew, cross country, cross country skiing, fencing, football, golf, ice hockey, lacrosse, sailing, soccer, squash, softball, swimming-diving, tennis, track & field, volleyball, water polo, wrestling
Women's Non-aid: alpine skiing, basketball, crew, cross country, cross country skiing, fencing, field hockey, golf, ice hockey, lacrosse, sailing, soccer, squash, softball, swimming-diving, tennis, track & field, volleyball, water polo

HOLY CROSS COLLEGE
1 College Street
Worcester, MA 01610
(508) 793-2583 Contact: Jeff Nelson
Unspecified athletic aid available
M: basketball, football. Men's Non-aid: baseball, crew, cross country, golf, ice hockey, indoor track, lacrosse, soccer, swimming-diving, tennis, track & field
W: basketball, cross country, field hockey, indoor track, lacrosse, soccer, softball, swimming-diving, tennis, track & field, volleyball. Women's Non-aid: crew

MASSACHUSETTS BAY COMMUNITY COLLEGE
47 Flagg Drive
Framingham, MA 01701
2-year college
(508) 875-5300 Contact: Alan Harrison
Men's Non-aid: baseball, basketball
Women's Non-aid: basketball, softball, volleyball

MASSACHUSETTS INSTITUTE OF TECHNOLOGY
P.O. Box D
Cambridge, MA 02139-4307

(617) 253-7946 Contact: Roger F. Crosley
Men's Non-aid: alpine skiing, baseball, basketball, crew, cross country, cross country skiing, diving, fencing, football, golf, gymnastics, indoor track, lacrosse, riflery, sailing, soccer, squash, swimming, swimming-diving, tennis, track & field, wrestling
Women's Non-aid: alpine skiing, basketball, crew, cross country, cross country skiing, diving, fencing, field hockey, gymnastics, lacrosse, riflery, sailing, soccer, softball, swimming, swimming-diving, tennis, track & field, volleyball

MASSASOIT COMMUNITY COLLEGE
1 Massasoit Boulevard
Brockton, MA 02402
2-year college
(617) 588-9100 Contact: Bruce Langlan
Unspecified athletic aid available
M: baseball, basketball, soccer
W: soccer, softball

MERRIMACK COLLEGE
315 Turnpike Street
North Andover, MA 01845
(508) 837-5345 Contact: Jim Seavey
Men's Aid (#/$): 10/$150,000
Women's Aid (#/$): 5/$75,000
M: baseball, ice hockey, soccer. Men's Non-aid: cross country, golf, lacrosse, tennis
W: basketball, soccer, softball. Women's Non-aid: cross country, field hockey, tennis, volleyball

MOUNT HOLYOKE COLLEGE
Kendall Hall
South Hadley, MA 01075
(413) 538-2276 Contact: Janice Savitz
Women's Non-aid: basketball, crew, cross country, diving, equestrian, field hockey, indoor track, soccer, softball, squash, swimming, swimming-diving, tennis, track & field, volleyball

MT. WACHUSETT COMMUNITY COLLEGE
Gardner, MA 01440
2-year college
(508) 632-6600 Contact: Dr. Richard G. Rollins
Men's Non-aid: baseball, basketball, cross country, tennis
Women's Non-aid: basketball, cross country, softball, tennis

NICHOLS COLLEGE
Dudley Hill
Dudley, MA 01570
(508) 943-1560 X. 101 Contact: Bob Flannery
Men's Non-aid: baseball, basketball, field hockey, football, golf, ice hockey, lacrosse, soccer, softball, tennis, track & field

NORTH ADAMS STATE COLLEGE
Church Street
North Adams, MA 01247
(413) 664-4511 X. 357 Contact: Tim Kelly
Unspecified athletic aid available
M: alpine skiing, baseball, basketball, cross country, ice hockey, soccer, softball, tennis
W: alpine skiing, baseball, basketball, cross country, soccer, softball, tennis, volleyball

NORTHEASTERN UNIVERSITY
360 Huntington Avenue
Boston, MA 02115
(617) 437-2691 Contact: Jack Grinold
Men's Aid (#/$): 31/$317,130
Women's Aid (#/$): 22/$225,060
No sports information provided

QUINSIGAMOND COLLEGE
670 West Boylston Street
Worcester, MA 01606
2-year college
(508) 853-2300 X. 266 Contact: Barry Glinski
Men's Non-aid: baseball, basketball, golf
Women's Non-aid: golf, softball

REGIS COLLEGE
235 Wellesley Street Boulevard
Weston, MA 02193
(617) 893-1820 X. 2303 Contact: Dr. Judy Burling
Women's Non-aid: basketball, cross country, diving, soccer, softball, swimming-diving, tennis, volleyball

SALEM STATE COLLEGE
225 Canal Street
O'Keefe Sports Center
Salem, MA 01970
(508) 741-6549 Contact: Thomas Roundy
Men's Non-aid: baseball, basketball, cross country, golf, ice hockey, sailing, soccer, swimming, tennis, track & field
Women's Non-aid: basketball, cross country, field hockey, gymnastics, sailing, soccer, softball, swimming, tennis, track & field, volleyball

SMITH COLLEGE
Ainsworth Gym
Northampton, MA 01063
(413) 585-2703 Contact: Carole A. Grills
Women's Non-aid: alpine skiing, crew, cross country, equestrian, field hockey, indoor track, lacrosse, soccer, softball, squash, swimming-diving, tennis, track & field, volleyball

SOUTHEASTERN MASSACHUSETTS UNIVERSITY
Old Westport Road
North Dartmouth, MA 02747
(617) 999-8727 Contact: William Gathright
Men's Non-aid: baseball, basketball, cross country, fencing, golf, ice hockey, indoor track, soccer, swimming, swimming-diving, tennis, track & field
Women's Non-aid: basketball, cross country, fencing, field hockey, indoor track, softball, swimming, swimming-diving, tennis, track & field, volleyball

SPRINGFIELD COLLEGE
263 Alden Street
Springfield, MA 01109
(413) 788-3341 Contact: Ken Cerino
Men's Non-aid: baseball, basketball, cross country, diving, football, golf, gymnastics, indoor track, lacrosse, soccer, swimming, swimming-diving, tennis, track & field, volleyball, wrestling
Women's Non-aid: basketball, cross country, diving, field hockey, golf, gymnastics, indoor track, lacrosse, soccer, softball, swimming, swimming-diving, tennis, track & field, volleyball

SPRINGFIELD TECHNICAL COMMUNITY COLLEGE
1 Armory Square
Springfield, MA 01105
2-year college
(413) 781-7822 Contact: J. Vincent Grassetti
Unspecified athletic aid available
M: baseball, basketball, soccer
W: basketball, softball

STONEHILL COLLEGE
320 Washington Street
North Easton, MA 02356
(508) 230-1347 Contact: Eileen O'Leary
Men's Aid (#/$): 12/$200,700
Women's Aid (#/$): 12/$200,700
M: basketball. Men's Non-aid: baseball, cross country, equestrian, football, ice hockey, indoor track, sailing, soccer, tennis, track & field
W: basketball. Women's Non-aid: cross country, equestrian, indoor track, sailing, soccer, softball, tennis, track & field, volleyball

SUFFOLK UNIVERSITY
8 Ashburton Place
Boston, MA 02108
(617) 573-8447 Contact: Louis B. Connelly
Men's Non-aid: baseball, basketball, cross country, golf, ice hockey, soccer, tennis
Women's Non-aid: basketball, cross country, golf, squash, tennis

TUFTS UNIVERSITY
Cousens Gym
College Avenue

Medford, MA 02155
(617) 628-5000 Contact: Mike Friedman
Men's Non-aid: baseball, basketball, crew, cross country, diving, football, golf, ice hockey, indoor track, lacrosse, soccer, squash, swimming, swimming-diving, tennis, track & field
Women's Non-aid: basketball, crew, cross country, diving, field hockey, indoor track, lacrosse, sailing, soccer, softball, squash, swimming, swimming-diving, tennis, track & field, volleyball

UNIVERSITY OF LOWELL
One University Avenue
Lowell, MA 01854
(508) 934-2306 Contact: B.L. Elfring
Men's Aid (#/$): 92/$492,432
Women's Aid (#/$): 48/$207,687
Restrictions and notes: All athletic aid restricted to Massachusetts residents except hockey and basketball.
M: baseball, basketball, cross country, golf, ice hockey, indoor track, soccer, swimming, swimming-diving, tennis, track & field, wrestling. Men's Non-aid: crew, football
W: basketball, cross country, field hockey, indoor track, softball, tennis, track & field, volleyball. Women's Non-aid: crew

UNIVERSITY OF MASSACHUSETTS (AMHERST)
255A Boyden Building
Amherst, MA 01003
(413) 545-2439 Contact: Howard Davis
Unspecified athletic aid available
M: baseball, basketball, cross country, diving, football, gymnastics, indoor track, lacrosse, soccer, swimming, swimming-diving, track & field
W: basketball, cross country, diving, field hockey, gymnastics, indoor track, lacrosse, soccer, softball, swimming, swimming-diving, track & field, volleyball

UNIVERSITY OF MASSACHUSETTS (BOSTON)
Harbor Campus
Boston, MA 02125
(617) 287-7815 Contact: Kevin Dolan
Men's Non-aid: baseball, basketball, cross country, football, ice hockey, indoor track, lacrosse, soccer, swimming, swimming-diving, tennis, track & field, wrestling
Women's Non-aid: basketball, cross country, indoor track, softball, swimming, swimming-diving, track & field

WELLESLEY COLLEGE
Wellesley Sports Center
Wellesley, MA 02181
(617) 235-0320 Contact: Glenna Fortier
Women's Non-aid: basketball, crew, cross country, diving, fencing, field hockey, lacrosse, soccer, squash, swimming, swimming-diving, tennis, volleyball

WESTERN NEW ENGLAND COLLEGE
1215 Wilbraham Road
Springfield, MA 01119
(413) 782-1227 Contact: Gene Gumbs
Men's Non-aid: alpine skiing, baseball, basketball, bowling, football, golf, ice hockey, lacrosse, soccer, tennis, volleyball, wrestling
Women's Non-aid: alpine skiing, basketball, bowling, field hockey, soccer, softball, tennis, volleyball

WESTFIELD STATE COLLEGE
Western Avenue
Westfield, MA 01086
(413) 568-3311 X. 433 Contact: Mickey Curtis
Men's Non-aid: badminton, baseball, basketball, field hockey, ice hockey, sailing, tennis
Women's Non-aid: basketball, cross country, field hockey, indoor track, soccer, softball, swimming-diving, track & field

WILLIAMS COLLEGE
P.O. Box 676
Williamstown, MA 01267
(413) 597-4982 Contact: Dick Quinn

Men's Non-aid: baseball, basketball, crew, cross country, cross country skiing, diving, football, golf, ice hockey, indoor track, lacrosse, soccer, squash, swimming, swimming-diving, tennis, track & field, volleyball, wrestling
Women's Non-aid: basketball, crew, cross country, cross country skiing, diving, indoor track, lacrosse, soccer, softball, squash, swimming, swimming-diving, tennis, track & field, volleyball

WORCESTER STATE COLLEGE
Worcester, MA 01602
(508) 793-8056 Contact: Susan Hafner
Unspecified athletic aid available
M: baseball, basketball, cross country, football, golf, ice hockey, indoor track, tennis, track & field
Women's Non-aid: baseball, basketball, cross country, field hockey, indoor track, softball, tennis, track & field, volleyball

Michigan

ADRIAN COLLEGE
110 South Madison Street
Adrian, MI 49221
(517) 265-5161 X. 4323 Contact: Darcy Gifford
Men's Non-aid: baseball, basketball, cross country, football, golf, soccer, swimming-diving, tennis, track & field
Women's Non-aid: basketball, cross country, golf, soccer, softball, swimming-diving, tennis, track & field, volleyball

ALBION COLLEGE
611 East Porter
Albion, MI 49224
(517) 629-0434 Contact: J. Robin Hartman
Men's Non-aid: baseball, basketball, cross country, football, golf, soccer, swimming-diving, tennis, track & field
Women's Non-aid: basketball, cross country, field hockey, softball, swimming-diving, tennis, track & field, volleyball

ALMA COLLEGE
614 West Superior Street
Alma, MI 48801
(517) 463-7323 Contact: Greg Baadte
Men's Non-aid: baseball, basketball, cross country, field hockey, football, golf, soccer, softball, swimming-diving, tennis, track & field, volleyball
Women's Non-aid: baseball, basketball, cross country, field hockey, softball, swimming-diving, tennis, track & field, volleyball

AQUINAS COLLEGE
1607 Robinson Road, SE
Grand Rapids, MI 49506
(616) 459-8281 X. 3120 Contact: Marie Mell-Reikow
Unspecified athletic aid available
Restrictions and notes: Awarded by academic/athletic financial formula. No athlete can receive more than $2,500 per sport.
M: baseball, basketball, cross country, golf, indoor track, soccer, tennis, track & field
W: basketball, cross country, indoor track, soccer, softball, tennis, track & field, volleyball

CALVIN COLLEGE
3201 Burton SE
Grand Rapids, MI 49546
(616) 957-6475 Contact: Phil de Haan
Men's Non-aid: baseball, basketball, cross country, diving, golf, soccer, swimming, tennis, track & field
Women's Non-aid: basketball, cross country, diving, golf, soccer, softball, swimming, tennis, track & field, volleyball

CENTRAL MICHIGAN UNIVERSITY
108 West Hall
Mount Pleasant, MI 48859
(517) 774-3277

Contact: Fred Stabley, Jr.
Men's Aid (#/$): 45/$177,529
Women's Aid (#/$): 24/$91,455
M: baseball, basketball, cross country, football, indoor track, soccer, track & field, wrestling
W: basketball, cross country, field hockey, gymnastics, indoor track, softball, track & field, volleyball

CONCORDIA COLLEGE
4090 Geddes Road
Ann Arbor, MI 48105
(313) 995-7344 Contact: Chuck Boerger
Men's Aid (#/$): 27/$32,000
Women's Aid (#/$): 30/$33,800
M: baseball, basketball, soccer, track & field
W: basketball, softball, track & field, volleyball

DELTA COLLEGE
University Center, MI 48710
2-year college
(517) 686-9025 Contact: Chuck Lord
Unspecified athletic aid available
M: basketball, soccer. Men's Non-aid: golf, tennis
W: basketball, softball, volleyball

DETROIT COLLEGE OF BUSINESS
4801 Oakman Boulevard
Dearborn, MI 48126
(313) 581-4400 Contact: Kevin Brazell
Men's Aid (#/$): 16/$77,760
M: golf, soccer

EASTERN MICHIGAN UNIVERSITY
200 Bowen Fieldhouse
Ypsilanti, MI 48197
(313) 487-0317 Contact: James Streeter
Men's Aid (#/$): 147/$975,452
Women's Aid (#/$): 79/$521,894
M: baseball, basketball, cross country, diving, football, golf, gymnastics, indoor track, soccer, swimming, swimming-diving, tennis, track & field, wrestling
W: basketball, cross country, diving, field hockey, gymnastics, indoor track, softball, swimming, swimming-diving, tennis, track & field, volleyball

FERRIS STATE COLLEGE
901 South State Street
110 West Building
Big Rapids, MI 49307
(616) 592-2331 Contact: Ted Halm
Men's Aid ($): $427,500
Women's Aid ($): $156,605
M: baseball, basketball, cross country, football, ice hockey, indoor track, swimming-diving, tennis, track & field, wrestling. Men's Non-aid: golf
W: basketball, cross country, indoor track, softball, swimming-diving, tennis, track & field, volleyball. Women's Non-aid: golf

GLEN OAKS COMMUNITY COLLEGE
62249 Shimmel Road
Centreville, MI 49032
2-year college
(616) 467-9945 Contact: Heather Teadt
Men's Aid (#/$): 25/unspecified $
Women's Aid (#/$): 20/unspecified $
M: baseball, basketball, golf
W: basketball, volleyball

GRAND RAPIDS BAPTIST COLLEGE AND SEMINARY
1001 East Beltline, N.E.
Grand Rapids, MI 49505
(616) 949-5300 X. 313 Contact: John F. VerBerkmoes
Men's Aid (#/$): 17/$18,888
Women's Aid (#/$): 6/$10,550
M: baseball, basketball, soccer
W: basketball, softball, volleyball

GRAND RAPIDS JUNIOR COLLEGE
143 Bostwick, NE
Grand Rapids, MI 49503
2-year college
(616) 771-3990 Contact: Rick Vanderveen
Unspecified athletic aid available

M: baseball, basketball, cross country, football, swimming-diving, tennis, wrestling
W: basketball, cross country, softball, swimming-diving, tennis, volleyball

GRAND VALLEY STATE COLLEGE
1 Campus Drive
Allendale, MI 49401
(616) 895-3275 Contact: Don Thomas
Unspecified athletic aid available
M: basketball, football, wrestling.
Men's Non-aid: baseball, cross country, indoor track, swimming-diving, track & field
W: basketball, softball, volleyball.
Women's Non-aid: cross country, indoor track, swimming-diving, track & field

HENRY FORD COMMUNITY COLLEGE
5101 Evergreen
Dearborn, MI 48128
2-year college
(313) 845-9647 Contact: Nancy Bryden
Men's Aid (#/$): 32/unspecified $
Women's Aid (#/$): 37/unspecified $
M: baseball, basketball, golf, tennis
W: basketball, softball, tennis, volleyball

HIGHLAND PARK COMMUNITY COLLEGE
Glendale at Third Avenue
Highland Park, MI 48203
2-year college
(313) 252-0475 Contact: Glen Donahue
Unspecified athletic aid available
M: baseball, basketball, tennis
W: basketball, cross country

HILLSDALE COLLEGE
201 Oak Street
Hillsdale, MI 49242
(517) 437-7364 Contact: Brian Boyse
Men's Aid (#/$): 23/$114,096
Women's Aid (#/$): 23/$114,096
M: baseball, basketball, cross country, football, indoor track, track & field.
Men's Non-aid: golf, tennis
W: basketball, cross country, indoor track, softball, swimming, track & field, volleyball. Women's Non-aid: tennis

HOPE COLLEGE
137 East 12th Street
Holland, MI 49423
(616) 394-7860 Contact: Tom Renner
Men's Non-aid: baseball, basketball, cross country, diving, football, golf, soccer, swimming, swimming-diving, tennis, track & field, water polo
Women's Non-aid: basketball, cross country, diving, field hockey, softball, swimming, swimming-diving, tennis, track & field, volleyball

JORDAN COLLEGE
3488 North Jennings Street
Flint, MI 48504
2-year college
(313) 789-0520 Contact: Victor Porter
Men's Aid (#/$): 13/$19,000
Women's Aid (#/$): 11/unspecified $
M: basketball
W: basketball

KALAMAZOO COLLEGE
1200 Academy Street
Kalamazoo, MI 49007
(616) 383-8584 Contact: John Greenhoe
Men's Non-aid: baseball, basketball, cross country, diving, football, golf, soccer, swimming, swimming-diving, tennis
Women's Non-aid: basketball, cross country, diving, field hockey, soccer, swimming, swimming-diving, tennis, volleyball

KALAMAZOO VALLEY COMMUNITY COLLEGE
6767 West "O" Avenue
Kalamazoo, MI 49009
2-year college
(616) 372-5395 Contact: Dick Shilts
Men's Aid (#/$): 31/$25,307
Women's Aid (#/$): 36/$26,236
Restrictions and notes: Tuition and fee aid only.

M: baseball, basketball, golf, tennis
W: basketball, softball, tennis, volleyball

LAKE MICHIGAN COLLEGE
2755 East Napier Avenue
Benton Harbor, MI 49022
2-year college
(616) 927-8165 Contact: Kathy Leitke
Men's Aid (#/$): 24/unspecified $
Women's Aid (#/$): 26/unspecified $
M: baseball, basketball, golf
W: basketball, softball, volleyball

LAKE SUPERIOR STATE UNIVERSITY
Norris Center
Sault Sainte Marie, MI 49783
(906) 635-2601 Contact: Scott Managhan
Men's Aid (#/$): 13/$58,633
Women's Aid (#/$): 13/$19,253
M: basketball, cross country, golf, ice hockey, tennis, wrestling. Men's Non-aid: indoor track, track & field
W: basketball, cross country, softball, tennis, volleyball. Women's Non-aid: indoor track, track & field

LANSING COMMUNITY COLLEGE
P.O. Box 40010
Lansing, MI 48901-7210
2-year college
(517) 483-1227 Contact: Walt Lingo
Men's Non-aid: basketball, cross country, golf
Women's Non-aid: basketball, cross country, golf, softball, volleyball

MACOMB COMMUNITY COLLEGE
14500 East 12 Mile Road
Warren, MI 48093-3896
2-year college
(313) 445-7208 Contact: Nancy Kosinski
Unspecified athletic aid available
M: baseball, basketball, cross country, golf, indoor track, soccer, tennis, track & field
W: cross country, indoor track, softball, tennis, track & field, volleyball

MADONNA UNIVERSITY
36600 Schoolcraft
Livonia, MI 48150
(313) 591-5036 Contact: Chris Ziegler
Unspecified athletic aid available
M: baseball, basketball, golf
W: basketball, softball, volleyball

MICHIGAN CHRISTIAN COLLEGE
800 West Avon Road
Rochester, MI 48306
2-year college
(313) 651-5800 Contact: Bill Shinsky
Unspecified athletic aid available
M: baseball, basketball, cross country, soccer, track & field
W: basketball, cross country, softball, track & field, volleyball

MICHIGAN STATE UNIVERSITY
223 Jenison Field House
East Lansing, MI 48824
(517) 355-9710 Contact: Charles Wilson
Unspecified athletic aid available
M: baseball, basketball, cross country, football, golf, gymnastics, ice hockey, lacrosse, soccer, swimming-diving, tennis, track & field, wrestling. Men's Non-aid: fencing
W: basketball, cross country, field hockey, golf, gymnastics, soccer, softball, swimming-diving, tennis, track & field, volleyball

MICHIGAN TECHNOLOGICAL UNIVERSITY
1400 Townsend Drive
SDC Room 233
Houghton, MI 49931-1295
(906) 487-2350 Contact: Dave Fischer
Men's Aid (#/$): 26/$79,389
Women's Aid (#/$): 8/$24,427
M: basketball, football, ice hockey. Men's Non-aid: cross country, cross country skiing, tennis, track & field
W: basketball, volleyball. Women's Non-aid: cross country, cross country skiing, tennis, track & field

MOTT COMMUNITY COLLEGE
1401 East Court Street
Flint, MI 48502

2-year college
(313) 762-0417 Contact: Richard Zanetta
Unspecified athletic aid available
M: baseball, basketball, golf
W: basketball, softball, volleyball

MUSKEGON COMMUNITY COLLEGE
221 South Quarterline Road
Muskegon, MI 49442
2-year college
(616) 777-0381 Contact: J. Paul King
Men's Aid (#/$): 46/$28,700
Women's Aid (#/$): 35/$24,500
M: baseball, basketball, golf, wrestling
W: basketball, golf, softball, volleyball

NORTHERN MICHIGAN UNIVERSITY
607 Cohodas Building
Marquette, MI 49855
(906) 227-1012 Contact: Jim Pinar
Men's Aid (#/$): 69.9/$530,482
Women's Aid (#/$): 31.6/$228,599
M: basketball, cross country, cross country skiing, football, ice hockey. Men's Non-aid: golf
W: basketball, cross country, cross country skiing, diving, swimming, swimming-diving, volleyball. Women's Non-aid: tennis

NORTHWOOD INSTITUTE
3225 Cook Road
Midland, MI 48640
(517) 837-4239 Contact: Fritz Reznor
Unspecified athletic aid available
M: baseball, basketball, football, indoor track, tennis, track & field. Men's Non-aid: golf
W: basketball, indoor track, softball, track & field, volleyball

OAKLAND COMMUNITY COLLEGE
Auburn Hills Campus
2900 Featherstone Road
Auburn Hills, MI 48057
2-year college
(313) 340-6662 Contact: Prentice Ryan
Men's Aid (#/$): 22/$11,154
Women's Aid (#/$): 46/$18,846
M: basketball, cross country, golf, tennis
W: basketball, cross country, softball, tennis, volleyball

OAKLAND UNIVERSITY
Lepley Sports Center
Rochester, MI 48309-4401
(313) 370-4008 Contact: Andrew Glantzman
Men's Aid (#/$): 10/$25,909
Women's Aid (#/$): 8/$29,153
M: basketball, cross country, diving, golf, soccer, swimming, tennis
W: basketball, diving, swimming, tennis, volleyball

OLIVET COLLEGE
News and Information Department
Olivet, MI 49076
(616) 749-7657 Contact: Jerry Rashid
Men's Non-aid: baseball, basketball, cross country, football, golf, soccer, tennis, track & field, wrestling
Women's Non-aid: basketball, field hockey, softball, tennis, volleyball

SAGINAW VALLEY STATE COLLEGE
2250 Pierce Road
University Center, MI 48710
(517) 790-4053 Contact: Thomas Waske
Men's Aid (#/$): 42/$76,821
Women's Aid (#/$): 16/$30,693
M: baseball, basketball, bowling, cross country, football, golf, indoor track, track & field
W: basketball, indoor track, softball, tennis, track & field, volleyball

SAINT MARY'S COLLEGE
3535 Indian Trail
Orchard Lake, MI 48324
(313) 683-0508 Contact: Darrell Brockway
Women's Non-aid: basketball, fencing, soccer, softball, swimming-diving, tennis, track & field, volleyball

SCHOOLCRAFT COLLEGE
18600 Haggerty Road
Livonia, MI 48152
2-year college
(313) 462-4400 Contact: Dr. Martin C. Nowak
Men's Aid (#/$): 28/$18,500
Women's Aid (#/$): 29/$18,500
M: basketball, golf, soccer
W: basketball, cross country, soccer, volleyball

SIENA HEIGHTS COLLEGE
1247 East Siena Heights Drive
Adrian, MI 49221
(517) 263-0731 X. 216 Contact: Scott McClure
Men's Aid (#/$): 160/$175,893
Women's Aid (#/$): 113/$127,895
M: baseball, basketball, cross country, golf, soccer, tennis, track & field
W: basketball, cross country, soccer, softball, tennis, track & field, volleyball

SOUTHWESTERN MICHIGAN JUNIOR COLLEGE
589001 Cherry Grove Road
Dowagiac, MI 49047
2-year college
(616) 782-5113 Contact: Ronald Gunn
Unspecified athletic aid available
M: baseball, basketball, cross country, golf, indoor track, track & field, wrestling
W: basketball, cross country, indoor track, softball, track & field, volleyball

SPRING ARBOR COLLEGE
College Street
Spring Arbor, MI 49283
(517) 750-1200 Contact: Robert Miller
Unspecified athletic aid available
M: baseball, basketball, cross country, indoor track, soccer, tennis, track & field
W: basketball, cross country, indoor track, softball, track & field, volleyball

UNIVERSITY OF DETROIT MERCY
4001 West McNichols Road
Detroit, MI 48221
(313) 933-1745 Contact: Mark Engel
Unspecified athletic aid available
Restrictions and notes: Full scholarships available in basketball, partial tuition scholarships available in all other sports.
M: baseball, basketball, cross country, fencing, golf, indoor track, soccer, tennis, track & field
W: basketball, cross country, equestrian, indoor track, soccer, softball, tennis, track & field

UNIVERSITY OF MICHIGAN
1000 South State Street
Ann Arbor, MI 48109-2201
(313) 763-4423 Contact: Bruce Madej
Men's Aid (#/$): 189.8/$3,301,000
Women's Aid (#/$): 102.4/$1,645,000
M: baseball, basketball, cross country, football, golf, gymnastics, ice hockey, indoor track, swimming-diving, track & field, wrestling
W: basketball, cross country, field hockey, golf, gymnastics, indoor track, softball, swimming-diving, track & field

WAYNE STATE UNIVERSITY
101 Matthaei Building
Detroit, MI 48202-3489
(313) 577-7542 Contact: Richard Thompson, Jr.
Unspecified athletic aid available
M: baseball, basketball, cross country, diving, fencing, football, golf, swimming, swimming-diving, tennis
W: basketball, diving, fencing, softball, swimming, swimming-diving, tennis, volleyball

WESTERN MICHIGAN UNIVERSITY
102 West Hall
Kalamazoo, MI 49008
(616) 387-8620 Contact: Kathy B. Beauregard
Men's Aid (#/$): 152/unspecified $
Women's Aid (#/$): 66/unspecified $
M: baseball, basketball, cross country, football, gymnastics, ice hockey, indoor track, soccer, tennis, track & field

W: basketball, cross country, gymnastics, indoor track, softball, tennis, track & field, volleyball

Minnesota

ANOKA-RAMSEY COLLEGE
11200 Mississippi Boulevard, NW
Coon Rapids, MN 55433
2-year college
(612) 422-3522
Men's Non-aid: baseball, basketball, football, wrestling
Women's Non-aid: basketball, softball, volleyball

ARROWHEAD COMMUNITY COLLEGE
1515 East 25th Street
Hibbing, MN 55746
2-year college
(218) 262-6748 Contact: Dick Varichak
Men's Non-aid: baseball, basketball, football, ice hockey, tennis
Women's Non-aid: basketball, softball, tennis, volleyball

AUGSBURG COLLEGE
731 21st Avenue South
Minneapolis, MN 55454
(612) 330-1677 Contact: Gene McGivern
Men's Non-aid: baseball, basketball, cross country, football, ice hockey, indoor track, soccer, track & field, wrestling
Women's Non-aid: basketball, cross country, indoor track, soccer, softball, track & field

AUSTIN COMMUNITY COLLEGE
1600 8th Avenue, NW
Austin, MN 55912-1470
2-year college
(507) 433-0543 Contact: David Lillemon
Men's Non-aid: baseball, basketball, diving, football, golf, rodeo, soccer, softball, tennis, track & field, water polo
Women's Non-aid: basketball, diving, martial arts, rodeo, softball, tennis, volleyball

BEMIDJI STATE UNIVERSITY
1500 Birchmont NE
Bemidji, MN 56601-2699
(218) 755-2071 Contact: John Schullo
Men's Aid (#/$): 60/$41,300
Women's Aid (#/$): 45/$26,976
M: basketball, football
W: basketball, track & field, volleyball

BETHANY LUTHERAN COLLEGE
734 Marsh Street
Mankato, MN 56001
2-year college
(507) 625-2977 Contact: Lyle Jones
Men's Aid (#/$): 60/$72,000
Women's Aid (#/$): 60/$72,000
M: baseball, basketball, soccer
W: basketball, softball, volleyball

BETHEL COLLEGE
3900 Bethel Drive
St. Paul, MN 55112
(612) 638-6394 Contact: Daniel C. Nelson
Men's Non-aid: baseball, basketball, cross country, football, golf, ice hockey, indoor track, soccer, tennis, track & field
Women's Non-aid: basketball, cross country, indoor track, tennis, track & field, volleyball

BRAINERD COMMUNITY COLLEGE
College Drive
Brainerd, MN 56401
2-year college
(218) 828-2504 Contact: Terry Larson
Men's Non-aid: baseball, basketball, football, tennis, wrestling
Women's Non-aid: softball, tennis, volleyball

CARLETON COLLEGE
One North College Street
Northfield, MN 55057

(507) 663-4183 Contact: Joe Hargis
Men's Non-aid: alpine skiing, baseball, basketball, cross country, cross country skiing, diving, football, golf, indoor track, soccer, swimming, swimming-diving, tennis, track & field, volleyball, wrestling
Women's Non-aid: alpine skiing, basketball, cross country, cross country skiing, diving, golf, indoor track, soccer, swimming, swimming-diving, tennis, track & field, volleyball

COLLEGE OF ST. BENEDICT
37 South College Avenue
St. Joesph, MN 56374-2099
(612) 363-5073 Contact: Mike Durbin
Women's Non-aid: basketball, cross country, diving, soccer, softball, swimming, tennis, volleyball

COLLEGE OF ST. SCHOLASTICA
Duluth, MN 55811
(218) 723-6397 Contact: Tim Rutka
Men's Non-aid: basketball, cross country, ice hockey, soccer, tennis
Women's Non-aid: basketball, cross country, softball, tennis, volleyball

CONCORDIA COLLEGE
901 South 8th Street
Moorhead, MN 56562
(218) 299-3194 Contact: Jerry Pyle
Men's Non-aid: baseball, basketball, soccer, track & field
Women's Non-aid: basketball, softball, track & field, volleyball

CONCORDIA COLLEGE
275 North Syndicate
St. Paul, MN 55104
(612) 641-8893 Contact: Mike Streitz
Men's Non-aid: badminton, baseball, basketball, bowling, football, golf, soccer, tennis, track & field, wrestling
Women's Non-aid: basketball, softball, tennis, track & field, volleyball

FERGUS FALLS COMMUNITY COLLEGE
Fergus Falls, MN 56537
2-year college
(218) 739-7538 Contact: Dave Retzlaff
Men's Non-aid: baseball, basketball, football, golf, track & field
Women's Non-aid: basketball, golf, softball, tennis, volleyball

GUSTAVUS ADOLPHUS COLLEGE
800 College Avenue
St. Peter, MN 56082
(507) 933-7647 Contact: Tim Kennedy
Men's Non-aid: baseball, basketball, cross country, football, golf, ice hockey, indoor track, soccer, swimming, swimming-diving, tennis, track & field
Women's Non-aid: basketball, cross country, golf, gymnastics, indoor track, soccer, softball, swimming, swimming-diving, tennis, track & field, volleyball

HAMLINE UNIVERSITY
1536 Hewitt Avenue
St. Paul, MN 55104
(612) 641-2280 Contact: Richard Manderfeld
Men's Non-aid: baseball, basketball, cross country, diving, football, golf, ice hockey, indoor track, soccer, softball, swimming-diving, track & field, wrestling
Women's Non-aid: basketball, cross country, diving, gymnastics, indoor track, softball, swimming-diving, track & field, volleyball

HIBBING COMMUNITY COLLEGE
1515 East 25th Street
Hibbing, MN 55746
2-year college
(218) 262-6749 Contact: Anna Van Tasser
Men's Non-aid: baseball, basketball, football, ice hockey
Women's Non-aid: basketball, softball, volleyball

INVER HILLS COMMUNITY COLLEGE
8445 College Trail
Inver Grove Heights, MN 55076
2-year college

(612) 450-8501 Contact: Steve Dove
Men's Non-aid: baseball, basketball, football, golf, track & field
Women's Non-aid: basketball, softball, track & field, volleyball

MACALESTER COLLEGE
1600 Grand Avenue
St. Paul, MN 55105-1899
(612) 696-6214 Contact: Andy Johnson
Men's Non-aid: baseball, basketball, cross country, diving, football, golf, indoor track, soccer, swimming-diving, tennis, track & field
Women's Non-aid: basketball, cross country, golf, indoor track, soccer, softball, swimming-diving, tennis, track & field, volleyball

MANKATO STATE UNIVERSITY
Box 28, MSU
Mankato, MN 56001
(507) 389-2625 Contact: Paul Allan
Men's Aid (#/$): 66/unspecified $
Women's Aid (#/$): 55/unspecified $
M: baseball, basketball, cross country, diving, football, golf, ice hockey, indoor track, swimming, swimming-diving, tennis, track & field, wrestling
W: basketball, cross country, diving, golf, indoor track, softball, swimming, swimming-diving, tennis, track & field, volleyball

MINNEAPOLIS COMMUNITY COLLEGE
1501 Hennepin Avenue
Minneapolis, MN 55403
2-year college
(612) 341-7070 Contact: Jay Pivec
Men's Non-aid: basketball, golf
Women's Non-aid: basketball, golf

MOORHEAD STATE UNIVERSITY
Moorhead, MN 56563
(218) 236-2113 Contact: Larry Scott
Men's Aid (#/$): 218/$51,800
Women's Aid (#/$): 114/$34,533
M: basketball, cross country, football, indoor track, track & field, wrestling.
Men's Non-aid: golf
W: basketball, cross country, golf, indoor track, softball, tennis, track & field, volleyball

NORTH HENNEPIN COMMUNITY COLLEGE
7411 85th Avenue North
Minneapolis, MN 55445
2-year college
(612) 424-0811 Contact: Glenn Young
Men's Non-aid: baseball, football, golf, tennis
Women's Non-aid: golf, softball, tennis, volleyball

NORTHLAND COMMUNITY COLLEGE
1101 Highway One East
Thief River Falls, MN 56701
2-year college
(218) 681-2181 Contact: Rick Nelson
Men's Non-aid: baseball, basketball, football
Women's Non-aid: basketball, softball, volleyball

NORTHWESTERN COLLEGE
St. Paul, MN 55113
(612) 631-5321 Contact: Richard Blatchley
Men's Non-aid: baseball, basketball, cross country, football, golf, soccer, softball, tennis, track & field, wrestling
Women's Non-aid: baseball, basketball, softball, track & field, volleyball

RAINY RIVER COMMUNITY COLLEGE
Highway 11-71
International Falls, MN 56649
2-year college
(218) 285-2241 Contact: Dave Horner
Men's Non-aid: basketball, golf, ice hockey, track & field
Women's Non-aid: basketball, softball, track & field, volleyball

ROCHESTER COMMUNITY COLLEGE
851 30th Avenue SE
Rochester, MN 55904

2-year college
(507) 285-7218 Contact: Tom Floyd
Men's Non-aid: baseball, basketball, football, golf, tennis, wrestling
Women's Non-aid: basketball, golf, softball, tennis, volleyball

SAINT CLOUD STATE UNIVERSITY

720 Fourth Avenue South
St. Cloud, MN 56301-4498
(612) 255-2141 Contact: Anne Abicht
Men's Aid (#/$): 75/$363,000
Women's Aid (#/$): 50/$95,000
M: baseball, basketball, cross country, diving, football, golf, ice hockey, indoor track, swimming, swimming-diving, tennis, track & field, wrestling
W: basketball, diving, indoor track, softball, swimming-diving, tennis, track & field, volleyball. Women's Non-aid: cross country, golf

SAINT JOHN'S UNIVERSITY

Wimmer Hall 208
Collegeville, MN 56321
(612) 363-2595 Contact: Tom Nelson
Men's Non-aid: baseball, basketball, cross country, diving, football, golf, ice hockey, indoor track, soccer, swimming, tennis, track & field, wrestling

SAINT OLAF COLLEGE

1520 St. Olaf Avenue
Northfield, MN 55057-1098
(507) 646-3834 Contact: Nancy Droen Moe
Men's Non-aid: alpine skiing, baseball, basketball, cross country, cross country skiing, diving, football, golf, ice hockey, indoor track, soccer, swimming-diving, tennis, track & field, wrestling
Women's Non-aid: alpine skiing, basketball, cross country, cross country skiing, diving, golf, indoor track, soccer, softball, swimming-diving, tennis, track & field, volleyball

SOUTHWEST STATE UNIVERSITY

1501 State Street
Marshall, MN 56258
(507) 537-7177 Contact: Bob Otterson
Unspecified athletic aid available
M: baseball, basketball, football, wrestling. Men's Non-aid: cross country, indoor track, track & field
W: basketball, softball, tennis, volleyball. Women's Non-aid: cross country, indoor track, track & field

UNIVERSITY OF MINNESOTA

10 University, c/o Athletics
Duluth, MN 55812-2496
(218) 726-8191 Contact: Bob Nygaard
Unspecified athletic aid available
M: baseball, basketball, cross country, football, ice hockey, indoor track, tennis, track & field, wrestling
W: basketball, cross country, indoor track, softball, tennis, track & field, volleyball

UNIVERSITY OF MINNESOTA

516 15th Avenue, S.E.
Minneapolis, MN 55455
(612) 625-4090 Contact: Bob Peterson
Unspecified athletic aid available
M: baseball, basketball, cross country, football, golf, ice hockey, indoor track, tennis, track & field, wrestling
W: basketball, cross country, football, ice hockey, indoor track, softball, tennis, track & field, volleyball

UNIVERSITY OF MINNESOTA

4th and College Avenue
Morris, MN 56267
(612) 589-6050 Contact: Judy Riley
Men's Non-aid: baseball, basketball, cross country, football, golf, tennis, track & field, wrestling
Women's Non-aid: basketball, golf, softball, tennis, track & field, volleyball

UNIVERSITY OF ST. THOMAS

Mail #4008
2115 Summit Avenue

St. Paul, MN 55105
(612) 962-5000 Contact: Greg Capell
Men's Non-aid: baseball, basketball, cross country, diving, football, golf, ice hockey, indoor track, soccer, swimming, swimming-diving, tennis, track & field, wrestling
Women's Non-aid: basketball, cross country, diving, golf, indoor track, soccer, softball, swimming, swimming-diving, tennis, track & field, volleyball

WINONA STATE UNIVERSITY
P.O. Box 5838
Winona, MN 55987-5838
(507) 457-5576 Contact: Daryl Henderson
Unspecified athletic aid available
M: baseball, basketball, cross country, football, golf, indoor track, tennis, track & field
W: basketball, cross country, golf, gymnastics, indoor track, softball, tennis, track & field, volleyball

WORTHINGTON COMMUNITY COLLEGE
Worthington, MN 56187
2-year college
(507) 732-2107 Contact: Arlo Mogck
Unspecified athletic aid available
Restrictions and notes: Athletic aid provides free books for all men and women student-athletes.
M: basketball, football, wrestling
W: basketball, volleyball

Mississippi

ALCORN STATE UNIVERSITY
P.O. Box 510-ASU
Lorman, MS 39096
(601) 877-6466 Contact: Augusta "Gus" Howard
Unspecified athletic aid available
M: baseball, basketball, cross country, football, golf, indoor track, track & field
W: basketball, cross country, tennis, track & field, volleyball

BELHAVEN COLLEGE
1500 Peachtree Street
Jackson, MS 39202
(601) 968-5933 Contact: Linda Phillips
Unspecified athletic aid available
M: baseball, basketball, soccer, softball, tennis
W: basketball. Women's Non-aid: baseball, softball

BLUE MOUNTAIN COLLEGE
Box 336
Blue Mountain, MS 38610
(601) 685-4771 Contact: Johnnie Armstrong
Women's Aid (#/$): 17/unspecified $
W: basketball, tennis

COAHOMA JUNIOR COLLEGE
Route 1, Box 616
Clarksdale, MS 38614
2-year college
(601) 627-2571 Contact: John Mayo
Unspecified athletic aid available
M: basketball, football. Men's Non-aid: baseball, golf, track & field
W: basketball. Women's Non-aid: softball

COPIAH-LINCOLN COMMUNITY COLLEGE
P.O. Box 649
Wesson, MS 39191
2-year college
(601) 643-5101 Contact: Ray Ishee
Unspecified athletic aid available
M: basketball, football. Men's Non-aid: baseball, golf, tennis, track & field

DELTA STATE UNIVERSITY
P.O. Box D-3, DSU
Cleveland, MS 38733
(601) 846-4677 Contact: Jody Correro
Men's Aid (#/$): 63/$35,604

Women's Aid (#/$): 16/$26,113
M: baseball, basketball, football, golf, swimming-diving, tennis
W: basketball, cross country, softball, swimming-diving, tennis

HINDS COMMUNITY COLLEGE
P.O. Box 1286
Raymond, MS 39154
2-year college
(601) 857-3362 Contact: Bob Hodges
Unspecified athletic aid available
M: basketball, football. Men's Non-aid: baseball, golf, synchronized swimming, track & field
W: basketball. Women's Non-aid: softball, synchronized swimming

HINDS COMMUNITY COLLEGE
Utica Campus
Utica, MS 39175
2-year college
(601) 885-6062 Contact: Earl Joe Nelson
Unspecified athletic aid available
M: basketball. Men's Non-aid: baseball, tennis
W: basketball. Women's Non-aid: tennis

HOLMES JUNIOR COLLEGE
P.O. Box 367
Goodman, MS 39079
2-year college
(601) 472-2312 Contact: James G. Williams
Unspecified athletic aid available
M: baseball, basketball, football. Men's Non-aid: track & field
W: basketball

ITAWAMBA COMMUNITY COLLEGE
602 West Hill Street
Fulton, MS 38843
2-year college
(601) 862-3101 Contact: Donna Thomas
Men's Aid (#/$): 53/unspecified $
Women's Aid (#/$): 10/unspecified $
M: baseball, basketball, football
W: basketball

JACKSON STATE UNIVERSITY
P.O. Box 17490
Jackson, MS 39217-0390
(601) 968-2273 Contact: Sam Jefferson
Unspecified athletic aid available
M: baseball, basketball, cross country, football, golf, indoor track, tennis, track & field
W: basketball, cross country, indoor track, tennis, track & field, volleyball

JONES COUNTY JUNIOR COLLEGE
1000 South Court Street
Ellisville, MS 39437
2-year college
(601) 477-4032 Contact: Rebecca Patrick
Unspecified athletic aid available
M: basketball, football. Men's Non-aid: baseball, golf, tennis, track & field
W: basketball. Women's Non-aid: tennis

MARY HOLMES COLLEGE
Highway 50 West
West Point, MS 39773
2-year college
(601) 494-6820 Contact: Joe N. Nimock
Unspecified athletic aid available
M: baseball, basketball. Men's Non-aid: cross country
W: baseball, basketball. Women's Non-aid: cross country, softball

MISSISSIPPI COLLEGE
Box 4003
Clinton, MS 39058
(601) 925-3255 Contact: Norman H. Gough
Unspecified athletic aid available
M: baseball, basketball, cross country, football, golf, tennis, track & field
W: basketball, softball, tennis, volleyball

MISSISSIPPI DELTA JUNIOR COLLEGE
Moorhead, MS 38761
2-year college

(601) 246-5631 Contact: Joe Wilson
Men's Aid (#/$): 94/$84,600
Women's Aid (#/$): 15/$13,500
M: baseball, basketball, football. Men's Non-aid: track & field
W: basketball, softball. Women's Non-aid: tennis

MISSISSIPPI GULF COAST JUNIOR COLLEGE
P.O. Box 64
Perkinston, MS 39573
2-year college
(601) 928-5211 Contact: Winfred Moncrief
Unspecified athletic aid available
M: basketball, football. Men's Non-aid: baseball, golf, tennis, track & field
W: basketball. Women's Non-aid: softball, tennis

MISSISSIPPI STATE UNIVERSITY
M.S.U. Athletic Department,
P.O. Box 5327
Mississippi State, MS 39762
(601) 325-2808 Contact: David Boles
Unspecified athletic aid available
M: baseball, basketball, cross country, football, golf, indoor track, tennis, track & field. Men's Non-aid: bowling, fencing, martial arts, power lifting, riflery, rodeo, rugby, soccer, water skiing, weightlifting
W: basketball, golf, indoor track, softball, tennis, track & field, volleyball. Women's Non-aid: bowling, martial arts, power lifting, riflery, rodeo, water skiing, weightlifting

MISSISSIPPI UNIVERSITY FOR WOMEN
Box 1636
Columbus, MS 39701
(601) 329-7119 Contact: Sharon Stephens
Unspecified athletic aid available
W: basketball, softball, tennis, volleyball

MISSISSIPPI VALLEY STATE UNIVERSITY
P.O. Box 743
Itta Bena, MS 38941
(601) 254-6641 Contact: Chuck Prophet
Unspecified athletic aid available
M: baseball, basketball, cross country, football, golf, indoor track, tennis, track & field. Men's Non-aid: diving, gymnastics, martial arts, power lifting, swimming, volleyball
W: basketball, cross country, golf, indoor track, tennis, track & field, volleyball. Women's Non-aid: diving, softball

NORTHEAST MISSISSIPPI COMMUNITY COLLEGE
Cunningham Boulevard
Booneville, MS 38829
2-year college
(601) 728-7751 Contact: Mark Lindsey
Unspecified athletic aid available
M: basketball, football. Men's Non-aid: baseball, tennis, track & field
W: basketball. Women's Non-aid: softball, tennis

NORTHWEST MISSISSIPPI COMMUNITY COLLEGE
P.O. Box HH
Senatobia, MS 38668
2-year college
(601) 562-3276 Contact: Mr. Brett Brown
Unspecified athletic aid available
M: basketball, football. Men's Non-aid: baseball, tennis
W: basketball. Women's Non-aid: softball, tennis

RUST COLLEGE
150 Rust Avenue
Holly Springs, MS 38635
(601) 252-8000 Contact: Paula Clark
Unspecified athletic aid available
M: baseball, basketball, cross country, tennis, track & field
W: basketball, cross country, tennis, track & field

TOUGALOO COLLEGE
Tougaloo, MS 39174
(601) 977-7766 Contact: Janis H. Evans
Men's Aid (#/$): 14/$32,745
Women's Aid (#/$): 12/$26,210
M: basketball
W: basketball

UNIVERSITY OF MISSISSIPPI
P.O. Box 217
Oxford, MS 38677
(601) 232-7522 Contact: Langston Rogers
Unspecified athletic aid available
M: baseball, basketball, cross country, football, golf, indoor track, tennis, track & field
W: basketball, cross country, golf, tennis, track & field, volleyball

UNIVERSITY OF SOUTHERN MISSISSIPPI
Box 5161
Hattiesburg, MS 39406-5161
(601) 266-4503 Contact: M.R. Napier
Men's Aid (#/$): 144/$733,536
Women's Aid (#/$): 57/$290,358
M: baseball, basketball, cross country, football, golf, indoor track, tennis, track & field, volleyball
W: basketball, cross country, golf, indoor track, tennis, track & field, volleyball

Missouri

AVILA COLLEGE
11901 Wornall Road
Kansas City, MO 64145
(816) 942-8400 X. 223 Contact: Cynthia A. Butler
Men's Aid (#/$): 75/$173,050
Women's Aid (#/$): 36/$88,700
M: baseball, basketball, soccer
W: basketball, softball, volleyball

BAPTIST BIBLE COLLEGE
628 East Kearney
Springfield, MO 65802
(417) 869-6000 Contact: Dick Bemarkt
Men's Non-aid: basketball
Women's Non-aid: volleyball

CENTRAL METHODIST COLLEGE
411 Central Methodist Square
Fayette, MO 65248
(816) 248-3391 Contact: Roberta L. Knipp
Aid (#/$): 335/$425,138 (M & W)
M: baseball, basketball, cross country, football, golf, soccer, tennis, track & field, volleyball
W: basketball, cross country, golf, soccer, softball, tennis, track & field, volleyball

CENTRAL MISSOURI STATE UNIVERSITY
Room 203, Multipurpose Building
Warrensburg, MO 64093
(816) 543-4312 Contact: Bill Turnage
Men's Aid (#/$): 68/$320,670
Women's Aid (#/$): 31/$145,290
M: baseball, basketball, cross country, football, indoor track, track & field, wrestling. Men's Non-aid: golf
W: basketball, cross country, indoor track, softball, track & field, volleyball

COLLEGE OF THE OZARKS
Point Lookout, MO 65726
(417) 334-6411 Contact: Al Waller
Men's Aid (#/$): 24/$38,400
Women's Aid (#/$): 24/$38,400
Restrictions and notes: All students must participate in a work program of 15 hours per week plus 2-40 hour work weeks during vacation.
M: baseball, basketball
W: basketball. Women's Non-aid: volleyball

COLUMBIA COLLEGE
1001 Rogers Street
Columbia, MO 65216
(314) 875-7362 Contact: Mary Lou Eldridge
Men's Aid (#/$): 44/$195,341
Women's Aid (#/$): 32/$148,162

M: basketball, soccer. Men's Non-aid: golf
W: softball, volleyball

CONCORDIA SEMINARY
801 DeMun Avenue
St. Louis, MO 63105
(314) 725-2629, Contact: Mark Shaltanis
Men's Non-aid: bowling, tennis
Women's Non-aid: bowling, tennis

CROWDER COLLEGE
601 Laclede
Neosho, MO 64850
2-year college
(417) 451-5530 Contact: Gary Roark
Men's Aid (#/$): 10/unspecified $
Women's Aid (#/$): 10/unspecified $
M: baseball
W: basketball, softball

CULVER-STOCKTON COLLEGE
1 College Hill
Canton, MO 63435
(314) 288-5221 Contact: John Schield
Unspecified athletic aid available
M: baseball, basketball, football, golf, tennis
W: basketball, golf, softball, tennis, volleyball

DRURY COLLEGE
900 North Benton Avenue
Springfield, MO 65802
(417) 865-8731 Contact: Dan Cashel
Men's Aid (#/$): 30/$41,900
Women's Aid (#/$): 27/$36,200
Restrictions and notes: Full grants only in basketball.
M: basketball, golf, soccer, swimming-diving, tennis. Men's Non-aid: volleyball

EAST CENTRAL COLLEGE
P.O. Box 529
Union, MO 63084
2-year college
(314) 583-5193 Contact: Ruth Dace
Unspecified athletic aid available
M: baseball, basketball, soccer
W: basketball, softball, volleyball

EVANGEL COLLEGE
1111 N. Glenstone
Springfield, MO 65802
(417) 865-2811 X. 260 Contact: David Fillmore
Unspecified athletic aid available
M: baseball, basketball, football
W: basketball, tennis, volleyball

HANNIBAL-LAGRANGE COLLEGE
2800 Palmrya Road
Hannibal, MO 63401
(314) 221-3675 X. 279 Contact: Dean Schoonover
Unspecified athletic aid available
M: baseball, basketball, golf
W: softball, volleyball

HARRIS-STOWE STATE COLLEGE
3026 LaClede
St. Louis, MO 63103
(314) 533-3366 X. 305 Contact: James Velten
Men's Aid (#/$): 18/$25,272
Women's Aid (#/$): 18/$25,272
M: baseball, basketball, soccer
W: basketball, track & field, volleyball

JEFFERSON COLLEGE
Hillsboro, MO 63050
2-year college
(314) 789-3951 Contact: Harold R. Oetting
Men's Aid (#/$): 28/$28,000
Women's Aid (#/$): 20/$28,000
M: baseball, tennis
W: basketball, volleyball

KEMPER MILITARY SCHOOL
701 Third Street
Boonville, MO 65233
2-year college
(816) 882-5623 Contact: Janet Gaddis
Men's Aid (#/$): 96/$321,225
M: baseball, basketball, football

LINCOLN UNIVERSITY
820 Chestnut Street
Jefferson City, MO 65102-6156

(314) 681-6156 Contact: Arnol Woods
Men's Non-aid: baseball, basketball, cross country, indoor track, soccer, tennis, track & field
Women's Non-aid: basketball, tennis, track & field, volleyball

LINDENWOOD COLLEGE
209 South Kingshighway
St. Charles, MO 63301
(314) 949-4923 Contact: Pam Jones Williams
Unspecified athletic aid available
M: basketball, soccer
W: basketball, soccer. Women's Non-aid: softball

MARYVILLE UNIVERSITY
13550 Conway Road
St. Louis, MO 63141
(314) 576-9312 Contact: Lonnie Folks
Men's Non-aid: baseball, basketball, cross country, soccer, tennis, track & field
Women's Non-aid: basketball, cross country, soccer, softball, tennis, track & field, volleyball

MINERAL AREA COLLEGE
P.O. Box 1000
Flat River, MO 63601
2-year college
(314) 431-4593 Contact: Bob Sechrest
Unspecified athletic aid available
M: baseball, basketball
W: basketball, volleyball

MISSOURI BAPTIST COLLEGE
12542 Conway Road
St. Louis, MO 63141
(314) 434-1115 X. 216 Contact: Helen Vincent
Men's Aid (#/$): 93/$147,000
Women's Aid (#/$): 50/$95,000
M: baseball, basketball, soccer. Men's Non-aid: golf
W: basketball, soccer, softball, volleyball

MISSOURI SOUTHERN STATE COLLEGE
3950 Newman Road
Joplin, MO 64801-1595
(417) 625-9359 Contact: Jim Frazier
Men's Aid (#/$): 68/$289,816
Women's Aid (#/$): 31/$132,122
Restrictions and notes: Athletic aid based on 16 credit hours and includes room/board/instate tuition. M: contact Jim Frazier. W: contact Sallie Beard.
M: baseball, basketball, cross country, football, golf, indoor track, soccer, track & field
W: basketball, cheerleading, cross country, indoor track, softball, tennis, track & field, volleyball

MISSOURI VALLEY COLLEGE
500 East College
Marshall, MO 65340
(816) 886-6924 Contact: Gayle Carter
Unspecified athletic aid available
M: baseball, basketball, cross country, football, golf, indoor track, soccer, track & field
W: basketball, cross country, golf, indoor track, soccer, softball, track & field, volleyball

MISSOURI WESTERN STATE COLLEGE
4525 Downs Drive
St. Joseph, MO 64507
(816) 271-4481 Contact: Ed Harris
Men's Aid (#/$): 51/$204,000
Women's Aid (#/$): 25/$100,000
Restrictions and notes: Most athletic aid is partial scholarships.
M: baseball, basketball, football, golf
W: basketball, softball, tennis, volleyball

NORTH CENTRAL MISSOURI COLLEGE
Main Street
Trenton, MO 64683
2-year college
(816) 359-3948 Contact: Robert Shields
Men's Aid (#/$): 15/$11,137
Women's Aid (#/$): 15/$11,137
M: baseball, softball
W: soccer

NORTHEAST MISSOURI STATE UNIVERSITY
112 McClain Hall
Kirksville, MO 63501
(816) 785-4276 Contact: William Cable
Unspecified athletic aid available
M: baseball, basketball, cross country, football, golf, soccer, tennis, track & field. Men's Non-aid: swimming-diving
W: basketball, cross country, golf, softball, swimming-diving, tennis, track & field, volleyball. Women's Non-aid: soccer

NORTHWEST MISSOURI STATE UNIVERSITY
Sports Information Office
Maryville, MO 64468
(816) 562-1118 Contact: Larry Cain
Men's Aid (#/$): 31/$63,314
Women's Aid (#/$): 15/$29,400
M: baseball, basketball, cross country, football, indoor track, tennis, track & field
W: basketball, cross country, indoor track, softball, tennis, track & field, volleyball

PARK COLLEGE
8700 River Park Drive, Box 44
Parkville, MO 64152
(816) 741-2000 X. 290 Contact: Ms. Pat Hollenbeck
Men's Aid (#/$): 78/$233,108
Women's Aid (#/$): 66/$175,717
M: basketball, cross country, equestrian, soccer, track & field, volleyball
W: basketball, cross country, equestrian, soccer, track & field, volleyball

PENN VALLEY COMMUNITY COLLEGE
3201 Southwest Trafficway
Kansas City, MO 64111
2-year college
(816) 932-7600 Contact: Fred Pohlman
Men's Aid (#/$): 16/$20,000
M: basketball, golf
W: volleyball

ROCKHURST COLLEGE
1100 Rockhurst Road
Kansas City, MO 64110
(816) 926-4141 Contact: Sid Bordman
Unspecified athletic aid available
M: basketball, soccer. Men's Non-aid: cross country
W: basketball, volleyball. Women's Non-aid: cross country

SAINT LOUIS UNIVERSITY
221 North Grand Boulevard
St. Louis, MO 63103
(314) 658-2524 Contact: Doug McIlhagga
Men's Aid (#/$): 20/$169,600
Women's Aid (#/$): 10/$84,800
M: baseball, basketball, soccer, swimming-diving, tennis. Men's Non-aid: cross country, golf, riflery
W: basketball, field hockey, softball, swimming-diving, tennis, volleyball

SOUTHEAST MISSOURI STATE UNIVERSITY
1 University Plaza
Cape Girardeau, MO 63701
(314) 651-2294 Contact: Ron Hines
Unspecified athletic aid available
M: baseball, basketball, cross country, football, indoor track, soccer, track & field
W: basketball, cross country, gymnastics, indoor track, softball, track & field, volleyball

SOUTHWEST BAPTIST UNIVERSITY
1601 South Springfield
Bolivar, MO 65613
(417) 326-1799 Contact: Christopher Johnson
Men's Aid (#/$): 65/$584,740
Women's Aid (#/$): 26/$233,896
M: baseball, basketball, cross country, football, golf, indoor track, tennis, track & field
W: basketball, cross country, indoor track, softball, tennis, track & field, volleyball

SOUTHWEST MISSOURI STATE UNIVERSITY
901 South National
Springfield, MO 65804
(417) 836-5402 Contact: Mark Stillwell
Men's Aid (#/$): 45/$168,438
Women's Aid (#/$): 21/$95,438
M: baseball, basketball, cross country, football, golf, indoor track, soccer, swimming, swimming-diving, tennis, track & field, wrestling. Men's Non-aid: riflery, rodeo
W: basketball, cross country, field hockey, golf, indoor track, softball, tennis, track & field, volleyball

ST. LOUIS COMMUNITY COLLEGE—FOREST PARK
5600 Oakland Avenue
St. Louis, MO 63110
2-year college
(314) 644-9100 Contact: Russ Dippold
Unspecified athletic aid available
M: baseball, basketball, soccer, wrestling
W: baseball, squash, volleyball

ST. LOUIS COMMUNITY COLLEGE—FLORISSANT VALLEY
3400 Pershall Road
St. Louis, MO 63135
2-year college
(314) 595-4275 Contact: Bill Miller
Unspecified athletic aid available
Restrictions and notes: 41 athletic scholarships available totalling $36,408.
M: baseball, basketball, soccer, wrestling
W: softball, volleyball

STATE FAIR COMMUNITY COLLEGE
1900 Clarendon Road
Sedalia, MO 65301
2-year college
(816) 826-9635 Contact: Bill Barton
Unspecified athletic aid available
M: baseball, basketball, golf
W: basketball, soccer

THREE RIVERS COMMUNITY COLLEGE
Three Rivers Boulevard
Poplar Bluff, MO 63901
2-year college
(314) 686-4101 Contact: Gene Bess
Unspecified athletic aid available
M: baseball, basketball, golf
W: basketball, volleyball

UNIVERSITY OF MISSOURI
8001 Natural Bridge
St. Louis, MO 63121
(314) 553-5641
Unspecified athletic aid available
M: baseball, basketball, cross country, football, golf, indoor track, swimming, swimming-diving, track & field, wrestling
W: cross country, golf, gymnastics, indoor track, softball, swimming, swimming-diving, track & field, volleyball

UNIVERSITY OF MISSOURI (COLUMBIA)
374 Hearnes
Columbia, MO 65211
(314) 882-6501 Contact: Bob Brendel
Men's Aid (#/$): 217/$1,062,863
Women's Aid (#/$): 117/$498,103
M: crew, basketball, cross country, diving, football, golf, indoor track, swimming, swimming-diving, track & field, wrestling. Men's Non-aid: tennis
W: basketball, cross country, diving, golf, gymnastics, indoor track, softball, swimming, swimming-diving, track & field, volleyball. Women's Non-aid: tennis

UNIVERSITY OF MISSOURI (KANSAS CITY)
5100 Rockhill Road
Kansas City, MO 64110
(816) 276-2712 Contact: Barney Turk
Unspecified athletic aid available
M: basketball. Men's Non-aid: golf, tennis

W: basketball. Women's Non-aid: golf, tennis

UNIVERSITY OF MISSOURI (ROLLA)
Multipurpose Building
Rolla, MO 65401
(314) 341-4175 Contact: John Kean
Men's Aid (#/$): 41.5/$280,050
Women's Aid (#/$): 11/$73,700
M: baseball, basketball, cross country, football, golf, soccer, swimming
W: basketball, cross country, soccer, softball

WASHINGTON UNIVERSITY
One Brooklings Drive
St. Louis, MO 63130-4890
(314) 935-5077 Contact: Michael Wolf
Men's Non-aid: baseball, basketball, cross country, football, golf, soccer, softball, swimming-diving, tennis, track & field, wrestling
Women's Non-aid: basketball, cross country, swimming-diving, tennis, track & field, volleyball

WEBSTER UNIVERSITY
470 East Lockwood Avenue
St. Louis, MO 63119-3194
(314) 968-7174 Contact: Bob Delaney
Men's Non-aid: baseball, basketball, soccer, tennis
Women's Non-aid: basketball, cross country, tennis, volleyball

WENTWORTH MILITARY ACADEMY AND JUNIOR COLLEGE
18th & Washington
Lexington, MO 64067
2-year college
(816) 259-2221 Contact: Bob Florence
Unspecified athletic aid available
M: basketball

WILLIAM JEWELL COLLEGE
500 College Hill
Liberty, MO 64068
(816) 781-7700 X. 5146 Contact: Sue Armstrong
Men's Aid (#/$): 228/$245,175
Women's Aid (#/$): 105/$60,100
M: baseball, basketball, cross country, football, golf, indoor track, soccer, tennis, track & field, wrestling
W: basketball, cross country, diving, indoor track, softball, tennis, track & field, volleyball

WILLIAM WOODS COLLEGE
200 West 12th Street
Fulton, MO 65251
(314) 592-4387 Contact: Roger Ternes
Unspecified athletic aid available
Restrictions and notes: William Woods is an all-women's college that provides full and partial tuition scholarships.
W: basketball, soccer, softball, swimming-diving, tennis, volleyball

Montana

CARROLL COLLEGE
North Benton Avenue
Helena, MT 59625
(406) 447-5411 Contact: Peggy Stebbins
Men's Aid (#/$): 81/$299,258
Women's Aid (#/$): 35/$169,120
M: basketball, football
W: basketball, volleyball

DAWSON COMMUNITY COLLEGE
P.O. Box 421
Glendive, MT 59330
2-year college
(406) 365-3396 Contact: Joyce Ayre
Men's Aid (#/$): 15/$21,050
Women's Aid (#/$): 15/$21,050
M: basketball, rodeo. Men's Non-aid: equestrian
W: basketball, rodeo. Women's Non-aid: equestrian

EASTERN MONTANA COLLEGE
1500 North 30th
Billings, MT 59101-0298

(406) 657-2269 Contact: Farrel Stewart
Unspecified athletic aid available
M: basketball, golf, gymnastics, tennis, volleyball
W: basketball, golf, tennis, volleyball

MILES COMMUNITY COLLEGE
2715 Dickinson
Miles City, MT 59301
2-year college
(406) 232-3031 Contact: Dan Connors
Men's Aid (#/$): 25/unspecified $
Women's Aid (#/$): 30/unspecified $
M: basketball, rodeo
W: basketball, rodeo, volleyball

MONTANA COLLEGE OF MINERAL SCIENCE AND TECHNOLOGY
West Park Street
Butte, MT 59701
(406) 496-4266 Contact: Dennis Grose
Unspecified athletic aid available
M: basketball, football, swimming, wrestling
W: basketball, swimming, volleyball

MONTANA STATE UNIVERSITY
416 Culbertson Hall
Bozeman, MT 59717
(406) 994-5133 Contact: Bill Lamberty
Unspecified athletic aid available
M: alpine skiing, basketball, cross country, cross country skiing, football, indoor track, rodeo, tennis, track & field, wrestling
W: alpine skiing, basketball, cross country, cross country skiing, gymnastics, indoor track, rodeo, tennis, track & field, volleyball

NORTHERN MONTANA COLLEGE
P.O. Box 7751
Havre, MT 59501
(406) 265-3761 Contact: Tom Heck
Men's Aid (#/$): 24/unspecified $
Women's Aid (#/$): 24/unspecified $
M: basketball, wrestling
W: basketball, volleyball

ROCKY MOUNTAIN COLLEGE
1511 Poly Drive
Billings, MT 59102
(406) 657-1105 Contact: Shelley Pingree
Unspecified athletic aid available
M: basketball, football
W: basketball, volleyball

UNIVERSITY OF MONTANA
Adams Field House
Missoula, MT 59812
(406) 243-6899 Contact: Dave Guffey
Men's Aid (#/$): 130/$603,523
Women's Aid (#/$): 52/$187,228
M: baseball, crew, field hockey, ice hockey, swimming, tennis, track & field
W: basketball, cross country, indoor track, tennis, track & field, volleyball

WESTERN MONTANA COLLEGE
Campus Box 32
Dillon, MT 59725
(406) 683-7201 Contact: Wally Feldt
Unspecified athletic aid available
M: basketball, football, track & field, wrestling. Men's Non-aid: cross country, swimming
W: basketball, track & field, volleyball. Women's Non-aid: cross country, swimming

Nebraska

BELLEVUE COLLEGE
Galvin Road and Harvell Drive
Bellevue, NE 68005
(402) 293-3781 Contact:
Roy A. Smith, Jr.
Men's Aid (#/$): 71/$46,545
Women's Aid (#/$): 12/$8,000
M: baseball, basketball, softball
W: baseball, softball, volleyball

CENTRAL COMMUNITY COLLEGE
P.O. Box 1027
Columbus, NE 68601
2-year college

(402) 564-7132 Contact: Jack Gutierrez
Men's Aid (#/$): 24/$20,000
Women's Aid (#/$): 24/$20,000
Restrictions and notes: Full tuition waivers (12 per sport)
M: basketball, soccer
W: basketball, volleyball

CHADRON STATE COLLEGE
Tenth and Main
Chadron, NE 69337
(308) 432-6212 Contact: Con Marshall
Men's Aid (#/$): 70/unspecified $
Women's Aid (#/$): 40/unspecified $
M: basketball, football, indoor track, rodeo, track & field, wrestling
W: basketball, golf, indoor track, track & field, volleyball

COLLEGE OF ST. MARY
1901 South 72nd Street
Omaha, NE 68124
(402) 399-2451 Contact: Ron Romine
Women's Aid (#/$): 37/$89,705
W: softball, tennis, volleyball

CONCORDIA TEACHERS COLLEGE
800 N. Columbia Avenue
Seward, NE 68434
(402) 643-7270 Contact: Judy J. Williams
Unspecified athletic aid available
M: baseball, basketball, cross country, football, golf, indoor track, soccer, swimming, swimming-diving, tennis, track & field
W: basketball, cross country, golf, indoor track, softball, swimming, swimming-diving, tennis, track & field, volleyball

CREIGHTON UNIVERSITY
24th and California
Vinardi Athletic Center
Omaha, NE 68178
(402) 280-2488 Contact: Kevin Sarver
Unspecified athletic aid available
M: baseball, basketball. Men's Non-aid: cross country, golf, swimming, tennis
W: basketball, softball. Women's Non-aid: cross country, golf, swimming, tennis

DANA COLLEGE
2848 College Drive
Blair, NE 68008-1099
(402) 426-7293 Contact: Dr. Leo McKillip
Men's Aid (#/$): 125/$282,725
Women's Aid (#/$): 58/$132,430
M: baseball, basketball, football, wrestling. Men's Non-aid: golf, tennis, track & field
W: basketball, softball. Women's Non-aid: golf, tennis, track & field

DOANE COLLEGE
1014 Boswell Avenue
Crete, NE 68333
(402) 826-8248 Contact: Andy McCallister
Unspecified athletic aid available
M: basketball, cross country, football, indoor track, track & field. Men's Non-aid: golf, tennis
W: basketball, cross country, indoor track, tennis, track & field, volleyball. Women's Non-aid: golf, softball

HASTINGS COLLEGE
7th and Turner
Hastings, NE 68901
(402) 463-2402 Contact: Ian Roberts
Men's Aid (#/$): 249/$525,245
Women's Aid (#/$): 74/$145,912
M: baseball, basketball, cross country, football, golf, indoor track, tennis, track & field
W: basketball, cross country, golf, indoor track, softball, tennis, track & field, volleyball

MCCOOK COMMUNITY COLLEGE
1205 East Third
McCook, NE 69001
2-year college
(308) 345-6303 Contact: Robert Christie
Unspecified athletic aid available
M: basketball, golf
W: basketball, volleyball

MIDLAND LUTHERAN COLLEGE
900 North Clarkson
Fremont, NE 68025
(402) 721-5480 X. 6059 Contact: Keith Kramme
Unspecified athletic aid available
Restrictions and notes: All athletic aid based on need.
M: baseball, basketball, cross country, football, golf, indoor track, tennis, track & field
W: basketball, cross country, golf, indoor track, softball, tennis, track & field, volleyball

MID-PLAINS COMMUNITY COLLEGE
State Farm Road
North Platte, NE 69101
2-year college
(308) 532-8980 Contact: Dr. Darrel Hildebrand
Men's Aid (#/$): 15/unspecified $
Women's Aid (#/$): 30/unspecified $
M: basketball
W: basketball, volleyball

NEBRASKA WESLEYAN UNIVERSITY
5000 St. Paul Avenue
Lincoln, NE 68504-2796
(402) 465-2151 Contact: Jim Angele
Men's Non-aid: baseball, basketball, cross country, football, golf, softball, tennis, track & field, volleyball

PERU STATE COLLEGE
RR 1, Box 10
Peru, NE 68421
(402) 872-2276 Contact: Vince Henzel
Men's Aid (#/$): 12/$51,000
Women's Aid (#/$): 8/$39,000
M: baseball, basketball, football
W: basketball, softball, volleyball

SOUTHEAST COMMUNITY COLLEGE
Route 2, Box 35A
Beatrice, NE 68310
2-year college
(402) 228-3468
Contact: Dan Johnson
Unspecified athletic aid available
M: basketball, golf
W: basketball, softball, volleyball

UNIVERSITY OF NEBRASKA
60th and Dodge
Omaha, NE 68182
(402) 554-8514
Contact: Dick Beechner
Unspecified athletic aid available
M: baseball, basketball, cross country, football, golf, indoor track, tennis, track & field, wrestling
W: diving, swimming, swimming-diving, tennis, track & field, volleyball

UNIVERSITY OF NEBRASKA (KEARNEY)
905 West 25th Street
Kearney, NE 68849
(308) 234-8520
Contact: Mr. Pat McTee
Unspecified athletic aid available
M: baseball, basketball, cheerleading, cross country, football, golf, tennis, track & field, wrestling
W: basketball, cheerleading, cross country, diving, softball, swimming, tennis, track & field, volleyball

UNIVERSITY OF NEBRASKA (LINCOLN)
116 South Stadium
Lincoln, NE 68588-0123
(402) 472-5959 Contact: Don Bryant
Unspecified athletic aid available
M: baseball, basketball, cross country, diving, football, golf, gymnastics, indoor track, swimming, swimming-diving, tennis, track & field, wrestling
W: basketball, cross country, diving, golf, gymnastics, indoor track, softball, swimming, swimming-diving, tennis, track & field, volleyball

WAYNE STATE COLLEGE
Wayne, NE 68787
(402) 375-7326 Contact: Mike Meighen

Unspecified athletic aid available
M: baseball, basketball, football. Men's Non-aid: indoor track, track & field
W: basketball, softball, track & field, volleyball. Women's Non-aid: indoor track

WESTERN NEBRASKA COMMUNITY COLLEGE
1601 E. 27th Street
Scottsbluff, NE 69361
2-year college
(308) 635-3606 Contact: John Perry
Unspecified athletic aid available
M: basketball, golf
W: basketball, volleyball

Nevada

SIERRA NEVADA COLLEGE
P.O. Box 4269
Incline Village, NV 89450
(702) 831-1314 Contact: Laura Whitelaw
Men's Non-aid: alpine skiing, cross country, cross country skiing
Women's Non-aid: alpine skiing, cross country, cross country skiing

UNIVERSITY OF NEVADA
4505 Maryland Parkway
Las Vegas, NV 89154
(702) 739-3207 Contact: Joseph A. Hawk
Unspecified athletic aid available
M: baseball, basketball, cross country, diving, football, golf, soccer, swimming, swimming-diving, tennis
W: cross country, diving, indoor track, softball, swimming, swimming-diving, tennis, track & field

UNIVERSITY OF NEVADA (RENO)
Mall Stop 232
Reno, NV 89557
(702) 784-4600 Contact: Paul Stuart
Men's Aid (#/$): 113.7/$1,036,276
Women's Aid (#/$): 52.3/$451,000
M: baseball, basketball, cross country, football, golf, tennis, track & field
W: basketball, cross country, swimming, tennis, track & field, volleyball

New Hampshire

COLBY-SAWYER COLLEGE
Main Street
New London, NH 03257
(603) 526-2010 X. 414 Contact: Bill Warnken
Men's Non-aid: alpine skiing, basketball, cross country skiing, equestrian, soccer, tennis
Women's Non-aid: alpine skiing, basketball, cross country skiing, equestrian, lacrosse, soccer, tennis, volleyball

DARTMOUTH COLLEGE
110 Alumni Gym
Hanover, NH 03755
(603) 646-2468 Contact: Kathy Slattery
Men's Non-aid: alpine skiing, baseball, basketball, crew, cross country, cross country skiing, diving, equestrian, football, golf, gymnastics, ice hockey, indoor track, lacrosse, riflery, sailing, soccer, squash, swimming, tennis, track & field
Women's Non-aid: alpine skiing, basketball, crew, cross country, cross country skiing, diving, equestrian, field hockey, golf, ice hockey, indoor track, lacrosse, riflery, sailing, soccer, squash, swimming, tennis, track & field

FRANKLIN PIERCE COLLEGE
College Road, P.O. Box 60
Rindge, NH 03461
(603) 899-4180 Contact: Susan Howard
Unspecified athletic aid available
M: baseball, basketball, soccer, tennis. Men's Non-aid: alpine skiing, cross country, golf, sailing

W: basketball, soccer, softball. Women's Non-aid: alpine skiing, sailing, tennis

HESSER COLLEGE
25 Lowell Street
Manchester, NH 03101
2-year college
(603) 668-6660 Contact: Gary LeSuer
Men's Non-aid: basketball, soccer
Women's Non-aid: softball, volleyball

KEENE STATE COLLEGE
229 Main Street
Keene, NH 03431
(603) 358-2280 Contact: Patricia Blodgett
Unspecified athletic aid available
M: alpine skiing, baseball, basketball, cross country, cross country skiing, diving, soccer, swimming, track & field
W: alpine skiing, basketball, cross country, cross country skiing, diving, field hockey, soccer, softball, swimming, track & field, volleyball

NEW HAMPSHIRE COLLEGE
2500 North River Road
Manchester, NH 03104-1045
(603) 645-9626 Contact: Tom McDermott
Unspecified athletic aid available
M: baseball, basketball, soccer, tennis. Men's Non-aid: ice hockey, lacrosse
W: basketball, soccer, softball, tennis, volleyball

PLYMOUTH STATE COLLEGE
Holderness Road
Plymouth, NH 03264
(603) 535-2477 Contact: Mike Moffett
Men's Non-aid: alpine skiing, badminton, basketball, football, ice hockey, lacrosse, soccer, tennis, wrestling
Women's Non-aid: alpine skiing, basketball, field hockey, lacrosse, soccer, softball, swimming-diving, tennis

SAINT ANSELM COLLEGE
87 St. Anselm Drive
Manchester, NH 03102-1310
(603) 641-7810 Contact: Kristopher L. Russell
Men's Aid (#/$): 7/$83,236
Women's Aid (#/$): 2/$19,350
M: basketball, ice hockey. Men's Non-aid: baseball, cross country, golf, lacrosse, soccer, tennis
W: basketball. Women's Non-aid: cross country, golf, soccer, squash, tennis

UNIVERSITY OF NEW HAMPSHIRE
224 Field House
Durham, NH 03824
(603) 862-2585 Contact: Joe Pagnotta
Unspecified athletic aid available
M: basketball, football, ice hockey. Men's Non-aid: alpine skiing, baseball, cross country, cross country skiing, golf, indoor track, lacrosse, soccer, swimming-diving, tennis, track & field, wrestling
W: basketball, field hockey, gymnastics, ice hockey, soccer. Women's Non-aid: alpine skiing, cross country, cross country skiing, indoor track, lacrosse, swimming-diving, tennis, track & field

New Jersey

ATLANTIC COMMUNITY COLLEGE
5100 Black Horse Pike
Mays Landing, NJ 08330
2-year college
(609) 343-5024 Contact: Bobby Royal
Men's Non-aid: archery, baseball, basketball, cross country, golf, soccer, tennis
Women's Non-aid: archery, basketball, cross country, golf, squash, tennis

BERGEN COMMUNITY COLLEGE
Paramus Road
Paramus, NJ 07652-1595
2-year college
(201) 447-7182 Contact: Bob Thompson
Unspecified athletic aid available

M: cross country, track & field. Men's Non-aid: baseball, basketball, golf, soccer, wrestling
W: cross country, track & field. Women's Non-aid: basketball, softball, volleyball

BLOOMFIELD COLLEGE
Franklin Street
Bloomfield, NJ 07003
(201) 748-9000 X. 362 Contact: Al Restaino
Men's Aid (#/$): 6/$60,000
Women's Aid (#/$): 4/$60,000
M: baseball, basketball, soccer. Men's Non-aid: lacrosse
W: basketball, softball. Women's Non-aid: volleyball

CALDWELL COLLEGE
Ryerson Avenue
Caldwell, NJ 07006
(201) 228-4424 Contact: Mark Kitchin
Unspecified athletic aid available
M: basketball
W: basketball, volleyball

CENTENARY COLLEGE
400 Jefferson Street
Hackettstown, NJ 07840
(908) 852-1400 X. 350 Contact: Kim Adamson
Men's Aid (#/$): 30/$122,100
Women's Aid (#/$): 8/$36,000
M: basketball, equestrian, soccer
W: basketball, equestrian, soccer, softball, volleyball

DREW UNIVERSITY
36 Madison Avenue
Madison, NJ 07940-4015
(201) 408-3574 Contact: Ernie Larossa
Men's Non-aid: baseball, basketball, cross country, equestrian, fencing, lacrosse, soccer, tennis
Women's Non-aid: basketball, cross country, equestrian, fencing, field hockey, lacrosse, tennis

FAIRLEIGH DICKINSON UNIVERSITY (MADISON)
285 Madison Avenue
Madison, NJ 07940
(201) 593-8965 Contact: Tom Bonerbo
Men's Non-aid: baseball, basketball, football, golf, lacrosse, soccer, tennis
Women's Non-aid: basketball, field hockey, softball, tennis, volleyball

FAIRLEIGH DICKINSON UNIVERSITY (TEANECK)
Rothman Center
Teaneck, NJ 07666
(201) 692-2149 Contact: Carmine Faccenda
Unspecified athletic aid available
M: baseball, basketball, cross country, golf, indoor track, lacrosse, soccer, tennis, track & field
W: basketball, cross country, fencing, indoor track, softball, tennis, track & field. Women's Non-aid: equestrian

FAIRLEIGH DICKINSON UNIVERSITY (RUTHERFORD)
217 Montross Avenue R 10 A
Rutherford, NJ 07070
(201) 460-5225 Contact: Joyce Heavey
Unspecified athletic aid available
M: baseball, basketball, cross country, equestrian, golf, soccer, tennis, track & field
W: basketball, cross country, equestrian, fencing, tennis, track & field, volleyball

GEORGIAN COURT COLLEGE
900 Lakewood
Lakewood, NJ 08701-2697
(908) 364-2200 X. 258 Contact: Sister Francesca Holly
Women's Aid (#/$): 35/$70,000
W: basketball, cross country, martial arts, softball, volleyball

GLOUCESTER COUNTY COLLEGE
Tanyard Road
Sewell, NJ 08080
2-year college
(609) 468-5000 X. 273 Contact: Richard H. Smith
Men's Non-aid: baseball, basketball, cross country, indoor track, soccer, tennis, track & field, wrestling

Women's Non-aid: cross country, tennis, track & field

KEAN COLLEGE OF NEW JERSEY
Morris Avenue
Union, NJ 07083
(908) 527-2939 Contact: Adam Fenton
Men's Non-aid: baseball, basketball, football, golf, ice hockey, lacrosse, soccer, tennis, wrestling
Women's Non-aid: basketball, field hockey, soccer, softball, swimming-diving, tennis, volleyball

MERCER COUNTY COMMUNITY COLLEGE
P.O. Box B
Trenton, NJ 08690
2-year college
(609) 586-4800 X. 740 Contact: Douglas S. Kokoskie
Unspecified athletic aid available
M: baseball, basketball, indoor track, soccer, tennis, track & field
W: basketball, indoor track, soccer, softball, track & field

MIDDLESEX COUNTY COLLEGE
155 Mill Road
Edison, NJ 08818
2-year college
(908) 548-6000 X. 3558 Contact: Rober Zifchak
Men's Aid (#/$): 2/$2,400
Women's Aid (#/$): 3/$3,600
Restrictions and notes: Athletic aid restricted to Middlesex County residents with H.S. GPA of 2.0 or better.
M: cheerleading, track & field. Men's Non-aid: baseball, basketball, cross country, golf, soccer
W: softball. Women's Non-aid: basketball, cross country, tennis, track & field

MONMOUTH COLLEGE
Cedar Avenue
West Long Branch, NJ 07764
(908) 571-3415 Contact: Bernie Greenberg
Unspecified athletic aid available
M: baseball, basketball, cross country, diving, soccer, swimming, tennis, track & field. Men's Non-aid: golf, indoor track, water polo
W: basketball, diving, soccer, softball, swimming. Women's Non-aid: tennis, track & field

MONTCLAIR STATE COLLEGE
1 Normal Avenue
Upper Montclair, NJ 07043
(201) 893-5249 Contact: Al Langer
Men's Non-aid: baseball, basketball, cross country, football, golf, indoor track, lacrosse, soccer, swimming, swimming-diving, tennis, track & field, water polo, wrestling
Women's Non-aid: basketball, cross country, field hockey, gymnastics, indoor track, softball, swimming, swimming-diving, tennis, track & field

NEW JERSEY INSTITUTE OF TECHNOLOGY
323 King Boulevard
Newark, NJ 07102
(201) 596-3479 Contact: Mary R. Hurdle
Men's Non-aid: baseball, basketball, bowling, ice hockey, riflery, soccer, tennis, volleyball
Women's Non-aid: softball, tennis

OCEAN COUNTY COLLEGE
College Drive
P.O. Box 2001
Toms River, NJ 08754-2001
2-year college
(908) 255-0345 Contact: John Stauff
Men's Non-aid: baseball, basketball, cross country, golf, ice hockey, soccer, swimming-diving, tennis, track & field
Women's Non-aid: basketball, cross country, field hockey, golf, softball, swimming-diving, tennis, track & field

PASSAIC COUNTY COMMUNITY COLLEGE
One College Boulevard
Paterson, NJ 07509

2-year college
(201) 684-5570 Contact: Nate Malachi
Men's Non-aid: basketball, cross country skiing, soccer
Women's Non-aid: basketball, cross country skiing

PRINCETON UNIVERSITY
P.O. Box 71
Room 9, Jadwin Gym
Princeton, NJ 08544-0071
(609) 258-3568 Contact: Kurt Kehl
Men's Non-aid: baseball, basketball, crew, cross country, fencing, football, golf, ice hockey, lacrosse, soccer, squash, swimming-diving, tennis, track & field, wrestling
Women's Non-aid: baseball, basketball, crew, cross country, field hockey, ice hockey, lacrosse, soccer, squash, swimming-diving, tennis, track & field, volleyball

RAMAPO COLLEGE
505 Ramapo Valley Road
Mahwah, NJ 07430-1630
(201) 529-7675 Contact: Mike Ricciardi
Men's Non-aid: baseball, basketball, cross country, football, golf, soccer, tennis, track & field, volleyball
Women's Non-aid: basketball, cross country, softball, tennis, track & field, volleyball

RIDER COLLEGE
2083 Lawrenceville Road
Lawrenceville, NJ 08648-3099
(609) 896-5138 Contact: Bud Focht
Unspecified athletic aid available
M: baseball, basketball, cross country, diving, golf, riflery, soccer, swimming, tennis, track & field, wrestling
W: basketball, diving, field hockey, riflery, softball, swimming, tennis, volleyball

ROWAN COLLEGE OF NEW JERSEY
201 Millica Road
Glassboro, NJ 08028
(609) 863-7080 Contact: Sheila Stevenson
Men's Non-aid: baseball, basketball, football, soccer, swimming-diving, tennis, track & field
Women's Non-aid: basketball, cross country, field hockey, lacrosse, softball, swimming-diving, tennis, track & field

RUTGERS, CAMDEN COLLEGE OF ARTS AND SCIENCES
Third and Linden Streets
Camden, NJ 08102
(609) 225-6193 Contact: Wilbur Wilson
Men's Non-aid: baseball, basketball, diving, golf, soccer, swimming, tennis, wrestling
Women's Non-aid: basketball, cheerleading, cross country, diving, softball, swimming, tennis

RUTGERS, COLLEGE AVENUE CAMPUS
Records Hall, Room 140
New Brunswick, NJ 08903
(908) 932-7755 Contact: Carl Buck
Unspecified athletic aid available
M: football. Men's Non-aid: baseball, basketball, cheerleading, crew, cross country, diving, fencing, golf, lacrosse, soccer, swimming, tennis, track & field, wrestling
Women's Non-aid: cheerleading, crew, diving, fencing, field hockey, golf, gymnastics, lacrosse, soccer, swimming, tennis, track & field, volleyball

RUTGERS, NEWARK COLLEGE OF ARTS AND SCIENCES
Newark, NJ 08903
(201) 932-7755 Contact: Carl Buck
Unspecified athletic aid available
M: volleyball. Men's Non-aid: baseball, basketball, fencing, wrestling
Women's Non-aid: basketball, fencing, golf, softball

SAINT PETER'S COLLEGE
2641 Kennedy Boulevard
Jersey City, NJ 07306

(201) 915-9101 Contact: Tim Camp
Men's Aid (#/$): 47/$450,000
Women's Aid (#/$): 45/$440,000
Restrictions and notes: Aid amounts represent equivalents. Most is tuition only. Full scholarships (NCAA allowable expenses) in basketball.
M: baseball, basketball, cross country, diving, golf, indoor track, soccer, swimming, swimming-diving, tennis, track & field. Men's Non-aid: bowling, football, water polo
W: basketball, cross country, diving, indoor track, soccer, softball, swimming, swimming-diving, tennis, track & field, volleyball

SETON HALL UNIVERSITY
400 South Orange Avenue
South Orange, NJ 07079
(201) 761-9493 Contact: John Wooding
Men's Aid (#/$): 74/$1,300,000
Women's Aid (#/$): 65/$1,000,000
M: baseball, basketball, cross country, golf, indoor track, soccer, swimming, swimming-diving, tennis, track & field, wrestling
W: basketball, cross country, indoor track, softball, swimming, swimming-diving, tennis, track & field, volleyball

STEVENS INSTITUTE OF TECHNOLOGY
Castle Point Station
Hoboken, NJ 07030
(201) 420-5690 Contact: John S. Lyon
Men's Non-aid: baseball, basketball, cross country, fencing, lacrosse, soccer, squash, tennis, volleyball, wrestling
Women's Non-aid: cross country, fencing, tennis, volleyball

TRENTON STATE COLLEGE
Hillwood Lakes CN 4700
Trenton, NJ 08650-4700
(609) 771-2517/2368 Contact: Peter G. Manetas
Men's Non-aid: baseball, basketball, cross country, football, golf, soccer, tennis, track & field, wrestling
Women's Non-aid: basketball, cross country, field hockey, gymnastics, lacrosse, softball, swimming, tennis, track & field

UNION COUNTY COLLEGE
1033 Springfield Avenue
Cranford, NJ 07016
2-year college
(908) 709-7093 Contact: Fred Perry
Women's Aid (#/$): 6/$9,000
Men's Non-aid: baseball, basketball, golf, soccer
W: basketball. Women's Non-aid: softball

WILLIAM PATTERSON COLLEGE
300 Pompton Road
Wayne, NJ 07470
(201) 595-2705 Contact: Joe Martinelli
Men's Non-aid: baseball, basketball, bowling, cross country, diving, fencing, football, golf, ice hockey, indoor track, soccer, swimming, swimming-diving, track & field
Women's Non-aid: basketball, bowling, cross country, diving, fencing, field hockey, indoor track, softball, swimming, swimming-diving, tennis, track & field, volleyball

New Mexico

COLLEGE OF THE SOUTHWEST
6610 Lovington Highway
Hobbs, NM 88240
(505) 392-6561 Contact: Glenna Ohaver
Men's Aid (#/$): 39/$35,630
Women's Aid (#/$): 12/$15,650
M: baseball, soccer
W: soccer

EASTERN NEW MEXICO UNIVERSITY
Station 6
Portales, NM 88130

(505) 562-2153 Contact: B.B. Lees
Unspecified athletic aid available
M: baseball, basketball, football, riflery, rodeo
W: basketball, riflery, rodeo, tennis, volleyball

NEW MEXICO HIGHLANDS UNIVERSITY
Rodgers Administration Building
Las Vegas, NM 87701
(505) 454-3318 Contact: Darlene Ortiz
Men's Aid (#/$): 44/unspecified $
Women's Aid (#/$): 20/unspecified $
M: baseball, basketball, cross country, football
W: basketball, cross country, softball, volleyball

NEW MEXICO JUNIOR COLLEGE
5317 Lovington Highway
Hobbs, NM 88240
2-year college
(505) 392-4510 Contact: Ray Birmingham
Unspecified athletic aid available
M: basketball, cross country, golf, rodeo, track & field
W: basketball, rodeo

NEW MEXICO STATE UNIVERSITY
Box 3001, Department 5100
Las Cruces, NM 88003
(505) 646-4105 Contact: Greeley W. Myers
Unspecified athletic aid available
M: baseball, basketball, cross country, diving, football, golf, swimming, tennis, track & field
W: basketball, cross country, diving, golf, softball, swimming, tennis, track & field, volleyball

UNIVERSITY OF NEW MEXICO
Mesa Vista North
Albuquerque, NM 87131
(505) 277-5017 Contact: John Whiteside
Men's Aid (#/$): 247/$1,328,238
Women's Aid (#/$): 100/$530,455
M: alpine skiing, baseball, basketball, cross country, football, golf, gymnastics, soccer, swimming, tennis, track & field, wrestling
W: alpine skiing, basketball, cross country, golf, softball, swimming, tennis, track & field, volleyball

WESTERN NEW MEXICO UNIVERSITY
Box 680
Silver City, NM 88061
(505) 538-6173 Contact: Charles P. Kelly
Unspecified athletic aid available
M: baseball, basketball, football, track & field
W: basketball, softball, track & field, volleyball

New York

ADELPHI UNIVERSITY
South Avenue
Woodruff Hall
Garden City, NY 11530
(516) 877-4236 Contact: S. Andrew Baumbach
Men's Aid (#/$): 19/$117,277
Women's Aid (#/$): 12/$96,888
M: baseball, basketball, lacrosse, soccer. Men's Non-aid: cross country, golf, tennis
W: basketball, soccer, softball, swimming. Women's Non-aid: cross country, tennis, volleyball

ADIRONDACK COLLEGE
Bay Road
Queensbury, NY 12804
2-year college
(518) 793-5994 Contact: Robert L. Harris
Men's Non-aid: alpine skiing, basketball, bowling, golf, soccer, tennis
Women's Non-aid: alpine skiing,

basketball, bowling, soccer, softball, tennis, volleyball

ALFRED UNIVERSITY
P.O. Box 578
Alfred, NY 14802
(607) 871-2106 Contact: Patrick Gillespie
Men's Non-aid: alpine skiing, basketball, cross country, diving, equestrian, football, indoor track, lacrosse, soccer, swimming, swimming-diving, track & field
Women's Non-aid: alpine skiing, basketball, cross country, diving, equestrian, indoor track, soccer, swimming, swimming-diving, tennis, track & field, volleyball

BARD COLLEGE
Stevenson Gymnasium
Annadale-on-Hudson, NY 12504
(914) 758-7530 Contact: Joel Tomson
Men's Non-aid: basketball, cross country, soccer, tennis, volleyball
Women's Non-aid: basketball, cross country, softball, tennis, volleyball

BRONX COMMUNITY COLLEGE
181 Street & University Avenue
Bronx, NY 10453
2-year college
(212) 220-6020 Contact: Michael Steuerman
Men's Non-aid: baseball, basketball, cross country, indoor track, soccer, track & field
Women's Non-aid: basketball, cross country, indoor track, softball, track & field, volleyball

BROOKLYN COLLEGE—CITY UNIVERSITY OF NEW YORK
Bedford Avenue
Brooklyn, NY 11210
(718) 780-5574 Contact: Lenn Margolis
Men's Non-aid: football
Women's Non-aid: volleyball

BROOME COMMUNITY COLLEGE
P.O. Box 1017
Binghamton, NY 13902
2-year college
(607) 778-5000 Contact: Dan Minch
Men's Non-aid: baseball, basketball, cross country, golf, ice hockey, soccer, tennis, wrestling
Women's Non-aid: bowling, cross country skiing, softball, volleyball

BRYANT & STRATTON BUSINESS INSTITUTE
1028 Main Street
Buffalo, NY 14202
2-year college
(716) 884-9120 Contact: Michael R. Roach
Men's Non-aid: basketball

BUFFALO STATE COLLEGE
1300 Elmwood Avenue
Buffalo, NY 14222
(716) 878-6030 Contact: Keith A. Bullion
Men's Non-aid: basketball, cross country, diving, football, indoor track, soccer, swimming-diving, tennis, track & field
Women's Non-aid: basketball, cross country, diving, indoor track, soccer, softball, swimming-diving, tennis, track & field, volleyball

BUFFALO STATE UNIVERSITY (NEW YORK)
103 Alumni Arena
Buffalo, NY 14260
(716) 636-3178 Contact: Tom Koller
Men's Non-aid: baseball, basketball, cross country, football, golf, ice hockey, indoor track, soccer, swimming-diving, tennis, track & field, wrestling
Women's Non-aid: basketball, cross country, field hockey, indoor track, soccer, softball, swimming-diving, tennis, track & field, volleyball

CANISIUS COLLEGE
2001 Main Street
Buffalo, NY 14208
(716) 888-2977 Contact: John Maddock
Men's Aid (#/$): 50/$500,000

Women's Aid (#/$): 40/$350,000
M: baseball, basketball, cross country, golf, ice hockey, indoor track, lacrosse, riflery, soccer, swimming, tennis.
Men's Non-aid: crew, football
W: basketball, cross country, indoor track, riflery, soccer, swimming, tennis, volleyball. Women's Non-aid: crew

CAYUGA COUNTY COMMUNITY COLLEGE
Franklin Street
Auburn, NY 13021
2-year college
(315) 255-1743 Contact: Charles Steveskey
Men's Non-aid: basketball, cross country, golf, indoor track, martial arts, power lifting, racquetball, tennis, track & field
Women's Non-aid: basketball, cross country, indoor track, racquetball, softball, tennis, track & field, volleyball

CITY COLLEGE OF NEW YORK
Athletic Department
138th Street and Covent Avenue
(212) 650-8228 Contact: John Araouzos
Men's Non-aid: baseball, basketball, cross country, fencing, gymnastics, indoor track, lacrosse, soccer, swimming, tennis, track & field, wrestling
Women's Non-aid: basketball, cross country, fencing, gymnastics, indoor track, softball, tennis, track & field, volleyball

CLARKSON UNIVERSITY
Alumni Gym
Potsdam, NY 13699-5830
(312) 268-6673 Contact: Gary Mikel
Men's Aid (#/$): 20/$400,000
Restrictions and notes: All athletic aid for Division I ice hockey
M: ice hockey. Men's Non-aid: alpine skiing, baseball, basketball, cross country, cross country skiing, diving, golf, lacrosse, soccer, swimming, swimming-diving, tennis
Women's Non-aid: alpine skiing, basketball, cross country, cross country skiing, diving, golf, lacrosse, soccer, swimming, swimming-diving, tennis, volleyball

CLINTON COMMUNITY COLLEGE
1000 Lincoln Boulevard
Plattsburgh, NY 12901
2-year college
(518) 561-6650 Contact: Athletic Department
Unspecified athletic aid available
M: baseball, basketball
W: volleyball

COLGATE UNIVERSITY
13 Oak Street
Hamilton, NY 13346
(315) 824-7602 Contact: Bob Cornell
Restrictions and notes: All aid awarded on the basis of need
Men's Non-aid: baseball, basketball, cross country, diving, football, golf, ice hockey, indoor track, lacrosse, soccer, swimming, tennis, track & field
Women's Non-aid: basketball, cross country, diving, field hockey, indoor track, lacrosse, soccer, softball, swimming, tennis, track & field, volleyball

COLLEGE OF NEW ROCHELLE
Castle Place
New Rochelle, NY 10805
(914) 654-5225 Contact: Dr. Ronald Pollack
Women's Non-aid: basketball, cross country, softball, swimming, tennis, volleyball

COLLEGE OF ST. ROSE
432 Western Avenue
Albany, NY 12203
(518) 454-5168 Contact: Jean E. Cossey
Unspecified athletic aid available
M: baseball, basketball, cross country, soccer, tennis. Men's Non-aid: bowling
W: cross country, soccer, softball, swimming-diving, tennis, volleyball.
Women's Non-aid: basketball, bowling

COLUMBIA-GREENE COMMUNITY COLLEGE
Box 1000
Hudson, NY 12534
2-year college
(518) 828-3181 Contact: Ron Gabriele
Men's Non-aid: baseball, basketball, bowling, cross country, soccer
Women's Non-aid: basketball, bowling, cross country, softball, volleyball

COLUMBIA UNIVERSITY
116th Street and Broadway
Dodge Fitness Center
New York, NY 10027
(212) 854-2154 Contact: Suzanne Clair
Men's Non-aid: baseball, basketball, crew, cross country, diving, fencing, football, golf, indoor track, soccer, swimming, swimming-diving, tennis, track & field, wrestling
Women's Non-aid: archery, basketball, crew, cross country, diving, fencing, indoor track, soccer, swimming, swimming-diving, tennis, track & field, volleyball

COMMUNITY COLLEGE OF THE FINGER LAKES
Lincoln Hill
Canandaigua, NY 14424
2-year college
(716) 394-6425 Contact: Putt Moore
Men's Non-aid: baseball, basketball, cross country, soccer
Women's Non-aid: basketball, cross country, soccer, softball

CONCORDIA COLLEGE
171 White Plains Road
Bronxville, NY 10708
(914) 337-9300 X. 2155 Contact: Gloria Henning
Unspecified athletic aid available
M: baseball, basketball, cross country, soccer, tennis, volleyball
W: basketball, cross country, softball, tennis, volleyball

CORNELL UNIVERSITY
P.O. Box 729
Ithaca, NY 14851
(607) 255-3752 Contact: Dave Wohlhueter
Men's Non-aid: alpine skiing, baseball, basketball, crew, cross country, cross country skiing, diving, fencing, football, golf, gymnastics, ice hockey, indoor track, lacrosse, polo, riflery, sailing, soccer, squash, swimming, swimming-diving, tennis, wrestling
Women's Non-aid: basketball, crew, cross country, diving, fencing, field hockey, gymnastics, ice hockey, indoor track, lacrosse, polo, riflery, sailing, soccer, swimming, swimming-diving, tennis, track & field, volleyball

DAEMEN COLLEGE
4380 Main Street
Amherst, NY 14226
(716) 839-8254 Contact: Helen Lukasik
Men's Aid (#/$): 8/$73,498
Women's Aid (#/$): 3/$26,905
M: basketball
W: basketball

DOMINICAN COLLEGE OF BLAUVELT
10 Western Highway
Orangeburg, NY 10962
(914) 359-7800 X. 225 Contact: Eileen Felske
Men's Aid (#/$): 8/$15,000
Women's Aid (#/$): 5/$12,000
M: basketball, soccer. Men's Non-aid: baseball
W: basketball, volleyball. Women's Non-aid: softball

DOWLING COLLEGE
Oakdale, NY 11769
(516) 589-6100 Contact: Diane Kazanecki
Unspecified athletic aid available
M: baseball, basketball, golf, soccer, tennis. Men's Non-aid: lacrosse, martial arts, racquetball, sailing
W: basketball, golf, softball, tennis, volleyball. Women's Non-aid: racquetball, sailing

DUTCHESS JUNIOR COLLEGE
53 Pendell Road
Poughkeepsie, NY 12601-1595

2-year college
(914) 471-4500 X. 1201 Contact: Mike Brown
Men's Non-aid: archery, baseball, basketball, bowling, golf, soccer, tennis
Women's Non-aid: basketball, bowling, golf, soccer, softball, tennis, volleyball

D'YOUVILLE COLLEGE
320 Porter Avenue
Buffalo, NY 14201
(716) 881-7600 Contact: Ronald Dannecker
Unspecified athletic aid available
M: basketball
W: basketball, volleyball

ELIZABETH SETON SCHOOL OF IONA COLLEGE
1061 North Broadway
Yonkers, NY 10701
2-year college
(914) 969-4000 X. 272 Contact: Candy Hack
Unspecified athletic aid available
M: basketball. Men's Non-aid: bowling, cross country
Women's Non-aid: basketball, bowling, cross country

ELMIRA COLLEGE
P.O. Box 881
Park Place
Elmira, NY 14901
(607) 734-3911 X. 301 Contact: Marti Whitmore
Men's Non-aid: basketball, golf, ice hockey, soccer, tennis
Women's Non-aid: basketball, soccer, softball, tennis, volleyball

FASHION INSTITUTE OF TECHNOLOGY
227 West 27th Street
New York, NY 10001
2-year college
(212) 760-7724 Contact: Nancy Yeldin
Men's Non-aid: alpine skiing, basketball, bowling, tennis
Women's Non-aid: alpine skiing, bowling, tennis, volleyball

FORDHAM UNIVERSITY
East Fordham Road
Bronx, NY 10458
(212) 579-2445 Contact: Joe Favorito
Unspecified athletic aid available
M: baseball, basketball, cross country, diving, football, golf, indoor track, soccer, swimming, swimming-diving, tennis, track & field, water polo. Men's Non-aid: crew, ice hockey, lacrosse, volleyball, wrestling
W: baseball, basketball, cross country, diving, indoor track, softball, swimming, swimming-diving, tennis, track & field, volleyball. Women's Non-aid: crew, soccer

FULTON-MONTGOMERY COMMUNITY COLLEGE
Route 67
Johnstown, NY 12095
2-year college
(518) 762-4651 X. 280 Contact: Dav Jarvis
Men's Non-aid: baseball, basketball, bowling, cross country, soccer, track & field, wrestling
Women's Non-aid: cross country, softball, track & field, volleyball

GENESEE COMMUNITY COLLEGE
Box 718
Batavia, NY 14020
2-year college
(716) 343-0055 X. 216 Contact: Anthony P. Cory
Men's Aid (#/$): 8/$6,000
Women's Aid (#/$): 8/$6,000
M: baseball, basketball, soccer, volleyball
W: basketball, soccer, softball, volleyball

HAMILTON COLLEGE
198 College Hill Road
Clinton, NY 13323
(315) 859-4685 Contact: Alan D. Brazier
Men's Non-aid: baseball, basketball, cross country, diving, football, golf, ice hockey, indoor track, lacrosse, soccer,

squash, swimming, swimming-diving, tennis, track & field
Women's Non-aid: basketball, cross country, diving, field hockey, golf, ice hockey, indoor track, lacrosse, soccer, squash, softball, swimming, swimming-diving, tennis, track & field, volleyball

HARTWICK COLLEGE
Binder PE Building
Oneonta, NY 13820
(607) 432-4703 Contact: Robert McKinney
Unspecified athletic aid available
M: soccer. Men's Non-aid: baseball, basketball, cross country, golf, indoor track, lacrosse, swimming-diving, tennis, track & field
Women's Non-aid: basketball, cross country, field hockey, golf, indoor track, lacrosse, soccer, swimming-diving, tennis, track & field

HERKIMER COUNTY COMMUNITY COLLEGE
Reservoir Road
Herkimer, NY 13350
2-year college
(315) 866-0300 X. 255 Contact: Sid Fox
Men's Non-aid: baseball, basketball, bowling, lacrosse, soccer, track & field
Women's Non-aid: basketball, field hockey, soccer, softball, tennis, track & field

HILBERT COLLEGE
5200 South Park Avenue
Hamburg, NY 14075
2-year college
(716) 649-7900 Contact: John W. Kissel
Unspecified athletic aid available
M: baseball, basketball, soccer
W: basketball, soccer, softball, volleyball

HOFSTRA UNIVERSITY
1000 Hempstead Turnpike
Hempstead, NY 11550
(516) 463-6750 Contact: Jim Garvey
Men's Aid (#/$): 38/unspecified $
Women's Aid (#/$): 30/unspecified $
M: baseball, basketball, cross country, football, golf, lacrosse, soccer, tennis, wrestling
W: basketball, cross country, field hockey, lacrosse, soccer, softball, tennis, volleyball

HOUGHTON COLLEGE
One Willard Avenue
Houghton, NY 14744
(716) 567-9328 Contact: Robert Brown
Unspecified athletic aid available
M: basketball, cheerleading, cross country, soccer, track & field
W: basketball, cheerleading, cross country, field hockey, soccer, track & field, volleyball

HUDSON VALLEY COMMUNITY COLLEGE
80 Vandenburg Avenue
Troy, NY 12180
2-year college
(518) 270-1542 Contact: John Della Contrada
Men's Non-aid: baseball, basketball, bowling, cross country, football, golf, indoor track, lacrosse, soccer, tennis, track & field
Women's Non-aid: bowling, softball, tennis, track & field, volleyball

HUNTER COLLEGE OF THE CITY UNIVERSITY OF NEW YORK
695 Park Avenue
New York, NY 10021
(212) 772-4631 Contact: Zak Ivkovic
Men's Non-aid: baseball, basketball, cheerleading, cross country, fencing, soccer, tennis, track & field, volleyball, wrestling
Women's Non-aid: basketball, cheerleading, cross country, diving, fencing, softball, swimming, tennis, track & field, volleyball

IONA COLLEGE
715 North Avenue
New Rochelle, NY 10801-1890

(914) 633-2334 Contact: David Torromeo
Unspecified athletic aid available
M: baseball, basketball, cross country, golf, indoor track, soccer, tennis, track & field. Men's Non-aid: crew, diving, football, ice hockey, lacrosse, rugby, swimming, swimming-diving, water polo
W: basketball, cross country, diving, indoor track, rugby, soccer, softball, swimming, swimming-diving, tennis, track & field, volleyball. Women's Non-aid: crew, lacrosse

ITHACA COLLEGE

953 Danby Road
Ithaca, NY 14850
(607) 274-3825 Contact: Pete Moore
Men's Non-aid: baseball, basketball, crew, cross country, football, golf, indoor track, lacrosse, soccer, swimming-diving, tennis, track & field, wrestling
Women's Non-aid: basketball, crew, cross country, field hockey, gymnastics, indoor track, lacrosse, soccer, softball, swimming-diving, tennis, track & field, volleyball

JEFFERSON COMMUNITY COLLEGE

Outer Coffeen Street
Watertown, NY 13601
2-year college
(315) 782-2248 Contact: Robert Williams
Unspecified athletic aid available
M: lacrosse, soccer. Men's Non-aid: baseball, basketball, golf
W: soccer, softball, volleyball. Women's Non-aid: basketball, cheerleading, golf

JUNIOR COLLEGE OF ALBANY

140 New Scotland Avenue
Albany, NY 12208
2-year college
(518) 445-1753 Contact: Bill Toowey
Men's Aid (#/$): 13/$30,000
M: basketball

THE KING'S COLLEGE

P.O Box 567
Briarcliff Manor, NY 10510
(914) 944-5662 Contact: Frederic Rowley
Unspecified athletic aid available
M: baseball, basketball, cross country, soccer, track & field
W: basketball, cross country, field hockey, softball, track & field, volleyball

LE MOYNE COLLEGE

Springfield Road
Syracuse, NY 13214
(315) 445-4412 Contact: Kim Bouck
Men's Aid (#/$): 13/$54,430
Women's Aid (#/$): 8/$15,700
M: baseball, basketball, cross country, golf, indoor track, soccer, tennis. Men's Non-aid: lacrosse
W: basketball, cross country, soccer, softball, tennis, volleyball

LONG ISLAND UNIVERSITY (BROOKLYN)

University Plaza
Brooklyn, NY 11201
(718) 403-1037 Contact: Rose Iannicelli
Unspecified athletic aid available
M: baseball, basketball, cross country, golf, gymnastics, indoor track, soccer, tennis, track & field
W: basketball, cross country, gymnastics, indoor track, softball, tennis, track & field

LONG ISLAND UNIVERSITY (C.W. POST CAMPUS)

Brookville, NY 11548
(516) 299-2338 Contact: Joanne Graziano
Men's Aid (#/$): 188/$741,473
Women's Aid (#/$): 68/$185,834
M: baseball, basketball, lacrosse, soccer, track & field.
Men's Non-aid: football
W: basketball, field hockey, softball, volleyball.
Women's Non-aid: tennis, track & field

LONG ISLAND UNIVERSITY (SOUTHHAMPTON CAMPUS)
239 Montauk Highway
Southampton, NY 11968
(516) 283-4000 X. 321 Contact: Susan M. Taylor
Men's Aid (#/$): 41/$221,355
Women's Aid (#/$): 42/$155,736
M: basketball, soccer, volleyball. Men's Non-aid: lacrosse
W: basketball, soccer, softball, volleyball

MANHATTAN COLLEGE
Sports Information Office
Riverdale, NY 10471
(212) 920-0228 Contact: Jeff Bernstein
Unspecified athletic aid available
M: basketball, cross country, track & field. Men's Non-aid: baseball, crew, golf, ice hockey, soccer, softball, swimming-diving, tennis, wrestling
W: basketball. Women's Non-aid: baseball, crew, cross country, softball, swimming-diving, volleyball

MANHATTAN COMMUNITY COLLEGE
199 Chambers Street
New York, NY 10007
2-year college
(212) 346-8000 Contact: Richard Packard
Men's Non-aid: baseball, basketball, soccer

MANHATTANVILLE COLLEGE
125 Purchase Street
Purchase, NY 10577
(914) 694-2200 X. 289 Contact: Susan Eichner
Men's Non-aid: baseball, basketball, lacrosse, rugby, soccer, tennis
Women's Non-aid: basketball, diving, field hockey, soccer, softball, swimming, swimming-diving, tennis, volleyball

MARIST COLLEGE
McCann Center North Road
Poughkeepsie, NY 12601
(914) 575-3000 X. 2322 Contact: Dan Sullivan
Men's Aid (#/$): 32/$505,600
Women's Aid (#/$): 25.5/$402,900
M: baseball, basketball, cross country, indoor track, lacrosse, soccer, swimming-diving, tennis, track & field.
Men's Non-aid: crew, football
W: basketball, cross country, indoor track, softball, swimming-diving, tennis, track & field, volleyball.
Women's Non-aid: crew

MERCY COLLEGE
555 Broadway
Dobbs Ferry, NY 10522
(914) 693-4500 X. 281 Contact: Steve Balsan
Unspecified athletic aid available
M: baseball, basketball, cross country, golf, soccer, softball, tennis
W: baseball, basketball, cross country, golf, soccer, softball, tennis, volleyball

MOHAWK VALLEY COMMUNITY COLLEGE
1101 Sherman Drive
Utica, NY 13501
2-year college
(315) 792-5352 Contact: Robert Jorgensen
Men's Non-aid: baseball, basketball, bowling, cross country, golf, ice hockey, indoor track, soccer, tennis, track & field, wrestling
Women's Non-aid: basketball, bowling, cross country, indoor track, soccer, softball, tennis, track & field, volleyball

MOLLOY COLLEGE
1000 Hempstead Avenue
Rockville Center, NY 11570
(516) 678-5000 Contact: Bob Houlihan
Unspecified athletic aid available
M: badminton, baseball, crew, diving, football
W: basketball, equestrian, tennis, volleyball. Women's Non-aid: soccer

NASSAU COMMUNITY COLLEGE
Stewart Avenue
Garden City, NY 11530

2-year college
(516) 222-7522 Contact: Michael Pelliccia
Men's Non-aid: baseball, basketball, bowling, cross country, football, golf, indoor track, lacrosse, soccer, tennis, track & field, wrestling
Women's Non-aid: basketball, bowling, cross country, indoor track, soccer, softball, tennis, track & field, volleyball

NAZARETH COLLEGE
4245 East Avenue
Rochester, NY 14610-3790
(716) 586-2525 X. 375 Contact: Joe Seil
Men's Non-aid: basketball, diving, golf, lacrosse, soccer, swimming, tennis
Women's Non-aid: basketball, diving, golf, soccer, softball, swimming, tennis, volleyball

NEW YORK INSTITUTE OF TECHNOLOGY
Northern Boulevard
Old Westbury, NY 11568
(516) 686-7626 Contact: Joseph Hennie
Unspecified athletic aid available
M: baseball, basketball, indoor track, soccer, softball, track & field, volleyball

NEW YORK STATE UNIVERSITY INSTITUTE OF TECHNOLOGY
P.O. Box 3050 Marcy Campus
Utica, NY 13504-3050
(315) 792-7134 Contact: Kevin Grimmer
Men's Non-aid: baseball, basketball, golf, soccer
Women's Non-aid: basketball, soccer, softball, volleyball

NEW YORK UNIVERSITY
Jerome S. Coles Sports and Recreational Center
New York, NY 10012
(212) 598-9310 Contact: Janice Quinn
Men's Non-aid: basketball, cross country, fencing, golf, soccer, swimming-diving, tennis, track & field, wrestling
Women's Non-aid: basketball, cross country, fencing, swimming-diving, tennis, volleyball

NIAGARA COUNTY COMMUNITY COLLEGE
3111 Saunders Settlement Road
Sanborn, NY 14132
2-year college
(716) 731-3271 X. 517 Contact: Pat Murray
Men's Non-aid: baseball, basketball, bowling, cross country, wrestling
Women's Non-aid: cross country, softball, volleyball

NIAGARA UNIVERSITY
Niagara University, NY 14109
(716) 285-1212 X. 205 Contact: Mike Jankowski
Unspecified athletic aid available
Restrictions and notes: Tuition only scholarships in all sports except basketball.
M: baseball, basketball, cross country, diving, golf, soccer, swimming, swimming-diving, tennis
W: basketball, cross country, diving, soccer, softball, swimming, swimming-diving, tennis, volleyball

NORTH COUNTRY COMMUNITY COLLEGE
20 Winona Avenue
Saranac Lake, NY 12983
2-year college
(518) 891-2915 Contact: Robert Hudak
Unspecified athletic aid available
M: alpine skiing. Men's Non-aid: basketball, ice hockey, soccer
W: alpine skiing. Women's Non-aid: basketball, soccer, softball

NYACK COLLEGE
South Boulevard
Nyack, NY 10960
(914) 358-1710 X. 151 Contact: Evelyn Stolarski
Men's Aid (#/$): 12/$22,975
Women's Aid (#/$): 12/$18,901

M: basketball, soccer. Men's Non-aid: baseball, volleyball
W: basketball, softball, volleyball. Women's Non-aid: cheerleading, soccer

ORANGE COUNTY COMMUNITY COLLEGE

115 South Street
Middletown, NY 10940
2-year college
(914) 344-6222 Contact: Marie Dulzer
Men's Non-aid: baseball, basketball, golf, soccer, tennis
Women's Non-aid: basketball, soccer, softball, tennis, volleyball

PACE UNIVERSITY

861 Bedford Road
Pleasantville, NY 10570
(914) 773-3411 Contact: John Balkam
Unspecified athletic aid available
Restrictions and notes: All Pace University branch campuses administrated in Pleasantville.
M: baseball, basketball, cross country, indoor track, track & field. Men's Non-aid: bowling, football, ice hockey, lacrosse, tennis, volleyball
W: basketball, cross country, indoor track, softball, tennis, track & field, volleyball. Women's Non-aid: bowling

POLYTECHNIC UNIVERSITY (BROOKLYN CAMPUS)

333 Jay Street
Brooklyn, NY 11201
(718) 260-3100 Contact: Ellen Hartigan
Men's Non-aid: baseball, basketball, cross country, lacrosse, martial arts, soccer, tennis
Women's Non-aid: martial arts, volleyball

QUEENSBOROUGH COMMUNITY COLLEGE

Bayside, NY 11364
2-year college
(212) 631-6323 Contact: Steve Weingard
Men's Non-aid: archery, baseball, basketball, cross country, soccer, swimming, swimming-diving, tennis, track & field
Women's Non-aid: archery, basketball, cross country, softball, swimming, swimming-diving, tennis, track & field

QUEENS COLLEGE

Kessena Boulevard
Flushing, NY 11367
(718) 520-7026 Contact: Bob Greenburg
Unspecified athletic aid available
M: baseball, basketball, cross country, diving, indoor track, soccer, swimming, tennis, track & field, water polo. Men's Non-aid: bowling, golf, lacrosse, volleyball
W: basketball, cross country, diving, indoor track, softball, swimming, tennis, track & field, volleyball

RENSSELAER POLYTECHNIC INSTITUTE

Eighth Street
Troy, NY 12190-3590
(518) 276-6536 Contact: Alan Shibley
Unspecified athletic aid available
M: ice hockey. Men's Non-aid: baseball, basketball, cross country, diving, football, golf, indoor track, lacrosse, soccer, swimming, swimming-diving, tennis, track & field
Women's Non-aid: basketball, cross country, diving, field hockey, soccer, softball, swimming, swimming-diving, tennis

ROBERTS WESLEYAN COLLEGE

2301 Westside Drive
Rochester, NY 14624-1997
(716) 594-9471 Contact: Thomas Seagren
Unspecified athletic aid available
M: basketball, cross country, indoor track, soccer, track & field. Men's Non-aid: baseball, tennis
W: basketball, cross country, indoor track, soccer, softball, track & field, volleyball. Women's Non-aid: tennis

ROCHESTER INSTITUTE OF TECHNOLOGY
One Lomb Memorial Drive
Rochester, NY 14623
(716) 475-6154 Contact: J. Roger Dykes
Men's Non-aid: baseball, basketball, cross country, ice hockey, indoor track, lacrosse, soccer, swimming, swimming-diving, tennis, track & field, wrestling
Women's Non-aid: cross country, ice hockey, soccer, softball, swimming, swimming-diving, tennis, track & field, volleyball

ROCKLAND COMMUNITY COLLEGE
145 College Road
Suffern, NY 10901
2-year college
(914) 356-4650 Contact: Howard Pierson
Unspecified athletic aid available
M: baseball, basketball, golf, soccer, tennis
W: basketball, softball, tennis, volleyball

ST. BONAVENTURE UNIVERSITY
Box G
St. Bonaventure, NY 14778
(716) 375-2319 Contact: Jim Engelhardt
Men's Aid (#/$): 17/$422,140
Women's Aid (#/$): 12/$88,213
M: baseball, basketball, diving, soccer, swimming, swimming-diving, tennis. Men's Non-aid: cross country, golf, lacrosse
W: basketball, diving, softball, swimming, swimming-diving, tennis, volleyball. Women's Non-aid: cross country, golf, soccer

SAINT FRANCIS COLLEGE
180 Remsen Street
Brooklyn, NY 11201
(718) 522-2300 X. 885 Contact: Patrick Horne
Men's Aid (#/$): 22/$20,000
Women's Aid (#/$): 22/$20,000
M: baseball, basketball, soccer, softball, swimming-diving, tennis. Men's Non-aid: cross country, water polo
W: basketball, swimming-diving, volleyball. Women's Non-aid: cross country, tennis

SAINT JOHN FISHER COLLEGE
3690 East Avenue
Rochester, NY 14618
(716) 385-8113 Contact: Michele Morano
Men's Non-aid: baseball, basketball, cross country, football, golf, soccer, tennis
Women's Non-aid: basketball, cross country, softball, soccer, tennis, volleyball

SAINT JOHN'S UNIVERSITY
Grand Central and Utopia Parkways
Jamaica, NY 11439
(718) 990-6367 Contact: Frank Racaniello
Men's Aid (#/$): 54/$371,771
Women's Aid (#/$): 20/$107,591
M: baseball, basketball, bowling, cross country, diving, fencing, golf, indoor track, lacrosse, soccer, swimming, swimming-diving, tennis, track & field. Men's Non-aid: crew, equestrian, football, ice hockey
W: basketball, bowling, cross country, diving, fencing, golf, softball, swimming, swimming-diving, synchronized swimming, tennis, track & field. Women's Non-aid: football

SAINT LAWRENCE UNIVERSITY
Augsbury Gymnasium
Canton, NY 13617
(315) 379-5588 Contact: Wally Johnson
Men's Non-aid: alpine skiing, baseball, basketball, cross country, cross country skiing, diving, equestrian, football, ice hockey, indoor track, lacrosse, soccer, swimming, swimming-diving, tennis, track & field, wrestling
Women's Non-aid: alpine skiing, basketball, cross country, cross country skiing, diving, equestrian, field hockey,

ice hockey, indoor track, lacrosse, soccer, swimming, swimming-diving, tennis, track & field, volleyball

SAINT THOMAS AQUINAS COLLEGE
Route 340
Sparkill, NY 10976
(914) 359-9500 Contact: Michael A. Madden
Men's Aid (#/$): 12/unspecified $
Women's Aid (#/$): 7/unspecified $
Restrictions and notes: Athletic aid for tuition only.
M: baseball, basketball, cross country, golf
W: basketball, softball, volleyball.
Women's Non-aid: soccer

SIENA COLLEGE
515 Loudon Road
Alumni Recreation Center
Loudonville, NY 12211
(518) 783-2551 Contact: John D'Argenio
Men's Aid (#/$): 17/$231,000
Women's Aid (#/$): 17/$231,000
M: basketball, soccer. Men's Non-aid: baseball, cross country, football, golf, indoor track, lacrosse, tennis
W: basketball, soccer. Women's Non-aid: cross country, field hockey, indoor track, softball, tennis, volleyball

SKIDMORE COLLEGE
North Broadway
Saratoga, NY 12866
(518) 584-5000 X. 2725
Contact: Bill Jones
Men's Non-aid: alpine skiing, baseball, basketball, crew, equestrian, golf, ice hockey, lacrosse, polo, soccer, tennis
Women's Non-aid: alpine skiing, basketball, crew, diving, equestrian, field hockey, ice hockey, lacrosse, polo, soccer, swimming, swimming-diving, tennis, volleyball

STATE UNIVERSITY OF NEW YORK
Delhi, NY 13753
2-year college
(607) 746-4111 Contact: Gary Cole
Men's Non-aid: basketball, cross country, golf, indoor track, soccer, track & field
Women's Non-aid: basketball, cross country, indoor track, soccer, track & field

STATE UNIVERSITY OF NEW YORK (ALBANY)
1400 Washington Avenue
Albany, NY 12222
(518) 442-3055 Contact: Vinny Reda
Men's Non-aid: baseball, basketball, cross country, diving, football, indoor track, lacrosse, soccer, swimming, swimming-diving, tennis, track & field, wrestling
Women's Non-aid: basketball, cross country, gymnastics, indoor track, soccer, softball, swimming-diving, tennis, track & field, volleyball

STATE UNIVERSITY OF NEW YORK (BINGHAMTON)
P.O. Box 6000
Binghamton, NY 13902-6000
(607) 777-4255 Contact: Dr. Joel Thirer
Men's Non-aid: baseball, basketball, diving, golf, soccer, swimming, swimming-diving, tennis, track & field, wrestling
Women's Non-aid: basketball, cross country, diving, soccer, softball, swimming, swimming-diving, tennis, track & field, volleyball

STATE UNIVERSITY OF NEW YORK (BUFFALO)
Buffalo, NY 14214
(716) 831-3724 Contact: Michael Randall
Men's Non-aid: basketball, cross country, diving, football, golf, swimming, tennis, track & field
Women's Non-aid: basketball, cross country, diving, soccer, softball, swimming, tennis, track & field, volleyball

STATE UNIVERSITY OF NEW YORK (PLATTSBURGH)

Memorial Hall 218
Plattsburgh, NY 12901
(518) 564-4148 Contact: Julie A. Terrizzi
Men's Non-aid: basketball, cross country, ice hockey, indoor track, soccer, swimming-diving, tennis, track & field
Women's Non-aid: basketball, cross country, indoor track, soccer, swimming-diving, tennis, track & field, volleyball

STATE UNIVERSITY OF NEW YORK (STONY BROOK)

Nicolls Road
Stony Brook, NY 11794
(516) 246-6790
Men's Non-aid: baseball, basketball, cross country, football, indoor track, lacrosse, soccer, squash, swimming, swimming-diving, tennis, track & field
Women's Non-aid: basketball, cross country, indoor track, soccer, softball, swimming-diving, tennis, track & field, volleyball

STATE UNIVERSITY OF NEW YORK COLLEGE (BROCKPORT)

318 Allen Building
Brockport, NY 14420
(716) 395-2380 Contact: Mike Andriatch
Men's Non-aid: baseball, basketball, cross country, diving, football, ice hockey, indoor track, soccer, swimming, swimming-diving, track & field, wrestling
Women's Non-aid: basketball, cross country, diving, field hockey, gymnastics, indoor track, soccer, softball, swimming, swimming-diving, tennis, track & field, volleyball

STATE UNIVERSITY OF NEW YORK COLLEGE (CORTLAND)

P.O. Box 2000
Cortland, NY 13045
(607) 753-5673 Contact: Peter Koryzno
Men's Non-aid: baseball, basketball, cross country, football, gymnastics, ice hockey, indoor track, lacrosse, soccer, swimming-diving, track & field, wrestling
Women's Non-aid: basketball, cross country, field hockey, gymnastics, indoor track, lacrosse, soccer, softball, swimming-diving, tennis, track & field, volleyball

STATE UNIVERSITY OF NEW YORK COLLEGE (FREDONIA)

Dods Hall
Fredonia, NY 14063
(716) 673-3108 Contact: Michael Conley
Men's Non-aid: baseball, basketball, cross country, ice hockey, indoor track, soccer, swimming, tennis, track & field
Women's Non-aid: basketball, cross country, indoor track, soccer, tennis, track & field, volleyball

STATE UNIVERSITY OF NEW YORK COLLEGE (GENESEO)

Alumni Fieldhouse
Geneseo, NY 144[illegible]4
(716) 245-5436 Contact: Fred Bright
Men's Non-aid: basketball, cross country, ice hockey, lacrosse, soccer, swimming, swimming-diving, track & field
Women's Non-aid: basketball, cross country, soccer, softball, swimming, swimming-diving, track & field, volleyball

STATE UNIVERSITY OF NEW YORK COLLEGE (NEW PALTZ)

Elting Gymnasium
New Paltz, NY 12561
(914) 257-3250 Contact: Daniel Sistarenik
Men's Non-aid: baseball, basketball, cross country, golf, soccer, swimming-diving, tennis, volleyball
Women's Non-aid: basketball, cross country, golf, soccer, softball, tennis, volleyball

STATE UNIVERSITY OF NEW YORK COLLEGE (OSWEGO)
202 Laker Hall
Oswego, NY 13126
(315) 341-4280 Contact: Dr. Sandra L. Moore
Men's Non-aid: baseball, basketball, cross country, diving, golf, ice hockey, lacrosse, soccer, swimming, swimming-diving, tennis, wrestling
Women's Non-aid: basketball, cross country, diving, field hockey, soccer, softball, swimming, swimming-diving, tennis, volleyball

STATE UNIVERSITY OF NEW YORK COLLEGE (POTSDAM)
Raymond Hall 320
Potsdam, NY 13676
(315) 267-2000 Contact: Karen O'Brien
Men's Non-aid: basketball, cross country, ice hockey, lacrosse, soccer, swimming, swimming-diving, wrestling
Women's Non-aid: basketball, cross country, field hockey, swimming, swimming-diving, tennis, volleyball

STATE UNIVERSITY OF NEW YORK COLLEGE (PURCHASE)
735 Anderson Hill Road
Purchase, NY 10577-1400
(914) 251-6355 Contact: Emillie B. Devine
Men's Non-aid: basketball, fencing, soccer
Women's Non-aid: tennis, ultimate frisbee, volleyball

STATE UNIVERSITY OF NEW YORK MARITIME COLLEGE
Fort Schuyler Bronx, NY 10465
(212) 409-7331 Contact: Kathy Hewitt
Men's Non-aid: baseball, basketball, crew, cross country, football, golf, ice hockey, lacrosse, riflery, rugby, sailing, soccer, swimming, tennis, volleyball
Women's Non-aid: basketball, crew, softball, tennis, volleyball

SUFFOLK COUNTY COMMUNITY COLLEGE
533 College Road
Selden, NY 11784
2-year college
(516) 732-2929 Contact: David L. Ross
Men's Non-aid: baseball, basketball, bowling, cross country, golf, lacrosse, soccer, tennis, track & field
Women's Non-aid: basketball, bowling, soccer, squash, softball, tennis, track & field, volleyball

SYRACUSE UNIVERSITY
Manley Field House
Syracuse, NY 13244-5020
(315) 443-2608 Contact: Larry Kimball
Unspecified athletic aid available
M: basketball, crew, cross country, football, gymnastics, indoor track, lacrosse, soccer, swimming diving, track & field, wrestling
W: basketball, crew, cross country, field hockey, indoor track, swimming-diving, tennis, track & field, volleyball

UNION COLLEGE
17 South Lane
Schenectady, NY 12308
(518) 370-6170 Contact: George Cuttita
Men's Non-aid: baseball, basketball, cross country, football, golf, ice hockey, indoor track, lacrosse, soccer, swimming, tennis, track & field
Women's Non-aid: basketball, cross country, field hockey, indoor track, lacrosse, soccer, softball, swimming, tennis, track & field, volleyball

VASSAR COLLEGE
Raymond Avenue
Poughkeepsie, NY 12601
(914) 437-7469 Contact: Susan Colodny
Men's Non-aid: basketball, cross country, fencing, soccer, squash, swimming-diving, tennis, volleyball
Women's Non-aid: basketball, cross country, fencing, field hockey, soccer, squash, swimming-diving, tennis, volleyball

VILLA MARIA COLLEGE
240 Pine Ridge Road
Buffalo, NY 14225
2-year college
(716) 896-0700 Contact: Ron Griffin

Men's Aid (#/$): 9/$37,000
Women's Aid (#/$): 11/$43,000
Restrictions and notes: New York students must apply for New York State aid and the scholarship is for tuition not covered by the state aid.
M: basketball
W: volleyball

WAGNER COLLEGE
631 Howard Avenue
Staten Island, NY 10301
(718) 390-3227 Contact: Scott Morse
Unspecified athletic aid available
M: baseball, basketball, cross country, golf, indoor track, tennis, track & field, wrestling
W: basketball, cross country, indoor track, softball, tennis, track & field, volleyball

YESHIVA UNIVERSITY
500 West 185th Street
New York, NY 10033
(212) 960-5269 Contact: Jack Nussbaum
Men's Non-aid: basketball, cross country, fencing, golf, tennis, volleyball, wrestling
Women's Non-aid: volleyball

YORK COLLEGE (CUNY)
Brewer Boulevard
Jamaica, NY 11451
(718) 262-2230 Contact: Adolphus Frazier
Men's Non-aid: basketball, cross country, indoor track, soccer, tennis, track & field, volleyball
Women's Non-aid: basketball, cheerleading, cross country, indoor track, track & field, volleyball

North Carolina

APPALACHIAN STATE UNIVERSITY
Second Floor
Broome-Kirk Gymnasium
Boone, NC 28608
(704) 262-3080 Contact: Rick Covington
Men's Aid (#/$): 166/$657,624
Women's Aid (#/$): 73/$179,916
M: baseball, basketball, cross country, football, golf, indoor track, soccer, tennis, track & field, wrestling
W: basketball, cross country, field hockey, golf, indoor track, tennis, track & field, volleyball

BARBER-SCOTIA COLLEGE
145 Cabarrus Avenue
Concord, NC 28025
(704) 786-5171 Contact: Dr. William Madrey
Unspecified athletic aid available
Restrictions and notes: Partial aid, based on need.
M: basketball, cross country, tennis, track & field. Men's Non-aid: indoor track
W: basketball, cross country, softball, tennis, track & field, volleyball. Women's Non-aid: indoor track

BARTON COLLEGE
West Lee Street
Wilson, NC 27893
(919) 399-6517 Contact: Gary W. Hall
Men's Aid (#/$): 18/$170,048
Women's Aid (#/$): 11/$106,887
M: baseball, basketball, golf, soccer, tennis
W: basketball, softball, tennis, volleyball

BELMONT ABBEY COLLEGE
Mount Holly Road
Belmont, NC 28012
(704) 825-6718 Contact: Eileen T. Dills
Men's Aid (#/$): 16.5/$198,689
Women's Aid (#/$): 7/$84,298
M: baseball, basketball, golf, soccer, tennis. Men's Non-aid: cross country
W: basketball, cross country, tennis, volleyball

BLANTON JUNIOR COLLEGE
126 College Street
Asheville, NC 28801
2-year college

(704) 252-7346 Contact: Doug Allen
Unspecified athletic aid available
M: basketball, cross country

BREVARD COLLEGE
400 North Broad Street
Brevard, NC 28712
2-year college
(704) 883-8292 Contact: Norm Witek
Unspecified athletic aid available
M: basketball, cross country, indoor track, soccer, tennis, track & field
W: basketball, cross country, indoor track, soccer, tennis, track & field

CAMPBELL UNIVERSITY
P.O. Box 10
Buies Creek, NC 27506
(919) 893-4111 Contact: Stan Cole
Men's Aid (#/$): 50/unspecified $
Women's Aid (#/$): 45/unspecified $
M: baseball, basketball, cross country, golf, soccer, tennis, track & field, wrestling
W: basketball, cross country, golf, soccer, softball, tennis, track & field, volleyball

CATAWBA COLLEGE
2300 West Innes Street
Salisbury, NC 28144
(704) 637-4720 Contact: Dennis Davidson
Men's Aid (#/$): 48/$547,200
Women's Aid (#/$): 16/$182,400
Restrictions and notes: 25 of men's scholarships are for football.
M: baseball, basketball, cross country, football, golf, soccer, tennis
W: basketball, cross country, field hockey, soccer, softball, tennis, volleyball

CHOWAN COLLEGE
Jones Drive
Murfreesboro, NC 27855
2-year college
(919) 398-4101 Contact: Jack Goldberg
Unspecified athletic aid available
M: baseball, basketball, football, golf, wrestling. Men's Non-aid: tennis
W: basketball, softball, volleyball. Women's Non-aid: tennis

COASTAL CAROLINA COMMUNITY COLLEGE
444 Western Boulevard
Jacksonville, NC 28540
2-year college
(919) 455-1221 X. 260 Contact: C. Ronald Cox
Unspecified athletic aid available
M: golf, softball, tennis
W: softball, tennis

DAVIDSON COLLEGE
P.O. Box 1750
Davidson, NC 28036
(704) 892-2374 Contact: Emil Parker
Men's Aid (#/$): 15/$300,000
Women's Aid (#/$): 19/$380,000
M: basketball, tennis. Men's Non-aid: baseball, cross country, diving, football, golf, indoor track, soccer, swimming, track & field
W: basketball, cross country, diving, field hockey, indoor track, soccer, swimming-diving, tennis, track & field, volleyball. Women's Non-aid: lacrosse

DUKE UNIVERSITY
115 Cameron Indoor Stadium
Durham, NC 27706
(919) 684-2633 Contact: Mike Cragg
Unspecified athletic aid available
M: baseball, basketball, football, golf, lacrosse, soccer, tennis, wrestling. Men's Non-aid: cross country, fencing, indoor track, swimming-diving, track & field
W: basketball, cross country, field hockey, golf, indoor track, tennis, track & field, volleyball. Women's Non-aid: fencing, swimming-diving

EAST CAROLINA UNIVERSITY
Sports Medicine Building
Greenville, NC 27834-4353
(919) 757-4522 Contact: Charles Bloom
Men's Aid (#/$): 142/$1,300,000
Women's Aid (#/$): 36/$250,000

M: baseball, basketball, cross country, football, golf, indoor track, soccer, swimming-diving, tennis, track & field
W: basketball, cross country, indoor track, softball, swimming-diving, tennis, track & field, volleyball

ELIZABETH CITY STATE UNIVERSITY
1704 Weeksville Road
Campus Box 900
Elizabeth City, NC 27909
(919) 335-3518 Contact: Glen Mason
Men's Aid (#/$): 52/$239,000
Women's Aid (#/$): 12/$39,000
M: basketball, football. Men's Non-aid: baseball, cross country, track & field
W: basketball. Women's Non-aid: cross country, softball, track & field

ELON COLLEGE
Campus Box 2500
Elon College, NC 27244
(919) 584-2420 Contact: Clay Hassard
Unspecified athletic aid available
Restrictions and notes: 61.5 equivalent grants for 12 sports (men and women).
M: baseball, basketball, football, golf, soccer, tennis, track & field
W: basketball, soccer, softball, tennis, volleyball

FAYETTEVILLE STATE UNIVERSITY
1200 Murchison Road
Fayetteville, NC 28301-4298
(919) 486-1325 Contact: Mae Ellen Graves
Unspecified athletic aid available
Restrictions and notes: Must file for Title IV federal funds using a need analysis application.
M: basketball, cross country, football, golf
W: basketball, cross country, golf, softball, volleyball

GARDNER-WEBB COLLEGE
P.O. Box 804
Boiling Springs, NC 28017
(704) 434-2361 Contact: Tim Vaughn
Unspecified athletic aid available
M: baseball, basketball, football, golf, tennis. Men's Non-aid: cross country, track & field
W: basketball, tennis, volleyball. Women's Non-aid: softball

GREENSBORO COLLEGE
815 West Market Street
Greensboro, NC 27401-1875
(919) 271-2217 Contact: Katharine Bonisolli
Men's Non-aid: basketball, golf, soccer, tennis
Women's Non-aid: basketball, softball, tennis, volleyball

HIGH POINT UNIVERSITY
University Station
High Point, NC 27262-3598
(919) 841-9105 Contact: Woody Gibson
Men's Aid (#/$): 21.5/$232,200
Women's Aid (#/$): 13/$140,400
M: baseball, basketball, cross country, golf, soccer, tennis, track & field
W: basketball, cross country, soccer, tennis, volleyball. Women's Non-aid: field hockey

JOHNSON C. SMITH UNIVERSITY
100 Beatties Ford Road
Charlotte, NC 28216
(704) 378-1035 Contact: Carolyn B. Smith
Unspecified athletic aid available
M: basketball, cross country, football, golf, indoor track, tennis, track & field
W: basketball, cross country, indoor track, track & field. Women's Non-aid: softball

LEES-MCRAE COLLEGE
Banner Elk, NC 28604
(704) 898-5241 Contact: Don Baker
Men's Aid (#/$): 27.5/$253,960
Women's Aid (#/$): 9.75/$90,055
M: alpine skiing, basketball, football, soccer, tennis
W: alpine skiing, basketball, soccer, tennis, volleyball

LENOIR COMMUNITY COLLEGE
P.O. Box 188
Kinston, NC 28501
2-year college
(919) 527-6223 Contact: Keith Spence
Unspecified athletic aid available
M: baseball, basketball, golf

LENOIR-RHYNE COLLEGE
LRC Box 7221
Hickory, NC 28603
(704) 328-7174 Contact: Thomas Neff
Unspecified athletic aid available
M: basketball, cross country, football, golf, soccer, softball, tennis, track & field, volleyball
W: basketball, cross country, football, golf, soccer, softball, tennis, track & field, volleyball

LIVINGSTONE COLLEGE
701 West Monroe Street
Salisbury, NC 28144
(704) 633-7960 Contact: Annie L. Pruitt
Unspecified athletic aid available
M: basketball, football, golf, tennis, wrestling. Men's Non-aid: track & field
W: basketball, tennis. Women's Non-aid: track & field

LOUISBURG COLLEGE
Louisburg, NC 27549
2-year college
(919) 496-2521 Contact: Elliott Avent
Unspecified athletic aid available
M: basketball. Men's Non-aid: baseball, golf
W: basketball, volleyball

MARS HILL COLLEGE
Main Street
Mars Hill, NC 28754
(704) 689-1373 Contact: Greg Seller
Men's Aid (#/$): 43.6/$458,010
Women's Aid (#/$): 12.2/$127,995
M: baseball, basketball, cross country, football, golf, soccer, tennis
W: basketball, cross country, soccer, softball, tennis, volleyball

MITCHELL COMMUNITY COLLEGE
West Broad Street
Statesville, NC 28677
2-year college
(704) 873-2201 Contact: Bill Moose
Unspecified athletic aid available
M: basketball, golf, tennis

MONTREAT-ANDERSON COLLEGE
P.O. Box 1267
Montreat, NC 28757
(704) 669-8011 Contact: Lisa H. Lankford
Unspecified athletic aid available
M: baseball, basketball, soccer
W: softball, volleyball

MOUNT OLIVE COLLEGE
College Hall Athletic Facility
Mount Olive, NC 28365
(919) 658-9772 Contact: George F. Whitfield
Men's Aid (#/$): 17.5/$168,875
Women's Aid (#/$): 11/$106,150
M: baseball, basketball, golf, soccer, tennis
W: basketball, softball, tennis, volleyball

NORTH CAROLINA A AND T STATE UNIVERSITY
Office of Financial Aid
Dowdy Administration Building
1601 East Market Street
Greensboro, NC 27411
(919) 334-7973 Contact: Dolores Davis
Unspecified athletic aid available
M: baseball, basketball, cross country, football, indoor track, tennis, track & field, wrestling
W: basketball, indoor track, softball, tennis, track & field, volleyball

NORTH CAROLINA CENTRAL UNIVERSITY
P.O. Box 197411
Durham, NC 27707

(919) 560-6202 Contact: Lola T. McKnight
Unspecified athletic aid available
M: basketball, cross country, football, indoor track, tennis, track & field
W: basketball, indoor track, softball, tennis, track & field, volleyball. Women's Non-aid: cross country

NORTH CAROLINA STATE UNIVERSITY

Box 8501
Raleigh, NC 27695-8501
(919) 737-2102 Contact: Mark Bockelman
Men's Aid (#/$): 53/$246,823
Women's Aid (#/$): 22/$140,553
M: baseball, basketball, cross country, football, golf, gymnastics, riflery, soccer, swimming-diving, tennis, track & field, wrestling. Men's Non-aid: fencing
W: basketball, cross country, golf, gymnastics, riflery, soccer, swimming-diving, tennis, track & field, volleyball. Women's Non-aid: fencing

NORTH CAROLINA WESLEYAN COLLEGE

3400 North Wesleyan Boulevard
Rocky Mount, NC 27804
(919) 977-7171 Contact: Patrick Baker
Men's Non-aid: baseball, basketball, soccer, tennis
Women's Non-aid: basketball, soccer, squash, volleyball

PEMBROKE STATE UNIVERSITY

College Road
Pembroke, NC 28372-1510
(919) 521-6370 Contact: Gary Spitler
Men's Aid (#/$): 27/$94,500
Women's Aid (#/$): 22/$77,000
M: baseball, basketball, cross country, golf, soccer, track & field, wrestling
W: basketball, cross country, softball, volleyball

PFEIFFER COLLEGE

P.O. Box 960
Misenheimer, NC 28109
(704) 463-7343 Contact: Ruby B. Mason
Unspecified athletic aid available
M: baseball, basketball, cross country, golf, soccer, tennis, wrestling. Men's Non-aid: lacrosse
W: basketball, diving, field hockey, softball, swimming, swimming-diving, tennis, volleyball

QUEENS COLLEGE

1900 Selwyn Avenue
Charlotte, NC 28274
(704) 337-2225 Contact: Dale Layer
Men's Aid (#/$): 16/$230,400
Women's Aid (#/$): 16/$230,400
M: basketball, golf, soccer, tennis
W: basketball, soccer, tennis, volleyball

SAINT ANDREWS PRESBYTERIAN COLLEGE

1700 Dogwood Mile
Laurinburg, NC 28352-5589
(919) 276-3652 X. 376 Contact: David Malcolm
Men's Non-aid: baseball, basketball, cross country, equestrian, golf, soccer, softball, tennis, track & field
Women's Non-aid: baseball, basketball, cross country, equestrian, softball, tennis, track & field, volleyball

SAINT AUGUSTINE'S COLLEGE

1315 Oakwood Avenue
Raleigh, NC 27611
(919) 828-4451 X. 381 Contact: Sherri Avent
Men's Aid (#/$): 85/$313,188
Women's Aid (#/$): 79/$282,364
M: baseball, basketball, golf, soccer, tennis, track & field
W: basketball, softball, track & field, volleyball

SOUTHEASTERN COMMUNITY COLLEGE

P.O. Box 151
Whiteville, NC 28472
2-year college

(919) 642-7141 Contact: Robert Brooks
Men's Aid (#/$): 10/$5,000
Women's Aid (#/$): 5/$2,940
M: baseball
W: softball

UNIVERSITY OF NORTH CAROLINA (ASHEVILLE)
One University Heights
Asheville, NC 28804
(704) 258-6459 Contact: Mike Gore
Men's Aid (#/$): 8/$25,673
Women's Aid (#/$): 7/$7,832
M: baseball, basketball, cross country, football, golf, indoor track, lacrosse, soccer, swimming, swimming-diving, tennis, track & field, wrestling. Men's Non-aid: fencing
W: basketball, cross country, field hockey, golf, gymnastics, lacrosse, soccer, softball, swimming, swimming-diving, tennis, track & field, volleyball. Women's Non-aid: fencing

UNIVERSITY OF NORTH CAROLINA (CHAPEL HILL)
P.O. Box 2126
Chapel Hill, NC 27514
(919) 962-2123 Contact: Rick Brewer
Unspecified athletic aid available
M: baseball, basketball, cross country, football, golf, indoor track, lacrosse, soccer, swimming, swimming-diving, tennis, track & field, wrestling. Men's Non-aid: fencing
W: basketball, cross country, field hockey, golf, gymnastics, lacrosse, soccer, softball, swimming, swimming-diving, tennis, track & field, volleyball. Women's Non-aid: fencing

UNIVERSITY OF NORTH CAROLINA (CHARLOTTE)
Highway 49
Charlotte, NC 28223
704) 547-4937 Contact: Thomas Whitestone
Men's Aid (#/$): 86/$372,460
Women's Aid (#/$): 56/$263,400
M: baseball, basketball, cross country, golf, soccer, tennis, track & field
W: basketball, cross country, softball, tennis, track & field, volleyball

UNIVERSITY OF NORTH CAROLINA (GREENSBORO)
HHP Building
Greensboro, NC 27412-5001
(919) 334-5615 Contact: Ty Buckner
Men's Aid (#/$): 19/$49,741
Women's Aid (#/$): 14/$38,675
M: basketball, golf, soccer, tennis
W: basketball, softball, tennis, volleyball

UNIVERSITY OF NORTH CAROLINA (WILMINGTON)
Track Coliseum
Wilmington, NC 28403
(919) 395-3236 Contact: Joe Browning
Men's Aid (#/$): 22/$41,601
Women's Aid (#/$): 24/$49,106
M: baseball, basketball, cross country, golf, soccer, swimming-diving, tennis, track & field
W: basketball, cross country, golf, softball, swimming-diving, tennis, track & field, volleyball

WAKE FOREST UNIVERSITY
P.O. Box 7426
Winston-Salem, NC 27109
(919) 759-5640 Contact: John Justus
Men's Aid (#/$): 51/$534,000
Women's Aid (#/$): 16/$119,000
M: baseball, basketball, cross country, football, golf, indoor track, soccer, tennis
W: basketball, cross country, field hockey, golf, indoor track, tennis

WARREN WILSON COLLEGE
701 WWC Road
Swannanoa, NC 28778
(704) 298-3325 X. 401 Contact: Robert Somerville

Men's Non-aid: baseball, basketball, cross country, soccer, swimming
Women's Non-aid: basketball, cross country, soccer, softball, swimming

WESTERN CAROLINA UNIVERSITY
2517 Ramsey Center
Cullowhee, NC 28723
(704) 227-7171 Contact: Steve White
Men's Aid (#/$): 91.3/$487,082
Women's Aid (#/$): 27.4/$132,349
M: baseball, basketball, football, golf, indoor track, tennis, track & field
W: basketball, cross country, indoor track, tennis, track & field, volleyball

WILKES COLLEGE
P.O. Box 120
Wilkesboro, NC 28697
2-year college
(919) 667-7137 Contact: Kathron Richards
Aid (#/$): 12/$37,400 (M & W)
M: wrestling. Men's Non-aid: baseball, basketball, cross country, football, golf, soccer, tennis
W: basketball, field hockey, softball, tennis, volleyball

WINGATE COLLEGE
Campus Box 3051
Wingate, NC 28174
(704) 233-8186 Contact: David Sherwood
Unspecified athletic aid available
M: baseball, basketball, football, golf, soccer, tennis
W: basketball, softball, tennis, volleyball

WINSTON-SALEM STATE UNIVERSITY
601 Martin Luther King Jr. Drive
Winston-Salem, NC 27110
(919) 750-2143 Contact: Joseph V. Valls
Unspecified athletic aid available
M: basketball, cross country, football, tennis, track & field, wrestling. Men's Non-aid: golf, indoor track, swimming
W: basketball, cross country, softball, tennis, track & field, volleyball.
Women's Non-aid: indoor track, swimming

North Dakota

BISMARCK STATE COLLEGE
1500 Edwards Avenue
Bismarck, ND 58501
2-year college
(701) 224-5456 Contact: Ed Kringstad
Men's Aid (#/$): 15/$14,350
Women's Aid (#/$): 17/$15,178
M: basketball, wrestling. Men's Non-aid: cross country, golf, rodeo, tennis, track & field
W: basketball. Women's Non-aid: cross country, golf, rodeo, tennis, track & field

DICKINSON STATE UNIVERSITY
P.O. Box 291
Dickinson, ND 58601
(701) 227-2371 Contact: LaVern Jessen
Unspecified athletic aid available
M: baseball, basketball, cross country, football, golf, indoor track, rodeo, tennis, track & field, wrestling
W: basketball, cross country, indoor track, rodeo, tennis, track & field, volleyball

JAMESTOWN COLLEGE
Box 6081
Jamestown, ND 58401
(701) 252-3467 Contact: Jerry Meyer
Unspecified athletic aid available
M: baseball, basketball, cross country, football, indoor track, track & field, wrestling.
W: basketball, cross country, indoor track, softball, track & field, volleyball

MAYVILLE STATE COLLEGE
330 Third Street, NE
Mayville, ND 58257
(701) 786-4834 Contact: Brad Tastad
Unspecified athletic aid available
M: baseball, basketball, football, wrestling
W: basketball, softball, volleyball

MINOT STATE
500 University Avenue West
Minot, ND 58701
(701) 857-3272 Contact: Duane Sweep
Men's Aid (#/$): 80/$50,000
Women's Aid (#/$): 45/$40,000
Restrictions and notes: Tuition and fee athletic award limits are applicable.
M: basketball, cross country, football, indoor track, track & field. Men's Non-aid: golf, tennis
W: basketball, cross country, indoor track, tennis, track & field, volleyball. Women's Non-aid: football

NORTH DAKOTA STATE
College of Science
Wahpeton, ND 58076
2-year college
(701) 671-2281 Contact: Blayne Helgeson
Unspecified athletic aid available
M: basketball, football, indoor track, track & field, wrestling. Men's Non-aid: cross country, golf, tennis
W: basketball, indoor track, track & field, volleyball. Women's Non-aid: cross country, golf, tennis

NORTH DAKOTA STATE UNIVERSITY
P.O. Box 5034
Fargo, ND 58105
(701) 237-8331 Contact: George A. Ellis
Unspecified athletic aid available
M: baseball, basketball, cross country, football, indoor track, track & field, wrestling. Men's Non-aid: golf
W: basketball, cross country, indoor track, track & field, volleyball. Women's Non-aid: softball

NORTH DAKOTA STATE UNIVERSITY (BOTTINEAU)
First and Simrall
Bottineau, ND 58318
2-year college
(701) 228-2277 Contact: Pete Toews
Men's Aid (#/$): 42/$13,450
Women's Aid (#/$): 16/$5,650
M: baseball, basketball, ice hockey
W: basketball, volleyball

UNIVERSITY OF MARY
7500 University Drive
Bismarck, ND 58504
(701) 255-7500 Contact: Stacy Herron
Men's Aid (#/$): 150/$250,000
Women's Aid (#/$): 150/$250,000
M: basketball, cross country, football, indoor track, tennis, track & field, wrestling
W: basketball, cross country, indoor track, softball, tennis, track & field, volleyball

UNIVERSITY OF NORTH DAKOTA
P.O. Box 8175
Grand Forks, ND 58202
(701) 777-2234 Contact: Pete Oliszozak
Men's Aid (#/$): 83/$460,000
Women's Aid (#/$): 29/$158,000
M: baseball, basketball, cross country, diving, football, ice hockey, indoor track, swimming, swimming-diving, track & field, wrestling. Men's Non-aid: golf
W: basketball, cross country, diving, indoor track, softball, swimming, swimming-diving, track & field, volleyball

UNIVERSITY OF NORTH DAKOTA (LAKE REGION)
1801 North College Drive
Devils Lake, ND 58307
2-year college
(701) 662-1600 Contact: Doug Darling
Men's Aid (#/$): 8/$12,500
Women's Aid (#/$): 15/$12,500
M: basketball
W: basketball, volleyball

VALLEY CITY STATE UNIVERSITY
Valley City, ND 58072
(701) 845-7412 Contact: Betty Kuss Schumacher
Unspecified athletic aid available
M: baseball, basketball, cross country, football, golf, tennis, track & field, volleyball
W: basketball, cheerleading, cross country, softball, tennis, track & field, volleyball

Ohio

ASHLAND COLLEGE
Athletic Department
Ashland, OH 44805
(419) 289-5442 Contact: Paul Martello
Men's Aid (#/$): 71/unspecified $
Women's Aid (#/$): 34/unspecified $
M: baseball, basketball, cross country, diving, football, indoor track, swimming, track & field, wrestling.
Men's Non-aid: golf, soccer, tennis
W: basketball, cross country, diving, indoor track, softball, swimming, track & field, volleyball. Women's Non-aid: tennis

BLUFFTON COLLEGE
280 West College Avenue
Bluffton, OH 45817
(419) 358-3241 Contact: Ron Geiser
Men's Non-aid: baseball, basketball, cross country, football, golf, soccer, tennis, track & field
Women's Non-aid: basketball, cross country, soccer, softball, tennis, track & field, volleyball

BOWLING GREEN STATE UNIVERSITY
Athletic Department
Stadium East
Bowling Green, OH 43403
(419) 372-7076 Contact: Steve Barr
Men's Aid (#/$): 50/$262,287
Women's Aid (#/$): 29/$115,585
M: baseball, basketball, cross country, diving, football, golf, ice hockey, soccer, swimming, tennis, track & field
W: basketball, cross country, diving, golf, gymnastics, softball, swimming, tennis, track & field, volleyball

CAPITAL UNIVERSITY
2199 East Main Street
Columbus, OH 43209-2394
(614) 236-6174 Contact: David Graham
Men's Non-aid: baseball, basketball, football, golf, soccer, tennis, wrestling
Women's Non-aid: basketball, softball, tennis, volleyball

CASE WESTERN RESERVE UNIVERSITY
10900 Euclid Avenue
Emerson PE Center
Cleveland, OH 44106-7223
(216) 368-6517 Contact: Sue Herdle
Men's Non-aid: baseball, basketball, cross country, diving, fencing, football, golf, indoor track, soccer, swimming, swimming-diving, tennis, track & field, wrestling
Women's Non-aid: basketball, cross country, diving, fencing, indoor track, soccer, swimming, swimming-diving, tennis, track & field, volleyball

CEDARVILLE COLLEGE
Box 601
Cedarville, OH 45314
(513) 766-7766 Contact: Mark Womack
Men's Aid (#/$): 11.6/$110,000
Women's Aid (#/$): 2.1/$22,000
M: baseball, basketball, cross country, golf, indoor track, soccer, tennis, track & field
W: basketball, cross country, indoor track, softball, tennis, track & field, volleyball

CENTRAL STATE UNIVERSITY
University Communications
Wilberforce, OH 45384
(513) 376-6142 Contact: Ed Chamness

Unspecified athletic aid available
M: baseball, basketball, football, indoor track, volleyball. Men's Non-aid: track & field

CINCINNATI TECHNICAL COLLEGE
3520 Central Parkway
Cincinnnati, OH 45223
2-year college
(513) 559-1556 Contact: Michelle Imhoff
Unspecified athletic aid available
M: basketball

CLARK STATE COLLEGE
570 East Leffels Lane
Springfield, OH 45505
2-year college
(513) 328-6056 Contact: Lynn M. Rector
Men's Aid (#/$): 15/$9,500
Women's Aid (#/$): 20/$12,000
M: basketball, golf
W: basketball, volleyball

CLEVELAND STATE UNIVERSITY
East 18th and Prospect Avenue
Cleveland, OH 44115
(216) 687-4818 Contact: Merle Levin
Men's Aid (#/$): 120/$389,000
Women's Aid (#/$): 53/$191,593
M: baseball, basketball, diving, fencing, golf, indoor track, soccer, swimming, swimming-diving, tennis, track & field, wrestling. Men's Non-aid: bowling, martial arts, sailing, water polo
W: basketball, cross country, diving, fencing, golf, indoor track, softball, swimming, swimming-diving, tennis, track & field, volleyball. Women's Non-aid: martial arts, sailing

COLLEGE OF MOUNT ST. JOSEPH
5701 Neeb Road
Mount St. Joseph, OH 45051
(513) 244-4311 Contact: Dane Neumeister
Women's Aid (#/$): 6/$20,000
W: basketball, volleyball

THE COLLEGE OF WOOSTER
Office of News Service
Wooster, OH 44691
(216) 263-2374 Contact: John P. Finn
Men's Non-aid: baseball, basketball, cross country, diving, football, golf, indoor track, lacrosse, soccer, swimming, tennis, track & field
Women's Non-aid: basketball, cross country, diving, field hockey, indoor track, lacrosse, soccer, swimming, tennis, track & field, volleyball

COLUMBUS STATE COMMUNITY COLLEGE
500 East Spring Street
Columbus, OH 43215
2-year college
(614) 227-2637 Contact: Tom Habegger
Men's Non-aid: baseball, basketball, cross country, golf, soccer
Women's Non-aid: cross country, equestrian, golf, softball, volleyball

CUYAHOGA COMMUNITY COLLEGE
2900 Community Avenue
Cleveland, OH 44115
2-year college
(216) 987-4180 Contact: Dr. Dennis Smith
Unspecified athletic aid available
M: basketball, soccer, track & field
W: basketball, soccer, track & field

CUYHOGA COMMUNITY COLLEGE
4250 Richmond Road
Highland Hills Village, OH 44122
2-year college
(216) 987-2075 Contact: Jan Schmidt
Unspecified athletic aid available
M: basketball, golf
W: basketball, volleyball

CUYAHOGA COMMUNITY COLLEGE
11000 Pleasant Valley Road
Parma, OH 44130
2-year college

(216) 987-5134 Contact: Dolores A. Sistrunk
Unspecified athletic aid available
M: baseball, track & field
W: softball, track & field

DEFIANCE COLLEGE
701 North Clinton Street
Defiance, OH 43512
(419) 783-2346 Contact: Cindy Elliott
Men's Non-aid: baseball, basketball, cheerleading, cross country, golf, soccer, tennis, track & field
Women's Non-aid: basketball, cheerleading, cross country, softball, track & field, volleyball

DENISON UNIVERSITY
Granville, OH 43023
(614) 587-6279 Contact: Marilyn Gilbert
Men's Non-aid: baseball, basketball, cross country, diving, football, golf, indoor track, lacrosse, soccer, swimming, tennis, track & field
Women's Non-aid: basketball, cross country, diving, field hockey, indoor track, lacrosse, soccer, softball, swimming, tennis, track & field

DYKE COLLEGE
112 Prospect Avenue
Cleveland, OH 44115
(216) 696-9000 Contact: Rusty Rogers
Unspecified athletic aid available
M: basketball
W: basketball

HEIDELBERG COLLEGE
67 Greenfield Street
Tiffin, OH 44883
(419) 448-2140 Contact: Dick Edmond
Women's Non-aid: baseball, basketball, cheerleading, cross country, football, golf, indoor track, soccer, softball, tennis, track & field, volleyball, wrestling

HIRAM COLLEGE
Jesse Smith House
Hiram, OH 44234
(216) 569-5288 Contact: Tim Bryan
Men's Non-aid: baseball, basketball, cross country, diving, football, golf, indoor track, soccer, swimming, tennis, track & field
Women's Non-aid: basketball, cross country, diving, indoor track, soccer, softball, swimming, tennis, track & field, volleyball

JOHN CARROLL UNIVERSITY
20700 North Park Boulevard
University Heights, OH 44118
(216) 397-4676 Contact: Christopher Wenzler
Men's Non-aid: baseball, basketball, cross country, football, golf, indoor track, soccer, swimming-diving, tennis, track & field, wrestling
Women's Non-aid: basketball, cross country, indoor track, softball, swimming-diving, tennis, track & field, volleyball

KENT STATE UNIVERSITY (ASHTABULA)
3325 West 13th Street
Ashtabula, OH 44004
2-year college
(216) 964-3322 Contact: Robert M. Dulak
Unspecified athletic aid available
M: baseball, basketball, cross country, football, golf, gymnastics, ice hockey, swimming, swimming-diving, track & field, wrestling
W: basketball, cross country, field hockey, gymnastics, softball, swimming, swimming-diving, track & field, volleyball

KENT STATE UNIVERSITY (EAST LIVERPOOL)
400 East 4th Street
East Liverpool, OH 43920
2-year college
(216) 385-3805 Contact: Darwin Smith
Men's Non-aid: baseball, basketball, golf, tennis
Women's Non-aid: basketball, tennis, volleyball

KENT STATE UNIVERSITY (KENT)
185 Memorial Athletic and Convocation Center
Kent, OH 44242-0001
(216) 672-5976 Contact: Judy Devine
Men's Aid (#/$): 161/unspecified $
Women's Aid (#/$): 68/unspecified $
M: baseball, basketball, cross country, football, golf, gymnastics, ice hockey, indoor track, track & field, wrestling
W: basketball, cross country, field hockey, gymnastics, indoor track, softball, track & field, volleyball

KENT STATE UNIVERSITY (NEW PHILADELPHIA)
University Drive NE
New Philadelphia, OH 44663
2-year college
(216) 339-3391 X. 243 Contact: Doyle W. Bolyard
Unspecified athletic aid available
M: baseball, basketball, cross country, football, golf, gymnastics, ice hockey, swimming, swimming-diving, track & field, wrestling
W: basketball, cross country, field hockey, gymnastics, softball, swimming, swimming-diving, track & field, volleyball

KENT STATE UNIVERSITY (WARREN)
4314 Mahoning Avenue NW
Warren, OH 44483
2-year college
(216) 847-0571 X. 246 Contact: William Sandora
Unspecified athletic aid available
M: baseball, basketball, cross country, football, golf, gymnastics, ice hockey, swimming, swimming-diving, track & field, wrestling
W: basketball, cross country, field hockey, gymnastics, softball, swimming, swimming-diving, track & field, volleyball

KENYON COLLEGE
Gambier, OH 43022
(614) 427-5000 Contact: Craig Daugherty
Men's Non-aid: baseball, basketball, cross country, diving, football, golf, indoor track, lacrosse, soccer, swimming, tennis, track & field
Women's Non-aid: basketball, cross country, diving, field hockey, golf, indoor track, lacrosse, soccer, swimming, tennis, track & field

LAKE ERIE COLLEGE
391 Washington Street
Painesville, OH 44077
(216) 639-7861 Contact: David Poorman
Men's Aid (#/$): $25,000
Women's Aid (#/$): $25,000
M: basketball
W: basketball, softball, volleyball

MALONE COLLEGE
515 25th Street, NW
Canton, OH 44709
(216) 489-7379 Contact: Mark W. Bankert
Men's Aid (#/$): 110/$82,500
Women's Aid (#/$): 60/$45,000
M: baseball, basketball, cross country, golf, indoor track, soccer, tennis, track & field
W: basketball, cross country, indoor track, softball, tennis, track & field, volleyball

MARIETTA COLLEGE
Box C96
Marietta, OH 45750
(614) 374-4674 Contact: Mike McNamara
Men's Non-aid: baseball, basketball, crew, cross country, football, golf, indoor track, lacrosse, soccer, tennis, track & field
Women's Non-aid: basketball, crew, cross country, field hockey, softball, tennis, track & field, volleyball

MIAMI UNIVERSITY
210 Millett Hall
Oxford, OH 45056
(513) 529-4327 Contact: Kent Cherrington

Men's Aid (#/$): 156/unspecified $
Women's Aid (#/$): 68/unspecified $
M: baseball, basketball, cross country, football, golf, ice hockey, swimming-diving, tennis, track & field, wrestling.
Men's Non-aid: soccer
W: basketball, cross country, field hockey, softball, swimming-diving, tennis, track & field, volleyball

MOUNT UNION COLLEGE
1972 Clark Avenue
Alliance, OH 44601
(216) 823-6093 Contact: Michael De Matteis
Men's Non-aid: baseball, basketball, cross country, football, golf, lacrosse, soccer, softball, swimming-diving, tennis, track & field, wrestling
Women's Non-aid: baseball, cross country, softball, swimming-diving, tennis, track & field, volleyball

MOUNT VERNON NAZARENE COLLEGE
800 Martinsburg Road
Mount Vernon, OH 43050
(614) 397-1244 X. 310 Contact: Paul Furey
Unspecified athletic aid available
M: baseball, basketball, soccer, tennis
W: basketball, softball, volleyball

MUSKINGUM COLLEGE
Public Relations Office
New Concord, OH 43762
(614) 826-8134 Contact: Kathy Normansell
Men's Non-aid: baseball, basketball, cross country, football, golf, indoor track, soccer, tennis, track & field, wrestling
Women's Non-aid: basketball, cheerleading, cross country, indoor track, soccer, softball, tennis, track & field, volleyball

NOTRE DAME COLLEGE OF OHIO
South Euclid, OH 44121
(216) 381-1680 X. 283 Contact: Debby Ghezzi
Women's Aid (#/$): 20/$57,000
W: basketball, softball, volleyball

OBERLIN COLLEGE
105 Philips PE Center
Oberlin, OH 44074
(216) 775-8503 Contact: Scott A. Wargo
Men's Non-aid: baseball, basketball, cross country, football, indoor track, lacrosse, soccer, swimming, swimming-diving, tennis, track & field
Women's Non-aid: basketball, cross country, field hockey, indoor track, lacrosse, soccer, swimming, swimming-diving, tennis, track & field, volleyball

OHIO DOMINICAN COLLEGE
1216 Sunbury Road
Columbus, OH 43219
(614) 253-2741 Contact: Cynthia A. Diller
Men's Aid (#/$): 39/$28,985
Women's Aid (#/$): 38/$31,500
M: baseball, basketball, soccer
W: basketball, softball, volleyball

OHIO NORTHERN UNIVERSITY
South Main Street
Ada, OH 45810
(419) 772-2046 Contact: Cort Reynolds
Men's Non-aid: baseball, basketball, cross country, diving, football, golf, indoor track, soccer, swimming, swimming-diving, tennis, track & field, wrestling
Women's Non-aid: basketball, diving, softball, swimming, swimming-diving, tennis, track & field, volleyball

OHIO STATE UNIVERSITY
410 Woody Hayes Drive
124 St. John Arena
Columbus, OH 43210
(614) 292-6861 Contact: Steve Snapp
Men's Aid ($): unspecified #/$1,668,381
Women's Aid ($): unspecified #/$1,018,482
M: baseball, basketball, cross country, diving, football, golf, gymnastics, ice hockey, indoor track, soccer,

swimming, swimming-diving, tennis, track & field, volleyball, wrestling. Men's Non-aid: fencing, lacrosse, riflery
W: basketball, cross country, diving, fencing, field hockey, golf, gymnastics, indoor track, softball, swimming, swimming-diving, synchronized swimming, tennis, track & field, volleyball. Women's Non-aid: riflery

OHIO UNIVERSITY
105 Convocation Center
Athens, OH 45701
(614) 593-1298 Contact: Glenn Coble
Men's Aid (#/$): 158/$644,475
Women's Aid (#/$): 158/$644,475
M: baseball, basketball, cross country, diving, football, golf, indoor track, swimming-diving, tennis, track & field, wrestling
W: basketball, cross country, diving, field hockey, indoor track, softball, swimming-diving, tennis, track & field, volleyball

OHIO WESLEYAN UNIVERSITY
Mowry Center
Delaware, OH 43015
(614) 368-3340 Contact: Mark Beckenbach
Men's Non-aid: baseball, basketball, cross country, football, golf, lacrosse, soccer, softball, swimming-diving, tennis, track & field
Women's Non-aid: basketball, cross country, field hockey, lacrosse, swimming-diving, tennis, track & field, volleyball

OTTERBEIN COLLEGE
141 West Park
Westerville, OH 43081
(614) 898-1600 Contact: Ed Syguda
Men's Non-aid: baseball, basketball, cross country, equestrian, football, golf, indoor track, soccer, tennis, track & field
Women's Non-aid: basketball, cross country, equestrian, indoor track, soccer, softball, tennis, track & field, volleyball

SHAWNEE STATE COLLEGE
940 Second Street
Portsmouth, OH 45662
2-year college
(614) 354-3205 Contact: Tom Bowman
Unspecified athletic aid available
M: basketball
W: basketball

SHAWNEE STATE UNIVERSITY
940 Second Street
Portsmouth, OH 45662
(614) 354-3205 Contact: Eugene D. Wilson
Unspecified athletic aid available
M: basketball, golf, soccer, tennis. Men's Non-aid: cross country, track & field
W: basketball, softball, tennis, volleyball. Women's Non-aid: cross country, track & field

SINCLAIR COMMUNITY COLLEGE
444 West Third Street
Dayton, OH 45402
2-year college
(513) 226-2730 Contact: Donald Cundiff
Men's Aid (#/$): 35/$17,000
Women's Aid (#/$): 24/$12,000
M: baseball, basketball, golf, tennis
W: basketball, tennis, volleyball

TIFFIN UNIVERSITY
155 Miami Street
Tiffin, OH 44883
(419) 447-6444 Contact: Beverly Riedy
Men's Aid (#/$): 92/$171,000
Women's Aid (#/$): 36/$45,000
Men's Non-aid: baseball, basketball, cross country, soccer
Women's Non-aid: basketball, cross country, volleyball

UNIVERSITY OF AKRON
Carroll Street
James A. Rhodes Arena
Akron, OH 44325-5201
(216) 972-7468 Contact: Mac Yates

Unspecified athletic aid available
M: baseball, basketball, cross country, football, golf, soccer, tennis, track & field. Men's Non-aid: riflery
W: basketball, cross country, softball, tennis, track & field, volleyball

UNIVERSITY OF CINCINNATI
309 Laurence Hall
Cincinnati, OH 45221-0021
(513) 556-5191 Contact: Tom Hathaway
Unspecified athletic aid available
M: baseball, basketball, cross country, diving, football, golf, indoor track, soccer, swimming, swimming-diving, tennis, track & field
W: basketball, cross country, diving, golf, soccer, swimming, swimming-diving, tennis, volleyball

UNIVERSITY OF DAYTON
300 College Park
Dayton, OH 45469
(513) 229-4460 Contact: Doug Hauschild
Men's Aid (#/$): 27/$378,000
Women's Aid (#/$): 24/$336,000
M: baseball, basketball, soccer. Men's Non-aid: cross country, football, golf, tennis, water polo, wrestling
W: basketball, soccer, volleyball. Women's Non-aid: cross country, golf, softball, tennis

UNIVERSITY OF FINDLAY
1000 North Main Street
Findlay, OH 45840
(419) 424-4727 Contact: David Faiella
Unspecified athletic aid available
M: baseball, basketball, cross country, diving, football, golf, indoor track, soccer, swimming, tennis, track & field, wrestling
W: basketball, cross country, diving, indoor track, soccer, softball, swimming, tennis, track & field, volleyball

UNIVERSITY OF RIO GRANDE
218 North Atwood Street
Rio Grande, OH 45674
(614) 245-5353 Contact: Kevin E. Kelly
Unspecified athletic aid available
M: baseball, basketball, cheerleading, cross country, soccer, track & field
W: basketball, cheerleading, softball, track & field, volleyball

UNIVERSITY OF TOLEDO
2801 West Bancroft Street
Toledo, OH 43606-3390
(419) 537-3790 Contact: John McNamara
Unspecified athletic aid available
M: baseball, basketball, cross country, diving, football, golf, indoor track, swimming, swimming-diving, tennis, track & field, wrestling
W: basketball, cross country, field hockey, indoor track, softball, tennis, track & field, volleyball

URBANA UNIVERSITY
One College Way
Urbana, OH 43078
(513) 652-1301 Contact: Ron Bolender
Unspecified athletic aid available
M: baseball, basketball, cheerleading, cross country, golf, indoor track, track & field
W: basketball, cheerleading, cross country, golf, indoor track, softball, track & field

WALSH COLLEGE
2020 Easton Street NW
Canton, OH 44720
(216) 499-7090 X. 512 Contact: Jim Clark
Unspecified athletic aid available
M: baseball, basketball, cross country, golf, soccer, tennis, track & field
W: basketball, cross country, softball, tennis, track & field, volleyball. Women's Non-aid: synchronized swimming

WILMINGTON COLLEGE
Pyle Center, Box 1265
Wilmington, OH 45177
(513) 382-6661 X. 314 Contact: Kara Hitchens

Men's Non-aid: baseball, basketball, cross country, football, golf, soccer, tennis, track & field, wrestling
Women's Non-aid: basketball, cross country, soccer, softball, tennis, track & field, volleyball

WRIGHT STATE UNIVERSITY
Nutter Center
Dayton, OH 45435
(513) 873-2771 Contact: Peggy Wynkoop
Men's Aid (#/$): 46.5/$384,429
Women's Aid (#/$): 34.4/$285,386
M: baseball, basketball, cross country, golf, soccer, swimming, swimming-diving, tennis
W: basketball, cross country, soccer, softball, swimming, swimming-diving, tennis, volleyball

XAVIER UNIVERSITY
3800 Victory Parway
Cincinnati, OH 45207
(513) 745-3416 Contact: Tom Eiser
Unspecified athletic aid available
M: basketball. Men's Non-aid: cross country
W: basketball. Women's Non-aid: cross country

YOUNGSTOWN STATE UNIVERSITY
410 Wick Avenue
Youngstown, OH 44555-0001
(216) 742-3501 Contact: William T. Collins, Jr.
Men's Non-aid: baseball, basketball, cross country, diving, football, golf, soccer, swimming, tennis, track & field
Women's Non-aid: basketball, cross country, diving, softball, swimming, tennis, track & field, volleyball

Oklahoma

BACONE JUNIOR COLLEGE
Muskogee, OK 74403
2-year college
(918) 683-4581 Contact: Bill Barnett
Unspecified athletic aid available
M: baseball, basketball. Men's Non-aid: cross country, track & field
W: basketball, softball. Women's Non-aid: cross country, track & field

BARTLESVILLE WESLEYAN
2201 Silver Lake Road
Bartlesville, OK 74006
(918) 335-6219 Contact: Brian L. Jenner
Unspecified athletic aid available
M: basketball, soccer
W: basketball

CAMERON UNIVERSITY
2800 Gore Boulevard
Lawton, OK 73505
(405) 581-2303 Contact: Hank Bradley
Men's Aid (#/$): 66/$130,000
Women's Aid (#/$): 34/$67,000
M: baseball, basketball, football, golf
W: basketball, softball, tennis, volleyball

CARL ALBERT JUNIOR COLLEGE
1507 South McKenna
Poteau, OK 74953-5208
2-year college
(918) 647-8660 Contact: Bill San Millan
Unspecified athletic aid available
M: baseball, basketball
W: basketball

CONNORS STATE COLLEGE
1000 College Road
Warner, OK 74469
2-year college
(918) 463-2931 X. 249 Contact: Gary Snyder
Unspecified athletic aid available
M: baseball, basketball, tennis
W: basketball, softball, tennis

EAST CENTRAL UNIVERSITY
East 14th Street
Ada, OK 74820-6899
(405) 332-8000 X. 258 Contact: John Long
Unspecified athletic aid available

M: basketball, football. Men's Non-aid: baseball, golf, tennis, track & field
W: basketball, tennis

EASTERN OKLAHOMA STATE COLLEGE
Wilburton, OK 74578
2-year college
(918) 465-2361 Contact: Anna Vee Hill
Unspecified athletic aid available
M: baseball, basketball, cross country, indoor track, rodeo, track & field. Men's Non-aid: gymnastics, swimming, tennis
W: basketball, cross country, indoor track, track & field. Women's Non-aid: gymnastics, swimming, tennis

LANGSTON UNIVERSITY
P.O. Box 175
Langston, OK 73050
(405) 466-3243 Contact: James W. Hillard Jr.
Unspecified athletic aid available
M: basketball, football. Men's Non-aid: track & field
W: basketball. Women's Non-aid: track & field

NORTHEASTERN STATE UNIVERSITY
600 North Grand Avenue
Tahlequah, OK 74464-2399
(918) 456-5511 Contact: Doug Quinn
Men's Aid: (#/$): 32/$108,800
Women's Aid: (#/$): 10/$34,000
M: basketball, football. Men's Non-Aid: baseball, golf, soccer, tennis, track & field
W: basketball, softball. Women's Non-Aid: tennis

NORTHWESTERN OKLAHOMA STATE UNIVERSITY
Oklahoma Boulevard
Alva, OK 73717
(405) 327-1700 X. 405 Contact: Justin Tinder
Unspecified athletic aid available
M: baseball, basketball, football, rodeo. Men's Non-aid: golf, power lifting, tennis
W: basketball. Women's Non-aid: golf, tennis

OKLAHOMA BAPTIST UNIVERSITY
Box 61738 OBU
Shawnee, OK 74801
(405) 878-2105 Contact: Marty O'Gwynn
Men's Aid (#/$): 33/$256,245
Women's Aid (#/$): 14/$108,710
M: baseball, basketball, cross country, tennis, track & field
W: basketball, softball

OKLAHOMA CHRISTIAN UNIVERSITY OF SCIENCE & ART
Box 11000
Oklahoma City, OK 73136
(405) 425-5000 Contact: Larry Hollingsworth
Men's Aid (#/$): 40/$308,500
Women's Aid (#/$): 12.5/$94,675
M: baseball, basketball, cross country, indoor track, soccer, tennis, track & field
W: basketball, cross country, indoor track, track & field

OKLAHOMA CITY UNIVERSITY
2501 North Blackwelder
Oklahoma City, OK 73106
(405) 521-5211 Contact: Vicki Hendrickson
Men's Aid (#/$): 46/$431,730
Women's Aid (#/$): 31/$292,190
M: baseball, basketball, golf, soccer, tennis
W: basketball, softball, tennis

OKLAHOMA STATE UNIVERSITY
202 Gallagher Iba Arena
Stillwater, OK 74078-0300
(405) 744-5749 Contact: Steve Buzzard
Men's Aid (#/$): 198/$1,061,496
Women's Aid (#/$): 53/$301,731
M: baseball, basketball, cross country, football, golf, indoor track, tennis, track & field, wrestling

W: basketball, cross country, golf, indoor track, softball, tennis, track & field

ORAL ROBERTS UNIVERSITY
7777 South Lewis Avenue
Tulsa, OK 74171
(918) 495-7102 Contact: Bob Brooks
Men's Aid (#/$): 68/$600,000
Women's Aid (#/$): 46/$500,000
M: baseball, basketball, cross country, golf, indoor track, soccer, swimming, tennis
W: basketball, cross country, golf, indoor track, tennis, volleyball

PANHANDLE STATE UNIVERSITY
P.O. Box 430
Goodwell, OK 73939
(405) 349-2611 X. 224 Contact: M.C. Rider
Unspecified athletic aid available
M: basketball, cross country, football, track & field
W: basketball, cheerleading, cross country, track & field

PHILLIPS UNIVERSITY
100 South University Avenue
Enid, OK 73701
(405) 237-4433 Contact: Shawn Martin
Unspecified athletic aid available
M: baseball, basketball, soccer, tennis
W: basketball

ROSE STATE JUNIOR COLLEGE
6420 SE 15th Street
Midwest City, OK 73110
2-year college
(405) 733-7350 Contact: Les Berryhill
Unspecified athletic aid available
M: baseball, basketball. Men's Non-aid: diving, gymnastics, swimming, swimming-diving, tennis, weightlifting
W: basketball. Women's Non-aid: diving, gymnastics, swimming, swimming-diving, tennis, weightlifting

SEMINOLE JUNIOR COLLEGE
P.O. Box 351
Seminole, OK 74868
2-year college
(405) 382-9950 Contact: Jim Cook
Unspecified athletic aid available
M: baseball, basketball
W: basketball

SOUTHEASTERN OKLAHOMA STATE UNIVERSITY
University Boulevard
Durant, OK 74701
(405) 924-0121 X. 406 Contact: Sherry Foster
Men's Aid (#/$): 95/$139,578
Women's Aid (#/$): 15/$22,551
M: baseball, basketball, equestrian, football, golf, rodeo, tennis, track & field
W: basketball, equestrian, golf, rodeo, tennis, track & field

SOUTHERN NAZARENE UNIVERSITY
6729 NW 39th Expressway
Bethany, OK 73008
(405) 789-6400 Contact: Diana Lee
Men's Aid (#/$): 19.2/$166,448
Women's Aid (#/$): 15/$129,417
M: basketball, soccer
W: basketball, volleyball

SOUTHWESTERN OKLAHOMA STATE UNIVERSITY
100 Campus Drive
Weatherford, OK 73096
(405) 772-6611 X. 3786 Contact: Larry Hollingworth
Men's Aid (#/$): 45/$135,000
Women's Aid (#/$): 10/$30,000
M: baseball, basketball, football, golf, tennis, track & field
W: basketball, tennis

ST. GREGORY'S COLLEGE
1900 West MacArthur
Shawnee, OK 74801
2-year college
(405) 273-9870 Contact: Alan Wilson
Unspecified athletic aid available
M: basketball. Men's Non-aid: fencing, golf, tennis

W: basketball. Women's Non-aid: fencing, tennis

UNIVERSITY OF CENTRAL OKLAHOMA
100 North University Drive
Edmond, OK 73034
(405) 341-2980 X. 2142 Contact: John "Skip" Wagnon
Men's Aid (#/$): 85/$340,789
Women's Aid (#/$): 27/$107,575
M: baseball, basketball, cross country, football, golf, indoor track, tennis, track & field, wrestling
W: basketball, cross country, indoor track, softball, tennis, track & field, volleyball

UNIVERSITY OF OKLAHOMA
Memorial Stadium
Norman, OK 73019
(405) 325-8231 Contact: Mike Treps
Unspecified athletic aid available
M: baseball, basketball, cross country, football, golf, gymnastics, indoor track, tennis, track & field, wrestling
W: basketball, cross country, golf, gymnastics, indoor track, softball, tennis, track & field, volleyball

UNIVERSITY OF TULSA
600 South College Avenue
Tulsa, OK 74104
(918) 631-2383 Contact: David Wentling
Men's Aid (#/$): 129/$1,686,675
Women's Aid (#/$): 36/$470,700
M: basketball, cross country, football, golf, indoor track, soccer, tennis, track & field
W: cross country, golf, indoor track, soccer, softball, tennis, track & field, volleyball

Oregon

BLUE MOUNTAIN COLLEGE
P.O. Box 100
Pendleton, OR 97801
2-year college
(503) 276-1260 Contact: Larry Bartee
Unspecified athletic aid available
M: basketball, tennis, track & field.
Men's Non-aid: baseball
W: basketball, tennis, track & field, volleyball

CHEMEKETA COMMUNITY COLLEGE
4000 Lancaster Drive
Salem, OR 97303
2-year college
(503) 399-5081 Contact: Ward Paldanius
Unspecified athletic aid available
M: basketball, track & field
W: basketball, track & field, volleyball

CLACKAMAS COMMUNITY COLLEGE
19600 South Molalla Avenue
Oregon City, OR 97045
2-year college
(503) 657-6958 X. 2435 Contact: Mike Hodges
Unspecified athletic aid available
M: baseball, basketball, cross country, track & field, wrestling
W: basketball, cross country, softball, track & field, volleyball

COLUMBIA CHRISTIAN COLLEGE
Portland, OR 97220
(503) 257-1209 Contact: Terry Fields
Unspecified athletic aid available
M: basketball. Men's Non-aid: soccer
W: volleyball. Women's Non-aid: basketball

EASTERN OREGON STATE COLLEGE
1410 L Street
La Grande, OR 97850-2899
(503) 962-3326 Contact: Bob Evans
Men's Non-aid: alpine skiing, baseball, basketball, cross country, cross country skiing, football, softball
Women's Non-aid: alpine skiing, basketball, cross country, cross country skiing, volleyball

GEORGE FOX COLLEGE
414 North Meridian Street
Newberg, OR 97132
(503) 538-8383 Contact: Barry Hubbell
Men's Aid (#/$): 174/$235,150
Women's Aid (#/$): 157/$156,250
M: baseball, basketball, cross country, soccer, track & field
W: basketball, cross country, soccer, softball, track & field, volleyball

LANE COMMUNITY COLLEGE
4000 East 30th Avenue
Eugene, OR 97405
2-year college
(503) 726-2215 Contact: Sue Thompson
Men's Aid (#/$): 33/$9,504
Women's Aid (#/$): 33/$9,504
Restrictions and notes: Aid offered only to athletes from AK, HI, WA, OR, CA, ID, MT, and British Columbia.
M: basketball, track & field
W: basketball, track & field

LEWIS AND CLARK COLLEGE
0615 S.W. Palatine Hill Road
Portland, OR 97219
(503) 768-7067 Contact: Steve Wallo
Men's Non-aid: baseball, basketball, cross country, football, golf, soccer, swimming-diving, tennis, track & field
Women's Non-aid: basketball, cross country, soccer, softball, swimming-diving, tennis, track & field, volleyball

LINFIELD COLLEGE
900 South Baker
McMinnville, OR 97128-8947
(503) 472-9978 X. 439 Contact: Kelly Bird
Men's Non-aid: baseball, basketball, cross country, football, golf, soccer, swimming, tennis, track & field, wrestling
Women's Non-aid: basketball, cross country, soccer, softball, swimming, tennis, track & field, volleyball

MULTNOMAH SCHOOL OF THE BIBLE
8435 Glisan, NE
Portland, OR 97220
2-year college
(503) 255-0332 Contact: Stan Hansen
Men's Non-aid: basketball, soccer, tennis
Women's Non-aid: volleyball

OREGON INSTITUTE OF TECHNOLOGY
3201 Campus Drive
Klamath Falls, OR 97601
(503) 885-1000 X. 224 Contact: John C. Huntley
Men's Non-aid: baseball, basketball, football, wrestling
Women's Non-aid: basketball, softball, volleyball

OREGON STATE UNIVERSITY
103 Gill Coliseum
Corvallis, OR 97331
(503) 737-3720 Contact: Hal Cowan
Unspecified athletic aid available
M: baseball, basketball, cross country, football, golf, softball, track & field, wrestling. Men's Non-aid: crew
W: baseball, basketball, cross country, golf, gymnastics, softball, swimming-diving, track & field, volleyball. Women's Non-aid: crew, tennis

PACIFIC UNIVERSITY
2043 College Way
Forest Grove, OR 97116
(503) 357-6151 Contact: Ken Schumann
Men's Non-aid: baseball, basketball, cross country, golf, handball, soccer, tennis, track & field, wrestling
Women's Non-aid: basketball, cross country, golf, handball, soccer, softball, tennis, track & field, volleyball

PORTLAND STATE UNIVERSITY
P.O. Box 751
Portland, OR 97207
(503) 725-2525 Contact: Larry Sellers
Men's Aid (#/$): 106/$371,716
Women's Aid (#/$): 38/$128,844
M: baseball, cross country, football, golf, track & field, wrestling
W: basketball, cross country, softball, tennis, track & field, volleyball

SOUTHERN OREGON STATE COLLEGE
1250 Siskiyou Boulevard
Ashland, OR 97520
(503) 552-6411 Contact: Al Blaszak
Men's Non-aid: basketball, cross country, football, indoor track, soccer, swimming, tennis, track & field, water polo, wrestling
Women's Non-aid: basketball, cross country, indoor track, soccer, swimming, tennis, track & field, volleyball, water polo

SOUTHWESTERN OREGON COMMUNITY COLLEGE
1988 Newmark
Coos Bay, OR 97420
2-year college
(503) 888-2525 Contact: John Speasl
Men's Aid: (#/$): 45/$14,580
Women's Aid: (#/$): 48/$15,552
Unspecified athletic aid available
M: basketball, track & field wrestling
W: basketball, volleyball

UMPQUA COLLEGE
P.O. Box 967
Roseburg, OR 97470
2-year college
(503) 440-4600 Contact: Cy Perkins
Unspecified athletic aid available
M: basketball, cross country, track & field
W: basketball, cross country, track & field, volleyball

UNIVERSITY OF OREGON
Casanova Center
Eugene, OR 97403
(503) 346-5488 Contact: Steve Hellyer
Men's Aid (#/$): 151/$785,027
Women's Aid (#/$): 90/$557,472
M: basketball, cross country, football, golf, tennis, track & field, wrestling
W: basketball, cross country, golf, softball, tennis, track & field, volleyball

UNIVERSITY OF PORTLAND
5000 North Williamette Boulevard
Portland, OR 97203-5798
(503) 283-7117 Contact: Steve Walker
Unspecified athletic aid available
M: baseball, basketball, cross country, golf, soccer, tennis, track & field
W: basketball, cross country, soccer, tennis, track & field, volleyball

WARNER PACIFIC COLLEGE
2219 SE 68th Street
Portland, OR 97215
(503) 775-4366 Contact: John Eakman
Men's Aid (#/$): 10/$11,600
Women's Aid (#/$): 6/$8,350
M: basketball, soccer
W: basketball, volleyball. Women's Non-aid: softball

WESTERN OREGON STATE COLLEGE
AD 308
Monmouth, OR 97361-1394
(503) 838-8308 Contact: Steve Weaver
Men's Non-aid: baseball, basketball, cross country, football, indoor track, track & field
Women's Non-aid: basketball, cross country, indoor track, softball, track & field, volleyball

WILLAMETTE UNIVERSITY
900 State Street
Salem, OR 97301
(503) 370-6110 Contact: Cliff Voliva
Men's Non-aid: baseball, basketball, cross country, diving, football, golf, indoor track, lacrosse, soccer, swimming, swimming-diving, tennis, track & field, weightlifting
Women's Non-aid: basketball, cross country, diving, indoor track, softball, swimming, swimming-diving, tennis, track & field, volleyball

Pennsylvania

ALBRIGHT COLLEGE
P.O. Box 15234
Reading, PA 19612-5234

(215) 921-2381 Contact: Elliot Tannenbaum
Men's Non-aid: baseball, basketball, cross country, football, golf, soccer, tennis, track & field, wrestling
Women's Non-aid: badminton, basketball, cross country, field hockey, softball, tennis, track & field, volleyball

ALLEGHENY CCAC
808 Ridge Avenue
Pittsburgh, PA 15212-6097
2-year college
(412) 237-2633
Men's Aid (#/$): 8/$11,558
Women's Aid (#/$): 6/$8,668
M: baseball, basketball, soccer, tennis
W: basketball, tennis

ALLEGHENY COLLEGE
P.O. Box 40
Meadville, PA 16335
(814) 332-6755 Contact: Steve Mest
Men's Non-aid: baseball, basketball, cross country, diving, football, golf, indoor track, soccer, swimming, swimming-diving, tennis, track & field
Women's Non-aid: basketball, cross country, diving, indoor track, soccer, softball, swimming, swimming-diving, tennis, track & field, volleyball

ALLENTOWN COLLEGE
2755 Station Avenue
Center Valley, PA 18034-9568
(215) 282-1100 Contact: John Gump
Men's Non-aid: baseball, basketball, cross country, soccer, tennis
Women's Non-aid: basketball, cross country, softball, tennis, volleyball

ALVERNIA COLLEGE
400 Saint Bernardine Street
Reading, PA 19607
(215) 777-5411 X. 275 Contact: Vali G. Heist
Unspecified athletic aid available
M: baseball, basketball, cross country. Men's Non-aid: golf
W: softball, volleyball. Women's Non-aid: basketball, cross country

BLOOMSBURG UNIVERSITY
Waller Administration Building
Bloomsburg, PA 17815
(717) 389-4413 Contact: Jim Hollister
Men's Aid ($): $143,085
Women's Aid ($): $103,068
M: baseball, basketball, football, swimming-diving, tennis, wrestling.
Men's Non-aid: cross country, soccer, track & field
W: basketball, diving, field hockey, soccer, softball, swimming, tennis.
Women's Non-aid: cross country, track & field

BRYN MAWR COLLEGE
Bern/Schwartz Gymnasium
Bryn Mawr, PA 19010
(215) 526-7348 Contact: Diane DiBonaventuro
Men's Non-aid: badminton, basketball
Women's Non-aid: badminton, basketball, cross country, field hockey, lacrosse, soccer, swimming, tennis, volleyball

BUCKNELL UNIVERSITY
Davis Gym
Lewisburg, PA 17837
(717) 524-1227 Contact: Bo Smolka
Restrictions and notes: All aid is need based and is granted through the Financial Aid Office.
Men's Non-aid: baseball, basketball, crew, cross country, field hockey, football, golf, indoor track, lacrosse, soccer, swimming, tennis, track & field, water polo, wrestling
Women's Non-aid: basketball, crew, cross country, indoor track, lacrosse, soccer, softball, swimming, tennis, track & field, volleyball

BUCKS COUNTY COMMUNITY COLLEGE
Swamp Road
Newton, PA 19030
2-year college
(215) 968-8450 Contact: Louis Pacchioli
Men's Non-aid: baseball, basketball,

cross country, equestrian, golf, soccer, tennis
Women's Non-aid: basketball, cross country, equestrian, golf, soccer, softball, tennis

BUTLER COUNTY COMMUNITY COLLEGE
P.O. Box 1203
Butler, PA 16003-1203
2-year college
(412) 287-8711 Contact: Charles W. Dunaway
Men's Non-aid: baseball, basketball, golf, racquetball, tennis
Women's Non-aid: softball, tennis, volleyball

CABRINI COLLEGE
610 King of Prussia Road
Radnor, PA 19087
(215) 971-8387 Contact: Dennis Wise
Men's Non-aid: baseball, basketball, cross country, soccer, softball, tennis, track & field
Women's Non-aid: baseball, basketball, cross country, field hockey, softball, tennis, track & field, volleyball

CALIFORNIA UNIVERSITY
Hamer Hall
California, PA 15419
(412) 938-4552 Contact: Bruce Wald
Men's Aid (#/$): 40/$200,000
Women's Aid (#/$): 30/$145,000
M: baseball, basketball, cross country, football, soccer, track & field, wrestling. Men's Non-aid: basketball, cross country, soccer, softball, tennis, track & field, volleyball

CARLOW COLLEGE
Pittsburgh, PA 15213
(412) 578-6058 Contact: Natalie Friedman
Women's Aid (#/$): 20/$45,400
W: basketball, cross country, volleyball. Women's Non-aid: crew

CARNEGIE-MELLON UNIVERSITY
5000 Forbes Avenue
Pittsburgh, PA 15213
(412) 268-3087 Contact: Bruce Gerson
Men's Non-aid: basketball, cross country, football, indoor track, soccer, swimming, tennis, track & field
Women's Non-aid: basketball, cross country, indoor track, soccer, swimming, tennis, track & field, volleyball

CHEYNEY UNIVERSITY OF PENNSYLVANIA
Creek Road
Cheyney, PA 19319
(215) 399-2025 Contact: George Heaslip
Men's Non-aid: basketball, cross country, football, soccer, tennis, track & field, wrestling
Women's Non-aid: basketball, soccer, tennis, track & field, volleyball

CLARION UNIVERSITY
974 Wood Street
Alumni House
Clarion, PA 16214
(814) 226-2334 Contact: Rich Herman
Unspecified athletic aid available
M: baseball, basketball, cheerleading, cross country, diving, football, golf, swimming, track & field, wrestling
W: basketball, cross country, diving, softball, swimming, tennis, track & field, volleyball

COLLEGE OF ALLEGHENY COUNTY
1750 Clairton Road
West Mifflin, PA 15212
2-year college
(412) 469-6245 Contact: Lee Frank
Men's Aid (#/$): 6/$7,200
Women's Aid (#/$): 2/$2,400
M: baseball, basketball. Men's Non-aid: bowling, golf, ice hockey, tennis
W: softball. Women's Non-aid: bowling, golf, tennis

DELAWARE COUNTY COMMUNITY COLLEGE
Route 252 & Media Line Road
Media, PA 19063

2-year college
(215) 359-5047 Contact: Cheryl Massnau
Men's Non-aid: baseball, basketball, cross country, softball, tennis
Women's Non-aid: cross country, softball

DELAWARE VALLEY COLLEGE
700 East Butler Avenue
Doylestown, PA 18901
(215) 345-1500 X. 2937 Contact: Matt Levy
Men's Non-aid: baseball, basketball, cross country, football, golf, soccer, track & field, wrestling
Women's Non-aid: basketball, cross country, field hockey, softball, track & field, volleyball

DICKINSON COLLEGE
Kline Life/Sports Center
Carlisle, PA 17013-2896
(717) 245-1652 Contact: Larry L. Shenk
Men's Non-aid: baseball, basketball, cross country, football, golf, indoor track, lacrosse, soccer, swimming, tennis, track & field
Women's Non-aid: basketball, cross country, field hockey, indoor track, lacrosse, soccer, softball, swimming, tennis, track & field, volleyball

DREXEL UNIVERSITY
32nd and Chestnut Streets
Building #14-318
Philadelphia, PA 19104
(215) 590-8946 Contact: Rob Wilson
Unspecified athletic aid available
M: baseball, basketball, cross country, diving, indoor track, lacrosse, soccer, swimming, swimming-diving, track & field, wrestling. Men's Non-aid: crew, golf, tennis
W: basketball, diving, field hockey, lacrosse, softball, swimming, swimming-diving, volleyball. Women's Non-aid: crew, tennis

DUQUESNE UNIVERSITY
A.J. Palumbo Center
Pittsburgh, PA 15282
(412) 434-6564 Contact: Nellie King
Men's Aid (#/$): 25/$75,781
Women's Aid (#/$): 14/$76,989
M: baseball, basketball, cross country, swimming, tennis
W: basketball, swimming, tennis, volleyball. Women's Non-aid: cross country, track & field

EASTERN COLLEGE
10 Fairview Drive
St. Davids, PA 19087
(215) 341-5937 Contact: Trish English
Men's Non-aid: baseball, basketball, cross country, soccer, tennis
Women's Non-aid: basketball, cross country, field hockey, lacrosse, soccer, softball, tennis, volleyball

EAST STROUDSBURG UNIVERSITY
Koehler Fieldhouse
Office 9
East Stroudsburg, PA 18301
(717) 424-3312 Contact: Peter Nevins
Men's Aid (#/$): 9/$10,800
Women's Aid (#/$): 1/$1,250
M: basketball, football, soccer, wrestling. Men's Non-aid: baseball, cross country, golf, gymnastics, indoor track, swimming-diving, tennis, track & field, volleyball
W: basketball, softball. Women's Non-aid: cross country, field hockey, gymnastics, indoor track, lacrosse, swimming-diving, tennis, track & field, volleyball

EDINBORO UNIVERSITY OF PENNSYLVANIA
RT 6N
Edinboro, PA 16444
(814) 732-2811 Contact: Todd B. Jay
Men's Aid (#/$): 34/$65,733
Women's Aid (#/$): 30/$17,836
M: basketball, cross country, football, wrestling. Men's Non-aid: baseball, soccer, swimming-diving, tennis, track & field, volleyball
W: basketball, cross country. Women's

Non-aid: softball, swimming-diving, tennis, track & field

ELIZABETHTOWN COLLEGE
One Alpha Drive
Elizabethtown, PA 17022-2298
(717) 367-1151 X. 311 Contact: Brad Brubaker
Men's Non-aid: baseball, basketball, cross country, diving, soccer, swimming, swimming-diving, tennis, wrestling
Women's Non-aid: basketball, cross country, diving, field hockey, softball, swimming, swimming-diving, tennis, volleyball

FRANKLIN & MARSHALL COLLEGE
P.O. Box 3003
Lancaster, PA 17604-3003
(717) 291-3838 Contact: Tom Byrnes
Men's Non-aid: baseball, basketball, crew, cross country, field hockey, football, golf, ice hockey, indoor track, lacrosse, soccer, squash, swimming, tennis, track & field, wrestling
Women's Non-aid: basketball, crew, cross country, field hockey, indoor track, lacrosse, soccer, softball, squash, swimming, tennis, track & field, volleyball

GANNON COLLEGE
University Square
Erie, PA 16541
(814) 871-7418 Contact: Bud Elwell
Unspecified athletic aid available
M: baseball, basketball, cross country, diving, football, golf, swimming, swimming-diving, tennis, wrestling.
Men's Non-aid: football
W: basketball, cross country, diving, softball, swimming, swimming-diving, tennis, volleyball

GENEVA COLLEGE
College Avenue
Beaver Falls, PA 15010
(412) 847-6521 Contact: Mark D. Weinstein
Men's Aid (#/$): 111/$308,499
Women's Aid (#/$): 59/$106,214
M: baseball, basketball. Men's Non-aid: cheerleading, cross country, football, indoor track, soccer, tennis, track & field
W: basketball, volleyball. Women's Non-aid: cheerleading, cross country, indoor track, soccer, softball, tennis, track & field, volleyball

GETTYSBURG COLLEGE
North Washington Street
Gettysburg, PA 17325
(717) 337-6527 Contact: Robert Kenworthy
Restrictions and notes: Financial aid strictly based on need.
Men's Non-aid: baseball, basketball, cross country, football, golf, indoor track, lacrosse, soccer, swimming, tennis, track & field, wrestling
Women's Non-aid: basketball, cross country, field hockey, golf, indoor track, lacrosse, soccer, softball, swimming, tennis, track & field

GROVE CITY COLLEGE
100 Campus Drive
Grove City, PA 16127-2104
(412) 458-2000 Contact: Joe Klimchak
Men's Non-aid: baseball, basketball, bowling, cross country, football, golf, soccer, softball, swimming-diving, tennis, track & field
Women's Non-aid: baseball, basketball, cross country, softball, swimming-diving, tennis, track & field, volleyball

HAVERFORD COLLEGE
370 Lancaster Avenue
Haverford, PA 19041
(215) 896-1117 Contact: Jeremy Edwards
Men's Non-aid: baseball, basketball, cross country, fencing, indoor track, lacrosse, soccer, tennis, track & field, wrestling
Women's Non-aid: basketball, field hockey, lacrosse, soccer, tennis, volleyball

HOLY FAMILY COLLEGE
Office of Financial Aid
Grant and Frankford Avenues
Philadelphia, PA 19114
(215) 637-7700 X. 234 Contact: Anna M. Raffaele
Men's Aid (#/$): 25/$87,400
Women's Aid (#/$): 26/$82,200
M: basketball, soccer
W: basketball, soccer

INDIANA UNIVERSITY OF PENNSYLVANIA
102 Memorial Field House
Indiana, PA 15705
(412) 357-2747 Contact: Larry Judge
Men's Aid (#/$): 44/$62,000
Women's Aid (#/$): 44/$62,000
M: basketball, football. Men's Non-aid: baseball, cross country, golf, riflery, soccer, swimming-diving, tennis, track & field
W: basketball, cross country, gymnastics, track & field. Women's Non-aid: field hockey, softball, swimming-diving, tennis, volleyball

JUNIATA COLLEGE
18th and Moore Streets
Huntingdon, PA 16652
(814) 643-4310 X. 230 Contact: Joe Scialabba
Men's Non-aid: baseball, basketball, cross country, football, golf, soccer, softball, swimming-diving, tennis, track & field, wrestling
Women's Non-aid: baseball, basketball, cross country, field hockey, golf, softball, swimming-diving, tennis, track & field, volleyball

KEYSTONE JUNIOR COLLEGE
La Plume, PA 18440-0200
2-year college
(717) 945-5142 Contact: Dennis Mishko
Men's Non-aid: baseball, basketball, soccer, tennis, wrestling
Women's Non-aid: basketball, field hockey, softball

KING'S COLLEGE
133 North Main Street
Wilkes-Barre, PA 18711
(717) 826-5900 Contact: John Engel
Men's Non-aid: baseball, basketball, cross country, diving, golf, riflery, soccer, swimming, swimming-diving, tennis, wrestling
Women's Non-aid: basketball, cross country, diving, riflery, softball, swimming, swimming-diving, tennis, volleyball

KUTZTOWN UNIVERSITY
College Hill
Kutztown, PA 19530
(215) 683-4095 Contact: Clark Yeaczr
Men's Aid ($): $81,500
Women's Aid ($): $57,500
M: basketball, cross country, diving, football, indoor track, soccer, swimming, tennis, track & field, wrestling. Men's Non-aid: baseball
W: basketball, cross country, diving, field hockey, indoor track, soccer, softball, swimming, tennis, track & field, volleyball

LACKAWANNA JUNIOR COLLEGE
901 Prospect Avenue
Scranton, PA 18505
2-year college
(717) 961-7818 Contact: Tim Dempsey
Men's Aid (#/$): 33/$40,000
Women's Aid (#/$): 26/$33,000
Restrictions and notes: Scholarships only cover tuition and fees.
M: baseball, basketball, golf
W: basketball, cheerleading, softball, volleyball

LAFAYETTE COLLEGE
17 Watson Hall
Easton, PA 18042
(215) 250-5122 Contact: Steve Pulver
Men's Non-aid: baseball, basketball, crew, cross country, fencing, football, golf, indoor track, lacrosse, power lifting, rugby, soccer, swimming,

swimming-diving, tennis, track & field, weightlifting, wrestling
Women's Non-aid: basketball, cross country, fencing, field hockey, indoor track, lacrosse, softball, swimming, swimming-diving, tennis, track & field, volleyball

LA ROCHE COLLEGE
9000 Babcock Boulevard
Pittsburgh, PA 15237
(412) 367-9275 Contact: Lynn M. Butler
Men's Non-aid: baseball, basketball, soccer
Women's Non-aid: basketball, softball, volleyball

LA SALLE UNIVERSITY
1900 West Olney Avenue
Philadelphia, PA 19141
(215) 951-1605 Contact: Michael Felici
Unspecified athletic aid available
M: baseball, basketball, crew, cross country, indoor track, soccer, swimming-diving, tennis, track & field. Men's Non-aid: wrestling
W: basketball, cross country, field hockey, indoor track, squash, softball, swimming-diving, tennis, track & field, volleyball. Women's Non-aid: crew

LEBANON VALLEY COLLEGE
101 North College Avenue
Annville, PA 17003
(717) 867-6033 Contact: John Dearner
Unspecified athletic aid available
M: baseball, basketball, cross country, football, golf, soccer, track & field, wrestling
W: basketball, cross country, field hockey, softball, track & field

LEHIGH COUNTY COMMUNITY COLLEGE
4525 Education Park Drive
Schnecksville, PA 18078
2-year college
(215) 799-1155 Contact: Douglas Stewart
Men's Non-aid: basketball, golf, tennis
Women's Non-aid: golf, tennis, volleyball

LEHIGH UNIVERSITY
436 Brodhead Avenue
Bethlehem, PA 18015
(215) 758-3174 Contact: Glenn Hofmann
Unspecified athletic aid available
M: wrestling. Men's Non-aid: baseball, basketball, cross country, football, golf, ice hockey, indoor track, lacrosse, riflery, soccer, squash, swimming, swimming-diving, tennis, track & field
Women's Non-aid: basketball, cross country, field hockey, lacrosse, riflery, softball, swimming, swimming-diving, tennis, volleyball

LOCK HAVEN UNIVERSITY OF PENNSYLVANIA
Akeley Hall
Lock Haven, PA 17745
(717) 893-2350 Contact: Pat Donghia
Unspecified athletic aid available
M: basketball, football, soccer, wrestling
W: basketball, field hockey

LYCOMING COLLEGE
Academy Street
Williamsport, PA 17701
(717) 321-4020 Contact: Jerry Zufelt
Men's Non-aid: basketball, cross country, football, golf, soccer, swimming-diving, tennis, track & field, wrestling
Women's Non-aid: basketball, cross country, field hockey, swimming-diving, tennis, track & field

MANSFIELD UNIVERSITY
Doane Center
Mansfield, PA 16933
(717) 662-4845 Contact: Steve McCloskey
Unspecified athletic aid available
M: baseball, basketball, cross country,

football, indoor track, track & field, wrestling
W: basketball, cross country, diving, field hockey, indoor track, softball, swimming, swimming-diving, track & field

MARYWOOD COLLEGE
Adams Avenue
Scranton, PA 18509
(717) 348-6259 Contact: Jack Seitzinger
Men's Non-aid: basketball, tennis
Women's Non-aid: basketball, field hockey, softball, tennis, volleyball

MERCYHURST COLLEGE
501 East 38th Street
Erie, PA 16546
(814) 824-2228 Contact: Pete Russo
Men's Aid (#/$): $330,000
Women's Aid (#/$): $210,000
M: baseball, basketball, crew, cross country, golf, soccer, tennis. Men's Non-aid: football, ice hockey
W: basketball, crew, cross country, soccer, softball, tennis, volleyball

MESSIAH COLLEGE
Grantham, PA 17027
(717) 766-2511 Contact: Michael D'Virgilio
Men's Non-aid: baseball, basketball, cross country, soccer, track & field, wrestling
Women's Non-aid: basketball, cross country, field hockey, softball, track & field, volleyball

MILLERSVILLE UNIVERSITY
207 North George Street
Alumni House
Millersville, PA 17551-0302
(717) 872-3100 Contact: Greg Wright
Men's Aid (#/$): 18/$129,728
Women's Aid (#/$): 5/$34,575
Restrictions and notes: All scholarships distributed as partial allocations.
M: baseball, basketball, cross country, football, golf, soccer, tennis, track & field, wrestling
W: basketball, cross country, field hockey, lacrosse, softball, swimming-diving, tennis, track & field, volleyball

MORAVIAN COLLEGE
1200 Main Street
Bethlehem, PA 18018
(215) 861-1365 Contact: Don Cunningham
Men's Non-aid: baseball, basketball, cross country, equestrian, football, golf, ice hockey, indoor track, soccer, tennis, track & field, wrestling
Women's Non-aid: basketball, cross country, equestrian, field hockey, indoor track, tennis, volleyball

MT. ALOYSIUS COLLEGE
One College Drive
Cresson, PA 16630
2-year college
(814) 886-4131 Contact: Dr. Judith Newton
Unspecified athletic aid available
M: basketball
W: basketball

MUHLENBERG COLLEGE
2400 Chew Street
Allentown, PA 18104
(215) 821-3232 Contact: Gracia Perilli
Men's Non-aid: baseball, basketball, cross country, football, golf, soccer, tennis, track & field, wrestling
Women's Non-aid: baseball, crew, fencing, indoor track, sailing, soccer, synchronized swimming, tennis, volleyball

NORTHEASTERN CHRISTIAN JUNIOR COLLEGE
1860 Montgomery Avenue
Villanova, PA 19085
2-year college
(215) 525-6780 Contact: Natillie Garner
Unspecified athletic aid available
M: basketball, bowling, golf, soccer, volleyball
W: basketball, bowling, golf, volleyball

PENN STATE UNIVERSITY
147 Shenango Avenue
Sharon, PA 16146

2-year college
(412) 983-5800 Contact: Shelley Vadino
Men's Non-aid: baseball, basketball
Women's Non-aid: basketball, softball, volleyball

PENN STATE UNIVERSITY
104 Physical Education Building
Abington, PA 19001
2-year college
(215) 881-7445 Contact: Kristin Shearer
Men's Non-aid: baseball, basketball, golf, soccer, tennis
Women's Non-aid: basketball, field hockey, softball, tennis, volleyball

PENN STATE UNIVERSITY
P.O. Box 7009
Tulpehocken Road
Reading, PA 19610
2-year college
(215) 320-4882 Contacy: William Sutherland
Men's Non-aid: basketball, soccer, tennis
Women's Non-aid: tennis, volleyball

PENNSYLVANIA STATE UNIVERSITY
234 Recreation Building
University Park, PA 16802
(814) 865-1757 Contact: L. Budd Thalman
Unspecified athletic aid available
M: baseball, basketball, cross country, football, gymnastics, indoor track, soccer, swimming-diving, tennis, track & field, wrestling. Men's Non-aid: fencing, lacrosse, volleyball
W: basketball, cross country, field hockey, golf, gymnastics, indoor track, softball, swimming-diving, tennis, track & field, volleyball. Women's Non-aid: fencing, lacrosse

PENNSYLVANIA STATE UNIVERSITY (BEHREND COLLEGE)
Station Road
Erie, PA 16563-0107
(814) 898-6322 Contact: Dan Gallegos
Men's Non-aid: baseball, basketball, golf, soccer, tennis, volleyball
Women's Non-aid: basketball, softball, tennis, volleyball

PHILADELPHIA COLLEGE OF PHARMACY AND SCIENCE
43rd and Kingsessing
Philadelphia, PA 19104
(215) 596-8894 Contact: Beverly S. Hayden
Men's Aid (#/$): 3/$9,000
Women's Aid (#/$): 3/$2,200
Athletic programs not specified

PHILADELPHIA COLLEGE OF TEXTILE AND SCIENCE
School House Lane and Henry Avenue
Philadelphia, PA 19144
(215) 951-2720 Contact: Tom Shirley
Men's Aid ($): $377,254
Women's Aid ($): $193,974
M: baseball, basketball, soccer, tennis
W: basketball, soccer, softball, tennis

PHILADELPHIA COMMUNITY COLLEGE
1700 Spring Garden Street
Philadelphia, PA 19130
2-year college
(215) 988-9006 Contact: James Burton
Men's Non-aid: basketball, cross country, soccer, softball, tennis
Women's Non-aid: basketball, cross country, softball, tennis, volleyball

POINT PARK COLLEGE
201 Wood Street
Pittsburgh, PA 15522-1984
(412) 392-3849 Contact: Mark Cohen
Unspecified athletic aid available
M: baseball, basketball, soccer
W: basketball, softball

ROBERT MORRIS COLLEGE
Narrows Run Road
Coraopolis, PA 15108
(412) 262-8315 Contact: Marty Galosi
Men's Aid (#/$): 25/$66,000

Women's Aid (#/$): 17/$42,100
M: basketball, cross country, golf, indoor track, soccer, tennis, track & field
W: basketball, cross country, soccer, softball, tennis, track & field, volleyball

SAINT FRANCIS COLLEGE
Maurice Stokes Building
Loretto, PA 15940
(814) 472-3128 Contact: Kevin Southard
Men's Aid (#/$): 28/unspecified $
Women's Aid (#/$): 28/unspecified $
M: basketball, cross country, golf, indoor track, soccer, tennis, track & field, volleyball. Men's Non-aid: football
W: basketball, cross country, golf, indoor track, soccer, softball, tennis, track & field, volleyball

SAINT JOSEPH'S UNIVERSITY
5600 City Avenue
Philadelphia, PA 19131
(215) 660-1704 Contact: Ken Krsolovic
Unspecified athletic aid available
M: baseball, basketball, cross country, golf, indoor track, soccer, tennis, track & field. Men's Non-aid: crew, lacrosse
W: basketball, cross country, field hockey, indoor track, softball, tennis, track & field. Women's Non-aid: crew, lacrosse

SAINT VINCENT COLLEGE
Latrobe, PA 15650
(412) 539-9761 Contact: Kristen M. Zawacki
Men's Aid ($): $22,250
Women's Aid ($): $22,250
M: baseball, basketball, cross country, lacrosse, soccer, tennis
W: basketball, cross country, softball, volleyball

SETON HILL COLLEGE
Greensburg, PA 15601
(412) 834-2200 Contact: Mary Phillip Aaron
Women's Aid (#/$): 41/$111,892
W: basketball, soccer, softball, tennis, volleyball. Women's Non-aid: cross country, equestrian

SHIPPENSBURG UNIVERSITY OF PENNSYLVANIA
North Prince Street
Shippensburg, PA 17257
(717) 532-1201 Contact: John Alosi
Unspecified athletic aid available
M: baseball, basketball, cross country, diving, football, golf, indoor track, soccer, swimming, tennis, track & field, wrestling
W: basketball, cross country, diving, indoor track, lacrosse, softball, swimming, tennis, track & field, volleyball. Women's Non-aid: field hockey

SLIPPERY ROCK UNIVERSITY OF PENNSYLVANIA
103 Morrow Field House
Slippery Rock, PA 16057-1324
(412) 738-2777 Contact: John R. Carpenter
Men's Aid (#/$): 125/$165,698
Women's Aid (#/$): 52/$57,860
M: baseball, basketball, cross country, football, golf, soccer, swimming-diving, tennis, track & field, wrestling. Men's Non-aid: water polo
W: basketball, cross country, softball, swimming-diving, tennis, track & field, volleyball. Women's Non-aid: field hockey

SWARTHMORE COLLEGE
Athletics Department
Swarthmore, PA 19081
(215) 328-8206 Contact: Mike Greenstone
Men's Non-aid: baseball, basketball, cross country, football, golf, indoor track, lacrosse, soccer, swimming, tennis, track & field, wrestling
Women's Non-aid: badminton, basketball, cross country, field hockey, indoor track, lacrosse, soccer, softball, swimming, tennis, track & field, volleyball

TEMPLE UNIVERSITY
McGonigle Hall 101
Philadelphia, PA 19122
(215) 787-7445 Contact: Al Shrier
Unspecified athletic aid available
M: baseball, basketball, crew, football, golf, gymnastics, soccer, tennis, track & field
W: basketball, fencing, field hockey, gymnastics, lacrosse, softball, tennis, track & field, volleyball

UNIVERSITY OF PENNSYLVANIA
Weightman Hall South
Philadelphia, PA 19104-6322
(215) 898-6128 Contact: Gail Stasulli
Men's Non-aid: baseball, basketball, crew, cross country, fencing, football, indoor track, lacrosse, soccer, squash, swimming-diving, tennis, track & field, wrestling
Women's Non-aid: basketball, crew, cross country, fencing, field hockey, gymnastics, indoor track, lacrosse, squash, softball, swimming-diving, tennis, track & field, volleyball

UNIVERSITY OF PITTSBURGH
P.O. Box 7436
Pittsburgh, PA 15213
(814) 362-7555 Contact: Philip J. Alletto
Unspecified athletic aid available
M: baseball, basketball, cross country, football, gymnastics, indoor track, soccer, swimming, swimming-diving, track & field, wrestling. Men's Non-aid: tennis
W: cross country, gymnastics, indoor track, swimming, swimming-diving, track & field, volleyball. Women's Non-aid: tennis

UNIVERSITY OF PITTSBURGH (BRADFORD)
300 Campus Drive
Bradford, PA 16701
(814) 362-7550 Contact: Philip J. Alletto
Men's Aid (#/$): 10/$50,000
Women's Aid (#/$): 10/$20,000
M: basketball. Men's Non-aid: cross country, soccer
W: basketball. Women's Non-aid: cross country, volleyball

UNIVERSITY OF PITTSBURGH (JOHNSTOWN)
Johnstown, PA 15904
(814) 269-7045 Contact: Thomas Wonders
Unspecified athletic aid available
M: baseball, basketball, wrestling. Men's Non-aid: cross country, golf, indoor track, soccer, track & field
W: basketball, cross country, indoor track, track & field. Women's Non-aid: volleyball

UNIVERSITY OF SCRANTON
John Long Center
Scranton, PA 18510-4650
(717) 941-7571 Contact: Kenneth Buntz
Men's Non-aid: baseball, basketball, cross country, golf, ice hockey, lacrosse, soccer, swimming, swimming-diving, tennis, wrestling
Women's Non-aid: basketball, cross country, field hockey, sailing, softball, swimming-diving, tennis, volleyball

URSINUS COLLEGE
Main Street
Collegeville, PA 19426-1000
(215) 489-4111 X. 2282 Contact: David M. Sherman
Men's Non-aid: baseball, basketball, cross country, football, golf, indoor track, soccer, swimming, tennis, track & field, volleyball, wrestling
Women's Non-aid: basketball, cross country, field hockey, gymnastics, indoor track, lacrosse, softball, swimming, tennis, track & field, volleyball

VALLEY FORGE CHRISTIAN COLLEGE
Box 782
Phoenixville, PA 19460
(215) 935-0450 Contact: Dan Boothman

Men's Non-aid: basketball, soccer
Women's Non-aid: basketball, softball, volleyball

VILLANOVA UNIVERSITY
Lancaster and Ithan Avenues
Villanova, PA 19085-1674
(215) 645-4120 Contact: James H. Delorenzo
Men's Aid (#/$): 122/$2,196,543
Women's Aid (#/$): 55/$926,132
M: baseball, basketball, cross country, football, soccer, swimming-diving. Men's Non-aid: crew, golf, ice hockey, lacrosse, rugby, tennis, volleyball, water polo
W: basketball, cross country, field hockey, soccer, softball, swimming-diving, volleyball. Women's Non-aid: crew, lacrosse, tennis

WASHINGTON AND JEFFERSON COLLEGE
45 South Lincoln Street
Washington, PA 15301
(412) 223-6074 Contact: Susan Isola
Men's Non-aid: baseball, basketball, cross country, football, golf, soccer, swimming-diving, tennis, track & field, wrestling
Women's Non-aid: basketball, cross country, soccer, softball, swimming-diving, tennis, volleyball

WEST CHESTER UNIVERSITY
Hollinger Fieldhouse
West Chester, PA 19383
(215) 436-3317 Contact: Cynthia Ryder
Aid ($): $154,000
Restrictions and notes: Partial athletic grants are offered.
M: baseball, basketball, cross country, diving, football, golf, lacrosse, soccer, swimming, track & field. Men's Non-aid: indoor track, tennis
W: basketball, cross country, diving, field hockey, gymnastics, lacrosse, soccer, softball, swimming, track & field, volleyball. Women's Non-aid: indoor track, tennis

WESTMINSTER COLLEGE
New Wilmington, PA 16172
(412) 946-7190 Contact: Dan Irwin
Unspecified athletic aid available
M: basketball, football. Men's Non-aid: baseball, cross country, golf, soccer, swimming, swimming-diving, tennis, track & field
W: basketball, softball, tennis, volleyball

WILKES UNIVERSITY
P.O. Box 111
Wilkes-Barre, PA 18766
(717) 831-4777 Contact: Tom McGuire
Men's Aid (#/$): 1/unspecified $
M: wrestling. Men's Non-aid: baseball, basketball, cross country, football, golf, soccer, tennis, wrestling
Women's Non-aid: basketball, cross country, field hockey, soccer, softball, tennis

WILLIAMSON TRADE SCHOOL
106 South New Middletown
Media, PA 19063
2-year college
(215) 566-2815 Contact: Dale H. Plummer
Men's Aid (#/$): 230/$2,300,000
Restrictions and notes: All students accepted at Williamson are on full scholarships worth $10,000 per year.
M: baseball, basketball, cross country, football, soccer, wrestling

WILSON COLLEGE
Phil Avenue
Chambersburg, PA 17201
(717) 264-4141 Contact: Lori Frey
Women's Non-aid: equestrian, field hockey, softball, tennis, volleyball

YORK COLLEGE OF PENNSYLVANIA
Country Club Road
York, PA 17403
(717) 846-7788 Contact: Calvin Williams
Men's Non-aid: baseball, basketball,

diving, golf, soccer, swimming, swimming-diving, tennis, track & field, wrestling
Women's Non-aid: basketball, diving, field hockey, softball, swimming, swimming-diving, tennis, volleyball

Puerto Rico

BAYAMON CENTRAL UNIVERSITY
Bayamon, PR 00621
(809) 786-3030 X. 263 Contact: Henry Mirand Vazquez
Men's Aid (#/$): 124/$45,000
Women's Aid (#/$): 70/$25,000
M: basketball, track & field, volleyball.
Men's Non-aid: bowling, power lifting, weightlifting
W: basketball, track & field, volleyball.
Women's Non-aid: bowling, power lifting, weightlifting

CATHOLIC UNIVERSITY OF PUERTO RICO
Las Americas Avenue
Station 6
Ponce, PR 00732
(809) 841-2000 Contact: Ms. Frau
Unspecified athletic aid available
M: basketball, cross country, martial arts, softball, swimming, tennis, track & field, volleyball, water polo, weightlifting, wrestling
W: basketball, cross country, martial arts, softball, swimming, tennis, track & field, volleyball

UNIVERSITY OF PUERTO RICO
Cayey University College
Cayey, PR 00633
(809) 738-2161 Contact: Josefina Hernandez
Men's Non-aid: basketball, cross country, soccer, softball, swimming, tennis, track & field, volleyball, water polo, weightlifting, wrestling
Women's Non-aid: basketball, cross country, tennis, track & field, volleyball

UNIVERSITY OF PUERTO RICO (BAYAMON)
Bayamon, PR 00619
(809) 786-2885 Contact: Sonia Llavona
Unspecified athletic aid available
M: basketball, cross country, tennis, track & field, volleyball, weightlifting, wrestling
W: basketball, cross country, tennis, track & field, volleyball, weightlifting, wrestling

UNIVERSITY OF PUERTO RICO (PONCE)
Ponce, PR 00732
(809) 844-8181 Contact: Carmelo Vega Montes
Men's Aid (#/$): 49/$22,560
Women's Aid (#/$): 30/$13,620
M: basketball, cross country, tennis, track & field, volleyball, weightlifting
W: basketball, cross country, tennis, track & field, volleyball, weightlifting

Rhode Island

BROWN UNIVERSITY
Box 1932
Providence, RI 02912
(401) 863-2219 Contact: Christopher Humm
Men's Non-aid: baseball, basketball, crew, cross country, football, golf, ice hockey, indoor track, lacrosse, soccer, swimming-diving, tennis, track & field, wrestling
Women's Non-aid: basketball, crew, cross country, field hockey, gymnastics, ice hockey, indoor track, lacrosse, soccer, squash, softball, swimming-diving, tennis, track & field, volleyball

BRYANT COLLEGE
450 Douglas Pike
Smithfield, RI 02917

(401) 232-6020 Contact: James C. Dorian
Men's Aid (#/$): 11/$192,935
Women's Aid (#/$): 11/$168,427
M: basketball. Men's Non-aid: baseball, bowling, cross country, golf, soccer, tennis, track & field
W: bowling. Women's Non-aid: cross country, soccer, softball, tennis, track & field, volleyball

COMMUNITY COLLEGE OF RHODE ISLAND
1762 Louisquisset Pike
Lincoln, RI 02865-4585
2-year college
(401) 333-7313 Contact: Israel Siperstein
Men's Non-aid: baseball, basketball, cross country, golf, ice hockey, soccer, tennis, weightlifting
Women's Non-aid: basketball, cross country, softball, tennis, volleyball, weightlifting

PROVIDENCE COLLEGE
River Avenue
Providence, RI 02918
(401) 865-2272 Contact: Gregg Burke
Men's Aid (#/$): 27/$244,000
Women's Aid (#/$): 31/$311,000
M: baseball, basketball, cross country, ice hockey, soccer, softball, swimming-diving, tennis, track & field. Men's Non-aid: golf, lacrosse
W: baseball, basketball, cross country, field hockey, lacrosse, soccer, softball, swimming-diving, tennis, track & field, volleyball. Women's Non-aid: ice hockey

RHODE ISLAND COLLEGE
600 Mount Pleasant Avenue
Providence, RI 02908
(401) 456-8516 Contact: Edward J. Vaillancourt
Men's Non-aid: baseball, basketball, cross country, indoor track, soccer, tennis, track & field, wrestling
Women's Non-aid: basketball, cross country, gymnastics, indoor track, softball, tennis, track & field, volleyball

SALVE REGINA COLLEGE
100 Ochre Point Avenue
Newport, RI 02840
(401) 847-6650 Contact: Joyce M. Yarrow
Men's Non-aid: baseball, basketball, cross country, golf, indoor track, soccer, tennis, track & field
Women's Non-aid: basketball, cross country, golf, indoor track, soccer, softball, tennis, track & field

UNIVERSITY OF RHODE ISLAND
207 Keaney Gymnasium
Kingston, RI 02881
(401) 792-2409 Contact: Jim Norman
Unspecified athletic aid available
M: baseball, basketball, field hockey, football, gymnastics, indoor track, soccer, softball, swimming-diving, track & field, volleyball. Men's Non-aid: crew, cross country, golf, ice hockey, lacrosse, rugby, sailing, tennis, water polo, wrestling
W: basketball, cross country, field hockey, gymnastics, indoor track, soccer, softball, swimming-diving, track & field, volleyball. Women's Non-aid: sailing, tennis

South Carolina

ALLEN UNIVERSITY
1530 Harden Street
Columbia, SC 29204
(803) 254-4165 Contact: Napolean E. Coleman II
Men's Aid (#/$): 37/$2,200
M: baseball, basketball, cross country, track & field

ANDERSON COLLEGE
316 Boulevard
Anderson, SC 29621

(803) 231-2070 Contact: James L. Owens
Men's Aid (#/$): 23/unspecified $
Women's Aid (#/$): 15/unspecified $
M: baseball, basketball, cross country, golf, indoor track, soccer, tennis, track & field, wrestling
W: basketball, soccer, softball, tennis, volleyball

BENEDICT COLLEGE
Harden Street
Columbia, SC 29204
(803) 253-5105 Contact: Wayne Sumpter
Unspecified athletic aid available
M: baseball, basketball, cross country, indoor track, tennis, track & field
W: basketball, softball, tennis, track & field, volleyball

CENTRAL WESLEYAN COLLEGE
One Wesleyan Drive
Central, SC 29630
(803) 639-2453 Contact: D.W. Hamilton
Men's Aid (#/$): 60/$166,155
Women's Aid (#/$): 27/$120,840
M: baseball, basketball, golf, soccer.
Men's Non-aid: cheerleading
W: basketball, softball, volleyball.
Women's Non-aid: cheerleading

CHARLESTON SOUTHERN UNIVERSITY
P.O. Box 10087
Charleston, SC 29411
(803) 797-4117 Contact: Ellen C. Green
Unspecified athletic aid available
M: baseball, basketball, cross country, golf, indoor track, soccer, tennis, track & field
W: basketball, cross country, indoor track, softball, tennis, track & field, volleyball

THE CITADEL
Citadel Station
Charleston, SC 29409
(803) 792-5120 Contact: Josh Baker
Unspecified athletic aid available
M: baseball, basketball, cross country, football, golf, riflery, soccer, tennis, track & field, wrestling

CLAFLIN COLLEGE
700 College Avenue
Orangeburg, SC 29115
(803) 534-2710 X. 334 Contact: Yvonne C. Claflin
Unspecified athletic aid available
M: basketball, track & field
W: basketball, squash, track & field

CLEMSON UNIVERSITY
P.O. Box 632
Clemson, SC 29633
(803) 656-2114 Contact: Tim Bourret
Men's Aid (#/$): 11/unspecified $
Women's Aid (#/$): 7/unspecified $
M: baseball, basketball, cross country, football, golf, indoor track, soccer, swimming-diving, tennis, track & field, wrestling
W: cross country, indoor track, swimming-diving, tennis, track & field, volleyball

COASTAL CAROLINA COLLEGE
P.O. Box 1954
Conway, SC 29527
(803) 349-2822 Contact: Jeff Dannelly
Unspecified athletic aid available
M: baseball, basketball, cross country, golf, soccer, tennis
W: basketball, cross country, golf, softball, tennis, volleyball

COKER COLLEGE
College Avenue
Hartsville, SC 29550
(803) 383-8073 Contact: Greg Grissom
Men's Aid (#/$): 14/$177,136
Women's Aid (#/$): 10/$124,579
M: baseball, basketball, golf, soccer, tennis
W: basketball, soccer, softball, tennis, volleyball

COLLEGE OF CHARLESTON
66 George Street
Charleston, SC 29424

(803) 792-5465 Contact: Tony Ciuffo
Men's Aid (#/$): 44/$352,000
Women's Aid (#/$): 30/$240,000
M: baseball, basketball, cross country, diving, golf, soccer, swimming, swimming-diving, tennis. Men's Non-aid: equestrian, sailing
W: basketball, cross country, diving, golf, softball, swimming, swimming-diving, tennis, volleyball. Women's Non-aid: equestrian, sailing

COLUMBIA COLLEGE
1301 Columbia College Drive
Columbia, SC 29203
(803) 786-3644 Contact: Doris L. Harrel
Women's Aid (#/$): 22/$29,150
W: tennis, volleyball

CONVERSE COLLEGE
580 East Main Street
Spartanburg, SC 29301-0006
(803) 596-9702 Contact: Patricia Chandler
Unspecified athletic aid available
W: basketball, tennis, volleyball. Women's Non-aid: equestrian, synchronized swimming

ERSKINE COLLEGE
Due West, SC 29639
(803) 379-8895 Contact: Dot Carter
Unspecified athletic aid available
M: baseball, basketball, cross country, golf, soccer, tennis
W: basketball, soccer, softball, tennis, volleyball

FRANCIS MARION UNIVERSITY
P.O. Box 100547
Florence, SC 29501-0547
(803) 661-1222 Contact: Michael G. Hawkins
Men's Aid (#/$): 27/$154,010
Women's Aid (#/$): 13/$75,683
M: baseball, basketball, cross country, golf, soccer, tennis, track & field
W: basketball, cross country, softball, tennis, volleyball

FURMAN UNIVERSITY
Poinsett Highway
Greenville, SC 29613
(803) 294-2061 Contact: Hunter Reid
Unspecified athletic aid available
M: baseball, basketball, cross country, diving, football, golf, soccer, swimming, swimming-diving, tennis, track & field. Men's Non-aid: wrestling
W: basketball, golf, softball, swimming-diving, tennis, volleyball. Women's Non-aid: cross country

LANDER COLLEGE
P.O. Box 6005
Greenwood, SC 29649
(803) 229-8316 Contact: Bob Stoner
Men's Aid (#/$): 53/$90,397
Women's Aid (#/$): 39/$61,729
M: basketball, cross country, soccer, tennis
W: basketball, cross country, softball, tennis

LIMESTONE COLLEGE
1115 College Drive
Gaffney, SC 29340
(803) 489-7151 X. 311 Contact: Virginia Hickey
Unspecified athletic aid available
M: baseball, basketball, cheerleading, golf, lacrosse, soccer, tennis
W: basketball, cheerleading, soccer, softball, tennis, volleyball

NEWBERRY COLLEGE
2100 College Street
Newberry, SC 29108
(803) 321-5169 Contact: Patrick Stewart
Men's Aid (#/$): 44/$486,500
Women's Aid (#/$): 8/$84,500
M: baseball, basketball, football, golf, tennis
W: basketball, softball, tennis, volleyball

NORTH GREENVILLE COLLEGE
P.O. Box 1892
Tigerville, SC 29688
2-year college

(803) 895-1410 Contact: Jan McDonald
Men's Aid (#/$): 15.5/$144,150
Women's Aid (#/$): 6.2/$57,660
M: baseball, basketball, football, golf, tennis
W: basketball, softball, volleyball

PRESBYTERIAN COLLEGE
South Broad Street
Clinton, SC 29325
(803) 833-8252 Contact: David Hibbard
Men's Aid (#/$): 41.7/$600,229
Women's Aid (#/$): 11.5/$165,531
M: baseball, basketball, football, golf, soccer, tennis. Men's Non-aid: cheerleading, track & field
W: basketball, soccer, tennis, volleyball. Women's Non-aid: cheerleading

SOUTH CAROLINA STATE COLLEGE
300 College Street NE
Orangeburg, SC 29117-0001
(803) 536-7060 Contact: William P. Hamilton
Men's Aid (#/$): 107/$555,758
Women's Aid (#/$): 39/$202,566
M: basketball, cross country, football, golf, indoor track, tennis, track & field. Men's Non-aid: baseball
W: basketball, cross country, indoor track, tennis, track & field, volleyball

SPARTANBURG METHODIST
1200 Textile Road
Spartanburg, SC 29301-0009
2-year college
(803) 587-4213 Contact: Kevin Good
Unspecified athletic aid available
M: baseball, basketball, golf, soccer
W: basketball, softball, volleyball

UNIVERSITY OF SOUTH CAROLINA
Coastal Carolina College
Myrtle Beach, SC 29578
(803) 347-3161 Contact: Molly A. Bethea-Floyd
Unspecified athletic aid available
M: baseball, basketball, cross country, diving, football, golf, soccer, swimming, swimming-diving, tennis, track & field
W: basketball, diving, golf, softball, swimming, swimming-diving, tennis, volleyball

UNIVERSITY OF SOUTH CAROLINA
Rosewood Drive
Columbia, SC 29208
(803) 777-5204 Contact: Kelly Tharp
Men's Aid (#/$): 70/$212,548
Women's Aid (#/$): 19/$74,238
M: baseball, basketball, cross country, diving, football, golf, soccer, swimming, swimming-diving, tennis, track & field
W: basketball, diving, golf, softball, swimming, swimming-diving, tennis, volleyball

UNIVERSITY OF SOUTH CAROLINA (AIKEN)
171 University Parkway
Aiken, SC 29801
(803) 648-6851 Contact: A. Glenn Shumpert
Men's Aid (#/$): 22.26/$93,640
Women's Aid (#/$): 12.23/$46,372
M: baseball, basketball, cross country, golf, soccer, tennis
W: basketball, cross country, softball, volleyball

UNIVERSITY OF SOUTH CAROLINA (SPARTANBURG)
800 University Way
Spartanburg, SC 29303-9982
(803) 599-2129 Contact: Michael F. MacEachern
Men's Aid (#/$): 23/unspecified $
Women's Aid (#/$): 15/unspecified $
Restrictions and notes: The amounts are equivalencies, and as such are divided among many athletes.
M: baseball, basketball, cross country, soccer, tennis
W: basketball, softball, tennis, volleyball

WINTHROP UNIVERSITY
Department of Athletics
Eden Terrace
Rock Hill, SC 29733
(803) 323-2129 Contact: Jack Frost
Men's Aid (#/$): 39/$246,948
Women's Aid (#/$): 26/$164,632
Restrictions and notes: School has women's Dance Team program.
M: baseball, basketball, cross country, golf, soccer, tennis, track & field. Men's Non-aid: cheerleading
W: basketball, cross country, golf, softball, tennis, track & field, volleyball. Women's Non-aid: cheerleading

WOFFORD COLLEGE
429 North Church Street
Spartanburg, SC 29303-3663
(803) 597-4093 Contact: Mark Cohen
Men's Aid (#/$): 54.5/unspecified $
Women's Aid (#/$): 6.5/unspecified $
Restrictions and notes: The total athletic endowment was $1,635,924. Gifts to the endowment have totaled $1,140,043 during the past three years.
M: baseball, basketball, football, golf, soccer, tennis. Men's Non-aid: cross country
W: basketball, tennis, volleyball. Women's Non-aid: cross country

South Dakota

AUGUSTANA COLLEGE
29th and Summit Avenue
Sioux Falls, SD 57197
(605) 336-5216 Contact: F. Eugene Linton
Men's Aid (#/$): 60/$730,800
Women's Aid (#/$): 25/$304,500
M: baseball, basketball, cross country, football, indoor track, track & field, wrestling. Men's Non-aid: golf, tennis
W: basketball, cross country, indoor track, softball, track & field, volleyball. Women's Non-aid: golf, tennis

BLACK HILLS STATE UNIVERSITY
Box 9512
Spearfish, SD 57799-9512
(605) 642-6445 Contact: John R. Buxton
Unspecified athletic aid available
M: basketball, cheerleading, cross country, football, indoor track, track & field
W: basketball, cheerleading, cross country, ice hockey, track & field, volleyball

DAKOTA STATE UNIVERSITY
820 North Washington
Madison, SD 57042
(605) 256-5152 Contact: Sandra Paul
Unspecified athletic aid available
M: basketball, cross country, football, indoor track, track & field
W: basketball, cross country, indoor track, track & field, volleyball

DAKOTA WESLEYAN UNIVERSITY
1200 West University Boulevard
Mitchell, SD 57301
(605) 995-2654 Contact: Deb Henriksen
Men's Aid (#/$): 60/$100,000
Women's Aid (#/$): 40/$70,000
M: baseball, basketball, cross country, football, track & field
W: basketball, cross country, golf, track & field, vollleyball

HURON UNIVERSITY
9th and Ohio
Huron, SD 57350
(605) 352-8721 Contact: Vern Tate
Unspecified athletic aid available
M: basketball, cross country, football, golf, wrestling
W: basketball, cross country, golf, volleyball

MOUNT MARTY COLLEGE
1100 West 5th
Yankton, SD 57078

(605) 668-1589 Contact: Don Buehrer
Men's Aid (#/$): 6.6/$65,633
Women's Aid (#/$): 5.3/$52,930
M: baseball, basketball. Men's Non-aid: golf, soccer
W: basketball, volleyball. Women's Non-aid: golf

NORTHERN STATE UNIVERSITY
1200 South Jay
Aberdeen, SD 57401
(605) 622-7748 Contact: Deb Smith
Men's Aid (#/$): 21/$39,030
Women's Aid (#/$): 33/$60,614
M: basketball, cross country, football, wrestling. Men's Non-aid: baseball, golf, tennis
W: basketball, cross country, golf, softball, tennis, volleyball

SIOUX FALLS COLLEGE
1501 South Prairie Avenue
Sioux Falls, SD 57105
(605) 331-6623 Contact: Glen Poppinga
Men's Aid (#/$): 106/$117,567
Women's Aid (#/$): 38/$33,700
M: basketball, cross country, football, tennis, track & field
W: basketball, cross country, tennis, track & field, volleyball

SOUTH DAKOTA SCHOOL OF MINES AND TECHNOLOGY
501 East Saint Joesph
Rapid City, SD 57701
(605) 394-2351 Contact: Tom Rudebusch
Men's Aid (#/$): 58/$40,000
Women's Aid (#/$): 32/$16,000
M: basketball, cross country, football, tennis, track & field
W: basketball, cross country, track & field, volleyball

SOUTH DAKOTA STATE UNIVERSITY
Box 2820
Brookings, SD 57007-1497
(605) 688-4623 Contact: Ron Lenz
Unspecified athletic aid available
M: baseball, basketball, cross country, football, indoor track, track & field, wrestling. Men's Non-aid: swimming
W: basketball, cross country, indoor track, softball, swimming, track & field, volleyball. Women's Non-aid: golf

UNIVERSITY OF SOUTH DAKOTA
414 East Cherry Street
Vermillion, SD 57069
(605) 677-5927 Contact: Kyle Johnson
Men's Aid (#/$): 55.3/$280,382
Women's Aid (#/$): 22.5/$112,101
Restrictions and notes: Aid figures based on full tuition equivalents.
M: baseball, basketball, cross country, football, indoor track, swimming-diving, tennis, track & field
W: basketball, cross country, indoor track, softball, swimming-diving, tennis, track & field, volleyball

Tennessee

AQUINAS JUNIOR COLLEGE
4210 Harding Road
Nashville, TN 37205
2-year college
(615) 297-7653 Contact: Charles Anderson
Men's Aid (#/$): 16/$160,000
Restrictions and notes: Athletic aid in form of tuition only.
M: baseball, basketball

AUSTIN PEAY STATE UNIVERSITY
P.O. Box 4515
Clarksville, TN 37044
(615) 648-7561 Contact: Brad Kirtley
Men's Aid (#/$): 89/$547,857
Women's Aid (#/$): 29/$200,926
Restrictions and notes: Aid amounts based on full equated scholaships.
M: baseball, basketball, cross country, football, golf, tennis, track & field

W: basketball, cross country, indoor track, softball, tennis, track & field, volleyball

BELMONT COLLEGE
Belmont Boulevard
Nashville, TN 37203
(615) 385-6420 Contact: Kenneth Sidwell
Men's Aid (#/$): 25/$250,000
Women's Aid (#/$): 20/$200,000
M: baseball, basketball, cross country, soccer, tennis, track & field. Men's Non-aid: golf
W: basketball, cross country, softball, tennis, track & field, volleyball. Women's Non-aid: golf

BETHEL COLLEGE
Cherry Street
McKenzie, TN 38201
(901) 352-5321 Contact: James R. Shannon, Jr.
Unspecified athletic aid available
M: baseball, basketball, golf
W: basketball, tennis

BRISTOL UNIVERSITY
1241 Volunteer Parkway
P.O. Box 4366
Bristol, TN 37620
(615) 968-1442 Contact: Gill Payne
Unspecified athletic aid available
M: baseball, basketball, golf
W: basketball

CARSON-NEWMAN COLLEGE
Campus Box 2009
Jefferson City, TN 37760
(615) 471-3477 Contact: Steve Cotton
Unspecified athletic aid available
M: baseball, basketball, cross country, football, golf, tennis, track & field, wrestling. Men's Non-aid: soccer
W: basketball, cross country, softball, tennis, track & field, volleyball

CHRISTIAN BROTHERS COLLEGE
650 East Parkway Street
Memphis, TN 38104
(901) 722-0307 Contact: Sandi Mayo
Men's Aid (#/$): 40/$164,387
Women's Aid (#/$): 26/$74,513
M: baseball, basketball, soccer
W: basketball, soccer, volleyball

CLEVELAND STATE COMMUNITY COLLEGE
P.O. Box 3570
Cleveland, TN 37320-3570
2-year college
(615) 472-7141 Contact: Jim Cigliano
Unspecified athletic aid available
M: baseball, basketball
W: basketball

DAVID LIPSCOMB COLLEGE
3901 Granny White Pike
Nashville, TN 37204-3951
(615) 269-1791 Contact: Shirley Slatton
Men's Aid (#/$): 58/$319,625
Women's Aid (#/$): 22/$116,211
M: baseball, basketball, cross country, golf, tennis, track & field
W: basketball, cross country, tennis, track & field

DYERSBURG STATE COMMUNITY COLLEGE
Lake Road
Dyersburg, TN 38024
2-year college
(901) 285-6910 Contact: Barry Young
Unspecified athletic aid available
M: baseball, basketball. Men's Non-aid: basketball

EAST TENNESSEE STATE UNIVERSITY
P.O. Box 21730A
Johnson City, TN 37614
(615) 929-4220 Contact: John Cathey
Unspecified athletic aid available
M: baseball, basketball, cross country, football, golf, indoor track, tennis, track & field
W: basketball, cross country, indoor track, tennis, track & field

FISK UNIVERSITY
17th Avenue North
Nashville, TN 37203

(615) 329-8735 Contact: Annette Miller
Men's Non-aid: basketball, cross country, soccer, track & field
Women's Non-aid: basketball, cross country, track & field, volleyball

FREED-HARDEMAN COLLEGE
158 East Main
Henderson, TN 38340
(901) 989-6048 Contact: Mike McCutchen
Men's Aid (#/$): 40/$170,000
Women's Aid (#/$): 25/$127,500
M: baseball, basketball, golf, tennis
W: basketball, softball, tennis, volleyball

HIWASSEE COLLEGE
Hiwassee Road
Madisonville, TN 37354
2-year college
(615) 442-4807 Contact: Eugene Kiger
Men's Aid (#/$): 11/$75,000
Women's Aid (#/$): 11/$75,000
M: baseball, basketball. Men's Non-aid: equestrian
W: basketball, softball. Women's Non-aid: equestrian

JACKSON STATE COMMUNITY COLLEGE
2046 North Parkway
Jackson, TN 38301
2-year college
(901) 424-3520 Contact: Jack Martin
Unspecified athletic aid available
M: baseball, basketball
W: basketball

KING COLLEGE
1350 King College Road
Bristol, TN 37620–2699
(615) 652-4726 Contact: Mildred B. Greeson
Men's Aid (#/$): 53/$158,000
Women's Aid (#/$): 28/$90,054
M: baseball, basketball, cross country, golf, soccer, tennis
W: baseball, basketball, cross country, softball, tennis, volleyball

KNOXVILLE COLLEGE
901 College Street
Knoxville, TN 37921
(615) 524-6525 Contact: Carol Scott
Men's Non-aid: basketball, football, indoor track, tennis, track & field
Women's Non-aid: basketball, football, indoor track, tennis, track & field

LAMBUTH UNIVERSITY
705 Lambuth Boulevard
Jackson, TN 38301
(901) 425-3330 Contact: Brad Jones
Men's Aid (#/$): 39/unspecified $
Women's Aid (#/$): 36/unspecified $
M: badminton, baseball, football, sailing, tennis. Men's Non-aid: field hockey
W: basketball, soccer, softball, tennis, volleyball

LEE COLLEGE
Ocoee Street
Cleveland, TN 37311
(615) 472-2111 X. 330 Contact: Michael Ellis
Men's Aid (#/$): 47/$153,775
Women's Aid (#/$): 38/$106,605
M: basketball, golf, soccer, tennis
W: basketball, softball, tennis, volleyball. Women's Non-aid: soccer

LEMOYNE-OWEN COLLEGE
807 Walker Avenue
Memphis, TN 38126
(901) 942-7326 Contact: Eddie Cook
Men's Non-aid: baseball, basketball, track & field
Women's Non-aid: basketball

LINCOLN MEMORIAL UNIVERSITY
Cumberland Gap Parkway
Harrogate, TN 37752
(615) 869-6236 Contact: Tom Amis
Men's Aid ($): $245,000
Women's Aid ($): $145,000
M: baseball, basketball, cross country, golf, soccer, tennis
W: basketball, cross country, softball, tennis, volleyball

MARYVILLE COLLEGE
Court Street
Maryville, TN 37801
(615) 981-8291 Contact: Wes Moore
Men's Non-aid: baseball, basketball, football, soccer, tennis
Women's Non-aid: basketball, softball, tennis, volleyball

MEMPHIS STATE UNIVERSITY
205 Athletic Office Building
Memphis, TN 38152
(901) 678-2337 Contact: Bob Winn
Unspecified athletic aid available
M: baseball, basketball, cross country, football, golf, indoor track, soccer, tennis, track & field
W: basketball, cross country, golf, indoor track, tennis, volleyball

MIDDLE TENNESSEE STATE UNIVERSITY
MTSU Box 20
Murfreesboro, TN 37132
(615) 898-2450 Contact: Ed Given
Men's Aid (#/$): 117/$675,444
Women's Aid (#/$): 43/$228,996
M: baseball, basketball, cross country, football, golf, indoor track, tennis, track & field. Men's Non-aid: riflery
W: basketball, cross country, indoor track, softball, tennis, track & field, volleyball. Women's Non-aid: riflery

MILLIGAN COLLEGE
P.O. Box 101
Milligan College, TN 37682
(615) 929-0116 X. 132 Contact: Paul Bader
Unspecified athletic aid available
M: baseball, basketball, tennis
W: basketball, softball, tennis, volleyball

MOTLOW STATE COMMUNITY COLLEGE
P.O. Box 88100
Tullahoma, TN 37388-8100
2-year college
(615) 455-8511 Contact: Charle Coffey
Men's Aid (#/$): 10/$20,000
Women's Aid (#/$): 5/$10,000
M: baseball, basketball. Men's Non-aid: golf
W: basketball

ROANE STATE COMMUNITY COLLEGE
Patton Lane
Harriman, TN 37748
2-year college
(615) 354-3000 Contact: Valerie Privett
Men's Aid (#/$): 4/$2,000
Women's Aid (#/$): 4/$2,000
M: baseball, basketball
W: basketball

SHELBY STATE COMMUNITY COLLEGE
P.O. Box 40568
Memphis, TN 38174-0568
2-year college
(901) 528-6754 Contact: Bob Canada
Unspecified athletic aid available
M: baseball, basketball, golf
W: basketball

TENNESSEE STATE UNIVERSITY
3500 John A. Merritt Boulevard
Nashville, TN 37209
(615) 320-3440 Contact: Homer R. Wheaton
Unspecified athletic aid available
M: baseball, basketball, football, indoor track, swimming, track & field
W: basketball, indoor track, track & field

TENNESSEE TECHNOLOGICAL UNIVERSITY
P.O. Box 5057
Cookeville, TN 38505
(615) 372-3088 Contact: Rob Schabert
Men's Aid (#/$): 141/$521,377
Women's Aid (#/$): 47/$102,852
M: baseball, basketball, cross country, football, golf, indoor track, riflery, tennis
W: basketball, cross country, golf, indoor track, riflery, softball, tennis, volleyball

TENNESSEE TEMPLE UNIVERSITY
1815 Union Avenue
Chattanooga, TN 37404
(615) 493-4100 Contact: Randy Stem
Unspecified athletic aid available
M: baseball, basketball, soccer. Men's Non-aid: bowling
W: basketball, volleyball. Women's Non-aid: softball

TENNESSEE WESLEYAN COLLEGE
P.O. Box 40
Athens, TN 371-0400
(615) 745-7504 Contact: Wayne Norfleet
Unspecified athletic aid available
M: baseball, basketball, soccer. Men's Non-aid: football, golf, tennis
W: basketball, tennis. Women's Non-aid: soccer, softball

TREVECCA NAZARENE COLLEGE
333 Murfreesboro Road
Nashville, TN 37203
(615) 248-1271 Contact: Susan Harris
Men's Aid (#/$): 57/$146,651
Women's Aid (#/$): 29/$45,721
M: baseball, basketball
W: softball, volleyball

TUSCULUM COLLEGE
P.O. Box 5049
Greeneville, TN 37743
(615) 636-7312 Contact: Diane L. Keasling
Unspecified athletic aid available
M: baseball, basketball, soccer. Men's Non-aid: golf, tennis
W: basketball, softball, volleyball. Women's Non-aid: tennis

UNION UNIVERSITY
Highway 45 Bypass
Jackson, TN 38305
(901) 668-1818 X. 211 Contact: Don Morris
Men's Aid (#/$): 4/$7,500

UNIVERSITY OF TENNESSEE
615 McCallie Avenue
Chattanooga, TN 37402-2598
(615) 755-4618 Contact: Neil Magnussen
Unspecified athletic aid available
M: baseball, basketball, cross country, diving, football, golf, indoor track, swimming, swimming-diving, tennis, track & field. Men's Non-aid: soccer
W: basketball, cross country, diving, indoor track, swimming, swimming-diving, tennis, track & field, volleyball

UNIVERSITY OF TENNESSEE (KNOXVILLE)
1720 Volunteer Boulevard
Knoxville, TN 37901-5016
(615) 974-1212 Contact: Bud Ford
Unspecified athletic aid available
M: baseball, basketball, cross country, diving, football, golf, indoor track, swimming, swimming-diving, tennis, track & field. Men's Non-aid: crew, ice hockey, soccer
W: basketball, cross country, diving, golf, indoor track, swimming, swimming-diving, tennis, track & field, volleyball

UNIVERSITY OF TENNESSEE (MARTIN)
304 Administration
Martin, TN 38238-5070
(901) 587-7630 Contact: Lee Wilmot
Unspecified athletic aid available
M: baseball, basketball, cross country, football, golf, riflery, tennis, track & field
W: basketball, cross country, riflery, softball, tennis, track & field, volleyball

VANDERBILT UNIVERSITY
2601 Jess Neely Drive
Nashville, TN 37203
(615) 322-4121 Contact: Lew Harris
Men's Aid (#/$): 46/$688,095
Women's Aid (#/$): 19/$188,541
M: baseball, basketball, football, golf, soccer, tennis. Men's Non-aid: cross country
W: basketball, cross country, golf, indoor track, soccer, tennis, track & field

WALTERS STATE COMMUNITY COLLEGE
500 South Davy Crockett Parkway
Morristown, TN 37813
2-year college
(615) 581-2121 X. 429 Contact: Bill Brittain
Unspecified athletic aid available
M: baseball, basketball, tennis. Men's Non-aid: golf
W: basketball

Texas

ABILENE CHRISTIAN UNIVERSITY
P.O. Box 7795
Abilene, TX 79699
(915) 674-2693 Contact: Garner Roberts
Men's Aid (#/$): 71/$710,000
Women's Aid (#/$): 36/$360,000
M: basketball, cross country, football, golf, tennis, track & field
W: basketball, cross country, indoor track, tennis, track & field, volleyball

ANGELINA COLLEGE
P.O. Box 1768
Lufkin, TX 75902-1768
2-year college
(409) 633-5282 Contact: Jim Twogig
Unspecified athletic aid available
M: baseball, basketball
W: basketball

ANGELO STATE UNIVERSITY
P.O. Box 11021
ASU Station
San Angelo, TX 76909
(915) 942-2248 Contact: Frank Rudnicki
Unspecified athletic aid available
M: basketball, cross country, football, golf, tennis, track & field
W: basketball, cross country, tennis, track & field, volleyball

AUSTIN COLLEGE
900 N. Grand Avenue
Sherman, TX 75090
(903) 813-2318 Contact: Charlene Rowland
Men's Non-aid: baseball, basketball, diving, football, golf, rodeo, soccer, softball, tennis, track & field, water polo
Women's Non-aid: basketball, diving, martial arts, rodeo, softball, tennis, volleyball

BAYLOR UNIVERSITY
3031 Dutton Avenue
Waco, TX 76711
(817) 755-1234 Contact: Maxey Parrish
Unspecified athletic aid available
M: baseball, basketball, cross country, football, golf, indoor track, tennis, track & field
W: basketball, cross country, indoor track, softball, tennis, track & field, volleyball

CONCORDIA LUTHERAN COLLEGE
Interstate 35 North
Austin, TX 78705
(512) 452-7661 Contact: Lynette Heckmann
Men's Aid ($): $75,000
Women's Aid ($): $75,000
M: baseball, basketball, tennis. Men's Non-aid: golf
W: basketball, tennis, volleyball. Women's Non-aid: golf

COOKE COUNTY JUNIOR COLLEGE
1525 California Street
Gainesville, TX 76240
2-year college
(817) 668-7731 X. 254 Contact: Rodger Boyce
Unspecified athletic aid available
M: basketball
W: tennis, volleyball

DALLAS BAPTIST UNIVERSITY
7777 West Kiest
Dallas, TX 75211
(214) 333-5112 Contact: Wayne Poage
Men's Aid (#/$): 12/$150,000

Women's Aid (#/$): 7/$35,000
M: baseball. Men's Non-aid: golf, soccer
W: volleyball

EAST TEXAS BAPTIST UNIVERSITY
1209 North Grove
Marshall, TX 75670
(903) 935-7963 X. 231 Contact: Brad Livingston
Unspecified athletic aid available
M: baseball, basketball. Men's Non-aid: tennis
W: basketball, volleyball. Women's Non-aid: tennis

EAST TEXAS STATE UNIVERSITY
ETSU Station
Commerce, TX 75429
(903) 886-5131 Contact: Bill Powers
Unspecified athletic aid available
M: basketball, cross country, football, golf, tennis, track & field
W: basketball, cross country, tennis, track & field, volleyball

EASTFIELD COLLEGE
3737 Motley Drive
Mesquite, TX 75150
2-year college
(214) 324-7643 Contact: Bob Flickner
Men's Non-aid: baseball, basketball, golf, softball, tennis
Women's Non-aid: softball, tennis, volleyball

FRANK PHILLIPS COLLEGE
Box 5118
Borger, TX 79007-5118
2-year college
(806) 274-5311 Contact: Garry McGregory
Men's Aid (#/$): 29/$72,872
Women's Aid (#/$): 13/$33,124
M: baseball, basketball, rodeo
W: basketball, rodeo

GRAYSON COUNTY COLLEGE
6101 Highway 691
Denison, TX 75020
2-year college
(214) 465-6030 Contact: Roy Jackson
Unspecified athletic aid available
M: basketball, golf, tennis
W: basketball, tennis

HARDIN-SIMMONS UNIVERSITY
Drawer H, HSU
Abilene, TX 79698
(915) 670-1273 Contact: Kevin Carson
Unspecified athletic aid available
M: baseball, basketball, golf, riflery, soccer, tennis
W: cross country, golf, riflery, soccer, tennis, volleyball

HOUSTON BAPTIST UNIVERSITY
7502 Fondern Road
Houston, TX 77074
(713) 774-7661 Contact: Ken Rogers
Unspecified athletic aid available
M: basketball, cross country, golf, gymnastics, indoor track, soccer, tennis, track & field
W: cross country, gymnastics, indoor track, soccer, track & field, volleyball

HOWARD PAYNE UNIVERSITY
1000 Fisk
Brownwood, TX 76801
(915) 643-2502 Contact: Mike Blackwell
Unspecified athletic aid available
M: basketball, cross country, football, golf, indoor track
W: basketball, tennis, volleyball. Women's Non-aid: cross country

HUSTON-TILLOTSON COLLEGE
1820 East 8th Street
Austin, TX 78702
(512) 476-7421 Contact: Jackie Wilson
Unspecified athletic aid available
M: baseball, basketball, golf, tennis
W: basketball, tennis, volleyball

INCARNATE WORD COLLEGE
4301 Broadway
San Antonio, TX 78209
(512) 829-3828 Contact: Charles Olmstead
Unspecified athletic aid available

M: baseball, basketball, cross country, golf, soccer, tennis
W: basketball, cross country, soccer, softball, tennis, volleyball

JACKSONVILLE COLLEGE
Pine Street
Jacksonville, TX 75766
2-year college
(903) 586-2518 Contact: Vernon Harton
Unspecified athletic aid available
M: basketball, golf

KILGORE COLLEGE
1100 Broadway
Kilgor, TX 75662
2-year college
(903) 983-8181 Contact: Archie Whitfield
Men's Aid (#/$): 50/unspecified $
Women's Aid (#/$): 15/unspecified $
M: basketball, football
W: basketball

LAMAR UNIVERSITY
Box 10066 LU Station
Beaumont, TX 77710
(409) 880-8329 Contact: Rush Wood
Men's Aid (#/$): 32/$120,000
Women's Aid (#/$): 16/$60,000
M: baseball, basketball, cross country, football, golf, indoor track, tennis, track & field
W: basketball, cross country, golf, indoor track, softball, tennis, track & field, volleyball

LEE COLLEGE
P.O. Box 818
Baytown, TX 77522-0818
2-year college
(713) 425-6487 Contact: Brenda Gentry
Men's Aid (#/$): 50/$86,200
Women's Aid (#/$): 25/$30,100
M: baseball, basketball
W: volleyball

LETOURNEAU COLLEGE
P.O. Box 7001
Longview, TX 75607
(903) 753-0231 Contact: Willard D. Rusk
Unspecified athletic aid available
M: baseball, basketball, cross country, soccer, track & field
W: cross country, tennis

LUBBOCK CHRISTIAN COLLEGE
5601 West 19th Street
Lubbock, TX 79407
(806) 792-3221 Contact: Marcus Wilson
Unspecified athletic aid available
M: baseball, basketball, cross country, indoor track, track & field. Men's Non-aid: soccer
W: basketball, cross country, indoor track, track & field, volleyball

MCLENNAN COMMUNITY COLLEGE
1400 College Drive
Waco, TX 76708
2-year college
(817) 750-3657 Contact: Ken DeWeese
Unspecified athletic aid available
M: baseball, basketball, tennis
W: basketball, tennis

MIDLAND COLLEGE
3600 North Garfield
Midland, TX 79705-6399
2-year college
(915) 685-4575 Contact: Delnor Poss
Men's Aid (#/$): 18/unspecified $
M: basketball, golf

MIDWESTERN STATE UNIVERSITY
3400 Taft
Wichita Falls, TX 76308
(817) 692-1332 Contact: Harve Allen
Men's Aid (#/$): 36/$96,000
Women's Aid (#/$): 14/$40,000
M: basketball, soccer. Men's Non-aid: field hockey, golf, tennis, track & field
W: basketball. Women's Non-aid: tennis, track & field, volleyball

NAVARRO COLLEGE
3200 West 7th Avenue
Corsicana, TX 75110

2-year college
(903) 874-6508 Contact: Bob McElroy
Unspecified athletic aid available
M: baseball, basketball, football, tennis
W: tennis

NORTHWOOD INSTITUTE (TEXAS CAMPUS)
1114 West Farm Market Road
Cedar Hill, TX 75104
(214) 291-1541 Contact: Al Williams
Unspecified athletic aid available
M: baseball, basketball, football, indoor track, tennis, track & field. Men's Non-aid: golf
W: basketball, indoor track, softball, track & field, volleyball

ODESSA COLLEGE
201 West University
Odessa, TX 79764
2-year college
(915) 335-6567 Contact: Barry Rodenhaver
Unspecified athletic aid available
M: basketball, golf, indoor track, rodeo, tennis, track & field

PAN AMERICAN UNIVERSITY
1200 West University
Edinburg, TX 78539
(512) 381-2221 Contact: Jim McKone
Men's Aid (#/$): 41.2/$222,727
Women's Aid (#/$): 25.4/$136,231
M: baseball, basketball, cross country, golf, tennis, track & field. Men's Non-aid: indoor track, soccer
W: basketball, cross country, indoor track, tennis, track & field, volleyball

PANOLA JUNIOR COLLEGE
West Panola Street
Carthage, TX 75633
2-year college
(903) 693-2062 Contact: Brenda Allums
Unspecified athletic aid available
M: baseball, basketball
W: basketball

PARIS JUNIOR COLLEGE
2400 Clarksville Street
Paris, TX 75460
2-year college
(903) 784-9218 Contact: Don C. Wilhelm
Men's Aid (#/$): 48/unspecified $
Women's Aid (#/$): 16/unspecified $
M: baseball, basketball, cheerleading, golf
W: basketball, cheerleading

PRAIRIE VIEW A & M UNIVERSITY
Prairie View, TX 77446-2610
(409) 857-2423 Contact: A.D. James, Jr.
Unspecified athletic aid available
M: baseball, basketball, cross country, football, golf, track & field. Men's Non-aid: indoor track, rodeo, tennis
W: basketball, cross country, track & field. Women's Non-aid: indoor track, tennis, volleyball

RICE UNIVERSITY
P.O. Box 1892
Houston, TX 77251-1892
(713) 527-4034 Contact: Bill Cousins
Unspecified athletic aid available
M: baseball, basketball, cross country, football, golf, indoor track, tennis, track & field. Men's Non-aid: swimming-diving
W: basketball, cross country, indoor track, swimming, tennis, track & field, volleyball

SAINT EDWARD'S UNIVERSITY
3001 South Congress Avenue
Austin, TX 78704
(512) 448-8525 Contact: Doris F. Constantine
Men's Aid (#/$): 25.5/$239,088
Women's Aid (#/$): 23.5/$220,336
M: baseball, basketball, golf, soccer, tennis
W: basketball, soccer, softball, tennis, volleyball

SAINT MARY'S UNIVERSITY
One Camino Santa Maria
San Antonio, TX 78228
(512) 436-3141 Contact: David R. Krause

Unspecified athletic aid available
M: baseball, basketball. Men's Non-aid: golf, soccer, tennis
W: basketball, softball, volleyball. Women's Non-aid: tennis

SAM HOUSTON STATE UNIVERSITY
1700 Sam Houston Avenue
Huntsville, TX 77340
(409) 294-1111 Contact: Rick Campbell
Aid (#/$): 55/$54,000 (M&W)
M: baseball, basketball, football, golf, rodeo, soccer, tennis
W: basketball, rodeo, softball, tennis, volleyball. Women's Non-aid: track & field

SCHREINER COLLEGE
Kerrville, TX 78028
(512) 896-5411 Contact: Jeff R. Scofield
Men's Aid (#/$): 53/$180,983
Women's Aid (#/$): 39/$144,434
M: baseball, basketball, soccer, tennis. Men's Non-aid: cross country
W: basketball, soccer, tennis, volleyball. Women's Non-aid: cross country

SOUTH PLAINS COMMUNITY COLLEGE
1400 College Avenue
Levelland, TX 79336
2-year college
(806) 894-9611 X. 210 Contact: Stephen John
Unspecified athletic aid available
M: basketball, cross country, golf, indoor track, tennis, track & field. Men's Non-aid: rodeo
W: basketball, tennis. Women's Non-aid: rodeo

SOUTHERN METHODIST UNIVERSITY
6024 Airline Road
Dallas, TX 75275
(214) 692-2883 Contact: Ed Wisneski
Unspecified athletic aid available
M: basketball, cross country, diving, football, golf, indoor track, soccer, swimming, swimming-diving, tennis, track & field
W: basketball, diving, golf, swimming, swimming-diving, tennis. Women's Non-aid: cross country, indoor track, soccer, track & field

SOUTHWESTERN UNIVERSITY
P.O. Box 6273, SU Station
Georgetown, TX 78626
(512) 863-1381 Contact: Carla Lowryine
Men's Non-aid: baseball, basketball, cross country, golf, tennis
Women's Non-aid: basketball, cross country, golf, tennis, volleyball

SOUTHWEST TEXAS STATE UNIVERSITY
Jowers Center
San Marcos, TX 78666-4616
(512) 245-2315 Contact: Tony Brubaker
Unspecified athletic aid available
M: baseball, basketball, cross country, football, golf, tennis, track & field
W: basketball, cross country, softball, tennis, track & field, volleyball

STEPHEN F. AUSTIN STATE UNIVERSITY
P.O. Box 13010, SFA Station
Nacogdoches, TX 75962-3010
(409) 568-2606 Contact: Greg Fort
Unspecified athletic aid available
M: baseball, basketball, cross country, football, golf, indoor track, track & field
W: basketball, cross country, indoor track, softball, track & field, volleyball

ST. PHILIP'S COLLEGE
2111 Nevada Street
San Antonio, TX 78203
2-year college
(512) 531-3240 Contact: Jim Dalglish
Unspecified athletic aid available
M: basketball
W: volleyball

SUL ROSS STATE UNIVERSITY
Box C-112 Alpine
Alpine, TX 79832

(915) 837-8061 Contact: Lee Sleeper
Unspecified athletic aid available
M: rodeo. Men's Non-aid: baseball, basketball, football, golf, tennis, track & field
W: rodeo. Women's Non-aid: basketball, golf, tennis, track & field, volleyball

TARLETON STATE UNIVERSITY
P.O. Box T-309
Stephenville, TX 76402
(817) 968-9077 Contact: Reed Richmond
Men's Non-aid: baseball, basketball, cross country, football, golf, indoor track, rodeo, tennis, track & field
Women's Non-aid: basketball, cross country, indoor track, rodeo, tennis, track & field, volleyball

TEMPLE JUNIOR COLLEGE
2600 South First Street
Temple, TX 76504
2-year college
(817) 773-9961 Contact: Danny Scott
Men's Aid (#/$): 22/unspecified $
Women's Aid (#/$): 22/unspecified $
M: basketball, golf, tennis
W: basketball, tennis

TEXARKANA COLLEGE
2500 North Robinson Road
Texarkana, TX 75599
2-year college
(903) 838-4541 X. 373 Contact: Don Woods
Men's Aid (#/$): 16/unspecified $
M: baseball, golf

TEXAS A & I UNIVERSITY
Campus Box 114
Kingsville, TX 78363
(512) 595-3908 Contact: Fred Nuesch
Men's Aid (#/$): 158/$1,106,000
Women's Aid (#/$): 82/$530,800
M: baseball, basketball, cross country, diving, football, golf, indoor track, swimming, swimming-diving, tennis, track & field. Men's Non-aid: riflery
W: basketball, cross country, diving, golf, indoor track, softball, swimming, swimming-diving, tennis, track & field, volleyball. Women's Non-aid: riflery, soccer

TEXAS A & M UNIVERSITY
Joe Routt Boulevard
College Station, TX 77843-1228
(409) 845-5725 Contact: Alan Cannon
Men's Aid (#/$): 56/$168,000
Women's Aid (#/$): 26/$65,000
M: baseball, basketball, cross country, football, golf, indoor track, swimming, swimming-diving, tennis, track & field. Men's Non-aid: riflery
W: basketball, cross country, golf, indoor track, softball, swimming, swimming-diving, tennis, track & field, volleyball. Women's Non-aid: soccer

TEXAS CHRISTIAN UNIVERSITY
P.O. Box 32924
Fort Worth, TX 76129
(817) 921-7969 Contact: Glen Stone
Men's Aid (#/$): 30/$321,200
Women's Aid (#/$): 8/$77,600
M: baseball, basketball, cross country, diving, football, golf, swimming, swimming-diving, tennis, track & field. Men's Non-aid: riflery, soccer
W: basketball, cross country, golf, swimming, swimming-diving, tennis, track & field. Women's Non-aid: riflery, soccer

TEXAS LUTHERAN COLLEGE
1000 West Court Street
Seguin, TX 78155
(512) 372-8134 Contact: Henry Lehnhoff
Men's Aid (#/$): 68/$190,810
Women's Aid (#/$): 38/$152,030
M: baseball, basketball, golf, soccer, tennis
W: basketball, softball, tennis, volleyball

TEXAS SOUTHERN UNIVERSITY
Houston, TX 77004
(713) 527-7208 Contact: Yancy Beavers
Unspecified athletic aid available

M: baseball, basketball, cross country, football, golf, indoor track, soccer, tennis, track & field, volleyball
W: basketball, cross country, indoor track, tennis, track & field, volleyball

TEXAS SOUTHMOST JUNIOR COLLEGE
80 Fort Brown
Brownsville, TX 78520
2-year college
(512) 544-8293 Contact: Arnie Aluarez
Unspecified athletic aid available
M: baseball
W: volleyball

TEXAS TECH UNIVERSITY
P.O. Box 4199
Lubbock, TX 79409
(806) 742-2770 Contact: Joe Hornaday
Unspecified athletic aid available
M: baseball, basketball, cross country, football, golf, indoor track, tennis, track & field. Men's Non-aid: gymnastics, lacrosse, rodeo, soccer
W: basketball, cross country, golf, indoor track, tennis, track & field, volleyball. Women's Non-aid: gymnastics, rodeo

TEXAS WESLEYAN COLLEGE
Fort Worth, TX 76105
(817) 531-4420 Contact: Marie Ferrier
Unspecified athletic aid available
M: baseball, basketball, golf
W: basketball, volleyball

TEXAS WOMAN'S UNIVERSITY
P.O. Box 22628
Denton, TX 76204-0909
(817) 898-2378 Contact: Judy Southard
Women's Aid (#/$): 45/$90,000
W: basketball, gymnastics, tennis, volleyball

TRINITY UNIVERSITY
715 Stadium Drive
San Antonio, TX 78212
(512) 736-8447 Contact: James Hill
Unspecified athletic aid available
M: tennis. Men's Non-aid: baseball, basketball, football, golf, riflery, soccer
W: tennis. Women's Non-aid: basketball, riflery, soccer, softball, volleyball

TYLER JUNIOR COLLEGE
P.O. Box 9020
Tyler, TX 75711
2-year college
(903) 510-2458 Contact: Billy Jack Doggett
Unspecified athletic aid available
M: basketball, golf, football, soccer, tennis
W: basketball, tennis

UNIVERSITY OF DALLAS
1845 East Northgate
Irving, TX 75062
(214) 721-5209 Contact: Patty Danko
Men's Non-aid: basketball, golf, tennis
Women's Non-aid: basketball, tennis, volleyball

UNIVERSITY OF HOUSTON
3855 Holman
Houston, TX 77204-5121
(713) 743-9379 Contact: Bill McGillis
Men's Aid (#/$): 124/$620,000
Women's Aid (#/$): 43/$215,000
M: baseball, basketball, cross country, football, golf, indoor track, track & field
W: basketball, cross country, diving, indoor track, swimming, swimming-diving, tennis, track & field, volleyball

UNIVERSITY OF MARY HARDIN-BAYLOR
VMHB Station Box 8010
Belton, TX 76513
(817) 939-4517 Contact: James Cohagan
Men's Aid (#/$): 20/unspecified $
Women's Aid (#/$): 20/unspecified $
M: baseball, basketball, golf, soccer, tennis
W: basketball, softball, tennis, volleyball

UNIVERSITY OF NORTH TEXAS
P.O. Box 13917
Denton, TX 76203-3917

(817) 565-2664 Contact: Brian Briscoe
Men's Aid (#/$): 165/$482,000
Women's Aid (#/$): 56/$138,000
M: basketball, cross country, football, golf, indoor track, soccer, tennis, track & field
W: basketball, cross country, golf, indoor track, tennis, track & field, volleyball

UNIVERSITY OF TEXAS (ARLINGTON)
Box 19079
Arlington, TX 76019
(817) 273-2239 Contact: Jim Patterson
Men's Aid (#/$): 16/$49,190
Women's Aid (#/$): 17/$66,220
M: baseball, basketball, cross country, golf, indoor track, tennis, track & field. Men's Non-aid: riflery
W: basketball, indoor track, softball, tennis, track & field, volleyball. Women's Non-aid: riflery

UNIVERSITY OF TEXAS (AUSTIN)
P.O. Box 7399
Austin, TX 78713
(512) 471-7437 Contact: Bill Little
Unspecified athletic aid available
M: baseball, basketball, cross country, diving, football, golf, indoor track, swimming, swimming-diving, tennis, track & field
W: basketball, cross country, diving, golf, swimming, tennis, track & field, volleyball

UNIVERSITY OF TEXAS (EL PASO)
500 West University
El Paso, TX 79968
(915) 747-5330 Contact: Eddie Mullens
Men's Aid (#/$): 149/$1,141,140
Women's Aid (#/$): 44/$413,016
M: basketball, cross country, football, golf, indoor track, riflery, tennis, track & field
W: basketball, cross country, golf, indoor track, riflery, tennis, track & field, volleyball

UNIVERSITY OF TEXAS (PAN AMERICAN)
1201 West University
Edinburg, TX 78539
(512) 381-2501 Contact: Arnold Trejo
Men's Aid (#/$): 113/$231,197
Women's Aid (#/$): 46/$118,231
M: baseball, basketball, cross country, golf, soccer, tennis, track & field
W: basketball, cross country, tennis, track & field, volleyball

UNIVERSITY OF TEXAS (SAN ANTONIO)
6900 North Loop 1604E
San Antonio, TX 78285
(512) 691-4635 Contact: Sonny Gonzales
Men's Aid (#/$): 28/$51,904
Women's Aid (#/$): 25/$46,853
M: basketball, cross country, golf, indoor track, riflery, soccer, tennis, track & field. Men's Non-aid: volleyball
W: basketball, cross country, indoor track, riflery, tennis, track & field, volleyball

WAYLAND BAPTIST UNIVERSITY
Campus Box 321
1900 West 7th Street
Plainview, TX 79072
(806) 296-5521 Contact: Greg Feris
Unspecified athletic aid available
M: basketball, cross country, indoor track, track & field
W: basketball, cross country, indoor track, track & field

WEST TEXAS STATE UNIVERSITY
P.O. Box 939
Canyon, TX 79016
(806) 656-2055 Contact: Lynda Tinsley
Unspecified athletic aid available
M: basketball, football, riflery, tennis
W: basketball, riflery, tennis, volleyball

WESTERN TEXAS COLLEGE
6200 College Avenue
Snyder, TX 79549
2-year college

(915) 573-8511 Contact: Milton Ham
Unspecified athletic aid available
M: basketball, golf, rodeo
W: basketball, rodeo

WHARTON COUNTY JUNIOR COLLEGE
911 Boling Highway
Wharton, TX 77488
2-year college
(409) 532-4563 Contact: Gene Bahnsen
Unspecified athletic aid available
M: rodeo, tennis
W: rodeo, tennis, volleyball

Utah

BRIGHAM YOUNG UNIVERSITY
30 SFH
Provo, UT 84602
(801) 378-4909 Contact: Ralph R. Zobell
Unspecified athletic aid available
M: baseball, basketball, cross country, diving, football, golf, gymnastics, indoor track, soccer, swimming, tennis, track & field, wrestling
W: basketball, cross country, diving, golf, gymnastics, indoor track, swimming, tennis, track & field, volleyball

DIXIE COLLEGE
225 South 700 East
St. George, UT 84770
2-year college
(801) 673-4811 X. 420 Contact: Jason Glover
Unspecified athletic aid available
M: baseball, basketball, football, tennis
W: basketball, softball, volleyball

SNOW COLLEGE
150 College Avenue
Ephraim, UT 84627
2-year college
(801) 283-4021 Contact: Bob Trythall
Men's Aid (#/$): 129/$35,760
Women's Aid (#/$): 30/$6,000
M: baseball, basketball, football. Men's Non-aid: alpine skiing, archery, badminton, bowling, cross country skiing, equestrian, golf, power lifting, racquetball, soccer, softball, swimming, tennis, volleyball, weightlifting
W: basketball, softball, volleyball. Women's Non-aid: alpine skiing, archery, badminton, bowling, cross country skiing, equestrian, golf, power lifting, racquetball, soccer, softball, swimming, tennis, volleyball, weightlifting

SOUTHERN UTAH UNIVERSITY
351 West Center Street
Cedar City, UT 84720
(801) 586-7752 Contact: Jim Robinson
Unspecified athletic aid available
M: baseball, basketball, cross country, football, golf, track & field
W: basketball, cross country, gymnastics, softball, track & field, volleyball

UNIVERSITY OF UTAH
Huntsman Center
Salt Lake City, UT 84112
(801) 581-3511 Contact: Liz Abel
Men's Aid (#/$): 166/$1,045,186
Women's Aid (#/$): 92/$492,845
M: alpine skiing, baseball, basketball, cross country, cross country skiing, football, golf, indoor track, swimming-diving, tennis, track & field
W: alpine skiing, basketball, cross country, cross country skiing, gymnastics, indoor track, softball, swimming-diving, tennis, track & field, volleyball

UTAH STATE UNIVERSITY
Athletics Spectrum Annex, VMC 7400
Logan, UT 84322
(801) 750-1361 Contact: Craig Hislop
Unspecified athletic aid available
M: baseball, basketball, cross country, football, golf, indoor track, tennis, track & field, wrestling. Men's Non-aid: rodeo, rugby
W: basketball, cross country,

gymnastics, indoor track, softball, volleyball

WEBER STATE COLLEGE
3750 Harrison Boulevard
Ogden, UT 84408-2702
(801) 626-6010 Contact: Brad Larsen
Unspecified athletic aid available
M: basketball, cross country, football, golf, tennis, track & field, wrestling.
Men's Non-aid: rodeo
W: basketball, cross country, golf, tennis, track & field, volleyball.
Women's Non-aid: rodeo

Vermont

CASTLETON STATE COLLEGE
Box 227
Castleton, VT 05735
(802) 468-5611 X. 286 Contact: Ken Moulton
Men's Non-aid: alpine skiing, baseball, basketball, cross country, cross country skiing, lacrosse, soccer, tennis
Women's Non-aid: alpine skiing, basketball, cross country, cross country skiing, field hockey, lacrosse, soccer, softball, tennis

CHAMPLAIN COLLEGE
P.O. Box 670
Burlington, VT 05402
2-year college
(802) 658-0800 X. 2547 Contact: Robert Tipson
Unspecified athletic aid available
M: basketball. Men's Non-aid: alpine skiing, cross country skiing, golf, soccer
W: field hockey. Women's Non-aid: alpine skiing, cross country skiing, golf, softball

GREEN MOUNTAIN COLLEGE
College Street
Poultney, VT 05764
(802) 287-9313 X. 210 Contact: Richard Hendrickson
Unspecified athletic aid available
M: basketball, soccer
W: basketball, soccer, softball.
Women's Non-aid: volleyball

JOHNSON STATE COLLEGE
College Road
Johnson, VT 05656
(802) 635-2356 X. 380 Contact: Elizabeth A. Flynn
Men's Non-aid: alpine skiing, baseball, basketball, cross country, cross country skiing, soccer, tennis
Women's Non-aid: alpine skiing, basketball, cross country, cross country skiing, soccer, softball

LYNDON STATE COLLEGE
Vail Hill
Lyndonville, VT 05851
(802) 626-9371 Contact: Skip Pound
Men's Non-aid: baseball, basketball, cross country, soccer, tennis
Women's Non-aid: basketball, cheerleading, cross country, soccer, softball, tennis

MIDDLEBURY COLLEGE
Memorial Fieldhouse
Middlebury, VT 05753
(802) 388-3711 Contact: Thomas Lawson
Unspecified athletic aid available
M: alpine skiing, cross country, ice hockey. Men's Non-Aid: baseball, basketball, cross country, football, golf, lacrosse, soccer, swimming-diving, tennis, track & field
W: alpine skiing, cross country skiing, ice hockey. Women's Non-Aid: basketball, cross country, field hockey, lacrosse, soccer, squash, swimming-diving, tennis, track & field

NORWICH UNIVERSITY
Main Street
Northfield, VT 05663
(802) 485-2015 Contact: Debra Hintz
Men's Non-aid: baseball, basketball, cross country, cross country skiing, diving, football, golf, ice hockey,

indoor track, lacrosse, riflery, rugby, sailing, soccer, swimming, swimming-diving, track & field, wrestling
Women's Non-aid: basketball, cross country, cross country skiing, diving, golf, indoor track, riflery, rugby, sailing, soccer, softball, swimming, swimming-diving, track & field

SAINT MICHAEL'S COLLEGE
Winooski Park
Colchester, VT 05439
(802) 655-2000 X. 2537 Contact: Christopher Kenney
Unspecified athletic aid available
M: basketball. Men's Non-aid: alpine skiing, cross country, cross country skiing, golf, ice hockey, lacrosse, soccer, swimming-diving, tennis
W: basketball. Women's Non-aid: alpine skiing, cross country, cross country skiing, field hockey, golf, lacrosse, soccer, swimming-diving, tennis, volleyball

UNIVERSITY OF VERMONT
86 South Williams Street
Burlington, VT 05401
(802) 656-1109 Contact: Dick Whittier
Unspecified athletic aid available
M: alpine skiing, basketball, cross country skiing, ice hockey, soccer. Men's Non-aid: baseball, cross country, golf, gymnastics, indoor track, lacrosse, swimming, swimming-diving, tennis, track & field
W: alpine skiing, basketball, cross country, cross country skiing, soccer. Women's Non-aid: field hockey, gymnastics, indoor track, lacrosse, softball, swimming, swimming-diving, tennis, track & field, volleyball

Virginia

APPRENTICE SCHOOL
4101 Washington Avenue
Newport News, VA 23607
(804) 380-2613 Contact: Horace Underwood
Men's Non-aid: baseball, basketball, cross country, football, golf, soccer, tennis, track & field, wrestling
Women's Non-aid: softball, track & field, volleyball

AVERETT COLLEGE
420 West Main Street
Danville, VA 24541
(804) 791-5645 Contact: Linda W. Shields
Men's Non-aid: basketball, golf, soccer, tennis
Women's Non-aid: basketball, softball, tennis, volleyball

BLUEFIELD COLLEGE
3000 College Drive
Bluefield, VA 24605
(703) 326-4214 Contact: Nina Wilburn
Unspecified athletic aid available
M: baseball, basketball, golf. Men's Non-aid: bowling
W: basketball

BRIDGEWATER COLLEGE
East College Street
Bridgewater, VA 22812
(703) 828-2501 X. 404 Contact: Rob Washburn
Men's Non-aid: baseball, basketball, cross country, football, golf, indoor track, soccer, tennis, track & field
Women's Non-aid: basketball, cheerleading, cross country, field hockey, indoor track, lacrosse, softball, tennis, track & field

CHRISTOPHER NEWPORT COLLEGE
50 Shoe Lane
Newport News, VA 23606
(804) 594-7382 Contact: Wayne Block
Men's Non-aid: baseball, basketball, cross country, golf, indoor track, sailing, soccer, tennis, track & field
Women's Non-aid: basketball, cross country, indoor track, sailing, softball, tennis, track & field, volleyball

CLINCH VALLEY COLLEGE
College Avenue
Wise, VA 24293
(703) 328-0140 Contact: Russell B. Necessary
Unspecified athletic aid available
M: baseball, basketball, golf, tennis
W: basketball, tennis

COLLEGE OF WILLIAM AND MARY
P.O. Box 399
Williamsburg, VA 23185
(804) 221-3344 Contact: Jean Elliot
Unspecified athletic aid available
M: baseball, basketball, cross country, football, gymnastics, indoor track, soccer, tennis, track & field, wrestling. Men's Non-aid: diving, fencing, golf, swimming, swimming-diving
W: basketball, cross country, field hockey, gymnastics, indoor track, lacrosse, soccer, tennis, track & field, volleyball. Women's Non-aid: diving, golf, swimming, swimming-diving

EASTERN MENNONITE COLLEGE
1200 Park Road
Harrisonburg, VA 22801
(703) 432-4137 Contact: David Schrock
Men's Non-aid: baseball, basketball, cross country, soccer, track & field
Women's Non-aid: basketball, cross country, field hockey, softball, track & field, volleyball

EMORY AND HENRY COLLEGE
Emory, VA 24327
(703) 944-4121 Contact: Nathan Graybeal
Men's Non-aid: baseball, basketball, football, tennis, track & field
Women's Non-aid: basketball, tennis, track & field, volleyball

FERRUM COLLEGE
Public Relations
Ferrum, VA 24088
(703) 365-4306 Contact: Gary Holden
Men's Non-aid: baseball, basketball, equestrian, football, golf, soccer, tennis
Women's Non-aid: basketball, equestrian, golf, soccer, softball, tennis, volleyball

GEORGE MASON UNIVERSITY
4400 University Drive
Fairfax, VA 22030-4444
(703) 993-3260 Contact: Carl Sell, Jr.
Unspecified athletic aid available
M: baseball, basketball, cross country, golf, indoor track, soccer, tennis, track & field, volleyball, wrestling
W: basketball, cross country, indoor track, soccer, softball, tennis, track & field, volleyball

HAMPDEN-SYDNEY COLLEGE
P.O. Box 698
Hampden-Sydney, VA 23943
(804) 223-6156 Contact: Dean E. Hybl
Men's Non-aid: baseball, basketball, cross country, football, golf, lacrosse, soccer, tennis, wrestling

HAMPTON UNIVERSITY
Office of Sports Information
Hampton, VA 23668
(804) 727-5757 Contact: LeCounte Conaway
Unspecified athletic aid available
M: basketball, football, indoor track, tennis, track & field. Men's Non-aid: cross country, golf, wrestling
W: basketball, indoor track, track & field. Women's Non-aid: baseball, cross country, volleyball

JAMES MADISON UNIVERSITY
Sports Media Relations
Harrisonburg, VA 22807
(703) 568-6154 Contact: Gary Michael
Unspecified athletic aid available
M: baseball, basketball, cross country, football, golf, gymnastics, indoor track, soccer, swimming-diving, tennis, track & field, wrestling. Men's Non-aid: archery
W: basketball, cross country, field hockey, golf, gymnastics, indoor track, lacrosse, swimming-diving, tennis, track

& field, volleyball. Women's Non-aid: archery, fencing

LIBERTY UNIVERSITY
P.O. Box 20000
Lynchburg, VA 24506
(804) 582-2292 Contact: Mitch Goodman
Men's Aid (#/$): 127/$1,325,880
Women's Aid (#/$): 33/$344,520
Restrictions and notes: Aid available for Athletic Training and Sports Information in addition to the listed sports programs.
M: baseball, basketball, cheerleading, cross country, football, golf, indoor track, soccer, tennis, track & field, wrestling
W: basketball, cheerleading, cross country, indoor track, soccer, track & field, volleyball

LONGWOOD COLLEGE
Sports Information
Farmville, VA 23909
(804) 395-2097 Contact: Hoke Currie
Men's Aid (#/$): 18/$133,000
Women's Aid (#/$): 18/$133,000
M: baseball, basketball, golf, soccer, wrestling. Men's Non-aid: tennis
W: basketball, field hockey, golf, softball, tennis. Women's Non-aid: lacrosse

LYNCHBURG COLLEGE
1501 Lakeside Drive
Lynchburg, VA 24501
(804) 522-8286 Contact: Lee Ashby
Men's Non-aid: baseball, basketball, cross country, equestrian, golf, indoor track, lacrosse, soccer, tennis, track & field, water polo
Women's Non-aid: basketball, cross country, equestrian, field hockey, indoor track, lacrosse, softball, tennis, track & field, volleyball

MARY BALDWIN COLLEGE
Director of Athletics
Staunton, VA 24401
(703) 887-7161 Contact: Mary Ann Kasselmann
Women's Non-aid: basketball, field hockey, swimming, swimming-diving, tennis, volleyball

MARYMOUNT UNIVERSITY
2807 North Glebe Road
Arlington, VA 22207
(703) 284-1515 Contact: Webb Hatch
Men's Non-aid: basketball, golf, lacrosse, soccer, swimming, tennis
Women's Non-aid: basketball, soccer, swimming, tennis, volleyball

MARY WASHINGTON COLLEGE
Room 106A, Goolrick Hall
Fredericksburg, VA 22401
(703) 899-4378 Contact: Vince Benigni
Men's Non-aid: baseball, basketball, cross country, equestrian, indoor track, softball, soccer, swimming, tennis, track & field
Women's Non-aid: basketball, cross country, equestrian, field hockey, indoor track, lacrosse, soccer, softball, swimming, tennis, track & field, volleyball

NORFOLK STATE UNIVERSITY
2401 Corprew Avenue
Norfolk, VA 23504
(804) 623-8152 Contact: Kenny Snelling
Unspecified athletic aid available
M: baseball, basketball, cross country, football, indoor track, track & field, wrestling
W: basketball, cross country, indoor track, softball, track & field

OLD DOMINION UNIVERSITY
Athletic Administration
Building 136
Norfolk, VA 23529-0201
(804) 683-3372
Contact: Carol Hudson, Jr.
Unspecified athletic aid available
M: baseball, basketball, cross country, golf, soccer, swimming, tennis, wrestling. Men's Non-aid: sailing
W: basketball, cross country, field

hockey, lacrosse, swimming, tennis. Women's Non-aid: sailing

RADFORD UNIVERSITY
P.O. Box 5760
Radford, VA 24142
(703) 831-5211 Contact: Rick Rogers
Unspecified athletic aid available
M: baseball, basketball, cross country, golf, gymnastics, lacrosse, soccer, tennis
W: basketball, cross country, field hockey, gymnastics, soccer, tennis, volleyball

RANDOLPH-MACON COLLEGE
P.O. Box 5005
Ashland, VA 23005-5505
(804) 798-8372 X. 513 Contact: Todd Hilder
Unspecified athletic aid available
M: basketball, soccer. Men's Non-aid: baseball, football, golf, lacrosse, tennis
W: basketball. Women's Non-aid: field hockey, lacrosse, soccer, tennis

ROANOKE COLLEGE
Room 225, East Center
Salem, VA 24153
(703) 375-2344 Contact: Howard Wimmer
Men's Non-aid: basketball, cross country, golf, lacrosse, soccer, tennis, track & field
Women's Non-aid: basketball, cross country, field hockey, lacrosse, swimming-diving, tennis, volleyball

SAINT PAUL'S COLLEGE
406 Windsor Avenue
Lawrenceville, VA 23868
(804) 848-2001 Contact: Monique Jones
Unspecified athletic aid available
M: basketball, cross country, football, track & field. Men's Non-aid: badminton, indoor track
W: basketball, softball, track & field, volleyball

SWEET BRIAR COLLEGE
P.O. Box F
Sweet Briar, VA 24595
(804) 381-6330 Contact: Elizabeth B. Irvine
Restrictions and notes: No athletic aid but college policy guarantees 100% of need-based aid.
Women's Non-aid: basketball, diving, equestrian, field hockey, lacrosse, soccer, swimming, swimming-diving, tennis, volleyball

UNIVERSITY OF RICHMOND
Robins Center
Richmond, VA 23173
(804) 289-8363 Contact: Barry Barnum
Aid (#/$): 52/$547,042 (M&W)
M: baseball, basketball, field hockey, football, golf, soccer, tennis. Men's Non-aid: cross country, diving, indoor track, swimming, swimming-diving, track & field, water polo
W: basketball, field hockey, lacrosse, tennis. Women's Non-aid: cross country, diving, indoor track, swimming, swimming-diving, synchronized swimming, track & field

UNIVERSITY OF VIRGINIA
P.O. Box 3785
Charlottesville, VA 22903
(804) 982-5500 Contact: Rich Murray
Men's Aid (#/$): 172/$2,036,172
Women's Aid (#/$): 73.1/$916,515
M: baseball, basketball, cross country, football, golf, indoor track, lacrosse, soccer, swimming-diving, tennis, track & field, wrestling
W: basketball, cross country, field hockey, indoor track, lacrosse, soccer, softball, swimming-diving, tennis, track & field, volleyball

VIRGINIA COMMONWEALTH UNIVERSITY
VCU Box 2003
Richmond, VA 23284-2003
(804) 367-8818 Contact: Mark Halstead
Men's Aid (#/$): 88/$457,174
Women's Aid (#/$): 64/$345,457
M: baseball, basketball, cross country, golf, indoor track, soccer, tennis, track & field

W: basketball, cross country, field hockey, indoor track, tennis, track & field, volleyball

VIRGINIA INTERMONT COLLEGE
1013 Moore Street
Bristol, VA 24201
(703) 669-6101 Contact: Cathy Ramsey
Men's Aid (#/$): 46/$200,000
Women's Aid (#/$): 30/$100,000
M: baseball, basketball, tennis
W: basketball, tennis

VIRGINIA MILITARY INSTITUTE
303 Letcher Avenue
Lexington, VA 24450
(703) 464-7253 Contact: Mike Strickler
Unspecified athletic aid available
M: baseball, basketball, cross country, football, golf, indoor track, lacrosse, riflery, soccer, swimming, tennis, track & field, wrestling

VIRGINIA POLYTECHNIC INSTITUTE & STATE UNIVERSITY
222 Burruss Hall
Blacksburg, VA 24061-0222
(703) 231-5179 Contact: Dr. Martha Harder
Men's Aid (#/$): 244/$1,477,883
Women's Aid (#/$): 64/$396,921
M: baseball, basketball, cross country, football, golf, indoor track, soccer, tennis, track & field, wrestling
W: basketball, cross country, indoor track, tennis, track & field, volleyball

VIRGINIA STATE UNIVERSITY
P.O. Box 58
Petersburg, VA 23803
(804) 524-5028 Contact: George C. Goings
Unspecified athletic aid available
M: basketball, cross country, football, indoor track, track & field. Men's Non-aid: baseball, tennis
W: basketball, cross country, indoor track, track & field. Women's Non-aid: tennis, volleyball

VIRGINIA UNION UNIVERSITY
1500 North Lombardy Street
Richmond, VA 23220
(804) 257-5882 Contact: Phenie D. Golatt
Men's Aid (#/$): 38/unspecified $
Women's Aid (#/$): 7/unspecified $
M: basketball, cross country, football, golf, tennis, track & field
W: basketball, cross country, softball, track & field, volleyball

VIRGINIA WESLEYAN COLLEGE
Wesleyan Drive
Norfolk, VA 23502
(804) 461-3232 Contact: Steve Stocks
Men's Non-aid: baseball, basketball, golf, soccer, tennis
Women's Non-aid: basketball, soccer, softball, tennis

Washington

BELLEVUE COMMUNITY COLLEGE
3000 Landersholm Circle, SE
Bellevue, WA 98007-6484
2-year college
(206) 641-2391 Contact: Ray Washburn
Unspecified athletic aid available
M: baseball, basketball, softball
W: baseball, softball, volleyball

BIG BEND COMMUNITY COLLEGE
7662 Chanute Street
Moses Lake, WA 98837
2-year college
(509) 762-5351 Contact: Mark Poth
Unspecified athletic aid available
M: baseball. Men's Non-aid: basketball, wrestling
W: baseball, volleyball. Women's Non-aid: softball

CENTRAL WASHINGTON UNIVERSITY
214 Buillon Hill
Ellensburg, WA 98926
(509) 963-1485 Contact: Bob Guptill

Men's Non-aid: baseball, basketball, cross country, diving, football, golf, swimming, swimming-diving, tennis, track & field, wrestling
Women's Non-aid: basketball, cross country, diving, swimming, swimming-diving, tennis, track & field, volleyball

CLARK COLLEGE
1800 East McLoughlin Boulevard
Vancouver, WA 98663
2-year college
(206) 699-0268 Contact: Roger D. Daniels
Unspecified athletic aid available
M: baseball, basketball, golf
W: basketball, tennis, volleyball

COLUMBIA BASIN COMMUNITY COLLEGE
2600 North 20th Avenue
Pasco, WA 99301
2-year college
(509) 547-0511 X. 310 Contact: Lynda Meyers
Men's Aid (#/$): 36/$23,472
Women's Aid (#/$): 21/$12,639
M: baseball, basketball, golf, tennis
W: basketball, golf, tennis, volleyball

COMMUNITY COLLEGES OF SPOKANE
1810 North Greene Street
Spokane, WA 99207-5399
2-year college
(509) 533-7231 Contact: Michael R. Pidding
Unspecified athletic aid available
M: baseball, basketball, cross country, football, golf, soccer, tennis, track & field
W: basketball, cross country, gymnastics, softball, tennis, track & field, volleyball

EASTERN WASHINGTON UNIVERSITY
M5-66
Cheney, WA 99004-2499
(509) 359-6334 Contact: David Cook
Men's Aid (#/$): 87.5/$544,955
Women's Aid (#/$): 39.5/$234,197
M: basketball, cross country, football, golf, indoor track, tennis, track & field
W: basketball, cross country, golf, indoor track, tennis, track & field, volleyball

EDMONDS COMMUNITY COLLEGE
20000 68th Avenue West
Lynnwood, WA 98036
2-year college
(206) 771-1507 Contact: Mark B. Honey
Men's Aid (#/$): 53/$7,950
Women's Aid (#/$): 53/$7,950
M: baseball, basketball, soccer
W: basketball, softball, volleyball

EVERETT COMMUNITY COLLEGE
801 Wetmore Avenue
Everett, WA 98201
2-year college
(206) 388-9328 Contact: Larry Walker
Unspecified athletic aid available
M: basketball, cross country, golf, indoor track, soccer, tennis, track & field
W: basketball, cross country, golf, indoor track, tennis, track & field, volleyball

EVERGREEN STATE COLLEGE
CRC 302
Olympia, WA 98505
(206) 866-6000 X. 6538 Contact: Jan Smisek
Unspecified athletic aid available
Restrictions and notes: All athletic awards are in the form of tuition waivers. The awards are good for 1 year and must be reapplied for each year.
M: soccer, swimming
W: soccer, swimming

FORT STEILACOOM COMMUNITY COLLEGE
9401 Far West Drive, SW
Tacoma, WA 98498

2-year college
(206) 964-6614 Contact: Bill Doyle
Unspecified athletic aid available
M: baseball, basketball, soccer
W: basketball, softball, volleyball

GONZAGA UNIVERSITY
East 502 Boone Avenue
Spokane, WA 99258
(509) 328-4220 Contact: Mike Roth
Men's Aid (#/$): 29/$439,110
Women's Aid (#/$): 24/$362,610
M: baseball, basketball, cross country, soccer. Men's Non-aid: crew, golf, indoor track, tennis, track & field
W: basketball, cross country, volleyball. Women's Non-aid: crew, indoor track, soccer, tennis, track & field

GRAYS HARBOR COLLEGE
1620 Edward P. Smiith Drive
Aberdeen, WA 98520
2-year college
(206) 532-9020 Contact: Diane Smith
Unspecified athletic aid available
M: basketball, golf, soccer, track & field
W: basketball, golf, softball, track & field, volleyball

GREEN RIVER COMMUNITY COLLEGE
12401 320th Street, SE
Auburn, WA 98002
2-year college
(206) 833-9111 X. 434 Contact: Gary Hayes
Unspecified athletic aid available
M: baseball, basketball, cross country, golf, soccer, tennis, track & field
W: basketball, cross country, softball, tennis, track & field, volleyball

LOWER COLUMBIA COLLEGE
P.O. Box 3010
Longview, WA 98632
2-year college
(206) 577-2309 Contact: Gary Earnest
Men's Aid (#/$): 69/$10,350
Women's Aid (#/$): 38/$5,700
M: baseball, basketball, cross country, golf, soccer, wrestling
W: baseball, basketball, cross country, golf, softball, volleyball

OLYMPIC COLLEGE
1600 Chester Avenue
Bremerton, WA 98310
2-year college
(206) 478-4731 Contact: Dick Myers
Men's Aid (#/$): 51/$7,650
Women's Aid (#/$): 51/$7,650
M: baseball, basketball
W: basketball, softball, volleyball

PACIFIC LUTHERAN UNIVERSITY
Financial Aid
Tacoma, WA 98447
(206) 535-7161 Contact: Kay Soltis
Men's Aid (#/$): 291/$394,000
Women's Aid (#/$): 125/$253,000
M: alpine skiing, baseball, basketball, crew, cross country, cross country skiing, football, golf, soccer, swimming, tennis, track & field, wrestling
W: alpine skiing, basketball, crew, cross country, cross country skiing, soccer, softball, swimming, tennis, track & field, volleyball

SAINT MARTIN'S COLLEGE
Financial Aid Office
Lacey, WA 98503
(206) 438-4397 Contact: Marianna Deeken
Men's Aid (#/$): 16/$91,425
Women's Aid (#/$): 18/$64,430
M: basketball, golf
W: basketball, golf, volleyball

SEATTLE PACIFIC UNIVERSITY
3307 Third Avenue West
Seattle, WA 98119
(206) 281-2772 Contact: Frank MacDonald
Men's Aid (#/$): 17.1/$261,080
Women's Aid (#/$): 13.8/$211,212
M: basketball, cross country, soccer, track & field. Men's Non-aid: crew
W: basketball, cross country,

gymnastics, track & field, volleyball. Women's Non-aid: crew

SEATTLE UNIVERSITY
550 14th Avenue
Seattle, WA 98122
(206) 296-5915 Contact: Joe Sauvage
Men's Aid (#/$): $100,000
Women's Aid (#/$): $100,000
M: alpine skiing, basketball, cross country, soccer, tennis
W: alpine skiing, basketball, cross country, soccer, tennis

SHORELINE COMMUNITY COLLEGE
16101 Greenwood Avenue North
Seattle, WA 98133
2-year college
(206) 546-4745 Contact: Dan Pray
Men's Aid (#/$): 14/$2,100
Women's Aid (#/$): 36/$5,400
M: baseball, basketball, soccer, tennis
W: basketball, softball, tennis, volleyball

SKAGIT VALLEY COLLEGE
2405 College Way
Mount Vernon, WA 98273
2-year college
(206) 428-1203 Contact: Tomi Clarke
Unspecified athletic aid available
M: baseball, basketball, cross country, soccer, tennis
W: basketball, cross country, softball, tennis, volleyball

UNIVERSITY OF PUGET SOUND
1500 North Warner
Tacoma, WA 98416
(206) 756-3141 Contact: Robin Hamilton
Men's Aid (#/$): 31/$123,000
Women's Aid (#/$): 23/$47,000
M: baseball, basketball, cross country, football, golf, soccer, swimming, tennis, track & field. Men's Non-aid: alpine skiing, crew, cross country skiing
W: basketball, cross country, soccer, softball, swimming, tennis, track & field, volleyball. Women's Non-aid: alpine skiing, crew, cross country skiing

UNIVERSITY OF WASHINGTON
202 Graves Building
Seattle, WA 98195
(206) 543-2230 Contact: Jim Daves
Unspecified athletic aid available
M: baseball, basketball, cross country, football, golf, indoor track, soccer, swimming, swimming-diving, tennis, track & field. Men's Non-aid: bowling
W: basketball, cross country, golf, gymnastics, indoor track, softball, swimming, swimming-diving, tennis, track & field, volleyball. Women's Non-aid: bowling

WALLA WALLA COMMUNITY COLLEGE
500 Tausick Way
Walla Walla, WA 99362
2-year college
(509) 527-4306 Contact: Don Boen
Unspecified athletic aid available
M: basketball, football, golf, rodeo, tennis
W: basketball, rodeo, tennis, volleyball

WASHINGTON STATE UNIVERSITY
M-8 Bohler Gym
Pullman, WA 99164-1602
(509) 332-8309 Contact: Rod Commons
Men's Aid (#/$): 142/$1,250,556
Women's Aid (#/$): 112/$723,943
M: baseball, basketball, cross country, football, golf, tennis, track & field
W: basketball, crew, cross country, golf, soccer, swimming, tennis, volleyball

WESTERN WASHINGTON UNIVERSITY
516 High Street
Bellingham, WA 98225
(206) 676-3108 Contact: Paul Madison
Unspecified athletic aid available
M: basketball. Men's Non-aid: crew, football, golf, indoor track, soccer, softball, tennis, track & field, volleyball

W: basketball. Women's Non-aid: crew, football, golf, indoor track, soccer, softball, tennis, track & field, volleyball

WHITMAN COLLEGE
Sherwood Center
Walla Walla, WA 99362
(509) 527-5414 Contact: Neil McDonald
Men's Non-aid: alpine skiing, baseball, basketball, cross country, cross country skiing, golf, soccer, swimming-diving, tennis, track & field
Women's Non-aid: alpine skiing, basketball, cross country, cross country skiing, soccer, swimming-diving, tennis, track & field, volleyball

WHITWORTH COLLEGE
Whitworth Drive
Spokane, WA 99251
(509) 466-3235 Contact: Paul J. Merkel
Unspecified athletic aid available
Restrictions and notes: Non-athletic dollars awarded in sports based on need.
M: baseball, basketball, cross country, football, soccer, swimming, tennis, track & field
W: bowling, cross country, soccer, swimming, tennis, track & field, volleyball

YAKIMA VALLEY COLLEGE
West Nob Hill Boulevard
Yakima, WA 98902
2-year college
(509) 575-2423 Contact: Jerry Ward
Unspecified athletic aid available
M: baseball, basketball, football, tennis
W: basketball, softball, tennis, volleyball

West Virginia

ALDERSON-BROADDUS COLLEGE
P.O. Box 306
Philippi, WV 26416
(304) 457-1700 X. 250 Contact: Mamie R. Argo
Men's Aid (#/$): 34/$232,981
Women's Aid (#/$): 17/$80,216
Restrictions and notes: All recipients must apply for all federal and state funds first.
M: baseball, basketball, soccer. Men's Non-aid: cross country
W: basketball, volleyball. Women's Non-aid: cross country

BETHANY COLLEGE
Athletic Department
Bethany, WV 26032
(304) 829-7231 Contact: Sports Information Director
Men's Non-aid: baseball, basketball, cross country, football, golf, soccer, softball, swimming-diving, tennis, track & field
Women's Non-aid: baseball, basketball, cross country, field hockey, golf, softball, swimming-diving, tennis, track & field, volleyball

BLUEFIELD STATE COLLEGE
Rock Street
Bluefield, WV 24701
(304) 327-4022 Contact: Audrey Clay
Men's Aid (#/$): 47/$64,713
Women's Aid (#/$): 14/$19,457
M: baseball, basketball, cross country, golf, tennis
W: basketball, cheerleading, cross country, softball, tennis

CONCORD COLLEGE
P.O. Box 1000
Athens, WV 24712
(304) 384-5358 Contact: Patricia Harmon
Unspecified athletic aid available
M: basketball, football. Men's Non-aid: golf, tennis
W: basketball, volleyball. Women's Non-aid: softball, tennis

DAVIS & ELKINS COLLEGE
Sycamore Street
Elkins, WV 26241

(304) 636-1900 X. 252 Contact: Will Shaw
Unspecified athletic aid available
M: baseball, basketball, cross country, golf, soccer, tennis
W: basketball, cross country, field hockey, softball, tennis

FAIRMONT STATE COLLEGE
Locust Avenue
Fairmont, WV 26554
(304) 367-4213 Contact: William D. Shaffer
Men's Aid (#/$): 10/$29,400
Women's Aid (#/$): 4/$11,760
M: basketball, football, golf, swimming-diving, tennis
W: basketball, cross country, swimming-diving, tennis, volleyball

GLENVILLE STATE COLLEGE
200 High Street
Glenville, WV 26351
(304) 462-4102 Contact: Tina Cunningham
Men's Aid (#/$): 5/$12,430
Women's Aid (#/$): 3/$2,970
M: basketball, cross country, football, golf, track & field, weightlifting
W: basketball, cross country, track & field

MARSHALL UNIVERSITY
P.O. Box 1360
Huntington, WV 25715
(304) 696-5275 Contact: Gary Richter
Unspecified athletic aid available
M: baseball, basketball, cross country, football, golf, indoor track, soccer, swimming-diving, track & field
W: basketball, cross country, indoor track, tennis, track & field, volleyball

OHIO VALLEY COLLEGE
College Parkway
Parkersburg, WV 26101
2-year college
(800) 678-6780 Contact: Marty Davis
Men's Aid (#/$): 22/$11,500
Women's Aid (#/$): 15/$10,000
M: baseball, basketball
W: basketball, volleyball. Women's Non-aid: cheerleading

SALEM-TEIKYO UNIVERSITY
223 West Main Street
Salem, WV 26426
(304) 782-5205 Contact: Don Delgado
Unspecified athletic aid available
M: baseball, basketball. Men's Non-aid: golf, soccer, tennis
W: basketball, softball, volleyball. Women's Non-aid: tennis

SHEPHERD COLLEGE
HPER Center
Shepherdstown, WV 25443-1569
(304) 876-2511 X. 228 Contact: Michael Straley
Men's Aid (#/$): 18/$120,000
Women's Aid (#/$): 14/$40,000
M: basketball, football. Men's Non-aid: baseball, cross country, golf, soccer, tennis
W: basketball, volleyball. Women's Non-aid: cross country, golf, softball, tennis

UNIVERSITY OF CHARLESTON
2300 MacCorkle Avenue SE
Charleston, WV 25304
(800) 995-GOUC Contact: John Cyrus
Men's Aid (#/$): 63/$380,788
Women's Aid (#/$): 54/$269,872
M: baseball, basketball, crew, golf, soccer, tennis
W: basketball, crew, soccer, softball, tennis, volleyball

WEST LIBERTY STATE COLLEGE
West Liberty, WV 26074
(304) 336-8212 Contact: William Hanna
Men's Aid (#/$): 64/$198,400
Women's Aid (#/$): 17/$46,720
M: baseball, basketball, football, tennis. Men's Non-aid: cross country, golf, wrestling
W: baseball, soccer, synchronized swimming, volleyball

WEST VIRGINIA INSTITUTE OF TECHNOLOGY
Athletic Department
Montgomery, WV 25136

(304) 442-3308 Contact: Joe Lefkay
Men's Aid (#/$): 38/$50,000
Women's Aid (#/$): 12/$11,000
M: baseball, basketball, football, tennis
W: basketball, softball, tennis, volleyball

WEST VIRGINIA STATE COLLEGE
Campus Box 133
Institute, WV 25112
(304) 766-3131 Contact: Fred D. Black
Unspecified athletic aid available
M: basketball, football. Men's Non-aid: baseball, tennis, track & field
W: basketball. Women's Non-aid: tennis, track & field

WEST VIRGINIA UNIVERSITY
P.O. Box 877
107 Coliseum
Morgantown, WV 26506
(304) 293-2821 Contact: Shelly Poe
Men's Aid (#/$): 193/$1,386,259
Women's Aid (#/$): 57/$408,440
M: baseball, basketball, cross country, football, indoor track, riflery, soccer, swimming-diving, tennis, track & field, wrestling
W: basketball, cross country, gymnastics, indoor track, riflery, swimming-diving, tennis, track & field, volleyball

WEST VIRGINIA WESLEYAN COLLEGE
College Relations Office
Buckhannon, WV 26201
(304) 473-8487 Contact: John Scott
Unspecified athletic aid available
M: basketball, soccer. Men's Non-aid: baseball, cross country, football, golf, tennis, track & field
W: basketball, tennis. Women's Non-aid: cross country, softball, track & field

WHEELING JESUIT COLLEGE
316 Washington Avenue
Wheeling, WV 26003
(304) 243-2304 Contact: Su Saunders
Men's Aid (#/$): 36/$147,865
Women's Aid (#/$): 50/$109,842
M: basketball, cross country, golf, soccer
W: basketball, cross country, golf, soccer, volleyball

Wisconsin

BELOIT COLLEGE
700 College
Beloit, WI 53511
(608) 363-2229 Contact: Paul Erickson
Men's Non-aid: baseball, basketball, diving, football, golf, indoor track, soccer, swimming, swimming-diving, tennis, track & field
Women's Non-aid: basketball, diving, indoor track, soccer, softball, swimming, swimming-diving, tennis, track & field, volleyball

CARDINAL STRITCH COLLEGE
6801 North Yates Road
Milwaukee, WI 53217-3985
(414) 352-5400 X. 259 Contact: Denny Fox
Men's Non-aid: baseball, basketball, cheerleading
Women's Non-aid: basketball, cheerleading, softball, volleyball

CARROLL COLLEGE
100 North East Avenue
Waukesha, WI 53186
(414) 542-7297 Contact: Jane A. Lemke
Men's Non-aid: baseball, basketball, cross country, football, golf, indoor track, swimming, tennis, track & field, wrestling
Women's Non-aid: basketball, cross country, indoor track, swimming, tennis, track & field, volleyball

CARTHAGE COLLEGE
2001 Alford Park Drive
Kenosha, WI 53140

(414) 551-6627 Contact: Scott Pedersen
Men's Non-aid: baseball, basketball, cross country, football, golf, indoor track, swimming, tennis, track & field
Women's Non-aid: basketball, cross country, indoor track, softball, swimming, tennis, track & field, volleyball

CONCORDIA UNIVERSITY WISCONSIN
12800 North Lakeshore Drive
MeQuon, WI 53092
(414) 243-5700 Contact: R. Edward Schroeder
Unspecified athletic aid available
M: baseball, basketball, football. Men's Non-aid: tennis
W: basketball, softball. Women's Non-aid: tennis

EDGEWOOD COLLEGE
855 Woodrow Street
Madison, WI 53711
(608) 257-4861 Contact: Dave Smith
Men's Non-aid: baseball, basketball, golf, soccer, tennis
Women's Non-aid: basketball, golf, softball, tennis, volleyball

LAWRENCE UNIVERSITY
P.O. Box 599
Appleton, WI 54912
(414) 832-6590 Contact: Rick Peterson
Restrictions and notes: No athletic aid. 61% of 1992-93 students received need-based aid packages averaging $14,194.
Men's Non-aid: baseball, basketball, cross country, diving, fencing, football, golf, ice hockey, indoor track, soccer, swimming, swimming-diving, tennis, track & field, wrestling
Women's Non-aid: basketball, cross country, fencing, indoor track, soccer, softball, swimming, swimming-diving, tennis, track & field, volleyball

MADISON AREA TECHNICAL COLLEGE
3550 Anderson Street
Madison, WI 53704
2-year college
(608) 246-6098 Contact: Julie N. Do
Unspecified athletic aid available
M: baseball, basketball, wrestling.
Men's Non-aid: bowling, cross country, golf, tennis
W: basketball, softball, volleyball.
Women's Non-aid: bowling, cross country, golf, tennis

MARIAN COLLEGE
45 South National Avenue
Fond du Lac, WI 54935
(414) 923-7625 Contact: Brian Gillogly
Men's Non-aid: baseball, basketball, cross country, golf, soccer, tennis
Women's Non-aid: basketball, cross country, soccer, softball, tennis, volleyball

MARQUETTE UNIVERSITY
1212 West Wisconsin Avenue
Milwaukee, WI 53233
(414) 288-7447 Contact: Kathleen Hohl
Men's Aid (#/$): 33/$445,000
Women's Aid (#/$): 23/$306,000
M: basketball, cross country, golf, indoor track, soccer, tennis, track & field, wrestling
W: basketball, cross country, indoor track, soccer, tennis, track & field, volleyball

MILWAUKEE AREA TECHNOLOGY COLLEGE
700 West State Street
Milwaukee, WI 53233
2-year college
(414) 278-6448 Contact: Mike Basile
Unspecified athletic aid available
M: baseball, basketball, cross country, indoor track, soccer, track & field
W: basketball, cross country, indoor track, track & field

NORTHLAND COLLEGE
1411 Ellis Avenue
Ashland, WI 54806
(715) 682-1243 Contact: Steve Franklin
Unspecified athletic aid available

M: basketball, soccer
W: basketball, volleyball

RIPON COLLEGE
300 Seward Street
P.O. Box 248
Ripon, WI 54971
(414) 748-8101 Contact: Karri S. Verhelst
Men's Non-aid: baseball, basketball, cross country, football, golf, indoor track, soccer, swimming, swimming-diving, tennis, track & field
Women's Non-aid: basketball, cross country, indoor track, soccer, softball, swimming, swimming-diving, tennis, track & field, volleyball

SAINT NORBERT COLLEGE
Schuldes Sports Center
De Pere, WI 54115
(414) 337-4077 Contact: Larry Van Alstine
Men's Non-aid: baseball, basketball, cross country, football, golf, indoor track, soccer, tennis, track & field
Women's Non-aid: basketball, cross country, golf, indoor track, soccer, softball, tennis, track & field, volleyball

UNIVERSITY OF WISCONSIN (EAU CLAIRE)
P.O. Box 4004
Eau Claire, WI 54702-4004
(715) 836-4184 Contact: Tim Petermann
Men's Non-aid: baseball, basketball, cross country, diving, football, golf, ice hockey, indoor track, swimming, swimming-diving, tennis, track & field, wrestling
Women's Non-aid: basketball, cross country, diving, gymnastics, indoor track, soccer, softball, swimming, swimming-diving, tennis, track & field, volleyball

UNIVERSITY OF WISCONSIN (GREEN BAY)
Phoenix Sports Center
Green Bay, WI 54311-7001
(414) 465-2145 Contact: Terry Powers
Unspecified athletic aid available
M: basketball, soccer. Men's Non-aid: cross country, cross country skiing, diving, golf, sailing, swimming-diving, tennis
W: basketball. Women's Non-aid: cross country, cross country skiing, diving, golf, sailing, softball, swimming-diving, tennis, volleyball

UNIVERSITY OF WISCONSIN (LA CROSSE)
1725 State Street
La Crosse, WI 54601
(608) 785-8604 Contact: Al C. Stadthaus
Men's Non-aid: baseball, basketball, bowling, cross country, diving, football, golf, gymnastics, ice hockey, indoor track, rugby, swimming, swimming-diving, tennis, track & field, wrestling
Women's Non-aid: basketball, bowling, cross country, diving, gymnastics, indoor track, softball, swimming, swimming-diving, tennis, track & field, volleyball

UNIVERSITY OF WISCONSIN (MADISON)
1440 Monroe Street
Madison, WI 53706
(608) 263-5502 Contact: Tamara J. Flarup
Men's Aid (#/$): 242/$703,791
Women's Aid (#/$): 119/$1,460,134
Restrictions and notes: Football is $694,400 of the total Men's aid amount.
M: basketball, cross country, diving, football, golf, ice hockey, indoor track, soccer, swimming, swimming-diving, tennis, track & field, wrestling. Men's Non-aid: crew
W: basketball, cross country, diving, golf, indoor track, soccer, swimming, swimming-diving, tennis, track & field, volleyball

UNIVERSITY OF WISCONSIN (MILWAUKEE)
North Building P.O. Box 413
Milwaukee, WI 53201

(414) 229-4593 Contact: Paul Helgren
Men's Aid (#/$): 94/$374,255
Women's Aid (#/$): 94/$315,552
M: baseball, basketball, cross country, indoor track, soccer, swimming, swimming-diving, tennis, track & field, volleyball
W: basketball, cross country, indoor track, soccer, swimming, swimming-diving, tennis, track & field, volleyball

UNIVERSITY OF WISCONSIN (OSHKOSH)

108 Kolf Sports Center
Oshkosh, WI 54901
(414) 424-0365 Contact: Kennan Timm
Men's Non-aid: baseball, basketball, cross country, football, golf, gymnastics, indoor track, soccer, swimming-diving, tennis, track & field, wrestling
Women's Non-aid: basketball, cross country, gymnastics, indoor track, softball, swimming-diving, tennis, track & field, volleyball

UNIVERSITY OF WISCONSIN (PLATTEVILLE)

One University Plaza
Platteville, WI 53818
(608) 342-1574 Contact: Becky Bohm
Men's Non-aid: baseball, basketball, cross country, football, golf, indoor track, soccer, tennis, track & field, wrestling
Women's Non-aid: basketball, cross country, indoor track, softball, tennis, track & field, volleyball

UNIVERSITY OF WISCONSIN (RIVER FALLS)

Room 23, South Hall
River Falls, WI 54022
(715) 425-3846 Contact: Jim Thies
Men's Non-aid: baseball, basketball, cross country, football, golf, ice hockey, indoor track, swimming-diving, tennis, track & field, wrestling
Women's Non-aid: basketball, cross country, gymnastics, indoor track, softball, swimming-diving, tennis, track & field, volleyball

UNIVERSITY OF WISCONSIN (STEVENS POINT)

106 Student Service Building
Stevens Point, WI 54481
(715) 346-4771 Contact: Phillip C. George
Men's Non-aid: baseball, basketball, cross country, diving, football, golf, ice hockey, indoor track, swimming, tennis, track & field, wrestling
Women's Non-aid: basketball, cross country, diving, indoor track, soccer, softball, swimming, tennis, track & field, volleyball

UNIVERSITY OF WISCONSIN (STOUT)

210 Bowman Hall
Menomonie, WI 54751
(715) 232-1363 Contact: Howard Slinden
Men's Non-aid: baseball, basketball, cross country, diving, football, golf, indoor track, swimming, swimming-diving, tennis, track & field, wrestling
Women's Non-aid: basketball, cross country, diving, gymnastics, indoor track, swimming, swimming-diving, tennis, track & field, volleyball

UNIVERSITY OF WISCONSIN (SUPERIOR)

1800 Grand Avenue
Superior, WI 54880
(715) 394-8503 Contact: Lee Purdy
Men's Non-aid: baseball, basketball, cross country, football, golf, ice hockey, track & field, wrestling
Women's Non-aid: baseball, basketball, cross country, gymnastics, track & field, volleyball

VITERBO COLLEGE

815 South 9th Street
La Crosse, WI 54601
(608) 791-0487 Contact: Terry Norman
Men's Non-aid: baseball, basketball, soccer

Women's Non-aid: basketball, softball, volleyball

Wyoming

CENTRAL WYOMING COLLEGE
2660 Peck Avenue
Riverton, WY 82501
2-year college
(307) 856-9291 Contact: Carolyne Perry
Unspecified athletic aid available
M: basketball, rodeo
W: basketball, rodeo, volleyball

EASTERN WYOMING COLLEGE
3200 West C Street
Torrington, WY 82240
2-year college
(307) 532-7111 Contact: Holly Sims
Men's Aid (#/$): 12/unspecified $
Women's Aid (#/$): 12/unspecified $
M: basketball
W: volleyball

LARAMIE COUNTY COMMUNITY COLLEGE
1400 East College Drive
Cheyenne, WY 82001
2-year college
(307) 634-5853 Contact: Woody Halverson
Men's Non-aid: rodeo
Women's Non-aid: rodeo

NORTHWEST COLLEGE
Athletics
231 West 6th Street
Powell, WY 82435-1878
2-year college
(307) 754-6505 Contact: Ken Rochlitz
Unspecified athletic aid available
M: basketball, wrestling
W: basketball, volleyball

SHERIDAN COLLEGE
Athletic Department
Box 1500
Sheridan, WY 82801
2-year college
(307) 674-6446 Contact: Bruce Hoffman
Men's Aid (#/$): 12/$43,000
Women's Aid (#/$): 14/$42,000
M: basketball
W: basketball, volleyball

UNIVERSITY OF WYOMING
P.O. Box 3414
Laramie, WY 8207-3414
(307) 766-2256 Contact: Kevin M. McKinney
Men's Aid (#/$): 112/$213,600
Women's Aid (#/$): 38/$71,200
M: baseball, basketball, cross country, diving, football, golf, indoor track, swimming, swimming-diving, track & field, wrestling
W: basketball, cross country, diving, golf, indoor track, swimming, swimming-diving, track & field, volleyball

WESTERN WYOMING COMMUNITY COLLEGE
Box 428
Rock Springs, WY 82901
2-year college
(307) 382-1651 Contact: Dick Flores
Unspecified athletic aid available
M: basketball, tennis. Men's Non-aid: alpine skiing, bowling
W: basketball, tennis, volleyball. Women's Non-aid: alpine skiing, bowling

SPORT-BY-SPORT APPENDIX

Understanding the Appendix

The Appendix is an alphabetical list of sports programs and the colleges that offer each program. The state code for each college is also shown. (M) indicates that the program is only offered to men. (W) means it is offered to women, and (MW) indicates the program is offered to both men and women.

Keep in mind that this list mixes both scholarship and non-scholarship programs together. Thus, it is important to use the directory listings to determine which kind of scholarship is offered.

Sports Programs Listed

The following programs are included in the Appendix:

State Abbreviations

Alabama	AL
Alaska	AK
Arizona	AZ
Arkansas	AR
California	CA
Colorado	CO
Connecticut	CT
Delaware	DE
District of Columbia	DC
Florida	FL
Georgia	GA
Hawaii	HI
Idaho	ID
Illinois	IL
Indiana	IN
Iowa	IA
Kansas	KS
Kentucky	KY
Louisiana	LA
Maine	ME
Maryland	MD
Massachusetts	MA
Michigan	MI
Minnesota	MN
Mississippi	MS
Missouri	MO
Montana	MT
Nebraska	NE
Nevada	NV
New Hampshire	NH
New Jersey	NJ
New Mexico	NM
New York	NY
North Carolina	NC
North Dakota	ND
Ohio	OH
Oklahoma	OK
Oregon	OR
Pennsylvania	PA
Puerto Rico	PR
Rhode Island	RI
South Carolina	SC
South Dakota	SD
Tennessee	TN
Texas	TX
Utah	UT
Vermont	VT
Virginia	VA
Washington	WA
West Virginia	WV
Wisconsin	WI
Wyoming	WY

Alpine Skiing

Adirondack College, NY (MW)
Albertson College, ID (MW)
Alfred University, NY (MW)
Bates College, ME (MW)
Boston College, MA (MW)
Bowdoin College, ME (MW)
Carleton College, MN (MW)
Castleton State College, VT (MW)
Champlain College, VT (MW)
Clarkson University, NY (MW)
Colby-Sawyer College, NH (MW)
Colorado School of Mines, CO (MW)
Cornell University, NY (M)
Dartmouth College, NH (MW)
Eastern Oregon State College, OR (MW)
Fairfield University, CT (MW)
Fashion Institute of Technology, NY (MW)
Fort Lewis College, CO (W)
Franklin Pierce College, NH (MW)
Harvard University, MA (MW)
Johnson State College, VT (MW)
Keene State College, NH (MW)
Lees-McRae College, NC (MW)
Massachusetts Institute of Technology, MA (MW)
Middlebury College, VT (MW)
Montana State University, MT (MW)
Moorpark College, CA (MW)
North Adams State College, MA (MW)
North Country Community College, NY (MW)
Pacific Lutheran University, WA (MW)
Plymouth State College, NH (MW)
Saint Lawrence University, NY (MW)
Saint Michael's College, VT (MW)
Saint Olaf College, MN (MW)
Seattle University, WA (MW)
Sierra College, CA (MW)
Sierra Nevada College, NV (MW)
Skidmore College, NY (MW)
Smith College, MA (W)
Snow College, UT (MW)
University of Alaska, AK (MW)
University of Alaska Southeast, AK (MW)
University of Colorado, CO (MW)
University of Denver, CO (MW)
University of New Hampshire, NH (MW)
University of New Mexico, NM (MW)
University of Puget Sound, WA (MW)
University of Utah, UT (MW)
University of Vermont, VT (MW)
Western New England College, MA (MW)
Western State College, CO (MW)
Western Wyoming Community College, WY (MW)
Whitman College, WA (MW)

Archery

Arizona State University, AZ (MW)
Atlantic Community College, NJ (MW)
California State University (Long Beach), CA (MW)
Columbia University, NY (W)
Dalton College, GA (MW)
Dominican College, CA (W)
Dutchess Junior College, NY (M)
Glendale Community College, AZ (MW)
Goucher College, MD (MW)
Indiana State University, IN (MW)
James Madison University, VA (MW)
Johns Hopkins University, MD (M)
Navajo Community College, AZ (MW)
Pima Community College, AZ (MW)
Queensborough Community College, NY (MW)
Scottsdale Community College, AR (MW)
Snow College, UT (MW)

Badminton

Albright College, PA (W)
Arizona State University, AZ (MW)
Bryn Mawr College, PA (MW)
California State University (Long Beach), CA (MW)
Concordia College, MN (M)
Dalton College, GA (MW)
Goucher College, MD (MW)
Johns Hopkins University, MD (M)
Lambuth University, TN (M)
Molloy College, NY (M)
Moorpark College, CA (MW)
Plymouth State College, NH (M)
Roosevelt University, IL (MW)
Saint Paul's College, VA (M)
San Diego Mesa College, CA (MW)
Snow College, UT (MW)
Southern Connecticut State University, CT (W)
Swarthmore College, PA (W)
Westfield State College, MA (M)

Baseball

Adelphi University, NY (M)
Adrian College, MI (M)
Alabama State University, AL (M)
Albertson College, ID (M)
Albion College, MI (M)
Albright College, PA (M)
Alcorn State University, MS (M)
Alderson-Broaddus College, WV (M)
Alice Lloyd College, KY (M)
Allegheny CCAC, PA (M)
Allegheny College, PA (M)
Allen County College, KS (M)
Allentown College, PA (M)
Allen University, SC (M)
Alma College, MI (MW)
Alvernia College, PA (M)
American International College, MA (M)
American University, DC (M)
Amherst College, MA (M)
Anderson College, SC (M)
Anderson University, IN (M)
Andrew College, GA (M)
Angelina College, TX (M)
Anoka-Ramsey College, MN (M)
Appalachian State University, NC (M)
Apprentice School, VA (M)
Aquinas College, MI (M)
Aquinas Junior College, TN (M)
Arizona State University, AZ (M)
Arkansas College, AR (M)
Arkansas State University, AR (M)
Arkansas Tech University, AR (M)
Armstrong State College, GA (M)
Arrowhead Community College, MN (M)
Asbury College, KY (M)

Ashland College, OH (M)
Atlantic Community College, NJ (M)
Auburn University, AL (M)
Auburn University (Montgomery), AL (M)
Augsburg College, MN (M)
Augusta College, GA (M)
Augustana College, IL (M)
Augustana College, SD (M)
Aurora University, IL (M)
Austin College, TX (M)
Austin Community College, MN (M)
Austin Peay State University, TN (M)
Avila College, MO (M)
Azusa Pacific University, CA (M)
Babson College, MA (M)
Bacone Junior College, OK (M)
Baker University, KS (M)
Ball State University, IN (M)
Baltimore City Community College, MD (M)
Barry University, FL (M)
Barstow College, CA (M)
Barton College, NC (M)
Barton County College, KS (M)
Bates College, ME (M)
Baylor University, TX (M)
Becker College, MA (M)
Belhaven College, MS (MW)
Bellarmine College, KY (M)
Belleville Area College, IL (M)
Bellevue College, NE (MW)
Bellevue Community College, WA (MW)
Belmont Abbey College, NC (M)
Belmont College, TN (M)
Beloit College, WI (M)
Benedict College, SC (M)
Benedictine College, KS (M)
Bentley College, MA (M)
Bergen Community College, NJ (M)
Berry College, GA (M)
Bethany College, KS (MW)
Bethany College, WV (MW)
Bethany Lutheran College, MN (M)
Bethel College, IN (M)
Bethel College, MN (M)
Bethel College, TN (M)
Bethune-Cookman College, FL (M)
Big Bend Community College, WA (MW)
Biola University, CA (M)
Birmingham-Southern College, AL (M)
Bismarck State College, ND (MW)
Blackburn College, IL (M)
Black Hawk College, IL (M)
Bloomfield College, NJ (M)
Bloomsburg University, PA (M)
Bluefield College, VA (M)
Bluefield State College, WV (M)
Blue Mountain College, OR (M)
Bluffton College, OH (M)
Boston College, MA (M)
Boston University, MA (M)
Bowdoin College, ME (M)
Bowie State University, MD (M)
Bowling Green State University, OH (M)
Bradley University, IL (M)
Brainerd Community College, MN (M)
Brandeis University, MA (M)
Brevard College, FL (M)
Brewton Parker College, GA (M)
Briar Cliff College, IA (M)
Bridgewater College, VA (M)
Bridgewater State College, MA (M)
Brigham Young University, UT (M)
Bristol University, TN (M)
Bronx Community College, NY (M)
Broome Community College, NY (M)
Broward Community College, FL (MW)
Brown University, RI (M)
Bryant College, RI (M)
Bucknell University, PA (M)
Bucks County Community College, PA (M)
Buena Vista College, IA (M)
Buffalo State University (New York), NY (M)
Bunker Hill Community College, MA (MW)
Butler County Community College, KS (M)
Butler County Community College, PA (M)
Butte College, CA (M)
Cabrillo College, CA (M)
Cabrini College, PA (MW)
California Baptist College, CA (M)
California Institute of Technology, CA (M)
California Lutheran University, CA (M)
California Polytechnic State University, CA (M)
California State Polytechnic University, CA (M)
California State University, CA (M)
California State University (Chico), CA (M)
California State University (Dominguez Hills), CA (M)
California State University (Fresno), CA (M)
California State University (Fullerton), CA (M)
California State University (Hayward), CA (M)
California State University (Long Beach), CA (M)
California State University (Los Angeles), CA (M)
California State University (Northridge), CA (M)
California State University (Sacramento), CA (M)
California State University (San Bernardino), CA (M)
California University, PA (M)
Calvin College, MI (M)
Cameron University, OK (M)
Campbellsville College, KY (M)
Campbell University, NC (M)
Canisius College, NY (M)
Capital University, OH (M)
Cardinal Stritch College, WI (M)
Carl Albert Junior College, OK (M)
Carleton College, MN (M)
Carroll College, WI (M)
Carson-Newman College, TN (M)
Carthage College, WI (M)
Case Western Reserve University, OH (M)
Castleton State College, VT (M)
Catawba College, NC (M)
Catholic University of America, DC (M)
Catonsville Community College, MD (M)
Cecil Community College, MD (M)
Cedarville College, OH (M)
Centenary College, LA (M)
Central Arizona College, AZ (M)
Central College, IA (M)
Central College, KS (M)
Central Connecticut State University, CT (M)
Central Florida Community College, FL (M)
Central Methodist College, MO (M)
Central Michigan University, MI (M)
Central Missouri State University, MO (M)
Central State University, OH (M)

Central Washington University, WA (M)
Central Wesleyan College, SC (M)
Cerritos College, CA (M)
Chaffey College, CA (M)
Chapman University, CA (M)
Charles County Community College, MD (M)
Charleston Southern University, SC (M)
Chattahoochee Valley Community College, AL (M)
Chicago State University, IL (M)
Chipola Junior College, FL (M)
Chowan College, NC (M)
Christian Brothers College, TN (M)
Christopher Newport College, VA (M)
Citadel, SC (M)
City College of New York, NY (M)
City College of San Francisco, CA (MW)
Clackamas Community College, OR (M)
Clarion University, PA (M)
Clark College, WA (M)
Clarkson University, NY (M)
Clark University, MA (M)
Clemson University, SC (M)
Cleveland State Community College, TN (M)
Cleveland State University, OH (M)
Clinch Valley College, VA (M)
Clinton Community College, NY (M)
Cloud County Community College, KS (M)
Coahoma Junior College, MS (M)
Coastal Carolina College, SC (M)
Cochise County Community College, AZ (M)
Coe College, IA (M)
Coffeyville Community College, KS (M)
Coker College, SC (M)
Colby Community College, KS (M)
Colgate University, NY (M)
College of Allegheny County, PA (M)
College of Charleston, SC (M)
College of Charleston, SC (M)
College of Idaho, ID (M)
College of Southern Idaho, ID (M)
College of St. Francis, IL (M)
College of St. Rose, NY (M)
College of William and Mary, VA (M)
College of the Desert, CA (M)
College of the Ozarks, MO (M)
College of the Redwoods, CA (M)
College of the Sequoias, CA (M)
College of Wooster, OH (M)
Colorado College, CO (M)
Colorado Northwestern Community College, CO (M)
Colorado School of Mines, CO (MW)
Columbia Basin Community College, WA (M)
Columbia-Greene Community College, NY (M)
Columbia University, NY (M)
Columbus College, GA (M)
Columbus State Community College, OH (M)
Community College of Rhode Island, RI (M)
Community College of the Finger Lakes, NY (M)
Community Colleges of Spokane, WA (M)
Compton Community College, CA (M)
Concordia College, MI (M)
Concordia College (Moorhead), MN (M)
Concordia College (St. Paul), MN (M)
Concordia College, NY (M)
Concordia Lutheran College, TX (M)
Concordia Teachers College, NE (M)
Concordia University, IL (M)
Concordia University Wisconsin, WI (M)
Connors State College, OK (M)
Contra Costa College, CA (M)
Copiah-Lincoln Community College, MS (M)
Coppin State College, MD (M)
Cornell College, IA (M)
Cornell University, NY (M)
Cosummes River College, CA (M)
Cowley County Community College, KS (M)
Creighton University, NE (M)
Crowder College, MO (M)
Cuesta College, CA (M)
Culver-Stockton College, MO (M)
Cumberland College, KY (M)
Curry College, MA (M)
Cuyahoga Community College, OH (M)
Dakota Wesleyan University, SD (M)
Dallas Baptist University, TX (M)
Dana College, NE (M)
Dartmouth College, NH (M)
David Lipscomb College, TN (M)
Davidson College, NC (M)
Davis & Elkins College, WV (M)
Dean Junior College, MA (M)
De Anza Community College, CA (M)
Defiance College, OH (M)
Delaware County Community College, PA (M)
Delaware Valley College, PA (M)
Delgado College, LA (M)
Delta State University, MS (M)
Denison University, OH (M)
De Pauw University, IN (MW)
Des Moines Area Community College, IA (M)
Diablo Valley Community College, CA (M)
Dickinson College, PA (M)
Dickinson State University, ND (M)
Dixie College, UT (M)
Doane College, NE (M)
Dodge City Community College, KS (M)
Dominican College of Blauvelt, NY (M)
Dowling College, NY (M)
Drew University, NJ (M)
Drexel University, PA (M)
Duke University, NC (M)
Dundalk Community College, MD (M)
Duquesne University, PA (M)
Dutchess Junior College, NY (M)
Dyersburg State Community College, TN (M)
Earlham College, IN (M)
East Carolina University, NC (M)
East Central College, MO (M)
East Central University, OK (M)
Eastern College, PA (M)
Eastern Connecticut State University, CT (MW)
Eastern Illinois University, IL (M)
Eastern Kentucky University, KY (M)
Eastern Mennonite College, VA (M)
Eastern Michigan University, MI (M)
Eastern Nazarene College, MA (M)
Eastern New Mexico University, NM (M)
Eastern Oklahoma State College, OR (M)
Eastern Oregon State College, OR (M)
Eastfield College, TX (M)

East Los Angeles Community College, CA (M)
East Stroudsburg University, PA (M)
East Tennessee State University, TN (M)
East Texas Baptist University, TX (M)
Edgewood College, WI (M)
Edinboro University of Pennsylvania, PA (M)
Edison Community College, FL (M)
Edmonds Community College, WA (M)
Edward Waters College, FL (M)
El Camino College, CA (M)
Elgin Community College, IL (M)
Elizabeth City State University, NC (M)
Elizabethtown College, PA (M)
Elmhurst College, IL (M)
Elon College, NC (M)
Emerson College, MA (M)
Emory and Henry College, VA (M)
Emporia State University, KS (M)
Enterprise State Junior College, AL (M)
Erskine College, SC (M)
Essex Community College, MD (M)
Evangel College, MO (M)
Fairfield University, CT (M)
Fairleigh Dickinson University (Madison), NJ (M)
Farleigh Dickinson University (Teaneck), NJ (M)
Fairleigh Dickinson University (Rutherford), NJ (M)
Faulkner University, AL (M)
Fergus Falls Community College, MN (M)
Ferris State College, MI (M)
Ferrum College, VA (M)
Fitchburg State College, MA (M)
Flagler College, FL (M)
Florida A & M University, FL (M)
Florida Atlantic University, FL (M)
Florida College, FL (M)
Florida Institute of Technology, FL (M)
Florida International University, FL (M)
Florida Memorial College, FL (M)
Florida Southern College, FL (M)
Florida State University, FL (M)
Foothill College, CA (M)
Fordham University, NY (MW)
Fort Hays State University, KS (M)
Fort Scott College, KS (M)
Fort Steilacoom Community College, WA (M)
Fort Valley State College, GA (M)
Francis Marion University, SC (M)
Franklin & Marshall College, PA (M)
Franklin Pierce College, NH (M)
Frank Phillips College, TX (M)
Frederick Community College, MD (W)
Freed-Hardeman College, TN (M)
Fresno City College, CA (M)
Friends University, KS (M)
Fullerton College, CA (M)
Fulton-Montgomery Community College, NY (M)
Furman University, SC (M)
Gadsden State Community College, AL (M)
Gannon College, PA (M)
Gardner-Webb College, NC (M)
Garrett Community College, MD (M)
Genesee Community College, NY (M)
Geneva College, PA (M)
George C. Wallace Community College, AL (M)
George Fox College, OR (M)
George Mason University, VA (M)
Georgetown College, KY (M)
George Washington University, DC (M)
Georgia College, GA (M)
Georgia Institute of Technology, GA (M)
Georgia Southern University, GA (M)
Georgia Southwestern College, GA (M)
Georgia State University, GA (M)
Gettysburg College, PA (M)
Glendale Community College, AZ (M)
Glendale Community College, CA (M)
Glen Oaks Community College, MI (M)
Gloucester County College, NJ (M)
Golden West College, (CA)
Gonzaga University, WA (M)
Gordon College, MA (M)
Goshen College, IN (M)
Grace College, IN (M)
Graceland College, IA (M)
Grambling State University, LA (M)
Grand Canyon College, AZ (M)
Grand Rapids Baptist College and Seminary, MI (M)
Grand Rapids Junior College, MI (M)
Grand Valley State College, MI (M)
Grand View College, IA (M)
Greenfield Community College, MA (M)
Green River Community College, WA (M)
Greenville College, IL (M)
Grinnel College, IA (M)
Grove City College, PA (MW)
Gulf Coast Community College, FL (M)
Gustavus Adolphus College, MN (M)
Hagerstown Junior College, MD (M)
Hamilton College, NY (M)
Hamline University, MN (M)
Hampden-Sydney College, VA (M)
Hampton University, VA (W)
Hannibal-Lagrange College, MO (M)
Hanover College, IN (M)
Harding University, AR (M)
Hardin-Simmons University, TX (M)
Harford Community College, MD (M)
Harper William Rainey College, IL (M)
Harris-Stowe State College, MO (M)
Hartwick College, NY (M)
Harvard University, MA (M)
Hastings College, NE (M)
Haverford College, PA (M)
Hawaii Pacific University, HI (M)
Heidelberg College, OH (W)
Henderson State University, AR (M)
Henry Ford Community College, MI (M)
Herkimer County Community College, NY (M)
Hibbing Community College, MN (M)
Highland Community College, KS (M)
Highland Park Community College, MI (M)
High Point University, NC (M)
Hilbert College, NY (M)
Hillsborough Community College, FL (M)
Hillsdale College, MI (M)
Hinds Community College (Raymund), MS (M)

Hinds Community College (Utica) MS (M)
Hiram College, OH (M)
Hiwassee College, TN (M)
Hofstra University, NY (M)
Holmes Junior College, MS (M)
Holy Cross College, MA (M)
Hope College, MI (M)
Howard University, DC (M)
Hudson Valley Community College, NY (M)
Hunter College of the City University of New York, NY (M)
Huntingdon College, AL (M)
Huntington College, IN (M)
Husson College, ME (M)
Huston-Tillotson College, TX (M)
Hutchinson College, KS (M)
Illinois Benedictine College, IL (M)
Illinois Central College, IL (M)
Illinois College, IL (M)
Illinois Institute of Technology, IL (M)
Illinois State University, IL (M)
Illinois Valley Community College, IL (M)
Illinois Wesleyan University, IL (M)
Incarnate Word College, TX (M)
Indiana State University, IN (M)
Indiana University, IN (M)
Indiana University of Pennsylvania, PA (M)
Indiana University-Purdue University, IN (M)
Indiana University-Purdue University (Fort Wayne), IN (M)
Indiana Wesleyan University, IN (M)
Indian Hills Community College, IA (M)
Indian River Community College, FL (M)
Inver Hills Community College, MN (M)
Iona College, NY (M)
Iowa State University of Science and Technology, IA (M)
Iowa Wesleyan College, IA (M)
Itawamba Community College, MS (M)
Ithaca College, NY (M)
Jackson State Community College, TN (M)
Jackson State University, MS (M)
Jacksonville State University, AL (M)
Jacksonville University, FL (M)
James Madison University, VA (M)
Jamestown College, ND (M)
Jefferson College, MO (M)
Jefferson Community College, NY (M)
Jefferson Davis Junior College, AL (M)
Jefferson State Junior College, AL (M)
John Carroll University, OH (M)
John C. Calhoun State College, AL (M)
Johns Hopkins University, MD (M)
Johnson County Community College, KS (M)
Johnson State College, VT (M)
Jones County Junior College, MS (M)
Juniata College, PA (MW)
Kalamazoo College, MI (M)
Kalamazoo Valley Community College, MI (M)
Kankakee Community College, IL (M)
Kansas City Kansas Community College, KS (M)
Kansas Newman College, KS (M)
Kansas State University, KS (M)
Kansas Wesleyan College, KS (M)
Kaskaskia Community College, IL (M)
Kean College of New Jersey, NJ (M)
Keene State College, NH (M)
Kemper Military School, MO (M)
Kennesaw State College, GA (M)
Kent State University (Kent), OH (M)
Kent State University (New Philadelphia), OH (M)
Kent State University (Warren), OH (M)
Kent State University (Ashtabula), OH (M)
Kent State University (East Liverpool), OH (M)
Kentucky Christian College, KY (M)
Kentucky State University, KY (M)
Kentucky Wesleyan College, KY (M)
Kenyon College, OH (M)
Keystone Junior College, PA (M)
King College, TN (MW)
King's College, NY (M)
King's College, PA (M)
Kirkwood Community College, IA (M)
Kishwaukee College, IL (M)
Knox College, IL (M)
Kutztown University, PA (M)
Labette Community College, KS (M)
Lackawanna Junior College, PA (M)
Lafayette College, PA (M)
Lake Land College, IL (M)
Lake Michigan College, MI (M)
Lamar Community College, CO (M)
Lamar University, TX (M)
Lambuth University, TN (M)
La Roche College, PA (M)
La Salle University, PA (M)
Lawrence University, WI (M)
Lebanon Valley College, PA (M)
Lee College, TX (M)
Lees Junior College, KY (M)
Lehigh University, PA (M)
Le Moyne College, NY (M)
LeMoyne-Owen College, TN (M)
Lenoir Community College, NC (M)
LeTourneau College, TX (M)
Lewis and Clark College, OR (M)
Lewis and Clark Community College, IL (M)
Lewis/Clark State College, ID (M)
Lewis University, IL (M)
Liberty University, VA (M)
Limestone College, SC (M)
Lincoln Christian College, IL (M)
Lincoln College, IL (M)
Lincoln Land Community College, IL (M)
Lincoln Memorial University, TN (M)
Lincoln University, MO (M)
Linfield College, OR (M)
Livingston University, AL (M)
Long Beach City College, CA (M)
Long Island University (Brooklyn), NY (M)
Long Island University (C.W. Post Campus), NY (M)
Longwood College, VA (M)
Loras College, IA (M)
Los Angeles Pierce Junior College, CA (M)
Los Angeles Valley College, CA (M)
Los Medanos College, CA (M)
Louisburg College, NC (M)
Louisiana State University (Baton Rouge), LA (M)

Louisiana State University (Alexandria), LA (M)
Louisiana Tech University, LA (M)
Lower Columbia College, WA (MW)
Loyola Marymount University, CA (M)
Lubbock Christian College, TX (M)
Luther College, IA (M)
Lynchburg College, VA (M)
Lyndon State College, VT (M)
Lynn University, FL (M)
Macalester College, MN (M)
Macomb Community College, MI (M)
Madison Area Technical College, WI (M)
Madonna University, MI (M)
Malone College, OH (M)
Manchester College, IN (M)
Manchester Community Technical College, CT (M)
Manhattan College, NY (MW)
Manhattan Community College, NY (M)
Manhattanville College, NY (M)
Mankato State University, MN (M)
Mansfield University, PA (M)
Maple Woods Community College, MO (M)
Marian College, IN (M)
Marian College, WI (M)
Marietta College, OH (M)
Marion Military Institute, AL (M)
Marist College, NY (M)
Marshall University, WV (M)
Mars Hill College, NC (M)
Mary Holmes College, MS (MW)
Maryville College, TN (M)
Maryville University, MO (M)
Mary Washington College, VA (M)
Massachusetts Bay Community College, MA (M)
Massachusetts Institute of Technology, MA (M)
Massasoit Community College, MA (M)
Master's College, CA (M)
Mayville State College, ND (M)
McHenry County College, IL (M)
McKendree College, IL (M)
McLennan Community College, TX (M)
McNeese State University, LA (M)
Memphis State University, TN (M)
Mercer County Community College, NJ (M)
Mercer University, GA (M)
Mercy College, NY (MW)
Mercyhurst College, PA (M)
Merrimack College, MA (M)
Mesa Community College, AZ (M)
Mesa State College, CO (M)
Messiah College, PA (M)
Metropolitan State College, CO (M)
Miami-Dade Community College (North), FL (M)
Miami-Dade Community College (South Campus), FL (M)
Miami-Dade Junior College, FL (M)
Miami University, OH (M)
Michigan Christian College, MI (M)
Michigan State University, MI (M)
Mid-America Nazarene College, KS (M)
Middlebury College, VT (M)
Middlesex County College, NJ (M)
Middle Tennessee State University, TN (M)
Midland Lutheran College, NE (M)
Miles College, AL (M)
Millersville University, PA (M)
Milligan College, TN (M)
Millikin University, IL (M)
Milwaukee Area Technology College, WI (M)
Mineral Area College, MO (M)
Mississippi College, MS (M)
Mississippi Delta Junior College, MS (M)
Mississippi Gulf Coast Junior College, MS (M)
Mississippi State University, MS (M)
Mississippi Valley State University, MS (M)
Missouri Baptist College, MO (M)
Missouri Southern State College, MO (M)
Missouri Valley College, MO (M)
Missouri Western State College, MO (M)
Mitchell College, CT (M)
Mobile College, AL (MW)
Modesto Junior College, CA (M)
Mohawk Valley Community College, NY (M)
Molloy College, NY (M)
Monmouth College, IL (M)
Monmouth College, NJ (M)
Montclair State College, NJ (M)
Montreat-Anderson College, NC (M)
Moorpark College, CA (MW)
Moraine Valley Community College, IL (M)
Moravian College, PA (M)
Morehead State University, KY (M)
Morgan State University, MD (M)
Morningside College, IA (MW)
Morton College, IL (M)
Motlow State Community College, TN (M)
Mott Community College, MI (M)
Mount Marty College, SD (M)
Mount Mercy College, IA (M)
Mount Olive College, NC (M)
Mount St. Mary College, MD (M)
Mount Union College, OH (MW)
Mount Vernon Nazarene College, OH (M)
Mt. San Antonio College, CA (M)
Mt. Wachusett Community College, MA (M)
Muhlenberg College, PA (MW)
Murray State University, KY (M)
Muskegon Community College, MI (M)
Muskingum College, OH (M)
Nassau Community College, NY (M)
Navarro College, TX (M)
Nebraska Wesleyan University, NE (M)
Newberry College, SC (M)
New Hampshire College, NH (M)
New Jersey Institute of Technology, NJ (M)
New Mexico Highlands University, NM (M)
New Mexico State University, NM (M)
New York Institute of Technology, NY (M)
New York State University Institute of Technology, NY (M)
Niagara County Community College, NY (M)
Niagara University, NY (M)
Nicholls State University, LA (M)
Nichols College, MA (M)
Norfolk State University, VA (M)
North Adams State College, MA (MW)

North Arkansas Community College, AR (M)
North Carolina A and T State University, NC (M)
North Carolina State University, NC (M)
North Carolina Wesleyan College, NC (M)
North Central College, IL (M)
North Central Missouri College, MO (M)
North Dakota State University, ND (M)
North Dakota State University (Bottineau), ND (M)
Northeastern Illinois University, IL (M)
Northeastern State University, OK (MW)
Northeast Louisiana University, LA (M)
Northeast Mississippi Community College, MS (M)
Northeast Missouri State University, MO (M)
Northern Illinois University, IL (M)
Northern Kentucky University, KY (M)
Northern State University, SD (M)
North Florida Junior College, FL (M)
North Greenville College, SC (M)
North Hennepin Community College, MN (M)
North Idaho College, ID (M)
North Iowa Area Community College, IA (M)
Northland Community College, MN (M)
Northwest Alabama State Community College, AL (M)
Northwestern College, IA (M)
Northwestern College, MN (MW)
Northwestern Oklahoma State University, OK (M)
Northwestern State University of Louisiana, LA (M)
Northwestern University, IL (M)
Northwest Mississippi Community College, MS (M)
Northwest Missouri State University, MO (M)
Northwest Nazarene College, ID (M)
Northwood Institute, MI (M)
Northwood Institute (Texas Campus), TX (M)
Norwich University, VT (M)
Nova University, FL (M)
Nyack College, NY (M)
Oakland City College, IN (M)
Oakton Community College, IL (M)
Oberlin College, OH (M)
Occidental College, CA (M)
Ocean County College, NJ (M)
Oglethorpe University, GA (M)
Ohio Dominican College, OH (M)
Ohio Northern University, OH (M)
Ohio State University, OH (M)
Ohio University, OH (M)
Ohio Valley College, WV (M)
Ohio Wesleyan University, OH (M)
Oklahoma Baptist University, OK (M)
Oklahoma Christian University of Science & Art, OK (M)
Oklahoma City University, OK (M)
Oklahoma State University, OK (M)
Old Dominion University, VA (M)
Olivet College, MI (M)
Olivet Nazarene University, IL (M)
Olney Central College, IL (M)
Olympic College, WA (M)
Oral Roberts University, OK (M)
Orange Coast College, CA (M)
Orange County Community College, NY (M)
Oregon Institute of Technology, OR (M)
Oregon State University, OR (MW)
Otero Junior College, CO (M)
Otterbein College, OH (M)
Ouachita Baptist University, AR (M)
Oxnard College, CA (M)
Pace University, NY (M)
Pacific Lutheran University, WA (M)
Pacific University, OR (M)
Paducah Community College, CA (M)
Paine College, GA (M)
Palm Beach Atlantic College, FL (M)
Palm Beach Community College, FL (M)
Palomar College, CA (M)
Pan American University, TX (M)
Panola Junior College, TX (M)
Paris Junior College, TX (M)
Parkland College, IL (M)
Pembroke State University, NC (M)
Penn State University (Abington), PA (M)
Penn State University (Sharon), PA (M)
Pennsylvania State University, PA (M)
Pennsylvania State University (Behrend College), PA (M)
Pensacola Junior College, FL (M)
Pepperdine University, CA (M)
Peru State College, NE (M)
Pfeiffer College, NC (M)
Philadelphia College of Textile and Science, PA (M)
Phillips University, OK (M)
Phoenix College, AZ (M)
Piedmont College, GA (M)
Pikeville College, KY (M)
Pima Community College, AZ (M)
Pittsburg State University, KS (M)
Point Loma Nazarene College, CA (M)
Point Park College, PA (M)
Polk Community College, FL (M)
Polytechnic University (Brooklyn Campus), NY (M)
Pomona-Pitzer Colleges, CA (M)
Portland State University, OR (M)
Prairie View A & M University, TX (M)
Pratt Community College, KS (M)
Presbyterian College, SC (M)
Prince George's Community College, MD (M)
Princeton University, NJ (MW)
Principia College, IL (M)
Providence College, RI (MW)
Purdue University, IN (M)
Queens College, NY (M)
Queensborough Community College, NY (M)
Quincy College, IL (M)
Quinnipiac College, CT (M)
Quinsigamond College, MA (M)
Radford University, VA (M)
Ramapo College, NJ (M)
Randolph-Macon College, VA (M)
Ranetto Santiago College, CA (M)
Regis University, CO (M)
Rend Lake, IL (MW)
Rensselaer Polytechnic Institute, NY (M)
Rhode Island College, RI (M)
Rice University, TX (M)
Ricks College, ID (M)
Rider College, NJ (M)
Ripon College, WI (M)
Riverside College, CA (M)
Roane State Community College, TN (M)

Roberts Wesleyan College, NY (M)
Rochester Community College, MN (M)
Rochester Institute of Technology, NY (M)
Rockland Community College, NY (M)
Rollins College, FL (M)
Rosary College, IL (M)
Rose-Hulman Institute of Technology, IN (M)
Rose State Junior College, OK (M)
Rowan College of New Jersey, NJ (M)
Rust College, MS (M)
Rutgers, Newark College of Arts and Sciences, NJ (M)
Sacred Heart University, CT (M)
Saddleback College, CA (M)
Saginaw Valley State College, MI (M)
Saint Ambrose College, IA (M)
Saint Andrews Presbyterian College, NC (MW)
Saint Anselm College, NH (M)
Saint Augustine's College, NC (M)
Saint Bonaventure University, NY (M)
Saint Cloud State University, MN (M)
Saint Edward's University, TX (M)
Saint Francis College, IN (M)
Saint Francis College, NY (M)
Saint John Fisher College, NY (M)
Saint John's University, MN (M)
Saint John's University, NY (M)
Saint Joseph's College, IN (M)
Saint Joseph's University, PA (M)
Saint Lawrence University, NY (M)
Saint Leo College, FL (M)
Saint Louis University, MO (M)
Saint Mary's College, MD (M)
Saint Mary's College of California, CA (M)
Saint Mary's University, TX (M)
Saint Norbert College, WI (M)
Saint Olaf College, MN (M)
Saint Peter's College, NJ (M)
Saint Thomas Aquinas College, NY (M)
Saint Thomas University, FL (M)
Saint Vincent College, PA (M)
Saint Xavier University, IL (M)
Salem State College, MA (M)
Salem-Teikyo University, WV (M)
Salve Regina College, RI (M)
Samford University, AL (M)
Sam Houston State University, TX (M)
San Bernardino Community College, CA (M)
San Diego City College, CA (M)
San Diego Mesa College, CA (MW)
San Diego State University, CA (M)
San Francisco State University, CA (M)
San Joaquin Delta College, CA (M)
San Jose State University, CA (M)
Santa Barbara City College, CA (M)
Santa Clara University, CA (M)
Santa Fe Community College, FL (M)
Santa Monica College, CA (MW)
Santa Rosa Junior College, CA (M)
Savannah State College, GA (M)
Schreiner College, TX (M)
Scottsdale Community College, AR (M)
Selma University, AL (M)
Seminole Community College, FL (M)
Seminole Junior College, OK (M)
Seton Hall University, NJ (M)
Seward County Community College, KS (M)
Shelby State Community College, TN (M)
Shepherd College, WV (M)
Shippensburg University of Pennsylvania, PA (M)
Shoreline Community College, WA (M)
Shorter College, AR (M)
Shorter College, GA (M)
Siena College, NY (M)
Siena Heights College, MI (M)
Sierra College, CA (M)
Simpson College, CA (M)
Sinclair Community College, OH (M)
Skagit Valley College, WA (M)
Skidmore College, NY (M)
Skyline College, CA (M)
Slippery Rock University of Pennsylvania, PA (M)
Snead State Community College, AL (M)
Snow College, UT (M)
Solano Community College, CA (M)
South Carolina State College, SC (M)
South Dakota State University, SD (M)
Southeastern Community College, IA (M)
Southeastern Community College, NC (M)
Southeastern Illinois College, IL (M)
Southeastern Louisiana University, LA (M)
Southeastern Massachusetts University, MA (M)
Southeastern Oklahoma State University, OK (M)
Southeastern Missouri State University, MO (M)
Southern Arkansas University, AR (M)
Southern California College, CA (M)
Southern College of Technology, GA (M)
Southern Connecticut State University, CT (MW)
Southern Illinois University, IL (M)
Southern Illinois University (Edwardsville), IL (M)
Southern Union State Junior College, AL (M)
Southern University and A & M College, LA (M)
Southern Utah University, UT (M)
Southwest, NM (M)
Southwest Baptist University, MO (M)
Southwestern College, CA (M)
Southwestern Michigan Junior College, MI (M)
Southwestern Oklahoma State University, OK (M)
Southwestern University, TX (M)
Southwest Missouri State University, MO (M)
Southwest State University, MN (M)
Southwest Texas State University, TX (M)
Spartanburg Methodist, SC (M)
Spoon River College, IL (M)
Spring Arbor College, MI (M)
Springfield College, MA (M)
Springfield Technical Community College, MA (M)
Spring Hill College, AL (M)
Stanford University, CA (M)
State Fair Community College, MO (M)
State University of New York (Albany), NY (M)

State University of New York (Binghamton), NY (M)
State University of New York (Stony Brook), NY (M)
State University of New York College (Brockport), NY (M)
State University of New York College (Cortland), NY (M)
State University of New York College (Fredonia), NY (M)
State University of New York College (New Paltz), NY (M)
State University of New York College (Oswego), NY (M)
State University of New York Maritime College, NY (M)
Stephen F. Austin State University, TX (M)
Sterling College, KS (MW)
Stetson University, FL (M)
Stevens Institute of Technology, NJ (M)
St. Johns River Community College, FL (M)
St. Louis Community College (Florissant Valley), MO (M)
St. Louis Community College (Forest Park), MO (MW)
St. Mary of the Plains College, KS (M)
Stonehill College, MA (M)
St. Petersburg Junior College, FL (M)
Sue Bennett College, KY (M)
Suffolk County Community College, NY (M)
Suffolk University, MA (M)
Sul Ross State University, TX (M)
Swarthmore College, PA (M)
Tabor College, KS (M)
Taft College, CA (M)
Talledaga College, AL (M)
Tampa College, FL (M)
Tarleton State University, TX (M)
Teikyo Marycrest University, IA (M)
Teikyo Post University, CT (MW)
Teikyo Westmar University, IA (M)
Temple University, PA (M)
Tennessee State University, TN (M)
Tennessee Technological University, TN (M)
Tennessee Temple University, TN (M)
Tennessee Wesleyan College, TN (M)
Texarkana College, TX (M)
Texas A & I University, TX (M)
Texas A & M University, TX (M)
Texas Christian University, TX (M)
Texas Lutheran College, TX (M)
Texas Southern University, TX (M)
Texas Southmost Junior College, TX (M)
Texas Tech University, TX (M)
Texas Wesleyan College, TX (M)
Thomas College, ME (MW)
Thomas More College, KY (M)
Three Rivers Community College, MO (M)
Tiffin University, OH (M)
Toccoa Falls College, GA (M)
Towson State University, MD (M)
Trenton State College, NJ (M)
Trevecca Nazarene College, TN (M)
Trinidad State Junior College, CO (M)
Trinity Christian College, IL (M)
Trinity College, CT (M)
Trinity College, IL (M)
Trinity University, TX (M)
Tri-State University, IN (M)
Triton College, IL (M)
Troy State University, AL (M)
Truett-McConnell Junior College, GA (M)
Tufts University, MA (M)
Tulane University, LA (M)
Tusculum College, TN (M)
Tuskegee University, AL (M)
Union College, KY (M)
Union College, NY (M)
Union County College, NJ (M)
University of Akron, OH (M)
University of Alabama (Birmingham), AL (M)
University of Alabama (Tuscaloosa), AL (M)
University of Arizona, AZ (M)
University of Arkansas (Fayetteville), AR (M)
University of Arkansas (Little Rock), AR (M)
University of Arkansas (Monticello), AR (M)
University of Bridgeport, CT (M)
University of California (Berkeley), CA (M)
University of California (Davis), CA (M)
University of California (Riverside), CA (M)
University of California (San Diego), CA (M)
University of California (Santa Barbara), CA (M)
University of California (UCLA), CA (M)
University of Central Arkansas, AR (M)
University of Central Florida, FL (M)
University of Central Oklahoma, OK (M)
University of Charleston, WV (M)
University of Chicago, IL (M)
University of Cincinnati, OH (M)
University of Connecticut, CT (M)
University of Dayton, OH (M)
University of Delaware, DE (M)
University of Denver, CO (M)
University of Detroit Mercy, MI (M)
University of Dubuque, IA (M)
University of Evansville, IN (M)
University of Findlay, OH (M)
University of Florida, FL (M)
University of Georgia, GA (M)
University of Hartford, CT (M)
University of Hawaii (Hilo), HI (M)
University of Hawaii (Manoa), HI (M)
University of Houston, TX (M)
University of Indianapolis, IN (M)
University of Indiana Southeast, IN (M)
University of Iowa, IA (M)
University of Kansas, KS (M)
University of Kentucky, KY (M)
University of La Verne, CA (M)
University of Louisville, KY (M)
University of Lowell, MA (M)
University of Maine, ME (M)
University of Maine (Presque Isle), ME (M)
University of Mary Hardin-Baylor, TX (M)
University of Maryland, MD (M)
University of Maryland (Baltimore County), MD (M)
University of Maryland (Eastern Shore), MD (M)
University of Massachusetts (Amherst), MA (M)
University of Massachusetts (Boston), MA (M)
University of Miami, FL (M)
University of Michigan, MI (M)
University of Minnesota (Duluth), MN (M)

University of Minnesota (Minneapolis), MN (M)
University of Minnesota (Morris), MN (M)
University of Mississippi, MS (M)
University of Missouri, MO (M)
University of Missouri (Rolla), MO (M)
University of Montana, MT (M)
University of Montevallo, AL (M)
University of Nebraska, NE (M)
University of Nebraska (Kearney), NE (M)
University of Nebraska (Lincoln), NE (M)
University of Nevada, NV (M)
University of Nevada (Reno), NV (M)
University of New Hampshire, NH (M)
University of New Haven, CT (M)
University of New Mexico, NM (M)
University of New Orleans, LA (M)
University of North Alabama, AL (M)
University of North Carolina (Asheville), NC (M)
University of North Carolina (Chapel Hill), NC (M)
University of North Carolina (Charlotte), NC (M)
University of North Carolina (Wilmington), NC (M)
University of North Dakota, ND (M)
University of Northern Colorado, CO (M)
University of Northern Iowa, IA (M)
University of Notre Dame, IN (M)
University of Oklahoma, OK (M)
University of Pennsylvania, PA (M)
University of Pittsburgh, PA (M)
University of Pittsburgh (Johnstown), PA (M)
University of Portland, OR (M)
University of Puget Sound, WA (M)
University of Redlands, CA (MW)
University of Rhode Island, RI (M)
University of Richmond, VA (M)
University of Rio Grande, OH (M)
University of San Diego, CA (M)
University of San Francisco, CA (M)
University of Scranton, PA (M)
University of South Alabama, AL (M)
University of South Carolina (Columbia), SC (M)
University of South Carolina (Myrtle Beach), SC (M)
University of South Carolina (Aiken), SC (M)
University of South Carolina (Spartanburg), SC (M)
University of South Dakota, SD (M)
University of Southern California, CA (M)
University of Southern Indiana, IN (M)
University of Southern Mississippi, MS (M)
University of South Florida, FL (M)
University of Southwestern Louisiana, LA (M)
University of St. Thomas, MN (M)
University of Tampa, FL (M)
University of Tennessee, TN (M)
University of Tennessee (Knoxville), TN (M)
University of Tennessee (Martin), TN (M)
University of Texas (Arlington), TX (M)
University of Texas (Austin), TX (M)
University of Texas (Pan American), TX (M)
University of the Pacific, CA (M)
University of Toledo, OH (M)
University of Utah, UT (M)
University of Vermont, VT (M)
University of Virginia, VA (M)
University of Washington, WA (M)
University of West Florida, FL (M)
University of Wisconsin (Eau Claire), WI (M)
University of Wisconsin (La Crosse), WI (M)
University of Wisconsin (Milwaukee), WI (M)
University of Wisconsin (Oshkosh), WI (M)
University of Wisconsin (Platteville), WI (M)
University of Wisconsin (River Falls), WI (M)
University of Wisconsin (Stevens Point), WI (M)
University of Wisconsin (Stout), WI (M)
University of Wisconsin (Superior), WI (MW)
University of Wyoming, WY (M)
Upper Iowa University, IA (M)
Urbana University, OH (M)
Ursinus College, PA (M)
U.S. International University, CA (M)
Utah State University, UT (M)
Valdosta State College, GA (M)
Valencia Community College, FL (M)
Valley City State University, ND (M)
Valparaiso University, IN (M)
Vanderbilt University, TN (M)
Ventura College, CA (M)
Villanova University, PA (M)
Vincennes University Junior College, IN (M)
Virginia Commonwealth University, VA (M)
Virginia Intermont College, VA (M)
Virginia Military Institute, VA (M)
Virginia Polytechnic Institute & State University, VA (M)
Virginia State University, VA (M)
Virginia Wesleyan College, VA (M)
Viterbo College, WI (M)
Wabash College, IN (M)
Wabash Valley College, IL (M)
Wagner College, NY (M)
Wake Forest University, NC (M)
Waldorf College, IA (M)
Wallace Community College (Selma), AL (M)
Wallace State Community College, AL (M)
Walsh College, OH (M)
Walters State Community College, TN (M)
Warner Southern College, FL (M)
Warren Wilson College, NC (M)
Wartburg College, IA (M)
Washburn University, KS (M)
Washington and Jefferson College, PA (M)
Washington College, MD (M)
Washington State University, WA (M)
Washington University, MO (M)
Waubonsee College, IL (M)
Wayne State College, NE (M)

Wayne State University, MI (M)
Webster University, MO (M)
Wesleyan University, CT (M)
Wesley College, DE (M)
Westark Community College, AR (M)
West Chester University, PA (M)
Western Carolina University, NC (M)
Western Connecticut State University, CT (M)
Western Illinois University, IL (M)
Western Kentucky University, KY (M)
Western Maryland College, MD (M)
Western Michigan University, MI (M)
Western New England College, MA (M)
Western New Mexico University, NM (M)
Western Oregon State College, OR (M)
Westfield State College, MA (M)
West Georgia College, GA (M)
West Liberty State College, WV (MW)
Westminster College, PA (M)
Westmont College, CA (M)
West Virginia Institute of Technology, WV (M)
West Virginia State College, WV (M)
West Virginia University, WV (M)
West Virginia Wesleyan College, WV (M)
Wheaton College, IL (M)
Whitman College, WA (M)
Whittier College, CA (M)
Whitworth College, WA (M)
Wichita State University, KS (M)
Wilkes College, NC (M)
Wilkes University, PA (M)
Willamette University, OR (M)
William Jewell College, MO (M)
William Patterson College, NJ (M)
William Penn College, IA (M)
William Rainey Harper College, IL (M)
Williams College, MA (M)
Williamson Trade School, PA (M)
Wilmington College, DE (M)
Wilmington College, OH (M)
Wingate College, NC (M)
Winona State University, MN (M)
Winthrop University, SC (M)
Wofford College, SC (M)
Worcester State College, MA (MW)
Wright State University, OH (M)
Yakima Valley College, WA (M)
Yale University, CT (M)
Yavapai College, AZ (M)
York College of Pennsylvania, PA (M)
Youngstown State University, OH (M)
Yuba Community College, CA (M)

Basketball

Abilene Christian University, TX (MW)
Adams State College, CO (MW)
Adelphi University, NY (MW)
Adirondack College, NY (MW)
Adrian College, MI (MW)
Alabama A & M University, AL (MW)
Alabama State University, AL (MW)
Albany State College, GA (MW)
Albertson College, ID (M)
Albion College, MI (MW)
Albright College, PA (MW)
Alcorn State University, MS (MW)
Alderson-Broaddus College, WV (MW)
Alfred University, NY (MW)
Alice Lloyd College, KY (MW)
Allegheny CCAC, PA (MW)
Allegheny College, PA (MW)
Allen County College, KS (MW)
Allentown College, PA (MW)
Allen University, SC (M)
Alma College, MI (MW)
Alvernia College, PA (MW)
American International College, MA (MW)
American University, DC (MW)
Amherst College, MA (MW)
Anderson College, SC (MW)
Anderson University, IN (MW)
Angelina College, TX (MW)
Angelo State University, TX (MW)
Anoka-Ramsey College, MN (MW)
Appalachian State University, NC (MW)
Apprentice School, VA (M)
Aquinas College, MI (MW)
Aquinas Junior College, TN (M)
Arizona State University, AZ (MW)
Arkansas College, AR (MW)
Arkansas State University, AR (MW)
Arkansas Tech University, AR (MW)
Armstrong State College, GA (MW)
Arrowhead Community College, MN (MW)
Asbury College, KY (MW)
Ashland College, OH (MW)
Assumption College, MA (MW)
Athens State College, AL (M)
Atlantic Community College, NJ (MW)
Atlantic Union College, MA (M)
Auburn University, AL (MW)
Auburn University (Montgomery), AL (MW)
Augsburg College, MN (MW)
Augusta College, GA (MW)
Augustana College, IL (MW)
Augustana College, SD (MW)
Aurora University, IL (MW)
Austin College, TX (MW)
Austin Community College, MN (MW)
Austin Peay State University, TN (MW)
Averett College, VA (MW)
Avila College, MO (MW)
Azusa Pacific University, CA (MW)
Babson College, MA (MW)
Bacone Junior College, OK (MW)
Baker University, KS (MW)
Ball State University, IN (MW)
Baltimore City Community College, MD (MW)
Baptist Bible College, MO (M)
Barber-Scotia College, NC (MW)
Bard College, NY (MW)
Barry University, FL (M)
Barstow College, CA (M)
Bartlesville Wesleyan, OK (MW)
Barton College, NC (MW)
Barton County College, KS (MW)
Bates College, ME (MW)
Bayamon Central University, PR (MW)
Baylor University, TX (MW)
Becker College, MA (MW)
Belhaven College, MS (MW)
Bellarmine College, KY (MW)
Belleville Area College, IL (MW)

Bellevue College, NE (M)
Bellevue Community College, WA (M)
Belmont Abbey College, NC (MW)
Belmont College, TN (MW)
Beloit College, WI (MW)
Bemidji State University, MN (MW)
Benedict College, SC (MW)
Benedictine College, KS (MW)
Bentley College, MA (MW)
Bergen Community College, NJ (MW)
Berry College, GA (MW)
Bethany College, KS (MW)
Bethany College, WV (MW)
Bethany Lutheran College, MN (MW)
Bethel College, IN (MW)
Bethel College, KS (MW)
Bethel College, MN (MW)
Bethel College, TN (MW)
Bethune-Cookman College, FL (MW)
Big Bend Community College, WA (M)
Biola University, CA (MW)
Birmingham-Southern College, AL (M)
Blackburn College, IL (MW)
Black Hawk College (Moline), IL (MW)
Black Hawk College (Kewanee), IL (MW)
Black Hills State University, SD (MW)
Blanton Junior College, NC (M)
Bloomfield College, NJ (MW)
Bloomsburg University, PA (MW)
Bluefield College, VA (MW)
Bluefield State College, WV (MW)
Blue Mountain College, MS (W)
Blue Mountain College, OR (MW)
Bluffton College, OH (MW)
Boise State University, ID (MW)
Boston College, MA (MW)
Boston University, MA (MW)
Bowdoin College, ME (MW)
Bowie State University, MD (MW)
Bowling Green State University, OH (MW)
Bradley University, IL (MW)
Brainerd Community College, MN (MW)
Brandeis University, MA (MW)
Brescia College, KY (MW)
Brevard College, FL (MW)
Brevard College, NC (MW)
Brewton Parker College, GA (MW)
Briar Cliff College, IA (MW)
Bridgewater College, VA (MW)
Bridgewater State College, MA (MW)
Brigham Young University, HI (M)
Brigham Young University, UT (MW)
Bristol University, TN (MW)
Bronx Community College, NY (MW)
Broome Community College, NY (M)
Broward Community College, FL (MW)
Brown University, RI (MW)
Brunswick Junior College, GA (M)
Bryant & Stratton Business Institute, NY (M)
Bryant College, RI (M)
Bryn Mawr College, PA (MW)
Bucknell University, PA (MW)
Bucks County Community College, PA (MW)
Buena Vista College, IA (MW)
Buffalo State College, NY (MW)
Buffalo State University (New York), NY (MW)
Bunker Hill Community College, MA (MW)
Butler County Community College, KS (M)
Butler County Community College, PA (M)
Butler University, IN (MW)
Butte College, CA (MW)
Cabrillo College, CA (MW)
Cabrini College, PA (MW)
Caldwell College, NJ (MW)
California Baptist College, CA (MW)
California Institute of Technology,k CA (M)
California Lutheran University, CA (MW)
California Maritime Academy, CA (M)
California Polytechnic State University, CA (MW)
California State Polytechnic University, CA (MW)
California State University, CA (MW)
California State University at Bakersfield, CA (M)
California State University (Chico), CA (MW)
California State University (Dominguez Hills), CA (MW)
California State University (Fresno), CA (MW)
California State University (Fullerton), CA (MW)
California State University (Hayward), CA (MW)
California State University (Long Beach), CA (MW)
California State University (Los Angeles), CA (MW)
California State University (Northridge), CA (MW)
California State University (Sacramento), CA (MW)
California State University (San Bernardino), CA (MW)
California University, PA (MW)
Calvin College, MI (MW)
Cameron University, OK (MW)
Campbellsville College, KY (MW)
Campbell University, NC (MW)
Canisius College, NY (MW)
Capital University, OH (MW)
Cardinal Stritch College, WI (MW)
Carl Albert Junior College, OK (MW)
Carleton College, MN (MW)
Carlow College, PA (W)
Carnegie-Mellon University, PA (MW)
Carroll College, MT (MW)
Carroll College, WI (MW)
Carson-Newman College, TN (MW)
Carthage College, WI (MW)
Case Western Reserve University, OH (MW)
Castleton State College, VT (MW)
Catawba College, NC (MW)
Catholic University of America, DC (MW)
Catholic University of Puerto Rico, PR (MW)
Catonsville Community College, MD (MW)
Cayuga County Community College, NY (MW)
Cecil Community College, MD (MW)
Cedarville College, OH (MW)
Centenary College, LA (M)
Centenary College, NJ (MW)
Central Arizona College, AZ (MW)
Central Baptist College, AR (MW)
Central College, IA (MW)
Central College, KS (MW)
Central Community College, NE (MW)
Central Connecticut State University, CT (MW)

Central Florida Community College, FL (MW)
Central Methodist College, MO (MW)
Central Michigan University, MI (MW)
Central Missouri State University, MO (MW)
Central State University, OH (M)
Central Washington University, WA (MW)
Central Wesleyan College, SC (MW)
Central Wyoming College, WY (MW)
Cerritos College, CA (M)
Chadron State College, NE (MW)
Chaffey College, CA (M)
Chaminade University, HI (M)
Champlain College, VT (M)
Chapman University, CA (MW)
Charles County Community College, MD (M)
Charleston Southern University, SC (MW)
Chattahoochee Valley Community College, AL (MW)
Chemeketa Community College, OR (MW)
Cheyney University of Pennsylvania, PA (MW)
Chicago State University, IL (MW)
Chipola Junior College, FL (MW)
Chowan College, NC (MW)
Christian Brothers College, TN (MW)
Christopher Newport College, VA (MW)
Cincinnati Technical College, OH (M)
Citadel, SC (M)
City College of New York, NY (MW)
City College of San Francisco, CA (MW)
City College of San Francisco, CA (MW)
Clackamas Community College, OR (MW)
Claflin College, SC (MW)
Clarion University, PA (MW)
Clark Atlanta University, GA (MW)
Clark College, WA (MW)
Clarkson University, NY (MW)
Clark State College, OH (MW)
Clark University, MA (MW)
Clemson University, SC (M)
Cleveland State Community College, TN (MW)
Cleveland State University, OH (MW)
Clinch Valley College, VA (MW)
Clinton Community College, IA (M)
Clinton Community College, NY (M)
Cloud County Community College, KS (MW)
Coahoma Junior College, MS (MW)
Coastal Carolina College, SC (MW)
Cochise County Community College, AZ (MW)
Coe College, IA (MW)
Coffeyville Community College, KS (MW)
Coker College, SC (MW)
Colby Community College, KS (MW)
Colby-Sawyer College, NH (MW)
Colgate University, NY (MW)
College of Allegheny County, PA (M)
College of Charleston, SC (MW)
College of Charleston, SC (MW)
College of Idaho, ID (M)
College of Mount St. Joseph, OH (W)
College of New Rochelle, NY (W)
College of Notre Dame, CA (MW)
College of Notre Dame of Maryland, MD (M)
College of Saint Mary, NE (W)
College of Southern Idaho, ID (MW)
College of St. Benedict, MN (W)
College of St. Francis, IL (MW)
College of St. Rose, NY (MW)
College of St. Scholastica, MN (MW)
College of the Desert, CA (MW)
College of the Ozarks, MO (MW)
College of the Redwoods, CA (MW)
College of the Sequoias, CA (MW)
College of William and Mary, VA (MW)
College of Wooster, OH (MW)
Colorado Christian University, CO (MW)
Colorado College, CO (MW)
Colorado Northwestern Community College, CO (MW)
Colorado School of Mines, CO (MW)
Colorado State University, CO (MW)
Columbia Basin Community College, WA (MW)
Columbia Christian College, OR (MW)
Columbia College, MO (M)
Columbia-Greene Community College, NY (MW)
Columbia Union College, MD (MW)
Columbia University, NY (MW)
Columbus College, GA (M)
Columbus State Community College, OH (M)
Community College of Rhode Island, RI (MW)
Community College of the Finger Lakes, NY (MW)
Community Colleges of Spokane, WA (MW)
Compton Community College, CA (MW)
Concord College, WV (MW)
Concordia College, MI (MW)
Concordia College (Moorhead), MN (MW)
Concordia College (St. Paul), MN (MW)
Concordia College, NY (MW)
Concordia Lutheran College, TX (MW)
Concordia Teachers College, NE (MW)
Concordia University, IL (MW)
Concordia University Wisconsin, WI (MW)
Connecticut College, CT (MW)
Connors State College, OK (MW)
Contra Costa College, CA (MW)
Converse College, SC (W)
Cooke County Junior College, TX (M)
Copiah-Lincoln Community College, MS (M)
Coppin State College, MD (MW)
Cornell College, IA (MW)
Cornell University, NY (MW)
Consummes River College, CA (M)
Covenant College, GA (MW)
Cowley County Community College, KS (MW)
Creighton University, NE (MW)
Crowder College, MO (W)
Cuesta College, CA (MW)
Culver-Stockton College, MO (MW)
Cumberland College, KY (MW)
Curry College, MA (MW)

Cuyahoga Community College (Cleveland), OH (MW)
Cuyahoga Community College (Highland Hills Village), OH (MW)
Daemen College, NY (MW)
Dakota State University, SD (MW)
Dakota Wesleyan University, SD (MW)
Dana College, NE (MW)
Danville Area Community College, IL (MW)
Dartmouth College, NH (MW)
David Lipscomb College, TN (MW)
Davidson College, NC (MW)
Davis & Elkins College, WV (MW)
Dawson Community College, MT (MW)
Daytona Beach Community College, FL (M)
Dean Junior College, MA (MW)
De Anza Community College, CA (MW)
Defiance College, OH (MW)
Delaware County Community College, PA (M)
Delaware State College, DE (MW)
Delaware Valley College, PA (MW)
Delgado College, LA (MW)
Delta College, MI (MW)
Delta State University, MS (MW)
Denison University, OH (MW)
DePaul University, IL (MW)
De Pauw University, IN (MW)
Des Moines Area Community College, IA (MW)
Diablo Valley Community College, CA (M)
Dickinson College, PA (MW)
Dickinson State University, ND (MW)
Dillard University, LA (MW)
Dixie College, UT (MW)
Doane College, NE (MW)
Dodge City Community College, KS (MW)
Dominican College, CA (M)
Dominican College of Blauvelt, NY (MW)
Dowling College, NY (MW)
Drake University, IA (MW)
Drew University, NJ (MW)
Drexel University, PA (MW)
Drury College, MO (M)
Duke University, NC (MW)
Dundalk Community College, MD (MW)
Duquesne University, PA (MW)
Dutchess Junior College, NY (MW)
Dyersburg State Community College, TN (M)
Dyke College, OH (MW)
D'Youville College, NY (MW)
Earlham College, IN (MW)
East Carolina University, NC (MW)
East Central College, MO (MW)
East Central University, OK (MW)
Eastern College, PA (MW)
Eastern Connecticut State University, CT (MW)
Eastern Illinois University, IL (MW)
Eastern Kentucky University, KY (MW)
Eastern Mennonite College, VA (MW)
Eastern Michigan University, MI (MW)
Eastern Montana College, MT (MW)
Eastern Nazarene College, MA (MW)
Eastern New Mexico University, NM (MW)
Eastern Oklahoma State College, OK (MW)
Eastern Oregon State College, OR (MW)
Eastern Washington University, WA (MW)
Eastern Wyoming College, WY (M)
Eastfield College, TX (M)
East Los Angeles Community College, CA (MW)
East Stroudsburg University, PA (MW)
East Tennessee State University, TN (MW)
East Texas Baptist University, TX (MW)
East Texas State University, TX (MW)
Edgewood College, WI (MW)
Edinboro University of Pennsylvania, PA (MW)
Edison Community College, FL (MW)
Edmonds Community College, WA (MW)
Edward Waters College, FL (MW)
El Camino College, CA (MW)
Elgin Community College, IL (MW)
Elizabeth City State University, NC (MW)
Elizabeth Seton School of Iona College, NY (MW)
Elizabethtown College, PA (MW)
Elmhurst College, IL (MW)
Elmira College, NY (MW)
Elon College, NC (MW)
Emerson College, MA (MW)
Emory and Henry College, VA (MW)
Emporia State University, KS (MW)
Enterprise State Junior College, AL (M)
Erskine College, SC (MW)
Essex Community College, MD (MW)
Eureka College, IL (MW)
Evangel College, MO (MW)
Everett Community College, WA (MW)
Fairfield University, CT (MW)
Fairleigh Dickinson University (Madison), NJ (MW)
Fairleigh Dickinson University (Teaneck), NJ (MW)
Fairleigh Dickinson University (Rutherford), NJ (MW)
Fairmont State College, WV (MW)
Fashion Institute of Technology, NY (M)
Faulkner University, AL (M)
Fayetteville State University, NC (MW)
Fergus Falls Community College, MN (MW)
Ferris State College, MI (MW)
Ferrum College, VA (MW)
Fisk University, TN (MW)
Fitchburg State College, MA (MW)
Flagler College, FL (MW)
Florida A & M University, FL (MW)
Florida Atlantic University, FL (W)
Florida College, FL (M)
Florida Institute of Technology, FL (MW)
Florida International University, FL (MW)
Florida Memorial College, FL (MW)
Florida Southern College, FL (MW)
Florida State University, FL (MW)
Foothill College, CA (MW)
Fordham University, NY (MW)
Fort Hays State University, KS (MW)
Fort Lewis College, CO (MW)
Fort Scott College, KS (MW)
Fort Steilacoom Community College, WA (MW)
Fort Valley State College, GA (MW)
Francis Marion University, SC (MW)

Franklin & Marshall College, PA (MW)
Franklin Pierce College, NH (MW)
Frank Phillips College, TX (MW)
Frederick Community College, MD (MW)
Freed-Hardeman College, TN (MW)
Fresno City College, CA (MW)
Fresno Pacific College, CA (MW)
Friends University, KS (MW)
Fullerton College, CA (MW)
Fulton-Montgomery Community College, NY (M)
Furman University, SC (MW)
Gadsden State Community College, AL (MW)
Gannon College, PA (MW)
Garden City Community College, KS (MW)
Gardner-Webb College, NC (MW)
Garrett Community College, MD (MW)
Genesee Community College, NY (MW)
Geneva College, PA (MW)
George C. Wallace Community College, AL (MW)
George Fox College, OR (MW)
George Mason University, VA (MW)
Georgetown College, KY (MW)
Georgetown University, DC (MW)
George Washington University, DC (MW)
Georgia College, GA (MW)
Georgia Institute of Technology, GA (MW)
Georgian Court College, NJ (W)
Georgia Southern University, GA (MW)
Georgia Southwestern College, GA (MW)
Georgia State University, GA (MW)
Gettysburg College, PA (MW)
Glendale Community College, AZ (MW)
Glendale Community College, CA (MW)
Glen Oaks Community College, MI (MW)
Glenville State College, WV (MW)
Gloucester County College, NJ (M)
Golden West College, CA (MW)
Gonzaga University, WA (MW)
Gordon College, MA (MW)
Goshen College, IN (MW)
Goucher College, MD (MW)
Grace College, IN (MW)
Graceland College, IA (MW)
Grambling State University, LA (MW)
Grand Canyon College, AZ (M)
Grand Rapids Baptist College and Seminary, MI (MW)
Grand Rapids Junior College, MI (MW)
Grand Valley State College, MI (MW)
Grand View College, IA (MW)
Grays Harbor College, WA (MW)
Grayson County College, TX (MW)
Greenfield Community College, MA (MW)
Green Mountain College, VT (MW)
Green River Community College, WA (MW)
Greensboro College, NC (MW)
Greenville College, IL (MW)
Grinnell College, IA (MW)
Grove City College, PA (MW)
Gulf Coast Community College, FL (M)
Gustavus Adolphus College, MN (MW)
Hagerstown Junior College, MD (MW)
Hamilton College, NY (MW)
Hamline University, MN (MW)
Hampden-Sydney College, VA (M)
Hampton University, VA (MW)
Hannibal-Lagrange College, MO (M)
Hanover College, IN (MW)
Harding University, AR (MW)
Hardin-Simmons University, TX (M)
Harford Community College, MD (MW)
Harper William Rainey College, IL (MW)
Harris-Stowe State College, MO (MW)
Hartwick College, NY (MW)
Harvard University, MA (MW)
Haskell Indian Junior College, KS (MW)
Hastings College, NE (MW)
Haverford College, PA (MW)
Hawaii Pacific University, HI (M)
Heidelberg College, OH (W)
Henderson State University, AR (MW)
Henry Ford Community College, MI (MW)
Herkimer County Community College, NY (MW)
Hesser College, NH (M)
Hibbing Community College, MN (MW)
Highland Community College, KS (MW)
Highland Park Community College, MI (MW)
High Point University, NC (MW)
Hilbert College, NY (MW)
Hillsborough Community College, FL (MW)
Hillsdale College, MI (MW)
Hinds Community College (Raymond), MS (MW)
Hinds Community College (Utica), MS (MW)
Hiram College, OH (MW)
Hiwassee College, TN (MW)
Hofstra University, NY (MW)
Holmes Junior College, MS (MW)
Holy Cross College, MA (MW)
Holy Family College, PA (MW)
Hood College, MD (W)
Hope College, MI (MW)
Houghton College, NY (MW)
Houston Baptist University, TX (M)
Howard Payne University, TX (MW)
Howard University, DC (MW)
Hudson Valley Community College, NY (M)
Humboldt State University, CA (MW)
Hunter College of the City University of New York, NY (MW)
Huntington College, IN (MW)
Huron University, SD (MW)
Husson College, ME (MW)
Huston-Tillotson College, TX (MW)
Hutchinson College, KS (MW)
Idaho State University, ID (MW)
Illinois Benedictine College, IL (MW)
Illinois Central College, IL (MW)
Illinois College, IL (MW)
Illinois Institute of Technology, IL (MW)
Illinois State University, IL (MW)
Illinois Valley Community College, IL (MW)
Illinois Wesleyan University, IL (MW)
Incarnate Word College, TX (MW)
Indiana Institute of Technology, IN (MW)
Indiana State University, IN (MW)

Indiana University, IN (MW)
Indiana University of Pennsylvania, PA (MW)
Indiana University-Purdue University, IN (MW)
Indiana University-Purdue University (Fort Wayne), IN (MW)
Indiana University (South Bend), IN (MW)
Indiana Wesleyan University, IN (MW)
Indian Hills Community College, IA (M)
Indian River Community College, FL (MW)
Inver Hills Community College, MN (MW)
Iona College, NY (MW)
Iowa State University of Science and Technology, IA (MW)
Iowa Wesleyan College, IA (MW)
Itawamba Community College, MS (MW)
Ithaca College, NY (MW)
Jackson State Community College, TN (MW)
Jackson State University, MS (MW)
Jacksonville College, TX (M)
Jacksonville State University, AL (MW)
Jacksonville University, FL (M)
James Madison University, VA (MW)
Jamestown College, ND (MW)
Jefferson College, MO (W)
Jefferson Community College, NY (MW)
Jefferson Davis Junior College, AL (MW)
Jefferson State Junior College, AL (M)
John Brown University, AR (MW)
John Carroll University, OH (MW)
John C. Calhoun State College, AL (MW)
Johns Hopkins University, MD (MW)
Johnson County Community College, KS (MW)
Johnson C. Smith University, NC (MW)
Johnson State College, VT (MW)
Jones County Junior College, MS (MW)
Jordan College, MI (M)
Judson College, AL (W)
Junianta College, PA (MW)
Junior College of Albany, NY (M)
Kalamazoo College, MI (MW)
Kalamazoo Valley Community College, MI (MW)
Kankakee Community College, IL (MW)
Kansas City Kansas Community College, KS (MW)
Kansas Newman College, KS (W)
Kansas Stae University, KS (MW)
Kansas Wesleyan College, KS (MW)
Kaskaskia Community College, IL (M)
Kean College of New Jersey, NJ (MW)
Keene State College, NH (MW)
Kemper Military School, MO (M)
Kennesaw State College, GA (MW)
Kent State University (Ashtabula), OH (MW)
Kent State University (East Liverpool), OH (MW)
Kent State University (Kent), OH (MW)
Kent State University (New Philadelphia), OH (MW)
Kent State University (Warren), OH (MW)
Kentucky Christian College, KY (MW)
Kentucky State University, KY (MW)
Kentucky Wesleyan College, KY (MW)
Kenyon College, OH (MW)
Keystone Junior College, PA (MW)
Kilgore College, TX (MW)
King College, TN (MW)
King's College, NY (MW)
King's College, PA (MW)
Kirkwood Community College, IA (MW)
Kishwaukee College, IL (MW)
Knox College, IL (MW)
Knoxville College, TN (MW)
Kutztown University, PA (MW)
Labette Community College, KS (MW)
Lackawanna Junior College, PA (MW)
Lafayette College, PA (MW)
Lake Erie College, OH (MW)
Lake Forest College, IL (MW)
Lake Land College, IL (MW)
Lake Michigan College, MI (MW)
Lake-Sumter Community College, FL (M)
Lake Superior State University, MI (MW)
Lamar Community College, CO (MW)
Lamar University, TX (MW)
Lambuth University, TN (W)
Lander College, SC (MW)
Lane Community College, OR (MW)
Langston University, OK (MW)
Lansing Community College, MI (MW)
La Roche College, PA (MW)
La Salle University, PA (MW)
Lawrence University, WI (MW)
Lebanon Valley College, PA (MW)
Lee College, TN (MW)
Lee College, TX (M)
Lees Junior College, KY (MW)
Lees-McRae College, NC (MW)
Lehigh County Community College, PA (M)
Lehigh University, PA (MW)
Le Moyne College, NY (MW)
LeMoyne-Owen College, TN (MW)
Lenoir Community College, NC (M)
Lenoir-Rhyne College, NC (MW)
LeTourneau College, TX (M)
Lewis and Clark College, OR (MW)
Lewis and Clark Community College, IL (MW)
Lewis/Clark State College, ID (MW)
Lewis University, IL (MW)
Liberty University, VA (MW)
Limestone College, SC (MW)
Lincoln Christian College, IL (MW)
Lincoln College, IL (MW)
Lincoln Land Community College, IL (MW)
Lincoln Memorial University, TN (MW)
Lincoln Trail College, IL (MW)
Lincoln University, MO (MW)
Lindenwood College, MO (MW)
Linfield College, OR (MW)
Livingstone College, NC (MW)
Livingston University, AL (MW)
Lock Haven University of Pennsylvania, PA (MW)
Long Beach City College, CA (MW)
Long Island University (Brooklyn), NY (MW)
Long Island University (CW. Post Campus), NY (MW)
Long Island University (South-

hampton Campus), NY (MW)
Longwood College, VA (MW)
Loras College, IA (MW)
Los Angeles Pierce Junior College, CA (MW)
Los Angeles Valley College, CA (M)
Los Medanos College, CA (MW)
Louisburg College, NC (MW)
Louisiana College, LA (MW)
Louisiana State University, LA (MW)
Louisiana State University, LA (MW)
Louisiana Tech University, LA (MW)
Lower Columbia College, WA (MW)
Loyola College, MD (MW)
Loyola Marymount University, CA (MW)
Loyola University, IL (MW)
Lubbock Christian College, TX (MW)
Luther College, IA (MW)
Lycoming College, PA (MW)
Lynchburg College, VA (MW)
Lynchburg College, VA (MW)
Lyndon State College, VT (MW)
Macalester College, MN (MW)
Macomb Community College, MI (M)
Madison Area Technical College, WI (MW)
Madonna University, MI (MW)
Malone College, OH (MW)
Manchester College, IN (MW)
Manchester Community Technical College, CT (MW)
Manhattan College, NY (MW)
Manhattan Community College, NY (M)
Manhattanville College, NY (MW)
Mankato State University, MN (MW)
Mansfield University, PA (MW)
Marian College, IN (MW)
Marian College, WI (MW)
Marietta College, OH (MW)
Marist College, NY (MW)
Marquette University, WI (MW)
Marshall University, WV (MW)
Mars Hill College, NC (MW)
Mary Baldwin College, VA (W)
Marycrest College, IA (MW)
Mary Holmes College, MS (MW)
Marymount University, VA (MW)
Maryville College, TN (MW)
Maryville University, MO (MW)
Mary Washington College, VA (MW)
Marywood College, PA (MW)
Massachusetts Bay Community College, MA (MW)
Massachusetts Institute of Technology, MA (MW)
Massasoit Community College, MA (M)
Master's College, CA (MW)
Mayville State College, ND (MW)
McCook Community College, NE (MW)
McHenry County College, IL (MW)
McKendree College, IL (MW)
McLennan Community College, TX (MW)
McNeese State University, LA (MW)
McPherson College, KS (MW)
Memphis State University, TN (MW)
Mercer County Community College, NJ (MW)
Mercer University, GA (MW)
Mercy College, NY (MW)
Mercyhurst College, PA (MW)
Merrimack College, MA (W)
Mesa Community College, AZ (MW)
Mesa State College, CO (M)
Messiah College, PA (MW)
Metropolitan State College, CO (MW)
Miami-Dade Community College (North), FL (MW)
Miami-Dade Community College (South), FL (MW)
Miami University, OH (MW)
Michigan Christian College, MI (MW)
Michigan State University, MI (MW)
Michigan Technological University, MI (MW)
Mid-America Nazarene College, KS (MW)
Middle Tennessee State University, TN (MW)
Middlebury College, VT (MW)
Middlesex County College, NJ (MW)
Midland College, TX (M)
Midland Lutheran College, NE (MW)
Mid-Plains Community College, NE (MW)
Midwestern State University, TX (MW)
Miles College, AL (MW)
Miles Community College, MT (MW)
Millersville University, PA (MW)
Milligan College, TN (MW)
Millikin University, IL (MW)
Milwaukee Area Technology College, WI (MW)
Mineral Area College, MO (MW)
Minneapolis Community College, MN (MW)
Minot State, ND (MW)
MiraCosta College, CA (M)
Mississippi College, MS (MW)
Mississippi Delta Junior College, MS (MW)
Mississippi Gulf Coast Junior College, MS (MW)
Mississippi State University, MS (MW)
Mississippi University for Women, MS (W)
Mississippi Valley State University, MS (MW)
Missouri Baptist College, MO (MW)
Missouri Southern State College, MO (MW)
Missouri Valley College, MO (MW)
Missouri Western State College, MO (MW)
Mitchell College, CT (M)
Mitchell Community College, NC (M)
Mobile College, AL (M)
Modesto Junior College, CA (MW)
Mohawk Valley Community College, NY (MW)
Molloy College, NY (W)
Monmouth College, IL (MW)
Monmouth Collee, NJ (MW)
Montana College of Mineral Science and Technology, MT (MW)
Montana State University, MT (MW)
Montclair State College, NJ (MW)
Montgomery College, MD (M)
Montreat-Anderson College, NC (M)
Moody Bible Institute, IL (MW)
Moorhead State University, MN (MW)
Moorpark College, CA (MW)
Moraine Valley Community College, IL (MW)
Moravian College, PA (MW)
Morehead State University, KY (MW)
Morehouse College, GA (M)
Morgan State University, MD (MW)
Morningside College, IA (MW)
Morton College, IL (MW)

Motlow State Community College, TN (MW)
Mott Community College, MI (MW)
Mount Holyoke College, MA (W)
Mount Marty College, SD (MW)
Mount Mercy College, IA (MW)
Mount Olive College, NC (MW)
Mount St. Mary College, MD (MW)
Mount Union College, OH (M)
Mount Vernon Nazarene College, OH (MW)
Mt. Aloysius College, PA (MW)
Mt. San Antonio College, CA (MW)
Mt. Wachusett Community College, MA (MW)
Muhlenberg College, PA (M)
Multnomah School of the Bible, OR (M)
Murray State University, KY (MW)
Muskegon Community College, MI (MW)
Muskingum College, OH (MW)
Nassau Community College, NY (MW)
National-Louis University, IL (W)
Navajo Community College, AZ (MW)
Navarro College, TX (M)
Nazareth College, NY (MW)
Nebraska Wesleyan University, NE (M)
Newberry College, SC (MW)
New Hampshire College, NH (MW)
New Jersey Institute of Technology, NJ (M)
New Mexico Highlands University, NM (MW)
New Mexico Junior College, NM (MW)
New Mexico State University, NM (MW)
New York Institute of Technology, NY (M)
New York State University Institute of Technology, NY (MW)
New York University, NY (MW)
Niagara County Community College, NY (M)
Niagara University, NY (MW)
Nicholls State University, LA (MW)
Nichols College, MA (M)
Norfolk State University, VA (MW)
North Adams State College, MA (MW)
North Arkansas Community College, AR (MW)
North Carolina A and T State University, NC (MW)
North Carolina Central University, NC (MW)
North Carolina State University, NC (MW)
North Carolina Wesleyan College, NC (MW)
North Central College, IL (MW)
North Country Community College, NY (MW)
North Dakota State, ND (MW)
North Dakota State University, ND (MW)
North Dakota State University (Bottineau), ND (MW)
Northeastern Christian Junior College, PA (MW)
Northeastern Illinois University, IL (MW)
Northeastern Junior College, CO (MW)
Northeastern State University, OK (MW)
Northeast Louisiana University, LA (MW)
Northeast Mississippi Community College, MS (MW)
Northeast Missouri State University, MO (MW)
Northern Arizona University, AZ (MW)
Northern Illinois University, IL (MW)
Northern Kentucky University, KY (MW)
Northern Michigan University, MI (MW)
Northern Montana College, MT (MW)
Northern State University, SD (MW)
North Florida Junior College, FL (MW)
North Georgia College, GA (MW)
North Greenville College, SC (MW)
North Idaho College, ID (M)
North Iowa Area Community College, IA (MW)
Northland College, WI (MW)
Northland Community College, MN (MW)
Northwest Alabama State Community College, AL (MW)
Northwest College, WY (MW)
Northwestern College, IA (MW)
Northwestern College, MN (MW)
Northwestern Oklahoma State University, OK
Northwestern State University of Louisiana, LA (MW)
Northwestern University, IL (MW)
Northwest Mississippi Community College, MS (MW)
Northwest Missouri State University, MO (MW)
Northwest Nazarene College, ID (MW)
Northwood Institute, MI (MW)
Northwood Institute (Texas Campus), TX (MW)
Norwich University, VT (MW)
Notre Dame College of Ohio, OH (W)
Nova University, FL (M)
Nyack College, NY (MW)
Oakland City College, IN (MW)
Oakland Community College, MI (MW)
Oakland University, MI (MW)
Oakton Community College, IL (MW)
Oberlin College, OH (MW)
Occidental College, CA (MW)
Ocean County College, NJ (MW)
Odessa College, TX (M)
Oglethorpe University, GA (MW)
Ohio Dominican College, OH (MW)
Ohio Northern University, OH (MW)
Ohio State University, OH (MW)
Ohio University, OH (MW)
Ohio Valley College, WV (MW)
Ohio Wesleyan University, OH (MW)
Oklahoma Baptist University, OK (MW)
Oklahoma Christian University of Science & Art, OK (MW)
Oklahoma City University, OK (MW)
Oklahoma State University, OK (MW)
Old Dominion University, VA (MW)
Olivet College, MI (MW)
Olivet Nazarene University, IL (MW)
Olney Central College, IL (MW)
Olympic College, WA (MW)
Oral Roberts University, OK (MW)
Orange Coast College, CA (MW)

Orange County Community College, NY (MW)
Oregon Institute of Technology, OR (MW)
Oregon State University, OR (MW)
Otero Junior College, CO (MW)
Ottawa University, KS (MW)
Otterbein College, OH (MW)
Ouachita Baptist University, AR (MW)
Oxnard College, CA (MW)
Pace University, NY (MW)
Pacific Lutheran University, WA (MW)
Pacific University, OR (MW)
Paducah Community College, CA (MW)
Paine College, GA (MW)
Palm Beach Atlantic College, FL (M)
Palm Beach Community College, FL (MW)
Palomar College, CA (MW)
Pan American University, TX (MW)
Panhandle State University, OK (MW)
Panola Junior College, TX (MW)
Paris Junior College, TX (MW)
Park College, MO (MW)
Parkland College, IL (MW)
Parks College of St. Louis University, IL (W)
Passaic County Community College, NJ (MW)
Pembroke State University, NC (MW)
Penn State University (Abington), PA (MW)
Penn State University (Reading), PA (MW)
Penn State University (Sharon), PA (M)
Pennsylvania State University, PA (MW)
Pennsylvania State University (Behrend College), PA (MW)
Penn Valley Community College, MO (M)
Pensacola Junior College, FL (MW)
Pepperdine University, CA (MW)
Peru State College, NE (MW)
Pfeiffer College, NC (MW)
Philadelphia College of Textile and Science, PA (MW)
Philadelphia Community College, PA (MW)
Phillips University, OK (MW)
Phoenix College, AZ (MW)
Piedmont College, GA (MW)
Pikeville College, KY (MW)
Pima Community College, AZ (MW)
Pittsburg State University, KS (MW)
Plymouth State College, NH (MW)
Point Loma Nazarene College, CA (MW)
Point Park College, PA (MW)
Polk Community College, FL (MW)
Polytechnic University (Brooklyn Campus), NY (M)
Pomona-Pitzer Colleges, CA (MW)
Portland State University, OR (W)
Prairie View A & M University, TX (MW)
Pratt Community College, KS (MW)
Presbyterian College, SC (MW)
Prince George's Community College, MD (MW)
Princeton University, NJ (MW)
Principia College, IL (MW)
Providence College, RI (MW)
Purdue University, IN (MW)
Purdue University (Calumet), IN (MW)
Queensborough Community College, NY (MW)
Queens College, NY (MW)
Queens College, NC (MW)
Quincy College, IL (MW)
Quinnipiac College, CT (MW)
Quinsigamond College, MA (M)
Radford University, VA (MW)
Rainy River Community College, MN (MW)
Ramapo College, NJ (MW)
Randolph-Macon College, VA (MW)
Ranetto Santiago College, CA (MW)
Regis College, MA (W)
Regis University, CO (MW)
Rend Lake,IL (M)
Rensselaer Polytechnic Institute, NY (MW)
Rhode Island College, RI (MW)
Rice University, TX (MW)
Ricks College, ID (MW)
Rider College, NJ (MW)
Ripon College, WI (MW)
Riverside College, CA (MW)
Roane State Community College, TN (MW)
Roanoke College, VA (MW)
Robert Morris College, PA (MW)
Roberts Wesleyan College, NY (MW)
Rochester Community College, MN (MW)
Rochester Institute of Technology, NY (M)
Rockhurst College, MO (MW)
Rockland Community College, NY (MW)
Rocky Mountain College, MT (MW)
Rollins College, FL (MW)
Roosevelt University, IL (M)
Rosary College, IL (MW)
Rose-Hulman Institute of Technology, IN (M)
Rose State Junior College, OK (MW)
Rowan College of New Jersey, NJ (MW)
Rust College, MS (MW)
Rutgers, Newark College of Arts and Sciences, NJ (MW)
Sacred Heart University, CT (M)
Saddleback College, CA (MW)
Saginaw Valley State College, MI (MW)
Saint Ambrose College, IA (MW)
Saint Andrews Presbyterian College, NC (MW)
Saint Anselm College, NH (MW)
Saint Augustine's College, NC (MW)
Saint Bonaventure University, NY (MW)
Saint Cloud State University, MN (MW)
Saint Edward's University, TX (MW)
Saint Francis College, IN (MW)
Saint Francis College, NY (MW)
Saint Francis College, PA (MW)
Saint John Fisher College, NY (MW)
Saint John's University, MN (M)
Saint John's University, NY (MW)
Saint Joseph's College, IN (MW)
Saint Joseph's University, PA (MW)
Saint Lawrence University, NY (MW)
Saint Leo College, FL (MW)
Saint Louis University, MO (MW)
Saint Martin's College, WA (MW)
Saint Mary College, KS (M)
Saint Mary's College, IN (W)
Saint Mary's College, MD (MW)
Saint Mary's College, MI (W)

Saint Mary's College of California, CA (MW)
Saint Mary's University, TX (MW)
Saint Michael's College, VT (MW)
Saint Norbert College, WI (MW)
Saint Olaf College, MN (MW)
Saint Paul's College, VA (MW)
Saint Peter's College, NJ (MW)
Saint Thomas Aquinas College, NY (MW)
Saint Thomas University, FL (M)
Saint Vincent College, PA (MW)
Saint Xavier University, IL (M)
Salem State College, MA (MW)
Salem-Teikyo University, WV (MW)
Salve Regina College, RI (MW)
Samford University, AL (M)
Sam Houston State University, TX (MW)
San Bernardino Community College, CA (MW)
San Diego City College, CA (MW)
San Diego Mesa College, CA (MW)
San Diego State University, CA (MW)
San Francisco State University, CA (MW)
San Joaquin Delta College, CA (MW)
San Jose State University, CA (MW)
Santa Barbara City College, CA (MW)
Santa Clara University, CA (MW)
Santa Fe Community College, FL (MW)
Santa Monica College, CA (MW)
Santa Rosa Junior College, CA (MW)
Sauk Valley College, IL (MW)
Savannah State College, GA (MW)
Schoolcraft College, MI (MW)
Schreiner College, TX (MW)
Scottsdale Community College, AR (MW)
Seattle Pacfiic University, WA (MW)
Seattle University, WA (MW)
Selma University, AL (MW)
Seminole Community College, FL (MW)
Seminole Junior College, OK (MW)
Seton Hall University, NJ (MW)
Seton Hill College, PA (W)
Seward County Community College, KS (MW)
Shawnee State College, OH (MW)
Shawnee State University, OH (MW)
Shelby State Community College, TN (MW)
Sheldon Jackson College, AK (MW)
Shepherd College, WV (MW)
Sheridan College, WY (MW)
Shippensburg University of Pennsylvania, PA (MW)
Shoreline Community College, WA (MW)
Shorter College, AR (MW)
Shorter College, GA (MW)
Siena College, NY (MW)
Siena Heights College, MI (MW)
Sierra College, CA (MW)
Simpson College, CA (MW)
Sinclair Community College, OH (MW)
Sioux Falls College, SD (MW)
Skagit Valley College, WA (MW)
Skidmore College, NY (MW)
Skyline College, CA (M)
Slippery Rock University of Pennsylvania, PA (MW)
Snead State Community College, AL (MW)
Snow College, UT (MW)
South Carolina State College, SC (MW)
South Dakota School of Mines and Technology, SD (MW)
South Dakota State University, SD (MW)
Southeast Community College, NE (MW)
Southeastern Community College, IA (MW)
Southeastern Illinois College, IL (MW)
Southeastern Louisiana University, LA (MW)
Southeastern Massachusetts University, MA (MW)
Southeastern Oklahoma State University, OK (MW)
Southeast Missouri State University, MO (MW)
Southern Arkansas University, AR (MW)
Southern California College, CA (MW)
Southern College of Technology, GA (M)
Southern Connecticut State University, CT (M)
Southern Illinois University, IL (MW)
Southern Illinois University (Edwardsville), IL (MW)
Southern Methodist University, TX (MW)
Southern Nazrene University, OK (MW)
Southern Oregon State College, OR (MW)
Southern Union State Junior College, AL (MW)
Southern University and A & M College, LA (MW)
Southern Utah University, UT (MW)
South Florida Community College, FL (M)
South Plains Community College, TX (MW)
Southwest Baptist University, MO (MW)
Southwestern College, CA (MW)
Southwestern College, KS (MW)
Southwestern Michigan Junior College, MI (MW)
Southwestern Oklahoma State University, OK (MW)
Southwestern Oregon Community College, OR (MW)
Southwestern University, TX (MW)
Southwest Missouri State University, MO (MW)
Southwest State University, MN (MW)
Southwest Texas State University, TX (MW)
Spartanburg Methodist, SC (MW)
Spoon River College, IL (MW)
Spring Arbor College, MI (MW)
Springfield College, MA (MW)
Springfield Technical Community College, MA (MW)
Spring Hill College, AL (MW)
Stanford University, CA (MW)
State Fair Community College, MO (MW)
State University of New York, NY (MW)
State University of New York (Albany), NY (MW)
State University of New York (Binghamton), NY (MW)
State University of New York (Buffalo), NY (MW)
State University of New York (Plattsburgh), NY (MW)
State University of New York (Stony Brook), NY (MW)
State University of New York College (Brockport), NY (MW)

State University of New York College (Cortland), NY (MW)
State University of New York College (Fredonia), NY (MW)
State University of New York College (Geneseo), NY (MW)
State University of New York College (New Paltz), NY (MW)
State University of New York College (Oswego), NY (MW)
State University of New York College (Potsdam), NY (MW)
State University of New York College (Purchase), NY (M)
State University of New York Maritime College, NY (MW)
St. Catherine College, KY (MW)
Stephen F. Austin State University, TX (MW)
Sterling College, KS (MW)
Stetson University, FL (MW)
Stevens Institute of Technology, NJ (M)
St. Gregory's College, OK (MW)
St. Johns River Community College, FL (M)
St. Louis Community College (Florissant Valley), MO (M)
St. Louis Community College (Forest Park), MO (M)
St. Mary of the Plains College, KS (MW)
Stonehill College, MA (MW)
St. Petersburg Junior College, FL (MW)
St. Philip's College, TX (M)
Sue Bennett College, KY (MW)
Suffolk County Community College, NY (MW)
Suffolk University, MA (MW)
Sul Ross State University, TX (MW)
Swarthmore College, PA (MW)
Sweet Briar College, VA (W)
Syracuse University, NY (MW)
Tabor College, KS (MW)
Talledaga College, AL (MW)
Tampa College, FL (MW)
Tarleton State University, TX (MW)
Teikyo Marycrest University, IA (MW)
Teikyo Post University, CT (MW)
Teikyo Westmar University, IA (MW)
Temple Junior College, TX (MW)
Temple University, PA (MW)
Tennessee State University, TN (MW)
Tennessee Technological University, TN (MW)
Tennessee Temple University, TN (MW)
Tennessee Wesleyan College, TN (MW)
Texas A & I University, TX (MW)
Texas A & M University, TX (MW)
Texas Christian University, TX (MW)
Texas Lutheran College, TX (MW)
Texas Southern University, TX (MW)
Texas Tech University, TX (MW)
Texas Wesleyan College, TX (MW)
Texas Woman's University, TX (W)
Thomas College, ME (MW)
Thomas More College, KY (MW)
Three Rivers Community College, MO (MW)
Tiffin University, OH (MW)
Toccoa Falls College, GA (MW)
Tougaloo College, MS (MW)
Towson State University, MD (MW)
Transylvania University, KY (MW)
Trenton State College, NJ (MW)
Trevecca Nazarene College, TN (M)
Trinidad State Junior College, CO (M)
Trinity Christian College, IL (MW)
Trinity University, TX (MW)
Tri-State University, IN (MW)
Triton College, IL (MW)
Troy State University, AL (M)
Truett-McConnell Junior College, GA (MW)
Tufts University, MA (MW)
Tulane University, LA (W)
Tusculum College, TN (MW)
Tuskegee University, AL (MW)
Tyler Junior College, TX (MW)
Umpqua College, OR (MW)
Union College, KY (MW)
Union College, NY (MW)
Union County College, NJ (MW)
Unity College, ME (M)
University of Akron, OH (MW)
University of Alabama (Birmingham), AL (MW)
University of Alabama (Huntsville), AL (MW)
University of Alabama (Tuscaloosa), AL (MW)
University of Alaska, AK (MW)
University of Alaska (Fairbanks), AK (MW)
University of Alaska Southeast, AK (MW)
University of Arizona, AZ (MW)
University of Arkansas (Fayetteville), AR (MW)
University of Arkansas (Little Rock), AR (M)
University of Arkansas (Monticello), AR (MW)
University of Arkansas (Pine Bluff), AR (MW)
University of Bridgeport, CT (MW)
University of California (Berkeley), CA (MW)
University of California (Davis) CA (MW)
University of California (Irvine), CA (MW)
University of California (Riverside), CA (MW)
University of California (San Diego), CA (MW)
University of California (Santa Barbara), CA (MW)
University of California (Santa Cruz), CA (MW)
University of California (UCLA), CA (MW)
University of Central Arkansas, AR (MW)
University of Central Florida, FL (MW)
University of Central Oklahoma, OK (MW)
University of Charleston, WV (MW)
University of Chicago, IL (MW)
University of Cincinnati, OH (MW)
University of Colorado, CO (MW)
University of Colorado (Colorado Springs), CO (MW)
University of Connecticut, CT (MW)
University of Dallas, TX (MW)
University of Dayton, OH (MW)
University of Delaware, DE (MW)
University of Denver, CO (MW)
University of Detroit Mercy, MI (MW)

University of Dubuque, IA (MW)
University of Evansville, IN (MW)
University of Findlay, OH (MW)
University of Florida, FL (MW)
University of Georgia, GA (M)
University of Guam, PA (MW)
University of Hartford, CT (MW)
University of Hawaii (Hilo), HI (M)
University of Hawaii (Manoa), HI (MW)
University of Houston, TX (MW)
University of Idaho, ID (MW)
University of Illinois, IL (MW)
University of Illinois (Urbana-Champaign), IL (MW)
University of Indianapolis, IN (MW)
University of Indiana Southeast, IN (MW)
University of Iowa, IA (MW)
University of Kansas, KS (MW)
University of Kentucky, KY (MW)
University of La Verne, CA (MW)
University of Louisville, KY (MW)
University of Lowell, MA (MW)
University of Maine, ME (MW)
University of Maine (Fort Kent), ME (MW)
University of Maine (Machias), ME (MW)
University of Maine (Presque Isle), ME (MW)
University of Mary, ND (MW)
University of Mary Hardin-Baylor, TX (MW)
University of Maryland, MD (MW)
University of Maryland (Baltimore County), MD (MW)
University of Maryland (Eastern Shore), MD (MW)
University of Massachusetts (Amherst), MA (MW)
University of Massachusetts (Boston), MA (MW)
University of Miami, FL (MW)
University of Michigan, MI (MW)
University of Minnesota (Duluth), MN (MW)
University of Minnesota (Minneapolis), MN (MW)
University of Minnesota (Morris), MN (MW)
University of Mississippi, MS (MW)
University of Missouri, MO (M)
University of Missouri (Columbia), MO (MW)
University of Missouri (Kansas City), MO (MW)
University of Missouri (Rolla), MO (MW)
University of Montana, MT (W)
University of Montevallo, AL (MW)
University of Nebraska, NE (M)
University of Nebraska (Kearney), NE (MW)
University of Nebraska (Lincoln), NE (MW)
University of Nevada, NV (M)
University of Nevada (Reno), NV (MW)
University of New England, ME (MW)
University of New Hampshire, NH (MW)
University of New Haven, CT (MW)
University of New Mexico, NM (MW)
University of New Orleans, LA (MW)
University of North Alabama, AL (MW)
University of North Carolina (Asheville), NC (MW)
University of North Carolina (Chapel Hill), NC (MW)
University of North Carolina (Charlotte), NC (MW)
University of North Carolina (Greensboro), NC (MW)
University of North Carolina (Wilmington), NC (MW)
University of North Dakota, ND (MW)
University of Northern Colorado, CO (MW)
University of Northern Iowa, IA (MW)
University of North Texas, TX (MW)
University of Notre Dame, IN (MW)
University of Oklahoma, OK (MW)
University of Oregon, OR (MW)
University of Pennsylvania, PA (MW)
University of Pittsburgh, PA (M)
University of Pittsburgh (Bradford), PA (MW)
University of Pittsburgh (Johnstown), PA (MW)
University of Portland, OR (MW)
University of Puerto Rico, PR (MW)
University of Puerto Rico (Bayamon), PR (MW)
University of Puerto Rico (Ponce), PR (MW)
University of Puget Sound, WA (MW)
University of Redlands, CA (MW)
University of Rhode Island, RI (MW)
University of Richmond, VA (MW)
University of Rio Grande, OH (MW)
University of San Diego, CA (MW)
University of San Francisco, CA (MW)
University of Scranton, PA (MW)
University of South Alabama, AL (MW)
University of South Carolina (Columbia), SC (MW)
University of South Carolina (Myrtle Beach), SC (MW)
University of South Carolina (Aiken), SC (MW)
University of South Carolina (Spartanburg), SC (MW)
University of South Dakota, SD (MW)
University of Southern California, CA (MW)
University of Southern Colorado, CO (MW)
University of Southern Indiana, IN (MW)
University of Southern Mississippi, MS (MW)
University of South Florida, FL (MW)
University of Southwestern Louisiana, LA (MW)
University of St. Thomas, MN (MW)
University of Tampa, FL (MW)
University of Tennessee, TN (MW)
University of Tennessee (Knoxville), TN (MW)
University of Tennessee (Martin), TN (MW)
University of Texas (Arlington), TX (MW)
University of Texas (Austin), TX (MW)
University of Texas (El Paso), TX (MW)
University of Texas (Pan American), TX (MW)

University of Texas (San Antonio), TX (MW)
University of the District of Columbia, DC (MW)
University of the Ozarks, AR (MW)
University of the Pacific, CA (MW)
University of Toledo, OH (MW)
University of Tulsa, OK (M)
University of Utah, UT (MW)
University of Vermont, VT (MW)
University of Virginia, VA (MW)
University of Washington, WA (MW)
University of West Florida, FL (W)
University of Wisconsin (Eau Claire), WI (MW)
University of Wisconsin (Green Bay), WI (MW)
University of Wisconsin (La Crosse), WI (MW)
University of Wisconsin (Madison), WI (MW)
University of Wisconsin (Milwaukee), WI (MW)
University of Wisconsin (Oshkosh), WI (MW)
University of Wisconsin (Platteville), WI (MW)
University of Wisconsin (River Falls), WI (MW)
University of Wisconsin (Stevens Point), WI (MW)
University of Wisconsin (Stout), WI (MW)
University of Wisconsin (Superior), WI (MW)
University of Wyoming, WY (MW)
Upper Iowa University, IA (MW)
Urbana University, OH (MW)
Ursinus College, PA (MW)
U.S. International University, CA (MW)
Utah State University, UT (MW)
Valdosta State College, GA (MW)
Valencia Community College, FL (MW)
Valley City State University, ND (MW)
Valley Forge Christian College, PA (MW)
Valparaiso University, IN (MW)
Vanderbilt University, TN (MW)
Vassar College, NY (MW)
Ventura College, CA (MW)
Villa Maria College, NY (M)
Villanova University, PA (MW)
Vincennes University Junior College, IN (MW)
Virginia Commonwealth University, VA (MW)
Virginia Intermont College, VA (MW)
Virginia Military Institute, VA (M)
Virginia Polytechnic Institute & State University, VA (MW)
Virginia State University, VA (MW)
Virginia Union University, VA (MW)
Virginia Wesleyan College, VA (MW)
Viterbo College, WI (MW)
Wabash College, IN (M)
Wabash Valley College, IL (MW)
Wagner College, NY (MW)
Wake Forest University, NC (MW)
Waldorf College, IA (MW)
Wallace Community College (Selma), AL (M)
Wallace State Community College, AL (MW)
Walla Walla Community College, WA (MW)
Walsh College, OH (MW)
Walters State Community College, TN (MW)
Warner Pacific College, OR (MW)
Warner Southern College, FL (MW)
Warren Wilson College, NC (MW)
Wartburg College, IA (MW)
Washburn University, KS (MW)
Washington and Jefferson College, PA (MW)
Washington College, MD (MW)
Washington State University, WA (MW)
Washington University, MO (MW)
Waubonsee College, IL (MW)
Wayland Baptist University, TX (MW)
Wayne State College, NE (MW)
Wayne State University, MI (MW)
Webber College, FL (MW)
Weber State College, UT (MW)
Webster University, MO (MW)
Wellesley College, MA (W)
Wentworth Military Academy and Junior College, MO (M)
Wesleyan University, CT (MW)
Wesley College, DE (MW)
Westark Community College, AR (MW)
West Chester University, PA (MW)
Western Carolina University, NC (MW)
Western Connecticut State University, CT (MW)
Western Illinois University, IL (MW)
Western Kentucky University, KY (M)
Western Maryland College, MD (MW)
Western Michigan University, MI (MW)
Western Montana College, MT (MW)
Western Nebraska Community College, NE (MW)
Western New England College, MA (MW)
Western New Mexico University, NM (MW)
Western Oregon State College, OR (MW)
Western State College, CO (MW)
Western Texas College, TX (MW)
Western Washington University, WA (MW)
Western Wyoming Community College, WY (MW)
Westfield State College, MA (MW)
West Georgia College, GA (MW)
West Liberty State College, WV (M)
Westminster College, PA (MW)
Westmont College, CA (M)
West Texas State University, TX (MW)
West Virginia Institute of Technology, WV (MW)
West Virginia State College, WV (MW)
West Virginia University, WV (MW)
West Virginia Wesleyan College, WV (MW)
Wheaton College, IL (MW)
Wheeling Jesuit College, WV (MW)
Whitman College, WA (MW)
Whittier College, CA (MW)
Whitworth College, WA (M)
Wichita State University, KS (MW)
Wilkes College, NC (MW)
Wilkes University, PA (MW)
Willamette University, OR (MW)

William Jewell College, MO (MW)
William Patterson College, NJ (MW)
William Penn College, IA (MW)
William Rainey Harper College, IL (MW)
Williams College, MA (MW)
Williamson Trade School, PA (M)
William Woods College, MO (W)
Wilmington College, DE (MW)
Wilmington College, OH (MW)
Wingate College, NC (MW)
Winona State University, MN (MW)
Winston-Salem State University, NC (MW)
Winthrop University, SC (MW)
Wofford College, SC (MW)
Worcester State College, MA (MW)
Worthington Community College, MN (MW)
Wright State University, OH (MW)
Xavier University, OH (MW)
Xavier University of Louisiana, LA (MW)
Yakima Valley College, WA (MW)
Yale University, CT (MW)
Yavapai College, AZ (W)
Yeshiva University, NY (M)
York College (CUNY), NY (MW)
York College of Pennsylvania, PA (MW)
Youngstown State University, OH (MW)
Yuba Community College, CA (M)

Bowling

Adirondack College, NY (MW)
Bayamon Central University, PR (MW)
Bluefield College, VA (M)
Broome Community College, NY (W)
Broward Community College, FL (MW)
Bryant College, RI (MW)
Catonsville Community College, MD (MW)
Cleveland State University, OH (M)
College of Allegheny County, PA (MW)
College of St. Rose, NY (MW)
Colorado School of Mines, CO (MW)
Columbia-Greene Community College, NY (MW)
Concordia College, MN (M)
Concordia Seminary, MO (MW)
Dalton College, GA (MW)
Dundalk Community College, MD (W)
Dutchess Junior College, NY (MW)
Elizabeth Seton School of Iona College, NY (MW)
Essex Community College, MD (MW)
Fashion Institute of Technology, NY (MW)
Fulton-Montgomery Community College, NY (M)
Goucher College, MD (MW)
Grove City College, PA (M)
Herkimer County Community College, NY (M)
Hudson Valley Community College, NY (MW)
Indiana State University, IN (MW)
Madison Area Technical Colledge, WI (MW)
Maple Woods Community College, MO (M)
Mississippi State University, MS (MW)
Mohawk Valley Community College, NY (MW)
Moorpark College, CA (MW)
Nassau Community College, NY (MW)
New Jersey Institute of Technology, NJ (M)
Niagara County Community College, NY (M)
Northeastern Christian Junior College, PA (MW)
Pace University, NY (MW)
Prince George's Community College, MD (MW)
Queens College, NY (M)
Roosevelt University, IL (MW)
Saginaw Valley State College, MI (M)
Saint John's University, NY (MW)
Saint Peter's College, NJ (M)
San Diego Mesa College, CA (MW)
Scottsdale Community College, AR (MW)
Selma University, AL (M)
Snow College, UT (MW)
Southeastern Community College, IA (M)
Suffolk County Community College, NY (MW)
Tennessee Temple University, TN (M)
University of Washington, WA (MW)
University of Wisconsin (La Crosse), WI (MW)
Vincennes University Junior College, IN (MW)
Western New England College, MA (MW)
Western Wyoming Community College, WY (MW)
Whitworth College, WA (W)
William Patterson College, NJ (MW)

Cheerleading

Auburn University (Montgomery), AL (M)
Barstow College, CA (MW)
Black Hills State University, SD (MW)
Bluefield State College, WV (W)
Bridgewater College, VA (W)
California State University (Fullerton), CA (MW)
Cardinal Stritch College, WI (MW)
Central Wesleyan College, SC (MW)
Clarion University, PA (M)
Clark Atlanta University, GA (W)
College of St. Francis, IL (W)
Defiance College, OH (MW)
Faulkner University, AL (MW)
Florida Institute of Technology, FL (MW)
Geneva College, PA (MW)
Heidelberg College, OH (W)
Houghton College, NY (MW)
Hunter College of the City University of New York, NY (MW)
Jefferson Community College, NY (W)
Lackawanna Junior College, PA (W)
Liberty University, VA (MW)
Limestone College, SC (MW)
Louisiana College, LA (MW)
Lyndon State College, VT (W)
Middlesex County College, NJ (M)
Missouri Southern State College, MO (W)
Muskingum College, OH (W)
Northeastern State University, OK (MW)
North Idaho College, ID (MW)
Nyack College, NY (W)
Ohio Valley College, WV (W)
Palm Beach Atlantic College, FL (W)
Panhandle State University, OK (W)

Paris Junior College, TX (MW)
Parkland College, IL (MW)
Pratt Community College, KS (MW)
Presbyterian College, SC (MW)
Quinnipiac College, CT (W)
Saint Leo College, FL (W)
Snead State Community College, AL (MW)
Sue Bennett College, KY (W)
Troy State University, AL (MW)
University of Indiana Southeast, IN (MW)
University of Maine, ME (MW)
University of Montevallo, AL (W)
University of Nebraska (Kearney), NE (MW)
University of Rio Grande, OH (MW)
University of the District of Columbia, DC (W)
Urbana University, OH (MW)
Valley City State University, ND (W)
Waldorf College, IA (W)
Wallace Community College (Selma), AL (MW)
Warner Southern College, FL (MW)
Wesley College, DE (MW)
Winthrop University, SC (MW)
York College (CUNY), NY (W)

Crew

Boston University, MA (MW)
Brown University, RI (MW)
Bucknell University, PA (MW)
California Maritime Academy, CA (M)
Canisius College, NY (MW)
Carlow College, PA (W)
City College of San Francisco, CA (MW)
Clark University, MA (MW)
Columbia University, NY (MW)
Connecticut College, CT (MW)
Cornell University, NY (MW)
Dartmouth College, NH (MW)
Drexel University, PA (MW)
Emory University, GA (M)
Fairfield University, CT (MW)
Florida Institute of Technology, FL (M)
Fordham University, NY (MW)
Franklin & Marshall College, PA (MW)
George Washington University, DC (MW)
Gonzaga University, WA (MW)
Harvard University, MA (MW)
Holy Cross College, MA (MW)
Iona College, NY (MW)
Ithaca College, NY (MW)
Jacksonville University, FL (MW)
Johns Hopkins University, MD (MW)
Lafayette College, PA (MW)
La Salle University, PA (MW)
Loyola Marymount University, CA (MW)
Manhattan College, NY (MW)
Marietta College, OH (MW)
Marist College, NY (MW)
Massachusetts Institute of Technology, MA (MW)
Mercyhurst College, PA (MW)
Mobile College, AL (W)
Molloy College, NY (M)
Mount Holyoke College, MA (W)
Muhlenberg College, PA (W)
Orange Coast College, CA (MW)
Oregon State University, OR (MW)
Pacific Lutheran University, WA (MW)
Princeton University, NJ (MW)
Rollins College, FL (MW)
Saint John's University, NY (M)
Saint Joseph's University, PA (MW)
Saint Mary's College of California, CA (MW)
Santa Clara University, CA (MW)
Seattle Pacific University, WA (MW)
Skidmore College, NY (MW)
Smith College, MA (W)
Stanford University, CA (MW)
State University of New York Maritime College, NY (MW)
Syracuse University, NY (MW)
Temple University, PA (M)
Trinity College, CT (MW)
Trinity College, IL (MW)
Tufts University, MA (MW)
University of Alabama (Huntsville), AL (MW)
University of California (Berkeley), CA (MW)
University of California (Irvine), CA (MW)
University of California (San Diego), CA (MW)
University of Charleston, WV (MW)
University of Lowell, MA (MW)
University of Missouri (Columbia), MO (M)
University of Montana, MT (M)
University of Pennsylvania, PA (MW)
University of Puget Sound, WA (MW)
University of Redlands, CA (MW)
University of Rhode Island, RI (M)
University of San Diego, CA (MW)
University of Southern California, CA (MW)
University of Tampa, FL (MW)
University of Tennessee (Knoxville), TN (M)
University of the Pacific, CA (MW)
University of Wisconsin (Madison), WI (M)
Villanova University, PA (MW)
Washington College, MD (M)
Washington State University, WA (W)
Webber College, FL (MW)
Wellesley College, MA (W)
Wesleyan University, CT (MW)
Western Washington University, WA (MW)
Williams College, MA (MW)
Yale University, CT (MW)

Cross Country

Abilene Christian University, TX (MW)
Adams State College, CO (MW)
Adelphi University, NY (MW)
Adrian College, MI (MW)
Agnes Scott College, GA (W)
Alabama A & M University, AL (MW)
Alabama State University, AL (MW)
Albany State College, GA (M)
Albion College, MI (MW)
Albright College, PA (MW)
Alcorn State University, MS (MW)
Alderson-Broaddus College, WV (MW)
Alfred University, NY (MW)
Allegheny College, PA (MW)
Allen County College, KS (MW)
Allentown College, PA (MW)
Allen University, SC (M)
Alma College, MI (MW)
Alvernia College, PA (MW)
American University, DC (MW)
Amherst College, MA (MW)

Anderson College, SC (M)
Anderson University, IN (MW)
Andrew College, GA (MW)
Angelo State University, TX (MW)
Appalachian State University, NC (MW)
Apprentice School, VA (M)
Aquinas College, MI (MW)
Arizona State University, AZ (MW)
Arkansas College, AR (MW)
Arkansas State University, AR (MW)
Armstrong State College, GA (MW)
Asbury College, KY (MW)
Ashland College, OH (MW)
Atlantic Community College, NJ (MW)
Auburn University, AL (MW)
Augsburg College, MN (MW)
Augusta College, GA (MW)
Augustana College, IL (MW)
Augustana College, SD (MW)
Austin Peay State University, TN (MW)
Azusa Pacific University, CA (MW)
Babson College, MA (MW)
Bacone Junior College, OK (MW)
Baker University, KS (MW)
Ball State University, IN (MW)
Baltimore City Community College, MD (MW)
Barber-Scotia College, NC (MW)
Bard College, NY (MW)
Barry University, FL (MW)
Barstow College, CA (M)
Barton County College, KS (MW)
Bates College, ME (MW)
Baylor University, TX (MW)
Bellarmine College, KY (MW)
Balmont Abbey College, NC (MW)
Belmont College, TN (MW)
Benedict College, SC (M)
Bentley College, MA (MW)
Bergen Community College, NJ (MW)
Berry College, GA (MW)
Bethany College, KS (MW)
Bethany College, WV (MW)
Bethel College, IN (MW)
Bethel College, MN (MW)
Bethune-Cookman College, FL (MW)
Biola University, CA (M)
Bismarck State College, ND (MW)
Blackburn College, IL (MW)
Black Hills State University, SD (MW)
Blanton Junior College, NC (M)
Bloomsburg University, PA (MW)
Bluefield State College, WV (MW)
Bluffton College, OH (MW)
Boston College, MA (MW)
Boston University, MA (MW)
Bowdoin College, ME (MW)
Bowie State University, MD (MW)
Bowling Green State University, OH (MW)
Bradley University, IL (MW)
Brandeis University, MA (MW)
Brevard College, FL (MW)
Brevard College, NC (MW)
Bridgewater College, VA (MW)
Bridgewater State College, MA (MW)
Brigham Young University, HI (MW)
Brigham Young University, UT (MW)
Bronx Community College, NY (MW)
Broome Community College, NY (M)
Brown University, RI (MW)
Bryant College, RI (MW)
Bryn Mawr College, PA (W)
Bucknell University, PA (MW)
Bucks County Community College, PA (MW)
Buena Vista College, IA (MW)
Buffalo State College, NY (MW)
Buffalo State University (New York), NY (MW)
Butler University, IN (MW)
Butte College, CA (MW)
Cabrillo College, CA (MW)
Cabrini College, PA (MW)
California Institute of Technology, CA (MW)
California Lutheran University, CA (MW)
California Polytechnic State University, CA (MW)
California State Polytechnic University, CA (MW)
California State University, CA (MW)
California State University (Chico), CA (MW)
California State University (Fresno), CA (MW)
California State University (Fullerton), CA (MW)
California State University (Hayward), CA (MW)
California State University (Long Beach), CA (MW)
California State University (Los Angeles), CA (MW)
California State University (Sacramento), CA (MW)
California State University (San Bernardino), CA (MW)
California University, PA (MW)
Calvin College, MI (MW)
Campbellsville College, KY (MW)
Campbell University, NC (MW)
Canisius College, NY (MW)
Carleton College, MN (MW)
Carlow College, PA (W)
Carnegie-Mellon University, PA (MW)
Carroll College, WI (MW)
Carson-Newman College, TN (MW)
Carthage College, WI (MW)
Case Western Reserve University, OH (MW)
Castleton State College, VT (MW)
Catawba College, NC (MW)
Catholic University of America, DC (MW)
Catholic University of Puerto Rico, PR (MW)
Catonsville Community College, MD (MW)
Cayuga County Community College, NY (MW)
Cedarville College, OH (MW)
Centenary College, LA (MW)
Central Arizona College, AZ (M)
Central College, IA (MW)
Central College, KS (MW)
Central Connecticut State University, CT (MW)
Central Methodist College, MO (MW)
Central Michigan University, MI (MW)
Central Missouri State University, MO (MW)
Central Washington University, WA (MW)
Cerritos College, CA (MW)
Chaminade University, HI (MW)
Chapman University, CA (M)
Charleston Southern University, SC (MW)
Cheyney University of Pennsylvania, PA (M)
Chicago State University, IL (MW)
Christopher Newport College, VA (MW)
Citadel, SC (M)
City College of New York, NY (MW)
City College of San Francisco, CA (MW)

Clackamas Community College, OR (MW)
Clarion University, PA (MW)
Clark Atlanta University, GA (W)
Clarkson University, NY (MW)
Clark University, MA (MW)
Clemson University, SC (MW)
Cleveland State University, OH (W)
Cloud County Community College, KS (MW)
Coastal Carolina College, SC (MW)
Coe College, IA (MW)
Colby Community College, KS (MW)
Colgate University, NY (MW)
College of Charleston, SC (MW)
College of New Rochelle, NY (W)
College of Notre Dame, CA (MW)
College of Notre Dame of Maryland, MD (MW)
College of Southern Idaho, ID (MW)
College of St. Benedict, MN (W)
College of St. Francis, IL (W)
College of St. Rose, NY (MW)
College of St. Scholastica, MN (MW)
College of the Desert, CA (MW)
College of the Redwoods, CA (MW)
College of the Sequoias, CA (MW)
College of William and Mary, VA (MW)
College of Wooster, OH (MW)
Colorado College, CO (MW)
Colorado School of Mines, CO (MW)
Colorado State University, CO (MW)
Columbia-Greene Community College, NY (MW)
Columbia Union College, MD (MW)
Columbia University, NY (MW)
Columbus College, GA (M)
Columbus State Community College, OH (MW)
Community College of Rhode Island, RI (MW)
Community College of the Finger Lakes, NY (MW)
Community Colleges of Spokane, WA (MW)
Compton Community College, CA (MW)
Concordia College, NY (MW)
Concordia Teachers College, NE (MW)
Concordia University, IL (MW)
Connecticut College, CT (MW)
Contra Costa College, CA (M)
Coppin State College, MD (MW)
Cornell College, IA (MW)
Cornell University, NY (MW)
Cosummes River College, CA (MW)
Covenant College, GA (MW)
Creighton University, NE (MW)
Cuesta College, CA (MW)
Cumberland College, KY (M)
Dakota State University, SD (MW)
Dakota Wesleyan University, SD (MW)
Danville Area Community College, IL (MW)
Dartmouth College, NH (MW)
David Lipscomb College, TN (MW)
Davidson College, NC (MW)
Davis & Elkins College, WV (MW)
De Anza Community College, CA (MW)
Defiance College, OH (MW)
Delaware County Community College, PA (MW)
Delaware State College, DE (MW)
Delaware Valley College, PA (MW)
Delta State University, MS (W)
Denison University, OH (MW)
DePaul University, IL (MW)
De Pauw University, IN (MW)
Diablo Valley Community College, CA (MW)
Dickinson College, PA (MW)
Dickinson State University, ND (MW)
Doane College, NE (MW)
Dominican College, CA (M)
Drake University, IA (MW)
Drew University, NJ (MW)
Drexel University, PA (M)
Duke University, NC (MW)
Duquesne University, PA (MW)
Earlham College, IN (MW)
East Carolina University, NC (MW)
Eastern College, PA (MW)
Eastern Connecticut State University, CT (MW)
Eastern Illinois University, IL (MW)
Eastern Kentucky University, KY (MW)
Eastern Mennonite College, VA (MW)
Eastern Michigan University, MI (MW)
Eastern Nazarene College, MA (MW)
Eastern Oklahoma College, OK (MW)
Eastern Oregon State College, OR (MW)
Eastern Washington University, WA (MW)
East Los Angeles Community College, CA (W)
East Stroudsburg University, PA (MW)
East Tennessee State University, TN (MW)
East Texas State University, TX (MW)
Edinboro University of Pennsylvania, PA (MW)
Edward Waters College, FL (MW)
El Camino College, CA (MW)
Elizabeth City State University, NC (MW)
Elizabeth Seton School of Iona College, NY (MW)
Elizabethtown College, PA (MW)
Elmhurst College, IL (MW)
Emory University, GA (MW)
Emporia State University, KS (MW)
Erskine College, SC (M)
Essex Community College, MD (MW)
Everett Community College, WA (MW)
Fairfield University, CT (MW)
Fairleigh Dickinson University, NJ (MW)
Fairleigh Dickinson University (Rutherford), NJ (MW)
Fairmont State College, WV (W)
Fayetteville State University, NC (MW)
Ferris State College, MI (MW)
Fisk University, TN (MW)
Fitchburg State College, MA (MW)
Flagler College, FL (MW)
Florida A & M University, FL (MW)
Florida Atlantic University, FL (MW)
Florida College, FL (W)
Florida Institute of Technology, FL (MW)
Florida International University, FL (MW)
Florida Memorial College, FL (MW)
Florida Southern College, FL (MW)
Florida State University, FL (MW)

Foothill College, CA (MW)
Fordham University, NY (MW)
Fort Hays State University, KS (MW)
Fort Lewis College, CO (MW)
Francis Marion University, SC (MW)
Franklin & Marshall College, PA (MW)
Franklin Pierce College, NH (M)
Fresno City College, CA (MW)
Fresno Pacific College, CA (MW)
Fullerton College, CA (MW)
Fulton-Montgomery Community College, NY (MW)
Furman University, SC (MW)
Gannon College, PA (MW)
Garden City Community College, KS (MW)
Gardner-Webb College, NC (M)
Geneva College, PA (MW)
George Fox College, OR (MW)
George-Mason University, VA (MW)
Georgetown College, KY (MW)
Georgetown University, DC (MW)
George Washington University, DC (MW)
Georgia Institute of Technology, GA (MW)
Georgian Court College, NJ (W)
Georgia Southern University, GA (MW)
Georgia State University, GA (MW)
Gettysburg College, PA (MW)
Glendale Community College, AZ (MW)
Glendale Community College, CA (MW)
Glenville State College, WV (MW)
Gloucester County College, NJ (MW)
Golden West College, CA (MW)
Gonzaga University, WA (MW)
Gordon College, MA (MW)
Goshen College, IN (MW)
Graceland College, IA (MW)
Grambling State University, LA (W)
Grand Rapids Junior College, MI (MW)
Grand Valley State College, MI (MW)
Grand View College, IA (MW)
Greenfield Community College, MA (MW)
Green River Community College, WA (MW)
Greenville College, IL (M)
Grinnell College, IA (MW)
Grove City College, PA (MW)
Gustavus Adolphus College, MN (MW)
Hagerstown Junior College, MD (MW)
Hamilton College, NY (MW)
Hamline University, MN (MW)
Hampden-Sydney College, VA (M)
Hampton University, VA (MW)
Hanover College, IN (MW)
Harding University, AR (MW)
Hardin-Simmons University, TX (W)
Harper William Rainey College, IL (MW)
Hartwick College, NY (MW)
Harvard University, MA (MW)
Haskell Indian Junior College, KS (MW)
Hastings College, NE (MW)
Haverford College, PA (M)
Hawaii Pacific University, HI (MW)
Heidelberg College, OH (W)
Henderson State University, AR (MW)
Highland Community College, KS (MW)
Highland Park Community College, MI (W)
High Point University, NC (MW)
Hillsdale College, MI (MW)
Hiram College, OH (MW)
Hofstra University, NY (MW)
Holy Cross College, MA (MW)
Hope College, MI (MW)
Houghton College, NY (MW)
Houston Baptist University, TX (MW)
Howard Payne University, TX (MW)
Hudson Valley Community College, NY (M)
Humboldt State University, CA (MW)
Hunter College of the City University of New York, NY (MW)
Huntington College, IN (MW)
Huron University, SD (MW)
Hutchinson College, KS (M)
Idaho State University, ID (MW)
Illinois Benedictine College, IL (MW)
Illinois College, IL (MW)
Illinois Institute of Technology, IL (MW)
Illinois State University, IL (MW)
Illinois Wesleyan University, IL (MW)
Incarnate Word College, TX (MW)
Indiana State University, IN (MW)
Indiana University of Pennsylvania, PA (MW)
Indiana University-Purdue University (Fort Wayne), IN (MW)
Indiana Wesleyan University, IN (MW)
Iona College, NY (MW)
Iowa State University of Science and Technology, IA (MW)
Iowa Wesleyan College, IA (MW)
Ithaca College, NY (MW)
Jackson State University, MS (MW)
Jacksonville University, FL (MW)
James Madison University, VA (MW)
Jamestown College, ND (MW)
John Carroll University, OH (MW)
Johns Hopkins University, MD (W)
Johnson County Community College, KS (MW)
Johnson C. Smith University, NC (MW)
Johnson State College, VT (MW)
Juniata College, PA (MW)
Kalamazoo College, MI (MW)
Kansas City Kansas Community College, KS (MW)
Kansas State University, KS (W)
Kansas Wesleyan College, KS (MW)
Kennesaw State College, GA (MW)
Keene State College, NH (MW)
Kent State University (Ashtabula), OH (MW)
Kent State University (Kent), OH (MW)
Kent State University (New Philadelphia), OH (MW)
Kent State University (Warren), OH (MW)
Kentucky State University, KY (MW)
Kenyon College, OH (MW)
King College, TN (MW)
King's College, NY (MW)
King's College, PA (MW)
Knox College, IL (MW)
Kutztown University, PA (MW)
Lafayette College, PA (MW)

Lake Land College, IL (MW)
Lake Superior State University, MI (MW)
Lamar University, TX (MW)
Lander College, SC (MW)
Lansing Community College, MI (MW)
La Salle University, PA (MW)
Lawrence University, WI (MW)
Lebanon Valley College, PA (MW)
Lees Junior College, KY (MW)
Lehigh University, PA (MW)
Le Moyne College, NY (MW)
Lenoir-Rhyne College, NC (MW)
LeTourneau College, TX (MW)
Lewis and Clark College, OR (MW)
Lewis University, IL (MW)
Liberty University, VA (MW)
Lincoln College, IL (M)
Lincoln Land Community College, IL (M)
Lincoln Memorial University, TN (MW)
Lincoln University, MO (M)
Linfield College, OR (MW)
Long Beach City College, CA (MW)
Long Island University (Brooklyn), NY (MW)
Loras College, IA (MW)
Los Angeles Pierce Junior College, CA (MW)
Los Angeles Valley College, CA (MW)
Louisiana State University (Alexandria), LA (MW)
Louisiana State University (Baton Rouge), LA (MW)
Louisiana Tech University, LA (MW)
Lower Columbia College, WA (MW)
Loyola College, MD (MW)
Loyola Marymount University, CA (MW)
Loyola University, IL (MW)
Lubbock Christian College, TX (MW)
Luther College, IA (MW)
Lycoming College, PA (MW)
Lynchburg College, VA (MW)
Lyndon State College, VT (MW)
Macalester College, MN (MW)
Macomb Community College, MI (MW)
Madison Area Technical College, WI (MW)
Malone College, OH (MW)
Manchester College, IN (MW)
Manhattan College, NY (MW)
Mankato State University, MN (MW)
Mansfield University, PA (MW)
Marian College, IN (MW)
Marian College, WI (MW)
Marietta College, OH (MW)
Marist College, NY (MW)
Marquette University, WI (MW)
Marshall University, WV (MW)
Mars Hill College, NC (MW)
Mary Holmes College, MS (MW)
Maryville University, MO (MW)
Mary Washington College, VA (MW)
Massachusetts Institute of Technology, MA (MW)
Master's College, CA (MW)
McNeese State University, LA (MW)
McPherson College, KS (MW)
Memphis State University, TN (MW)
Mercer University, GA (MW)
Mercy College, NY (MW)
Mercyhurst College, PA (MW)
Merrimack College, MA (MW)
Mesa Community College, AZ (MW)
Mesa State College, CO (W)
Messiah College, PA (MW)
Miami University, OH (MW)
Michigan Christian College, MI (MW)
Michigan State University, MI (MW)
Michigan Technological University, MI (MW)
Mid-America Nazarene College, KS (MW)
Middlebury College, VT (MW)
Middlesex County College, NJ (MW)
Middle Tennessee State University, TN (MW)
Midland Lutheran College, NE (MW)
Miles College, AL (MW)
Millersville University, PA (MW)
Millikin University, IL (MW)
Milwaukee Area Technology College, WI (MW)
Minot State, ND (MW)
MiraCosta College, CA (W)
Mississippi College, MS (M)
Mississippi State University, MS (M)
Mississippi Valley State University, MS (MW)
Missouri Southern State College, MO (MW)
Missouri Valley College, MO (MW)
Mobile College, AL (M)
Modesto Junior College, CA (MW)
Mohawk Valley Community College, NY (MW)
Monmouth College, IL (MW)
Monmouth College, NJ (M)
Montana State University, MT (MW)
Montclair State College, NJ (MW)
Moorhead State University, MN (MW)
Moorpark College, CA (MW)
Moravian College, PA (MW)
Morehead State University, KY (MW)
Morgan State University, MD (MW)
Morton College, IL (MW)
Mount Holyoke College, MA (W)
Mount Mercy College, IA (MW)
Mount St. Mary College, MD (MW)
Mount Union College, OH (MW)
Mt. San Antonio College, CA (MW)
Mt. Wachusett Community College, MA (MW)
Muhlenberg College, PA (M)
Murray State University, KY (MW)
Muskingum College, OH (MW)
Nassau Community College, NY (MW)
Navajo Community College, AZ (MW)
Nebraska Wesleyan University, NE (M)
New Mexico Highlands University, NM (MW)
New Mexico Junior College, NM (M)
New Mexico State University, NM (MW)
New York University, NY (MW)
Niagara County Community College, NY (MW)
Niagara University, NY (MW)
Nicholls State University, LA (MW)
Norfolk State University, VA (MW)
North Adams State College, MA (MW)
North Carolina A & T State University, NC (M)
North Carolina Central University, NC (MW)

North Carolina State University, NC (MW)
North Central College, IL (MW)
North Dakota State, ND (MW)
North Dakota State University, ND (MW)
Northeastern Illinois University, IL (MW)
Northeastern Junior College, CO (MW)
Northeast Louisiana University, LA (MW)
Northeast Missouri State University, MO (MW)
Northern Arizona University, AZ (MW)
Northern Kentucky University, KY (MW)
Northern Michigan University, MI (MW)
Northern State University, SD (MW)
North Idaho College, ID (MW)
Northwestern College, IA (MW)
Northwestern College, MN (M)
Northwestern University, IL (MW)
Northwest Missouri State University, MO (MW)
Norwich University, VT (MW)
Nova University, FL (MW)
Oakland Community College, MI (MW)
Oakland University, MI (M)
Oakton Community College, IL (MW)
Oberlin College, OH (MW)
Occidental College, CA (MW)
Ocean County College, NJ (MW)
Oglethorpe University, GA (MW)
Ohio Northern University, OH (M)
Ohio State University, OH (MW)
Ohio University, OH (MW)
Ohio Wesleyan University, OH (MW)
Oklahoma Baptist University, OK (M)
Oklahoma Christian University of Science & Art, OK (MW)
Oklahoma State University, OK (MW)
Old Dominion University, VA (MW)
Olivet College, MI (M)
Olivet Nazarene University, IL (MW)
Oral Roberts University, OK (MW)
Orange Coast College, CA (MW)
Oregon State University, OR (MW)
Ottawa University, KS (MW)
Otterbein College, OH (MW)
Ouachita Baptist University, AR (M)
Oxnard College, CA (MW)
Pace University, NY (MW)
Pace University (White Plains Campus), NY (MW)
Pacific Lutheran University, WA (MW)
Pacific University, OR (MW)
Paine College, GA (MW)
Pan American University, TX (MW)
Panhandle State University, OK (MW)
Park College, MO (MW)
Parkland College, IL (MW)
Pembroke State University, NC (MW)
Pennsylvania State University, PA (MW)
Pepperdine University, CA (MW)
Pfeiffer College, NC (M)
Philadelphia Community College, PA (MW)
Phoenix College, AZ (MW)
Piedmont College, GA (MW)
Pima Community College, AZ (MW)
Pittsburg State University, KS (MW)
Point Loma Nazarene College, CA (MW)
Polytechnic University (Brooklyn Campus), NY (M)
Pomona-Pitzer Colleges, CA (MW)
Portland State University, OR (MW)
Prairie View A & M University, TX (MW)
Pratt Community College, KS (MW)
Princeton University, NJ (MW)
Principia College, IL (MW)
Providence College, RI (MW)
Purdue University, IN (MW)
Queensborough Community College, NY (MW)
Queens College, NY (MW)
Quinnipiac College, CT (MW)
Radford University, VA (MW)
Ramapo College, NJ (MW)
Ranetto Santiago College, CA (MW)
Regis College, MA (W)
Rensselaer Polytechnic Institute, NY (MW)
Rhode Island College, RI (MW)
Rice University, TX (MW)
Ricks College, ID (MW)
Rider College, NJ (M)
Ripon College, WI (MW)
Riverside College, CA (MW)
Roanoke College, VA (MW)
Robert Morris College, PA (MW)
Roberts Wesleyan College, NY (MW)
Rochester Institute of Technology, NY (MW)
Rockhurst College, MO (MW)
Rollins College, FL (MW)
Roosevelt University, IL (M)
Rose-Hulman Institute of Technology, IN (M)
Rowan College of New Jersey, NJ (W)
Rust College, MS (MW)
Sacred Heart University, CT (MW)
Saddleback College, CA (MW)
Saginaw Valley State College, MI (M)
Saint Ambrose College, IA (M)
Saint Andrews Presbyterian College, NC (MW)
Saint Anselm College, NH (MW)
Saint Bonaventure University, NY (MW)
Saint Cloud State University, MN (MW)
Saint Francis College, IN (MW)
Saint Francis College, NY (MW)
Saint Francis College, PA (MW)
Saint John Fisher College, NY (MW)
Saint John's University, MN (M)
Saint John's University, NY (MW)
Saint Joseph's College, IN (MW)
Saint Joseph's University, PA (MW)
Saint Lawrence University, NY (MW)
Saint Leo College, FL (MW)
Saint Louis University, MO (M)
Saint Mary's College of California, CA (MW)
Saint Michael's College, VT (MW)
Saint Norbert College, WI (MW)
Saint Olaf College, MN (MW)
Saint Paul's College, VA (M)
Saint Peter's College, NJ (MW)
Saint Thomas Aquinas College, NY (M)
Saint Vincent College, PA (MW)
Salem State College, MA (MW)
Salve Regina College, RI (MW)
Samford University, AL (M)
San Bernardino Community College, CA (MW)

San Diego City College, CA (MW)
San Diego Mesa College, CA (MW)
San Diego State University, CA (MW)
San Francisco State University, CA (MW)
San Joaquin Delta College, CA (MW)
San Jose State University, CA (M)
Santa Barbara City College, CA (MW)
Santa Clara University, CA (MW)
Santa Monica College, CA (MW)
Santa Rosa Junior College, CA (MW)
Savannah State College, GA (W)
Schoolcraft College, MI (W)
Schreiner College, TX (MW)
Scottsdale Community College, AR (MW)
Seattle Pacific University, WA (MW)
Seattle University, WA (MW)
Seminole Community College, FL (M)
Seton Hall University, NJ (MW)
Seton Hill College, PA (W)
Shawnee State University, OH (MW)
Shepherd College, WV (MW)
Shippensburg University of Pennsylvania, PA (MW)
Shorter College, GA (MW)
Siena College, NY (MW)
Siena Heights College, MI (MW)
Sierra College, CA (MW)
Sierra Nevada College, NV (MW)
Simpson College, CA (MW)
Sioux Falls College, SD (MW)
Skagit Valley College, WA (MW)
Skyline College, CA (MW)
Slippery Rock University of Pennsylvania, PA (MW)
Smith College, MA (W)
Snead State Community College, AL (W)
South Carolina State College, SC (MW)
South Dakota School of Mines and Technology, SD (MW)
South Dakota State University, SD (MW)
Southeastern Louisiana University, LA (MW)
Southeastern Massachusetts University, MA (MW)
Southeast Missouri State University, MO (MW)
Southern Arkansas University, AR (M)
Southern California College, CA (MW)
Southern Connecticut State University, CT (MW)
Southern Illinois University, IL (MW)
Southern Illinois University (Edwardsville), IL (MW)
Southern Methodist University, TX (MW)
Southern Oregon State College, OR (MW)
Southern University and A & M College, LA (MW)
Southern Utah University, UT (MW)
South Plains Community College, TX (M)
Southwest Baptist University, MO (MW)
Southwestern College, KS (MW)
Southwestern Michigan Junior College, MI (MW)
Southwestern University, TX (MW)
Southwest Missouri State University, MO (MW)
Southwest State University, MN (MW)
Southwest Texas State University, TX (MW)
Spoon River College, IL (MW)
Spring Arbor College, MI (MW)
Springfield College, MA (MW)
State University of New York, NY (MW)
State University of New York (Albany), NY (MW)
State University of New York (Binghamton), NY (W)
State University of New York (Buffalo), NY (MW)
State University of New York (Plattsburgh), NY (MW)
State University of New York (Stony Brook), NY (MW)
State University of New York College (Brockport), NY (MW)
State University of New York College (Cortland), NY (MW)
State University of New York College (Fredonia), NY (MW)
State University of New York College (Geneseo), NY (MW)
State University of New York College (New Paltz), NY (MW)
State University of New York College (Oswego), NY (MW)
State University of New York College (Potsdam), NY (MW)
State University of New York Maritime College, NY (M)
St. Catherine College, KY (M)
Stephen F. Austin State University, TX (MW)
Stetson University, FL (MW)
Stevens Institute of Technology, NJ (MW)
Stonehill College, MA (MW)
Sue Bennett College, KY (MW)
Suffolk County Community College, NY (M)
Suffolk University, MA (MW)
Swarthmore College, PA (MW)
Syracuse University, NY (MW)
Taft College, CA (MW)
Talledaga College, AL (MW)
Tampa College, FL (MW)
Tarleton State University, TX (MW)
Teikyo Marycrest University, IA (MW)
Tennessee Technological University, TN (MW)
Texas A & I University, TX (MW)
Texas A & M University, TX (MW)
Texas Christian University, TX (MW)
Texas Southern University, TX (MW)
Texas Tech University, TX (MW)
Tiffin University, OH (MW)
Toccoa Falls College, GA (M)
Towson State University, MD (MW)
Trenton State College, NJ (MW)
Trinity College, CT (MW)
Trinity College, IL (MW)
Tri-State University, IN (W)
Troy State University, AL (MW)
Tufts University, MA (MW)
Tulane University, LA (MW)
Tuskegee University, AL (MW)
Umpqua College, OR (MW)
Union College, NY (MW)
Unity College, ME (M)
University of Akron, OH (MW)
University of Alabama (Birmingham), AL (MW)
University of Alabama (Huntsville), AL (MW)
University of Alabama (Tuscaloosa), AL (MW)
University of Alaska, AK (M)
University of Alaska (Fairbanks), AK (MW)
University of Arizona, AZ (MW)

University of Arkansas (Fayetteville), AR (MW)
University of Arkansas (Little Rock), AR (W)
University of Arkansas (Monticello), AR (MW)
University of Arkansas (Pine Bluff), AR (MW)
University of California (Berkeley), CA (MW)
University of California (Davis), CA (MW)
University of California (Irvine), CA (MW)
University of California (Riverside), CA (MW)
University of California (San Diego), CA (M)
University of California (Santa Barbara), CA (MW)
University of California (Santa Cruz), CA (MW)
University of California (UCLA), CA (MW)
University of Central Arkansas, AR (MW)
University of Central Florida, FL (MW)
University of Central Oklahoma, OK (MW)
University of Chicago, IL (MW)
University of Cincinnati, OH (MW)
University of Colorado, CO (MW)
University of Connecticut, CT (MW)
University of Dayton, OH (MW)
University of Delaware, DE (MW)
University of Detroit Mercy, MI (MW)
University of Dubuque, IA (MW)
University of Evansville, IN (MW)
University of Findlay, OH (MW)
University of Florida, FL (W)
University of Georgia, GA (MW)
University of Hartford, CT (MW)
University of Hawaii (Hilo), HI (MW)
University of Hawaii (Manoa), HI (W)
University of Houston, TX (MW)
University of Idaho, ID (MW)
University of Illinois, IL (MW)
University of Illinois (Urbana-Champaign), IL (MW)
University of Indianapolis, IN (MW)
University of Iowa, IA (M)
University of Kansas, KS (MW)
University of Kentucky, KY (MW)
University of La Verne, CA (MW)
University of Louisville, KY (MW)
University of Lowell, MA (MW)
University of Maine, ME (MW)
University of Maine (Presque Isle), ME (MW)
University of Mary, ND (MW)
University of Maryland, MD (MW)
University of Maryland (Baltimore County), MD (MW)
University of Maryland (Eastern Shore), MD (MW)
University of Massachusetts (Amherst), MA (MW)
University of Massachusetts (Boston), MA (MW)
University of Miami, FL (MW)
University of Michigan, MI (MW)
University of Minnesota (Duluth), MN (MW)
University of Minnesota (Minneapolis), MN (MW)
University of Minnesota (Morris), MN (M)
University of Mississippi, MS (MW)
University of Missouri, MO (MW)
University of Missouri (Columbia), MO (MW)
University of Missouri (Rolla), MO (MW)
University of Montana, MT (W)
University of Nebraska, NE (M)
University of Nebraska (Kearney), NE (MW)
University of Nebraska (Lincoln), NE (MW)
University of Nevada, NV (MW)
University of Nevada (Reno), NV (MW)
University of New Hampshire, NH (MW)
University of New Haven, CT (M)
University of New Mexico, NM (MW)
University of New Orleans, LA (MW)
University of North Alabama, AL (MW)
University of North Carolina (Asheville), NC (MW)
University of North Carolina (Chapel Hill), NC (MW)
University of North Carolina (Charlotte), NC (MW)
University of North Carolina (Wilmington), NC (MW)
University of North Dakota, ND (MW)
University of Northern Iowa, IA (MW)
University of North Florida, FL (MW)
University of North Texas, TX (MW)
University of Notre Dame, IN (MW)
University of Oklahoma, OK (MW)
University of Oregon, OR (MW)
University of Pennsylvania, PA (MW)
University of Pittsburgh, PA (MW)
University of Pittsburgh (Bradford), PA (MW)
University of Pittsburgh (Johnstown), PA (MW)
University of Portland, OR (MW)
University of Puerto Rico, PR (MW)
University of Puerto Rico (Bayamon), PR (MW)
University of Puerto Rico (Ponce), PR (MW)
University of Puget Sound, WA (MW)
University of Rhode Island, RI (MW)
University of Richmond, VA (MW)
University of Rio Grande, OH (M)
University of San Diego, CA (MW)
University of San Francisco, CA (MW)
University of Scranton, PA (MW)
University of South Alabama, AL (MW)
University of South Carolina, SC (M)
University of South Carolina (Aiken), SC (MW)
University of South Carolina (Spartanburg), SC (M)
University of South Dakota, SD (MW)
University of Southern California, CA (MW)
University of Southern Colorado, CO (MW)
University of Southern Indiana, IN (MW)
University of Southern Mississippi, MS (MW)
University of South Florida, FL (MW)

University of Southwestern Louisiana, LA (MW)
University of St. Thomas, MN (MW)
University of Tampa, FL (MW)
University of Tennessee, TN (MW)
University of Tennessee (Knoxville), TN (MW)
University of Tennessee (Martin), TN (MW)
University of Texas (Arlington), TX (M)
University of Texas (Austin), TX (MW)
University of Texas (El Paso), TX (MW)
University of Texas (Pan American), TX (MW)
University of Texas (San Antonio), TX (MW)
University of the District of Columbia, DC (MW)
University of the Pacific, CA (W)
University of Toledo, OH (MW)
University of Tulsa, OK (MW)
University of Utah, UT (MW)
University of Vermont, VT (MW)
University of Virginia, VA (MW)
University of Washington, WA (MW)
University of Wisconsin (Eau Claire), WI (MW)
University of Wisconsin (Green Bay), WI (MW)
University of Wisconsin (La Crosse), WI (MW)
University of Wisconsin (Madison), WI (MW)
University of Wisconsin (Milwaukee), WI (MW)
University of Wisconsin (Oshkosh), WI (MW)
University of Wisconsin (Platteville), WI (MW)
University of Wisconson (River Falls), WI (MW)
University of Wisconson (Stevens Point), WI (MW)
University of Wisconsin (Stout), WI (MW)
University of Wisconson (Superior), WI (MW)
University of Wyoming, WY (MW)
Upper Iowa University, IA (MW)
Urbana University, OH (MW)
Ursinus College, PA (MW)
U.S. International University, CA (MW)
Utah State University, UT (MW)
Valdosta State College, GA (MW)
Valley City State University, ND (MW)
Valparaiso University, IN (M)
Vanderbilt University, TN (MW)
Vassar College, NY (MW)
Ventura College, CA (MW)
Villanova University, PA (MW)
Vincennes University Junior College, IN (MW)
Virginia Commonwealth University, VA (MW)
Virginia Military Institute, VA (M)
Virginia Polytechnic Institute & State University, VA (MW)
Virginia State University, VA (MW)
Virginia Union University, VA (MW)
Wabash College, IN (M)
Wagner College, NY (MW)
Wake Forest University, NC (MW)
Walsh College, OH (MW)
Warren Wilson College, NC (MW)
Wartburg College, IA (MW)
Washington and Jefferson College, PA (MW)
Washington State University, WA (MW)
Washington University, MO (MW)
Waubonsee College, IL (M)
Wayland Baptist University, TX (MW)
Wayne State University, MI (M)
Webber College, FL (MW)
Weber State College, UT (MW)
Webster University, MO (W)
Wellesley College, MA (W)
Wesleyan University, CT (MW)
West Chester University, PA (MW)
Western Carolina University, NC (W)
Western Illinois University, IL (MW)
Western Kentucky University, KY (MW)
Western Maryland College, MD (MW)
Western Michigan University, MI (MW)
Western Montana College, MT (MW)
Western Oregon State College, OR (MW)
Western State College, CO (MW)
Westfield State College, MA (W)
West Georgia College, GA (MW)
West Liberty State College, WV (M)
Westminster College, PA (M)
Westmont College, CA (MW)
West Virginia University, WV (MW)
West Virginia Wesleyan College, WV (MW)
Wheaton College, IL (MW)
Wheeling Jesuit College, WV (MW)
Whitman College, WA (MW)
Whittier College, CA (MW)
Whitworth College, WA (MW)
Wichita State University, KS (MW)
Wilkes College, NC (M)
Wilkes University, PA (MW)
Willamette University, OR (MW)
William Jewell College, MO (MW)
William Patterson College, NJ (MW)
William Penn College, IA (MW)
Williams College, MA (MW)
Williamson Trade School, PA (M)
Wilmington College, DE (M)
Wilmington College, OH (MW)
Winona State University, MN (MW)
Winston-Salem State University, NC (MW)
Winthrop University, SC (MW)
Wofford College, SC (MW)
Worcester State College, MA (MW)
Wright State University, OH (MW)
Xavier University, OH (MW)
Yale University, CT (MW)
Yeshiva University, NY (M)
York College (CUNY), NY (MW)
Youngstown State University, OH (MW)

Cross Country Skiing

Bates College, ME (MW)
Bowdoin College, ME (MW)
Broome Community College, NY (W)
Carleton College, MN (MW)
Castleton State College, VT (MW)
Champlain College, VT (MW)
Clarkson University, NY (MW)
Colby-Sawyer College, NH (MW)
College of Idaho, ID (MW)

Colorado School of Mines, CO (MW)
Cornell University, NY (M)
Dartmouth College, NH (MW)
Eastern Oregon State College, OR (MW)
Harvard University, MA (MW)
Johnson State College, VT (MW)
Keene State College, NH (MW)
Massachusetts Institute of Technology, MA (MW)
Mesa State College, CO (W)
Michigan Technological University, MI (MW)
Middlebury College, VT (MW)
Montana State University, MT (MW)
Northern Michigan University, MI (MW)
North Iowa Area Community College, IA (MW)
Norwich University, VT (MW)
Pacific Lutheran University, WA (MW)
Passaic County Community College, NJ (MW)
Saint Lawrence University, NY (MW)
Saint Michael's College, VT (MW)
Saint Olaf College, MN (MW)
Samford University, AL (W)
Sierra College, CA (MW)
Sierra Nevada College, NV (MW)
Snow College, UT (MW)
University of Alaska, AK (MW)
University of Alaska (Fairbanks), AK (MW)
University of Colordao, CO (MW)
University of New Hampshire, NH (MW)
University of Puget Sound, WA (MW)
University of Utah, UT (MW)
University of Vermont, VT (MW)
University of Wisconsin (Green Bay), WI (MW)
Western State College, CO (MW)
Whitman College, WA (MW)
Williams College, MA (MW)

Diving

Alfred University, NY (MW)
Allegheny College, PA (MW)
Arizona State University, AZ (MW)
Ashland College, OH (MW)
Auburn University, AL (MW)
Augustana College, IL (M)
Austin College, TX (MW)
Austin Community College, MN (MW)
Babson College, MA (MW)
Beloit College, WI (MW)
Bloomsburg University, PA (W)
Boston College, MA (MW)
Boston University, MA (MW)
Bowdoin College, ME (MW)
Bowling Green State University, OH (MW)
Brigham Young University, UT (MW)
Broward Community College, FL (MW)
Buena Vista College, IA (MW)
Buffalo State College, NY (MW)
California State University (Hayward), CA (MW)
California State University (Los Angeles), CA (MW)
California State University (Sacramento), CA (MW)
Calvin College, MI (MW)
Carleton College, MN (MW)
Case Western Reserve University, OH (MW)
Catonsville Community College, MD (MW)
Central Connecticut State University, CT (MW)
Central Washington University, WA (MW)
Chaffey College, CA (MW)
Clarion University, PA (MW)
Clarkson University, NY (MW)
Clark University, MA (MW)
Cleveland State University, OH (MW)
Colgate University, NY (MW)
College of Charleston, SC (MW)
College of St. Benedict, MN (W)
College of the Sequoias, CA (MW)
College of William and Mary, VA (MW)
College of Wooster, OH (MW)
Colorado School of Mines, CO (MW)
Colorado State University, CO (W)
Columbia University, NY (MW)
Cornell University, NY (MW)
Dartmouth College, NH (MW)
Davidson College, NC (MW)
De Anza Community College, CA (MW)
Denison University, OH (MW)
Diablo Valley Community College, CA (MW)
Drexel University, PA (MW)
Eastern Illinois University, IL (MW)
Eastern Michigan University, MI (MW)
El Camino College, CA (MW)
Elizabethtown College, PA (MW)
Eureka College, IL (MW)
Fairfield University, CT (MW)
Florida State University, FL (MW)
Fordham University, NY (MW)
Furman University, SC (M)
Gannon College, PA (MW)
George Washington University, DC (MW)
Grinnell College, IA (MW)
Hamilton College, NY (MW)
Hamline University, MN (MW)
Harper William Rainey College, IL (MW)
Henderson State University, AR (M)
Hiram College, OH (MW)
Hood College, MD (W)
Hope College, MI (MW)
Hunter College of the City University of New York, NY (W)
Illinois Benedictine College, IL (MW)
Illinois Institute of Technology, IL (MW)
Illinois Wesleyan University, IL (MW)
Iona College, NY (MW)
Johns Hopkins University, MD (W)
Kalamazoo College, MI (MW)
Keene State College, NH (MW)
Kenyon College, OH (MW)
King's College, PA (MW)
Knox College, IL (MW)
Kutztown University, PA (MW)
Lake Forest College, IL (MW)
Lawrence University, WI (M)
Loras College, IA (MW)
Louisiana State University, LA (MW)
Loyola College, MD (MW)
Macalester College, MN (M)
Manhattanville College, NY (W)
Mankato State University, MN (MW)
Mansfield University, PA (W)
Massachusetts Institute of Technology, MA (MW)
Miami-Dade Community College (South Campus), FL (MW)
Millikin University, IL (M)

Mississippi Valley State University, MS (MW)
Molloy College, NY (M)
Monmouth College, NJ (MW)
Montgomery College, MD (MW)
Morehead State University, KY (MW)
Mount Holyoke College, MA (W)
Mt. San Antonio College, CA (M)
Nazareth College, NY (MW)
New Mexico State University, NM (MW)
Niagara University, NY (MW)
Northeast Louisiana University, LA (MW)
Northern Arizona University, AZ (W)
Northern Michigan University, MI (W)
Norwich University, VT (MW)
Oakland University, MI (MW)
Occidental College, CA (MW)
Ohio Northern University, OH (MW)
Ohio State University, OH (MW)
Ohio University, OH (MW)
Orange Coast College, CA (MW)
Ouachita Baptist University, AR (MW)
Palomar College, CA (MW)
Pfeiffer College, NC (W)
Pomona-Pitzer Colleges, CA (MW)
Principia College, IL (MW)
Queens College, NY (MW)
Ranetto Santiago College, CA (MW)
Regis College, MA (W)
Rensselaer Polytechnic Institute, NY (MW)
Rider College, NJ (MW)
Rose-Hulman Institute of Technology, IN (M)
Rose State Junior College, OK (MW)
Saddleback College, CA (MW)
Saint Bonaventure University, NY (MW)
Saint Cloud State University, MN (MW)
Saint John's University, MN (M)
Saint John's University, NY (MW)
Saint Lawrence University, NY (MW)
Saint Olaf College, MN (MW)
Saint Peter's College, NJ (MW)
San Diego Mesa College, CA (MW)
Shippensburg University of Pennsylvania, PA (MW)
Sierra College, CA (MW)
Skidmore College, NY (W)
Southern Methodist University, TX (MW)
Springfield College, MA (MW)
State University of New York (Albany), NY (M)
State University of New York (Binghamton), NY (MW)
State University of New York (Buffalo), NY (MW)
State University of New York College (Brockport), NY (MW)
State University of New York College (Oswego), NY (MW)
Sweet Briar College, VA (W)
Texas A & I University, TX (MW)
Texas Christian University, TX (M)
Tufts University, MA (MW)
University of Arkansas (Fayetteville), AR (W)
University of Arkansas (Little Rock), AR (M)
University of California (Berkeley), CA (W)
University of California (Irvine), CA (MW)
University of California (Riverside), CA (MW)
University of California (San Diego), CA (MW)
University of California (Santa Barbara), CA (MW)
University of California (UCLA), CA (MW)
University of Central Arkansas, AR (MW)
University of Chicago, IL (MW)
University of Cincinnati, OH (MW)
University of Connecticut, CT (M)
University of Findlay, OH (MW)
University of Georgia, GA (MW)
University of Houston, TX (W)
University of Illinois, IL (MW)
University of Illinois (Urbana-Champaign), IL (MW)
University of Iowa, IA (M)
University of Kansas, KS (MW)
University of Kentucky, KY (MW)
University of Louisville, KY (MW)
University of Maine, ME (MW)
University of Maryland, MD (MW)
University of Maryland (Baltimore County), MD (MW)
University of Massachusetts (Amherst), MA (MW)
University of Miami, FL (MW)
University of Missouri (Columbia), MO (MW)
University of Nebraska, NE (W)
University of Nebraska (Kearney), NE (W)
University of Nebraska (Lincoln), NE (MW)
University of Nevada, NV (MW)
University of North Dakota, ND (MW)
University of Richmond, VA (MW)
University of South Carolina (Columbia), SC (MW)
University of South Carolina (Myrtle Beach), SC (MW)
University of Southern California, CA (MW)
University of St. Thomas, MN (MW)
University of Tennessee, TN (MW)
University of Tennessee (Knoxville), TN (MW)
University of Texas (Austin), TX (MW)
University of Toledo, OH (M)
University of Wisconsin (Eau Claire), WI (MW)
University of Wisconsin (Green Bay), WI (MW)
University of Wisconsin (La Crosse), WI (MW)
University of Wisconsin (Madison), WI (MW)
University of Wisconsin (Stevens Point), WI (MW)
University of Wisconson (Stout), WI (MW)
University of Wyoming, WY (MW)
Valparaiso University, IN (MW)
Vincennes University Junior College, IN (MW)
Wabash College, IN (M)
Wayne State University, MI (MW)
Wellesley College, MA (W)
West Chester University, PA (MW)
Western Kentucky University, KY (M)
Whittier College, CA (MW)
Willamette University, OR (MW)
William Jewell College, MO (W)
William Patterson College, NJ (MW)
Williams College, MA (MW)
Yale University, CT (MW)

York College of Pennsylvania, PA (MW)
Youngstown State University, OH (MW)

Equestrian

Alfred University, NY (MW)
Becker College, MA (MW)
Bucks County Community College, PA (MW)
Centenary College, NJ (MW)
Colby-Sawyer College, NH (MW)
College of Charleston, SC (MW)
Columbus State Community College, OH (W)
Converse College, SC (W)
Dartmouth College, NH (MW)
Dawson Community College, MT (MW)
Drew University, NJ (MW)
Fairleigh Dickinson University, NJ (W)
Fairleigh Dickinson University (Rutherford), NJ (MW)
Ferrum College, VA (MW)
Goucher College, MD (MW)
Henderson State University, AR (W)
Hiwassee College, TN (MW)
Lynchburg College, VA (MW)
Mary Washington College, VA (MW)
Molloy College, NY (W)
Moorpark College, CA (MW)
Moravian College, PA (MW)
Mount Holyoke College, MA (W)
Otterbein College, OH (MW)
Pace University, NY (W)
Park College, MO (MW)
Saint Andrews Presbyterian College, NC (MW)
Saint John's University, NY (M)
Saint Lawrence University, NY (MW)
Seton Hill College, PA (W)
Skidmore College, NY (MW)
Smith College, MA (W)
Snow College, UT (MW)
Southeastern Oklahoma State University, OK (MW)
Stonehill College, MA (MW)
Sweet Briar College, VA (W)
Teikyo Post University, CT (MW)
University of Detroit Mercy, MI (W)
Wilson College, PA (W)

Fencing

Boston College, MA (W)
Brandeis University, MA (MW)
California Institute of Technology, CA (MW)
California State University (Fullerton), CA (MW)
California State University (Long Beach), CA (MW)
Case Western Reserve University, OH (MW)
City College of New York, NY (MW)
Cleveland State University, OH (MW)
College of William and Mary, VA (M)
Columbia University, NY (MW)
Cornell University, NY (MW)
Dalton College, GA (MW)
Dominican College, CA (MW)
Drew University, NJ (MW)
Duke University, NC (MW)
Fairfield University, CT (MW)
Fairleigh Dickinson University, NJ (W)
Fairleigh Dickinson University (Rutherford), NJ (W)
Florida Atlantic University, FL (MW)
Goucher College, MD (MW)
Harvard University, MA (MW)
Haverford College, PA (M)
Hunter College of the City University of New York, NY (MW)
James Madison University, VA (W)
Johns Hopkins University, MD (W)
Lafayette College, PA (MW)
Lawrence University, WI (MW)
Massachusetts Institute of Technology, MA (MW)
Miami-Dade Community College (North), FL (MW)
Michigan State University, MI (M)
Mississippi State University, MS (M)
Muhlenberg College, PA (W)
New York University, NY (MW)
North Carolina State University, NC (MW)
Northwestern University, IL (MW)
Ohio State University, OH (MW)
Pace University, NY (M)
Pace University (White Plains Campus), NY (MW)
Pennsylvania State University, PA (MW)
Princeton University, NJ (M)
Rutgers, Newark College of Arts and Sciences, NJ (MW)
Saint John's University, NY (MW)
Saint Mary's College, IN (W)
Saint Mary's College, MI (W)
San Diego Mesa College, CA (MW)
Scottsdale Community College, AR (MW)
Southeastern Massachusetts University, MA (MW)
Stanford University, CA (MW)
State University of New York College (Purchase), NY (M)
Stevens Institute of Technology, NJ (MW)
St. Gregory's College, OK (MW)
Temple University, PA (W)
Trinity College, CT (MW)
Trinity College, IL (MW)
Tri-State University, IN (MW)
University of California (San Diego), CA (MW)
University of Chicago, IL (MW)
University of Detroit Mercy, MI (M)
University of Illinois, IL (M)
University of Illinois (Urbana-Champaign), IL (M)
University of North Carolina (Asheville), NC (MW)
University of North Carolina (Chapel Hill), NC (MW)
University of Notre Dame, IN (MW)
University of Pennsylvania, PA (MW)
Vassar College, NY (MW)
Wayne State University, MI (MW)
Wellesley College, MA (W)
Western Connecticut State University, CT (MW)
William Patterson College, NJ (MW)
Yale University, CT (MW)
Yeshiva University, NY (M)

Field Hockey

Albion College, MI (W)
Albright College, PA (W)
Alma College, MI (MW)
American University, DC (W)
Amherst College, MA (W)
Appalachian State University, NC (W)
Babson College, MA (W)
Ball State University, IN (W)
Bates College, ME (W)

Becker College, MA (W)
Bellarmine College, KY (W)
Bentley College, MA (W)
Bethany College, KS (W)
Bethany College, WV (W)
Bloomsburg University, PA (W)
Boston College, MA (W)
Boston University, MA (W)
Bowdoin College, ME (W)
Bridgewater College, VA (W)
Bridgewater State College, MA (W)
Brown University, RI (W)
Bryn Mawr College, PA (W)
Bucknell University, PA (M)
Buffalo State University (New York), NY (W)
Cabrini College, PA (W)
California State University (Chico), CA (W)
Castleton State College, VT (W)
Catawba College, NC (W)
Catholic University of America, DC (W)
Central Michigan University, MI (W)
Champlain College, VT (W)
Clark University, MA (W)
Colgate University, NY (W)
College of William and Mary, VA (W)
College of Wooster, OH (W)
Connecticut College, CT (W)
Cornell University, NY (W)
Dartmouth College, NH (W)
Davidson College, NC (W)
Davis & Elkins College, WV (W)
Dean Junior College, MA (W)
Delaware Valley College, PA (W)
Denison University, OH (W)
De Pauw University, IN (W)
Dickinson College, PA (W)
Drew University, NJ (W)
Drexel University, PA (W)
Duke University, NC (W)
Earlham College, IN (W)
Eastern College, PA (W)
Eastern Mennonite College, VA (W)
Eastern Michigan University, MI (W)
East Stroudsburg University, PA (W)
Elizabethtown College, PA (W)
Essex Community College, MD (W)
Fairfield University, CT (W)
Fairleigh Dickinson University, NJ (W)
Fitchburg State College, MA (W)
Franklin & Marshall College, PA (MW)
Gettysburg College, PA (W)
Gordon College, MA (W)
Goucher College, MD (MW)
Hamilton College, NY (W)
Hanover College, IN (W)
Harford Community College, MD (W)
Hartwick College, NY (W)
Harvard University, MA (W)
Haverford College, PA (W)
Herkimer County Community College, NY (W)
High Point University, NC (W)
Hofstra University, NY (W)
Holy Cross College, MA (W)
Hood College, MD (W)
Hope College, MI (W)
Houghton College, NY (W)
Indiana University of Pennsylvania, PA (W)
Ithaca College, NY (W)
James Madison University, VA (W)
Johns Hopkins University, MD (W)
Juniata College, PA (W)
Kalamazoo, College, MI (W)
Kean College of New Jersey, NJ (W)
Keene State College, NH (W)
Kent State University (Ashtabula), OH (W)
Kent State University (Kent), OH (W)
Kent State University (New Philadelphia), OH (W)
Kent State University (Warren), OH (W)
Kenyon College, OH (W)
Keystone Junior College, PA (W)
King's College, NY (W)
Kutztown University, PA (W)
Lafayette College, PA (W)
Lambuth University, TN (M)
La Salle University, PA (W)
Lebanon Valley College, PA (W)
Lehigh University, PA (W)
Lock Haven University of Pennsylvania, PA (W)
Long Island University (C. W. Post Campus), NY (W)
Longwood College, VA (W)
Luther College, IA (W)
Lycoming College, PA (W)
Lynchburg College, VA (W)
Manhattanville College, NY (W)
Mansfield University, PA (W)
Marietta College, OH (W)
Mary Baldwin College, VA (W)
Mary Washington College, VA (W)
Marywood College, PA (W)
Massachusetts Institute of Technology, MA (W)
Merrimack College, MA (W)
Messiah College, PA (W)
Miami University, OH (W)
Michigan State University, MI (W)
Middlebury College, VT (W)
Midwestern State University, TX (M)
Millersville University, PA (W)
Mitchell College, CT (M)
Montclair State College, NJ (W)
Moorpark College, CA (MW)
Moravian College, PA (W)
Mount Holyoke College, MA (W)
Nichols College, MA (M)
Northwestern University, IL (W)
Oberlin College, OH (W)
Ocean County College, NJ (W)
Ohio State University, OH (W)
Ohio University, OH (W)
Ohio Wesleyan University, OH (W)
Old Dominion University, VA (W)
Olivet College, MI (W)
Penn State University, PA (W)
Pennsylvania State University, PA (W)
Pfeiffer College, NC (W)
Plymouth State College, NH (W)
Princeton University, NJ (W)
Providence College, RI (W)
Purdue University, IN (W)
Radford University, VA (W)
Randolph-Macon College, VA (W)
Rensselaer Polytechnic Institute, NY (W)
Rider College, NJ (W)
Roanoke College, VA (W)
Rowan College of New Jersey, NJ (W)
Saint Joseph's University, PA (W)
Saint Lawrence University, NY (W)
Saint Louis University, MO (W)
Saint Michael's College, VT (W)
Salem State College, MA (W)
San Jose State University, CA (W)
Shippensburg University of Pennsylvania, PA (W)
Siena College, NY (W)
Skidmore College, NY (W)
Slippery Rock University of Pennsylvania, PA (W)
Smith College, MA (W)
Southeastern Massachusetts University, MA (W)

Southern Connecticut State University, CT (W)
Southwest Missouri State University, MO (W)
Springfield College, MA (W)
Stanford University, CA (W)
State University of New York College (Brockport), NY (W)
State University of New York College (Cortland), NY (W)
State University of New York College (Oswego), NY (W)
State University of New York College (Potsdam), NY (W)
Swarthmore College, PA (W)
Sweet Briar College, VA (W)
Syracuse University, NY (W)
Temple University, PA (W)
Towson State University, MD (W)
Transylvania University, KY (W)
Trenton State College, NJ (W)
Trinity College, CT (W)
Trinity College, IL (W)
Tufts University, MA (W)
Union College, NY (W)
University of California (Berkeley), CA (W)
University of Connecticut, CT (W)
University of Delaware, DE (W)
University of Iowa, IA (MW)
University of Louisville, KY (W)
University of Lowell, MA (W)
University of Maine, ME (W)
University of Maryland, MD (W)
University of Massachusetts (Amherst), MA (W)
University of Michigan, MI (W)
University of Montana, MT (M)
University of New Hampshire, NH (W)
University of North Carolina (Asheville), NC (W)
University of North Carolina (Chapel Hill), NC (W)
University of Pennsylvania, PA (W)
University of Rhode Island, RI (MW)
University of Richmond, VA (MW)
University of Scranton, PA (W)
University of the Pacific, CA (W)
University of Toledo, OH (W)
University of Vermont, VT (W)
University of Virginia, VA (W)
Ursinus College, PA (W)
Valparaiso University, IN (W)
Vassar College, NY (W)
Villanova University, PA (W)
Virginia Commonwealth University, VA (W)
Wake Forest University, NC (W)
Washington College, MD (W)
Wellesley College, MA (W)
Wesleyan University, CT (W)
West Chester University, PA (W)
Western Connecticut State University, CT (W)
Western Maryland College, MD (W)
Western New England College, MA (W)
Westfield State College, MA (MW)
Wilkes College, NC (W)
Wilkes University, PA (W)
William Patterson College, NJ (W)
Wilson College, PA (W)
Worcester State College, MA (W)
Yale University, CT (W)
York College of Pennsylvania, PA (W)

Football

Abilene Christian University, TX (M)
Adams State College, CO (M)
Adrian College, MI (M)
Alabama A & M University, AL (M)
Alabama State University, AL (M)
Albany State College, GA (M)
Albion College, MI (M)
Albright College, PA (M)
Alcorn State University, MS (M)
Alfred University, NY (M)
Allegheny College, PA (M)
Alma College, MI (M)
American International College, MA (M)
Amherst College, MA (M)
Anderson University, IN (M)
Angelo State University, TX (M)
Anoka-Ramsey College, MN (M)
Appalachian State University, NC (M)
Apprentice School, VA (M)
Arizona State University, AZ (M)
Arkansas State University, AR (M)
Arkansas Tech University, AR (M)
Arrowhead Community College, MN (M)
Ashland College, OH (M)
Auburn University, AL (M)
Augsburg College, MN (M)
Augustana College, IL (M)
Augustana College, SD (M)
Aurora University, IL (M)
Austin College, TX (M)
Austin Community College, MN (M)
Austin Peay State University, TN (M)
Azusa Pacific University, CA (M)
Baker University, KS (M)
Ball State University, IN (M)
Bates College, ME (M)
Baylor University, TX (M)
Beloit College, WI (M)
Bemidji State University, MN (M)
Benedictine College, KS (M)
Bethany College, KS (M)
Bethany College, WV (M)
Bethel College, KS (M)
Bethel College, MN (M)
Bethune-Cookman College, FL (M)
Black Hills State University, SD (M)
Bloomsburg University, PA (M)
Bluffton College, OH (M)
Boise State University, ID (M)
Boston College, MA (M)
Boston University, MA (M)
Bowdoin College, ME (M)
Bowie State University, MD (M)
Bowling Green State University, OH (M)
Brainerd Community College, MN (M)
Bridgewater College, VA (M)
Bridgewater State College, MA (M)
Brigham Young University, UT (M)
Brooklyn College—City University of New York, NY (M)
Brown University, RI (M)
Bucknell University, PA (M)
Buena Vista College, IA (M)
Buffalo State College, NY (M)
Buffalo State University (New York), NY (M)
Butler University, IN (M)
Butte College, CA (M)
Cabrillo College, CA (M)
California Lutheran University, CA (M)
California Polytechnic State University, CA (M)
California State University (Chico), CA (M)

California State University (Fresno), CA (M)
California State University (Fullerton), CA (M)
California State University (Hayward), CA (M)
California State University (Long Beach), CA (M)
California State University (Northridge), CA (M)
California State University (Sacramento), CA (M)
California University, PA (M)
Cameron University, OK (M)
Campbellsville College, KY (M)
Canisius College, NY (M)
Capital University, OH (M)
Carleton College, MN (M)
Carnegie-Mellon University, PA (M)
Carroll College, MT (M)
Carroll College, WI (M)
Carson-Newman College, TN (M)
Carthage College, WI (M)
Case Western Reserve University, OH (M)
Catawba College, NC (M)
Catholic University of America, DC (M)
Central College, IA (M)
Central College, KS (M)
Central Connecticut State University, CT (M)
Central Methodist College, MO (M)
Central Michigan University, MI (M)
Central Missouri State University, MO (M)
Central State University, OH (M)
Central Washington University, WA (M)
Cerritos College, CA (M)
Chadron State College, NE (M)
Chaffey College, CA (M)
Cheyney University of Pennsylvania, PA (M)
Chowan College, NC (M)
Citadel, SC (M)
City College of San Francisco, CA (M)
Clarion University, PA (M)
Clark Atlanta University, GA (M)
Clemson University, SC (M)
Coahoma Junior College, MS (M)
Coe College, IA (MW)
Coffeyville Community College, KS (M)
Colgate University, NY (M)
College of St. Francis, IL (M)
College of the Desert, CA (M)
College of the Redwoods, CA (M)
College of the Sequoias, CA (M)
College of William and Mary, VA (M)
College of Wooster, OH (M)
Colorado College, CO (M)
Colorado School of Mines, CO (MW)
Colorado State University, CO (M)
Columbia University, NY (M)
Community Colleges of Spokane, WA (M)
Compton Community College, CA (M)
Concord College, WV (M)
Concordia College, MN (M)
Concordia Teachers College, NE (M)
Concordia University, IL (M)
Concordia University Wisconsin, WI (M)
Contra Costa College, CA (M)
Copiah-Lincoln Community College, MS (M)
Cornell College, IA (M)
Cornell University, NY (M)
Culver-Stockton College, MO (M)
Cumberland College, KY (M)
Curry College, MA (M)
Dakota State University, SD (M)
Dakota Wesleyan University, SD (M)
Dana College, NE (M)
Dartmouth College, NH (M)
Davidson College, NC (M)
Dean Junior College, MA (M)
De Anza Community College, CA (M)
Delaware State College, DE (M)
Delaware Valley College, PA (M)
Delta State University, MS (M)
Denison University, OH (M)
De Pauw University, IN (M)
Diablo Valley Community College, CA (M)
Dickinson College, PA (M)
Dickinson State University, ND (M)
Dixie College, UT (M)
Doane College, NE (M)
Dodge City Community College, KS (M)
Drake University, IA (M)
Duke University, NC (M)
Earlham College, IN (M)
East Carolina University, NC (M)
East Central University, OK (M)
Eastern Illinois University, IL (M)
Eastern Kentucky University, KY (M)
Eastern Michigan University, MI (M)
Eastern New Mexico University, NM (M)
Eastern Oregon State College, OR (M)
Eastern Washington University, WA (M)
East Stroudsburg University, PA (M)
East Tennessee State University, TN (M)
East Texas State University, TX (M)
Edinboro University of Pennsylvania, PA (M)
El Camino College, CA (M)
Elizabeth City State University, NC (M)
Elmhurst College, IL (M)
Elon College, NC (M)
Emory and Henry College, VA (M)
Emporia State University, KS (M)
Eureka College, IL (M)
Evangel College, MO (M)
Fairleigh Dickinson University, NJ (M)
Fairmont State College, WV (M)
Fayetteville State University, NC (M)
Fergus Falls Community College, MN (M)
Ferris State College, MI (M)
Ferrum College, VA (M)
Fitchburg State College, MA (M)
Florida A & M University, FL (M)
Florida Southern College, FL (M)
Florida State University, FL (M)
Fordham University, NY (M)
Fort Hays State University, KS (M)
Fort Lewis College, CO (M)
Fort Scott College, KS (M)
Fort Valley State College, GA (M)
Franklin & Marshall College, PA (M)
Fresno City College, CA (M)
Friends University, KS (M)
Fullerton College, CA (M)
Furman University, SC (M)
Gannon College, PA (MW)
Garden City Community College, KS (M)
Gardner-Webb College, NC (M)

Geneva College, PA (M)
Georgetown College, KY (M)
Georgia Institute of Technology, GA (M)
Georgia Military College, GA (M)
Georgia Southern University, GA (M)
Georgia Southwestern College, GA (M)
Gettysburg College, PA (M)
Glendale Community College, AZ (M)
Glendale Community College, CA (M)
Glenville State College, WV (M)
Golden West College, CA (M)
Graceland College, IA (M)
Grambling State University, LA (M)
Grand Rapids Junior College, MI (M)
Grand Valley State College, MI (M)
Grinnell College, IA (M)
Grove City College, PA (M)
Gustavus Adolphus College, MN (M)
Hamilton College, NY (M)
Hamline University, MN (M)
Hampden-Sydney College, VA (M)
Hampton University, VA (M)
Hanover College, IN (M)
Harding University, AR (M)
Harper William Rainey College, IL (M)
Harvard University, MA (M)
Haskell Indian Junior College, KS (M)
Hastings College, NE (M)
Heidelberg College, OH (W)
Henderson State University, AR (M)
Hibbing Community College, MN (M)
Highland Community College, KS (M)
Hillsdale College, MI (M)
Hinds Community College, MS (M)
Hiram College, OH (M)
Hofstra University, NY (M)
Holmes Junior College, MS (M)
Holy Cross College, MA (M)
Hope College, MI (M)
Howard Payne University, TX (M)
Howard University, DC (M)
Hudson Valley Community College, NY (M)
Humboldt State University, CA (M)
Huron University, SD (M)
Hutchinson College, KS (M)
Idaho State University, ID (M)
Illinois Benedictine College, IL (M)
Illinois College, IL (M)
Illinois State University, IL (M)
Illinois Valley Community College, IL (M)
Illinois Wesleyan University, IL (M)
Indiana State University, IN (M)
Indiana University, IN (M)
Indiana University of Pennsylvania, PA (M)
Inver Hills Community College, MN (M)
Iona College, NY (M)
Iowa State University of Science and Technology, IA (M)
Iowa Wesleyan College, IA (M)
Itawamba Community College, MS (M)
Ithaca College, NY (M)
Jackson State University, MS (M)
Jacksonville State University, AL (M)
James Madison University, VA (M)
Jamestown College, ND (M)
John Carroll University, OH (M)
Johnson C. Smith University, NC (M)
Jones County Junior College, MS (M)
Juniata College, PA (M)
Kalamazoo College, MI (M)
Kansas State University, KS (M)
Kansas Wesleyan College, KS (M)
Kean College of New Jersey, NJ (M)
Kemper Military School, MO (M)
Kent State University (Ashtabula), OH (M)
Kent State University (Kent), OH (M)
Kent State University (New Philadelphia), OH (M)
Kent State University (Warren), OH (M)
Kentucky State University, KY (M)
Kentucky Wesleyan College, KY (M)
Kenyon College, OH (M)
Kilgore College, TX (M)
Knox College, IL (M)
Knoxville College, TN (MW)
Kutztown University, PA (M)
Lafayette College, PA (M)
Lake Forest College, IL (M)
Lamar University, TX (M)
Lambuth University, TN (M)
Langston University, OK (M)
Lawrence University, WI (M)
Lebanon Valley College, PA (M)
Lees-McRae College, NC (M)
Lehigh University, PA (M)
Lenoir-Rhyne College, NC (MW)
Lewis and Clark College, OR (M)
Liberty University, VA (M)
Linfield College, OR (M)
Livingstone College, NC (M)
Livingston University, AL (M)
Lock Haven University of Pennsylvania, PA (M)
Long Beach City College, CA (M)
Long Island University (C. W. Post Campus), NY (M)
Loras College, IA (M)
Los Angeles Pierce Junior College, CA (M)
Los Angeles Valley College, CA (M)
Los Medanos College, CA (M)
Louisiana State University (Alexandria), LA (M)
Louisiana State University (Baton Rouge), LA (M)
Louisiana Tech University, LA (M)
Luther College, IA (M)
Lycoming College, PA (M)
Macalester College, MN (M)
Manchester College, IN (M)
Mankato State University, MN (M)
Mansfield University, PA (M)
Marietta College, OH (M)
Marion Military Institute, AL (M)
Marist College, NY (M)
Marshall University, WV (M)
Mars Hill College, NC (M)
Maryville College, TN (M)
Massachusetts Institute of Technology, MA (M)
Mayville State College, ND (M)
McNeese State University, LA (M)
McPherson College, KS (M)
Memphis State University, TN (M)
Mercyhurst College, PA (M)
Mesa State College, CO (M)
Miami University, OH (M)
Michigan State University, MI (M)
Michigan Technological University, MI (M)
Mid-America Nazarene College, KS (M)
Middlebury College, VT (M)

Middle Tennessee State University, TN (M)
Midland Lutheran College, NE (M)
Millersville University, PA (M)
Millikin University, IL (M)
Minot State, ND (MW)
Mississippi College, MS (M)
Mississippi Delta Junior College, MS (M)
Mississippi Gulf Coast Junior College, MS (M)
Mississippi State University, MS (M)
Mississippi Valley State University, MS (M)
Missouri Southern State College, MO (M)
Missouri Valley College, MO (M)
Missouri Western State College, MO (M)
Modesto Junior College, CA (M)
Molloy College, NY (M)
Monmouth College, IL (M)
Montana College of Mineral Science and Technology, MT (M)
Montana State University, MT (M)
Montclair State College, NJ (M)
Moorhead State University, MN (M)
Moorpark College, CA (M)
Moraine Valley Community College, IL (M)
Moravian College, PA (M)
Morehead State University, KY (M)
Morehouse College, GA (M)
Morgan State University, MD (M)
Morningside College, IA (M)
Mount Union College, OH (M)
Mt. San Antonio College, CA (M)
Muhlenberg College, PA (M)
Murray State University, KY (M)
Muskingum College, OH (M)
Nassau Community College, NY (M)
Navarro College, TX (M)
Nebraska Wesleyan University, NE (M)
Newberry College, SC (M)
New Mexico Highlands University, NM (M)
New Mexico State University, NM (M)
Nicholls State University, LA (M)
Nichols College, MA (M)
Norfolk State University, VA (M)
North Carolina A and T State University, NC (M)
North Carolina Central University, NC (M)
North Carolina State University, NC (M)
North Central College, IL (M)
North Dakota State, ND (M)
North Dakota State University, ND (M)
Northeastern Illinois University, IL (M)
Northeastern State University, OK (W)
Northeast Louisiana University, LA (M)
Northeast Mississippi Community College, MS (M)
Northeast Missouri State University, MO (M)
Northern Arizona University, AZ (M)
Northern Illinois University, IL (M)
Northern Michigan University, MI (M)
Northern State University, SD (M)
North Greenville College, SC (M)
North Hennepin Community College, MN (M)
North Iowa Area Community College, IA (M)
Northland Community College, MN (M)
Northwestern College, IA (M)
Northwestern College, MN (M)
Northwestern Oklahoma State University, OK (M)
Northwestern State University of Louisiana, LA (M)
Northwestern University, IL (M)
Northwest Mississippi Community College, MS (M)
Northwest Missouri State University, MO (M)
Northwood Institute, MI (M)
Northwood Institute (Texas Campus), TX (M)
Norwich University, VT (M)
Oberlin College, OH (M)
Occidental College, CA (M)
Ohio Northern University, OH (M)
Ohio State University, OH (M)
Ohio University, OH (M)
Ohio Wesleyan University, OH (M)
Oklahoma State University, OK (M)
Olivet College, MI (M)
Olivet Nazarene University, IL (M)
Orange Coast College, CA (MW)
Oregon Institute of Technology, OR (M)
Oregon State University, OR (M)
Ottawa University, KS (M)
Otterbein College, OH (M)
Pace University, NY (M)
Pacific Lutheran University, WA (M)
Palomar College, CA (M)
Panhandle State University, OK (M)
Pennsylvania State University, PA (M)
Peru State College, NE (M)
Phoenix College, AZ (M)
Pittsburg State University, KS (M)
Plymouth State College, NH (M)
Pomona-Pitzer Colleges, CA (M)
Portland State University, OR (M)
Prairie View A & M University, TX (M)
Presbyterian College, SC (M)
Princeton University, NJ (M)
Principia College, IL (M)
Purdue University, IN (M)
Ramapo College, NJ (M)
Randolph-Macon College, VA (M)
Ranetto Santiago College, CA (M)
Rensselaer Polytechnic Institute, NY (M)
Rice University, TX (M)
Ricks College, ID (M)
Ripon College, WI (M)
Riverside College, CA (M)
Rochester Community College, MN (M)
Rocky Mountain College, MT (M)
Rose-Hulman Institute of Technology, IN (M)
Rowan College of New Jersey, NJ (M)
Saddleback College, CA (M)
Saginaw Valley State College, MI (M)
Saint Ambrose College, IA (M)
Saint Cloud State University, MN (M)
Saint Francis College, PA (M)
Saint John Fisher College, NY (M)
Saint John's University, MN (M)
Saint John's University, NY (MW)
Saint Joseph's College, IN (M)
Saint Lawrence University, NY (M)
Saint Mary's College of California, CA (M)

Saint Norbert College, WI (M)
Saint Olaf College, MN (M)
Saint Paul's College, VA (M)
Saint Peter's College, NJ (M)
Samford University, AL (M)
Sam Houston State University, TX (M)
San Bernardino Community College, CA (M)
San Diego City College, CA (M)
San Diego Mesa College, CA (MW)
San Diego State University, CA (M)
San Francisco State University, CA (M)
San Joaquin Delta College, CA (M)
San Jose State University, CA (M)
Santa Barbara City College, CA (M)
Santa Clara University, CA (M)
Santa Monico College, CA (M)
Santa Rosa Junior College, CA (M)
Savannah State College, GA (M)
Scottsdale Community College, AR (M)
Shepherd College, WV (M)
Shippensburg University of Pennsylvania, PA (M)
Siena College, NY (M)
Sierra College, CA (M)
Simpson College, CA (M)
Sioux Falls College, SD (M)
Slippery Rock University of Pennsylvania, PA (M)
Snow College, UT (M)
Solano Community College, CA (M)
South Carolina State College, SC (M)
South Dakota School of Mines and Technology, SD (M)
South Dakota State University, SD (M)
Southeastern Oklahoma State University, OK (M)
Southeast Missouri State University, MO (M)
Southern Arkansas University, AR (M)
Southern Connecticut State University, CT (M)
Southern Illinois University, IL (M)
Southern Methodist University, TX (M)
Southern Oregon State College, OR (M)
Southern University and A & M College, LA (M)
Southern Utah University, UT (M)
Southwest Baptist University, MO (M)
Southwestern College, CA (M)
Southwestern College, KS (M)
Southwest Missouri State University, MO (M)
Southwest State University, MN (M)
Southwest Texas State University, TX (M)
Springfield College, MA (M)
Stanford University, CA (M)
State University of New York (Albany), NY (M)
State University of New York (Buffalo), NY (M)
State University of New York (Stony Brook), NY (M)
State University of New York College (Brockport), NY (M)
State University of New York College (Cortland), NY (M)
State University of New York Maritime College, NY (M)
Stephen F. Austin State University, TX (M)
Sterling College, KS (M)
St. Mary of the Plains College, KS (M)
Stonehill College, MA (M)
Sul Ross State University, TX (M)
Swarthmore College, PA (M)
Syracuse University, NY (M)
Tabor College, KS (M)
Taft College, CA (M)
Tarleton State University, TX (M)
Teikyo Westmar University, IA (M)
Temple University, PA (M)
Tennessee State University, TN (M)
Tennessee Technological University, TN (M)
Tennessee Wesleyan College, TN (M)
Texas A & I University, TX (M)
Texas A & M University, TX (M)
Texas Christian University, TX (M)
Texas Southern University, TX (M)
Texas Tech University, TX (M)
Towson State University, MD (M)
Trenton State College, NJ (M)
Trinity College, CT (M)
Trinity College, IL (M)
Trinity University, TX (M)
Triton College, IL (M)
Troy State University, AL (M)
Tufts University, MA (M)
Tulane University, LA (M)
Tuskegee University, AL (M)
Tyler Junior College, TX (M)
Union College, NY (M)
University of Akron, OH (M)
University of Alabama (Tuscaloosa), AL (M)
University of Arizona, AZ (M)
University of Arkansas (Fayetteville), AR (M)
University of Arkansas (Monticello), AR (M)
University of Arkansas (Pine Bluff), AR (M)
University of California (Berkeley), CA (M)
University of California (Davis), CA (M)
University of California (UCLA), CA (M)
University of Central Arkansas, AR (M)
University of Central Florida, FL (M)
University of Central Oklahoma, OK (M)
University of Chicago, IL (M)
University of Cincinnati, OH (M)
University of Colorado, CO (M)
University of Connecticut, CT (M)
University of Dayton, OH (M)
University of Delaware, DE (M)
University of Dubuque, IA (M)
University of Findlay, OH (M)
University of Florida, FL (M)
University of Georgia, GA (M)
University of Guam, PA (M)
University of Hawaii (Manoa), HI (M)
University of Houston, TX (M)
University of Idaho, ID (M)
University of Illinois, IL (M)
University of Illinois (Urbana-Champaign), IL (M)
University of Indianapolis, IN (M)
University of Iowa, IA (M)
University of Kansas, KS (M)
University of Kentucky, KY (M)
University of La Verne, CA (M)
University of Louisville, KY (M)
University of Lowell, MA (M)
University of Maine, ME (M)
University of Mary, ND (M)
University of Maryland, MD (M)
University of Massachusetts (Amherst), MA (M)
University of Massachusetts (Boston), MA (M)
University of Miami, FL (M)

University of Michigan, MI (M)
University of Minnesota (Duluth), MN (M)
University of Minnesota (Minneapolis), MN (MW)
University of Minnesota (Morris), MN (M)
University of Mississippi, MS (M)
University of Missouri, MO (M)
University of Missouri (Columbia), MO (M)
University of Missouri (Rolla), MO (M)
University of Nebraska, NE (M)
University of Nebraska (Kearney), NE (M)
University of Nebraska (Lincoln), NE (M)
University of Nevada, NV (M)
University of Nevada (Reno), NV (M)
University of New Hampshire, NH (M)
University of New Haven, CT (M)
University of New Mexico, NM (M)
University of North Alabama, AL (M)
University of North Carolina (Asheville), NC (M)
University of North Carolina (Chapel Hill), NC (M)
University of North Dakota, ND (M)
University of Northern Colorado, CO (M)
University of Northern Iowa, IA (M)
University of North Texas, TX (M)
University of Notre Dame, IN (M)
University of Oklahoma, OK (M)
University of Oregon, OR (M)
University of Pennsylvania, PA (M)
University of Pittsburgh, PA (M)
University of Puget Sound, WA (M)
University of Redlands, CA (M)
University of Rhode Island, RI (M)
University of Richmond, VA (M)
University of San Diego, CA (M)
University of South Carolina (Columbia), SC (M)
University of South Carolina (Myrtle Beach), SC (M)
University of South Dakota, SD (M)
University of Southern California, CA (M)
University of Southern Mississippi, MS (M)
University of Southwestern Louisiana, LA (M)
University of St. Thomas, MN (M)
University of Tennessee, TN (M)
University of Tennessee (Knoxville), TN (M)
University of Tennessee (Martin), TN (M)
University of Texas (Austin), TX (M)
University of Texas (El Paso), TX (M)
University of the District of Columbia, DC (M)
University of the Pacific, CA (M)
University of Toledo, OH (M)
University of Tulsa, OK (M)
University of Utah, UT (M)
University of Virginia, VA (M)
University of Washington, WA (M)
University of Wisconsin (Eau Claire), WI (M)
University of Wisconsin (La Crosse), WI (M)
University of Wisconsin (Madison), WI (M)
University of Wisconsin (Oshkosh), WI (M)
University of Wisconsin (Platteville), WI (M)
University of Wisconsin (River Falls), WI (M)
University of Wisconsin (Stevens Point), WI (M)
University of Wisconsin (Stout), WI (M)
University of Wisconson (Superior), WI (M)
University of Wyoming, WY (M)
Upper Iowa University, IA (M)
Ursinus College, PA (M)
Utah State University, UT (M)
Valdosta State College, GA (M)
Valley City State University, ND (M)
Valparaiso University, IN (M)
Vanderbilt University, TN (M)
Ventura College, CA (M)
Villanova University, PA (M)
Virginia Military Institute, VA (M)
Virginia Polytechnic Institute & State University, VA (M)
Virginia State University, VA (M)
Virginia Union University, VA (M)
Wabash College, IN (M)
Wake Forest University, NC (M)
Waldorf College, IA (M)
Walla Walla Community College, WA (M)
Wartburg College, IA (M)
Washburn University, KS (M)
Washington and Jefferson College, PA (M)
Washington State University, WA (M)
Washington University, MO (M)
Wayne State College, NE (M)
Wayne State University, MI (M)
Weber State College, UT (M)
Wesleyan University, CT (M)
Wesley College, DE (M)
West Chester University, PA (M)
Western Carolina University, NC (M)
Western Connecticut State University, CT (M)
Western Kentucky University, KY (M)
Western Maryland College, MD (M)
Western Michigan University, MI (M)
Western Montana College, MT (M)
Western New England College, MA (M)
Western New Mexico University, NM (M)
Western Oregon State College, OR (M)
Western State College, CO (M)
Western Washington University, WA (MW)
West Georgia College, GA (M)
West Liberty State College, WV (M)
Westminster College, PA (M)
West Texas State University, TX (M)
West Virginia Institute of Technology, WV (M)
West Virginia University, WV (M)
West Virginia Wesleyan College, WV (M)
Wheaton College, IL (M)
Whittier College, CA (M)
Whitworth College, WA (M)
Wilkes College, NC (M)
Wilkes University, PA (M)
Willamette University, OR (M)
William Jewell College, MO (M)

William Patterson College, NJ (M)
William Penn College, IA (M)
William Rainey Harper College, IL (M)
Williams College, MA (M)
Williamson Trade School, PA (M)
Wilmington College, DE (M)
Wilmington College, OH (M)
Wingate College, NC (M)
Winona State University, MN (M)
Winston-Salem State University, NC (M)
Wofford College, SC (M)
Worcester State College, MA (M)
Worthington Community College, MN (M)
Yakima Valley College, WA (M)
Yale University, CT (MW)
Youngstown State University, OH (M)
Yuba Community College, CA (M)

Golf

Abilene Christian University, TX (M)
Adams State College, CO (M)
Adelphi University, NY (M)
Adirondack College, NY (M)
Adrian College, MI (MW)
Alabama State University, AL (M)
Albion College, MI (M)
Albright College, PA (M)
Alcorn State University, MS (M)
Allegheny College, PA (M)
Allen County College, KS (M)
Alma College, MI (M)
Alvernia College, PA (M)
American International College, MA (M)
American University, DC (M)
Amherst College, MA (MW)
Anderson College, SC (M)
Anderson University, IN (M)
Angelo State University, TX (M)
Appalachian State University, NC (MW)
Apprentice School, VA (M)
Aquinas College, MI (M)
Arizona State University, AZ (MW)
Arkansas College, AR (MW)
Arkansas State University, AR (MW)
Arkansas Tech University, AR (M)
Ashland College, OH (M)
Atlantic Community College, NJ (MW)
Auburn University, AL (MW)
Augusta College, GA (M)
Augustana College, IL (M)
Augustana College, SD (MW)
Aurora University, IL (MW)
Austin College, TX (M)
Austin Community College, MN (M)
Austin Peay State University, TN (M)
Averett College, VA (M)
Babson College, MA (M)
Baker University, KS (M)
Ball State University, IN (M)
Barry University, FL (M)
Barton College, NC (M)
Barton County College, KS (M)
Bates College, ME (MW)
Baylor University, TX (M)
Bellarmine College, KY (M)
Belmont Abbey College, NC (M)
Belmont College, TN (MW)
Beloit College, WI (M)
Benedictine College, KS (MW)
Bentley College, MA (M)
Bergen Community College, NJ (M)
Berry College, GA (M)
Bethany College, KS (MW)
Bethany College, WV (MW)
Bethel College, IN (M)
Bethel College, MN (M)
Bethel College, TN (M)
Bethune-Cookman College, FL (MW)
Bismarck State College, ND (MW)
Blackburn College, IL (M)
Black Hawk College, IL (M)
Bluefield College, VA (M)
Bluefield State College, WV (M)
Bluffton College, OH (M)
Boise State University, ID (MW)
Boston College, MA (MW)
Boston University, MA (M)
Bowdoin College, ME (MW)
Bowling Green State University, OH (MW)
Bradley University, IL (MW)
Brescia College, KY (M)
Briar Cliff College, IA (MW)
Bridgewater College, VA (M)
Brigham Young University, UT (MW)
Bristol University, TN (M)
Broome Community College, NY (M)
Broward Community College, FL (MW)
Brown University, RI (M)
Bryant College, RI (M)
Bucknell University, PA (M)
Bucks County Community College, PA (MW)
Buena Vista College, IA (MW)
Buffalo State University (New York), NY (M)
Butler County Community College, KS (M)
Butler County Community College, PA (M)
Butler University, IN (M)
Butte College, CA (M)
Cabrillo College, CA (M)
California Institute of Technology, CA (MW)
California Lutheran University, CA (M)
California State University, CA (M)
California State University (Dominguez Hills), CA (M)
California State University (Fresno), CA (M)
California State University (Long Beach), CA (MW)
California State University (Northridge), CA (M)
California State University (Sacramento), CA (MW)
California State University (San Bernardino), CA (M)
Calvin College, MI (MW)
Cameron University, OK (M)
Campbellsville College, KY (MW)
Campbell University, NC (MW)
Canisius College, NY (M)
Capital University, OH (M)
Carleton College, MN (MW)
Carroll College, WI (M)
Carson-Newman College, TN (M)
Carthage College, WI (M)
Case Western Reserve University, OH (M)
Catawba College, NC (M)
Catholic University of America, DC (M)
Cayuga County Community College, NY (M)
Cedarville College, OH (M)
Centenary College, LA (M)
Central College, IA (MW)
Central College, KS (MW)
Central Connecticut State University, CT (M)
Central Methodist College, MO (MW)
Central Missouri State University, MO (M)
Central Washington University, WA (M)
Central Wesleyan College, SC (M)
Cerritos College, CA (M)
Chadron State College, NE (W)

Chaffey College, CA (MW)
Champlain College, VT (MW)
Charles County Community College, MD (M)
Charleston Southern University, SC (M)
Chicago State University, IL (M)
Chowan College, NC (M)
Christopher Newport College, VA (M)
Citadel, SC (M)
Clarion University, PA (M)
Clark College, WA (M)
Clark State College, OH (M)
Clarkson University, NY (MW)
Clark University, MA (MW)
Clemson University, SC (M)
Cleveland State University, OH (MW)
Clinch Valley College, VA (M)
Cloud County Community College, KS (M)
Coahoma Junior College, MS (M)
Coastal Carolina College, SC (MW)
Coastal Carolina Community College, NC (M)
Coe College, IA (M)
Coffeyville Community College, KS (M)
Coker College, SC (M)
Colgate University, NY (M)
College of Allegheny County, PA (MW)
College of Charleston, SC (MW)
College of St. Francis, IL (M)
College of the Desert, CA (M)
College of the Redwoods, CA (M)
College of the Sequoias, CA (M)
College of William and Mary, VA (MW)
College of Wooster, OH (M)
Colorado Colege, CO (M)
Colorado School of Mines, CO (MW)
Colorado State University, CO (MW)
Columbia Basin Community College, WA (MW)
Columbia College, MO (M)
Columbia University, NY (M)
Columbus College, GA (M)
Columbus State Community College, OH (MW)
Community College of Rhode Island, RI (M)
Community Colleges of Spokane, WA (M)
Concord College, WV (M)
Concordia College, MN (M)
Concordia Lutheran College, TX (MW)
Concordia Teachers College, NE (MW)
Copiah-Lincoln Community College, MS (M)
Cornell College, IA (M)
Cornell University, NY (M)
Creighton University, NE (MW)
Cuesta College, CA (M)
Culver-Stockton College, MO (MW)
Cumberland College, KY (M)
Cuyahoga Community College, OH (M)
Dallas Baptist University, TX (M)
Dalton College, GA (MW)
Dana College, NE (MW)
Danville Area Community College, IL (MW)
Dartmouth College, NH (MW)
David Lipscomb College, TN (M)
Davidson College, NC (M)
Davis & Elkins College, WV (M)
De Anza Community College, CA (M)
Defiance College, OH (M)
Delaware Valley College, PA (M)
Delta College, MI (M)
Delta State University, MS (M)
Denison University, OH (M)
DePaul University, IL (M)
De Pauw University, IN (MW)
Detroit College of Business, MI (M)
Dickinson College, PA (M)
Dickinson State University, ND (M)
Doane College, NE (MW)
Dodge City Community College, KS (M)
Dowling College, NY (MW)
Drake University, IA (M)
Drexel University, PA (M)
Drury College, MO (M)
Duke University, NC (MW)
Dutchess Junior College, NY (MW)
Earlham College, IN (M)
East Carolina University, NC (M)
East Central University, OK (M)
Eastern Kentucky University, KY (M)
Eastern Michigan University, MI (M)
Eastern Montana College, MT (MW)
Eastern Washington University, WA (MW)
Eastfield College, TX (M)
East Stroudsburg University, PA (M)
East Tennessee State University, TN (M)
East Texas State University, TX (M)
Edgewood College, WI (MW)
Edison Community College, FL (M)
El Camino College, CA (M)
Elgin Community College, IL (MW)
Elmhurst College, IL (M)
Elmira College, NY (M)
Elon College, NC (M)
Emerson College, MA (M)
Emporia State University, KS (M)
Erskine College, SC (M)
Essex Community College, MD (M)
Eureka College, IL (M)
Everett Community College, WA (MW)
Fairfield University, CT (M)
Fairleigh Dickinson University (Madison), NJ (M)
Fairleigh Dickinson University (Rutherford), NJ (M)
Fairleigh Dickinson University (Teaneck), NJ (M)
Fairmont State College, WV (M)
Fayetteville State University, NC (MW)
Fergus Falls Community College, MN (MW)
Ferris State College, MI (MW)
Ferrum College, VA (MW)
Flagler College, FL (M)
Florida A & M University, FL (M)
Florida Atlantic University, FL (M)
Florida College, FL (M)
Florida International University, FL (MW)
Florida Southern College, FL (MW)
Florida State University, FL (MW)
Foothill College, CA (M)
Fordham University, NY (M)
Fort Hays State University, KS (M)
Fort Lewis College, CO (M)
Francis Marion University, SC (M)
Franklin & Marshall College, PA (M)
Franklin Pierce College, NH (M)
Frederick Community College, MD (MW)
Freed-Hardeman College, TN (M)
Fresno City College, CA (M)
Fullerton College, CA (M)
Furman University, SC (MW)

Gannon College, PA (M)
Garden City Community College, KS (M)
Gardner-Webb College, NC (M)
George C. Wallace Community College, AL (M)
George Mason University, VA (M)
Georgetown College, KY (M)
Georgetown University, DC (M)
George Washington University, DC (M)
Georgia College, GA (M)
Georgia Institute of Technology, GA (M)
Georgia Southern University, GA (M)
Georgia State University, GA (MW)
Gettysburg College, PA (MW)
Glendale Community College, AZ (M)
Glen Oaks Community College, MI (M)
Glenville State College, WV (M)
Golden West College, CA (M)
Gonzaga University, WA (M)
Goucher College, MD (MW)
Grace College, IN (M)
Grambling State University, LA (MW)
Grand Canyon College, AZ (M)
Grand View College, IA (MW)
Grays Harbor College, WA (MW)
Grayson County College, TX (M)
Greenfield Community College, MA (MW)
Green River Community College, WA (M)
Greensboro College, NC (M)
Greenville College, IL (M)
Grinnell College, IA (M)
Grove City College, PA (M)
Gustavus Adolphus College, MN (MW)
Hamilton College, NY (MW)
Hamline University, MN (M)
Hampden-Sydney College, VA (M)
Hampton University, VA (M)
Hannibal-Lagrange College, MO (M)
Hanover College, IN (M)
Harding University, AR (M)
Hardin-Simmons University, TX (MW)
Hartwick College, NY (MW)
Harvard University, MA (MW)
Haskell Indian Junior College, KS (MW)
Hastings College, NE (MW)
Heidelberg College, OH (W)
Henderson State University, AR (M)
Henry Ford Community College, MI (M)
High Point University, NC (M)
Hillsdale College, MI (M)
Hinds Community College, MS (M)
Hiram College, OH (M)
Hofstra University, NY (M)
Holy Cross College, MA (M)
Hope College, MI (M)
Houston Baptist University, TX (M)
Howard Payne University, TX (M)
Hudson Valley Community College, NY (M)
Huntingdon College, AL (M)
Huntington College, IN (M)
Huron University, SD (MW)
Husson College, ME (M)
Huston-Tillotson College, TX (M)
Hutchinson College, KS (M)
Idaho State University, ID (M)
Illinois Benedictine College, IL (MW)
Illinois Central College, IL (M)
Illinois College, IL (MW)
Illinois State University, IL (MW)
Illinois Wesleyan University, IL (M)
Incarnate Word College, TX (M)
Indiana University, IN (MW)
Indiana University of Pennsylvania, PA (M)
Indiana University-Purdue University (Fort Wayne), IN (M)
Indiana Wesleyan University, IN (M)
Indian River Community College, FL (M)
Inver Hills Community College, MN (M)
Iona College, NY (M)
Iowa State University of Science and Technology, IA (MW)
Ithaca College, NY (M)
Jackson State University, MS (M)
Jacksonville University, FL (MW)
Jacksonville College, TX (M)
Jacksonville State University, AL (M)
James Madison University, VA (MW)
Jefferson Community College, NY (MW)
John Carroll University, OH (M)
Johnson County Community College, KS (M)
Johnson C. Smith University, NC (M)
Jones County Junior College, MS (M)
Judson College, AL (W)
Juniata College, PA (MW)
Kalamazoo College, MI (M)
Kalamazoo Valley Community College, MI (M)
Kansas City Kansas Community College, KS (M)
Kansas Newman College, KS (M)
Kansas State University, KS (MW)
Kean College of New Jersey, NJ (M)
Kennesaw State College, GA (M)
Kent State University (Ashtabula), OH (M)
Kent State University (East Liverpool), OH (M)
Kent State University (Kent), OH (M)
Kent State University (New Philadelphia), OH (M)
Kent State University (Warren), OH (M)
Kentucky State University, KY (MW)
Kentucky Wesleyan College, KY (M)
Kenyon College, OH (MW)
King College, TN (M)
King's College, PA (M)
Kishwaukee College, IL (MW)
Knox College, IL (M)
Lackawanna Junior College, PA (M)
Lafayette College, PA (M)
Lake Michigan College, MI (M)
Lake-Sumter Community College, FL (MW)
Lake Superior State University, MI (M)
Lamar University, TX (MW)
Lansing Community College, MI (MW)
Lawrence University, WI (M)
Lebanon Valley College, PA (M)
Lee College, TN (M)
Lehigh County Community College, PA (MW)
Lehigh University, PA (M)
Le Moyne College, NY (M)
Lenoir Community College, NC (M)
Lenoir-Rhyne College, NC (MW)
Lewis and Clark College, OR (M)
Lewis University, IL (M)

Liberty University, VA (M)
Limestone College, SC (M)
Lincoln College, IL (M)
Lincoln Land Community College, IL (M)
Lincoln Memorial University, TN (M)
Lincoln Trail College, IL (M)
Linfield College, OR (M)
Livingstone College, NC (M)
Long Beach City College, CA (M)
Long Island University (Brooklyn), NY (M)
Longwood College, VA (MW)
Loras College, IA (MW)
Los Angeles Pierce Junior College, CA (M)
Louisburg College, NC (M)
Louisiana State University (Alexandria), LA (MW)
Louisiana State University (Baton Rouge), LA (MW)
Louisiana Tech University, LA (M)
Lower Columbia College, WA (MW)
Loyola College, MD (M)
Loyola Marymount University, CA (M)
Loyola University, IL (M)
Luther College, IA (MW)
Lycoming College, PA (M)
Lynchburg College, VA (M)
Lynn University, FL (MW)
Macalester College, MN (MW)
Macomb Community College, MI (M)
Madison Area Technical College, WI (MW)
Madonna University, MI (M)
Malone College, OH (M)
Manchester College, IN (M)
Manhattan College, NY (M)
Mankato State University, MN (MW)
Maple Woods Community College, MO (M)
Marian College, IN (M)
Marian College, WI (M)
Marietta College, OH (M)
Marion Military Institute, AL (M)
Marquette University, WI (M)
Marshall University, WV (M)
Mars Hill College, NC (M)
Marymount University, VA (M)
Massachusetts Institute of Technology, MA (M)
McCook Community College, NE (M)
McKendree College, IL (MW)
McNeese State University, LA (M)
McPherson College, KS (MW)
Memphis State University, TN (MW)
Mercer University, GA (MW)
Mercy College, NY (MW)
Mercyhurst College, PA (M)
Merrimack College, MA (M)
Mesa Community College, AZ (M)
Miami University, OH (M)
Michigan State University, MI (MW)
Middlebury College, VT (M)
Middlesex County College, NJ (M)
Middle Tennessee State University, TN (M)
Midland College, TX (M)
Midland Lutheran College, NE (MW)
Midwestern State University, TX (M)
Millersville University, PA (M)
Millikin University, IL (M)
Minneapolis Community College, MN (MW)
Minot State, ND (M)
Mississippi College, MS (M)
Mississippi Gulf Coast Junior College, MS (M)
Mississippi State University, MS (MW)
Mississippi Valley State University, MS (MW)
Missouri Baptist College, MO (M)
Missouri Southern State College, MO (M)
Missouri Valley College, MO (MW)
Missouri Western State College, MO (M)
Mitchell College, CT (MW)
Mitchell Community College, NC (M)
Mobile College, AL (M)
Modesto Junior College, CA (M)
Mohawk Valley Community College, NY (M)
Monmouth College, NJ (M)
Montclair State College, NJ (M)
Moorhead State University, MN (MW)
Moorpark College, CA (MW)
Moraine Valley Community College, IL (M)
Moravian College, PA (M)
Morehead State University, KY (M)
Morningside College, IA (MW)
Morton College, IL (M)
Motlow State Community College, TN (M)
Mott Community College, MI (M)
Mount Marty College, SD (MW)
Mount Mercy College, IA (MW)
Mount Olive College, NC (M)
Mount St. Mary College, MD (M)
Mount Union College, OH (M)
Mt. San Antonio College, CA (M)
Muhlenberg College, PA (M)
Murray State University, KY (M)
Muskegon Community College, MI (MW)
Muskingum College, OH (M)
Nassau Community College, NY (M)
Nazareth College, NY (MW)
Nebraska Wesleyan University, NE (M)
Newberry College, SC (M)
New Mexico Junior College, NM (M)
New Mexico State University, NM (MW)
New York State University Institute of Technology, NY (M)
New York University, NY (M)
Niagara University, NY (M)
Nichols College, MA (M)
North Carolina State University, NC (MW)
North Central College, IL (M)
North Dakota State, ND (MW)
North Dakota State University, ND (M)
Northeastern Christian Junior College, PA (MW)
Northeastern Illinois University, IL (M)
Northeastern State University, OK (MW)
Northeast Louisiana University, LA (M)
Northeast Missouri State University, MO (MW)
Northern Illinois University, IL (MW)
Northern Kentucky University, KY (M)
Northern Michigan University, MI (M)
Northern State University, SD (MW)
North Greenville College, SC (M)
North Hennepin Community College, MN (MW)
North Iowa Area Community College, IA (M)
Northwestern College, IA (MW)
Northwestern College, MN (M)
Northwestern Oklahoma State University, OH (MW)

Northwestern State University of Louisiana, LA (M)
Northwestern University, IL (M)
Northwood Institute, MI (M)
Northwood Institute (Texas Campus), TX (M)
Norwich University, VT (MW)
Nova University, FL (M)
Oakland Community College, MI (M)
Oakland University, MI (M)
Oakton Community College, IL (M)
Occidental College, CA (M)
Ocean County College, NJ (MW)
Odessa College, TX (M)
Ohio Northern University, OH (M)
Ohio State University, OH (MW)
Ohio University, OH (M)
Ohio Wesleyan University, OH (M)
Oklahoma City University, OK (M)
Oklahoma State University, OK (MW)
Old Dominion University, VA (M)
Olivet College, MI (M)
Olivet Nazarene University, IL (M)
Oral Roberts University, OK (MW)
Orange Coast College, CA (MW)
Orange County Community College, NY (M)
Oregon State University, OR (MW)
Ottawa University, KS (MW)
Otterbein College, OH (M)
Ouachita Baptist University, AR (M)
Pace University, NY (MW)
Pace University (White Plains Campus), NY (MW)
Pacific Lutheran University, WA (M)
Pacific University, OR (MW)
Paducah Community College, CA (M)
Palomar College, CA (M)
Pan American University, TX (M)
Paris Junior College, TX (M)
Parkland College, IL (M)
Pembroke State University, NC (M)
Penn State University, PA (M)
Pennsylvania State University, PA (W)
Pennsylvania State University (Behrend College), PA (M)
Penn Valley Community College, MO (M)
Pepperdine University, CA (MW)
Pfeiffer College, NC (M)
Phoenix College, AZ (MW)
Piedmont College, GA (MW)
Pima Community College, AZ (M)
Pittsburg State University, KS (M)
Point Loma Nazarene College, CA (M)
Pomona-Pitzer Colleges, CA (M)
Portland State University, OR (M)
Prairie View A & M University, TX (M)
Presbyterian College, SC (M)
Prince George's Community College, MD (M)
Princeton University, NJ (M)
Providence College, RI (M)
Purdue University, IN (MW)
Queens College, NY (M)
Queens College, NC (M)
Quinnipiac College, CT (M)
Quinsigamond College, MA (MW)
Radford University, VA (M)
Rainy River Community College, MN (M)
Ramapo College, NJ (M)
Randolph-Macon College, VA (M)
Ranetto Santiago College, CA (M)
Regis University, CO (M)
Rend Lake, IL (M)
Rensselaer Polytechnic Institute, NY (M)
Rice University, TX (M)
Rider College, NJ (M)
Ripon College, WI (M)
Riverside College, CA (M)
Roanoke College, VA (M)
Robert Morris College, PA (M)
Rochester Community College, MN (MW)
Rockland Community College, NY (M)
Rollins College, FL (MW)
Roosevelt University, IL (M)
Rose-Hulman Institute of Technology, IN (M)
Rutgers, Newark College of Arts and Sciences, NJ (W)
Saddleback College, CA (M)
Saginaw Valley State College, MI (M)
Saint Ambrose College, IA (MW)
Saint Andrews Presbyterian College, NC (M)
Saint Anselm College, NH (MW)
Saint Augustine's College, NC (M)
Saint Bonaventure University, NY (MW)
Saint Cloud State University, MN (MW)
Saint Edward's University, TX (M)
Saint Francis College, PA (MW)
Saint John Fisher College, NY (M)
Saint John's University, MN (M)
Saint John's University, NY (MW)
Saint Joseph's College, IN (M)
Saint Joseph's University, PA (M)
Saint Louis University, MO (M)
Saint Martin's College, WA (MW)
Saint Mary's College of California, CA (M)
Saint Mary's University, TX (M)
Saint Michael's College, VT (MW)
Saint Norbert College, WI (MW)
Saint Olaf College, MN (MW)
Saint Peter's College, NJ (M)
Saint Thomas Aquinas College, NY (M)
Saint Thomas University, FL (M)
Salem State College, MA (M)
Salem-Teikyo University, WV (M)
Salve Regina College, RI (MW)
Samford University, AL (M)
Sam Houston State University, TX (M)
San Bernardino Community College, CA (M)
San Diego City College, CA (MW)
San Diego Mesa College, CA (MW)
San Joaquin Delta College, CA (M)
San Jose State University, CA (MW)
Santa Barbara City College, CA (M)
Santa Clara University, CA (MW)
Santa Rosa Junior College, CA (M)
Sauk Valley College, IL (M)
Schoolcraft College, MI (M)
Scottsdale Community College, AR (M)
Seton Hall University, NJ (M)

Shawnee State University, OH (M)
Shelby State Community College, TN (M)
Shepherd College, WV (MW)
Shippensburg University of Pennsylvania, PA (M)
Shorter College, AR (M)
Shorter College, GA (M)
Siena College, NY (M)
Siena Heights College, MI (M)
Sierra College, CA (MW)
Simpson College, CA (MW)
Sinclair Community College, OH (M)
Skidmore College, NY (M)
Slippery Rock University of Pennsylvania, PA (M)
Snead State Community College, AL (M)
Snow College, UT (MW)
South Carolina State College, SC (M)
South Dakota State University, SD (W)
Southeast Community College, NE (M)
Southeastern Community College, IA (M)
Southeastern Louisiana University, LA (M)
Southeastern Massachusetts University, MA (M)
Southeastern Oklahoma State University, OK (MW)
Southern Arkansas University, AR (M)
Southern Connecticut State University, CT (M)
Southern Illinois University, IL (MW)
Southern Illinois University (Edwardsville), IL (M)
Southern Methodist University, TX (MW)
Southern University and A & M College, LA (M)
Southern Utah University, UT (M)
South Plains Community College, TX (M)
Southwest Baptist University, MO (M)
Southwestern College, KS (MW)
Southwestern Michigan Junior College, MI (M)
Southwestern Oklahoma State University, OK (M)
Southwestern University, TX (MW)
Southwest Missouri State University, MO (MW)
Southwest Texas State University, TX (M)
Spartanburg Methodist, SC (M)
Spoon River College, IL (MW)
Springfield College, MA (MW)
Spring Hill College, AL (M)
Stanford University, CA (MW)
State Fair Community College, MO (M)
State University of New York, NY (M)
State University of New York (Binghamton), NY (M)
State University of New York (Buffalo), NY (M)
State University of New York College (New Paltz), NY (MW)
State University of New York College (Oswego), NY (M)
State University of New York Maritime College, NY (M)
Stephen F. Austin State University, TX (M)
Stetson University, FL (MW)
St. Gregory's College, OK (M)
St. Petersburg Junior College, FL (M)
Suffolk County Community College, NY (M)
Suffolk University, MA (MW)
Sul Ross State University, TX (MW)
Swarthmore College, PA (M)
Taft College, CA (M)
Talledaga College, AL (M)
Tampa College, FL (M)
Tarleton State University, TX (M)
Teikyo Westmar University, IA (MW)
Temple Junior College, TX (M)
Temple University, PA (M)
Tennessee Technological University, TN (MW)
Tennessee Wesleyan College, TN (M)
Texarkana College, TX (M)
Texas A & I University, TX (MW)
Texas A & M University, TX (MW)
Texas Christian University, TX (MW)
Texas Lutheran College, TX (M)
Texas Southern University, TX (M)
Texas Tech University, TX (MW)
Texas Wesleyan College, TX (M)
Thomas College, ME (MW)
Three Rivers Community College, MO (M)
Towson State University, MD (M)
Transylvania University, KY (M)
Trenton State College, NJ (M)
Trinidad State Junior College, CO (MW)
Trinity College, CT (M)
Trinity College, IL (M)
Trinity University, TX (M)
Tri-State University, IN (M)
Troy State University, AL (M)
Tufts University, MA (M)
Tulane University, LA (M)
Tusculum College, TN (M)
Tyler Junior College, TX (M)
Union College, NY (M)
Union County College, NJ (M)
University of Akron, OH (M)
University of Alabama (Birmingham), AL (MW)
University of Alabama (Huntsville), AL (M)
University of Alabama (Tuscaloosa), AL (MW)
University of Arizona, AZ (MW)
University of Arkansas (Fayetteville), AR (M)
University of Arkansas (Little Rock), AR (M)
University of Arkansas (Monticello), AR (MW)
University of Arkansas (Pine Bluff), AR (M)
University of Bridgeport, CT (M)
University of California (Berkeley), CA (M)
University of California (Davis), CA (M)
University of California (Irvine), CA (M)
University of California (San Diego), CA (MW)
University of California (Santa Barbara), CA (M)
University of California (UCLA), CA (MW)
University of Central Arkansas, AR (M)
University of Central Florida, FL (MW)
University of Central Oklahoma, OK (M)
University of Charleston, WV (M)
University of Cincinnati, OH (MW)
University of Colorado, CO (M)
University of Colorado (Colorado Springs), CO (M)
University of Connecticut, CT (M)
University of Dallas, TX (M)
University of Dayton, OH (MW)
University of Delaware, DE (M)
University of Denver, CO (M)

University of Detroit Mercy, MI (M)
University of Dubuque, IA (MW)
University of Findlay, OH (M)
University of Florida, FL (MW)
University of Georgia, GA (MW)
University of Hartford, CT (MW)
University of Hawaii (Hilo), HI (M)
University of Hawaii (Manoa), HI (MW)
University of Houston, TX (M)
University of Idaho, ID (M)
University of Illinois, IL (MW)
University of Illinois (Urbana-Champaign), IL (MW)
University of Indianapolis, IN (MW)
University of Iowa, IA (MW)
University of Kansas, KS (MW)
University of Kentucky, KY (MW)
University of La Verne, CA (M)
University of Louisville, KY (M)
University of Lowell, MA (M)
University of Maine, ME (M)
University of Mary Hardin-Baylor, TX (M)
University of Maryland, MD (M)
University of Maryland (Baltimore County), MD (M)
University of Maryland (Eastern Shore), MD (MW)
University of Miami, FL (MW)
University of Michigan, MI (MW)
University of Minnesota (Minneapolis), MN (M)
University of Minnesota (Morris), MN (MW)
University of Mississippi, MS (MW)
University of Missouri, MO (MW)
University of Missouri (Columbia), MO (MW)
University of Missouri (Kansas City), MO (MW)
University of Missouri (Rolla), MO (M)
University of Montevallo, AL (M)
University of Nebraska, NE (M)
University of Nebraska (Kearney), NE (M)
University of Nebraska (Lincoln), NE (MW)
University of Nevada, NV (M)
University of Nevada (Reno), NV (M)
University of New Hampshire, NH (M)
University of New Mexico, NM (MW)
University of New Orleans, LA (M)
University of North Alabama, AL (M)
University of North Carolina (Asheville), NC (MW)
University of North Carolina (Chapel Hill), NC (MW)
University of North Carolina (Charlotte), NC (M)
University of North Carolina (Greensboro), NC (M)
University of North Carolina (Wilmington), NC (MW)
University of North Dakota, ND (M)
University of Northern Iowa, IA (MW)
University of North Florida, FL (M)
University of North Texas, TX (MW)
University of Notre Dame, IN (MW)
University of Oklahoma, OK (MW)
University of Oregon, OR (MW)
University of Pittsburgh (Johnstown), PA (M)
University of Portland, OR (M)
University of Puget Sound, WA (M)
University of Redlands, CA (M)
University of Rhode Island, RI (M)
University of Richmond, VA (M)
University of San Diego, CA (M)
University of San Francisco, CA (MW)
University of Scranton, PA (M)
University of South Alabama, AL (MW)
University of South Carolina (Columbia), SC (MW)
University of South Carolina (Myrtle Beach), SC (MW)
University of South Carolina (Aiken), SC (M)
University of Southern California, CA (MW)
University of Southern Colorado, CO (M)
University of Southern Indiana, IN (M)
University of Southern Mississippi, MS (MW)
University of South Florida, FL (MW)
University of Southwestern Louisiana, LA (M)
University of St. Thomas, MN (MW)
University of Tampa, FL (M)
University of Tennessee, TN (M)
University of Tennessee (Knoxville), TN (MW)
University of Tennessee (Martin), TN (M)
University of Texas (Arlington), TX (M)
University of Texas (Austin), TX (MW)
University of Texas (El Paso), TX (MW)
University of Texas (Pan American), TX (M)
University of Texas (San Antonio), TX (M)
University of the Pacific, CA (M)
University of Toledo, OH (M)
University of Tulsa, OK (MW)
University of Utah, UT (M)
University of Vermont, VT (M)
University of Virginia, VA (M)
University of Washington, WA (MW)
University of West Florida, FL (M)
University of Wisconsin (Eau Claire), WI (M)
University of Wisconsin (Green Bay), WI (MW)
University of Wisconsin (La Crosse), WI (M)
University of Wisconsin (Madison), WI (MW)
University of Wisconsin (Oshkosh), WI (M)
University of Wisconsin (Platteville), WI (M)
University of Wisconsin (River Falls), WI (M)
University of Wisconsin (Stevens Point), WI (M)
University of Wisconsin (Stout), WI (M)
University of Wisconsin (Superior), WI (M)
University of Wyoming, WY (MW)
Upper Iowa University, IA (MW)
Urbana University, OH (MW)
Ursinus College, PA (M)
U.S. International University, CA (MW)
Utah State University, UT (M)
Valdosta State College, GA (M)
Valley City State University, ND (M)
Valparaiso University, IN (M)

Vanderbilt University, TN (MW)
Ventura College, CA (M)
Villanova University, PA (M)
Vincennes University Junior College, IN (M)
Virginia Commonwealth University, VA (M)
Virginia Military Institute, VA (M)
Virginia Polytechnic Institute & State University, VA (M)
Virginia Union University, VA (M)
Virginia Wesleyan College, VA (M)
Wabash College, IN (M)
Wabash Valley College, IL (M)
Wagner College, NY (M)
Wake Forest University, NC (MW)
Waldorf College, IA (MW)
Wallace State Community College, AL (M)
Walla Walla Community College, WA (M)
Walsh College, OH (M)
Walters State Community College, TN (M)
Wartburg College, IA (MW)
Washburn University, KS (M)
Washington and Jefferson College, PA (M)
Washington State University, WA (MW)
Washington University, MO (M)
Waubonsee College, IL (M)
Wayne State University, MI (M)
Webber College, FL (M)
Weber State College, UT (MW)
Wesleyan University, CT (M)
Wesley College, DE (MW)
West Chester University, PA (M)
Western Carolina University, NC (M)
Western Connecticut State University, CT (M)
Western Illinois University, IL (M)
Western Kentucky University, KY (MW)
Western Maryland College, MD (W)
Western Nebraska Community College, NE (M)
Western New England College, MA (M)
Western State College, CO (M)
Western Texas College, TX (M)
Western Washington University, WA (MW)
West Georgia College, GA (M)
West Liberty State College, WV (M)
Westminster College, PA (M)
West Virginia Wesleyan College, WV (M)
Wheaton College, IL (M)
Wheeling Jesuit College, WV (MW)
Whitman College, WA (M)
Whittier College, CA (M)
Wichita State University, KS (MW)
Wilkes College, NC (M)
Wilkes University, PA (M)
Willamette University, OR (M)
William Jewell College, MO (M)
William Patterson College, NJ (M)
William Penn College, IA (MW)
William Rainey Harper College, IL (M)
Williams College, MA (M)
Wilmington College, DE (M)
Wilmington College, OH (M)
Wingate College, NC (M)
Winona State University, MN (MW)
Winston-Salem State University, NC (M)
Winthrop University, SC (MW)
Wofford College, SC (M)
Worcester State College, MA (M)
Wright State University, OH (M)
Yale University, CT (MW)
Yeshiva University, NY (M)
York College of Pennsylvania, PA (M)
Youngstown State University, OH (M)

Gymnastics

Adams State College, CO (W)
Arizona State University, AZ (MW)
Auburn University, AL (W)
Ball State University, IN (W)
Boise State University, ID (W)
Bowling Green State University, OH (W)
Brigham Young University, UT (MW)
Brown University, RI (W)
California Polytechnic State University, CA (W)
California State University (Chico), CA (W)
California State University (Fullerton), CA (W)
California State University (Long Beach), CA (W)
California State University (Sacramento), CA (W)
Centenary College, LA (W)
Central Michigan University, MI (W)
City College of New York, NY (MW)
College of William and Mary, VA (MW)
Community College of Spokane, WA (W)
Connecticut College, CT (W)
Cornell University, NY (MW)
Dartmouth College, NH (M)
Eastern Michigan University, MI (MW)
Eastern Oklahoma State College, OK (MW)
East Stroudsburg University, PA (MW)
George Washington University, DC (W)
Georgia College, GA (W)
Gustavus Adolphus College, MN (W)
Hamline University, MN (W)
Houston Baptist University, TX (MW)
Illinois State University, IL (W)
Indiana State University, IN (W)
Indiana University of Pennsylvania, PA (W)
Iowa State University of Science and Technology, IA (MW)
Ithaca College, NY (W)
James Madison University, VA (MW)
Kent State University (Ashtabula), OH (MW)
Kent State University (Kent), OH (MW)
Kent State University (New Philadelphia), OH (MW)
Kent State University (Warren), OH (MW)
Long Island University (Brooklyn), NY (MW)
Los Angeles Pierce Junior College, CA (W)
Louisiana State University, LA (W)
Massachusetts Institute of Technology, MA (MW)
Michigan State University, MI (MW)
Mississippi Valley State University, MS (M)
Montana State University, MT (W)
Montclair State College, NJ (W)
North Carolina State University, NC (MW)

Northern Illinois University, IL (W)
Ohio State University, OH (MW)
Oregon State University, OR (W)
Pennsylvania State University, PA (MW)
Radford University, VA (MW)
Rhode Island College, RI (W)
Rose State Junior College, OK (MW)
Salem State College, MA (W)
Samford University, AL (W)
San Diego Mesa College, CA (MW)
San Jose State University, CA (MW)
Seattle Pacific University, WA (W)
Southeast Missouri State University, MO (W)
Southern Connecticut State University, CT (MW)
Southern Utah University, UT (W)
Springfield College, MA (MW)
Stanford University, CA (MW)
State University of New York (Albany), NY (W)
State University of New York College (Brockport), NY (W)
State University of New York College (Cortland), NY (MW)
Syracuse University, NY (M)
Temple University, PA (MW)
Texas Tech University, TX (MW)
Texas Woman's University, TX (W)
Towson State University, MD (W)
Trenton State College, NJ (W)
University of Alabama (Tuscaloosa), AL (W)
University of Alaska, AK (W)
University of Arizona, AZ (W)
University of Bridgeport, CT (W)
University of California (Berkeley), CA (MW)
University of California (Davis), CA (W)
University of California (Santa Barbara), CA (MW)
University of California (UCLA), CA (MW)
University of Connecticut, CT (W)
University of Denver, CO (W)
University of Florida, FL (W)
University of Georgia, GA (W)
University of Illinois, IL (MW)
University of Illinois (Urbana-Champaign), IL (MW)
University of Iowa, IA (MW)
University of Kentucky, KY (W)
University of Maryland, MD (W)
University of Massachusetts (Amherst), MA (MW)
University of Michigan, MI (MW)
University of Missouri, MO (W)
University of Missouri (Columbia), MO (W)
University of Nebraska (Lincoln), NE (MW)
University of New Hampshire, NH (W)
University of New Mexico, NM (M)
University of North Carolina (Asheville), NC (W)
University of Oklahoma, OK (MW)
University of Pennsylvania, PA (W)
University of Pittsburgh, PA (MW)
University of Rhode Island, RI (MW)
University of Utah, UT (W)
University of Vermont, VT (MW)
University of Washington, WA (W)
University of Wisconsin (Eau Claire), WI (W)
University of Wisconsin (La Crosse), WI (MW)
University of Wisconsin (Oshkosh), WI (MW)
University of Wisconsin (River Falls), WI (W)
University of Wisconsin (Stout), WI (W)
University of Wisconsin (Superior), WI (W)
Ursinus College, PA (W)
Utah State University, UT (W)
Valparaiso University, IN (W)
Ventura College, CA (W)
West Chester University, PA (W)
Western Michigan University, MI (MW)
West Virginia University, WV (W)
Winona State University, MN (W)
Yale University, CT (W)

Handball

Florida State University, FL (W)
Lake Forest College, IL (MW)
Pacific University, OR (MW)

Ice Hockey

American International College, MA (M)
Amherst College, MA (M)
Arrowhead Community College, MN (M)
Augsburg College, MN (M)
Babson College, MA (M)
Bentley College, MA (M)
Bethel College, MN (M)
Black Hills State University, SD (W)
Boston College, MA (M)
Boston University, MA (M)
Bowdoin College, ME (MW)
Bowling Green State University, OH (M)
Broome Community College, NY (M)
Brown University, RI (MW)
Buffalo State University (New York), NY (M)
Canisius College, NY (M)
Clarkson University, NY (M)
Colgate University, NY (M)
College of Allegheny County, PA (M)
College of St. Scholastica, MN (M)
Colorado College, CO (M)
Community College of Rhode Island, RI (M)
Connecticut College, CT (M)
Cornell College, IA (M)
Cornell University, NY (MW)
Curry College, MA (M)
Dartmouth College, NH (MW)
Elmira College, NY (M)
Emerson College, MA (M)
Fairfield University, CT (M)
Ferris State College, MI (M)
Fitchburg State College, MA (M)
Fordham University, NY (M)
Franklin & Marshall College, PA (M)
Gustavus Adolphus College, MN (M)
Hamilton College, NY (MW)
Hamline University, MN (M)
Harvard University, MA (MW)
Hibbing Community College, MN (M)
Holy Cross College, MA (M)
Iona College, NY (M)
Kean College of New Jersey, NJ (M)
Kent State University (Ashtabula), OH (M)
Kent State University (Kent), OH (M)
Kent State University (New Philadelphia), OH (M)
Kent State University (Warren), OH (M)

Lake Forest College, IL (M)
Lake Superior State University, MI (M)
Lawrence University, WI (M)
Lehigh University, PA (M)
Manhattan College, NY (M)
Mankato State University, MN (M)
Mercyhurst College, PA (M)
Merrimack College, MA (M)
Miami University, OH (M)
Michigan State University, MI (M)
Michigan Technological University, MI (M)
Middlebury College, VT (MW)
Mohawk Valley Community College, NY (M)
Moravian College, PA (M)
New Hampshire College, NH (M)
New Jersey Institute of Technology, NJ (M)
Nichols College, MA (M)
North Adams State College, MA (M)
North County Community College, NY (M)
North Dakota State University (Bottineau), ND (M)
Northern Arizona University, AZ (M)
Northern Michigan University, MI (M)
Norwich University, VT (M)
Ocean County College, NJ (M)
Ohio State University, OH (M)
Pace University, NY (M)
Plymouth State College, NH (M)
Princeton University, NJ (MW)
Providence College, RI (MW)
Quinnipiac College, CT (M)
Rainy River Community College, MN (M)
Rensselaer Polytechnic Institute, NY (M)
Rochester Institute of Technology, NY (MW)
Saint Anselm College, NH (M)
Saint Cloud State University, MN (M)
Saint John's University, MN (M)
Saint John's University, NY (M)
Saint Lawrence University, NY (MW)
Saint Michael's College, VT (M)
Saint Olaf College, MN (M)
Salem State College, MA (M)
Skidmore College, NY (MW)
Southeastern Massachusetts University, MA (M)
State University of New York (Plattsburgh), NY (M)
State University of New York College (Brockport), NY (M)
State University of New York College (Cortland), NY (M)
State University of New York College (Fredonia), NY (M)
State University of New York College (Geneseo), NY (M)
State University of New York College (Oswego), NY (M)
State University of New York College (Potsdam), NY (M)
State University of New York Maritime College, NY (M)
Stonehill College, MA (M)
Suffolk University, MA (M)
Trinity College, CT (M)
Trinity College, IL (M)
Tufts University, MA (M)
Union College, NY (M)
University of Alabama (Huntsville), AL (M)
University of Alaska, AK (M)
University of Alaska (Fairbanks), AK (M)
University of Connecticut, CT (M)
University of Denver, CO (M)
University of Lowell MA (M)
University of Maine, ME (M)
University of Massachusetts (Boston), MA (M)
University of Michigan, MI (M)
University of Minnesota (Duluth), MN (M)
University of Minnesota (Minneapolis), MN (MW)
University of Montana, MT (M)
University of New Hampshire, NH (MW)
University of North Dakota, ND (M)
University of Notre Dame, IN (M)
University of Rhode Island, RI (M)
University of Scranton, PA (M)
University of St. Thomas, MN (M)
University of Tennessee (Knoxville), TN (M)
University of Vermont, VT (M)
University of Wisconsin (Eau Claire), WI (M)
University of Wisconsin (La Crosse), WI (M)
University of Wisconsin (Madison), WI (M)
University of Wisconsin (River Falls), WI (M)
University of Wisconsin (Stevens Point), WI (M)
University of Wisconsin (Superior), WI (M)
U.S. International University, CA (M)
Villanova University, PA (M)
Wesleyan University, CT (MW)
Western Michigan University, MI (M)
Western New England College, MA (M)
William Patterson College, NJ (M)
Williams College, MA (M)
Worcester State College, MA (M)
Yale University, CT (MW)

Indoor Track

Abilene Christian University, TX (W)
Adams State College, CO (MW)
Alabama A & M University, AL (MW)
Alabama State University, AL (MW)
Alcorn State University, MS (M)
Alfred University, NY (MW)
Allegheny College, PA (MW)
Amherst College, MA (MW)
Anderson College, SC (M)
Anderson University, IN (MW)
Appalachian State University, NC (MW)
Aquinas College, MI (MW)
Arizona State University, AZ (MW)
Arkansas College, AR (MW)
Arkansas State University, AR (MW)
Ashland College, OH (MW)
Auburn University, AL (MW)
Augsburg College, MN (MW)
Augustana College, SD (MW)
Austin Peay State University, TN (W)
Azusa Pacific University, CA (MW)
Baker University, KS (MW)
Ball State University, IN (MW)
Baltimore City Community College, MD (MW)
Barber-Scotia College, NC (MW)
Barton County College, KS (MW)
Bates College, ME (MW)
Baylor University, TX (MW)
Bellarmine College, KY (MW)
Beloit College, WI (MW)
Benedict College, SC (M)
Benedictine College, KS (MW)
Bentley College, MA (MW)
Bethel College, KS (M)
Bethel College, MN (MW)

Bethune-Cookman College, FL (MW)
Black Hills State University, SD (M)
Boston College, MA (MW)
Boston University, MA (MW)
Bowdoin College, ME (MW)
Bowie State University, MD (MW)
Brandeis University, MA (MW)
Brevard College, FL (MW)
Brevard College, NC (MW)
Bridgewater College, VA (MW)
Brigham Young University, UT (MW)
Bronx Community College, NY (MW)
Brown University, RI (MW)
Bucknell University, PA (MW)
Buffalo State College, NY (MW)
Buffalo State University (New York), NY (MW)
Butler University, IN (MW)
California State University (Fresno), CA (MW)
Canisius College, NY (MW)
Carleton College, MN (MW)
Carnegie-Mellon University, PA (MW)
Carroll College, WI (MW)
Carthage College, WI (MW)
Case Western Reserve University, OH (MW)
Catonsville Community College, MD (MW)
Cayuga County Community College, NY (MW)
Cedarville College, OH (MW)
Central College, IA (MW)
Central College, KS (MW)
Central Connecticut State University, CT (MW)
Central Michigan University, MI (MW)
Central Missouri State University, MO (MW)
Central State University, OH (M)
Chadron State College, NE (MW)
Charleston Southern University, SC (MW)
Chicago State University, IL (MW)
Christopher Newport College, VA (MW)
City College of New York, NY (MW)
Clemson University, SC (MW)
Cleveland State University, OH (MW)
Cloud County Community College, KS (MW)
Coe College, IA (MW)
Colby Community College, KS (MW)
Colgate University, NY (MW)
College of William and Mary, VA (MW)
College of Wooster, OH (MW)
Colorado College, CO (MW)
Colorado School of Mines, CO (MW)
Columbia University, NY (MW)
Concordia Teachers College, NE (MW)
Coppin State College, MD (MW)
Cornell College, IA (MW)
Cornell University, NY (MW)
Dakota State University, SD (MW)
Dartmouth College, NH (MW)
Davidson College, NC (MW)
Delaware State College, DE (MW)
Denison University, OH (MW)
DePaul University, IL (MW)
Dickinson College, PA (MW)
Dickinson State University, ND (MW)
Doane College, NE (MW)
Drake University, IA (MW)
Drexel University, PA (M)
Duke University, NC (MW)
East Carolina University, NC (MW)
Eastern Illinois University, IL (MW)
Eastern Kentucky University, KY (MW)
Eastern Michigan University, MI (MW)
Eastern Oklahoma State College, OK (MW)
Eastern Washington University, WA (MW)
East Stroudsburg University, PA (MW)
East Tennessee State University, TN (MW)
Edward Waters College, FL (MW)
Elmhurst College, IL (MW)
Emporia State University, KS (MW)
Essex Community College, MD (M)
Everett Community College, WA (MW)
Fairleigh Dickinson University, NJ (MW)
Ferris State College, MI (MW)
Florida A & M University, FL (MW)
Florida Memorial College, FL (MW)
Florida Southern College, FL (MW)
Florida State University, FL (MW)
Fordham University, NY (MW)
Fort Hays State University, KS (MW)
Fort Scott College, KS (M)
Franklin & Marshall College, PA (MW)
Fresno Pacific College, CA (MW)
Garden City Community College, KS (MW)
Geneva College, PA (MW)
George Mason University, VA (MW)
Georgetown University, DC (MW)
Georgia Institute of Technology, GA (M)
Gettysburg College, PA (MW)
Gloucester County College, NJ (M)
Gonzaga University, WA (MW)
Grambling State University, LA (W)
Grand Valley State College, MI (MW)
Grinnell College, IA (MW)
Gustavus Adolphus College, MN (MW)
Hagerstown Junior College, MD (MW)
Hamilton College, NY (MW)
Hamline University, MN (MW)
Hampton University, VA (MW)
Harding University, AR (MW)
Hartwick College, NY (MW)
Hastings College, NE (MW)
Haverford College, PA (M)
Heidelberg College, OH (W)
Henderson State University, AR (M)
Highland Community College, KS (MW)
Hillsdale College, MI (MW)
Hiram College, OH (MW)
Holy Cross College, MA (MW)
Houston Baptist University, TX (MW)
Howard Payne University, TX (M)
Hudson Valley Community College, NY (M)
Idaho State University, ID (MW)
Illinois Benedictine College, IL (MW)
Illinois College, IL (MW)
Illinois State University, IL (MW)
Illinois Wesleyan University, IL (M)
Indiana State University, IN (M)

Iona College, NY (MW)
Iowa Wesleyan College, IA (MW)
Ithaca College, NY (MW)
Jackson State University, MS (MW)
James Madison University, VA (MW)
Jamestown College, ND (MW)
John Carroll University, OH (MW)
Johns Hopkins University, MD (MW)
Johnson County Community College, KS (MW)
Johnson C. Smith University, NC (MW)
Kansas State University, KS (MW)
Kansas Wesleyan College, KS (MW)
Kent State University, OH (MW)
Kentucky State University, KY (MW)
Kenyon College, OH (MW)
Knox College, IL (MW)
Knoxville College, TN (MW)
Kutztown University, PA (MW)
Lafayette College, PA (MW)
Lake Superior State University, MI (MW)
Lamar University, TX (MW)
La Salle University, PA (MW)
Lawrence University, WI (MW)
Lehigh University, PA (M)
Le Moyne College, NY (M)
Liberty University, VA (MW)
Lincoln Land Community College, IL (M)
Lincoln University, MO (M)
Long Island University (Brooklyn), NY (MW)
Loras College, IA (W)
Louisiana State University, LA (MW)
Louisiana Tech University, LA (MW)
Loyola University, IL (MW)
Lubbock Christian College, TX (MW)
Luther College, IA (MW)
Lynchburg College, VA (MW)
Macalester College, MN (MW)
Macomb Community College, MI (MW)
Malone College, OH (MW)
Manchester College, IN (MW)
Mankato State University, MN (MW)
Mansfield University, PA (MW)
Marietta College, OH (M)
Marist College, NY (MW)
Marquette University, WI (MW)
Marshall University, WV (MW)
Mary Washington College, VA (MW)
Massachusetts Institute of Technology, MA (M)
McPherson College, KS (MW)
Memphis State University, TN (MW)
Mercer County Community College, NJ (MW)
Mid-America Nazarene College, KS (MW)
Middle Tennessee State University, TN (MW)
Midland Lutheran College, NE (MW)
Millikin University, IL (MW)
Milwaukee Area Technology College, WI (MW)
Minot State, ND (MW)
Mississippi State University, MS (MW)
Mississippi Valley State University, MS (MW)
Missouri Southern State College, MO (MW)
Missouri Valley College, MO (MW)
Mohawk Valley Community College, NY (MW)
Monmouth College, IL (MW)
Monmouth College, NJ (M)
Montana State University, MT (MW)
Montclair State College, NJ (MW)
Moorhead State University, MN (MW)
Moravian College, PA (MW)
Morgan State University, MD (MW)
Mount Holyoke College, MA (W)
Mount St. Mary College, MD (MW)
Muhlenberg College, PA (W)
Murray State University, KY (MW)
Muskingum College, OH (MW)
Nassau Community College, NY (MW)
New York Institute of Technology, NY (M)
Norfolk State University, VA (MW)
North Carolina A and T State University, NC (MW)
North Carolina Central University, NC (MW)
North Central College, IL (MW)
North Dakota State, ND (MW)
North Dakota State University, ND (MW)
Northeastern Junior College, CO (MW)
Northeast Louisiana University, LA (MW)
Northern Arizona University, KAZ (MW)
Northwestern College, IA (MW)
Northwestern University, IL (MW)
Northwest Missouri State University, MO (MW)
Northwood Institute, MI (MW)
Northwood Institute (Texas Campus), TX (MW)
Norwich University, VT (MW)
Oakton Community College, IL (MW)
Oberlin College, OH (MW)
Odessa College, TX (M)
Ohio Northern University, OH (M)
Ohio State University, OH (MW)
Ohio University, OH (MW)
Oklahoma Christian University of Science & Art, OK (MW)
Oklahoma State University, OK (MW)
Oral Roberts University, OK (MW)
Otterbein College, OH (MW)
Ouachita Baptist University, AR (M)
Pace University, NY (MW)
Pan American University, kTX (MW)
Parkland College, IL (MW)
Pennsylvania State University, PA (MW)
Pittsburg State University, KS (MW)
Prairie View A & M University, TX (MW)
Pratt Community College, KS (MW)
Purdue University, IN (MW)
Queens College, NY (MW)
Rensselaer Polytechnic Institute, NY (M)
Rhode Island College, RI (MW)
Rice University, TX (MW)
Ricks College, ID (MW)
Ripon College, WI (MW)
Robert Morris College, PA (M)
Roberts Wesleyan College, NY (MW)
Rochester Institute of Technology, NY (M)
Rose-Hulman Institute of Technology, IN (M)
Saginaw Valley State College, MI (MW)

Saint Cloud State University, MN (MW)
Saint Francis College, PA (MW)
Saint John's University, MN (M)
Saint John's University, NY (M)
Saint Joseph's University, PA (MW)
Saint Lawrence University, NY (MW)
Saint Norbert College, WI (MW)
Saint Olaf College, MN (MW)
Saint Paul's College, VA (M)
Saint Peter's College, NJ (MW)
Salve Regina College, RI (MW)
Samford University, AL (MW)
Seton Hall University, NJ (MW)
Shippensburg University of Pennsylvania, PA (MW)
Siena College, NY (MW)
Simpson College, CA (MW)
Smith College, MA (W)
South Carolina State College, SC (MW)
South Dakota State University, SD (MW)
Southeastern Louisiana University, LA (MW)
Southeastern Massachusetts University, MA (MW)
Southeast Missouri State University, MO (MW)
Southern Arkansas University, AR (M)
Southern Illinois University, IL (MW)
Southern Methodist University, TX (MW)
Southern Oregon State College, OR (MW)
Southern University and A & M College, LA (MW)
South Plains Community College, TX (M)
Southwest Baptist University, MO (MW)
Southwestern College, KS (MW)
Southwestern Michigan Junior College, MI (MW)
Southwest Missouri State University, MO (MW)
Southwest State University, MN (MW)
Spoon River College, IL (MW)
Spring Arbor College, MI (MW)
Springfield College, MA (MW)
State University of New York, NY (MW)
State University of New York (Albany), NY (MW)
State University of New York (Plattsburgh), NY (MW)
State University of New York (Stony Brook), NY (MW)
State University of New York College (Brockport), NY (MW)
State University of New York College (Cortland), NY (MW)
State University of New York College (Fredonia), NY (MW)
Stephen F. Austin State University, TX (MW)
Stonehill College, MA (MW)
Swarthmore College, PA (MW)
Syracuse University, NY (MW)
Talladaga College, AL (MW)
Tarleton State University, TX (MW)
Teikyo Westmar University, IA (MW)
Tennessee State University, TN (MW)
Tennessee Technological University, TN (MW)
Texas A & I University, TX (MW)
Texas A & M University, TX (MW)
Texas Southern University, TX (MW)
Texas Tech University, TX (MW)
Towson State University, MD (MW)
Trinity College, CT (MW)
Trinity College, IL (MW)
Tri-State University, IN (MW)
Triton College, IL (MW)
Troy State University, AL (MW)
Tufts University, MA (MW)
Tuskegee University, AL (MW)
Union College, NY (MW)
University of Alabama (Tuscaloosa), AL (MW)
University of Arkansas (Fayettesville), AR (MW)
University of Arkansas (Pine Bluff), AR (W)
University of Central Arkansas, AR (MW)
University of Central Oklahoma, OK (MW)
University of Chicago, IL (MW)
University of Cincinnati, OH (M)
University of Colorado, CO (MW)
University of Connecticut, CT (MW)
University of Delaware, DE (MW)
University of Detroit Mercy, MI (MW)
University of Findlay, OH (MW)
University of Georgia, GA (MW)
University of Houston, TX (MW)
University of Idaho, I (MW)
University of Illinois, IL (MW)
University of Illinois (Urbana-Champaign), IL (MW)
University of Iowa, IA (M)
University of Kansas, KS (MW)
University of Kentucky, KY (MW)
University of Louisville, KY (MW)
University of Lowell, MA (MW)
University of Mary, ND (MW)
University of Maryland, MD (MW)
University of Maryland (Baltimore County), MD (MW)
University of Maryland (Eastern Shore), MD (MW)
University of Massachusetts (Amherst), MA (MW)
University of Massachusetts (Boston), MA (MW)
University of Michigan, MI (MW)
University of Minnesota, MN (Duluth), MN (MW)
University of Minnesota (Minneapolis), MN (MW)
University of Mississippi, MS (M)
University of Missouri, MO (MW)
University of Missouri (Columbia), MO (MW)
University of Montana, MT (W)
University of Nebraska, NE (M)
University of Nebraska (Lincoln), NE (MW)
University of Nevada, NV (W)
University of New Hampshire, NH (MW)
University of New Haven, CT (M)
University of New Orleans, LA (MW)
University of North Carolina (Asheville), NC (M)
University of North Carolina (Chapel Hill), NC (M)
University of North Dakota, ND (MW)
University of Northern Colorado, CO (MW)
University of Northern Iowa, IA (MW)

University of North Florida, FL (MW)
University of North Texas, TX (MW)
University of Notre Dame, IN (MW)
University of Oklahoma, OK (MW)
University of Pennsylvania, PA (MW)
University of Pittsburgh, PA (MW)
University of Pittsburgh (Johnstown), PA (MW)
University of Rhode Island, RI (MW)
University of Richmond, VA (MW)
University of South Alabama, AL (MW)
University of South Dakota, SD (MW)
University of Southern California, CA (MW)
University of Southern Colorado, CO (MW)
University of Southern Mississippi, MS (MW)
University of South Florida, FL (MW)
University of Southwestern Louisiana, LA (MW)
University of St. Thomas, MN (MW)
University of Tennessee, TN (MW)
University of Tennessee (Knoxville), TN (MW)
University of Texas (Arlington, TX (MW)
University of Texas (Austin), TX (M)
University of Texas (El Paso), TX (MW)
University of Texas (San Antonio), TX (MW)
University of Toledo, OH (MW)
University of Tulsa, OK (MW)
University of Utah, UT (MW)
University of Vermont, VT (MW)
University of Virginia, VA (MW)
University of Washington, WA (MW)
University of Wisconsin (Eau Claire), WI (MW)
University of Wisconsin (La Crosse), WI (MW)
University of Wisconsin (Madison), WI (MW)
University of Wisconsin (Milwaukee), WI (MW)
University of Wisconsin (Oshkosh), WI (MW)
University of Wisconsin (Platteville), WI (MW)
University of Wisconsin (River Falls), WI (MW)
University of Wisconsin (Stevens Point), WI (MW)
University of Wisconsin (Stout), WI (MW)
University of Wyoming, WY (MW)
Urbana University, OH (MW)
Ursinus College, PA (MW)
Utah State University, UT (MW)
Valparaiso University, IN (M)
Vanderbilt University, TN (W)
Vincennes University Junior College, IN (MW)
Virginia Commonwealth University, VA (MW)
Virginia Military Institute, Va (M)
Virginia Polytechnic Institute & State University, VA (MW)
Virginia State University, VA (MW)
Wagner College, NY (MW)
Wake Forest University, NC (MW)
Wartburg College, IA (MW)
Wayland Baptist University, TX (MW)
Wayne State College, NE (MW)
Wesleyan University, CT (MW)
West Chester University, PA (MW)
Western Carolina University, NC (MW)
Western Illinois University, IL (MW)
Western Kentucky University, KY (MW)
Western Michigan University, MI (MW)
Western Oregon State College, OR (MW)
Western Washington University, WA (MW)
Westfield State College, MA (W)
West Virginia University, WV (MW)
Wheaton College, IL(MW)
Wichita State University, KS (MW)
Willamette University, OR (MW)
William Jewell College, MO (MW)
William Patterson College, NJ (MW)
William Penn College, IA (MW)
Williams College, MA (MW)
Winona State University, MN (MW)
Winston-Salem State University, NC (MW)
Worcester State College, MA (MW)
Yale University, CT (MW)
York College (CUNY), NY (MW)

Lacrosse

Adelphi University, NY (M)
Alfred University, NY (M)
Amherst College, MA (MW)
Babson College, MA (MW)
Ball State University, IN (W)
Bates College, ME (MW)
Bloomfield College, NJ (M)
Boston College, MA (MW)
Bowdoin College, ME (MW)
Bridgewater College, VA (W)
Bridgewater State College, MA (W)
Brown University, RI (MW)
Bryn Mawr College, PA (W)
Bucknell University, PA (MW)
Butler University, IN (M)
Canisius College, NY (M)
Castleton State College, VT (MW)
Catholic University of America, DC (M)
Catonsville Community College, MD (M)
City College of New York, NY (M)
Clarkson University, NY (MW)
Colby-Sawyer College, NH (W)
Colgate University, NY (MW)
College of William and Mary, VA (W)
College of Wooster, OH (MW)
Colorado College, CO (M)
Colorado School of Mines, CO (M)
Connecticut College, CT (MW)
Cornell University, NY (MW)
Curry College, MA (M)
Dartmouth College, NH (MW)
Davidson College, NC (W)
Dean Junior College, MA (M)
Denison University, OH (MW)
Dickinson College, PA (MW)
Dowling College, NY (M)
Drew University, NJ (MW)
Drexel University, PA (MW)
Duke University, NC (M)
Earlham College, IN (W)
Eastern College, PA (W)
East Stroudsburg University, PA (W)
Essex Community College, MD (MW)
Fairfield University, CT (MW)

Fairleigh Dickinson University (Madison), NJ (M)
Fairleigh Dickinson University (Teaneck), NJ (M)
Fordham University, NY (M)
Franklin & Marshall College, PA (MW)
Georgetown University, DC (M)
Gettysburg College, PA (MW)
Goucher College, MD (W)
Hamilton College, NY (MW)
Hampden-Sydney College, VA (M)
Harford Community College, MD (MW)
Hartwick College, NY (MW)
Harvard University, MA (MW)
Haverford College, PA (MW)
Herkimer County Community College, NY (M)
Hofstra University, NY (MW)
Holy Cross College, MA (MW)
Hood College, MD (W)
Hudson Valley Community College, NY (M)
Iona College, NY (MW)
Ithaca College, NY (MW)
James Madison University, VA (W)
Jefferson Community College, NY (M)
Johns Hopkins University, MD (MW)
Kean College of New Jersey, NJ (M)
Kenyon College, OH (MW)
Lafayette kCollege, PA (MW)
Lake Forest College, IL (M)
Lehigh University, PA (MW)
Le Moyne College, NY (M)
Limestone College, SC (M)
Long Island University (C. W. Post Campus), NY (M)
Long Island University (Southhampton Campus), NY (M)
Longwood College, VA (W)
Loras College, IA (M)
Loyola College, MD (MW)
Lynchburg College, VA (MW)
Manhattanville College, NY (M)
Marietta College, OH (M)
Marist College, NY (M)
Marymount University, VA (M)
Mary Washington College, VA (W)
Massachusetts Institute of Technology, MA (MW)
Merrimack College, MA (M)
Michigan State University, MI (M)
Middlebury College, VT (MW)
Millersville University, PA (W)
Montclair State College, NJ (M)
Mount St. Mary College, MD (M)
Mount Union College, OH (M)
Nassau Community College, NY (M)
Nazareth College, NY (M)
New Hampshire College, NH (M)
Nichols College, MA (M)
Northwestern University, IL (W)
Norwich University, VT (M)
Oberlin College, OH (MW)
Ohio State University, OH (M)
Ohio Wesleyan University, OH (MW)
Old Dominion University, VA (W)
Pace University, NY (M)
Pace University (White Plains Campus), NY (M)
Pennsylvania State University, PA (MW)
Pfeiffer College, NC (M)
Plymouth State College, NH (MW)
Polytechnic University (Brooklyn Campus), NY (M)
Princeton University, NJ (MW)
Providence College, RI (MW)
Queens College, NY (M)
Quinnipiac College, CT (M)
Radford University, VA (M)
Randolph-Macon College, VA (MW)
Rensselaer Polytechnic Institute, NY (M)
Roanoke College, VA (MW)
Rochester Institute of Technology, NY (M)
Rowan College of New Jersey, NJ (W)
Saint Anselm College, NH (M)
Saint Bonaventure University, NY (M)
Saint John's University, NY (M)
Saint Joseph's University, PA (MW)
Saint Lawrence University, NY (MW)
Saint Mary's College, MD (MW)
Saint Mary's College of California, CA (MW)
Saint Michael's College, VT (MW)
Saint Thomas University, FL (M)
Saint Vincent College, PA (M)
Shippensburg University of Pennsylvania, PA (W)
Siena College, NY (M)
Skidmore College, NY (MW)
Smith College, MA (W)
Springfield College, MA (MW)
State University of New York (Albany), NY (M)
State University of New York (Stony Brook), NY (M)
State University of New York College (Cortland), NY (MW)
State University of New York College (Geneseo), NY (M)
State University of New York College (Oswego), NY (M)
State University of New York College (Potsdam), NY (M)
State University of New York Maritime College, NY (M)
Stevens Institute of Technology, NJ (M)
Suffolk County Community College, NY (M)
Swarthmore College, PA (MW)
Sweet Briar College, VA (W)
Syracuse University, NY (M)
Temple University, PA (W)
Texas Tech University, TX (M)
Towson State University, MD (MW)
Trenton State College, NJ (W)
Trinity College, CT (MW)
Trinity College, IL (MW)
Tufts University, MA (MW)
Union College, NY (MW)
University of Delaware, DE (MW)
University of Denver, CO (M)
University of Hartford, CT (M)
University of Maryland, MD (MW)
University of Maryland (Baltimore County), MD (MW)
University of Massachusetts (Amherst), MA (MW)
University of Massachusetts (Boston), MA (M)
University of New England, ME (M)
University of New Hampshire, NH (MW)
University of New Haven, CT (M)
University of North Carolina (Asheville), NC (MW)
University of North Carolina (Chapel Hill), NC (MW)
University of Notre Dame, IN (M)
University of Pennsylvania, PA (MW)
University of Rhode Island, RI (M)
University of Richmond, VA (W)
University of Scranton, PA (M)
University of Vermont, VT (MW)
University of Virginia, VA (MW)

University of the Pacific, CA (M)
Ursinus College, PA (W)
Villanova University, PA (MW)
Virginia Military Institute, VA (M)
Washington College, MD (MW)
Wellesley College, MA (W)
Wesleyan University, CT (MW)
Wesley College, DE (M)
West Chester University, PA (MW)
Western Maryland College, MD (MW)
Western New England College, MA (M)
Whittier College, CA (M)
Willamette University, OR (M)
Williams College, MA (MW)
Yale University, CT (MW)

Martial Arts

Austin College, TX (W)
Austin Community College, MN (W)
Catholic University of Puerto Rico, PR (MW)
Cayuga County Commuity College, NY (M)
Cleveland State University, OH (MW)
Dowling College, NY (M)
Georgian Court College, NJ (W)
Loras College, IA (MW)
Miami-Dade Community College (North), FL (MW)
Mississippi State University, MS (MW)
Mississippi Valley State University, MS (M)
Polytechnic University (Brooklyn Campus), NY (MW)
Roosevelt University, IL (MW)

Polo

Cornell University, NY (MW)
Skidmore College, NY (MW)

Power Lifting

Bayamon Central University, PR (MW)
Cayuga County Community College, NY (M)
Johns Hopkins University, MD (M)
Lafayette College, PA (M)
Louisiana Tech University, LA (MW)
Mississippi State University, MS (MW)
Mississippi Valley State University, MS (M)
Northwestern Oklahoma State University, OK (M)
Snow College, UT (MW)

Racquetball

Broward Community College, FL (MW)
Butler County Community College, KS (M)
Butler County Community College, PA (M)
Cayuga County Community College, NY (MW)
Dalton College, GA (MW)
Dowling College, NY (MW)
Goldey Beacom College, DE (W)
Goucher College, MD (MW)
Harper William Rainey College, IL (M)
Louisiana Tech University, LA (MW)
Maple Woods Community College, MO (M)
San Diego Mesa College, CA (MW)
Scottsdale Community College, AR (MW)
Snow College, UT (MW)

Riflery

Canisius College, NY (MW)
Centenary College, LA (MW)
Citadel, SC (M)
Cornell University, NY (MW)
Dartmouth College, NH (MW)
DePaul University, IL (MW)
Eastern New Mexico University, NM (MW)
Hardin-Simmons University, TX (MW)
Indiana University of Pennsylvania, PA (M)
Jacksonville State University, AL (M)
Jacksonville University, FL (MW)
Johns Hopkins University, MD (MW)
King's College, PA (MW)
Lehigh University, PA (MW)
Marion Military Institute, AL (M)
Massachusetts Institute of Technology, MA (MW)
Middle Tennessee State University, TN (MW)
Mississippi State University, MS (MW)
Morgan State University, MD (MW)
Murray State University, KY (MW)
New Jersey Institute of Technology, NJ (M)
Nicholls State University, LA (M)
North Carolina State University, NC (MW)
Northeastern Junior College, CO (MW)
North Georgia College, GA (MW)
Norwich University, VT (MW)
Ohio State University, OH (MW)
Rider College, NJ (MW)
Rose-Hulman Institute of Technology, (M)
Saint Louis University, MO (M)
Southwerst Missouri State University, MO (M)
State University of New York Maritime College, NY (M)
Tennessee Technological University, TN (MW)
Texas A & I University, TX (MW)
Texas A & M University, TX (M)
Texas Christian University, TX (MW)
Trinity University,TX (MW)
University of Akron, OH (M)
University of Alabama (Birmingham), AL (M)
University of Alaska (Fairbanks), AK (MW)
University of Alaska Southeast, AK (MW)
University of Kentucky, KY (MW)
University of San Francisco, CA (MW)
University of Tennessee (Martin), TN (MW)
University of Texas (Arlington), TX (MW)
University of Texas (El Paso), TX (MW)
University of Texas (San Antonio), TX (MW)
Virginia Military Institute, VA (M)
West Texas State University, TX (MW)
West Virginia University, WVV(MW)

Rodeo

Austin College, TX (MW)
Austin Community College, MN (MW)

Bismarck State College, ND (MW)
Central Arizona College, AZ (MW)
Central Wyoming College, WY (MW)
Chadron State College, NE (M)
Colby Community College, KS (MW)
College of Southern Idaho, ID (MW)
Dawson Community College, MT (MW)
Dickinson State University, ND (MW)
Dodge City Community College, KS (M)
Eastern New Mexico University, NM (MW)
Eastern Oklahoma State College, OK (M)
Fort Scott College, KS (MW)
Frank Phillips College, TX (MW)
Laramie County Community College, WY (MW)
Miles Community College, MT (MW)
Mississippi State University, MS (MW)
Montana State University, MT (MW)
Navajo Community College, AZ (MW)
New Mexico Junior College, NM (MW)
Northwestern Oklahoma State University, OK (M)
Odessa College, TX (M)
Otero Junior College, CO (MW)
Prairie View A & M University, TX (M)
Pratt Community College, KS (MW)
Sam Houston State University, TX (MW)
Southeastern Oklahoma State University, OK (MW)
Southern Arkansas University, AR (MW)
South Plains Community College, TX (MW)
Southwest Missouri State University, MO (M)
Sul Ross State University, TX (MW)
Tarleton State University, TX (MW)
Texas Tech University, TX (MW)
Utah State University, UT (M)
Walla Walla Community College, WA (MW)
Weber State College, UT (MW)
Western Texas College, TX (MW)
Wharton County Junior College, TX (MW)

Rugby

Brigham Young University, HI (M)
California State University (Long Beach), CA (M)
Fairfield University, CT (M)
Florida State University, FL (MW)
Iona College, NY (MW)
Lafayette College, PA (M)
Manhattanville College, NY (M)
Mississippi State University, MS (M)
Norwich University, VT (MW)
Saint Mary's College of California, CA (M)
State University of New York Maritime College, NY (M)
Trinity College, CT (MW)
Trinity College, IL (MW)
University of California (Berkeley), CA (M)
University of California (San Diego), CA (M)
University of Rhode Island, RI (M)
University of Wisconsin (La Crosse), WI (M)
University of the Pacific, CA (M)
Utah State University, UT (M)
Villanova University, PA (M)

Sailing

Boston College, MA (MW)
Bowdoin College, ME (MW)
Brandeis University, MA (MW)
Broward Community College, FL (MW)
California Institute of Technology, CA (MW)
California Maritime Academy, CA (M)
Christopher Newport College, VA (MW)
Cleveland State University, OH (MW)
College of Charleston, SC (MW)
Connecticut College, CT (MW)
Cornell University, NY (MW)
Dartmouth College, NH (MW)
Dowling College, NY (MW)
Fairfield University, CT (MW)
Franklin Pierce College, NH (MW)
Georgetown University, DC (MW)
Goucher College, MD (MW)
Harvard University, MA (MW)
Lambuth University, TN (M)
Massachusetts Institute of Technology, MA (MW)
Mercer University, GA (W)
Mitchell College, CT (MW)
Mobile College, AL (W)
Muhlenberg College, PA (W)
Norwich University, VT (MW)
Old Dominion University, VA (MW)
Orange Coast College, CA (MW)
Rollins College, FL (MW)
Saint Mary's College, MD (MW)
Salem State College, MA (MW)
Stanford University, CA (MW)
State University of New York Maritime College, NY (M)
Stonehill College, MA (MW)
Tufts University, MA (W)
University of California (Irvine), CA (MW)
University of California (San Diego), CA (MW)
University of California (Santa Cruz), CA (MW)
University of Hawaii (Manoa), HI (MW)
University of Rhode Island, RI (MW)
University of Scranton, PA (W)
University of Southern California, CA (MW)
University of Wisconsin (Green Bay), WI (MW)
Westfield State College, MA (M)

Soccer

Adelphi University, NY (MW)
Adirondack College, NY (MW)
Adrian College, MI (MW)
Alabama A & M University, AL (M)
Albertson College, ID (M)
Albion College, MI (M)
Albright College, PA (M)
Alderson-Broaddus College, WV (M)
Alfred University, NY (MW)
Allegheny CCAC, PA (M)
Allegheny College, PA (MW)
Allen County College, KS (M)
Allentown College, PA (M)
Alma College, MI (M)
American International College, MA (MW)
American University, DC (M)
Amherst College, MA (MW)
Anderson College, SC (MW)
Anderson University, IN (M)
Andrew College, GA (MW)
Appalachian State University, NC (M)

Apprentice School, VA (M)
Aquinas College, MI (MW)
Asbury College, KY (M)
Ashland College, OH (M)
Atlantic Community College, NJ (M)
Atlantic Union College, MA (M)
Auburn University (Montgomery), AL (M)
Augsburg College, MN (MW)
Augusta College, GA (M)
Augustana College, IL (M)
Aurora University, IL (M)
Austin College, TX (M)
Austin Community College, MN (M)
Averett College, VA (M)
Avila College, MO (M)
Azusa Pacific University, CA (M)
Babson College, MA (MW)
Baker University, KS (MW)
Bard College, NY (M)
Barry University, FL (MW)
Bartlesville Wesleyan, OK (M)
Barton College, NC (M)
Bates College, ME (MW)
Becker College, MA (MW)
Belhaven College, MS (M)
Bellarmine College, KY (MW)
Belmont Abbey College, NC (M)
Belmont College, TN (M)
Beloit College, WI (MW)
Benedictine College, KS (MW)
Bentley College, MA (M)
Bergen Community College, NJ (M)
Berry College, GA (MW)
Bethany College, KS (M)
Bethany College, WV (M)
Bethany Lutheran College, MN (M)
Bethel College, IN (M)
Bethel College, KS (MW)
Bethel College, MN (M)
Biola University, CA (M)
Birmingham-Southern College, AL (M)
Blackburn College, IL (M)
Bloomfield College, NJ (M)
Bloomsburg University, PA (MW)
Bluffton College, OH (MW)
Boston College, MA (MW)
Boston University, MA (M)
Bowdoin College, ME (MW)
Bowling Green State University, OH (M)
Bradley University, IL (MW)
Brandeis University, MA (MW)
Brescia College, KY (M)
Brevard College, FL (MW)
Brevard College, NC (MW)
Brewton Parker College, GA (M)
Bridgewater College, VA (M)
Bridgewater State College, MA (MW)
Brigham Young University, UT (M)
Bronx Community College, NY (M)
Broome Community College, NY (M)
Brown University, RI (MW)
Bryant College, RI (MW)
Bryn Mawr College, PA (W)
Bucknell University, PA (MW)
Bucks County Community College, PA (MW)
Buffalo State College, NY (MW)
Buffalo State University (New York), NY (MW)
Bunker Hill Community College, MA (MW)
Butler University, IN (MW)
Cabrillo College, CA (M)
Cabrini College, PA (M)
California Baptist College, CA (M)
California Institute of Technology, CA (MW)
California Lutheran University, CA (M)
California Maritime Academy, CA (M)
California Polytechnic State University, CA (M)
California State Polytechnic University, CA (MW)
California State University, CA (M)
California State University at Bakersfield, CA (M)
California State University (Chico), CA (MW)
California State University (Dominguez Hills), CA (MW)
California State University (Fresno), CA (M)
California State University (Fullerton), CA (M)
California State University (Hayward), CA (MW)
California State University (Long Beach), CA (W)
California State University (Los Angeles), CA (M)
California State University (Northridge), CA (M)
California State University (Sacramento), CA (M)
California State University (San Bernardino), CA (M)
California University, PA (MW)
Calvin College, MI (MW)
Campbellsville College, KY (M)
Campbell University, NC (MW)
Canisius College, NY (MW)
Capital University, OH (M)
Carleton College, MN (MW)
Carnegie-Mellon University, PA (MW)
Carson-Newman College, TN (M)
Case Western Reserve University, OH (MW)
Castleton State College, VT (MW)
Catawba College, NC (MW)
Catholic University of America, DC (M)
Catonsville Community College, MD (MW)
Cecil Community College, MD (M)
Cedarville College, OH (M)
Centenary College, LA (MW)
Centenary College, NJ (MW)
Central Community College, NE (M)
Central Connecticut State University, CT (M)
Central Methodist College, MO (MW)
Central Michigan University, MI (M)
Central Wesleyan College, SC (M)
Cerritos College, CA (M)
Champlain College, VT (M)
Chapman University, CA (MW)
Charles County Community College, MD (M)
Charleston Southern University, SC (M)
Cheyney University of Pennsylvania, PA (MW)
Chicago State University, IL (M)
Christian Brothers College, TN (MW)
Christopher Newport College, VA (M)
Citadel, SC (M)
City College of New York, NY (M)
City College of San Francisco, CA (M)
Clarkson University, NY (MW)
Clark University, MA (MW)
Clemson University, SC (M)
Cleveland State University, OH (M)
Cloud County Community College, KS (M)
Coastal Carolina College, SC (M)
Coe College, IA (MW)
Coker College, SC (MW)
Colby-Sawyer College, NH (MW)
Colgate University, NY (MW)
College of Charleston, SC (M)
College of Charleston, SC (M)

College of Idaho, ID (M)
College of Notre Dame, CA (M)
College of Notre Dame of Maryland, MD (M)
College of St. Benedict, MN (W)
College of St. Francis, IL (M)
College of St. Rose, NY (MW)
College of St. Scholastica, MN (M)
College of the Desert, CA (M)
College of William and Mary, VA (MW)
College of Wooster, OH (MW)
Colorado Christian University, CO (M)
Colorado College, CO (MW)
Colorado School of Mines, CO (M)
Columbia Christian College, OR (M)
Columbia College, MO (M)
Columbia-Green Community College, NY (M)
Columbia Union College, MD (M)
Columbia University, NY (MW)
Columbus College, GA (M)
Columbus State Community College, OH (M)
Community College of Rhode Island, RI (M)
Community College of the Finger Lakes, NY (MW)
Community Colleges of Spokane, WA (M)
Concordia College (Moorhead), MI (M)
Concordia College (St. Paul), MN (M)
Concordia College, MN (M)
Concordia College, NY (M)
Concordia Teachers College, NE (M)
Connecticut College, CT (MW)
Coppin State College, MD (M)
Cornell College, IA (MW)
Cornell University, NY (MW)
Cosummes River College, CA (M)
Covenant College, GA (M)
Curry College, MA (MW)
Cuyahoga Community College, OH (MW)
Dallas Baptist University, TX (M)
Dalton College, GA (MW)
Dartmouth College, NH (MW)
Davidson College, NC (MW)
Davis & Elkins College, WV (M)
Dean Junior College, MA (MW)
De Anza Community College, CA (M)
Defiance College, OH (M)
Delaware Valley College, PA (M)
Delta College, MI (M)
Denison University, OH (MW)
DePaul University, IL (M)
De Pauw University, IN (M)
Detroit College of Business, MI (M)
Dickinson College, PA (MW)
Dominican College of Blauvelt, NY (M)
Dowling College, NY (M)
Drake University, IA (M)
Drew University, NJ (M)
Drexel University, PA (M)
Drury College, MO (M)
Duke University, NC (M)
Dundalk Community College, MD (MW)
Dutchess Junior College, NY (MW)
Earlham College, IN (M)
East Carolina University, NC (M)
East Central College, MO (M)
Eastern College, PA (MW)
Eastern Connecticut State University, Ct (MW)
Eastern Illinois University, IL (M)
Eastern Mennonite College, VA (M)
Eastern Michigan University, MI (M)
Eastern Nazarene College, MA (M)
East Stroudsburg University, PA (M)
Edgewood College, WI (M)
Edinboro University of Pennsylvania, PA (M)
Edmonds Community College, WA (M)
El Camino College, Ca (MW)
Elizabethtown College, PA (M)
Elmira College, NY (MW)
Elon College, NC (MW)
Emerson College, MA (M)
Emory University, GA (M)
Erskine College, SC (MW)
Everett Community College, WA (M)
Evergreen State College, WA (MW)
Fairfield University, CT (MW)
Fairleigh Dickinson University (Madison), NJ (M)
Fairleigh Dickinson University (Teaneck), NJ (M)
Fairleigh Dickinson University (Rutherford), NJ (M)
Ferrum College, Va (MW)
Fisk University, TN (M)
Fitchburg State College, MA (M)
Flagler College, FL (M)
Florida Atlantic University, FL (M)
Florida International University, FL (MW)
Florida State University, FL (MW)
Foothill College, CA (M)
Fordham University, NY (MW)
Fort Lewis College, CO (M)
Fort Steilacoom Community College, WA (M)
Francis Marion University, SC (M)
Franklin & Marshall College, PA (MW)
Franklin Pierce College, NH (MW)
Frederick Community College, MD (W)
Fresno City College, CA (MW)
Fresno Pacific College, CA (M)
Friends University, KS (M)
Fullerton College, Ca (M)
Fulton-Montgomery Community College, NY (M)
Furman University, SC (M)
Garden City Community College, KS (M)
Genesee Community College, KS (M)
Genesee Community College, NY (MW)
Geneva College, PA (MW)
George Fox College, OR (MW)
George Mason University, VA (MW)
Georgetown College, KY (M)
George Washington University, DC (MW)
Georgia College, GA (M)
Georgia Southern University, GA (M)
Georgia State University, GA (M)
Gettysburg College, PA (MW)
Glendale Community College, AZ (M)
Glendale Community College, CA (M)
Gloucester County College, NJ (M)
Golden West College, CA (MW)
Goldey-Beacom College, DE (M)
Gonzaga University, WA (MW)
Gordon College, MA (MW)
Goshen College, IN (MW)
Goucher College, MD (W)
Grace College, IN (M)
Graceland College, IA (M)
Grand Canyon College, AZ (M)
Grand Rapids Baptist College and Seminary, MI (M)
Grand View College, IA (M)
Grays Harbor College, WA (M)

Greenfield Community College, MA (MW)
Green Mountain College, VT (MW)
Green River Community College, WA (M)
Greensboro College, NC (M)
Greenville College, IL (M)
Grinnell College, IA (M)
Grove City College, PA (M)
Gustavus Adolphus College, MN (MW)
Hagerstown Junior College, MD (M)
Hamilton College, NY (MW)
Hamline University, MN (M)
Hampden-Sydney College, VA (M)
Hanover College, IN (M)
Hardin-Simmons University, TX (MW)
Harford Community College, MD (M)
Harris-Stowe State College, MO (M)
Hartwick College, NY (MW)
Harvard University, MA (MW)
Haverford College, PA (MW)
Hawaii Pacific University, HI (M)
Heidelberg College, OH (W)
Herkimer County Community College, NY (MW)
Hesser College, NH (M)
High Point University, NC (MW)
Hilbert College, NY (MW)
Hiram College, OH (MW)
Hofstra University, NY (MW)
Holy Cross College, MA (MW)
Holy Family College, PA (MW)
Hope College, MI (M)
Houghton College, NY (MW)
Houston Baptist University, TX (MW)
Howard University, DC (M)
Hudson Valley Community College, NY (M)
Humboldt State University, CA (M)
Hunter College of the City University of New York, NY (M)
Huntingdon College, AL (MW)
Huntington College, IN (M)
Husson College, ME (M)
Illinois Benedictine College, IL (M)
Illinois College, IL (MW)
Illinois State University, IL (M)
Illinois Wesleyan University, IL (M)
Incarnate Word College, TX (MW)
Indiana University, IN (M)
Indiana University of Pennsylvania, PA (M)
Indiana University-Purdue University, IN (M)
Indiana University-Purdue University (Fort Wayne), IN (M)
Indiana Wesleyan University, IN (MW)
Iona College, NY (MW)
Ithaca College, NY (MW)
Jacksonville University, FL (MW)
James Madison University, VA (M)
Jefferson Community College, NY (MW)
John Brown University, AR (M)
John Carroll University, OH (M)
Johns Hopkins University, MD (MW)
Johnson County Community College, KS (M)
Johnson State College, VT (MW)
Juniata College, PA (M)
Kalamazoo College, MI (MW)
Kansas Newman College, KS (MW)
Kean College of New Jersey, NJ (MW)
Kennesaw State College, GA (M)
Keene State College, NH (MW)
Kentucky Christian College, KY (M)
Kentucky Wesleyan College, KY (M)
Kenyon College, OH (MW)
Keystone Junior College, PA (M)
King College, TN (M)
King's College, NY (M)
King's College, PA (M)
Kishwaukee College, IL (M)
Knox College, IL (M)
Kutztown University, PA (MW)
Lafayette College, PA (M)
Lake Forest College, IL (MW)
Lambuth University, TN (W)
Lander College, SC (M)
La Roche College, PA (M)
La Salle University, PA (M)
Lawrence University, WI (MW)
Lebanon Valley College, PA (M)
Lee College, TN (MW)
Lees-McRae College, NC (MW)
Lehigh University, PA (M)
Le Moyne College, NY (MW)
Lenoir-Rhyne College, NC (MW)
LeToumeau College, TX (M)
Lewis and Clark College, OR (MW)
Lewis and Clark Community College, IL (M)
Lewis University, IL (MW)
Liberty University, VA (MW)
Limestone College, SC (MW)
Lincoln Christian College, IL (M)
Lincoln College, IL (M)
Lincoln Land Community College, IL (M)
Lincoln Memorial University, TN (M)
Lincoln University, MO (M)
Lindenwood College, MO (MW)
Linfield College, OR (MW)
Lock Haven University of Pennsylvania, PA (M)
Long Beach City College, CA (MW)
Long Island University (Brooklyn), NY (M)
Long Island University (C. W. Post Campus), NY (M)
Long Island University (Southhampton Campus), NY (MW)
Longwood College, kVA (M)
Loras College, IA (M)
Los Angeles Pierce Junior College, CA (M)
Los Medanos College, CA (M)
Louisiana Tech University, LA (MW)
Lower Columbia College, WA (M)
Loyola College, MD (MW)
Loyola Marymount University, CA (MW)
Loyola University, IL (MW)
Lubbock Christian College, TX (M)
Lycoming College, PA (M)
Lynchburg College, VA (M)
Lyndon State College, VT (MW)
Lynn University, FL (MW)
Macalester College, MN (MW)
Macomb Community College, MI (M)
Malone College, OH (M)
Manchester College, IN (M)
Manchester Community Technical College, CT (M)
Manhattan College, NY (M)
Manhattan Community College, NY (M)
Manhattanville Community College, NY (M)
Marian College, IN (M)
Marian College, WI (MW)
Marietta College, OH (M)

Marist College, NY (M)
Marquette University, WI (MW)
Marshall University, WV (M)
Mars Hill College, NC (MW)
Marycrest College, IA (M)
Marymount College, CA (MW)
Marymount University, VA (MW)
Maryville College, TN (M)
Maryville University, MO (MW)
Mary Washington College, VA (MW)
Massachusetts Institute of Technology, MA (MW)
Massasoit Community College, MA (MW)
Master's College, CA (MW)
McHenry County College, IL (M)
McKendree College, IL (M)
Memphis State University, TN (M)
Mercer County Community College, NJ (MW)
Mercer University, GA (M)
Mercy College, NY (MW)
Mercyhurst College, PA (MW)
Merrimack College, MA (MW)
Mesa Community College, AZ (M)
Messiah College, PA (M)
Metropolitan State College, CO (MW)
Miami University, OH (M)
Miami-Dade Community College (North), FL (W)
Miami-Dade Community College (South Campus), FL (M)
Michigan Christian College, MI (M)
Michigan State University, MI (MW)
Mid-America Nazarene College, KS (M)
Middlebury College, VT (MW)
Middlesex County College, NJ (M)
Midwestern State University, TX (M)
Millersville University, PA (M)
Millikin University, IL (M)
Milwaukee Area Technology College, WI (M)
Mississippi State University, MS (M)
Missouri Baptist College, MO (MW)
Missouri Southern State College, MO (M)
Missouri Valley College, MO (MW)
Mitchell College, CT (MW)
Mobile College, AL (MW)
Modesto Junior College, CA (MW)
Mohawk Valley Community College, NY (MW)
Molloy College, NY (W)
Monmouth College, IL (M)
Monmouth College, NJ (MW)
Montclair State College, NJ (M)
Montgomery College, MD (M)
Montreat-Anderson College, NC (M)
Moody Bible Institute, IL (M)
Moorpark College, CA (MW)
Moraine Valley Community College, IL (M)
Moravian College, PA, (M)
Morehead State University, KY (MW)
Mount Holyoke College, MA (W)
Mount Marty College, SD (M)
Mount Mercy College, IA (M)
Mount Olive College, NC (M)
Mount St. Mary College, MD (MW)
Mount Union College, OH (M)
Mount Vernon Nazarene College, OH (M)
Mt. San Antonio College, CA (MW)
Muhlenberg College, PA (MW)
Multnomah School of the Bible, OR (M)
Muskingum College, OH (MW)
Nassau Community College, NY (MW)
National-Louis University, IL (M)
Nazareth College, NY (MW)
New Hampshire College, NH (MW)
New Jersey Institute of Technology, NJ (M)
New York Institute of Technology, NY (M)
New York State University Institute of Technology, NY (MW)
New York University, NY (M)
Niagara University, NY (MW)
Nicholls State University, LA (M)
Nichols College, MA (M)
North Adams State College, MA (MW)
North Carolina State University, NC (MW)
North Carolina Wesleyan College, NC (MW)
North Central College, IL (M)
North Central Missouri College, MO (W)
North Country Community College, NY (MW)
Northeastern Christian Junior College, PA (M)
Northeastern State University, OK (MW)
Northeast Missouri State University, MO (MW)
Northern Illinois University, IL (MW)
Northern Kentucky University, KY (M)
North Georgia College, GA (M)
Northland College, WE (M)
Northwestern College, MN (M)
Northwestern University, IL (M)
Northwest Nazarene College, ID (M)
Norwich University, VT (MW)
Nova University, FL (M)
Nyack College, NY (MW)
Oakland University, MI (M)
Oberlin College, OH (MW)
Occidental College, CA (MW)
Ocean County College, NJ (M)
Oglethorpe University, GA (MW)
Ohio Dominican College, OH (M)
Ohio Northern University, OH (M)
Ohio State University, OH (M)
Ohio Wesleyan University, OH (M)
Oklahoma Christian University of Science & Art, OK (M)
Oklahoma City University, OK (M)
Old Dominion University, VA (M)
Olivet College, MI (M)
Olivet Nazarene University, IL (M)
Oral Roberts University, OK (M)
Orange Coast College, CA (MW)
Orange County Community College, NY (MW)
Ottawa University, KS (M)
Otterbein College, OH (MW)
Oxnard College, CA (M)
Pace University, NY (M)
Pace University (White Plains Campus), NY (M)
Pacific Lutheran University, WA (MW)
Pacific University, OR (MW)
Palm Beach Atlantic College, FL (M)
Palomar College, CA (MW)
Pan American University, TX (M)
Park College, MO (MW)
Parks College of St. Louis University, IL (W)
Passaic County Community College, NJ (M)

Pembroke State University, NC (M)
Penn State University, PA (M)
Pennsylvania State University, PA (M)
Pennsylvania State University (Behrend College), PA (M)
Pepperdine University, CA (W)
Pfeiffer College, NC (M)
Philadelphia College of Textile and Science, PA (MW)
Philadelphia Community College, PA (M)
Phillips University, OK (M)
Phoenix College, AZ (M)
Piedmont College, GA (MW)
Plymouth State College, NH (MW)
Point Loma Nazarene College, NH (MW)
Point Park College, PA (M)
Polytechnic University (Brooklyn Campus), NY (M)
Pomona-Pitzer Colleges, CA (MW)
Presbyterian College, SC (MW)
Prince George's Community College, MD (M)
Princeton University, NJ (MW)
Principia College, IL (MW)
Providence College, RI (MW)
Purdue University (Calumet), IN (M)
Queensborough Community College, NY (M)
Queens College, NY (M)
Queens College, NC (MW)
Quincy College, IL (MW)
Quinnipiac College, CT (MW)
Radford University, VA (MW)
Ramapo College, NJ (M)
Randolph-Macon College, VA (MW)
Ranetto Santiago College, CA (M)
Regis College, MA (W)
Regis University, CO (MW)
Rensselaer Polytechnic Institute, NY (MW)
Rhode Island College, RI (M)
Rider College, NJ (M)
Ripon College, WI (MW)
Roanoke College, VA (M)
Robert Morris College, PA (MW)
Roberts Wesleyan College, NY (MW)
Rochester Institute of Technology, NY (MW)
Rockhurst College, MO (M)
Rockland Community College, NY (M)
Rollins College, FL (M)
Roosevelt University, IL (M)
Rosary College, IL (M)
Rose-Hulman Institute of Technology, IN (M)
Rowan College of New Jersey, NJ (M)
Sacred Heart University, CT (M)
Saint Andrews Presbyterian College, NC (M)
Saint Anselm College, NH (MW)
Saint Augustine's College, NC (M)
Saint Bonaventure University, NY (MW)
Saint Edward's University, TX (MW)
Saint Francis College, IN (M)
Saint Francis College, NY (M)
Saint Francis College, PA (MW)
Saint John Fisher College, NY (MW)
Saint John's University, MN (M)
Saint John's University, NY (M)
Saint Joseph's College, IN (M)
Saint Joseph's University, PA (M)
Saint Lawrence University, NY (MW)
Saint Leo College, FL (M)
Saint Louis University, MO (M)
Saint Mary College, KS (MW)
Saint Mary's College, IN (W)
Saint Mary's College, MD (MW)
Saint Mary's College, MI (W)
Saint Mary's College of California, CA (MW)
Saint Mary's University, TX (M)
Saint Michael's College, VT (MW)
Saint Norbert College, WI (MW)
Saint Olaf College, MN (MW)
Saint Peter's College, NJ (MW)
Saint Thomas Aquinas College, NY (W)
Saint Thomas University, FL (MW)
Saint Vincent College, PA (M)
Saint Xavier University, IL (M)
Salem State College, MA (MW)
Salem-Teikyo University, WV (M)
Salve Regina College, RI (MW)
Sam Houston State University, TX (M)
San Diego City College, CA (M)
San Diego Mesa College, CA (MW)
San Diego State University, CA (MW)
San Francisco State University, CA (MW)
San Joaquin Delta College, CA (M)
San Jose State University, CA (M)
Santa Barbara City College, CA (MW)
Santa Clara University, CA (MW)
Santa Monica College, CA (M)
Santa Rosa Junior College, CA (MW)
Sauk Valley College, IL (M)
Schoolcraft College, MI (MW)
Schreiner College, TX (MW)
Scottsdale Community College, AR (M)
Seattle Pacific University, WA (M)
Seattle University, WA (MW)
Seton Hall University, NJ (M)
Seton Hill College, PA (W)
Shawnee State University, OH (M)
Shepherd College, WV (M)
Shippensburg University of Pennsylvania, PA (M)
Shoreline Community College, WA (M)
Siena College, NY (MW)
Siena Heights College, MI (MW)
Skagit Valley College, WA (M)
Skidmore College, NY (MW)
Skyline College, CA (M)
Slippery Rock University of Pennsylvania, PA (M)
Smith College, MA (W)
Snow College, UT (MW)
Southeastern Massachusetts University, MA (M)
Southeast Missouri State University, MO (M)
Southern California College, CA (M)
Southern Connecticut State University, CT (M)
Southern Illinois University (Edwardsville), IL (MW)
Southern Methodist University, TX (MW)
Southern Nazarene University, OK (M)
Southern Oregon State College, OR (MW)
Southwest, NM (MW)
Southwestern College, CA (M)
Southwest Missouri State University, MO (M)
Spartanburg Methodist, SC (M)
Spring Arbor College, MI (M)
Springfield College, MA (MW)
Springfield Technical Community College, MA (M)
Stanford University, CA (MW)

State Fair Community College, MO (W)
State University of New York, NY (MW)
State University of New York (Albany), NY (MW)
State University of New York (Binghamton), NY (MW)
State University of New York (Buffalo), NY (W)
State University of New York (Plattsburgh), NY (MW)
State University of New York (Stony Brook), NY (MW)
State University of New York College (Brockport), NY (MW)
State University of New York College (Cortland), NY (MW)
State University of New York College (Fredonia), NY (MW)
State University of New York College (Geneseo), NY (MW)
State University of New York College (New Paltz), NY (MW)
State University of New York College (Oswego), NY (MW)
State University of New York College (Potsdam), NY (M)
State University of New York College (Purchase), NY (M)
State University of New York Maritime College, NY (M)
Stetson University, FL (MW)
Stevens Institute of Technology, NJ (M)
St. Louis Community College (Florissant Valley), MO (M)
St. Louis Community College (Forest Park), MO (M)
Stonehill College, MA (MW)
Sue Bennett College, KY (MW)
Suffolk County Community College, NY (MW)
Suffolk University, MA (M)
Swarthmore College, PA (MW)
Sweet Briar College, VA (W)
Syracuse University, NY (M)
Tabor College, KS (M)
Tampa College, FL (M)
Teikyo Marycrest University, IA (MW)
Teikyo Post University, CT (MW)
Teikyo Westmar University, IA (MW)
Temple University, PA (M)
Tennessee Temple University, TN (M)
Tennessee Wesleyan College, TN (MW)
Texas A & I University, TX (W)
Texas A & M University, TX (W)
Texas Christian University, TX (MW)
Texas Lutheran College, TX (M)
Texas Southern University, TX (M)
Texas Tech University, TX (M)
Thomas College, ME (MW)
Tiffin University, OH (M)
Toccoa Falls College, GA (M)
Towson State University, MD (M)
Transylvania University, KY (M)
Trenton State College, NJ (M)
Trinity Christian College, IL (M)
Trinity College, CT (MW)
Trinity College, IL (MW)
Trinity University, TX (MW)
Tri-State University, IN (MW)
Triton College, IL (M)
Truett-McConnell Junior College, GA (M)
Tufts University, MA (MW)
Tusculum College, TN (M)
Tyler Junior College, TX (M)
Union College, NY (MW)
Union County College, NJ (M)
Unity College, ME (M)
University of Akron, OH (M)
University of Alabama (Birmingham), AL (M)
University of Alabama (Huntsville), Al (M)
University of Arkansas (Fayetteville), AR (W)
University of Arkansas (Little Rock), AR (M)
University of Bridgeport, CT (MW)
University of California (Berkeley), CA (MW)
University of California (Davis), CA (MW)
University of California (Irvine), CA (MW)
University of California (San Diego), CA (MW)
University of California (Santa Barbara), CA (MW)
University of California (Santa Cruz), CA (M)
University of California (UCLA), CA (M)
University of Central Florida, FL (MW)
University of Charleston, WV (MW)
University of Cincinnati, OH (MW)
University of Colorado (Colorado Springs), CO (M)
University of Connecticut, CT (MW)
University of Dayton, OH (MW)
University of Delaware, DE (MW)
University of Denver, CO (MW)
University of Detroit Mercy, MI (MW)
University of Evansville, IN (MW)
University of Findlay, OH (MW)
University of Hartford, CT (MW)
University of Indianapolis, IN (M)
University of Kentucky, KY (MW)
University of La Verne, CA (M)
University of Louisville, KY (MW)
University of Lowell, MA (M)
University of Maine, ME (M)
University of Maine (Fort Kent), ME (W)
University of Maine (Machias), ME (MW)
University of Maine (Presque Isle), ME (MW)
University of Mary Hardin-Baylor, TX (M)
University of Maryland, MD (MW)
University of Maryland (Baltimore County), MD (MW)
University of Massachusetts (Amherst), MA (MW)
University of Massachusetts (Boston), MA (M)
University of Missouri (Rolla), MO (MW)
University of Nevada, NV (M)
University of New England, ME (M)
University of New Hampshire, NH (MW)
University of New Haven, CT (M)
University of New Mexico, NM (M)
University of North Carolina (Asheville), NC (MW)
University of North Carolina (Chapel Hill), NC (MW)
University of North Carolina (Charlotte), NC (M)
University of North Carolina (Greensboro), NC (M)
University of North Carolina (Wilmington), NC (M)
University of Northern Colorado, CO (W)

University of North Texas, TX (M)
University of Notre Dame, IN (MW)
University of Pennsylvania, PA (M)
University of Pittsburgh, PA (M)
University of Pittsburgh (Bradford), PA (M)
University of Pittsburgh (Johnstown), PA (M)
University of Portland, OR (MW)
University of Puerto Rico, PR (M)
University of Puget Sound, WA (MW)
University of Redlands, CA (MW)
University of Rhode Island, RI (MW)
University of Richmond, VA (M)
University of Rio Grande, OH (M)
University of San Diego, CA (M)
University of San Francisco, CA (MW)
University of Scranton, PA (M)
University of South Alabama, AL (M)
University of South Carolina, SC (M)
University of South Carolina (Aiken), SC (M)
University of South Carolina (Spartanburg), SC (M)
University of Southern Colorado, CO (M)
University of Southern Indiana, IN (M)
University of South Florida, FL (M)
University of St. Thomas, MN (MW)
University of Tampa, FL (M)
University of Tennessee, TN (M)
University of Tennessee (Knoxville), TN (M)
University of Texas (Pan American), TX (M)
University of Texas (San Antonio), TX (M)
University of the Pacific, CA (M)
University of Tulsa, OK (MW)
University of Vermont, VT (MW)
University of Virginia, VA (MW)
University of Washington, WA (M)
University of Wisconsin (Eau Claire), WI (W)
University of Wisconsin (Green Bay), WI (M)
University of Wisconsin (Madison), WI (MW)
University of Wisconsin (Milwaukee), WI (MW)
University of Wisconsin (Oshkosh), WI (M)
University of Wisconsin (Platteville), WI (M)
University of Wisconsin (Stevens Point), WI (W)
University of the District of Columbia, DC (M)
Ursinus College, PA (M)
U.S. International University, CA (M)
Valley Forge Christian College, PA (M)
Valparaiso University, IN (M)
Vanderbilt University, TN (MW)
Vassar College, NY (MW)
Villanova University, PA (MW)
Vincennes University Junior College, IN (M)
Virginia Commonwealth University, VA (M)
Virginia Military Institute, VA (M)
Virginia Polytechnic Institute & State University, VA (M)
Virginia Wesleyan College, VA (MW)
Viterbo College, WI (M)
Wabash College, IN (M)
Wake Forest University, NC (M)
Walsh College, OH (M)
Warner Pacific College, OR (M)
Warner Southern College, FL (M)
Warren Wilson College, NC (MW)
Wartburg College, IA (M)
Washington and Jefferson College, PA (MW)
Washington College, MD (M)
Washington State University, WA (W)
Washington University, MO (M)
Waubonsee College, IL (M)
Webber College, FL (MW)
Webster University, MO (M)
Wellesley College, MA (W)
Wesleyan University, CT (MW)
Wesley College, DE (M)
West Chester University, PA (MW)
Western Connecticut State University, CT (M)
Western Illinois University, IL (M)
Western Kentucky University, KY (M)
Western Maryland College, MD (MW)
Western Michigan University, MI (M)
Western New England College, MA (MW)
Western Washington University, WA (MW)
Westfield State College, MA (W)
West Liberty State College, WV (W)
Westminster College, PA (M)
Westmont College, CA (MW)
West Virginia University, WV (M)
West Virginia Wesleyan College, WV (M)
Wheaton College, IL (MW)
Wheeling Jesuit College, WV (MW)
Whitman College, WA (MW)
Whittier College, CA (MW)
Whitworth College, WA (MW)
Wilkes College, NC (M)
Wilkes University, OR (M)
Willamette University, OR (M)
William Jewell College, MO (M)
William Patterson College, NJ (M)
William Rainey Harper College, IL (M)
Williams College, MA (MW)
Williamson Trade School, PA (M)
William Woods College, MO (W)
Wilmington College, DE (MW)
Wilmington College, OH (MW)
Wingate College, NC (M)
Winthrop University, SC (M)
Wofford College, SC (M)
Wright State University, OH (MW)
Yale University, CT (MW)
York College (CUNY), NY (M)
York College of Pennsylvania, PA (M)
Youngstown State University, OH (M)

Softball

Adams State College, CO (W)
Adelphi University, NY (W)
Adirondack College, NY (W)
Adrian College, MI (W)
Albion College, MI (W)
Albright College, PA (W)
Alice Lloyd College, KY (W)
Allegheny College, KY (W)
Allen County College, KS (W)

Allentown College, PA (W)
Alma College, MI (MW)
Alvernia College, PA (W)
American International College, MA (W)
Anderson College, SC (W)
Anoka-Ramsey College, MN (W)
Apprentice School, VA (W)
Aquinas College, MI (W)
Arizona State University, AZ (W)
Arrowhead Community College, MN (W)
Asbury College, KY (W)
Ashland College, OH (W)
Athens State College, AL (W)
Augsburg College, MN (W)
Augusta College, GA (W)
Augustana College, IL (W)
Augustana College, SD (W)
Aurora University, IL (W)
Austin College, TX (MW)
Austin Community College, MN (MW)
Austin Peay State University, TN (W)
Averett College, VA (W)
Avila College, MO (W)
Azusa Pacific University, CA (W)
Babson College, MA (W)
Bacone Junior College, OK (W)
Baker University, KS (W)
Ball State University, IN (W)
Barber-Scotia College, NC (W)
Bard College, NY (W)
Barry University, FL (W)
Barstow College, CA (W)
Barton College, NC (W)
Barton County College, KS (W)
Bates College, ME (W)
Baylor University, TX (W)
Becker College, MA (W)
Belhaven College, MS (MW)
Bellarmine College, KY (W)
Belleville Area College, IL (W)
Bellevue College, NE (MW)
Bellevue Community College, WA (MW)
Belmont College, TN (W)
Beloit College, WI (W)
Benedict College, SC (W)
Benedictine College, KS (W)
Bentley College, MA (W)
Bergen Community College, NJ (W)
Bethany College, KS (MW)
Bethany College, WV (MW)
Bethany Lutheran College, MN (W)
Bethel College, IN (W)
Bethune-Cookman College, FL (W)
Big Bend Community College, WA (W)
Blackburn College, IL (MW)
Bloomfield College, NJ (W)
Bloomsburg University, PA (W)
Bluefield State College, WV (W)
Bluffton College, OH (W)
Boston College, MA (W)
Boston University, MA (W)
Bowdoin College, ME (W)
Bowie State University, MD (W)
Bowling Green State University, OH (W)
Bradley University, IL (MW)
Brainerd Community College, MN (W)
Brandeis University, MA (W)
Brevard College, FL (W)
Brewton Parker College, GA (W)
Briar Cliff College, IA (W)
Bridgewater College, VA (W)
Bronx Commuity College, NY (W)
Broome Community College, NY (W)
Broward Community College, FL (MW)
Brown University, RI (W)
Bryant College, RI (W)
Bucknell University, PA (W)
Bucks County Community College, PA (W)
Buena Vista College, IA (W)
Buffalo State College, NY (W)
Buffalo State University (New York), NY (W)
Bunker Hill Community College, KS (W)
Butler County Commuity College, KS (W)
Butler County Community College, PA (W)
Butler University, IN (W)
Butte College, CA (W)
Cabrillo College, CA (W)
Cabrini College, PA (MW)
California Baptist College, CA (W)
California Institute of Technology, CA (M)
California Lutheran University, CA (W)
California Polytechnic State University, CA (W)
California State Polytechnic University, CA (W)
California State University, CA (W)
California State University at Bakersfield, CA (W)
California State University (Chico), CA (W)
California State University (Dominguez Hills), CA (W)
California State University (Fresno), CA (W)
California State University (Fullerton), CA (W)
California State University (Hayward), CA (W)
California State University (Long Beach), CA (W)
California State University (Northridge), CA (W)
California State University (Sacramento), CA (W)
California State University (San Bernardino), CA (W)
California University, PA (M)
Calvin College, MI (W)
Cameron University, OK (W)
Campbellsville College, KY (W)
Campbell University, NC (W)
Capital University, OH (W)
Cardinal Stritch College, WI (W)
Carson-Newman College, TN (W)
Carthage College, WI (W)
Castleton State College, VT (W)
Catawba College, NC (W)
Catholic University of America, DC (W)
Catholic University of Puerto Rico, PR (MW)
Catonsville Community College, MD (W)
Cayuga County Community College, NY (W)
Cecil Community College, MD (W)
Cedarville College, OH (W)
Centenary College, LA (W)
Centenary College, NJ (W)
Central Arizona College, AZ (W)
Central College, IA (W)
Central College, KS (W)
Central Connecticut State University, CT (W)
Central Florida Community College, FL (W)
Central Methodist College, MO (W)
Central Michigan University, MI (W)
Central Missouri State University, MO (W)
Central Wesleyan College, SC (W)
Cerritos College, CA (W)
Chaffey College, CA (W)
Chaminade University, HI (W)
Champlain College, VT (W)
Chapman University, CA (W)
Charles County Community College, MD (W)

Charleston Southern University, SC (W)
Chattahoochee Valley Community College, AL (W)
Chicago State University, IL (W)
Chowan College, NC (W)
Christopher Newport College, VA (W)
City College of New York, NY (W)
Clackamas Community College, OR (W)
Clarion University, PA (W)
Clark University, MA (W)
Cleveland State University, OH (W)
Cloud County Community College, KS (W)
Coahoma Junior College, MS (W)
Coastal Carolina College, SC (W)
Coastal Carolina Community College, NC (MW)
Coe College, IA (W)
Coker College, SC (W)
Colby Community College, KS (W)
Colgate University, NY (W)
College of Allegheny County, PA (W)
College of Charleston, SC (W)
College of New Rochelle, NY (W)
College of Notre Dame, CA (W)
College of Notre Dame of Maryland, MD (W)
College of Saint Mary, NE (W)
College of St. Benedict, MN (W)
College of St. Francis, IL (W)
College of St. Mary, NE (W)
College of St. Rose, NY (W)
College of St. Scholastica, MN (W)
College of the Desert, CA (W)
College of the Redwoods, CA (W)
College of the Sequoias, CA (W)
Colorado Northwestern Community College, CO (W)
Colorado School of Mines, CO (W)
Columbia College, MO (W)
Columbia-Greene Community College, NY (W)
Columbia Union College, MD (W)
Columbus College, GA (W)
Columbus State Community College, OH (W)
Community College of Rhode Island, RI (W)
Community College of the Finger Lakes, NY (W)
Community Colleges of Spokane, WA (W)
Concord College, WV (W)
Concordia College, WV (W)
Concordia College (Duluth), MN (W)
Concordia College (St. Paul), MN (W)
Concordia College, NY (W)
Concordia Teachers College, NE (W)
Concordia University, IL (W)
Concordia University Wisconsin, WI (W)
Connors State College, OK (W)
Cornell College, IA (W)
Cosummes River College, CA (W)
Cowley County Community College, KS (W)
Creighton University, NE (W)
Crowder College, MO (W)
Cuesta College, CA (W)
Culver-Stockton College, MO (W)
Cumberland College, KY (W)
Curry College, MA (W)
Cuyahoga Community College, OH (W)
Dana College, NE (W)
Davis & Elkins College, WV (W)
Daytona Beach Community College, FL (W)
Dean Junior College, MA (W)
Defiance College, OH (W)
Delaware County Community College, PA (MW)
Delaware Valley College, PA (W)
Delta College, MI (W)
Delta State University, MS (W)
Denison University, OH (W)
DePaul University, IL (W)
De Pauw University, IN (MW)
Des Moines Area Community College, IA (W)
Diablo Valley Community College, CA (W)
Dickinson College, PA (W)
Dixie College, UT (W)
Doane College, NE (W)
Dodge City Community College, KS (W)
Dominican College of Blauvelt, NY (W)
Dowling College, NY (W)
Drake University, IA (W)
Drexel University, PA (W)
Dundalk Community College, MD (W)
Dutchess Junior College, NY (W)
Earlham College, IN (W)
East Carolina University, NC (W)
East Central College, MO (W)
Eastern College, PA (W)
Eastern Connecticut State University, CT (W)
Eastern Illinois University, IL (W)
Eastern Kentucky University, KY (W)
Eastern Mennonite College, VA (W)
Eastern Michigan University, MI (W)
Eastern Nazarene College, MA (W)
Eastern Oregon State College, OR (M)
Eastfield College, TX (MW)
East Stroudsburg University, PA (W)
Edgewood College, WI (W)
Edinboro University of Pennsylvania, PA (W)
Edison Community College, FL (W)
Edmonds Commuity College, WA (W)
Edward Waters College, FL (W)
El Camino College, CA (W)
Elgin Community College, IL (W)
Elizabeth City State University, NC (W)
Elizabethtown College, PA (W)
Elmhurst College, IL (W)
Elmira College, NY (W)
Elon College, NC (W)
Emerson College, MA (W)
Emporia State University, KS (W)
Enterprise State Junior College, AL (W)
Erskine College, SC (W)
Essex Community College, MD (M)
Eureka College, IL (W)
Fairfield University, CT (W)
Fairleigh Dickinson University (Madison), NJ (W)
Fairleigh Dickinson University (Teaneck), NJ (W)
Faulkner University, AL (W)
Fayetteville State University, NC (W)
Fergus Falls Community College, MN (W)
Ferris State College, MI (W)
Ferrum College, VA (W)
Fitchburg State College, MA (W)
Florida A & M University, FL (W)
Florida Institute of Technology, FL (W)

Florida Memorial College, FL (W)
Florida Southern College, FL (W)
Foothill College, CA (W)
Fordham University, NY (W)
Fort Lewis College, CO (W)
Fort Steilacoom Community College, WA (W)
Francis Marion University, SC (W)
Franklin & Marshall College, PA (W)
Franklin Pierce College, NH (W)
Frederick Community College, MD (M)
Freed-Hardeman College, TN (W)
Fresno City College, CA (W)
Friends University, KS (W)
Fullerton College, CA (W)
Fulton-Montgomery Community College, NY (W)
Furman University, SC (W)
Gadsden State Community College, AL (W)
Gannon College, PA (W)
Gardner-Webb College, NC (W)
Garrett Community College, MD (W)
Genesee Community College, NY (W)
Geneva College, PA (W)
George C. Wallace Community College, AL (W)
George Fox College, OR (W)
George Mason University, VA (W)
Georgetown College, KY (W)
Georgia College, GA (W)
Georgia Institute of Technology, GA (W)
Georgian Court College, NJ (W)
Georgia Southern University, GA (W)
Georgia Southwestern College, GA (W)
Georgia State University, GA (W)
Gettysburg College, PA (W)
Glendale Community College, AZ (W)
Golden West College, CA (W)
Goldey-Beacom College, DE (W)
Gordon College, MA (W)
Grace College, IN (W)
Graceland College, IA (W)
Grand Rapids Baptist College and Seminary, MI (W)
Grand Rapids Junior College, MI (W)
Grand Valley State College, MI (W)
Grand View College, IA (W)
Grays Harbor College, WA (W)
Greenfield Community College, MA (W)
Green Mountain College, VT (W)
Green River Community College, WA (W)
Greensboro College, NC (W)
Greenville College, IL (W)
Grinnell College, IA (W)
Grove City College, PA (MW)
Gulf Coast Community College, FL (W)
Gustavus Adolphus College, MN (W)
Hagerstown Junior College, MD (W)
Hamilton College, NY (W)
Hamline University, MN (MW)
Hannibal-Lagrange College, MO (W)
Hanover College, IN (W)
Harford Community College, MD (W)
Harper William Rainey College, IL (W)
Harvard University, MA (MW)
Hastings College, NE (W)
Hawaii Pacific University, HI (W)
Heidelberg College, OH (W)
Henry Ford Community College, MI (W)
Herkimer County Community College, NY (W)
Hesser College, NH (W)
Hibbing Community College, MN (W)
Highland Community College, KS (W)
Hilbert College, NY (W)
Hillsborough Community College, FL (W)
Hillsdale College, MI (W)
Hinds Community College, MS (W)
Hiram College, OH (W)
Hiwassee College, TN (W)
Hofstra University, NY (W)
Holy Cross College, MA (W)
Hope College, MI (W)
Hudson Valley Community College, NY (W)
Hunter College of the City University of New York, NY (W)
Huntingdon College, Al (W)
Huntington College, IN (W)
Husson College, ME (W)
Illinois Benedictine College, IL (W)
Illinois Central College, IL (W)
Illinois College, IL (W)
Illinois Institute of Technology, IL (W)
Illinois State University, IL (W)
Illinois Valley Community College, IL (W)
Illinois Wesleyan University, IL (W)
Incarnate Word College, TX (W)
Indiana State University, IN (W)
Indiana University, IN (W)
Indiana University of Pennsylvania, PA (W)
Indiana University-Purdue University, IN (W)
Indiana University-Purdue University (Fort Wayne), IN (W)
Indiana Wesleyan University, IN (W)
Inver Hills Community College, MN (W)
Iona College, NY (W)
Iowa State University of Science and Technology, IA (W)
Iowa Wesleyan College, IA (W)
Ithaca College, NY (W)
Jacksonville State University, AL (W)
Jamestown College, ND (W)
Jefferson Community College, NY (W)
Jefferson Davis Junior College, AL (W)
John Carroll University, OH (W)
John C. Calhoun State College, AL (W)
Johnson County Community College, KS (W)
Johnson C. Smith University, NC (W)
Johnson State College, VT (W)
Juniata College, PA (MW)
Kalamazoo Valley Community College, MI (W)
Kankakee Community College, IL (W)
Kansas City Kansas Community College, KS (W)
Kansas Newman College, KS (W)
Kansas Wesleyan College, KS (W)
Kaskaskia Community College, IL (W)
Kean College of New Jersey, NJ (W)
Kennesaw State College, GA (W)
Keene State College, NH (W)
Kent State University (Ashtabula), OH (W)

Kent State University (Kent), OH (W)
Kent State University (New Philadelphia), OH (W)
Kent State University (Warren), OH (W)
Kentucky State University, KY (W)
Kentucky Wesleyan College, KY (W)
Keystone Junior College, PA (W)
King College, TN (W)
King's College, NY (W)
King's College, PA (W)
Kirkwood Community College, IA (W)
Kishwaukee College, IL (W)
Knox College, IL (W)
Kutztown University, PA (W)
Lackawanna Junior College, PA (W)
Lafayette College, PA (W)
Lake Erie College, OH (W)
Lake Forest College, IL (W)
Lake Land College, IL (W)
Lake Michigan College, MI (W)
Lake Superior State University, MI (W)
Lamar University, TX (W)
Lambuth University, TN (W)
Lander College, SC (W)
Lansing Community College, MI (W)
La Roche College, PA (W)
La Salle University, PA (W)
Lawrence University, WI (W)
Lebanon Valley College, PA (W)
Lee College, TN (W)
Lees Junior College, KY (W)
Lehigh University, PA (W)
Le Moyne College, NY (W)
Lenoir-Rhyne College, NC (MW)
Lewis and Clark College, OR (W)
Lewis University, IL (W)
Limestone College, SC (W)
Lincoln College, IL (W)
Lincoln Land Community College, IL (W)
Lincoln Memorial University, TN (W)
Lincoln Trail College, IL (W)
Lindenwood College, IL (W)
Linfield College, OR (W)
Livingston University, KAL (W)
Long Beach City College, CA (W)
Long Island University (Brooklyn), NY (W)
Long Island University (C. W. Post Campus), NY (W)
Long Island University (Southhampton Campus), NY (W)
Longwood College, VA (W)
Loras College, VA (W)
Los Angeles Pierce Junior College, CA (W)
Los Angeles Valley College, CA (W)
Los Medanos College, CA (W)
Louisiana Tech University, LA (W)
Lower Columbia College, WA (W)
Loyola Marymount University, CA (W)
Luther College, IA (W)
Lynchburg College, VA (W)
Lyndon State College, VT (W)
Macalester College, MN (W)
Macomb Community College, MI (W)
Madison Area Technical College, WI (W)
Madonna University, MI (W)
Malone College, OH (W)
Manchester College, OH (W)
Manchester Community Technical College, CT (W)
Manhattan College, NY (MW)
Manhattanville College, NY (W)
Mankato State University, MN (W)
Mansfield University, PA (W)
Marian College, IN (W)
Marian College, WI (W)
Marietta College, OH (W)
Marist College, NY (W)
Mars Hill College, NC (W)
Mary Holmes College, MS (W)
Maryville College, TN (W)
Maryville University, MO (W)
Mary Washington College, VA (MW)
Marywood College, PA (W)
Massachusetts Bay Community College, MA (W)
Massachusetts Institute of Technology, MA (W)
Massasoit Community College, MA (W)
Mayville State College, ND (W)
McHenry County College, IL (W)
McKendree College, IL (W)
McNeese State University, LA (W)
Mercer County Community College, NJ (W)
Mercer University, GA (W)
Mercy College, NY (MW)
Mercyhurst College, PA (W)
Merrimack College, MA (W)
Mesa Community College, AZ (W)
Mesa State College, CO (W)
Messiah College, PA (W)
Metropolitan State College, CO (W)
Miami-Dade Community College (South Campus), FL (W)
Miami University, OH (W)
Michigan Christian College, MI (W)
Michigan State University, MI (W)
Mid-America Nazarene College, KS (W)
Middlesex County College, NJ (W)
Middle Tennessee State University, TN (W)
Midland Lutheran College, NE (W)
Millersville University, PA (W)
Milligan College, TN (W)
Millikin University, IL (W)
Mississippi College, MS (W)
Mississippi Delta Junior College, MS (W)
Mississippi Gulf Coast Junior College, MS (W)
Mississippi State University, MS (W)
Mississippi University For Women, MS (W)
Mississippi Valley State University, MS (W)
Missouri Baptist College, MO (W)
Missouri Southern State College, MO (W)
Missouri Valley College, MO (W)
Missouri Western State College, MO (W)
Mitchell College, CT (W)
Modesto Junior College, CA (W)
Mohawk Valley Community College, NY (W)
Monmouth College, IL (W)
Monmouth College, NJ (W)
Montclair State College, NJ (W)
Montreat-Anderson College, NC (W)
Moorhead State University, MN (W)
Moorpark College, CA (MW)
Moraine Valley Community College, IL (W)
Morehead State University, KY (W)
Morningside College, IA (MW)
Morton College, IL (W)
Mott Community College, MI (W)
Mount Holyoke College, MA (W)
Mount Mercy College, IA (W)
Mount Olive College, NC (W)

Mount St. Mary College, MD (W)
Mount Union College, OH (MW)
Mount Vernon Nazarene College, OH (W)
Mt. San Antonio College, CA (W)
Mt. Wachusett Community College, MA (W)
Muskegon Community College, MI (W)
Muskingum College, OH (W)
Nassau Community College, NY (W)
National-Louis University, IL (W)
Nazareth College, NY (W)
Nebraska Wesleyan University, NE (M)
Newberry College, SC (W)
New Hampshire College, NH (W)
New Jersey Institute of Technology, NJ (W)
New Mexico Highland University, NM (W)
New Mexico State University, NM (W)
New York Institute of Technology, NY (M)
New York State University Institute of Technology, NY (W)
Niagara County Community College, NY (W)
Niagara University, NY (W)
Nicholls State University, LA (W)
Nichols College, MA (M)
Norfolk State University, VA (W)
North Adams State College, MA (MW)
North Carolina A and T State University, NC (W)
North Carolina Central University, NC (W)
North Central College, IL (W)
North Central Missouri College, MO (M)
North County Community College, NY (W)
North Dakota State University, ND (W)
Northeastern Illinois University, IL (W)
Northeastern Junior College, CO (W)
Northeastern State University, OK (MW)
Northeast Louisiana University, LA (MW)
Northeast Mississippi Community College, MS (W)
Northeast Missouri State University, OK (MW)
Northern Illinois University, IL (W)
Northern Kentucky University, KY (W)
Northern State University, SD (W)
North Georgia College, GA (W)
North Greenville College, SC (W)
North Hennepin Community College, MN (W)
North Iowa Area Community College, IA (MW)
Northland Community College, MN (W)
Northwest Alabama State Community College, AL (W)
Northwestern College, IA (W)
Northwestern College, MN (MW)
Northwestern State University of Louisiana, LA (W)
Northwestern University, IL (W)
Northwest Mississippi Community College, MS (W)
Northwest Missouri State University, MO (W)
Northwood Institute, MI (W)
Northwood Institute (Texas Campus), TX (W)
Norwich University, VT (W)
Notre Dame College of Ohio, OH (W)
Nyack College, NY (W)
Oakland Community College, MI (W)
Oakton Community College, IL (W)
Ocean County College, NJ (W)
Ohio Dominican College, OH (W)
Ohio Northern University, OH (W)
Ohio State University, OH (W)
Ohio University, OH (W)
Ohio Wesleyan University, OH (M)
Oklahoma Baptist University, OK (W)
Oklahoma City University, OK (W)
Oklahoma State University, OK (W)
Olivet College, MI (W)
Olivet Nazarene University, IL (M)
Olney Central College, IL (W)
Olympic College, WA (W)
Orange Coast College, CA (W)
Orange County Community College, NY (W)
Oregon Institute of Technology, OR (W)
Oregon State University, OR (MW)
Otterbein College, OH (W)
Pace University, NY (W)
Pace University (White Plains Campus), NY (W)
Pacific Lutheran University, WA (W)
Pacific University, OR (W)
Paducah Community College, CA (W)
Paine College, GA (W)
Palm Beach Community College, FL (W)
Palomar College, CA (W)
Parkland College, IL (MW)
Pembroke State University, NC (W)
Penn State University (Abington), PA (W)
Penn State University (Sharon), PA (W)
Pennsylvania State University, PA (W)
Pennsylvania State University (Behrend College), PA (W)
Peru State College, NE (W)
Pfeiffer College, NC (W)
Philadelphia College of Textile and Science, PA (W)
Philadelphia Community College, PA (MW)
Phoenix College, AZ (W)
Piedmont College, GA (W)
Pikeville College, KY (W)
Pima Community College, AZ (W)
Pittsburg State University, KS (W)
Plymouth State College, NH (W)
Point Park College, PA (W)
Pomona-Pitzer Colleges, CA (W)
Portland State University, OR (W)
Prince George's Community College, MD (W)
Providence College, RI (MW)
Queensborough Community College, NY (W)
Queens College, NY (W)
Quincy College, IL (W)
Quinnipiac College, CT (W)
Quinsigamond College, MA (W)
Rainy River Community College, MN (W)
Ramapo College, NJ (W)
Ranetto Santiago College, CA (W)
Regis College, MA (W)
Regis University, CO (W)
Rend Lake, IL (W)
Rensselaer Polytechnic Institute, NY (W)
Rhode Island College, RI (W)
Rider College, NJ (W)
Ripon College, WI (W)

Riverside College, CA (W)
Robert Morris College, PA (W)
Roberts Wesleyan College, NY (W)
Rochester Community College, MN (W)
Rochester Institute of Technology, NY (W)
Rockland Community College, NY (W)
Rollins College, FL (W)
Rowan College of New Jersey, NJ (W)
Rutgers, Newark College of Arts and Sciences, NJ (W)
Sacred Heart University, CT (W)
Saddleback College, CA (W)
Saginaw Valley State College, MI (W)
Saint Ambrose College, IA (W)
Saint Andrews Presbyterian College, NC (MW)
Saint Augustine's College, NC (W)
Saint Bonaventure University, NY (W)
Saint Cloud State University, MN (W)
Saint Edward's University, TX (W)
Saint Francis College, IN (M)
Saint Francis College, NY (M)
Saint Francis College, PA (W)
Saint John Fisher College, NY (W)
Saint John's University, NY (W)
Saint Joseph's College, IN (W)
Saint Joseph's University, PA (W)
Saint Leo College, FL (W)
Saint Louis University, MO (W)
Saint Mary College, IN (W)
Saint Mary's College, IN (W)
Saint Mary's College, MI (W)
Saint Mary's College of California, CA (W)
Saint Mary's University, TX (W)
Saint Norbert College, MN (W)
Saint Olaf College, WI (W)
Saint Paul's College, VA (W)
Saint Peter's College, NJ (W)
Saint Thomas Aquinas College, NY (W)
Saint Thomas University, FL (W)
Saint Vincent College, PA (W)
Saint Xavier University, IL (W)
Salem State College, MA (W)
Salem-Teikyo University, WV (W)
Salve Regina College, RI (W)
Samford University, AL (W)
Sam Houston State University, TX (W)
San Bernardino Community College, CA (W)
San Diego City College, CA (W)
San Diego Mesa College, CA (MW)
San Diego State University, CA (W)
San Francisco State University, CA (W)
San Joaquin Delta College, CA (W)
San Jose State University, CA (W)
Santa Clara University, CA (W)
Santa FE Community College, FL (W)
Santa Monica College, CA (W)
Santa Rosa Junior College, CA (W)
Scottsdale Community College, AR (W)
Seminole Community College, FL (W)
Seton Hall University, NJ (W)
Seton Hill College, PA (W)
Shawnee State University, OH (W)
Shepherd College, WV (W)
Shippensburg University of Pennsylvania, PA (W)
Shoreline Community College, WA (W)
Shorter College, AR (W)
Shorter College, GA (W)
Siena College, NY (W)
Siena Heights College, MI (W)
Sierra College, CA (W)
Simpson College, CA (W)
Skagit Valley College, WA (W)
Skyline College, CA (W)
Slippery Rock University of Pennsylvania, PA (W)
Smith College, MA (W)
Snead State Community College, AL (W)
Snow College, UT (MW)
Solano Community College, CA (MW)
South Dakota State University, SD (W)
Southeast Community College, NE (W)
Southeastern Community College, NE (W)
Southeastern Illinois College, IL (W)
Southeastern Louisiana University, LA (W)
Southeastern Massachusetts University, MA (W)
Southeast Missouri State University, MO (W)
Southern California College, CA (W)
Southern Connecticut State University, CT (MW)
Southern Illinois University, IL (W)
Southern Illinois University (Edwardsville), IL (W)
Southern Utah University, UT (W)
Southwest Baptist University, MO (W)
Southwestern College, CA (W)
Southwestern Michigan Junior College, MI (W)
Southwest Missouri State University, MO (W)
Southwest State University, MN (W)
Southwest Texas State University, TX (W)
Spartanburg Methodist, SC (W)
Spoon River College, IL (W)
Spring Arbor College, MI (W)
Springfield College, MA (W)
Springfield Technical Community College, MA (W)
Spring Hill College, AL (M)
Stanford University, CA (W)
State University of New York (Albany), NY (W)
State University of New York (Binghamton), NY (W)
State University of New York (Buffalo), NY (W)
State University of New York (Stony Brook), NY (W)
State University of New York College (Brockport), NY (W)
State University of New York College (Cortland), NY (W)
State University of New York College (Geneseo), NY (W)
State University of New York College (New Paltz), NY (W)
State University of New York College (Oswego), NY (W)
State University of New York Maritime College, NY (W)
Stephen F. Austin State University, TX (W)
Sterling College, KS (MW)
Stetson University, FL (W)
St. Johns River Community College, FL (W)
St. Louis Community College (Florissant Valley), MO (W)
St. Mary of the Plains College, KS (W)
Stonehill College, MA (W)
St. Petersburg Junior College, FL (W)
Sue Bennett College, KY (MW)

Suffolk County Community College, NY (W)
Swarthmore College, PA (W)
Tabor College, KS (W)
Taft College, CA (W)
Tampa College, FL (W)
Teikyo Marycrest University, IA (W)
Teikyo Post University, CT (MW)
Teikyo Westmar University, IA (W)
Temple University, PA (W)
Tennessee Technological University, TN (W)
Tennessee Temple University, TN (W)
Tennessee Wesleyan College, TN (W)
Texas A & I University, TX (W)
Texas A & M University, TX (W)
Texas Lutheran College, TX (W)
Thomas College, ME (MW)
Thomas More College, KY (W)
Towson State University, MD (W)
Transylvania University, KY (W)
Trenton State College, NJ (W)
Trevecca Nazarene College, TN (W)
Trinity Christian College, IL (W)
Trinity College, CT (W)
Trinity College, IL (W)
Trinity University, TX (W)
Tri-State University, IN (W)
Triton College, IL (W)
Troy State University, AL (W)
Truett-McConnell Junior College, GA (W)
Tufts University, MA (W)
Tusculum College, TN (W)
Union College, KY (W)
Union College, NY (W)
Union County College, NJ (W)
University of Akron, OH (W)
University of Arizona, AZ (W)
University of Bridgeport, CT (W)
University of California (Berkeley), CA (W)
University of California (Davis), CA (W)
University of California (Riverside), CA (W)
University of California (San Diego), CA (W)
University of California (Santa Barbara), CA (W)
University of California (UCLA), CA (W)
University of Central Oklahoma, OK (W)
University of Charleston, WV (W)
University of Chicago, IL (W)
University of Colorado (Colorado Springs), CO (W)
University of Connecticut, CT (W)
University of Dayton, OH (W)
University of Delaware, DE (W)
University of Detroit Mercy, MI (W)
University of Dubuque, IA (W)
University of Evansville, IN (W)
University of Findlay, OH (W)
University of Hartford, CT (W)
University of Hawaii (Manoa), HI (W)
University of Indianapolis, IN (W)
University of Iowa, IA (MW)
University of Kansas, KS (W)
University of La Verne, CA (W)
University of Lowell, MA (W)
University of Maine (Presque Isle), ME (W)
University of Mary, ND (W)
University of Mary Hardin-Baylor, TX (W)
University of Maryland (Baltimore County), MD (W)
University of Massachusetts (Amherst), MA (W)
University of Massachusetts (Boston), MA (W)
University of Michigan, MI (W)
University of Minnesota (Duluth), MN (W)
University of Minnesota (Minneapolis), MN (W)
University of Minnesota (Morris), MN (W)
University of Missouri, MO (W)
University of Missouri (Columbia), MO (W)
University of Missouri (Rolla), MO (W)
University of Nebraska (Kearney), NY (W)
University of Nebraska (Lincoln), NE (W)
University of Nevada, NV (W)
University of New England, ME (W)
University of New Haven, CT (W)
University of Nex Mexico, NM (W)
University of North Alabama, AL (W)
University of North Carolina (Asheville), NC (W)
University of North Carolina (Chapel Hill), NC (W)
University of North Carolina (Charlotte), NC (W)
University of North Carolina (Greensboro), NC (W)
University of North Carolina (Wilmington), NC (W)
University of North Dakota, ND (W)
University of Northern Iowa, IA (W)
University of Notre Dame, IN (W)
University of Oklahoma, OK (W)
University of Oregon, OR (W)
University of Pennsylvania, PA (W)
University of Puerto Rico, PR (M)
University of Puget Sound, WA (W)
University of Redlands, CA (W)
University of Rhode Island, RI (MW)
University of Rio Grande, OH (W)
University of San Diego, CA (W)
University of Scranton, PA (W)
University of South Carolina, SC (W)
University of South Carolina (Aiken), SC (W)
University of South Carolina (Spartanburg), SC (W)
University of South Dakota, SD (W)
University of Southern Indiana, IN (W)
University of South Florida, FL (W)
University of Southwestern Louisiana, LA (W)
University of St. Thomas, MN (W)
University of Tampa, FL (W)
University of Tennessee (Martin), TN (W)
University of Texas (Arlington), TX (W)
University of the Pacific, CA (W)
University of Toledo, OH (W)
University of Tulsa, OK (W)
University of Utah, UT (W)
University of Vermont, VT (W)
University of Virginia, VA (W)
University of Washington, WA (MW)
University of West Florida, FL (W)
University of Wisconsin (Eau Claire), WI (W)

University of Wisconsin (Green Bay), WI (W)
University of Wisconsin (La Crosse), WI (W)
University of Wisconsin (Oshkosh), WI (W)
University of Wisconsin (Platteville), WI (W)
University of Wisconsin (River Falls), WI (W)
University of Wisconsin (Stevens Point), WI (W)
Upper Iowa University, IA (W)
Urbana University, OH (W)
Ursinus College, PA (W)
U.S. International University, CA (W)
Utah State University, UT (W)
Valdosta State College, GA (W)
Valencia Community College, FL (W)
Valley City State University, ND (W)
Valley Forge Christian College, PA (W)
Valparaiso University, IN (W)
Ventura College, CA (W)
Villanova University, PA (W)
Virginia Union University, VA (W)
Virginia Wesleyan College, VA (W)
Viterbo College, WI (W)
Wabash Valley College, IL (W)
Wagner College, NY (W)
Waldorf College, IA (W)
Wallace Community College (Selma), AL (W)
Walsh College, OH (W)
Warner Pacific College, OR (W)
Warren Wilson College, NC (W)
Wartburg College, IA (W)
Washburn University, KS (W)
Washington and Jefferson College, PA (W)
Washington College, MD (W)
Washington University, MO (M)
Waubonsee College, IL (W)
Wayne State College, NE (W)
Wayne State University, MI (W)
Webber College, FL (W)
Wesleyan University, CT (W)
Wesley College, DE (W)
West Chester University, PA (W)
Western Connecticut State University, CT (W)
Western Illinois University, IL (W)
Western Maryland College, MD (W)
Western Michigan University, MI (W)
Western New England College, MA (W)
Western New Mexico University, NM (W)
Western Oregon State College, OR (W)
Western Washington University, WA (MW)
Westfield State College, MA (W)
West Georgia College, GA (W)
Westminster College, PA (W)
West Virginia Institute of Technology, WV (W)
West Virginia Wesleyan College, WV (W)
Wheaton College, IL (W)
Whittier College, CA (W)
Wichita State University, KS (W)
Wilkes College, NC (W)
Wilkes University, PA (W)
Willamette University, OR (W)
William Jewell College, MO (W)
William Patterson College, NJ (W)
William Penn College, IA (W)
William Rainey Harper College, IL (W)
Williams College, MA (W)
William Woods College, MO (W)
Wilmington College, DE (W)
Wilmington College, OH (W)
Wilson College, PA (W)
Wingate College, NC (W)
Winona State University, MN (W)
Winston-Salem State University, NC (W)
Winthrop University, SC (W)
Worcester State College, MA (W)
Wright State University, OH (W)
Yakima Valley College, WA (W)
Yale University, CT (W)
York College of Pennsylvania, PA (W)
Youngstown State University, OH (W)
Yuba Community College, CA (W)

Squash

Amherst College, MA (MW)
Atlantic Community College, NJ (W)
Bates College, ME (MW)
Bowdoin College, ME (MW)
Brown University, RI (W)
Claflin College, SC (W)
Cornell University, NY (M)
Dartmouth College, NH (MW)
Franklin & Marshall College, PA (MW)
Hamilton College, NY (MW)
Harvard University, MA (MW)
Hawaii Pacific University, HI (M)
Johns Hopkins University, MD (W)
La Salle University, PA (W)
Lehigh University, PA (M)
Massachusetts Institute of Technology, MA (M)
Middlebury College, VT (W)
Mount Holyoke College, MA (W)
North Carolina Wesleyan College, NC (W)
Princeton University, NJ (MW)
Saint Anselm College, NH (W)
Smith College, MA (W)
State University of New York (Stony Brook), NY (M)
Stevens Institute of Technology, NJ (M)
St. Louis Community College (Forest Park), MO (W)
Suffolk County Community College, NY (W)
Suffolk University, MA (W)
Trinity College, CT (MW)
Trinity College, IL (MW)
Tufts University, MA (MW)
University of Pennsylvania, PA (MW)
Vassar College, NY (MW)
Wellesley College, MA (W)
Wesleyan University, CT (MW)
Williams College, MA (MW)
Yale University, CT (MW)

Swimming

Adelphi University, NY (W)
Alfred University, NY (MW)
Allegheny College, PA (MW)
Amherst College, MA (MW)
Arizona State University, AZ (MW)
Asbury College, KY (MW)
Ashland College, OH (MW)
Auburn University, AL (MW)
Augusta College, GA (W)
Babson College, MA (MW)
Beloit College, kWI (MW)
Bloomsburg University, PA (W)
Boston College, MA (MW)
Boston University, MA (MW)
Bowdoin College, ME (MW)
Bowling Green State University, OH (MW)
Bradley University, IL (MW)
Brandeis University, MA (MW)

Brevard College, FL (MW)
Bridgewater State College, MA (MW)
Brigham Young University, UT (MW)
Broward Community College, FL (MW)
Bryn Mawr College, PA (W)
Bucknell University, PA (MW)
Buena Vista College, IA (MW)
Butler University, IN (W)
Cabrillo College, CA (MW)
California State University at Bakersfield, CA (M)
California State University (Fresno), CA (MW)
California State University (Hayward), CA (MW)
California State University (Long Beach), CA (MW)
Californis State University (Los Angeles), CA (MW)
California State University (Sacramento), CA (MW)
Calvin College, MI (MW)
Campbellsville College, KY (MW)
Canisius College, NY (MW)
Carleton College, MN (MW)
Carnegie-Mellon University, PA (MW)
Carroll College, WI (MW)
Carthage College, WI (MW)
Case Western Reserve University, OH (MW)
Catholic University of Puerto Rico, PR (MW)
Catonsville Community College, MD (MW)
Central Connecticut State University, CT (MW)
Central Washington University, WA (MW)
Cerritos College, CA (MW)
Chaffey College, CA (MW)
City College of New York, NY (M)
Clarion University, PA (MW)
Clarkson University, NY (MW)
Clark University, MA (MW)
Cleveland State University, OH (MW)
Coe College, IA (MW)
Colgate University, NY (MW)
College of Charleston, SC (MW)
College of New Rochelle, NY (W)
College of St. Benedict, MN (W)
College of the Sequoias, CA (MW)
College of William and Mary, VA (MW)
College of Wooster, OH (MW)
Colorado College, CO (MW)
Colorado School of Mines, CO (MW)
Colorado State University, CO (W)
Columbia University, NY (MW)
Concordia Teachers College, NE (MW)
Connecticut College, CT (W)
Cornell College, IA (MW)
Cornell University, NY (MW)
Creighton University, NE (MW)
Dalton College, GA (MW)
Dartmouth College, NH (MW)
Davidson College, NC (M)
De Anza Community College, CA (MW)
Denison University, OH (MW)
Diablo Valley Community College, CA (MW)
Dickinson College, PA (MW)
Drexel University, PA (MW)
Duquesne University, PA (MW)
Eastern Illinois University, MI (MW)
Eastern Michigan University, MI (MW)
Eastern Oklahoma State College, OK (MW)
El Camino College, PA (MW)
Elizabethtown College, PA (MW)
Eureka College, IL (MW)
Evergreen State College, WA (MW)
Fairfield University, CT (MW)
Florida A & M University, FL (MW)
Florida State University, FL (MW)
Fordham University, NY (MW)
Franklin & Marshall College, PA (MW)
Fullerton College, CA (MW)
Furman University, SC (M)
Gannon College, PA (MW)
George Washington University, DC (MW)
Gettysburg College, PA (MW)
Golden West College, CA (MW)
Goucher College, MD (MW)
Grinnell College, IA (MW)
Gustavus Adolphus College, MN (MW)
Hamilton College, NY (MW)
Harper William Rainey College, IL (MW)
Hawaii Pacific University, HI (MW)
Henderson State University, AR (MW)
Hillsdale College, MI (W)
Hiram College, OH (MW)
Hood College, MD (W)
Hope College, MI (MW)
Howard University, DC (MW)
Humboldt State University, kCA (W)
Hunter College of the City University of New York, NY (W)
Illinois Benedictine College, IL (MW)
Illinois Institute of Technology, IL (MW)
Illinois Wesleyan University, IL (MW)
Indiana University, IN (MW)
Iona College, NY (MW)
Iowa State University of Science and Technology, IA (M)
Iowa Wesleyan College, IA (MW)
John Brown University, AR (MW)
Johns Hopkins University, MD (MW)
Kalamazoo College, MI (MW)
Keene State College, NH (MW)
Kent State University (Ashtabula), OH (MW)
Kent State University (New Philadelphia), OH (MW)
Kent State University (Warren), OH (MW)
Kenyon College, OH (MW)
King's College, PA (MW)
Kutztown University, PA (MW)
Lafayette College, PA (MW)
Lake Forest College, IL (MW)
Lawrence University, WI (MW)
Lehigh University, PA (MW)
Lincoln College, OR (MW)
Linfield College, OR (MW)
Long Beach City College, CA (MW)
Loras College, IA (MW)
Los Angeles Valley College, CA (MW)
Louisiana State University (Alexandria), LA (MW)
Louisiana State University (Baton Rouge), LA (MW)
Loyola College, MD (MW)
Loyola Marymount University, CA (W)
Loyola University, IL (W)
Manhattanville College, NY (W)
Mankato State University, MN (MW)
Mansfield University, PA (W)
Mary Baldwin College, VA (W)
Marymount University, VA (MW)

Mary Washington College, VA (MW)
Massachusetts Institute of Technology, MA (MW)
Metropolitan State College, CO (MW)
Miami-Dade Community College (South Campus), FL (MW)
Millikin University, IL (M)
Mississippi Valley State University, MS (M)
Monmouth College, NJ (MW)
Montana College of Mineral Science and Technology, MT (MW)
Montclair State College, NJ (MW)
Montgomery College, MD (MW)
Morehead State University, Ky (MW)
Mount Holyoke College, MA (W)
Mt. San Antonio College, CA (MW)
Nazareth College, NY (MW)
New Mexico State University, NM (MW)
Niagara University, NY (MW)
North Central College, IL (MW)
Northeast Louisiana University, LA (MW)
Northern Arizona University, AZ (MW)
Northern Michigan University, MI (W)
Norwich University, VT (MW)
Oakland University, MI (MW)
Oberlin College, OH (MW)
Occidental College, CA (MW)
Ohio Northern University, OH (MW)
Ohio State University, OH (MW)
Old Dominion University, VA (MW)
Oral Roberts University, OK (M)
Orange Coast College, CA (MW)
Ouachita Baptist University, AR (MW)
Pacific Lutheran University, WA (MW)
Palomar College, CA (MW)
Pepperdine University, CA (W)
Pfeiffer College, NC (W)
Pomona-Pitzer College, CA (MW)
Principia College, IL (MW)
Queensborough Community College, NY (MW)
Queens College, NY (MW)
Ranetto Santiago College, CA (MW)
Rensselaer Polytechnic Institute, NY (MW)
Rice University, TX (W)
Rider College, NJ (MW)
Ripon College, WI (MW)
Rochester Institute of Technology, IN (M)
Roosevelt University, IL (MW)
Rose-Hulman Institute of Technology, IN (M)
Rose State Junior College, OK (MW)
Saddleback College, CA (MW)
Saint Bonaventure University, NY (MW)
Saint Cloud State University, MN (M)
Saint John's University, MN (M)
Saint John's University, NY (MW)
Saint Lawrence University, NY (MW)
Saint Mary's College, MD (MW)
Saint Peter's College, NJ (MW)
Salem State College, MA (MW)
San Bernardino Community College, CA (MW)
San Diego Mesa College, CA (MW)
San Francisco State University, CA (MW)
San Joaquin Delta College, CA (MW)
San Jose State University, CA (W)
Santa Monica College, CA (MW)
Santa Rosa Junior College, CA (MW)
Seton Hall University, NJ (MW)
Shippensburg University of Pennsylvania, PA (MW)
Sierra College, CA (MW)
Skidmore College, NY (W)
Snow College, UT (MW)
Solano Community College, CA (M)
South Dakota State University, SD (MW)
Southeastern Massachusetts University, MA (MW)
Southern Methodist University, TX (MW)
Southern Oregon State College, OR (MW)
Southwest Missouri State University, MO (M)
Springfield College, MA (MW)
State University of New York (Albany), NY (M)
State University of New York (Binghamton), NY (MW)
State University of New York (Buffalo), NY (MW)
State University of New York (Stony Brook), NY (M)
State University of New York College (Brockport), NY (MW)
State University of New York College (Fredonia), NY (M)
State University of New York College (Geneseo), NY (MW)
State University of New York College (Oswego), NY (MW)
State University of New York College (Potsdam), NY (MW)
State University of New York Maritime College, NY (M)
Swarthmore College, PA (MW)
Sweet Briar College, VA (W)
Tampa College, FL (MW)
Tennessee State University, TN (M)
Texas A & I University, TX (MW)
Texas A & M University, TX (MW)
Texas Christian University, TX (MW)
Transylvania University, KY (MW)
Trenton State College, NJ (W)
Trinity College, CT (MW)
Trinity College, IL (MW)
Tufts University, MA (MW)
Tulane University, LA (MW)
Union College, KY (M)
Union College, NY (MW)
University of Alabama (Tuscaloosa), AL (MW)
University of Alaska, AK (M)
University of Arkansas (Fayetteville), AR (MW)
University of Arkansas (Little Rock), AR (MW)
University of California (Berkeley), CA (W)
University of California (Riverside), CA (MW)
University of California (San Diego), CA (MW)
University of California (Santa Barbara), CA (MW)
University of California (UCLA), CA (MW)
University of Central Arkansas, AR (MW)
University of Chicago, IL (MW)
University of Cincinnati, OH (MW)
University of Denver, CO (MW)
University of Evansville, IN (MW)
University of Findlay, OH (MW)

University of Georgia, GA (MW)
University of Houston, TX (W)
University of Illinois, IL (MW)
University of Illinois (Urbana-Champaign), IL (MW)
University of Iowa, IA (M)
University of Kansas, KS (MW)
University of Kentucky, KY (MW)
University of Louisville, KY (MW)
University of Lowell, MA (M)
University of Maine, ME (MW)
University of Maryland, MD (MW)
University of Maryland (Baltimore County), MD (MW)
University of Massachusetts (Amherst), MA (MW)
University of Massachusetts (Boston), MA (MW)
University of Miami, FL (MW)
University of Missouri, MO (MW)
University of Missouri (Columbia), MO (MW)
University of Missouri (Rolla), MO (M)
University of Nebraska, NE (W)
University of Nebraska (Kearney), NE (W)
University of Nebraska (Lincoln), NE (MW)
University of Nevada, NV (MW)
University of Nevada (Reno), NV (W)
University of New Mexico, NY (MW)
University of North Carolina (Asheville), NC (MW)
University of North Carolina (Chapel Hill), NC (MW)
University of North Dakota, ND (MW)
University of Pittsburgh, PA (MW)
University of Puerto Rico, PR (M)
University of Puget Sound, Wa (MW)
University of Redlands, CA (MW)
University of Richmond, Va (MW)
University of San Diego, CA (W)
University of Scranton, PA (M)
University of South Carolina, SC (MW)
University of Southern California, CA (MW)
University of St. Thomas, MN (MW)
University of Tampa, FL (MW)
University of Tennessee, TN (MW)
University of Tennessee (Knoxville), TN (MW)
University of Texas (Austin), TX (MW)
University of the Pacific, CA (MW)
University of Toledo, OH (M)
University of Vermont, VT (MW)
University of Washington, WA (MW)
University of Wisconsin (Eau Claire), WI (MW)
University of Wisconsin (La Crosse), WI (MW)
University of Wisconsin (Madison), WI (MW)
University of Wisconsin (Milwaukee), WI (MW)
University of Wisconsin (Stevens Point), WI (MW)
University of Wisconsin (Stout), WI (MW)
University of Wyoming, WY (MW)
Ursinus College, PA (MW)
Valparaiso University, IN (MW)
Ventura College, CA (MW)
Vincennes University Junior College, IN (MW)
Virginia Military Institute, VA (M)
Wabash College, IN (M)
Warren Wilson College, NC (MW)
Washington College, MD (MW)
Washinton State University, WA (W)
Wayne State University, MI (MW)
Wellesley College, MA (W)
Wesleyan University, CT (MW)
West Chester University, PA (MW)
Western Kentucky University, KY (M)
Western Maryland College, MD (MW)
Western Montana College, MT (MW)
Westminster College, PA (M)
Wheaton College, IL (MW)
Whittier College, CA (MW)
Whitworth College, WA (MW)
Willamette University, OR (MW)
William Patterson College, NJ (MW)
Williams College, MA (MW)
Winston-Salem State University, NC (MW)
Wright State University, OH (MW)
Yale University, Ct (MW)
York College of Pennsylvania, PA (MW)
Youngstown State University, OH (MW)

Swimming-Diving

Adrian College, MI (MW)
Albion College, MI (MW)
Alfred University, NY (MW)
Allegheny College, PA (MW)
Alma College, MI (MW)
American University, DC (MW)
Amherst College, MA (MW)
Arizona State University, AZ (MW)
Augusta College, GA (W)
Augustana College, IL (MW)
Ball State University, IN (MW)
Bates College, ME (MW)
Beloit College, WI (MW)
Bethany College, KS (MW)
Bethany College, WV (MW)
Blackburn College, IL (MW)
Bloomsburg University, PA (M)
Boston College, MA (MW)
Bowdoin College, ME (MW)
Brandeis University, MA (MW)
Broward Community College, FL (MW)
Brown University, RI (MW)
Buena Vista College, IA (MW)
Buffalo State College, NY (MW)
Buffalo State University (New York), NY (MW)
Cabrillo College, CA (M)
California Institute of Technology, CA (MW)
California State University at Bakersfield, CA (M)
California State University (Chico), CA (MW)
California State University (Hayward), CA (MW)
California State University (Long Beach), CA (MW)
California State University (Los Angeles), CA (MW)
California State University (Northridge), CA (MW)
California State University (Sacramento), CA (MW)
Carleton College, MN (MW)
Case Western Reserve University, OH (MW)

Catonsville Community College, MD (MW)
Central Connecticut State University, CT (MW)
Central Washington University, WA (MW)
Cerritos College, CA (MW)
Chaffey College, CA (MW)
City College of San Francisco, CA (MW)
Clarkson University, NY (MW)
Clark University, MA (MW)
Clemson University, SC (MW)
Cleveland State University, OH (MW)
College of Charleston, SC (MW)
College of St. Rose, NY (W)
College of the Sequoias, CA (MW)
College of William and Mary, VA (MW)
Colorado College, CO (MW)
Colorado School of Mines, CO (MW)
Colorado State University, CO (W)
Columbia University, NY (MW)
Concordia Teachers College, NE (MW)
Cornell College, IA (MW)
Cornell University, NY (MW)
Cuesta College, CA (MW)
Davidson College, NC (W)
Delta State University, MS (MW)
De Pauw University, IN (MW)
Drexel University, PA (MW)
Drury College, MO (M)
Duke University, NC (MW)
East Carolina University, NC (MW)
Eastern Michigan University, MI (MW)
East Stroudsburg University, PA (MW)
Edinboro University of Pennsylvania, PA (MW)
El Camino College, CA (MW)
Elizabethtown College, PA (MW)
Emory University, GA (MW)
Eureka College, IL (MW)
Fairfield University, CT (MW)
Fairmont State College, WV (MW)
Ferris State College, MI (MW)
Florida Atlantic University, FL (W)
Florida Southern College, FL (MW)
Florida State University, FL (MW)
Fordham University, NY (MW)
Fullerton College, CA (MW)
Furman University, SC (MW)
Gannon College, PA (MW)
Georgia Southern University, GA (MW)
Golden West College, CA (MW)
Grand Rapids Junior College, MI (MW)
Grand Valley State College, MI (MW)
Grinnell College, IA (MW)
Grove City College, PA (MW)
Gustavus Adolphus College, MN (MW)
Hamilton College, NY (MW)
Hamline University, MN (MW)
Harper William Rainey College, IL (MW)
Hartwick College, NY (MW)
Harvard University, MA (MW)
Henderson State University, AR (MW)
Holy Cross College, MA (MW)
Hope College, MI (MW)
Illinois Institute of Technology, IL (MW)
Illinois State University, IL (W)
Illinois Wesleyan University, IL (MW)
Indian River Community College, FL (MW)
Indiana University of Pennsylvania, PA (MW)
Iona College, NY (MW)
Ithaca College, NY (MW)
James Madison University, VA (MW)
John Carroll University, OH (MW)
Johns Hopkins University, MD (MW)
Juniata College, PA (MW)
Kalamazoo College, MI (MW)
Kean College of New Jersey, NJ (W)
Kent State University (Ashtabula), OH (MW)
Kent State University (New Philadelphia), OH (MW)
Kent State University (Warren), OH (MW)
King's College, PA (MW)
Knox College, IL (MW)
Lafayette College, PA (MW)
Lake Forest College, IL (MW)
La Salle University, PA (MW)
Lawrence University, WI (MW)
Lehigh University, PA (MW)
Lewis and Clark College, OR (MW)
Lincoln College, IL (MW)
Long Beach City College, CA (W)
Loras College, IA (MW)
Los Angeles Pierce Junior College, CA (MW)
Luther College, IA (MW)
Lycoming College, PA (MW)
Macalester College, MN (MW)
Manhattan College, NY (MW)
Manhattanville College, NY (W)
Mankato State University, MN (MW)
Mansfield University, PA (W)
Marist College, NY (MW)
Marshall University, WV (M)
Mary Baldwin College, VA (W)
Massachusetts Institute of Technology, MA (MW)
Miami University, OH (MW)
Michigan State University, MI (MW)
Middlebury College, VT (MW)
Millersville University, PA (W)
Millikin University, IL (W)
Modesto Junior College, CA (MW)
Montclair State College, NJ (MW)
Morehead State University, KY (MW)
Mount Holyoke College, MA (W)
Mount Union College, OH (MW)
Mt. San Antonio College, CA (MW)
New York University, NY (MW)
Niagara University, NY (MW)
North Carolina State University, NC (MW)
Northeast Missouri State University, MO (MW)
Northern Arizona University, AZ (W)
Northern Illinois University, IL (MW)
Northern Michigan University, MI (W)
Northwestern University, IL (MW)
Norwich University, VT (MW)
Oberlin College, OH (MW)
Occidental College, CA (MW)
Ocean County College, NJ (MW)
Ohio Northern University, OH (MW)
Ohio State University, OH (MW)
Ohio University, OH (MW)
Ohio Wesleyan University, OH (MW)
Orange Coast College, CA (MW)
Oregon State University, OR (W)
Ouachita Baptist University, AR (MW)

Palomar College, CA (MW)
Pennsylvania State University, PA (MW)
Pfeiffer College, NC (W)
Plymouth State College, NH (W)
Pomona-Pitzer Colleges, CA (MW)
Princeton University, NJ (MW)
Principia College, IL (MW)
Providence College, RI (MW)
Purdue University, IN (MW)
Queensborough Community College, NY (MW)
Ranetto Santiago College, CA (MW)
Regis College, MA (W)
Rensselaer Polytechnic Institute, NY (MW)
Rice University, TX (M)
Ripon College, WI (MW)
Riverside College, CA (MW)
Roanoke College, VA (W)
Rochester Institute of Technology, NY (MW)
Rose-Hulman Institue of Technology, IN (M)
Rose State Junior College, OK (MW)
Rowan College of New Jersey, NJ (MW)
Saddleback College, CA (MW)
Saint Bonaventure University, NY (MW)
Saint Cloud State University, MN (MW)
Saint Francis College, IN (MW)
Saint Francis College, NY (MW)
Saint John's University, NY (MW)
Saint Lawrence University, NY (MW)
Saint Louis University, MO (MW)
Saint Mary's College, IN (W)
Saint Mary's College, MI (W)
Saint Michael's College, VT (MW)
Saint Olaf College, MN (MW)
Saint Peter's College, NJ (MW)
San Diego Mesa College, CA (MW)
Seton Hall University, NJ (MW)
Sierra College, CA (MW)
Skidmore College, NY (W)
Slippery Rock University of Pennsylvania, PA (MW)
Smith College, MA (W)
Solano Community College, CA (W)
Southeastern Massachusetts University, MA (MW)
Southern Connecticut State University, CT (MW)
Southern Illinois University, IL (MW)
Southern Methodist University, TX (MW)
Southwest Missouri State University, MO (M)
Springfield College, MA (MW)
Stanford University, CA (MW)
State University of New York (Albany), NY (MW)
State University of New York (Binghamton), NY (MW)
State University of New York (Plattsburgh), NY (MW)
State University of New York (Stony Brook), NY (MW)
State University of New York College (Brockport), NY (MW)
State University of New York College (Cortland), NY (MW)
State University of New York College (Geneseo), NY (MW)
State University of New York College (New Paltz), NY (M)
State University of New York College (Oswego), NY (MW)
State University of New York College (Potsdam), NY (MW)
St. Petersburg Junior College, FL (MW)
Sweet Briar College, VA (W)
Syracuse University, NY (MW)
Texas A & I University, TX (MW)
Texas A & M University, TX (MW)
Texas Christian University, TX (MW)
Towson State University, MD (MW)
Trinity College, CT (MW)
Trinity College, IL (MW)
Triton College, IL (MW)
Tufts University, MA (MW)
Union College, KY (M)
University of Alabama (Tuscaloosa), AL (MW)
University of Alaska, AK (M)
University of Arizona, AZ (MW)
University of California (Berkeley), CA (MW)
University of California (Davis), CA (MW)
University of California (Irvine), CA (MW)
University of California (Riverside), CA (MW)
University of California (San Diego), CA (MW)
University of California (Santa Barbara), CA (MW)
University of California (UCLA), CA (MW)
University of Chicago, IL (MW)
University of Cincinnati, OH (MW)
University of Connecticut, CT (MW)
University of Delaware, DE (MW)
University of Florida, FL (MW)
University of Georgia, GA (MW)
University of Hawaii (Manoa), HI (MW)
University of Houston, TX (W)
University of Illinois, IL (MW)
University of Illinois (Urbana-Champaign), IL (MW)
University of Indianapolis, IN (MW)
University of Iowa, IA (MW)
University of Kansas, KS (MW)
University of Kentucky, KY (MW)
University of Lowell, MA (M)
University of Maryland, MD (MW)
University of Maryland (Baltimore County), MD (MW)
University of Massachusetts (Amherst), MA (MW)
University of Massachusetts (Boston), MA (MW)
University of Miami, FL (MW)
University of Michigan, MI (MW)
University of Missouri, MO (MW)
University of Missouri (Columbia), MO (MW)
University of Nebraska, NE (W)
University of Nebraska (Lincoln), NE (MW)
University of Nevada, NV (MW)
University of New Hampshire, NH (MW)
University of New Orleans, LA (MW)
University of North Carolina (Asheville), NC (MW)
University of North Carolina (Chapel Hill), NC (MW)
University of North Carolina (Wilmington), NC (MW)
University of North Dakota, ND (MW)
University of Northern Colorado, CO (W)
University of Northern Iowa, IA (MW)
University of Notre Dame, IN (MW)

University of Pennsylvania, PA (MW)
University of Pittsburgh, PA (MW)
University of Rhode Island, RI (MW)
University of Richmond, VA (MW)
University of Scranton, PA (MW)
University of South Carolina, SC (MW)
University of South Dakota, SD (MW)
University of St. Thomas, MN (MW)
University of Tennessee, TN (MW)
University of Tennessee (Knoxville), TN (MW)
University of Texas (Austin), TX (M)
University of Toledo, OH (M)
University of Utah, UT (MW)
University of Vermont, VT (MW)
University of Virginia, VA (MW)
University of Washington, WA (MW)
University of Wisconsin (Eau Claire), WI (MW)
University of Wisconsin (Green Bay), WI (MW)
University of Wisconsin (La Crosse), WI (MW)
University of Wisconsin (Madison), WI (MW)
University of Wisconsin (Milwaukee), WI (MW)
University of Wisconsin (Oshkosh), WI (MW)
University of Wisconsin (River Falls), WI (MW)
University of Wisconsin (Stout), WI (MW)
University of Wyoming, WY (MW)
Valparaiso University, IN (MW)
Vassar College, NY (MW)
Villanova University, PA (MW)
Vincennes University Junior College, IN (MW)
Wabash College, IN (M)
Washington and Jefferson College, PA (MW)
Washington University, MO (MW)
Wayne State University, MI (MW)
Wellesley College, MA (W)
Western Illinois University, IL (MW)
Western Kentucky University, KY (M)
Western State College, CO (W)
Westfield State College, MA (W)
Westminster College, PA (M)
West Virginia University, WV (MW)
Whitman College, WA (MW)
Whittier College, CA (MW)
Willamette University, OR (MW)
William Patterson College, NJ (MW)
William Rainey Harper College, IL (MW)
Williams College, MA (MW)
William Woods College, MO (W)
Wright State University, OH (MW)
Yale University, CT (MW)
York College of Pennsylvania, PA (MW)

Synchronized Swimming

Converse College, SC (W)
De Anza Community College, CA (W)
Florida State University, FL (W)
Goucher College, MD (MW)
Harper William Rainey College, IL (W)
Hinds Community College, MS (MW)
Luther College, IA (M)
Mobile College, AL (W)
Mt. San Antonio College, CA (W)
Muhlenberg College, PA (W)
Ohio State University, OH (W)
Saint John's University, NY (W)
University of Richmond, VA (W)
Walsh College, OH (W)
West Liberty State College, WV (W)

Tennis

Abilene Christian University, TX (MW)
Adelphi University, NY (MW)
Adirondack College, NY (MW)
Adrian College, MI (MW)
Agnes Scott College, GA (W)
Alabama A & M University, AL (M)
Alabama State University, AL (MW)
Albany State College, GA (MW)
Albertson College, ID (M)
Albion College, MI (MW)
Albright College, PA (MW)
Alcorn State University, MS (W)
Alfred University, NY (W)
Alice Lloyd College, KY (M)
Allegheny CCAC, PA (MW)
Allegheny College, PA (MW)
Allentown College, PA (MW)
Alma College, MI (MW)
American International College, MA (MW)
American University, DC (MW)
Amherst College, MA (MW)
Anderson College, SC (MW)
Anderson University, IN (MW)
Andrew College, GA (MW)
Angelo State University, TX (MW)
Appalachian State University, NC (MW)
Apprentice School, VA (M)
Aquinas College, MI (MW)
Arizona State University, AZ (MW)
Arkansas College, AR (MW)
Arkansas State University, AR (W)
Arkansas Tech University, AR (MW)
Armstrong State College, GA (MW)
Arrowhead Community College, MN (MW)
Asbury College, KY (MW)
Ashland College, OH (MW)
Atlantic Community College, NJ (MW)
Auburn University, AL (MW)
Auburn University (Montgomery), AL (MW)
Augusta College, GA (MW)
Augustana College, IL (MW)
Augustana College, SD (MW)
Aurora University, IL (MW)
Austin College, TX (MW)
Austin Community College, MN (MW)
Austin Peay State University, TN (MW)
Averett College, VA (MW)
Babson College, MA (MW)
Baker University, KS (MW)
Ball State University, IN (MW)
Barber-Scotia College, NY (MW)
Bard College, NY (MW)
Barry University, FL (MW)
Barstow College, CA (MW)
Barton College, NC (MW)
Barton County College, KS (W)
Bates College, ME (MW)
Baylor University, TX (MW)
Becker College, MA (M)
Belhaven College, MS (M)

Bellarmine College, KY (MW)
Belleville Area College, IL (MW)
Belmont Abbey College, NC (MW)
Belmont College, TN (MW)
Beloit College, WI (MW)
Benedict College, SC (MW)
Benedictine College, KS (MW)
Bentley College, MA (MW)
Berry College, GA (MW)
Bethany College, KS (MW)
Bethany College, WV (MW)
Bethel College, IN (MW)
Bethel College, KS (MW)
Bethel College, MN (MW)
Bethel College, TN (W)
Bethune-Cookman College, FL (MW)
Biola University, CA (W)
Birmingham-Southern College, AL (MW)
Bismarck State College, ND (MW)
Blackburn College, IL (MW)
Bloomsburg University, PA (MW)
Bluefield State College, WV (MW)
Blue Mountain College, MS (W)
Blue Mountain College, OR (MW)
Bluffton College, OH (MW)
Boise State University, ID (MW)
Boston College, MA (MW)
Boston University, MA (MW)
Bowdoin College, ME (MW)
Bowling Green State University, OH (MW)
Bradley University, IL (MW)
Brainerd Community College, MN (MW)
Brandeis University, MA (MW)
Brenau Women's University, GA (W)
Brevard College, NC (MW)
Brewton Parker College, GA (MW)
Bridgewater College, VA (MW)
Bridgewater State College, MA (MW)
Brigham Young University, HI (MW)
Brigham Young University, UT (MW)
Broome Community College, NY (M)
Broward Community College, FL (MW)
Brown University, RI (MW)
Brunswick Junior College, GA (MW)
Bryant College, RI (MW)
Bryn Mawr College, PA (W)
Bucknell University, PA (MW)
Bucks County Community College, PA (MW)
Buena Vista College, IA (MW)
Buffalo State College, NY (MW)
Buffalo State University (New York), NY (MW)
Butler County Community College, KS (MW)
Butler County Community College, PA (MW)
Butler University, IN (MW)
Butte College, CA (MW)
Cabrillo College, CA (M)
Cabrini College, PA (MW)
California Institute of Technology, CA (MW)
California Lutheran University, CA (MW)
California Polytechnic State University, CA (MW)
California State Polytechnic University, CA (MW)
California State University at Bakersfield, CA (W)
California State University (Fresno), CA (MW)
California State University (Fullerton), CA (W)
California State University (Hayward), CA (MW)
California State University (Long Beach), CA (MW)
California State University (Los Angeles), CA (MW)
California State University (Northridge), CA (W)
California State University (San Bernardino), CA (MW)
California University, PA (M)
Calvin College, MI (MW)
Cameron University, OK (W)
Campbellsville College, KY (MW)
Campbell University, NC (MW)
Canisius College, NY (MW)
Capital University, OH (MW)
Carleton College, MN (MW)
Carnegie-Mellon University, PA (MW)
Carroll College, WI (MW)
Carson-Newman College, TN (MW)
Carthage College, WI (MW)
Case Western Reserve University, OH (MW)
Castleton State College, VT (MW)
Catawba College, NC (MW)
Catholic University of America, DC (MW)
Catholic University of Puerto Rico, PR (MW)
Catonsville Community College, MD (MW)
Cayuga County Community College, NY (MW)
Cedarville College, OH (MW)
Centenary College, LA (MW)
Central College, IA (MW)
Central College, KS (MW)
Central Connecticut State University, CT (MW)
Central Methodist College, MO (MW)
Central Washington University, WA (MW)
Cerritos College, CA (MW)
Chaffey College, CA (W)
Chaminade University, HI (MW)
Chapman University, CA (M)
Charles County Community College, MD (MW)
Charleston Southern University, SC (MW)
Cheyney University of Pennsylvania, PA (MW)
Chicago State University, IL (M)
Chowan College, NC (MW)
Christopher Newport College, VA (MW)
Citadel, SC (M)
City College of New York, NY (MW)
City College of San Francisco, CA (MW)
Clarion University, PA (W)
Clark Atlanta University, GA (MW)
Clark College, WA (W)
Clarkson University, NY (MW)
Clark University, MA (MW)
Clemson University, SC (MW)
Cleveland State University, OH (MW)
Clinch Valley College, VA (MW)
Cloud County Community College, KS (MW)
Coastal Carolina College, SC (MW)
Coastal Carolina Community College, NC (MW)
Coe College, IA (W)
Coffeyville Community College, KS (MW)
Coker College, SC (MW)
Colby-Sawyer College, NH (MW)
Colgate University, NY (MW)
College of Allegheny County, PA (MW)
College of Charleston, SC (MW)
College of Idaho, ID (W)
College of New Rochelle, NY (W)
College of Notre Dame, CA (MW)
College of St. Benedict, MN (W)

College of St. Francis, IL (MW)
College of St. Mary, NY (W)
College of St. Rose, NY (MW)
College of St. Scholastica, MN (MW)
College of the Desert, CA (MW)
College of the Sequoias, CA (MW)
College of William and Mary, VA (MW)
College of Wooster, OH (MW)
Colorado College, CO (MW)
Colorado School of Mines, CO (MW)
Colorado State University, CO (MW)
Columbia Basin Community College, WA (MW)
Columbia College, SC (W)
Columbia Union College, MD (MW)
Columbia University, NY (MW)
Columbus College, GA (MW)
Community College of Rhode Island, RI (MW)
Community Colleges of Spokane, WA (MW)
Concord College, WV (MW)
Concordia College, MN (MW)
Concordia College, NY (MW)
Concordia Lutheran College, TX (MW)
Concordia Seminary MO (MW)
Concordia Teachers College, NE (MW)
Concordia University, IL (MW)
Concordia University Wisconsin, WI (MW)
Connecticut College, CT (MW)
Connors State College, OK (MW)
Contra Costa College, CA (MW)
Converse College, SC (W)
Cooke County Junior College, TX (W)
Copiah-Lincoln Community College, MS (M)
Coppin State College, MD (MW)
Cornell College, IA (MW)
Cornell University, NY (MW)
Cosummes River College, CA (MW)
Cowley County Community College, KS (M)
Creighton University, NE (MW)
Cuesta College, CA (MW)
Culver-Stockton College, MO (MW)
Cumberland College, KY (MW)
Curry College, MA (MW)
Dalton College, GA (MW)
Dana College, NE (MW)
Dartmouth College, NH (MW)
David Lipscomb College, TN (MW)
Davidson College, NC (MW)
Davis & Elkins College, WV (MW)
Dean Junior College, MA (MW)
De Anza Community College, CA (MW)
Defiance College, OH (M)
Delaware County Community College, PA (M)
Delaware State College, DE (MW)
Delta College, MI (M)
Delta State University, MS (MW)
Denison University, OH (MW)
DePaul University, IL (MW)
De Pauw University, IN (MW)
Diablo Valley Community College, CA (M)
Dickinson College, PA (MW)
Dickinson State University, ND (MW)
Dixie College, UT (M)
Doane College, NE (MW)
Dominican College, CA (MW)
Dowling College, NY (MW)
Drake University, IA (MW)
Drew University, NJ (MW)
Drexel University, PA (MW)
Drury College, MO (M)
Duke University, NC (MW)
Dundalk Community College, MD (MW)
Duquesne University, PA (MW)
Dutchess Junior College, NY (MW)
Earlham College, IN (MW)
East Carolina University, NC (MW)
East Central University, OK (MW)
Eastern College, PA (MW)
Eastern Illinois University, IL (MW)
Eastern Kentucky University, KY (MW)
Eastern Michigan University, MI (MW)
Eastern Montana College, MT (MW)
Eastern Nazarene College, MA (MW)
Eastern New Mexico University, NM (W)
Eastern Oklahoma State College, OK (MW)
Eastern Washington University, WA (MW)
Eastfeld College, TX (MW)
East Stroudsburg University, PA (MW)
East Tennessee State University, TN (MW)
East Texas Baptist University, TX (MW)
East Texas State University, TX (MW)
Edgewood College, WI (MW)
Edinboro University of Pennsylvania, PA (MW)
El Camino College, CA (MW)
Elgin Community College, IL (MW)
Elizabethtown College, PA (MW)
Elmhurst College, IL (MW)
Elmira College, NY (MW)
Elon College, NC (MW)
Emerson College, MA (W)
Emory University, GA (MW)
Emory and Henry College, VA (MW)
Emporia State University, KS (MW)
Enterprise State Junior College, AL (MW)
Erskine College, SC (MW)
Essex Community College, MD (MW)
Eureka College, IL (MW)
Evangel College, MO (W)
Everett Community College, WA (MW)
Fairfeld University, CT (MW)
Fairleigh Dickinson University (Madison), NJ (MW)
Fairleigh Dickinson University (Rutherford), NJ (MW)
Fairleigh Dickinson University (Teaneck), NJ (MW)
Fairmont State College, WV (MW)
Fashion Institute of Technology, NY (MW)
Fergus Falls Community College, MN (W)
Ferris State College, MI (MW)
Ferrum College, VA (MW)
Flagler College, FL (MW)
Florida A & M University, FL (MW)
Florida Atlantic University, FL (MW)
Florida Institute of Technology, FL (M)
Florida International University, FL (MW)
Florida Memorial College, FL (MW)
Florida Southern College, FL (MW)
Florida State University, FL (MW)
Foothill College, CA (MW)
Fordham University, NY (MW)
Fort Hays State University, KS (W)
Fort Scott College, KS (W)

Fort Valley State College, GA (MW)
Francis Marion University, SC (MW)
Franklin & Marshall College, PA (MW)
Franklin Pierce College, NH (MW)
Frederick Community College, MD (MW)
Freed-Hardeman College, TN (MW)
Fresno City College, CA (MW)
Fullerton College, CA (MW)
Furman University, SC (MW)
Gannon College, PA (MW)
Gardner-Webb College, NC (MW)
Garland County Community College, AR (MW)
Geneva College, PA (MW)
George Mason University, VA (MW)
Georgetown College, KY (MW)
Georgetown University, DC (W)
George Washington University, DC (MW)
Georgia College, GA (MW)
Georgia Institute of Technology, GA (MW)
Georgia Military College, GA (M)
Georgia Southern University, GA (MW)
Georgia Southwestern College, GA (MW)
Georgia State University, GA (MW)
Gettysburg College, PA (MW)
Glendale Community College, AZ (MW)
Glendale Community College, CA (MW)
Gloucester County College, NJ (MW)
Golden West College, CA (MW)
Gonzaga University, WA (MW)
Gordon College, MA (MW)
Goshen College, IN (MW)
Goucher College, MD (MW)
Grace College, IN (M)
Graceland College, IA (MW)
Grambling State University, LA (MW)
Grand Canyon College, AZ (MW)
Grand Rapids Junior College, MI (MW)
Grand View College, IA (MW)
Grayson County College, TX (MW)
Greensboro College, NC (MW)
Green River Community College, WA (MW)
Greenville College, IL (MW)
Grinnell College, IA (MW)
Grove City College, PA (MW)
Gustavus Adolphus College, MN (MW)
Hamilton College, NY (MW)
Hampden-Sydney College, VA (M)
Hampton University, VA (M)
Hanover College, IN (MW)
Harding University, AR (MW)
Hardin-Simmons University, TX (MW)
Harford Community College, MD (MW)
Harper William Rainey College, IL (MW)
Hartwick College, NY (MW)
Harvard University, MA (MW)
Hastings College, NE (MW)
Haverford College, PA (MW)
Hawaii Pacific University, HI (M)
Heidelberg College, OH (W)
Henderson State University, AR (MW)
Henry Ford Community College, MI (MW)
Herkimer County Community College, NY (W)
Highland Park Community College, MI (M)
High Point University, NC (MW)
Hillsborough Community College, FL (W)
Hillsdale College, MI (MW)
Hinds Community College, MS (MW)
Hiram College, OH (MW)
Hofstra University, NY (MW)
Holy Cross College, MA (MW)
Hood College, MD (W)
Hope College, MI (MW)
Houston Baptist University, TX (M)
Howard Payne University, TX (W)
Howard University, DC (MW)
Hudson Valley Community College, NY (MW)
Humboldt State University, CA (W)
Hunter College of the City University of New York, NY (MW)
Huntingdon College, AL (MW)
Huntington College, IN (MW)
Huston-Tillotson College, TX (MW)
Hutchinson College, KS (MW)
Idaho State University, ID (W)
Illinois Benedictine College, IL (MW)
Illinois College, IL (MW)
Illinois Institute of Technology, IL (MW)
Illinois State University, IL (MW)
Illinois Valley Community College, IL (MW)
Illinois Wesleyan University, IL (MW)
Incarnate Word College, TX (MW)
Indiana State University, IN (MW)
Indiana University, IN (MW)
Indiana University of Pennsylvania, PA (MW)
Indiana University-Purdue University, IN (M)
Indiana University-Purdue University (Fort Wayne), IN (MW)
Indiana Wesleyan University, IN (MW)
Indian River Community College, FL (MW)
Iona College, NY (MW)
Iowa State University of Science and Technology, IA (W)
Ithaca College, NY (MW)
Jackson State University, MS (MW)
Jacksonville State University, AL (MW)
Jacksonville University, FL (MW)
James Madison University, VA (MW)
Jefferson College, MO (M)
Jefferson Davis Junior College, AL (MW)
Jefferson State Junior College, AL (MW)
John Brown University, AR (MW)
John Carroll University, OH (MW)
Johns Hopkins University, MD (MW)
Johnson County Community College, KS (MW)
Johnson C. Smith University, NC (M)
Johnson State College, VT (M)
Jones County Junior College, MS (MW)
Judson College, AL (W)
Juniata College, PA (MW)
Kalamazoo College, MI (MW)
Kalamazoo Valley Community College, MI (MW)
Kankakee Community College, IL (M)
Kansas City Kansas Community College, KS (M)
Kansas State University, KS (W)
Kaskaskia Community College, IL (MW)

Kean College of New Jersey, NJ (MW)
Kent State University, OH (MW)
Kentucky State University, KY (MW)
Kentucky Wesleyan College, KY (W)
Kenyon College, OH (MW)
Keystone Junior College, PA (M)
King College, TN (MW)
King's College, PA (MW)
Knox College, IL (MW)
Knoxville College, TN (MW)
Kutztown University, PA (MW)
Labette Community College, KS (W)
Lafayette College, PA (MW)
Lake Forest College, IL (MW)
Lake Land College, IL (M)
Lake Superior State University, MI (MW)
Lamar University, TX (MW)
Lambuth University, TN (MW)
Lander College, SC (MW)
La Salle University, PA (MW)
Lawrence University, WI (MW)
Lee College, TN (MW)
Lees-McRae College, NC (MW)
Lehigh County Community College, PA (MW)
Lehigh University, PA (MW)
Le Moyne College, NY (MW)
Lenoir-Rhyne College, NC (MW)
LeTourneau College, TX (W)
Lewis and Clark College, OR (MW)
Lewis and Clark Community College, IL (MW)
Lewis/Clark State College, ID (MW)
Lewis University, IL (MW)
Liberty University, VA (M)
Limestone College, SC (MW)
Lincoln Christian College, IL (M)
Lincoln College, IL (MW)
Lincoln Memorial University, TN (MW)
Lincoln University, MO (MW)
Linfield College, OR (MW)
Livingstone College, NC (MW)
Livingston University, AL (MW)
Long Beach City College, CA (MW)
Long Island University (Brooklyn), NY (MW)
Long Island University (C.W. Post Campus), NY (W)
Longwood College, VA (MW)
Loras College, IA (MW)
Los Angeles Pierce Junior College, CA (MW)
Louisiana State University (Alexandria), LA (MW)
Louisiana State University (Baton Rouge), LA (MW)
Louisiana Tech University, LA (W)
Loyola College, MD (MW)
Loyola Marymount University, CA (MW)
Luther College, IA (MW)
Lycoming College, PA (MW)
Lynchburg College, VA (MW)
Lyndon State College, VT (MW)
Lynn University, FL (MW)
Macalester College, MN (MW)
Macomb Community College, MI (MW)
Madison Area Technical College, WI (MW)
Malone College, OH (MW)
Manchester College, IN (MW)
Manhattan College, NY (M)
Manhattanville College, NY (MW)
Mankato State University, MN (MW)
Marian College, IN (MW)
Marian College, WI (MW)
Marietta College, OH (MW)
Marion Military Institute, AL (M)
Marist College, NY (MW)
Marquette University, WI (MW)
Marshall University, WV (W)
Mars Hill College, NC (MW)
Mary Baldwin College, VA (W)
Marymount College, CA (MW)
Marymount University, VA (MW)
Maryville College, TN (MW)
Maryville University, MO (MW)
Mary Washington College, VA (MW)
Marywood College, PA (MW)
Massachusetts Institute of Technology, MA (MW)
McHenry County College, IL (MW)
McLennan Community College, TX (MW)
McPherson College, KS (MW)
Memphis State University, TN (MW)
Mercer County Community College, NJ (M)
Mercer University, GA (MW)
Mercy College, NY (MW)
Mercyhurst College, PA (MW)
Merrimack College, MA (MW)
Mesa Community College, AZ (MW)
Mesa State College, CO (MW)
Metropolitan State College, CO (MW)
Miami-Dade Community College (North), FL (MW)
Miami-Dade Community College (South Campus), FL (MW)
Miami-Dade Junior College, FL (MW)
Miami University, OH (MW)
Michigan State University, MI (MW)
Michigan Technological University, MI (MW)
Middlebury College, VT (MW)
Middlesex County College, NJ (W)
Middle Tennessee State University, TN (MW)
Midland Lutheran College, NE (MW)
Midwestern State University, TX (MW)
Millersville University, PA (MW)
Milligan College, TN (MW)
Millikin University, IL (MW)
Minot State, ND (MW)
MiraCosta College, CA (M)
Mississippi College, MS (MW)
Mississippi Delta Junior College, MS (W)
Mississippi Gulf Coast Junior College, MS (MW)
Mississippi State University, MS (MW)
Mississippi University For Women, MS (W)
Mississippi Valley State University, MS (MW)
Missouri Southern State College, MO (W)
Missouri Western State College, MO (W)
Mitchell College, CT (M)
Mitchell Community College, NC (M)
Mobile College, AL (M)
Modesto Junior College, CA (MW)
Mohawk Valley Community College, NY (MW)
Molloy College, NY (W)
Monmouth College, NJ (MW)
Montana State University, MT (MW)
Montclair State College, NJ (MW)
Montgomery College, MD (MW)
Moorhead State University, MN (W)
Moorpark College, CA (MW)
Moraine Valley Community College, IL (MW)
Moravian College, PA (MW)

Morehead State University, KY (MW)
Morehouse College, GA (M)
Morgan State University, MD (MW)
Morningside College, IA (MW)
Mount Holyoke College, MA (W)
Mount Olive College, NC (MW)
Mount St. Mary College, MD (MW)
Mount Union College, OH (MW)
Mount Vernon Nazarene College, OH (M)
Mt. San Antonio College, CA (M)
Mt. Wachusett Community College, MA (MW)
Muhlenberg College, PA (MW)
Multnomah School of the Bible, OR (M)
Murray State University, KY (MW)
Muskingum College, OH (MW)
Nassau Community College, NY (MW)
Navarro College, TX (MW)
Nazareth College, NY (MW)
Nebraska Wesleyan University, NE (M)
Newberry College, SC (MW)
New Hampshire College, NH (MW)
New Jersey Institute of Technology, NJ (MW)
New Mexico State University, NM (MW)
New York University, NY (MW)
Niagara University, NY (MW)
Nicholls State University, LA (W)
Nichols College, MA (M)
North Adams State College, MA (MW)
North Carolina A and T State University, NC (MW)
North Carolina Central University, NC (MW)
North Carolina State University, NC (MW)
North Carolina Wesleyan College, NC (M)
North Central College, IL (MW)
North Dakota State, ND (MW)
Northeastern Illinois University, IL (MW)
Northeastern Junior College, CO (MW)
Northeastern State University, OK (MW)
Northeast Louisiana University, LA (M)
Northeast Mississippi Community College, MS (MW)
Northeast Missouri State University, MO (MW)
Northern Arizona University, AZ (MW)
Northern Illinois University, IL (MW)
Northern Kentucky University, KY (MW)
Northern Michigan University, MI (W)
Northern State University, SD (MW)
North Georgia College, GA (MW)
North Greenville College, SC (M)
North Hennepin Community College, MN (MW)
Northwestern College, IA (MW)
Northwestern College, MN (M)
Northwestern Oklahoma State University, OK (MW)
Northwestern State University of Louisiana, LA (W)
Northwestern University, IL (MW)
Northwest Mississippi Community College, MS (MW)
Northwest Missouri State University, MO (MW)
Northwest Nazarene College, ID (W)
Northwood Institute, MI (M)
Northwood Institute (Texas Campus), TX (M)
Nova University FL (W)
Oakland Community College, MI (MW)
Oakland University, MI (MW)
Oakton Community College, IL (MW)
Oberlin College, OH (MW)
Occidental College, CA (MW)
Ocean County College, NJ (MW)
Odessa College, TX (M)
Oglethorpe University, GA (MW)
Ohio Northern University, OH (MW)
Ohio State University, OH (MW)
Ohio University, OH (MW)
Ohio Wesleyan University, OH (MW)
Okaloosa-Walton Junior College, FL (MW)
Oklahoma Baptist University, OK (M)
Oklahoma Christian University of Science & Art, OK (M)
Oklahoma City University, OK (MW)
Oklahoma State University, OK (MW)
Old Dominion University, VA (MW)
Olivet College, MI (MW)
Olivet Nazarene University, IL (MW)
Oral Roberts University, OK (MW)
Orange Coast College, CA (MW)
Orange County Community College, NY (MW)
Oregon State University, OR (W)
Ottawa University, KS (MW)
Otterbein College, OH (MW)
Ouachita Baptist University, AR (MW)
Pace University, NY (MW)
Pace University, NY (MW)
Pace University (White Plains Campus), NY (MW)
Pacific Lutheran University, WA (MW)
Pacific University, OR (MW)
Paducah Community College, CA (MW)
Palm Beach Community College, FL (MW)
Palomar College, CA (MW)
Pan American University, TX (MW)
Parkland College, IL (M)
Penn State University, PA (MW)
Penn State University, PA (MW)
Pennsylvania State University, PA (MW)
Pennsylvania State University (Behrend College), PA (MW)
Pepperdine University, CA (MW)
Pfeiffer College, NC (MW)
Philadelphia College of Textile and Science, PA (MW)
Philadelphia Community College, PA (MW)
Phillips University, OK (M)
Phoenix College, AZ (MW)
Piedmont College, GA (MW)
Pima Community College, AZ (MW)
Plymouth State College, NH (MW)
Point Loma Nazarene College, CA (MW)
Polytechnic University (Brooklyn Campus), NY (M)
Pomona-Pitzer Colleges, CA (MW)
Portland State University, OR (W)
Prairie View A & M University, TX (MW)

Pratt Community College, KS (MW)
Presbyterian College, SC (MW)
Prince George's Community College, MD (MW)
Princeton University, NJ (MW)
Principia College, IL (MW)
Providence College, RI (MW)
Purdue University, IN (MW)
Queensborough Community College, NY (MW)
Queens College, NY (MW)
Queens College, NC (MW)
Quinnipiac College, CT (MW)
Radford University, VA (MW)
Ramapo College, NJ (MW)
Randolph-Macon College, VA (MW)
Ranetto Santiago College, CA (MW)
Regis College, MA (W)
Regis University, CO (MW)
Rensselaer Polytechnic Institute, NY (MW)
Rhode Island College, RI (MW)
Rice University, TX (MW)
Rider College, NJ (MW)
Ripon College, WI (MW)
Riverside College, CA (MW)
Roanoke College, VA (MW)
Robert Morris College, PA (MW)
Roberts Wesleyan College, NY (MW)
Rochester Community College, MN (MW)
Rochester Institute of Technology, NY (MW)
Rockland Community College, NY (MW)
Rollins College, FL (MW)
Roosevelt University, IL (MW)
Rosary College, IL (MW)
Rose-Hulman Institute of Technology, IN (M)
Rose State Junior College, OK (MW)
Rowan College of New Jersey, NJ (MW)
Rust College, MS (MW)
Saddleback College, CA (MW)
Saginaw Valley State College, MI (W)
Saint Ambrose College, IA (MW)
Saint Andrews Presbyterian College, NC (MW)
Saint Anselm College, NH (MW)
Saint Augustine's College, NC (M)
Saint Bonaventure University, NY (MW)
Saint Cloud State University, MN (MW)
Saint Edward's University, TX (MW)
Saint Francis College, IN (MW)
Saint Francis College, NY (MW)
Saint Francis College, PA (MW)
Saint John Fisher College, NY (MW)
Saint John's University, MN (M)
Saint John's University, NY (MW)
Saint Joseph's College, IN (MW)
Saint Joseph's University, PA (MW)
Saint Lawrence University, NY (MW)
Saint Leo College, FL (MW)
Saint Louis University, MO (MW)
Saint Mary's College, IN (W)
Saint Mary's College, MD (MW)
Saint Mary's College, MI (W)
Saint Mary's College of California, CA (MW)
Saint Mary's University, TX (MW)
Saint Michael's College, VT (MW)
Saint Norbert College, WI (MW)
Saint Olaf College, MN (MW)
Saint Peter's College, NJ (MW)
Saint Thomas University, FL (W)
Saint Vincent College, PA (M)
Salem State College, MA (MW)
Salem-Teikyo University, WV (MW)
Salve Regina College, RI (MW)
Sam Houston State University, TX (MW)
San Bernardino Community College, CA (MW)
San Diego City College, CA (MW)
San Diego Mesa College, CA (MW)
San Diego State University, CA (MW)
San Joaquin Delta College, CA (MW)
San Jose State University, CA (MW)
Santa Barbara City College, CA (MW)
Santa Clara University, CA (MW)
Santa Monica College, CA (MW)
Santa Rosa Junior College, CA (MW)
Sauk Valley College, IL (MW)
Savannah State College, GA (W)
Schreiner College, TX (MW)
Scottsdale Community College, AR (MW)
Seattle University, WA (MW)
Seminole Community College, FL (MW)
Seton Hall University, NJ (MW)
Seton Hill College, PA (W)
Seward County Community College, KS (MW)
Shawnee State University, OH (MW)
Shepherd College, WV (MW)
Shippensburg University of Pennsylvania, PA (MW)
Shoreline Community College, WA (MW)
Shorter College, AR (M)
Shorter College, GA (MW)
Siena College, NY (MW)
Siena Heights College, MI (MW)
Sierra College, CA (MW)
Simpson College, CA (MW)
Sinclair Community College, OH (MW)
Sioux Falls College, SD (MW)
Skagit Valley College, WA (MW)
Skidmore College, NY (MW)
Slippery Rock University of Pennsylvania, PA (MW)
Smith College, MA (W)
Snead State Community College, AL (MW)
Snow College, UT (MW)
South Carolina State College, SC (MW)
South Dakota School of Mines and Technology, SD (M)
Southeastern Louisiana University, LA (MW)
Southeastern Massachusetts University, MA (MW)
Southeastern Oklahoma State University, OK (MW)
Southern Arkansas University, AR (MW)
Southern College of Technology, GA (MW)
Southern Connecticut State University, CT (MW)
Southern Illinois University, IL (MW)
Southern Illinois University (Edwardsville), IL (MW)
Southern Methodist University, TX (MW)
Southern Oregon State College, OR (MW)
Southern University and A & M College, LA (MW)

South Plains Community College, TX (MW)
Southwest Baptist University, MO (MW)
Southwestern College, CA (W)
Southwestern College, KS (MW)
Southwestern Oklahoma State University, OK (MW)
Southwestern University, TX (MW)
Southwest Missouri State University, MO (MW)
Southwest State University, MN (W)
Southwest Texas State University, TX (MW)
Spring Arbor College, MI (M)
Springfield College, MA (MW)
Spring Hill College, AL (MW)
Stanford University, CA (MW)
State University of New York (Albany), NY (MW)
State University of New York (Binghamton), NY (MW)
State University of New York (Buffalo), NY (MW)
State University of New York (Plattsburgh), NY (MW)
State University of New York (Stony Brook), NY (MW)
State University of New York College (Brockport), NY (W)
State University of New York College (Cortland), NY (W)
State University of New York College (Fredonia), NY (MW)
State University of New York College (New Paltz), NY (MW)
State University of New York College (Oswego), NY (MW)
State University of New York College (Potsdam), NY (W)
State University of New York College (Purchase), NY (W)
State University of New York Maritime College, NY (MW)
Sterling College, KS (MW)
Stetson University, FL (MW)
Stevens Institute of Technology, NJ (MW)
St. Gregory's College, OK (MW)
Stonehill College, MA (MW)
Suffolk County Community College, NY (MW)
Suffolk University, MA (MW)
Sul Ross State University, TX (MW)
Swarthmore College, PA (MW)
Sweet Briar College, VA (W)
Syracuse University, NY (W)
Tabor College, KS (MW)
Talledaga College, AL (MW)
Tampa College, FL (MW)
Tarleton State University, TX (MW)
Teikyo Westmar University, IA (M)
Temple Junior College, TX (MW)
Temple University, PA (MW)
Tennessee Technological University, TN (MW)
Tennessee Wesleyan College, TN (MW)
Texas A & I University, TX (MW)
Texas A & M University, TX (MW)
Texas Christian University, TX (MW)
Texas Lutheran College, TX (MW)
Texas Southern University, TX (MW)
Texas Tech University, TX (MW)
Texas Woman's University, TX (W)
Thomas College, ME (MW)
Thomas More College, KY (M)
Towson State University, MD (MW)
Transylvania University, KY (MW)
Trenton State College, NJ (MW)
Trinity College, CT (MW)
Trinity College, IL (MW)
Trinity University, TX (MW)
Tri-State University, IN (MW)
Troy State University, AL (MW)
Truett-McConnell Junior College, GA (MW)
Tufts University, MA (MW)
Tulane University, LA (MW)
Tusculum College, TN (MW)
Tuskegee University, AL (MW)
Tyler Junior College, TX (MW)
Union College, KY (M)
Union College, NY (MW)
University of Akron, OH (MW)
University of Alabama (Birmingham), AL (M)
University of Alabama (Huntsville), AL (MW)
University of Alabama (Tuscaloosa), AL (MW)
University of Arizona, AZ (MW)
University of Arkansas (Fayetteville), AR (MW)
University of Arkansas (Little Rock), AR (MW)
University of Arkansas (Pine Bluff), AR (M)
University of Bridgeport, CT (MW)
University of California (Berkeley), CA (MW)
University of California (Davis), CA (MW)
University of California (Irvine), CA (MW)
University of California (Riverside), CA (MW)
University of California (San Diego), CA (MW)
University of California (Santa Barbara), CA (MW)
University of California (Santa Cruz), CA (MW)
University of California (UCLA), CA (MW)
University of Central Arkansas, AR (MW)
University of Central Florida, FL (MW)
University of Central Oklahoma, OK (MW)
University of Charleston, WV (MW)
University of Chicago, IL (MW)
University of Cincinnati, OH (MW)
University of Colorado, CO (MW)
University of Colorado (Colorado Springs), CO (MW)
University of Connecticut, CT (MW)
University of Dallas, TX (MW)
University of Dayton, OH (MW)
University of Delaware, DE (MW)
University of Denver, CO (MW)
University of Detroit Mercy, MI (MW)
University of Dubuque, IA (MW)
University of Evansville, IN (MW)
University of Findlay, OH (MW)
University of Florida, FL (MW)
University of Georgia, GA (MW)
University of Hartford, CT (MW)
University of Hawaii (Hilo), HI (MW)
University of Hawaii (Manoa), HI (MW)
University of Houston, TX (W)
University of Idaho, ID (MW)
University of Illinois, IL (MW)
University of Illinois (Urbana-Champaign), IL (MW)

University of Indianapolis, IN (MW)
University of Iowa, IA (MW)
University of Kansas, KS (MW)
University of Kentucky, KY (MW)
University of La Verne, CA (MW)
University of Louisville, KY (MW)
University of Lowell, MA (MW)
University of Maine, ME (MW)
University of Mary, ND (MW)
University of Mary Hardin-Baylor, TX (MW)
University of Maryland, MD (MW)
University of Maryland (Baltimore County), MD (MW)
University of Maryland (Eastern Shore), MD (MW)
University of Massachusetts (Boston), MA (M)
University of Miami, FL (MW)
University of Minnesota (Duluth), MN (MW)
University of Minnesota (Minneapolis), MN (MW)
University of Minnesota (Morris), MN (MW)
University of Mississippi, MS (MW)
University of Missouri (Columbia), MO (MW)
University of Missouri (Kansas City), MO (MW)
University of Montana, MT (MW)
University of Nebraska, NE (MW)
University of Nebraska (Kearney), NE (MW)
University of Nebraska (Lincoln), NE (MW)
University of Nevada, NV (MW)
University of Nevada (Reno), NV (MW)
University of New Hampshire, NH (MW)
University of New Haven, CT (W)
University of New Mexico, NM (MW)
University of New Orleans, LA (W)
University of North Alabama, AL (MW)
University of North Carolina (Asheville), NC (MW)
University of North Carolina (Chapel Hill), NC (MW)
University of North Carolina (Charlotte), NC (MW)
University of North Carolina (Greensboro), NC (MW)
University of North Carolina (Wilmington), NC (MW)
University of Northern Colorado, CO (MW)
University of Northern Iowa, IA (MW)
University of North Florida, FL (MW)
University of North Texas, TX (MW)
University of Notre Dame, IN (MW)
University of Oklahoma, OK (MW)
University of Oregon, OR (MW)
University of Pennsylvania, PA (MW)
University of Pittsburgh, PA (MW)
University of Portland, OR (MW)
University of Puerto Rico, PR (MW)
University of Puerto Rico (Bayamon), PR (MW)
University of Puerto Rico (Ponce), PR (MW)
University of Puget Sound, WA (MW)
University of Redlands, CA (MW)
University of Rhode Island, RI (MW)
University of Richmond, VA (MW)
University of San Diego, CA (MW)
University of San Francisco, CA (MW)
University of Scranton, PA (MW)
University of South Alabama, AL (MW)
University of South Carolina, SC (MW)
University of South Carolina (Aiken), SC (M)
University of South Carolina (Spartanburg), SC (MW)
University of South Dakota, SD (MW)
University of Southern California, CA (MW)
University of Southern Colorado, CO (MW)
University of Southern Indiana, IN (MW)
University of Southern Mississippi, MS (MW)
University of South Florida, FL (MW)
University of Southwestern Louisiana, LA (MW)
University of St. Thomas, MN (MW)
University of Tampa, FL (MW)
University of Tennessee, TN (MW)
University of Tennessee (Knoxville), TN (MW)
University of Tennessee (Martin), TN (MW)
University of Texas (Arlington), TX (MW)
University of Texas (Austin), TX (MW)
University of Texas (El Paso), TX (MW)
University of Texas (Pan American), TX (MW)
University of Texas (San Antonio), TX (MW)
University of the District of Columbia, DC (MW)
University of the Pacific, CA (MW)
University of Toledo, OH (MW)
University of Tulsa, OK (MW)
University of Utah, UT (MW)
University of Vermont, VT (MW)
University of Virginia, VA (MW)
University of Washington, WA (MW)
University of West Florida, FL (MW)
University of Wisconsin (Eau Claire), WI (MW)
University of Wisconsin (Green Bay), WI (MW)
University of Wisconsin (La Crosse), WI (MW)
University of Wisconsin (Madison), WI (MW)
University of Wisconsin (Milwaukee), WI (MW)
University of Wisconsin (Oshkosh), WI (MW)
University of Wisconsin (Platteville), WI (MW)
University of Wisconsin (River Falls), WI (MW)
University of Wisconsin (Stevens Point), WI (MW)
University of Wisconsin (Stout), WI (MW)
Upper Iowa University, IA (MW)
Ursinus College, PA (MW)
U.S. International University of, CA (MW)
Utah State University, UT (M)
Valdosta State College, GA (MW)
Valley City State University, ND (MW)

Valparaiso University, IN (MW)
Vanderbilt University, TN (MW)
Vassar College, NY (MW)
Ventura College, CA (MW)
Villanova University, PA (MW)
Vincennes University Junior College, IN (M)
Virginia Commonwealth University, VA (MW)
Virginia Intermont College, VA (MW)
Virginia Military Institute, VA (M)
Virginia Polytechnic Institute & State University, VA (MW)
Virginia State University, VA (MW)
Virginia Union University, VA (M)
Virginia Wesleyan College, VA (MW)
Wabash College, IN (M)
Wabash Valley College, IL (M)
Wagner College, NY (MW)
Wake Forest University, NC (MW)
Wallace Community College (Selma), AL (MW)
Walla Walla Community College, WA (MW)
Walsh College, OH (MW)
Walters State Community College, TN (M)
Wartburg College, IA (MW)
Washburn University, KS (MW)
Washington and Jefferson College, PA (MW)
Washington College, MD (MW)
Washington State University, WA (MW)
Washington University, MO (MW)
Waubonsee College, IL (MW)
Wayne State University, MI (MW)
Webber College, FL (MW)
Weber State College, UT (MW)
Webster University, MO (MW)
Wellesley College, MA (W)
Wesleyan University, CT (MW)
Wesley College, DE (MW)
West Chester University, PA (MW)
Western Carolina University, NC (MW)
Western Connecticut State University, CT (MW)
Western Illinois University, IL (MW)
Western Kentucky University, KY (MW)
Western Maryland College, MD (MW)
Western Michigan University, MI (MW)
Western New England College, MA (MW)
Western Washington University, WA (MW)
Western Wyoming Community College, WY (MW)
Westfield State College, MA (M)
West Georgia College, GA (MW)
West Liberty State College, WV (M)
Westminster College, PA (MW)
Westmont College, CA (MW)
West Texas State University, TX (MW)
West Virginia Institute of Technology, WV (MW)
West Virginia State College, WV (MW)
West Virginia University, WV (MW)
West Virginia Wesleyan College, WV (MW)
Wharton County Junior College, TX (MW)
Wheaton College, IL (MW)
Whitman College, WA (MW)
Whittier College, CA (MW)
Whitworth College, WA (MW)
Wichita State University, KS (MW)
Wilkes College, NC (MW)
Wilkes University, PA (MW)
Willamette University, OR (MW)
William Jewell College, MO (MW)
William Patterson College, NJ (W)
William Penn College, IA (MW)
William Rainey Harper College, IL (MW)
Williams College, MA (MW)
William Woods College, MO (W)
Wilmington College, DE (M)
Wilmington College, OH (MW)
Wilson College, PA (W)
Wingate College, NC (MW)
Winona State University, MN (MW)
Winston-Salem State University, NC (MW)
Winthrop University, SC (MW)
Wofford College, SC (MW)
Worcester State College, MA (MW)
Wright State University, OH (MW)
Yakima Valley College, WA (MW)
Yale University, CT (MW)
Yeshiva University, NY (M)
York College (CUNY), NY (M)
York College of Pennsylvania, PA (MW)
Youngstown State University, OH (MW)
Yuba Community College, CA (MW)

Track & Field

Abilene Christian University, TX (MW)
Adams State College, CO (MW)
Adrian College, MI (MW)
Alabama A & M University, AL (MW)
Alabama State University, AL (MW)
Albany State College, GA (MW)
Albion College, MI (MW)
Albright College, PA (MW)
Alcorn State University, MS (MW)
Alfred University, NY (MW)
Allegheny College, PA (MW)
Allen County College, KS (MW)
Allen University, SC (M)
Alma College, MI (MW)
Amherst College, MA (MW)
Anderson College, SC (M)
Anderson University, IN (MW)
Angelo State University, TX (MW)
Appalachian State University, NC (MW)
Apprentice School, VA (MW)
Aquinas College, MI (MW)
Arizona State University, AZ (MW)
Arkansas College, AR (MW)
Arkansas State University, AR (MW)
Ashland College, OH (MW)
Auburn University, AL (MW)
Augsburg College, MN (MW)
Augustana College, IL (MW)
Augustana College, SD (MW)
Austin College, TX (M)
Austin Community College, MN (M)
Austin Peay State University, TN (MW)
Azusa Pacific University, CA (MW)
Bacone Junior College, OK (MW)
Baker University, KS (MW)

Ball State University, IN (MW)
Baltimore City Community College, MD (MW)
Barber-Scotia College, NC (MW)
Barton County College, KS (MW)
Bates College, ME (MW)
Bayamon Central University, PR (MW)
Baylor University, TX (MW)
Bellarmine College, KY (MW)
Belmont College, TN (MW)
Beloit College, WI (MW)
Bemidji State University, MN (W)
Benedict College, SC (MW)
Benedictine College, KS (MW)
Bentley College, MA (MW)
Bergen Community College, NJ (MW)
Bethany College, KS (MW)
Bethany College, WV (MW)
Bethel College, KS (MW)
Bethel College, MN (MW)
Bethune-Cookman College, FL (MW)
Biola University, CA (M)
Bismarck State College, ND (MW)
Blackburn College, IL (MW)
Black Hawk College, IL (MW)
Black Hills State University, SD (MW)
Bloomsburg University, PA (MW)
Blue Mountain College, OR (MW)
Bluffton College, OH (MW)
Boise State University, ID (MW)
Boston College, MA (MW)
Boston University, MA (MW)
Bowdoin College, ME (MW)
Bowie State University, MD (MW)
Bowling Green State University, OH (MW)
Brandeis University, MA (MW)
Brevard College, FL (MW)
Brevard College, NC (MW)
Bridgewater College, VA (MW)
Bridgewater State College, MA (MW)
Brigham Young University, UT (MW)
Bronx Community College, NY (MW)
Brown University, RI (MW)
Bryant College, RI (MW)
Bucknell University, PA (MW)
Buena Vista College, IA (MW)
Buffalo State College, NY (MW)
Buffalo State University (New York), NY (MW)
Butler University, IN (MW)
Butte College, CA (MW)
Cabrillo College, CA (MW)
Cabrini College, PA (MW)
California Institute of Technology, CA (MW)
California Lutheran University, CA (MW)
California Polytechnic State University, CA (MW)
California State Polytechnic University, CA (MW)
California State University, CA (MW)
California State University at Bakersfield, CA (MW)
California State University (Chico), CA (MW)
California State University (Fresno), CA (MW)
California State University (Fullerton), CA (MW)
California State University (Hayward), CA (MW)
California State University (Los Angeles), CA (MW)
California State University (Northridge), CA (MW)
California State University (Sacramento), CA (MW)
California University, PA (MW)
Calvin College, MI (MW)
Campbell University, NC (MW)
Carleton College, MN (MW)
Carnegie-Mellon University, PA (MW)
Carroll College, WI (MW)
Carson-Newman College, TN (MW)
Carthage College, WI (MW)
Case Western Reserve University, OH (MW)
Catholic University of America, DC (MW)
Catholic University of Puerto Rico, PR (MW)
Catonsville Community College, MD (MW)
Cayuga County Community College, NY (MW)
Cedarville College, OH (MW)
Central Arizona College, AZ (M)
Central College, IA (MW)
Central College, KS (MW)
Central Connecticut State University, CT (MW)
Central Methodist College, MO (MW)
Central Michigan University, MI (MW)
Central Missouri State University, MO (MW)
Central State University, OH (M)
Central Washington University, WA (MW)
Cerritos College, CA (MW)
Chadron State College, NE (MW)
Chaffey College, CA (MW)
Charleston Southern University, SC (MW)
Chemeketa Community College, OR (MW)
Cheyney University of Pennsylvania, PA (MW)
Chicago State University, IL (MW)
Christopher Newport College, VA (MW)
Citadel, SC (M)
City College of New York, NY (MW)
City College of San Francisco CA (MW)
Clackamas Community College, OR (MW)
Claflin College, SC (MW)
Clarion University, PA (MW)
Clark Atlanta University GA (MW)
Clark University, MA (MW)
Clemson University, SC (MW)
Cleveland State University, OH (MW)
Cloud County Community College, KS (MW)
Coahoma Junior College, MS (M)
Coe College, IA (M)
Coffeyville Community College, KS (MW)
Colby Community College, KS (MW)
Colgate University, NY (MW)
College of Notre Dame, CA (MW)
College of Southern Idaho, ID (MW)
College of the Desert, CA (MW)
College of the Redwoods, CA (MW)
College of the Sequoias, CA (MW)
College of William and Mary, VA (MW)
College of Wooster, OH (MW)
Colorado College, CO (MW)
Colorado School of Mines, CO (MW)
Colorado State University, CO (MW)
Columbia Union College, MD (MW)
Columbia University, NY (MW)
Community Colleges of Spokane, WA (MW)
Compton Community College, CA (MW)

Concordia College, MN (MW)
Concordia College (Moorhead), MN (MW)
Concordia College (St. Paul), MN (MW)
Concordia Teachers College, NE (MW)
Concordia University, IL (MW)
Connecticut College, CT (MW)
Contra Costa College, CA (MW)
Copiah-Lincoln Community College, MS (M)
Coppin State College, MD (MW)
Cornell College, IA (MW)
Cornell University, NY (MW)
Cosummes River College, CA (MW)
Cuesta College, CA (MW)
Cumberland College, KY (M)
Cuyahoga Community College, OH (MW)
Dakota State University, SD (MW)
Dakota Wesleyan University, SD (MW)
Dana College, NE (MW)
Dartmouth College, NH (MW)
David Lipscomb College, TN (MW)
Davidson College, NC (MW)
De Anza Community College, CA (MW)
Defiance College, OH (MW)
Delaware State College, DE (MW)
Delaware Valley College, PA (MW)
Denison University, OH (MW)
DePaul University, IL (MW)
De Pauw University, IN (MW)
Diablo Valley Community College, Ca (MW)
Dickinson College, PA (MW)
Dickinson State University, ND (MW)
Doane College, NE (MW)
Drake University, IA (MW)
Drexel University, PA (M)
Duke University, NC (MW)
Duquesne University, PA (W)
Earlham College, IN (MW)
East Carolina University, NC (MW)
East Central University, OK (M)
Eastern Connecticut State University, CT (MW)
Eastern Illinois University, IL (MW)
Eastern Kentucky University, KY (MW)
Eastern Mennonite College, VA (MW)
Eastern Michigan University, MI (MW)
Eastern Oklahoma State College, OK (MW)
Eastern Washington University, WA (MW)
East Los Angeles Community College, CA (W)
East Stroudsburg University, PA (MW)
East Tennessee State University, TN (MW)
East Texas State University, TX (MW)
Edinboro University of Pennsylvania, PA (MW)
Edward Waters College, FL (MW)
El Camino College, CA (MW)
Elizabeth City State University, NC (MW)
Elmhurst College, IL (MW)
Elon College, NC (M)
Emory and Henry College, VA (MW)
Emory University, GA (MW)
Emporia State University, KS (MW)
Essex Community College, MD (MW)
Eureka College, IL (MW)
Everett Community College, WA (MW)
Fairleigh Dickinson University, NJ (MW)
Fairleigh Dickinson University (Rutherford), NJ (MW)
Fergus Falls Community College, MN (M)
Ferris State College, MI (MW)
Fisk University, TN (MW)
Fitchburg State College, MA (MW)
Florida A & M University, FL (MW)
Florida Memorial College, FL (MW)
Florida Southern College, FL (MW)
Florida State University, FL (MW)
Foothill College, CA (MW)
Fordham University, NY (MW)
Fort Hays State University, KS (MW)
Fort Scott College, KS (M)
Fort Valley State College, GA (MW)
Francis Marion University, SC (M)
Franklin & Marshall College, PA (MW)
Frederick Community College, MD (MW)
Fresno City College, CA (MW)
Fresno Pacific College, CA (MW)
Fullerton College, CA (MW)
Fulton-Montgomery Community College, NY (MW)
Furman University, SC (M)
Garden City Community College, KS (MW)
Gardner-Webb College, NC (M)
Geneva College, PA (MW)
George Fox College, OR (MW)
George Mason University, VA (MW)
Georgetown University, DC (MW)
Georgia Institute of Technology, GA (MW)
Georgia Southern University, GA (W)
Gettysburg College, PA (MW)
Glendale Community College, AZ (MW)
Glendale Community College, CA (MW)
Glenville State College, WV (MW)
Gloucester County College, NJ (MW)
Golden West College, CA (MW)
Gonzaga University, WA (MW)
Goshen College, IN (MW)
Grace College, IN (MW)
Graceland College, IA (MW)
Grambling State University, LA (MW)
Grand Valley State College, MI (MW)
Grand View College, IA (MW)
Grays Harbor College, WA (MW)
Green River Community College, WA (MW)
Greenville College, IL (MW)
Grinnell College, IA (MW)
Grove City College, PA (MW)
Gustavus Adolphus College, MN (MW)
Hagerstown Junior College, MD (MW)
Hamilton College, NY (MW)
Hamline University, MN (MW)
Hampton University, VA (MW)
Hanover College, IN (MW)
Harding University, AR (MW)
Harper William Rainey College, IL (M)
Harris-Stowe State College, MO (W)
Hartwick College, NY (MW)
Harvard University, MA (MW)
Haskell Indian Junior College, KS (MW)
Hastings College, NE (MW)

Haverford College, PA (M)
Heidelberg College, OH (W)
Herkimer County Community College, NY (MW)
Highland Community College, KS (MW)
High Point University, NC (M)
Hillsdale College, MI (MW)
Hinds Community College, MS (M)
Hiram College, OH (MW)
Holmes Junior College, MS (M)
Holy Cross College, MA (MW)
Hope College, MI (MW)
Houghton College, NY (MW)
Houston Baptist University, TX (MW)
Howard University, DC (MW)
Hudson Valley Community College, NY (MW)
Humboldt State University, CA (MW)
Hunter College of the City University of New York, NY (MW)
Huntington College, IN (MW)
Hutchinson College, KS (MW)
Idaho State University, ID (MW)
Illinois Benedictine College, IL (MW)
Illinois College, IL (MW)
Illinois State University, IL (MW)
Illinois Valley Community College, IL (MW)
Illinois Wesleyan University, IL (MW)
Indiana State University, IN (MW)
Indiana University, IN (MW)
Indiana University of Pennsylvania, PA (MW)
Indiana Wesleyan University, IN (MW)
Inver Hills Community College, MN (MW)
Iona College, NY (MW)
Iowa State University of Science and Technology, IA (MW)
Iowa Wesleyan College, IA (MW)
Ithaca College, NY (MW)
Jackson State University, MS (MW)
James Madison University, VA (MW)
Jamestown College, ND (MW)
John Carroll University, OH (MW)
Johns Hopkins University, MD (MW)
Johnson County Community College, KS (MW)
Johnson C. Smith University, NC (MW)
Jones County Junior College, MS (M)
Juniata College, PA (MW)
Kansas City Kansas Community College, KS (MW)
Kansas State University, KS (MW)
Kansas Wesleyan College, KS (MW)
Kennesaw State College, GA (MW)
Keene State College, NH (MW)
Kent State University (Ashtabula), OH (MW)
Kent State University (Kent), OH (MW)
Kent State University (New Philadelphia), OH (MW)
Kent State University (Warren), OH (MW)
Kentucky State University, KY (MW)
Kenyon College, OH (MW)
King's College, NY (MW)
Knox College, IL (MW)
Knoxville College, TN (MW)
Kutztown University, PA (MW)
Lafayette College, PA (MW)
Lake Superior State University, MI (MW)
Lamar University, TX (MW)
Lane Community College, OR (MW)
Langston University, OK (MW)
La Salle University, PA (MW)
Lawrence University, WI (MW)
Lebanon Valley College, PA (MW)
Lehigh University, PA (M)
LeMoyne-Owen College, TN (M)
Lenoir-Rhyne College, NC (MW)
LeTourneau College, TX (M)
Lewis and Clark College, OR (MW)
Lewis University, IL (M)
Liberty University, VA (MW)
Lincoln Land Community College, IL (M)
Lincoln University, MO (MW)
Linfield College, OR (MW)
Livingstone College, NC (MW)
Long Beach City College, CA (MW)
Long Island University (Brooklyn), NY (MW)
Long Island University (C.W. Post Campus), NY (MW)
Loras College, IA (MW)
Los Angeles Pierce Junior College, CA (MW)
Los Angeles Valley College, CA (MW)
Louisiana State University (Alexandria), LA (MW)
Louisiana State University (Baton Rouge), LA (MW)
Louisiana Tech University, LA (MW)
Loyola University, IL (MW)
Lubbock Christian College, TX (MW)
Luther College, IA (MW)
Lycoming College, PA (MW)
Lynchburg College, VA (MW)
Macalester College, MN (MW)
Macomb Community College, MI (MW)
Malone College, OH (MW)
Manchester College, IN (MW)
Manhattan College, NY (M)
Mankato State University, MN (MW)
Mansfield University, PA (MW)
Marian College, IN (MW)
Marietta College, OH (MW)
Marist College, NY (MW)
Marquette University, WI (MW)
Marshall University, WV (MW)
Maryville University, MO (MW)
Mary Washington College, VA (MW)
Massachusetts Institute of Technology, MA (MW)
McNeese State University, LA (MW)
Memphis State University, TN (M)
Mercer County Community College, NJ (MW)
Mesa Community College, AZ (MW)
Messiah College, PA (MW)
Miami-Dade Community College (South Campus), FL (M)
Miami University, OH (MW)
Michigan Christian College, MI (MW)
Michigan State University, MI (MW)
Michigan Technological University, MI (MW)
Mid-America Nazarene College, KS (MW)
Middlebury College, VT (MW)
Middlesex County College, NJ (MW)
Middle Tennessee State University, TN (MW)
Midland Lutheran College, NE (MW)

Midwestern State University, TX (MW)
Miles College, AL (MW)
Millersville University, PA (MW)
Millikin University, IL (MW)
Milwaukee Area Technology College, WI (MW)
Minot State, ND (MW)
MiraCosta College, CA (W)
Mississippi College, MS (M)
Mississippi Delta Junior College, MS (M)
Mississippi Gulf Coast Junior College, MS (M)
Mississippi State University, MS (MW)
Mississippi Valley State University, MS (MW)
Missouri Southern State College, MO (MW)
Missouri Valley College, MO (MW)
Modesto Junior College, CA (MW)
Mohawk Valley Community College, NY (MW)
Monmouth College, IL (MW)
Monmouth College, NJ (MW)
Montana State University, MT (MW)
Montclair State College, NJ (MW)
Moorhead State University, MN (MW)
Moorpark College, CA (MW)
Moravian College, PA (M)
Morehouse College, GA (M)
Morgan State University, MD (MW)
Morningside College, IA (M)
Mount Holyoke College, MA (W)
Mount Mercy College, IA (MW)
Mount St. Mary College, MD (MW)
Mount Union College, OH (MW)
Mt. San Antonio College, CA (MW)
Muhlenberg College, PA (M)
Murray State University, KY (MW)
Muskingum College, OH (MW)
Nassau Community College, NY (MW)
Nebraska Wesleyan University, NE (M)
New Mexico Junior College, NM (M)
New Mexico State University, NM (MW)
New York Institute of Technology, NY (M)
New York University, NY (M)
Nicholls State University, LA (W)
Nichols College, MA (M)
Norfolk State University, VA (MW)
North Carolina A and T State University, NC (MW)
North Carolina Central University, NC (MW)
North Carolina State University, NC (MW)
North Central College, IL (MW)
North Dakota State, ND (MW)
North Dakota State University, ND (MW)
Northeastern Junior College, CO (MW)
Northeastern State University, OK (MW)
Northeast Louisiana University, LA. (MW)
Northeast Mississippi Community College, MS (M)
Northeast Missouri State University, MO (MW)
Northern Arizona University, AZ (MW)
North Idaho College, ID (MW)
Northwestern College, MN (MW)
Northwestern State University of Louisiana, LA (MW)
Northwestern University, IL (MW)
Northwest Missouri State University, MO (MW)
Northwest Nazarene College, ID (MW)
Northwood Institute, MI (MW)
Northwood Institute (Texas Campus), TX (MW)
Norwich University, VT (MW)
Oakton Community College, IL (MW)
Oberlin College, OH (MW)
Occidental College, CA (MW)
Ocean County College, NJ (MW)
Odessa College, TX (M)
Ohio Northern University, OH (MW)
Ohio State University, OH (MW)
Ohio University, OH (MW)
Ohio Wesleyan University, OH (MW)
Oklahoma Baptist University, OK (M)
Oklahoma Christian University of Science & Art, OK (MW)
Oklahoma State University, OK (MW)
Olivet College, MI (M)
Olivet Nazarene University, IL (MW)
Orange Coast College, CA (MW)
Oregon State University, OR (MW)
Ottawa University, KS (MW)
Otterbein College, OH (MW)
Ouachita Baptist University, AR (M)
Oxnard College, CA (MW)
Pace University, NY (MW)
Pacific Lutheran University, WA (MW)
Pacific University, OR (MW)
Paine College, GA (MW)
Pan American University, TX (MW)
Panhandle State University, OK (MW)
Park College, MO (MW)
Parkland College, IL (MW)
Pembroke State University, NC (M)
Pennsylvania State University, PA (MW)
Phoenix College, AZ (MW)
Pima Community College, AZ (MW)
Pittsburg State University, KS (MW)
Point Loma Nazarene College, CA (MW)
Pomona-Pitzer Colleges, CA (MW)
Portland State University, OR (MW)
Prairie View A & M University, TX (MW)
Pratt Community College, KS (MW)
Presbyterian College, SC (M)
Princeton University, NJ (MW)
Principia College, IL (MW)
Providence College, RI (MW)
Purdue University, IN (MW)
Queensborough Community College, NY (MW)
Queens College, NY (MW)
Rainy River Community College, MN (MW)
Ramapo College, NJ (MW)
Ranetto Santiago College, CA (MW)
Rensselaer Polytechnic Institute, NY (M)
Rhode Island College, RI (MW)
Rice University, TX (MW)
Ricks College, ID (MW)
Rider College, NJ (M)
Ripon College, WI (MW)
Riverside College, CA (MW)
Roanoke College, VA (M)
Robert Morris College, PA (MW)
Roberts Wesleyan College, NY (MW)

Rochester Institute of Technology, NY (MW)
Roosevelt University, IL (MW)
Rosary College, IL (M)
Rose-Hulman Institute of Technology, IN (M)
Rowan College of New Jersey, NJ (MW)
Rust College, MS (MW)
Saddleback College, CA (MW)
Saginaw Valley State College, MI (MW)
Saint Andrews Presbyterian College, NC (MW)
Saint Augustine's College, NC (MW)
Saint Cloud State University, MN (MW)
Saint Francis College, PA (MW)
Saint John Fisher College, NY (MW)
Saint John's University, MN (M)
Saint John's University, NY (MW)
Saint Joseph's College, IN (MW)
Saint Joseph's University, PA (MW)
Saint Lawrence University, NY (MW)
Saint Mary's College, IN (W)
Saint Mary's College, MI (W)
Saint Norbert College, WI (MW)
Saint Olaf College, MN (MW)
Saint Paul's College, VA (MW)
Saint Peter's College, NJ (MW)
Salem State College, MA (MW)
Salve Regina College, RI (MW)
Samford University, AL (MW)
Sam Houston State University, TX (W)
San Bernardino Community College, CA (MW)
San Diego City College, CA (MW)
San Diego Mesa College, CA (MW)
San Diego State University, CA (W)
San Francisco State University, CA (MW)
San Joaquin Delta College, CA (MW)
San Jose State University, CA (M)
Santa Barbara City College, CA (MW)
Santa Monica College, CA (MW)
Santa Rosa Junior College, CA (MW)
Savannah State College, CA (M)
Scottsdale Community College, AR (MW)
Seattle Pacific University, WA (MW)
Seminole Community College, FL (M)
Seton Hall University, NJ (MW)
Shawnee State University, OH (MW)
Shippensburg University of Pennsylvania, PA (MW)
Siena Heights College, MI (MW)
Simpson College, CA (MW)
Sioux Falls College, SD (MW)
Skyline College, CA (MW)
Slippery Rock University of Pennsylvania, PA (MW)
Smith College, MA (W)
Solano Community College, CA (MW)
South Carolina State College, SC (MW)
South Dakota School of Mines and Technology, SD (MW)
South Dakota State University, SD (MW)
Southeastern Louisiana University, LA (MW)
Southeastern Massachusetts University, MA (MW)
Southeastern Oklahoma State University, OK (MW)
Southeast Missouri State University, MO (MW)
Southern Arkansas University, AR (M)
Southern Connecticut State University, CT (MW)
Southern Illinois University, IL (MW)
Southern Illinois University, (Edwardsville), IL (MW)
Southern Methodist University, TX (MW)
Southern Oregon State College, OR (MW)
Southern University and A & M College, LA (MW)
Southern Utah University, UT (MW)
South Plains Community College, TX (M)
Southwest Baptist University, MO (MW)
Southwestern College, CA (MW)
Southwestern College, KS (MW)
Southwestern Michigan Junior College, MI (MW)
Southwestern Oklahoma State College, OK (M)
Southwestern Oregon Community College, OR (M)
Southwest Missouri State University, MO (MW)
Southwest State University, MN (MW)
Southwest Texas State University, TX (MW)
Spoon River College, IL (MW)
Spring Arbor College, MI (MW)
Springfield College, MA (MW)
Stanford University, CA (MW)
State University of New York, NY (MW)
State University of New York (Albany), NY (MW)
State University of New York (Binghamton), NY (MW)
State University of New York (Buffalo), NY (MW)
State University of New York (Plattsburgh), NY (MW)
State University of New York (Stony Brook), NY (MW)
State University of New York College (Brockport), NY (MW)
State University of New York College (Cortland), NY (MW)
State University of New York College (Fredonia), NY (MW)
State University of New York College (Geneseo), NY (MW)
Stephen F. Austin State University, TX (MW)
Sterling College, KS (MW)
Stetson University, FL (MW)
Stonehill College, MA (MW)
Suffolk County Community College, NY (MW)
Sul Ross State University, Tx (MW)
Swarthmore College, PA (MW)
Syracuse University, NY (MW)
Taft College, CA (MW)
Talledaga College, AL (MW)
Tarleton State University, TX (MW)
Teikyo Westmar University, IA (MW)
Temple University, PA (MW)
Tennessee State University, TN (MW)
Texas A & I University, TX (MW)
Texas A & M University, TX (MW)
Texas Christian University, TX (MW)
Texas Southern University, TX (MW)
Texas Tech University, TX (MW)
Towson State University, MD (MW)

Trenton State College, NJ (MW)
Trinity Christian College, IL (MW)
Trinity College, CT (MW)
Trinity College, IL (MW)
Tri-State University, IN (MW)
Triton College, IL (MW)
Troy State University, AL (MW)
Tufts University, MA (MW)
Tulane University, LA (MW)
Tuskegee University, AL (MW)
Umpqua College, OR (MW)
Union College, NY (MW)
University of Akron, OH (MW)
University of Alabama (Birmingham), AL (MW)
University of Alabama (Tuscaloosa), AL (MW)
University of Arizona, AZ (MW)
University of Arkansas (Fayetteville), AR (MW)
University of Arkansas (Monticello), AR (MW)
University of Arkansas (Pine Bluff), AR (MW)
University of California (Berkeley), CA (MW)
University of California (Davis), CA (MW)
University of California (Irvine), CA (MW)
University of California (Riverside), CA (MW)
University of California (San Diego), CA (MW)
University of California (Santa Barbara), CA (MW)
University of California (UCLA), CA (MW)
University of Central Arkansas, AR (MW)
University of Central Florida, FL (MW)
University of Central Oklahoma, OK (MW)
University of Chicago, IL (MW)
University of Cincinnati, OH (M)
University of Colorado, CO (MW)
University of Connecticut, CT (MW)
University of Delaware, DE (MW)
University of Detroit Mercy, MI (MW)
University of Dubuque, IA (MW)
University of Findlay, OH (MW)
University of Florida, FL (MW)
University of Georgia, GA (MW)
University of Hartford, CT (MW)
University of Houston, TX (MW)
University of Idaho, ID (MW)
University of Illinois, IL (MW)
University of Illinois (Urbana-Champaign), IL (MW)
University of Indianapolis, IN (MW)
University of Iowa, IA (MW)
University of Kansas, KS (MW)
University of Kentucky, KY (MW)
University of La Verne, CA (MW)
University of Louisville, KY (MW)
University of Lowell, MA (MW)
University of Maine, ME (MW)
University of Mary, ND (MW)
University of Maryland, MD (M)
University of Maryland (Baltimore County), MD (MW)
University of Maryland (Eastern Shore), MD (MW)
University of Massachusetts (Amherst), MA (MW)
University of Massachusetts (Boston), MA (MW)
University of Michigan, MI (MW)
University of Minnesota, MN (MW)
University of Mississippi, MS (MW)
University of Missouri, MD (MW)
University of Missouri (Columbia), MO (MW)
University of Montana, MT (MW)
University of Nebraska, NE (MW)
University of Nebraska (Kearney), NE (MW)
University of Nebraska (Lincoln), NE (MW)
University of Nevada, NV (W)
University of Nevada (Reno), NV (MW)
University of New Hampshire, NH (MW)
University of New Haven, CT (M)
University of New Mexico, NM (MW)
University of New Orleans, LA (MW)
University of North Carolina (Asheville), NC (MW)
University of North Carolina (Chapel Hill), NC (MW)
University of North Carolina (Charlotte), NC (MW)
University of North Carolina (Wilmington), NC (MW)
University of North Dakota, ND (MW)
University of Northern Colorado, CO (MW)
University of Northern Iowa, IA (MW)
University of North Florida, FL (MW)
University of North Texas, TX (MW)
University of Notre Dame, IN (MW)
University of Oklahoma, OK (MW)
University of Oregon, OR (MW)
University of Pennsylvania, PA (MW)
University of Pittsburgh, PA (MW)
University of Pittsburgh (Johnstown), PA (MW)
University of Portland, OR (MW)
University of Puerto Rico, PR (MW)
University of Puerto Rico (Bayamon), PR (MW)
University of Puerto Rico (Ponce), PR (MW)
University of Puget Sound, WA (MW)
University of Redlands, CA (MW)
University of Rhode Island, RI (MW)
University of Richmond, VA (MW)
University of Rio Grande, OH (MW)
University of South Alabama, AL (MW)
University of South Carolina, SC (M)
University of South Dakota, SD (MW)
University of Southern California, CA (MW)
University of Southern Colorado, CO (MW)
University of Southern Mississippi, MS (MW)
University of South Florida, FL (MW)
University of Southwestern Louisiana, LA (MW)
University of St. Thomas, MN (MW)

University of Tennessee, TN (MW)
University of Tennessee (Knoxville), TN (MW)
University of Tennessee (Martin), TN (MW)
University of Texas (Arlington), TX (MW)
University of Texas (Austin), TX (MW)
University of Texas (El Paso), TX (MW)
University of Texas (Pan American), TX (MW)
University of Texas (San Antonio), TX (MW)
University of the District of Columbia, DC (MW)
University of Toledo, OH (MW)
University of Tulsa, OK (MW)
University of Utah, UT (MW)
University of Vermont, VT (MW)
University of Virginia, VA (MW)
University of Washington, WA (MW)
University of Wisconsin (Eau Claire), WI (MW)
University of Wisconsin (La Crosse), WI (MW)
University of Wisconsin (Madison), WI (MW)
University of Wisconsin (Milwaukee), WI (MW)
University of Wisconsin (Oshkosh), WI (MW)
University of Wisconsin (Platteville), WI (MW)
University of Wisconsin (River Falls), WI (MW)
University of Wisconsin (Ste vens Point), WI (MW)
University of Wisconsin (Stout), WI (MW)
University of Wisconsin (Superior), WI (MW)
University of Wyoming, WY (MW)
Upper Iowa University, IA (MW)
Urbana University, OH (MW)
Ursinus College, PA (MW)
U.S. International University, CA (MW)
Utah State University, UT (M)
Valley City State University, ND (MW)
Valparaiso University, IN (M)
Vanderbilt University, TN (W)
Ventura College, CA (MW)
Vincennes University Junior College, IN (MW)
Virginia Commonwealth University, VA (MW)
Virginia Military Institute, VA (M)
Virginia Polytechnic Institute & State University, VA (MW)
Virginia State University, VA (MW)
Virginia Union University, VA (MW)
Wabash College, IN (M)
Wagner College, NY (MW)
Walsh College, OH (MW)
Wartburg College, IA (MW)
Washington and Jefferson College, PA (M)
Washington State University, WA (M)
Washington University, MO (MW)
Wayland Baptist University, TX (MW)
Wayne State College, NE (MW)
Weber State College, UT (MW)
Wesleyan University, CT (MW)
West Chester University, PA (MW)
Western Carolina University, NC (MW)
Western Illinois University, IL (MW)
Western Kentucky University, KY (MW)
Western Maryland College, MD (MW)
Western Michigan University, MI (MW)
Western Montana College, MT (MW)
Western New Mexico University, NM (MW)
Western Oregon State College, OR (MW)
Western State College, CO (MW)
Western Washington University, WA (MW)
Westfeld State College, MA (W)
Westminster College, PA (M)
Westmont College, CA (MW)
West Virginia State College, WV (MW)
West Virginia University, WV (MW)
West Virginia Wesleyan College, WV (MW)
Wheaton College, IL (MW)
Whitman College, WA (MW)
Whittier College, CA (MW)
Whitworth College, WA (MW)
Wichita State University, KS (MW)
Willamette University, OR (MW)
William Jewell College, MO (MW)
William Patterson College, NJ (MW)
William Penn College, IA (MW)
William Rainey Harper College, IL (MW)
Williams College, MA (MW)
Wilmington College, DE (MW)
Wilmington College, OH (MW)
Winona State University, MN (MW)
Winston-Salem State University, NC (MW)
Winthrop University, SC (MW)
Worcester State College, MA (MW)
Yale University, CT (MW)
York College (CUNY), NY (MW)
York College of Pennsylvania, PA (M)
Youngstown State University, OH (MW)
Yuba Community College, CA (MW)

Volleyball

Abilene Christian University, TX (W)
Adams State College, CO (W)
Adelphi University, NY (W)
Adirondack College, NY (W)
Adrian College, MI (W)
Alabama A & M University, AL (M)
Alabama State University, AL (W)
Albertson College, ID (W)
Albion College, MI (W)
Albright College, PA (W)
Alcorn State University, MS (W)
Alderson-Broaddus College, WV (W)
Alfred University, NY (W)
Allegheny College, PA (W)
Allen County College, KS (W)
Allentown College, PA (W)
Alma College, MI (MW)
Alvernia College, PA (W)
American International College, MA (W)
American University, DC (W)
Amherst College, MA (W)
Anderson College, SC (W)
Anderson University, IN (W)
Angelo State University, TX (W)
Anoka-Ramsey College, MN (W)

Appalachian State University, NC (W)
Apprentice School, VA (W)
Aquinas College, MI (W)
Arizona State University, AZ (W)
Arkansas State University, AR (W)
Arkansas Tech University AR (W)
Armstrong State College, GA (W)
Arrowhead Community College, MN (W)
Asbury College, KY (W)
Ashland College, OH (W)
Atlantic Union College, MA (W)
Auburn University, AL (W)
Augusta College, GA (W)
Augustana College, IL (W)
Augustana College, SD (W)
Aurora University, IL (W)
Austin College, TX (W)
Austin Community College, MN (W)
Austin Peay State University, TN (W)
Averett College, VA (W)
Avila College, MO (W)
Azusa Pacific University, CA (W)
Babson College, MA (W)
Baker University, KS (W)
Ball State University, IN (MW)
Baptist Bible College, MO (W)
Barber-Scotia College, NC (W)
Bard College, NY (MW)
Barstow College, CA (W)
Barton College, NC (W)
Barton County College, KS (W)
Bates College, ME (W)
Bayamon Central University, PR (MW)
Baylor University, TX (W)
Becker College, MA (W)
Bellarmine College, KY (W)
Belleville Area College, IL (W)
Bellevue College, NE (W)
Bellevue Community College, WA (W)
Belmont Abbey College, NC (W)
Belmont College, TN (W)
Beloit College, WI (W)
Bemidji State University, MN (W)
Benedict College, SC (W)
Benedictine College, KS (W)
Bentley College, MA (W)
Bergen Community College, NJ (W)
Bethany College, KS (W)
Bethany College, WV (W)
Bethany Lutheran College, MN (W)
Bethel College, IN (W)
Bethel College, KS (W)
Bethel College, MN (W)
Big Bend Community College, WA (W)
Biola University, CA (W)
Bismarck State College, ND (W)
Blackburn College, IL (W)
Black Hawk College, IL (W)
Black Hills State University, SD (W)
Bloomfield College, NJ (W)
Blue Mountain College, OR (W)
Bluffton College, OH (W)
Boise State University, ID (W)
Boston College, MA (W)
Bowdoin College, ME (W)
Bowie State University, MD (W)
Bowling Green State University, OH (W)
Bradley University, IL (MW)
Brainerd Community College, MN (W)
Brescia College, KY (W)
Brevard College, FL (W)
Briar Cliff College, IA (W)
Bridgewater State College, MA (W)
Brigham Young University, HI (W)
Brigham Young University, UT (W)
Bronx Community College, NY (W)
Brooklyn College–City University of New York, NY (W)
Broome Community College, NY (W)
Broward Community College, Fl (MW)
Brown University, RI (W)
Bryant College, RI (W)
Bryn Mawr College, PA (W)
Bucknell University, PA (W)
Buena Vista College, IA (W)
Buffalo State College, NY (W)
Buffalo State University (New York), NY (W)
Butler County Community College, KS (W)
Butler County Community College, PA (W)
Butler University, IN (W)
Butte College, CA (W)
Cabrillo College, CA (W)
Cabrini College, PA (W)
Caldwell College, NJ (W)
California Baptist College, CA (W)
California Lutheran University, CA (W)
California Maritime Academy, CA (M)
California Polytechnic State University, CA (W)
California State Polytechnic University, CA (W)
California State University, CA (W)
California State University at Bakersfield, CA (W)
California State University (Chico), CA (W)
California State University (Dominguez Hills), CA (W)
California State University (Fresno), CA (W)
California State University (Fullerton), CA (W)
California State University (Hayward), CA (W)
California State University (Long Beach), CA (MW)
California State University (Los Angeles), CA (MW)
California State University (Northridge), CA (MW)
California State University (Sacramento), CA (W)
California State University (San Bernardino), CA (W)
California University, PA (M)
Calvin College, MI (W)
Cameron University, OK (W)
Campbell University, NC (W)
Canisius College, NY (W)
Capital University, OH (W)
Cardinal Stritch College, WI (W)
Carleton College, MN (MW)
Carlow College, PA (W)
Carnegie-Mellon University, PA (W)
Carroll College, MT (W)
Carroll College, WI (W)
Carson-Newman College, TN (W)
Carthage College, WI (W)
Case Western Reserve University, OH (W)
Catawba College, NC (W)
Catholic University of America, DC (W)
Catholic University of Puerto Rico, PR (MW)
Catonsville Community College, MD (W)
Cayuga County Community College, NY (W)
Cecil Community College, MD (W)
Cedarville College, OH (W)
Centenary College, LA (W)
Centenary College, NJ (W)
Central Arizona College, AZ (W)
Central College, IA (W)
Central College, KS (W)
Central Community College, NE (W)

Central Connecticut State University, CT (W)
Central Methodist College, MO (MW)
Central Michigan University, MI (W)
Central Missouri State University, MO (W)
Central State University, OH (M)
Central Washington University, WA (W)
Central Wesleyan College, SC (W)
Central Wyoming College, WY (W)
Cerritos College, CA (W)
Chadron State College, NE (W)
Chaffey College, CA (W)
Chaminade University, HI (W)
Chapman University, CA (W)
Charles County Community College, MD (W)
Charleston Southern University, SC (W)
Chemeketa Community College, OR (W)
Cheyney University of Pennsylvania, PA (W)
Chicago State University, IL (W)
Chowan College, NC (W)
Christian Brothers College, TN (W)
Christopher Newport College, VA (W)
City College of New York, NY (W)
City College of San Francisco, CA (MW)
Clackamas Community College, OR (W)
Clarion University, PA (W)
Clark Atlanta University, GA (W)
Clark College, WA (W)
Clarkson University, NY (W)
Clark State College, OH (W)
Clark University, MA (W)
Clemson University, SC (W)
Cleveland State University, OH (W)
Clinton Community College, IA (W)
Clinton Community College, NY (W)
Cloud County Community College, KS (W)
Coastal Carolina College, SC (W)
Cochise County Community College, AZ (W)
Coe College, IA (W)
Coffeyville Community College, KS (W)
Coker College, SC (W)
Colby Community College, KS (W)
Colby-Sawyer College, NH (W)
Colgate University, NY (W)
College of Charleston, SC (W)
College of Idaho, ID (W)
College of Mount St. Joseph, OH (W)
College of New Rochelle, NY (W)
College of Notre Dame, CA (W)
College of Notre Dame of Maryland, MD (W)
College of Saint Mary, NE (W)
College of Southern Idaho, ID (W)
College of St. Benedict, MN (W)
College of St. Francis, IL (W)
College of St. Mary, NE (W)
College of St. Rose, NY (W)
College of St. Scholastica, MN (W)
College of the Desert, CA (W)
College of the Ozarks, MO (W)
College of the Redwoods, CA (W)
College of the Sequoias, CA (W)
College of William and Mary, VA (W)
College of Wooster, OH (W)
Colorado Christian University, CO (W)
Colorado College, CO (W)
Colorado Northwestern Community College, CO (W)
Colorado School of Mines, CO (W)
Colorado State University, CO (W)
Columbia Basin Community College, WA (W)
Columbia Christian College, OR (W)
Columbia College, MO (W)
Columbia College, SC (W)
Columbia-Greene Community College, NY (W)
Columbia Union College, MD (W)
Columbia University, NY (W)
Columbus College, GA (W)
Columbus State Community College, OH (W)
Community College of Rhode Island, RI (W)
Community Colleges of Spokane, WA (W)
Concord College, WV (W)
Concordia College, MI (W)
Concordia College (Moorhead), MN (W)
Concordia College (St. Paul), MN (W)
Concordia College, NY (MW)
Concordia Lutheran College, TX (W)
Concordia Teachers College, NE (W)
Concordia University, IL (W)
Connecticut College, CT (W)
Converse College, SC (W)
Cooke County Junior College, TX (W)
Coppin State College, MD (W)
Cornell College, IA (W)
Cornell University, NY (W)
Cosummes River College, CA (W)
Covenant College, GA (W)
Cowley County Community College, KS (W)
Cuesta College, CA (W)
Culver-Stockton College, MO (W)
Cumberland College, KY (W)
Dakota State University, SD (W)
Dakota Wesleyan University, SD (W)
Dallas Baptist University, TX (W)
Dalton College, GA (MW)
Davidson College, NC (W)
Defiance College, OH (W)
Delaware Valley College, PA (W)
Delta College, MI (W)
DePaul University, IL (W)
De Pauw University, IN (W)
Diablo Valley Community College, CA (W)
Dickinson College, PA (W)
Dickinson State University, ND (W)
Dixie College, UT (W)
Doane College, NE (W)
Dodge City Community College, KS (W)
Dominican College, CA (W)
Dominican College of Blauvelt, NY (W)
Dowling College, NY (W)
Drexel University, PA (W)
Drury College, MO (M)
Duke University, NC (W)
Dundalk Community College, MD (W)
Duquesne University, PA (W)
Dutchess Junior College, NY (W)
D'Youville College, NY (W)
Earlham College, IN (W)
East Carolina University, NC (W)
East Central College, MO (W)
Eastern College, PA (W)
Eastern Connecticut State University, CT (W)
Eastern Illinois University, IL (W)

Eastern Kentucky University, KY (W)
Eastern Mennonite College, VA (W)
Eastern Michigan University, MI (W)
Eastern Montana College, MT (MW)
Eastern Nazarene College, MA (W)
Eastern New Mexico University, NM (W)
Eastern Oregon State College, OR (W)
Eastern Washington University, WA (W)
Eastern Wyoming College, WY (W)
Eastfield College, TX (W)
East Los Angeles Community College, CA (W)
East Stroudsburg University, PA (MW)
East Texas Baptist University, TX (W)
East Texas State University, TX (W)
Edgewood College, WI (W)
Edinboro University of Pennsylvania, PA (M)
Edison Community College, FL (W)
Edmonds Community College, WA (W)
El Camino College, CA (MW)
Elgin Community College, IL (W)
Elizabethtown College, PA (W)
Elmhurst College, IL (W)
Elmira College, NY (W)
Elon College, NC (W)
Emerson College, MA (W)
Emory and Henry College, VA (W)
Emporia State University, KS (W)
Erskine College, SC (W)
Essex Community College, MD (W)
Eureka College, IL (W)
Evangel College, MO (W)
Everett Community College, WA (W)
Fairfield University, CT (W)
Fairleigh Dickinson University, NJ (W)
Fairleigh Dickinson University (Rutherford), NJ (W)
Fairmont State College, WV (W)
Fashion Institute of Technology, NY (W)
Fayetteville State University, NC (W)
Fergus Falls Community College, MN (W)
Ferris State College, MI (W)
Ferrum College, VA (W)
Fisk University, TN (W)
Fitchburg State College, MA (W)
Flagler College, FL (W)
Florida A & M University, FL (W)
Florida Institute of Technology, FL (W)
Florida International University, FL (W)
Florida Southern College, FL (W)
Florida State University, FL (W)
Foothill College, CA (W)
Fordham University, NY (MW)
Fort Hays State University, KS (W)
Fort Lewis College, CO (W)
Fort Scott College, KS (W)
Fort Steilacoom Community College, WA (W)
Fort Valley State College, GA (W)
Francis Marion University, SC (W)
Franklin & Marshall College, PA (W)
Frederick Community College, MD (M)
Freed-Hardeman College, TN (W)
Fresno City College, CA (W)
Fresno Pacific College, CA (W)
Friends University, KS (W)
Fullerton College, CA (W)
Fulton-Montgomery Community College, NY (W)
Furman University, SC (W)
Gannon College, PA (W)
Garden City Community College, KS (W)
Gardner-Webb College, NC (W)
Garrett Community College, MD (W)
Genesee Community College, NY (MW)
Geneva College, PA (MW)
George Fox College, OR (W)
George Mason University, VA (MW)
Georgetown College, KY (W)
Georgetown University, DC (W)
George Washington University, DC (W)
Georgia Institute of Technology, GA (W)
Georgian Court College, NJ (W)
Georgia Southern University, GA (W)
Georgia State University, GA (W)
Glendale Community College, AZ (W)
Glendale Community College, CA (W)
Glen Oaks Community College, MI (W)
Golden West College, CA (MW)
Gonzaga University, WA (W)
Gordon College, MA (W)
Goshen College, IN (W)
Goucher College, MD (MW)
Grace College, IN (W)
Graceland College, IA (MW)
Grambling State University, LA (W)
Grand Canyon College, AZ (W)
Grand Rapids Baptist College and Seminary, MI (W)
Grand Rapids Junior College, MI (W)
Grand Valley State College, MI (W)
Grand View College, IA (W)
Grays Harbor College, WA (W)
Greenfield Community College, MA (MW)
Green Mountain College, VT (W)
Green River Community College, WA (W)
Greensboro College, NC (W)
Greenville College, IL (W)
Grinnell College, IA (W)
Grove City College, PA (W)
Gustavus Adolphus College, MN (W)
Hagerstown Junior College, MD (W)
Hamilton College, NY (W)
Hamline University, MN (W)
Hampton University, VA (W)
Hannibal-Lagrange College, MO (W)
Hanover College, IN (W)
Harding University, AR (W)
Hardin-Simmons University, TX (W)
Harper William Rainey College, IL (W)
Harris-Stowe State College, MO (W)
Harvard University, MA (MW)
Hastings College, NE (W)
Haverford College, PA (W)
Hawaii Pacific University, HI (W)
Heidelberg College, OH (W)
Henderson State University, AR (W)
Henry Ford Community College, MI (W)
Hesser College, NH (W)
Hibbing Community College, MN (W)

Highland Community College, KS (W)
High Point University, NC (W)
Hilbert College, NY (W)
Hillsborough Community College, FL (W)
Hillsdale College, MI (W)
Hiram College, OH (W)
Hofstra University, NY (W)
Holy Cross College, MA (W)
Hood College, MD (W)
Hope College, MI (W)
Houghton College, NY (W)
Houston Baptist University, TX (W)
Howard Payne University, TX (W)
Howard University, DC (W)
Hudson Valley Community College, NY (W)
Humboldt State University, CA (W)
Hunter College of the City University of New York, NY (MW)
Huntingdon College, AL (W)
Huntington College, IN (W)
Huron University, SD (W)
Husson College, ME (W)
Huston-Tillotson College, TX (W)
Hutchinson College, KS (W)
Idaho State University, ID (W)
Illinois Benedictine College, IL (W)
Illinois Central College, IL (W)
Illinois College, IL (W)
Illinois Institute of Technology, IL (MW)
Illinois State University, IL (W)
Illinois Valley Community College, IL (W)
Illinois Wesleyan University, IL (W)
Incarnate Word College, TX (W)
Indiana State University, IN (W)
Indiana University, IN (W)
Indiana University of Pennsylvania, PA (W)
Indiana University-Purdue University, IN (W)
Indiana University-Purdue University (Fort Wayne), IN (MW)
Indiana Wesleyan University, IN (W)
Indian River Community College, FL (W)
Inver Hills Community College, MN (W)
Iona College, NY (W)
Iowa State University of Science and Technology, IA (W)
Iowa Wesleyan College, IA (W)
Ithaca College, NY (W)
Jackson State University, MS (W)
Jacksonville State University, AL (W)
Jacksonville University, FL (W)
James Madison University, VA (W)
Jamestown College, ND (W)
Jefferson College, MO (W)
Jefferson Community College, NY (W)
John Brown University, AR (W)
John Carroll University, OH (W)
Johns Hopkins University, MD (W)
Johnson County Community College, KS (W)
Juniata College, PA (W)
Kalamazoo College, MI (W)
Kalamazoo Valley Community College, MI (W)
Kankakee Community College, IL (W)
Kansas City Kansas Community College, KS (W)
Kansas Newman College, KS (W)
Kansas State University, KS (W)
Kansas Wesleyan College, KS (W)
Kaskaskia Community College, IL (W)
Kean College of New Jersey, NJ (W)
Keene State College, NH (W)
Kent State University (Ashtabula), OH (W)
Kent State University (East Liverpool), OH (W)
Kent State University (Kent), OH (W)
Kent State University (New Philadelphia), OH (W)
Kent State University (Warren), OH (W)
Kentucky State University, KY (W)
Kentucky Wesleyan College, KY (W)
King College, TN (W)
King's College, NY (W)
King's College, PA (W)
Kishwaukee College, IL (W)
Knox College, IL (W)
Kutztown University, PA (W)
Labette Community College, KS (MW)
Lackawanna Junior College, PA (W)
Lafayette College, PA (W)
Lake Erie College, OH (W)
Lake Forest College, IL (W)
Lake Land College, IL (W)
Lake Michigan College, MI (W)
Lake-Sumter Community College, FL (W)
Lake Superior State University, MI (W)
Lamar University, TX (W)
Lambuth University, TN (W)
Lansing Community College, MI (W)
La Roche College, PA (W)
La Salle University, PA (W)
Lawrence University, WI (W)
Lee College, TN (W)
Lee College, TX (W)
Lees-McRae College, NC (W)
Lehigh County Community College, PA (W)
Lehigh University, PA (W)
Le Moyne College, NY (W)
Lenoir-Rhyne College, NC (MW)
Lewis and Clark College, OR (W)
Lewis and Clark Community College, IL (W)
Lewis/Clark State College, ID (W)
Lewis University, IL (W)
Liberty University, VA (W)
Limestone College, SC (W)
Lincoln Christian College, IL (W)
Lincoln College, IL (W)
Lincoln Land Community College, IL (W)
Lincoln Memorial University, TN (W)
Lincoln Trail College, IL (W)
Lincoln University, MO (W)
Linfield College, OR (W)
Livingston University, AL (W)
Long Beach City College, CA (MW)
Long Island University (C.W. Post Campus), NY (W)
Long Island University (Southhampton Campus), NY (MW)
Los Angeles Pierce Junior College, CA (MW)
Louisburg College, NC (W)
Louisiana State University (Alexandria), LA (W)
Louisiana State University (Baton Rouge), LA (W)
Louisiana Tech University, LA (W)
Lower Columbia College, WA (W)
Loyola College, MD (W)
Loyola Marymount University, CA (MW)
Loyola University, IL (W)

Lubbock Christian College, TX (W)
Luther College, IA (W)
Lynchburg College, VA (W)
Macalester College, MN (W)
Macomb Community College, MI (W)
Madison Area Technical College, WI (W)
Madonna University, MI (W)
Malone College, OH (W)
Manchester College, IN (W)
Manhattan College, NY (W)
Manhattanville College, NY (W)
Mankato State University, MN (W)
Marian College, IN (W)
Marian College, WI (W)
Marietta College, OH (W)
Marist College, NY (W)
Marquette University, WI (W)
Marshall University, WV (W)
Mars Hill College, NC (W)
Mary Baldwin College, VA (W)
Marycrest College, IA (W)
Marymount University, VA (W)
Maryville College, TN (W)
Maryville University, MO (W)
Mary Washington College, VA (W)
Marywood College, PA (W)
Massachusetts Bay Community College, MA (W)
Massachusetts Institute of Technology, MA (MW)
Master's College, CA (W)
Mayville State College, ND (W)
McCook Community College, NE (W)
McHenry County College, IL (W)
McKendree College, IL (W)
McNeese State University, LA (W)
McPherson College, KS (W)
Memphis State University, TN (W)
Mercer University, GA (W)
Mercy College, NY (W)
Mercyhurst College, PA (W)
Merrimack College, MA (W)
Mesa Community College, AZ (W)
Mesa State College, CO (W)
Messiah College, PA (W)
Metropolitan State College, CO (W)
Miami-Dade Community College (South Campus), FL (W)
Miami-Dade Junior College, FL (W)
Miami University, OH (W)
Michigan Christian College, MI (W)
Michigan State University, MI (W)
Michigan Technological University, MI (W)
Mid-America Nazarene College, KS (W)
Middle Tennessee State University, TN (W)
Midland Lutheran College, NE (W)
Mid-Plains Community College, NE (W)
Midwestern State University, TX (W)
Miles College, AL (W)
Miles Community College, MT (W)
Millersville University, PA (W)
Milligan College, TN (W)
Millikin University, IL (W)
Mineral Area College, MO (W)
Minot State, ND (W)
Mississippi College, MS (W)
Mississippi State University, MS (W)
Mississippi University For Women, MS (MW)
Mississippi Valley State University, MS (W)
Missouri Baptist College, MO (W)
Missouri Southern State College, MO (W)
Missouri Valley College, MO (W)
Missouri Western State College, MO (W)
Mitchell College, CT (W)
Modesto Junior College, CA (W)
Mohawk Valley Community College, NY (W)
Molloy College, NY (W)
Monmouth College, IL (W)
Montana College of Mineral Science and Technology, MT (W)
Montana State University, MT (W)
Montgomery College, MD (W)
Montreat-Anderson College, NC (W)
Moody Bible Institute, IL (W)
Moorhead State University, MN (W)
Moorpark College, CA (MW)
Moraine Valley Community College, IL (W)
Moravian College, PA (W)
Morehead State University, KY (W)
Morgan State University, MD (W)
Morningside College, IA (W)
Mott Community College, MI (W)
Mount Holyoke College, MA (W)
Mount Marty College, SD (W)
Mount Mercy College, IA (W)
Mount Olive College, NC (W)
Mount Union College, OH (W)
Mount Vernon Nazarene College, OH (W)
Mt. San Antonio College, CA (MW)
Muhlenberg College, PA (W)
Multnomah School of the Bible, OR (W)
Murray State University, KY (W)
Muskegon Community College, MI (W)
Muskingum College, OH (W)
Nassau Community College, NY (W)
National-Louis University, IL (W)
Navajo Community College, AZ (W)
Nazareth College, NY (W)
Nebraska Wesleyan University, NE (M)
Newberry College, SC (W)
New Hampshire College, NH (W)
New Jersey Institute of Technology, NJ (M)
New Mexico Highlands University, NM (W)
New Mexico State University, NM (W)
New York Institute of Technology, NY (M)
New York State University Institute of Technology, NY (W)
New York University, NY (W)
Niagara County Community College, NY (W)
Niagara University, NY (W)
Nicholls State University, LA (W)
North Adams State College, MA (W)
North Arkansas Community College, AR (W)
North Carolina A and T State University, NC (W)
North Carolina Central University, NC (W)
North Carolina State University, NC (W)
North Carolina Wesleyan College, NC (W)
North Central College, IL (W)
North Dakota State, ND (W)
North Dakota State University, ND (W)
North Dakota State University (Bottineau), ND (W)

Northeastern Christian Junior College, PA (MW)
Northeastern Illinois University, IL (W)
Northeastern Junior College, CO (W)
Northeast Louisiana University, LA (W)
Northeast Missouri State University, MO (W)
Northern Arizona University, AZ (W)
Northern Illinois University, IL (W)
Northern Kentucky University, KY (W)
Northern Michigan University, MI (W)
Northern Montana College, MT (W)
Northern State University, SD (W)
North Greenville College, SC (W)
North Hennepin Community College, MN (W)
North Idaho College, ID (W)
North Iowa Area Community College, IA (MW)
Northland College, WI (W)
Northland Community College, MN (W)
Northwest College, WY (W)
Northwestern College, IA (W)
Northwestern College, MN (W)
Northwestern State University of Louisiana, LA (W)
Northwestern University, IL (W)
Northwest Missouri State University, MO (W)
Northwest Nazarene College, ID (W)
Northwood Institute, MI (W)
Northwood Institute (Texas Campus), TX (W)
Notre Dame College of Ohio, OH (W)
Nova University, FL (W)
Nyack College, NY (MW)
Oakland City College, IN (W)
Oakland Community College, MI (W)
Oakland University, MI (W)
Oakton Community College, IL (W)
Oberlin College, OH (W)
Occidental College, CA (W)
Oglethorpe University, GA (W)
Ohio Dominican College, OH (W)
Ohio Northern University, OH (W)
Ohio State University, OH (MW)
Ohio University, OH (W)
Ohio Valley College, WV (W)
Ohio Wesleyan University, OH (W)
Olivet College, MI (W)
Olivet Nazarene University, IL (W)
Olympic College, WA (W)
Oral Roberts University, OK (W)
Orange Coast College, CA (MW)
Orange County Community College, NY (W)
Oregon Institute of Technology, OR (W)
Oregon State University, OR (W)
Otero Junior College, CO (W)
Ottawa University, KS (W)
Otterbein College, OH (W)
Ouachita Baptist University, AR (W)
Oxnard College, CA (W)
Pace University, NY (MW)
Pace University (White Plains Campus), NY (W)
Pacific Lutheran University, WA (W)
Pacific University, OR (W)
Palm Beach Atlantic College, FL (W)
Palomar College, CA (W)
Pan American University, TX (W)
Park College, MO (MW)
Parkland College, IL (MW)
Pembroke State University, NC (W)
Penn State University, PA (W)
Pennsylvania State University, PA (MW)
Pennsylvania State University (Behrend College), PA (MW)
Penn Valley Community College, MO (W)
Pensacola Junior College, FL (W)
Pepperdine University, CA (MW)
Peru State College, NE (W)
Pfeiffer College, NC (W)
Philadelphia Community College, PA (W)
Phoenix College, AZ (W)
Pima Community College, AZ (W)
Pittsburg State University, KS (W)
Polk Community College, FL (W)
Polytechnic University (Brooklyn Campus), NY (W)
Pomona-Pitzer Colleges, CA (W)
Portland State University, OR (W)
Prairie View A & M University, TX (W)
Pratt Community College, KS (W)
Presbyterian College, SC (W)
Prince George's Community College, MD (W)
Princeton University, NJ (W)
Principia College, IL (W)
Providence College, RI (W)
Purdue University, IN (W)
Purdue University (Calumet), IN (W)
Queens College, NY (MW)
Queens College, NC (W)
Quincy College, IL (W)
Quinnipiac College, CT (W)
Radford University, VA (W)
Rainy River Community College, MN (W)
Ramapo College, NJ (MW)
Ranetto Santiago College, CA (W)
Regis College, MA (W)
Regis University, CO (W)
Rhode Island College, RI (W)
Rice University, TX (W)
Ricks College, ID (W)
Rider College, NJ (W)
Ripon College, WI (W)
Roanoke College, VA (W)
Robert Morris College, PA (W)
Roberts Wesleyan College, NY (W)
Rochester Community College, MN (W)
Rochester Institute of Technology, NY (W)
Rockhurst College, MO (W)
Rockland Community College, NY (W)
Rocky Mountain College, MT (W)
Rollins College, FL (W)
Roosevelt University, IL (W)
Rosary College, IL (W)
Rutgers, Newark College of Arts and Sciences, NJ (M)
Sacred Heart University, CT (MW)
Saddleback College, CA (W)
Saginaw Valley State College, MI (W)
Saint Ambrose College, IA (W)
Saint Andrews Presbyterian College, NC (W)
Saint Augustine's College, NC (W)
Saint Bonaventure University, NY (W)
Saint Cloud State University, MN (W)
Saint Edward's University, TX (W)
Saint Francis College, IN (W)
Saint Francis College, NY (W)

Saint Francis College, PA (MW)
Saint John Fisher College, NY (W)
Saint Lawrence University, NY (W)
Saint Leo College, FL (W)
Saint Louis University, MO (W)
Saint Martin's College, WA (W)
Saint Mary College, KS (W)
Saint Mary's College, IN (W)
Saint Mary's College, MD (W)
Saint Mary's College, MI (W)
Saint Mary's College of California, CA (W)
Saint Mary's University, TX (W)
Saint Michael's College, VT (W)
Saint Norbert College, WI (W)
Saint Olaf College, MN (W)
Saint Paul's College, VA (W)
Saint Peter's College, NJ (W)
Saint Thomas Aquinas College, NY (W)
Saint Vincent College, PA (W)
Saint Xavier University, IL (W)
Salem State College, MA (W)
Salem-Teikyo University, WV (W)
Samford University, AL (MW)
Sam Houston State University, TX (W)
San Bernardino Community College, CA (MW)
San Diego City College, CA (MW)
San Diego Mesa College, CA (MW)
San Diego State University, CA (MW)
San Francisco State University, CA (W)
San Joaquin Delta College, CA (W)
San Jose State University, CA (W)
Santa Barbara City College, CA (MW)
Santa Clara University, CA (W)
Santa Monica College, CA (MW)
Santa Rosa Junior College, CA (W)
Sauk Valley College, IL (W)
Savannah State College, GA (W)
Schoolcraft College, MI (W)
Schreiner College, TX (W)
Scottsdale Community College, AR (W)
Seattle Pacific University, WA (W)
Seminole Community College, FL (W)
Seton Hall University, NJ (W)
Seton Hill College, PA (W)
Seward County Community College, KS (W)
Shawnee State University, OH (W)
Shepherd College, WV (W)
Sheridan College, WY (W)
Shippensburg University of Pennsylvania, PA (W)
Shoreline Community College, WA (W)
Siena College, NY (W)
Siena Heights College, MI (W)
Sierra College, CA (W)
Simpson College, CA (W)
Sinclair Community College, OH (W)
Sioux Falls College, SD (W)
Skagit Valley College, WA (W)
Skidmore College, NY (W)
Skyline College, CA (W)
Slippery Rock University of Pennsylvania, PA (W)
Smith College, MA (W)
Snead State Community College, AL (W)
Snow College, UT (MW)
Solano Community College, CA (W)
South Carolina State College, SC (W)
South Dakota School of Mines and Technology, SD (W)
South Dakota State University, SD (W)
Southeast Community College, NE (W)
Southeastern Louisiana University, LA (W)
Southeastern Massachusetts University, MA (W)
Southeast Missouri State University, MO (W)
Southern Arkansas University, AR (W)
Southern California College, CA (W)
Southern Connecticut State University, CT (W)
Southern Illinois University, IL (W)
Southern Nazarene University, OK (W)
Souther Oregon State College, OR (W)
Southern University and A & M College, LA (W)
Southern Utah University, UT (W)
South Florida Community College, FL (W)
Southwest Baptist University, MO (W)
Southwestern College, CA (W)
Southwestern College, KS (W)
Southwestern Michigan Junior College, MI (W)
Southwestern Oregon Community College, OR (W)
Southwestern University, TX (W)
Southwest Missouri State University, MO (W)
Southwest State University, MN (W)
Southwest Texas State University, TX (W)
Spartanburg Methodist, SC (W)
Spoon River College, IL (W)
Spring Arbor College, MI (W)
Springfield College, MA (MW)
Stanford University, CA (MW)
State University of New York (Albany), NY (W)
State University of New York (Binghamton), NY (W)
State University of New York (Buffalo), NY (W)
State University of New York (Plattsburgh), NY (W)
State University of New York (Stony Brook), NY (W)
State University of New York College (Brockport), NY (W)
State University of New York College (Cortland), NY (W)
State University of New York College (Fredonia), NY (W)
State University of New York College (Geneseo), NY (W)
State University of New York College (New Paltz), NY (MW)
State University of New York College (Oswego), NY (W)
State University of New York College (Potsdam), NY (W)
State University of New York College (Purchase), NY (W)
State University of New York Maritime College, NY (MW)
Stephen F. Austin State University, TX (W)
Sterling College, KS (W)
Stetson University, FL (W)
Stevens Institute of Technology, NJ (MW)
St. Louis Community College (Florissant Valley), MO (W)
St. Louis Community College (Forest Park), MO (W)
St. Mary of the Plains College, KS (W)
Stonehill College, MA (W)
St. Philip's College, TX (W)
Sue Bennett College, KY (W)
Suffolk County Community College, NY (W)
Sul Ross State University, TX (W)

Swarthmore College, PA (W)
Sweet Briar College, VA (W)
Syracuse University, NY (W)
Tabor College, KS (W)
Taft College, CA (W)
Talledaga College, AL (W)
Tampa College, FL (W)
Tarleton State University, TX (W)
Teikyo Marycrest University, IA (W)
Teikyo Westmar University, IA (W)
Temple University, PA (W)
Tennessee Technological University, TN (W)
Tennessee Temple University, TN (W)
Texas A & I University, TX (W)
Texas A & M University, TX (W)
Texas Lutheran College, TX (W)
Texas Southern University, TX (MW)
Texas Southmost Junior College, TX (W)
Texas Tech University, TX (W)
Texas Wesleyan College, TX (W)
Texas Woman's University, TX (W)
Thomas More College, KY (W)
Three Rivers Community College, MO (W)
Tiffin University, OH (W)
Toccoa Falls College, GA (W)
Towson State University, MD (W)
Trevecca Nazarene College, TN (W)
Trinidad State Junior College, CO (W)
Trinity Christian College, IL (W)
Trinity College, CT (W)
Trinity College, IL (W)
Trinity University, TX (W)
Tri-State University, IN (MW)
Triton College, IL (W)
Troy State University, AL (W)
Truett-McConnell Junior College, GA (W)
Tufts University, MA (W)
Tulane University, LA (W)
Tusculum College, TN (W)
Tuskegee University, AL (W)
Umpqua College, OR (W)
Union College, NY (W)
Unity College, ME (W)
University of Akron, OH (W)
University of Alabama (Birmingham), AL (MW)
University of Alabama (Huntsville), AL (W)
University of Alabama (Tuscaloosa), AL (W)
University of Alaska, AK (W)
University of Alaska (Fairbanks), AK (W)
University of Arizona AZ (W)
University of Arkansas (Little Rock), AR (W)
University of Arkansas (Pine Bluff), AR (W)
University of Bridgeport, CT (MW)
University of California (Berkeley), CA (W)
University of California (Davis), CA (W)
University of California (Irvine), CA (MW)
University of California (Riverside), CA (MW)
University of California (San Diego), CA (MW)
University of California (Santa Barbara), CA (M)
University of California (Santa Cruz), CA (MW)
University of California (UCLA), CA (MW)
University of Central Arkansas, AR (W)
University of Central Florida, FL (W)
University of Central Oklahoma, OK (W)
University of Charleston, WV (W)
University of Chicago, IL (W)
University of Cincinnati, OH (W)
University of Colorado, CO (W)
University of Colorado (Colorado Springs), CO (W)
University of Connecticut, CT (W)
University of Dallas, TX (W)
University of Dayton, OH (W)
University of Delaware, DE (W)
University of Denver, CO (W)
University of Dubuque, IA (W)
University of Evansville, IN (W)
University of Findlay, OH (W)
University of Florida, FL (W)
University of Georgia, GA (W)
University of Guam, PA (MW)
University of Hartford, CT (W)
University of Hawaii (Hilo), HI (W)
University of Hawaii (Manoa), HI (MW)
University of Houston, TX (W)
University of Idaho, ID (W)
University of Illinois, IL (W)
University of Illinois (Urbana-Champaign), IL (W)
University of Indiana Southeast, IN (W)
University of Iowa, IA (MW)
University of Kansas, KS (W)
University of Kentucky, KY (W)
University of La Verne, CA (MW)
University of Louisville, KY (W)
University of Lowell, MA (W)
University of Maine (Fort Kent), ME (W)
University of Maine (Machias), ME (W)
University of Mary, ND (W)
University of Mary Hardin-Baylor, TX (W)
University of Maryland, MD (W)
University of Maryland (Baltimore County), MD (W)
University of Maryland (Eastern Shore), MD (W)
University of Massachusetts (Amherst), MA (W)
University of Minnesota (Duluth), MN (W)
University of Minnesota (Minneapolis), MN (W)
University of Minnesota (Morris), MN (W)
University of Mississippi, MS (W)
University of Missouri, MO (W)
University of Missouri (Columbia), MO (W)
University of Montana, MT (W)
University of Montevallo, AL (W)
University of Nebraska, NE (W)
University of Nebraska (Kearney), NE (W)
University of Nebraska (Lincoln), NE (W)
University of Nevada (Reno), NV (W)
University of New England, ME (W)
University of New Haven, CT (W)
University of New Mexico, NM (W)
University of New Orleans, LA (W)
University of North Alabama, AL (W)
University of North Carolina (Asheville), NC (W)
University of North Carolina (Chapel Hill), NC (W)

University of North Carolina (Charlotte), NC (W)
University of North Carolina (Greensboro), NC (W)
University of North Carolina (Wilmington), NC (W)
University of North Dakota, ND (W)
University of Northern Colorado, CO (W)
University of Northern Iowa, IA (W)
University of North Texas, TX (W)
University of Notre Dame, IN (W)
University of Oklahoma, OK (W)
University of Oregon, OR (W)
University of Pennsylvania, PA (W)
University of Pittsburgh, PA (W)
University of Pittsburgh (Bradford), PA (W)
University of Pittsburgh (Johnstown), PA (W)
University of Portland, OR (W)
University of Puerto Rico, PR (MW)
University of Puerto Rico (Bayamon), PR (MW)
University of Puerto Rico (Ponce), PR (MW)
University of Puget Sound, WA (W)
University of Redlands, CA (W)
University of Rhode Island, RI (MW)
University of Rio Grande, OH (W)
University of San Diego, CA (W)
University of San Francisco, CA (W)
University of Scranton, PA (W)
University of South Alabama, AL (W)
University of South Carolina, SC (W)
University of South Carolina, SC (W)
University of South Carolina (Aiken), SC (W)
University of South Carolina (Spartanburg), SC (W)
University of South Dakota, SD (W)
University of Southern California, CA (MW)
University of Southern Colorado, CO (W)
University of Southern Indiana, IN (W)
University of Southern Mississippi, MS (MW)
University of South Florida, FL (W)
University of Southwestern Louisiana, LA (W)
University of St. Thomas, MN (W)
University of Tampa, FL (W)
University of Tennessee, TN (W)
University of Tennessee (Knoxville), TN (W)
University of Tennessee (Martin), TN (W)
University of Texas (Arlington), TX (W)
University of Texas (Austin), TX (W)
University of Texas (El Paso), TX (W)
University of Texas (Pan American), TX (W)
University of Texas (San Antonio), TX (MW)
University of the District of Columbia, DC (W)
University of the Pacific, CA (W)
University of Toledo, OH (W)
University of Tulsa, OK (W)
University of Utah, UT (W)
University of Vermont, VT (W)
University of Virginia, VA (W)
University of Washington, WA (W)
University of Wisconsin (Eau Claire), WI (W)
University of Wisconsin (Green Bay), WI (W)
University of Wisconsin (La Crosse), WI (W)
University of Wisconsin (Madison), WI (W)
University of Wisconsin (Milwaukee), WI (MW)
University of Wisconsin (Oshkosh), WI (W)
University of Wisconsin (Platteville), WI (W)
University of Wisconsin (River Falls), WI (W)
University of Wisconsin (Stevens Point), WI (W)
University of Wisconsin (Stout), WI (W)
University of Wisconsin (Superior), WI (W)
University of Wyoming, WY (W)
Upper Iowa University, IA (W)
Ursinus College, PA (MW)
U.S. International University, CA (W)
Utah State University, UT (W)
Valley City State University, ND (MW)
Valley Forge Christian College, PA (W)
Valparaiso University, IN (W)
Vassar College, NY (MW)
Ventura College, CA (W)
Villa Maria College, NY (W)
Villanova University, PA (MW)
Vincennes University Junior College, IN (W)
Virginia Commonwealth University, VA (W)
Virginia Polytechnic Institute & State University, VA (W)
Virginia State University, VA (W)
Virginia Union University, VA (W)
Viterbo College, WI (W)
Wabash Valley College, IL (W)
Wagner College, NY (W)
Waldorf College, IA (W)
Walla Walla Community College, WA (W)
Walsh College, OH (W)
Warner Pacific College, OR (W)
Warner Southern College, FL (W)
Wartburg College, IA (W)
Washburn University, KS (W)
Washington and Jefferson College, PA (W)
Washington College, MD (W)
Washington State University, WA (W)
Washington University, MO (W)
Waubonsee College, IL (W)
Wayne State College, NE (W)
Wayne State University, MI (W)
Webber College, FL (W)
Weber State College, UT (W)
Webster University, MO (W)
Wellesley College, MA (W)
Wesleyan University, CT (W)
West Chester University, PA (W)
Western Carolina University, NC (W)
Western Connecticut State University, CT (W)
Western Illinois University, IL (W)
Western Kentucky University, KY (W)
Western Maryland College, MD (W)
Western Michigan University, MI (W)
Western Montana College, MT (W)
Western Nebraska Community College, NE (W)

Western New England College, MA (MW)
Western New Mexico University, NM (W)
Western Oregon State College, OR (W)
Western State College, CO (W)
Western Washington University, WA (MW)
Western Wyoming Community College, WY (W)
West Georgia College, GA (W)
West Liberty State College, WV (W)
Westminster College, PA (W)
Westmont College, CA (W)
West Texas State University, TX (W)
West Virginia Institute of Technology, WV (W)
West Virginia University, WV (W)
Wharton County Junior College, TX (W)
Wheaton College, IL (W)
Wheeling Jesuit College, WV (W)
Whitman College, WA (W)
Whittier College, CA (W)
Whitworth College, WA (W)
Wichita State University, KS (W)
Wilkes College, NC (W)
Willamette University, OR (W)
William Jewell College, MO (W)
William Patterson College, NJ (W)
William Penn College, IA (W)
William Rainey Harper College, IL (W)
Williams College, MA (MW)
William Woods College, MO (W)
Wilmington College, DE (W)
Wilmington College, OH (W)
Wilson College, PA (W)
Wingate College, NC (W)
Winona State University, MN (W)
Winston-Salem State University, NC (W)
Winthrop University, SC (W)
Wofford College, SC (W)
Worcester State College, MA (W)
Worthington Community College, MN (W)
Wright State University, OH (W)
Yakima Valley College, WA (W)
Yale University, CT (W)
Yavapai College, AZ (W)
Yeshiva University, NY (MW)
York College (CUNY), NY (MW)
York College of Pennsylvania, PA (W)
Youngstown State University, OH (W)
Yuba Community College, CA (W)

Water Polo

Austin College, TX (M)
Austin Community College, MN (M)
Bucknell University, PA (M)
Cabrillo College, CA (M)
California Institute of Technology, CA (MW)
California Maritime Academy, CA (M)
California State University (Fresno), CA (M)
California State University (Long Beach), CA (M)
Catholic University of Puerto Rico, PR (M)
Cerritos College, CA (M)
Chaffey College, CA (M)
Chaminade University, HI (M)
Chapman University, CA (M)
Cleveland State University, OH (M)
College of the Sequoias, CA (M)
Cuesta College, CA (M)
De Anza Community College, CA (M)
Diablo Valley Community College, CA (M)
El Camino College, CA (M)
Fordham University, NY (M)
Fullerton College, CA (M)
George Washington University, DC (M)
Golden West College, CA (M)
Harvard University, MA (MW)
Hope College, MI (M)
Iona College, NY (M)
Johns Hopkins University, MD (MW)
Long Beach City College, CA (M)
Los Angeles Pierce Junior College, CA (M)
Los Angeles Valley College, CA (M)
Loyola Marymount University, CA (M)
Lynchburg College, VA (M)
Massachusetts Institute of Technology, MA (M)
Modesto Junior College, CA (M)
Monmouth College, NJ (M)
Montclair State College, NJ (M)
Mt. San Antonio College, CA (M)
Occidental College, CA (M)
Orange Coast College, CA (M)
Paine College, GA (W)
Palomar College, CA (M)
Pepperdine University, CA (M)
Pomona-Pitzer College, CA (MW)
Queens College, NY (M)
Ranetto Santiago College, CA (M)
Riverside College, CA (MW)
Saddleback College, CA (M)
Saint Francis College, IN (M)
Saint Francis College, NY (M)
Saint Peter's College, NJ (M)
San Diego Mesa College, CA (MW)
San Joaquin Delta College, CA (M)
Santa Clara University, CA (M)
Santa Monica College, CA (M)
Santa Rosa Junior College, CA (M)
Sierra College, CA (M)
Slippery Rock University of Pennsylvania, PA (M)
Southern Oregon State College, OR (MW)
Stanford University, CA (M)
Trinity College, CT (MW)
Trinity College, IL (MW)
University of Arkansas (Little Rock), AR (M)
University of California (Berkeley), CA (M)
University of California (Davis), CA (M)
University of California (Irvine), CA (M)
University of California (Riverside), CA (MW)
University of California (San Diego), CA (MW)
University of California (Santa Barbara), CA (M)
University of California (UCLA), CA (M)
University of Dayton, OH (M)
University of Puerto Rico, PR (M)
University of Redlands, CA (M)
University of Rhode Island, RI (M)
University of Richmond, VA (M)
University of Southern California, CA (M)
University of the Pacific, CA (M)
Ventura College, CA (M)
Villanova University, PA (M)
Whittier College, CA (MW)
Yale University, CT (M)

Water Skiing

Florida State University, FL (MW)
Mississippi State University, MS (MW)
Rollins College, Fl (MW)

Weightlifting

Bayamon Central University, PR (MW)
Broward Community College, FL (MW)
Catholic University of Puerto Rico, PR (M)
Community College of Rhode Island, RI (MN)
Dalton College, GA (MW)
Glenville State College, WV (M)
Johnson County Community College, KS (M)
Lafayette College, PA (M)
Mississippi State University, MS (MW)
Moorpark College, CA (MW)
North Iowa Area Community College, IA (M)
Roosevelt University, IL (M)
Rose State Junior College, OK (MW)
Snow College, UT (MW)
University of Puerto Rico, PR (M)
University of Puerto Rico (Bayamon), PR (MW)
University of Puerto Rico (Ponce), PR (MW)
Willamette University, OR (M)

Wrestling

Adams State College, CO (M)
Albright College, PA (M)
American University, DC (M)
Anderson College, SC (M)
Anoka-Ramsey College, MN (M)
Appalachian State University, NC (M)
Apprentice School, VA (M)
Arizona State University, AZ (M)
Ashland College, OH (M)
Augsburg College, MN (M)
Augustana College, IL (M)
Augustana College, SD (M)
Bergen Community College, NJ (M)
Big Bend Community College, WA (M)
Bismarck State College, ND (M)
Bloomsburg University, PA (M)
Boise State University, ID (M)
Boston College, MA (M)
Boston University, MA (M)
Bowdoin College, ME (M)
Brainerd Community College, MN (M)
Bridgewater State College, MA (M)
Brigham Young University, UT (M)
Broome Community College, NY (M)
Brown University, RI (M)
Bucknell University, PA (M)
Buena Vista College, IA (M)
Buffalo State University (New York), NY (M)
Butte College, CA (M)
California Institute of Technology, CA (M)
California Polytechnic State University, CA (M)
California State University at Bakersfield, CA (M)
California State University (Chico), CA (M)
California State University (Fresno), CA (M)
California State University (Fullerton), CA (M)
California University, PA (M)
Campbell University, NC (M)
Capital University, OH (M)
Carleton College, MN (M)
Carroll College, WI (M)
Carson-Newman College, TN (M)
Case Western Reserve University, OH (M)
Catholic University of Puerto Rico, PR (M)
Central College, IA (M)
Central College, KS (M)
Central Connecticut State University, CT (M)
Central Michigan University, MI (M)
Central Missouri State University, MO (M)
Central Washington University, WA (M)
Cerritos College, CA (M)
Chadron State College, NE (M)
Cheyney University of Pennsylvania, PA (M)
Chicago State University, IL (M)
Chowan College, NC (M)
Citadel, SC (M)
City College of New York, NY (M)
Clackamas Community College, OR (M)
Clarion University, PA (M)
Clemson University, SC (M)
Cleveland State University, OH (M)
Coe College, IA (MW)
Colby Community College, KS (M)
College of William and Mary, VA (M)
Colorado Northwestern Community College, CO (M)
Colorado School of Mines, CO (M)
Columbia University, NY (M)
Concordia College, MN (M)
Concordia University, IL (M)
Coppin State College, MD (M)
Cornell College, IA (M)
Cornell University, NY (M)
Cuesta College, CA (M)
Dalton College, GA (M)
Dana College, NE (M)
Delaware State College, DE (M)
Delaware Valley College, PA (M)
De Pauw University, IN (M)
Diablo Valley Community College, CA (M)
Dickinson State University, ND (M)
Drake University, IA (M)
Drexel University, PA (M)
Duke University, NC (M)
Eastern Illinois University, IL (M)
Eastern Michigan University, MI (M)
East Stroudsburg University, PA (M)
Edinboro University of Pennsylvania, PA (M)
Elizabethtown College, PA (M)
Elmhurst College, IL (M)
Emerson College, MA (M)
Ferris State College, MI (M)
Fordham University, NY (M)
Fort Hays State University, KS (M)
Fort Lewis College, CO (M)
Franklin & Marshall College, PA (M)
Frederick Community College, MD (M)
Fresno City College, CA (M)
Fulton-Montgomery Community College, NY (M)
Furman University, SC (M)
Gannon College, PA (M)
Garden City Community College, KS (M)
George Mason University, VA (M)
Georgia State University, GA (M)
Gettysburg College, PA (M)
Gloucester County College, NJ (M)
Golden West College, CA (M)

Grand Rapids Junior College, MI (M)
Grand Valley State College, MI (M)
Hamline University, MN (M)
Hampden-Sydney College, VA (M)
Hampton University, VA (M)
Harper William Rainey College, IL (M)
Harvard University, MA (M)
Haverford College, PA (M)
Heidelberg College, OH (W)
Hofstra University, NY (M)
Howard University, DC (M)
Humboldt State University, CA (M)
Hunter College of the City University of New York, NY (M)
Huron University, SD (M)
Illinois College, IL (M)
Illinois State University, IL (M)
Indiana University, IN (M)
Iowa State University of Science and Technology, IA (M)
Ithaca College, NY (M)
James Madison University, VA (M)
Jamestown College, ND (M)
John Carroll University, OH (M)
Johns Hopkins University, MD (M)
Juniata College, PA (M)
Kean College of New Jersey, NJ (M)
Kent State University (Ashtabula), OH (M)
Kent State University (Kent), OH (M)
Kent State University (New Philadelphia), OH (M)
Kent State University (Warren), OH (M)
Keystone Junior College, PA (M)
King's College, PA (M)
Kirkwood Community College, IA (M)
Knox College, IL (M)
Kutztown University, PA (M)
Labette Community College, KS (M)
Lafayette College, PA (M)
Lake Superior State University, MI (M)
La Salle University, PA (M)
Lawrence University, WI (M)
Lebanon Valley College, PA (M)
Lehigh University, PA (M)
Liberty University, VA (M)
Lincoln College, IL (M)
Linfield College, OR (M)
Livingstone College, NC (M)
Lock Haven University of Pennsylvania, PA (M)
Longwood College, VA (M)
Loras College, IA (M)
Los Angeles Pierce Junior College, CA (M)
Lower Columbia College, WA (M)
Luther College, IA (M)
Lycoming College, PA (M)
Madison Area Technical College, WI (M)
Manhattan College, NY (M)
Mankato State University, MN (M)
Mansfield University, PA (M)
Marquette University, WI (M)
Massachusetts Institute of Technology, MA (M)
Mayville State College, ND (M)
Mesa State College, CO (M)
Messiah College, PA (M)
Miami University, OH (M)
Michigan State University, MI (M)
Millersville University, PA (M)
Millikin University, IL (M)
Modesto Junior College, CA (M)
Mohawk Valley Community College, NY (M)
Monmouth College, IL (M)
Montana College of Mineral Science and Technology, MT (M)
Montana State University, MT (M)
Montclair State College, NJ (M)
Moorhead State University, MN (M)
Moorpark College, CA (MW)
Moravian College, PA (M)
Morgan State University, MD (M)
Mount Union College, OH (M)
Mt. San Antonio College, CA (M)
Muhlenberg College, PA (M)
Muskegon Community College, MI (M)
Muskingum College, OH (M)
Nassau Community College, NY (M)
New York University, NY (M)
Niagara County Community College, NY (M)
Norfolk State University, VA (M)
North Carolina A and T State University, NC (M)
North Carolina State University, NC (M)
North Central College, IL (M)
North Dakota State, ND (M)
North Dakota State University, ND (M)
Northern Arizona University, AZ (M)
Northern Illinois University, IL (M)
Northern Montana College, MT (M)
Northern State University, SD (M)
North Idaho College, ID (M)
Northwest College, WY (M)
Northwestern College, IA (M)
Northwestern College, MN (M)
Northwestern University, IL (M)
Norwich University, VT (M)
Oakton Community College, IL (M)
Ohio Northern University, OH (M)
Ohio State University, OH (M)
Ohio University, OH (M)
Oklahoma State University, OK (M)
Old Dominion University, VA (M)
Olivet College, MI (M)
Olivet Nazarene University, IL (M)
Oregon Institute of Technology, OR (M)
Oregon State University, OR (M)
Pacific Lutheran University, WA (M)
Pacific University, OR (M)
Palomar College, CA (M)
Pembroke State University, NC (M)
Pennsylvania State University, PA (M)
Pfeiffer College, NC (M)
Phoenix College, AZ (M)
Pima Community College, AZ (M)
Plymouth State College, NH (M)
Portland State University, OR (M)
Princeton University, NJ (M)
Purdue University, IN (M)
Ranetto Santiago College, CA (M)
Rhode Island College, RI (M)
Ricks College, ID (M)
Rider College, NJ (M)
Rochester Community College, MN (M)
Rochester Institute of Technology, NY (M)
Rose-Hulman Institute of Technology, IN (M)
Rutgers, Newark College of Arts and Sciences, NJ (M)
Saint Cloud State University, MN (M)

Saint John's University, MN (M)
Saint Lawrence University, NY (M)
Saint Olaf College, MN (M)
San Bernardino Community College, CA (M)
San Diego City College, CA (M)
San Francisco State University, CA (M)
San Joaquin Delta College, CA (M)
San Jose State University, CA (M)
Santa Rosa Junior College, CA (M)
Seton Hall University, NJ (M)
Shippensburg University of Pennsylvania, PA (M)
Sierra College, CA (M)
Simpson College, CA (M)
Skyline College, CA (M)
Slippery Rock University of Pennsylvania, PA (M)
South Dakota State University, SD (M)
Southern Connecticut State University, CT (M)
Southern Illinois University (Edwardsville), IL (M)
Southern Oregon State College, OR (M)
Southwestern Michigan Junior College, MI (M)
Southwest Missouri State University, MO (M)
Southwest State University, MN (M)
Springfield College, MA (M)
Stanford University, CA (M)
State University of New York (Albany), NY (M)
State University of New York (Binghamton), NY (M)
State University of New York College (Brockport), NY (M)
State University of New York College (Cortland), NY (M)
State University of New York College (Oswego), NY (M)
State University of New York College (Pottsdam), NY (M)
Stevens Institute of Technology, NJ (M)
St. Louis Community College (Florissant Valley), MO (M)
St. Louis Community College (Forest Park), MO (M)
Swarthmore College, PA (M)
Syracuse University, NY (M)
Teikyo Westmar University, IA (M)
Trenton State College, NJ (M)
Trinity College, CT (M)
Trinity College, IL (M)
Triton College, IL (M)
University of California (Davis), CA (M)
University of Central Oklahoma, OK (M)
University of Chicago, IL (M)
University of Dayton, OH (M)
University of Dubuque, IA (M)
University of Findlay, OH (M)
University of Illinois, IL (M)
University of Illinois (Urbana-Champaign), IL (M)
University of Indianapolis, IN (M)
University of Iowa, IA (M)
University of La Verne, CA (M)
University of Lowell, MA (M)
University of Mary, ND (M)
University of Maryland, MD (M)
University of Massachusetts (Boston), MA (M)
University of Michigan, MI (M)
University of Minnesota (Duluth), MN (M)
University of Minnesota (Minneapolis), MN (M)
University of Minnesota (Morris), MN (M)
University of Missouri, MO (M)
University of Missouri (Columbia), MO (M)
University of Nebraska, NE (M)
University of Nebraska (Kearney), NE (M)
University of Nebraska (Lincoln), NE (M)
University of New Hampshire, NH (M)
University of New Mexico, NM (M)
University of North Carolina (Asheville), NC (M)
University of North Carolina (Chapel Hill), NC (M)
University of North Dakota, ND (M)
University of Northern Colorado, CO (M)
University of Northern Iowa, IA (M)
University of Oklahoma, OK (M)
University of Oregon, OR (M)
University of Pennsylvania, PA (M)
University of Pittsburgh, PA (M)
University of Pittsburgh (Johnstown), PA (M)
University of Puerto Rico, PR (M)
University of Puerto Rico (Bayamon), PR (MW)
University of Rhode Island, RI (M)
University of Scranton, PA (M)
University of Southern Colorado, CO (M)
University of St. Thomas, MN (M)
University of Toledo, OH (M)
University of Virginia, VA (M)
University of Wisconsin (Eau Claire), WI (M)
University of Wisconsin (La Crosse), WI (M)
University of Wisconsin (Madison), WI (M)
University of Wisconsin (Oshkosh), WI (M)
University of Wisconsin (Platteville), WI (M)
University of Wisconsin (River Falls), WI (M)
University of Wisconsin (Stevens Point), WI (M)
University of Wisconsin (Stout), WI (M)
University of Wisconsin (Superior), WI (M)
University of Wyoming, WY (M)
Upper Iowa University, IA (M)
Ursinus College, PA (M)
Utah State University, UT (M)
Valparaiso University, IN (M)
Virginia Military Institute, VA (M)
Virginia Polytechnic Institute & State University, VA (M)
Wabash College, IN (M)
Wagner College, NY (M)
Waldorf College, IA (M)
Wartburg College, IA (M)
Washington and Jefferson College, PA (M)
Washington University, MO (M)
Waubonsee College, IL (M)
Weber State College, UT (M)
Wesleyan University, CT (M)
Western Maryland College, MD (M)
Western Montana College, MT (M)
Western New England College, MA (M)
Western State College, CO (M)
West Liberty State College, WV (M)
West Virginia University, WV (M)
Wheaton College, IL (M)
Wilkes College, NC (M)
Wilkes University, PA (MW)

William Jewell College, MO (M)
William Penn College, IA (M)
William Rainey Harper College, IL (M)
Williams College, MA (M)
Williamson Trade School, PA (M)
Wilmington College, DE (M)
Wilmington College, OH (M)
Winston-Salem State University, NC (M)
Worthington Community College, MN (M)
Yale University, CT (M)
Yeshiva University, NY (M)
York College of Pennsylvania, PA (M)

SUGGESTED READINGS

Free Money for College
Laurie Blum
Facts On File
460 Park Avenue South
New York, New York 10016
(212) 683-2244

Lovejoy's College Guide
Charles T. Straughn II and
Barbarasue Lovejoy Straughn, Editors
Prentice Hall General Reference
15 Columbus Circle; New York, New York 10023
(212) 373-8500

Peterson's 1992 College Money Handbook
Ninth Edition
Peterson's Guides
Princeton, New Jersey
(609) 243-9111

INDEX

A

B

C

D

K

L

M

N

O

P

Q

R

S

V

W

X

Y